CW00503880

the chronology of pattern

1100 BCE 1400 1600 2000 1800

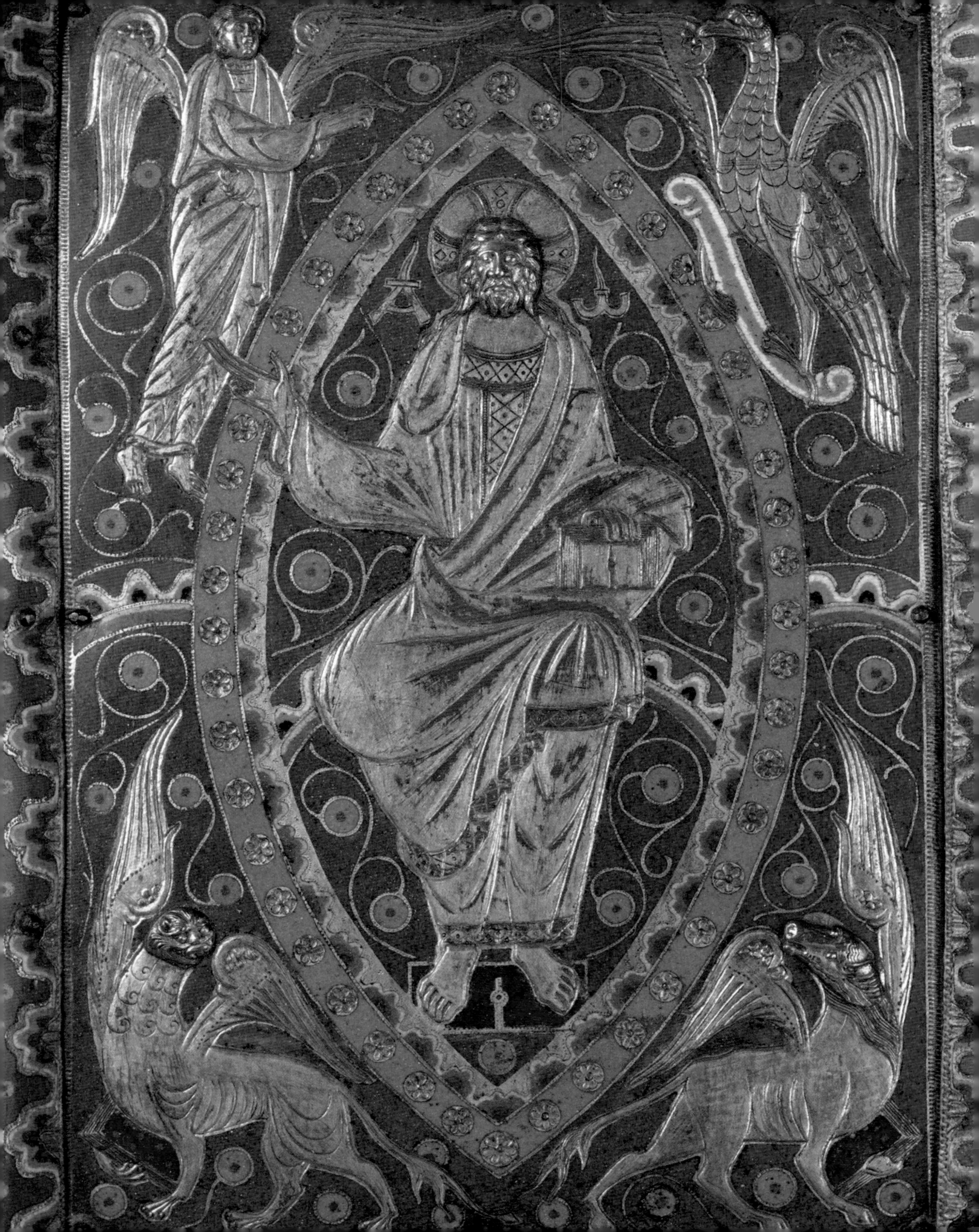

DIANA NEWALL &
CHRISTINA UNWIN

the chronology of pattern

PATTERN IN ART FROM LOTUS FLOWER
TO FLOWER POWER

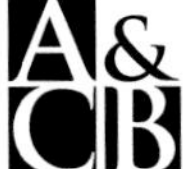

Dedication

This book is dedicated to Frances Pritchard and Grant Pooke

First published in 2011 by A&C Black,
an imprint of Bloomsbury Publishing Plc
36 Soho Square
London W1D 3QY, UK

www.acblack.com

British Library Cataloguing-in-Publication Data
A catalogue record for this book is available from the British Library

ISBN 978-1-4081-2641-7

This book was conceived,
designed and produced by

Ivy Press
210 High Street
Lewes
East Sussex BN7 2NS
United Kingdom

Creative Director: Peter Bridgewater
Publisher: Jason Hook
Editorial Director: Caroline Earle
Art Director: Michael Whitehead
Design: JC Lanaway
Picture Manager: Katie Greenwood
Assistant Editor: Jamie Pumfrey

Cover Design: James Watson
Cover Images: V&A Images

Typeset in Bembo and Helvetica Neue

Image Reproduction: Ivy Reproductions
Printed and bound in China

Contents

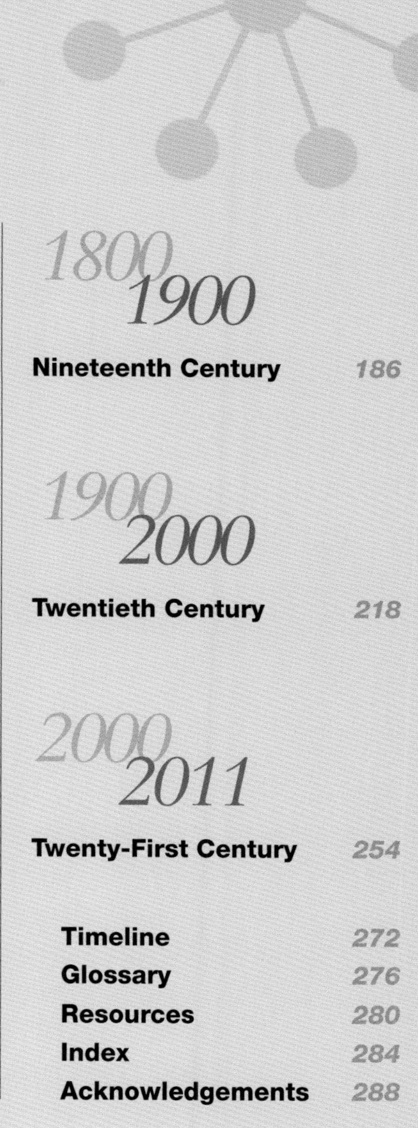

INTRODUCTION

Reading Patterns

This book will take the reader on a journey through 3,000 years of patterns. It shows how designs were created, reassessed, transformed and recycled in myriad styles and combinations through time. Taste, fashion, politics and ideas about the past and the future change continuously and are reflected by the creativity of artists and designers, who produce patterns in all media, both physical and virtual, within their own cultures and societies.

Patterns are composed of motifs that interrelate with each other as repeated, varied, alternating, symmetrical or asymmetrical shapes that are integral with the objects they decorate – clothing, jewellery, armour, textiles, wallpaper, furniture, ceramics, paintings, sculptures, and buildings.

Reading a pattern involves enquiring into the cultural and social context of its design and of the object it decorates – why was the object made or built; who designed, made or decorated it; who was permitted to see it; what was its function and the purpose of the pattern; and how did it relate to the interior or exterior world that surrounded it?

Patterned objects have agency – they engage and influence the viewer with the visual qualities of materials and technologies that enchant the eye. With their attributes of colour, shape and light-reflection, patterns can communicate ideas and emotions. People may also be merely wonderstruck by the virtuosity of the artist without necessarily understanding the function or historical context of the pattern. Patterns attract the viewer's gaze, but they also connect people to the decorated object and the social context in which it is, or was, seen or used. Patterns are important for human society, influencing the way people see objects. By encouraging the viewer to spend time looking, patterns ensure an unending interaction. This is important for a sense of appreciation or ownership but also for individual or group expressions of cultural or political status and power. For example, a decorated plate might reflect the taste of the owner or the society in which they live; its artistic qualities may signify wealth or power; and the origins of its patterns may be displaying connections to the past in order to communicate identity or status.

When motifs are combined, their individual power is magnified and the juxtaposition of different patterns within a design transforms their individual meaning and effect into something new. The repetition of individual, composite motifs, or

Seated Buddha 550–77, *Quyang, China*
This complex devotional object has been integrated with patterns of the natural form of the lotus flower, the spiritual symbol of flames, and religious figures representing the Buddha.

of whole sequences of forms, is vital to pattern-making, its impact and meaning. The way that patterns articulate the gaze over the surface of an object reflects the cultural thinking of the designer – for example, classical Greek lotus and palmette motifs in rows were redesigned by artists of early Iron Age Europe as abstract forms for patterns that flowed over surfaces in multiple ways.

Complex patterns can be read in different directions, at different levels and in different combinations, providing a multi-dimensional experience even with a two-dimensional design. For example, the complex layered arabesque patterns from the Middle East combine floral and geometric forms with almost infinite linkages of colours, shapes, motifs and repeats. The design of a pattern draws on a rich range of sources, influences and ideas, even if it is itself highly stylised or codified in apparently simple forms. The cultural, social and political environments of the people who commissioned and made objects gave rise to the psychological complexity, historical meaning, ritual symbolism and contemporary nuances inherent in the patterns that decorated them. The ways that instigators and producers of design have reacted to earlier or culturally remote patterns enable a rich continuity that, in turn, inspires the further exploration of materials and technologies.

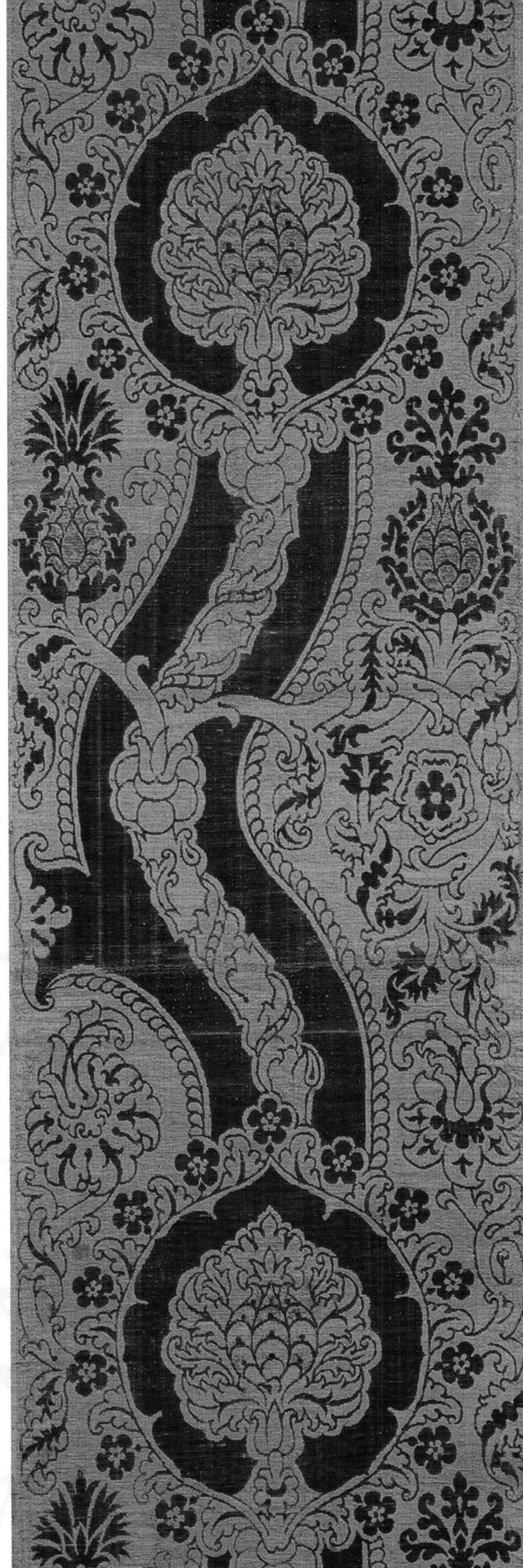

Brocade furnishing fabric, c. 1475, *Italy*
The patterns on luxury fabrics of the 15th century were intrinsic to their significance as symbols of power and status, whether for the Church, in an aristocratic house or as clothing.

INTRODUCTION

Interpreting Patterns

Patterns can be treated as 'texts' to be read and interpreted. Objects are decorated according to the cultural environments in which they are created, in turn influencing the societies in which they are seen or used. In many cases these two contexts were culturally different as patterned objects in the form of gifts or traded goods travelled across the world between societies. Patterned objects express complex relationships between themselves, their designers and their viewers, in a similar way to living things. The way in which a pattern is arranged on a surface – how it is animated – has great significance, along with its appropriateness and virtuosity in execution.

Social and cultural traditions, values and tastes also influence the design of a pattern, in relation to the artist and patron. Patterns reflect the natural and manufactured worlds with different degrees of reality and abstraction, or the transcendent and supernatural realms of spiritual beliefs. Patterns are created to have an intentional effect on the viewer, creating and transforming ideas that draw on the designer's individual and collective cultural experiences. This is seen in the patterned materials of many world cultures which are psychological expressions of the societies that produced them. For example, a motif such as the lotus in Egyptian culture carried an extensive range of meanings and symbolism which were foundational to its perceptions of identity and cosmic order. Patterns can also defend objects and social spaces from unwanted spiritual influences, applied as apotropaic – protective – designs in socially sensitive areas such as doorways and thresholds. They entrap with their complexities in the same way that the viewer's gaze is enrapt by the interplay of colour and form. In the modern era, the rise of the logo for corporate products and lifestyles is an incarnation of this defensive function – repeated as a pattern on an object, such as the GG motif of Guccio Gucci or the LV on Louis Vuitton luggage, this codified mark of identification and authentication acts as a powerful signifier for the luxury brand.

Fashion has a prominent place in the display and effects of pattern. Historically a reflector of status and power, it also showcases society's constantly changing ideas of appropriateness, desirability and beauty. The post-industrial period in Europe brought nostalgia for the past as well as enthusiasm for modernity, reflected in the design of patterns as well as the processes and materials with which they were made. The recycling of artistic concepts has always driven pattern-making and this, combined with parody and pastiche, has transformed design to express modernity in art

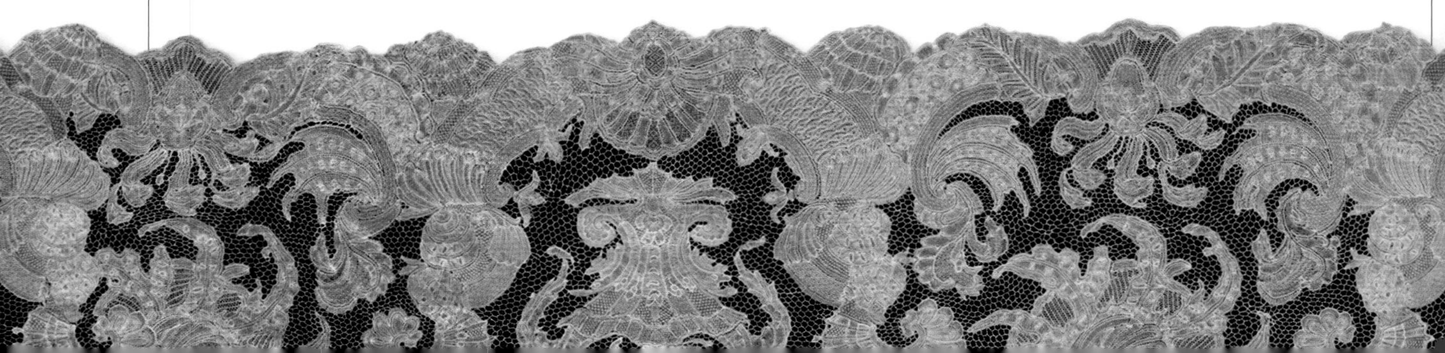

and architecture as a culturally rich and complex multi-dimensional stylistic force. The endless search for new and special ways to decorate and dress the body with pattern has meant that fashion has always been a phenomenon created by long-distance relationships. Exotic designs from faraway places have been held in high regard for their rarity and the prestige they confer on the wearer since the first diplomatic and trade routes linked the East with the West. Fashion's significance has been transformed in the modern world by the organisation on an international scale of the production of high-fashion objects that are transformed into goods for a global hierarchy of marketing outlets.

Design in the 21st century has been informed by ideas as much as by the attributes of physical materials. The development of computer software programs has enabled artists and designers to articulate and evaluate their concepts rapidly and easily in a virtual environment. This process, combined with an increasing knowledge of psychology, has led to the boundaries between design, form and the creative process becoming more fluid – pattern may come to be equated with the actual form of the object itself, as demonstrated by the 'Bird's Nest' Olympic stadium in Beijing, China. Craftworking has remained influential in the exploration of aesthetics and the expression of individual creativity. Designers working in all types of physical materials will continue to challenge their intrinsic properties, both referencing and transcending deeply ingrained historical influences and continually renewing the potential of their chosen materials.

Furnishing flounce, c. 1740, *Brussels, Belgium*
The technical process of lace-making took pattern-making to a new level and, before the advent of machine-making, symbolised the height of status and wealth.

'Calyx' furnishing fabric, Lucienne Day, 1951, *England*
In the 20th century, design focused on matching form to function but patterns continued to be developed and valued in stylised and joyful forms such as this.

INTRODUCTION

How to Use this Book

This book is organised into chapters covering time periods and centuries from c. 1100 BCE to 2011 CE. It explores types and developments of patterns and the objects on which they appear. The book draws on a rich variety of patterns and decorated objects from around the world to show how they were designed, were viewed and interacted with viewers through the centuries. The patterns are explored in three ways.

1 The main approach is to take a group of patterns and objects related by a specific theme, discussing their forms, origins, meanings, functions and relationships.

Pattern entry
Each pattern and object displayed is discussed in detail with an analysis of the forms and types of patterns and the context of the object.

Image
The pattern and object images have been chosen to exemplify particular types and forms of patterns within the scope of the theme on the page.

Dates
The date range at the top of the page is drawn from the objects discussed, even if the range spans more than a century.

Introduction text
The introduction text sets out the theme for the patterns and objects, providing an explanation of their relationships and historical context.

Quote
The quote has been selected to highlight particular issues relevant to the theme drawn from the work of experts and art historians writing in the field.

Elements of pattern
To summarise and clarify the patterns discussed on the page, the different elements and types of patterns are listed.

2 Where a work of art or architecture deserves a closer look, it receives detailed analysis of its different pattern elements.

Main image text
The caption for the main image describes its patterns, subject and context in more detail to provide a frame for the pattern details.

Image details
Images of the individual patterns visible on the image or scene are highlighted and enlarged so they can be studied in detail.

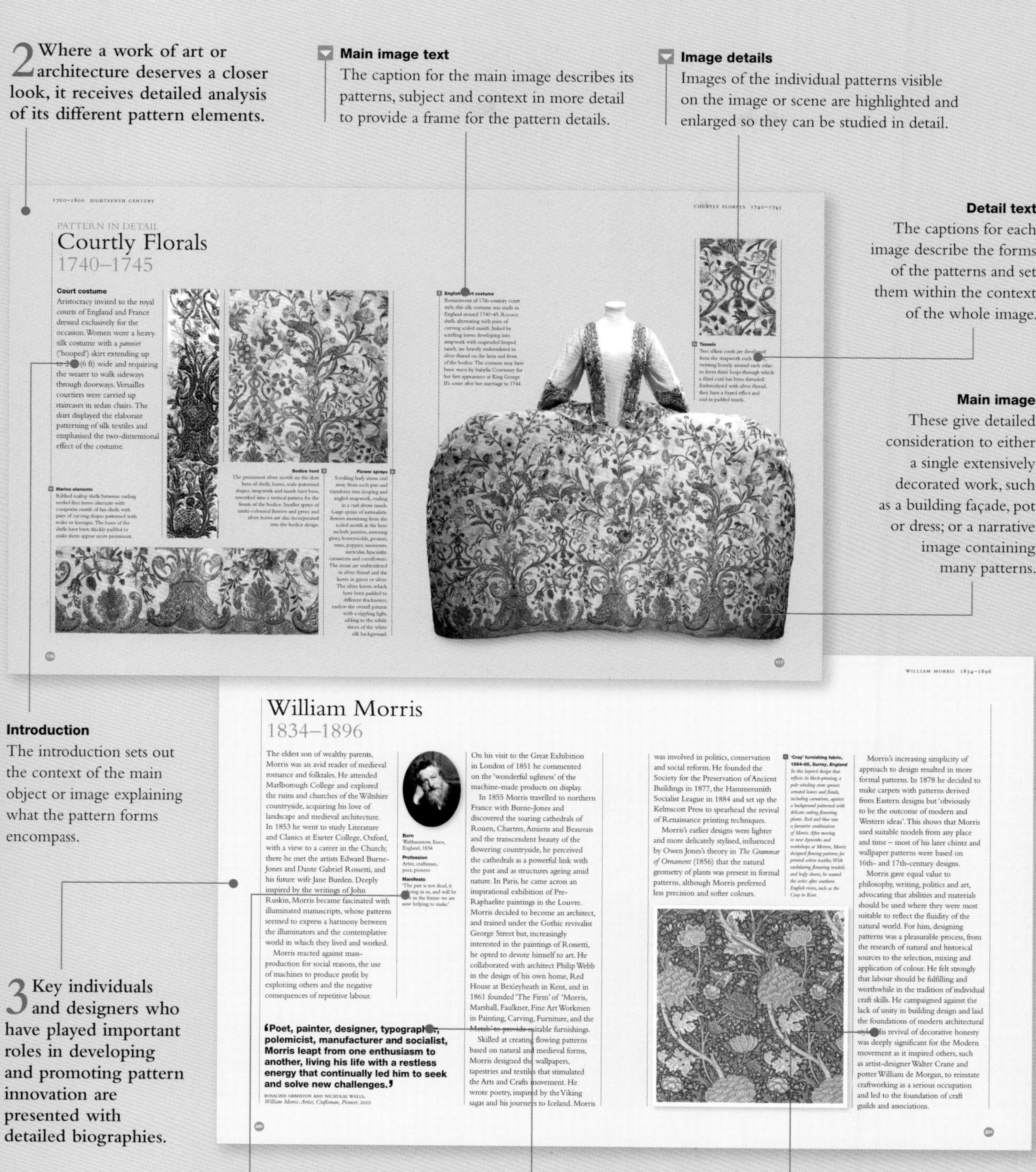

Detail text
The captions for each image describe the forms of the patterns and set them within the context of the whole image.

Main image
These give detailed consideration to either a single extensively decorated work, such as a building façade, pot or dress; or a narrative image containing many patterns.

Introduction
The introduction sets out the context of the main object or image explaining what the pattern forms encompass.

3 Key individuals and designers who have played important roles in developing and promoting pattern innovation are presented with detailed biographies.

Biography details at a glance
A key designer, artist or architect is introduced with a summarised biography giving their dates, location, profession and manifesto.

Quote
The quote for an individual provides a glimpse of the importance of their pattern forms and their pattern developments.

Main text
The life of the individual is explored in depth exploring their work, patterns and significance to design developments in the period in which they worked.

Looking at Patterns

Traditionally, patterns have been divided and categorised according to visual attributes such as structure or form. In this book, we avoid such generalisations by exploring individual pattern and object interrelationships in their cultural contexts to reveal their rich and many-layered meanings. This section is therefore aimed at providing some basic principles for how you might look at and explore patterns, while avoiding over-simplified groups.

Jar, 1395–1430, *Orvieto, Umbria, Italy*
The geometric patterns on this jar are matched by a sinuous plant pattern. The *chequy* heraldry pattern on the shield carries significance of status and family, whereas the hatched background and ribbon wave on the neck simply provide a contrast to the raised plants motif.

We are surrounded by patterns that reflect the ways we look at and process the world around us. They may be made up of repeated motifs or composed of variations and abstractions developed from a particular form or idea. They may be located on, within or beneath surfaces, designed to be seen on exteriors or interiors of buildings or objects, including places close to the human body such as underclothes or pocket linings. Patterns may be only seen by a specific individual in a private context, displayed by particular people in a private or public space, or exhibited fully in the public gaze at all times. Individually patterned objects such as painted ceramic tiles may be arranged in grids that form other patterns as part of the overall design. Other patterns may be closely related to the structure of an object, as in woven textiles and stone or brick walls.

Geometric patterns

Geometric patterns based on a grid of intersecting lines consist of straight-sided or curvilinear shapes subdividing space and form. These patterns may be clearly expressed as simple flat forms on an object, but they may represent complex cultural ideas and customs made bold by colour and design for display. More elaborate geometric patterns may be imbued with similar complexity of meaning but are designed according to different social artistic customs. Geometric patterns may have grids that are prominent in their design or only apparent on closer analysis. Stripes, lattices, checks, zigzags and intersecting circles display the grids on which they are based,

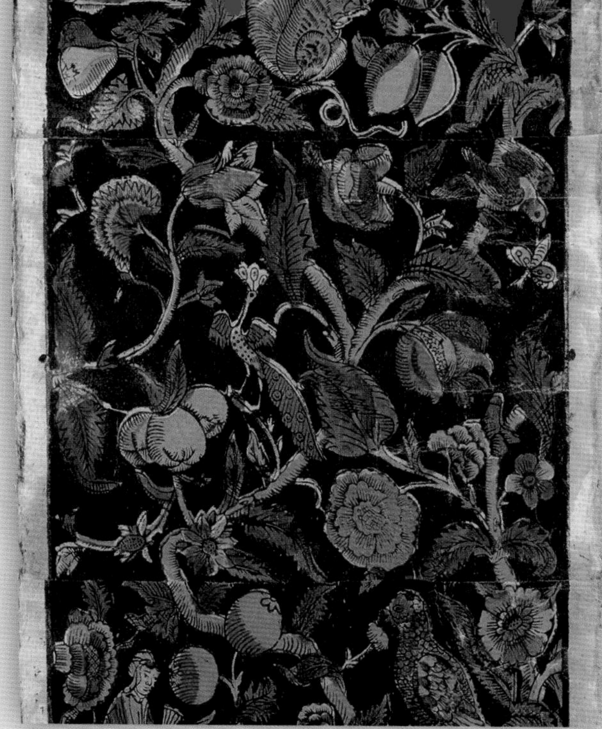

Print wallpaper, c. 1700, Ord House, *Northumberland, England*
The 18th century was a period when floral patterns and exotic motifs were particularly popular across the world. Initially stylised, floral representations became increasingly naturalistic, emulating the rich forms and textures of real blooms.

but the shapes created by them and between them produce visual networks of further patterns that can be read in different directions and at various levels. For example, a check pattern may be read as alternating coloured squares, interwoven bands or interlocking crosses.

Plant and animal forms

Plants have been a fundamental source of inspiration for pattern-makers. The flowing lines of root, stem, leaf, tendril, bud, flower and fruit have been transformed to create patterns of formal motifs, animated lush growing effects, closely observed naturalism and abstract design. The 'sacred tree' motif from the ancient Near East with its cosmological attributes – rooted in the earth and growing towards the sky – became a powerful device in the spirituality of pattern design for many Eastern and Western cultures, linking the earth with the heavens. Scientific enquiry into nature has inspired designs of plants as recognisable species – endowed with particular qualities. Flowers in particular were selected and transformed into motifs for building patterns.

Real and mythical animals have also been referenced widely in many cultures for pattern design. Inhabiting scrolling plants in patterns such as the Christian 'tree of life' that symbolised the interrelationship between living things and God, and between the Church and Christ, they vary from the naturalistic to the fantastical. Vines, ivy and acanthus leaves from Eastern and Mediterranean sources informed the designs of leaf scrolls, and plant and animal forms were used to create hybrid designs for animated patterns.

Patterns as identifiers

Patterns of personal identification, status and power were created for heraldic display, based on colours, metals and fur textures and including formalised plants, animals, people and objects. Heraldry has been incorporated into the decoration of many kinds of objects, such as textiles, ceramics, metalwork and architectural exteriors and interiors. Heraldic patterns and designs came to be affiliated with ideas of ancestry and heritage, qualities drawn upon by later designers who have built heraldic motifs into their work. Trademarks and logos are reincarnations of heraldic badges, making statements about the identity, authenticity and quality of branded objects.

1100 BCE 300 CE

Prehistory to Classical

Introduction

The patterns of the first millennium BCE encompass a wide range of forms and cultural contexts. Associated with the rituals of life and death, links and routes both across geographical territories and to the afterlife and the divine, patterns facilitated the mobility of thought and cultural meaning across physical and metaphysical boundaries.

The integration of patterns and their meaning with the forms, materials and function of the objects on which they were delineated were subject to formal rules. During the Late Bronze Age (c. 1300–750 BCE), long-distance journeys, trading and social networks linked peoples and ideas across Europe. This mobility was reflected in motifs and patterns, such as birds and wheel or sun motifs on bronze. Surviving patterns are often associated with high-status groups and individuals and with elite rituals to help ensure a privileged afterlife. In the last millennium of ancient Egypt, tomb painting focused on these rituals and the ubiquitous lotus and papyrus flowers carried the symbolic meaning of rejuvenation and new life, linked to the veneration of Osiris, the ruler of the underworld. In early Archaic Greece (750–700 BCE), geometric designs incorporated stylised human figures, animals and objects associated with events in life and death. Painted vessels had specific shapes and functions corresponding to the social rituals of life and death.

Patterns also conveyed attributes of the divine or spirit worlds. In the neo-Assyrian Empire (934–609 BCE), the motif of the 'sacred tree' – comprising lotuses, palmettes, pine cones, pomegranates, rosettes and guilloches (interwoven wavy lines) – was linked to a divine order placing the Assyrian kings as intermediaries between the earthly and the transcendent.

During the 8th and 7th centuries BCE, the palmette was introduced to Greece through contacts with Assyria, and the lotus flower and bud motif

Repeated complex motifs, elaborate interlace and undulating waves form unending rings of pattern and colour, ensnaring the viewer's gaze in the design and protecting the interior space of the vessel.

from Egypt began to appear in Greek designs. Alternating lotus and palmette patterns were combined with acanthus leaves to emphasise the vegetal effect. From the mid-5th century BCE, lotus flower and palmette motifs from classical Greek sources were reinterpreted by the metalworkers of the Iron Age. Half-lotuses, three-leaved motifs, comma leaves and triskeles were combined in order to create new dynamic patterning in bronze, iron and gold. Complex, multi-directional patterns, related to the reflective swirling properties of polished bronze, were applied to prestigious objects of display and ceremony, such as armour, weapons, wine vessels and mirrors.

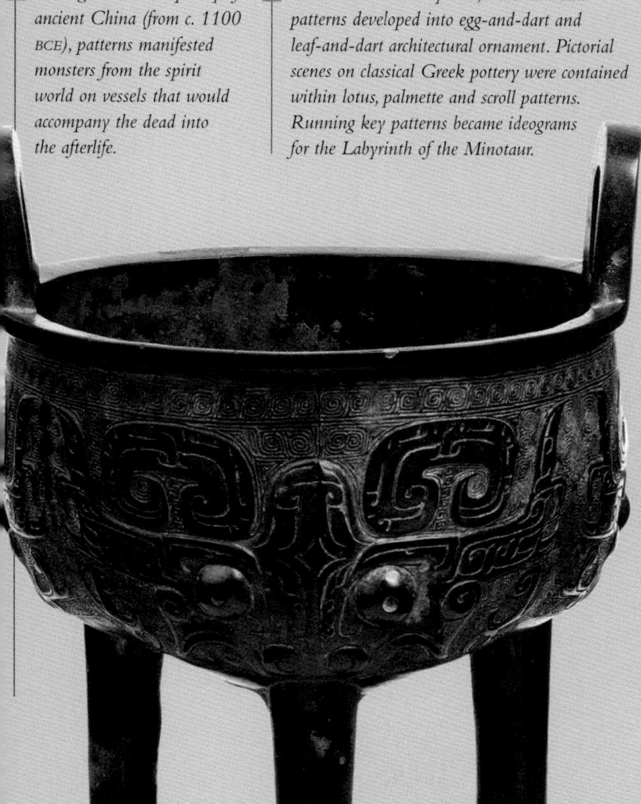

During the Zhou dynasty of ancient China (from c. 1100 BCE), patterns manifested monsters from the spirit world on vessels that would accompany the dead into the afterlife.

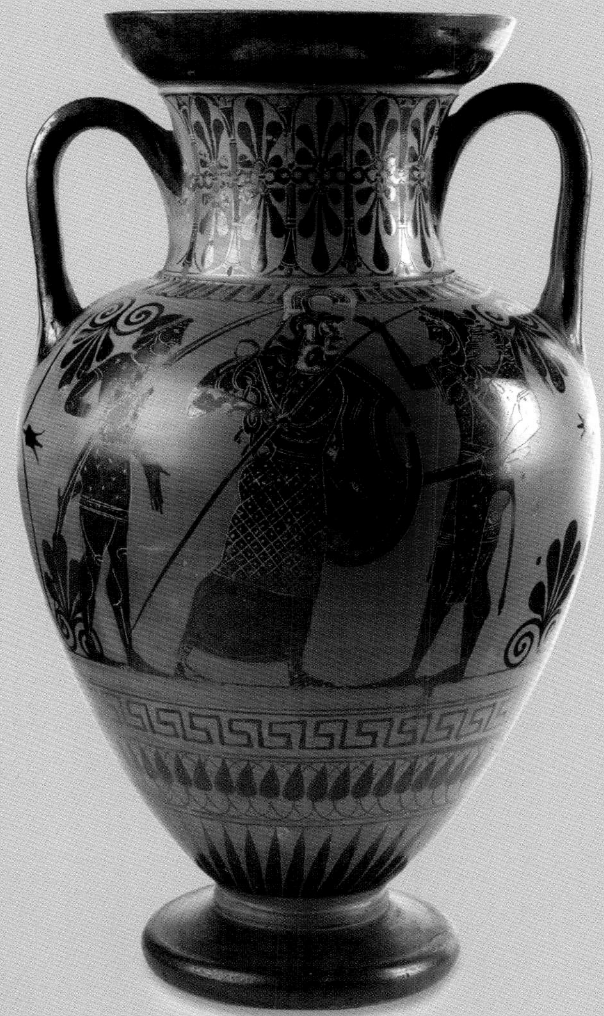

From the 6th century BCE, lotus-and-bud patterns developed into egg-and-dart and leaf-and-dart architectural ornament. Pictorial scenes on classical Greek pottery were contained within lotus, palmette and scroll patterns. Running key patterns became ideograms for the Labyrinth of the Minotaur.

The elaborate scrolling acanthus plants signified fertility and regeneration in the Roman Empire (44 BCE–476 CE), ornamenting the *Ara Pacis Augustae* altar, built in 13–9 BCE in Rome to herald the peaceful rule of the Emperor Augustus. Such patterns also decorated wall frescoes and floor mosaics in religious, public and private spaces.

In Roman Britain (1st to 4th century CE) mosaic floors demonstrated complex compositions of patterns in an interior setting. Patterns surrounding images of mythological figures, animals and drinking vessels protected these tokens of ritual and fortune.

Aristocratic Ceremonial Designs 1300 BCE–50 CE

Metalwork patterns in late Bronze Age and Iron Age Europe

In Late Bronze Age Europe (1300–750 BCE), new metalwork technologies expressed the power of aristocrats and warriors. Bronze drinking vessels, weapons, armour and extravagant body ornaments all bore patterns integrated with ceremonial power.

During the Early Iron Age (800–600 BCE), metalworkers combined different materials and techniques, perhaps in specialist workshops: engraving, compass work for circles and spirals, and casting objects with raised patterns and settings for glass or coral. From the mid-5th century BCE, specialist craftsworkers from central Europe exchanged ideas with Greek and Etruscan traders, producing the La Tène art of the later Iron Age.

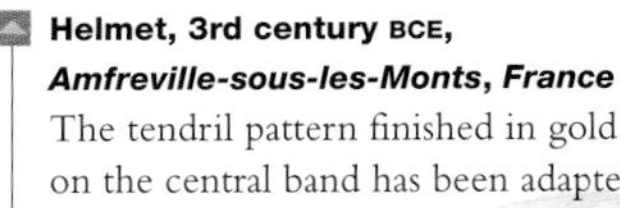

Helmet, 3rd century BCE,
Amfreville-sous-les-Monts, France
The tendril pattern finished in gold foil on the central band has been adapted from classical models of linear ornament, with three-sided triskeles allowing the pattern to flow visually in both directions. The sinuous patterns in iron openwork above and below were originally infilled with coloured glass enamel. Made by an armourer working for a high-ranking individual, this bronze helmet was worn as parade armour.

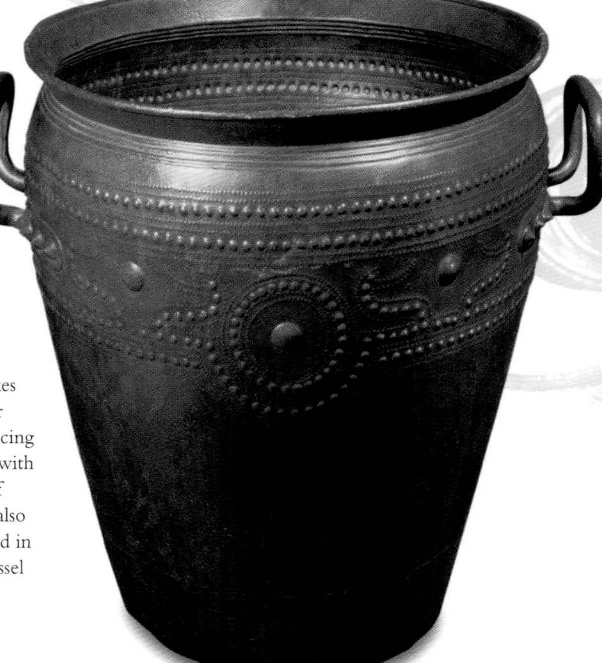

Drinking vessel, 1300–750 BCE,
Hajdúböszörmény, Hungary
The water birds may signify the journey from life to death, as prestigious artefacts were often ceremonially placed in rivers, lakes and marshes as gateways to other worlds. Patterns of water birds facing radiating sun or wheel symbols, with their special ritual associations of good luck and protection, were also displayed on body armour. Placed in the grave of an aristocrat, this vessel had been used for mixing and serving alcoholic drinks on ceremonial occasions.

ELEMENTS OF PATTERN

Late Bronze Age

- *water bird*
- *radiating sun or wheel*
- *dotted outlines*

Iron Age

- *fragmented and recomposed lotus and palmette*
- *comma leaf*
- *scrolling and linking tendril*
- *triskele articulating pattern in plural directions*
- *settings for precious coloured materials*

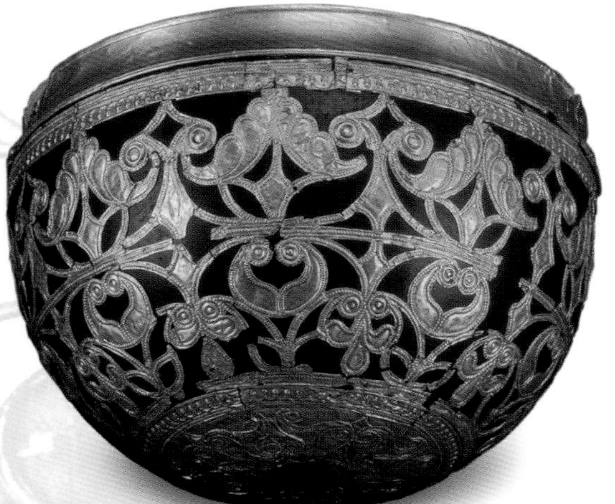

> **‘La Tène art reflects the complex interactions between Iron Age communities and the Roman and Greek world, marking the expression of new identities and symbolic practices.’**
>
> TOM MOORE, LECTURER IN ARCHAEOLOGY, DURHAM UNIVERSITY, 2010

Bowl mount, late 5th century BCE,
Schwarzenbach, Germany
Elements of lotus flower and palmette plant motifs on this openwork gilt bronze mount have been recomposed into a complex pattern designed to fit the curving surface of a wooden bowl. Outlines of embossed dots emphasise each element of the pattern. The bowl had been placed in the burial site of a wealthy individual.

Shield, late 2nd century BCE,
Battersea, London, England
Curling tendrils are visually controlled by triskeles to form flowing patterns of both loose and tight curvilinear design. The embossed curving ornament includes settings of red glass. Made for an aristocratic warrior as an object of display, this shield of La Tène bronze backed with leather or wood had been placed in the River Thames.

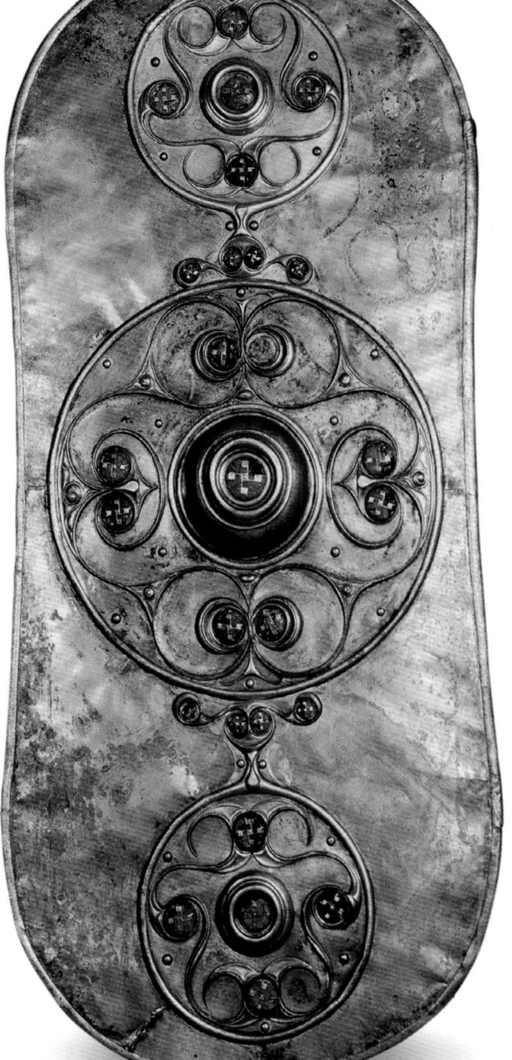

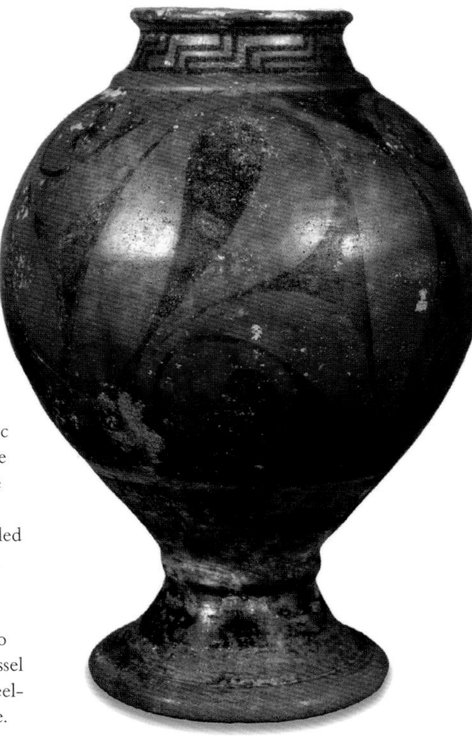

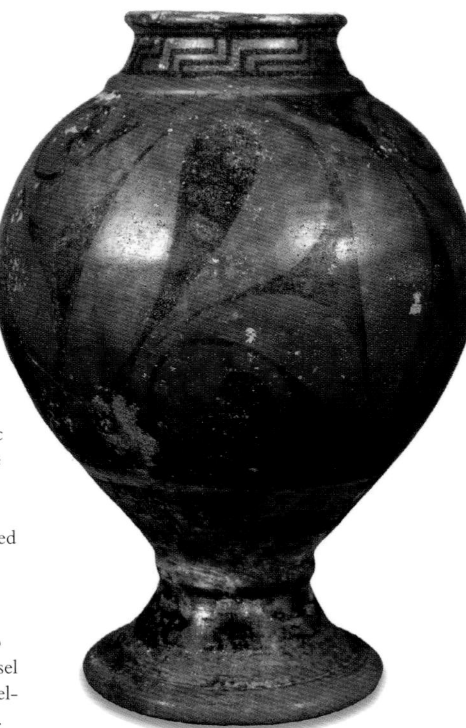

Pottery, 400–350 BCE,
Prunay, Marne, France
The neck of this pot is decorated with a geometric key pattern. In contrast, the pattern on the body of the pot is a repeating double scroll linked by tightly curled ends, based around a series of triskeles. Motifs from contemporary metalwork are here translated into two dimensions. This burial vessel is an example of early wheel-made pottery from Europe.

PATTERN IN DETAIL

Ancient Flower Power

950–900 BCE

Lotus and papyrus – eternal symbols of Egypt

The lotus and papyrus motifs represented plants that were fundamental to ancient Egyptian culture, politics and economy. Their stylised forms developed early in the Dynastic period (c. 3050–332 BCE) and were reproduced in all forms of painting, sculpture and architecture. Their distinctive long stem and flower-head forms provided the structure and decoration for columns and capitals, while the triangular flowers were adapted in various ways for patterning everyday objects, tomb walls and sarcophagi.

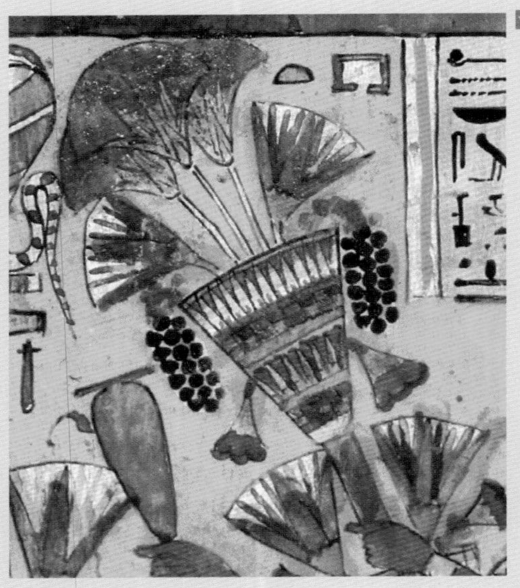

Lotus and papyrus
Lotus and papyrus are offered, in decorated lotus-shaped vessels, to the god Osiris, Egyptian ruler of the underworld. The motifs can be differentiated by the shape of the triangular flower heads – the lotus has the petals and green calyx (surrounding leaves) of the Egyptian white water lily (*Nymphaea lotus*) while the curved leading edge of the papyrus (*Cyperus papyrus*) represents the softer profile of its swaying flowers. Together the papyrus (new and vibrant life) and the lotus (rejuvenation) symbolise an individual's rebirth after death.

Chequered weave
The chequered pattern on Osiris's throne has a separating band between the squares suggesting that it was based on woven material. The characteristic colours – cream, green and terracotta – are combined here with blue-grey, which form the predominant colourings in the sarcophagus painting. Although part of the throne here, the pattern was used extensively as a decorative motif on coffins especially in the Late Period (664–332 BCE).

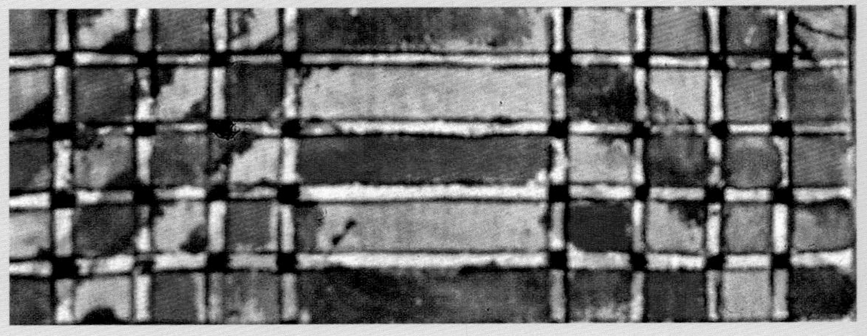

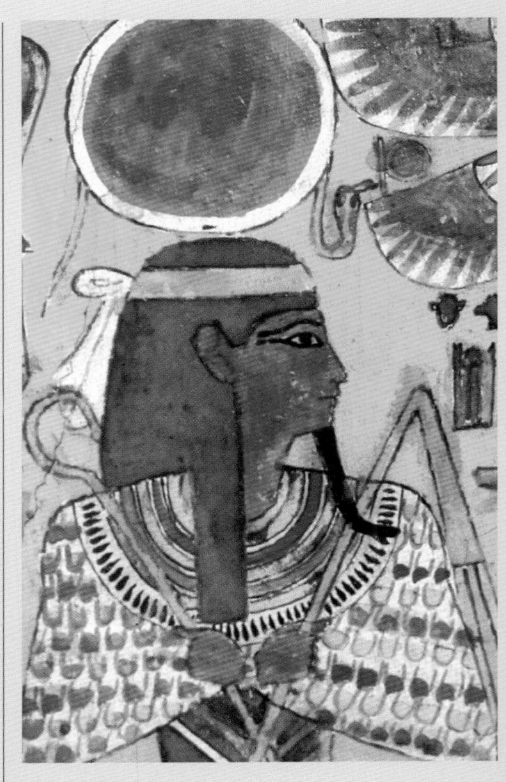

Petal and feather banding
The banded patterning on Osiris's collar is partly made up of the forms of petals laid in rows to create stripes. Underneath is a cape made of feathers, also arranged in rows to emulate the appearance of the wings of a sacred bird. The feather and petal patterns were commonly used as decorative features, especially on anthropomorphic coffins, such as that of Tutankhamen, when the motifs were rendered in inlaid gold.

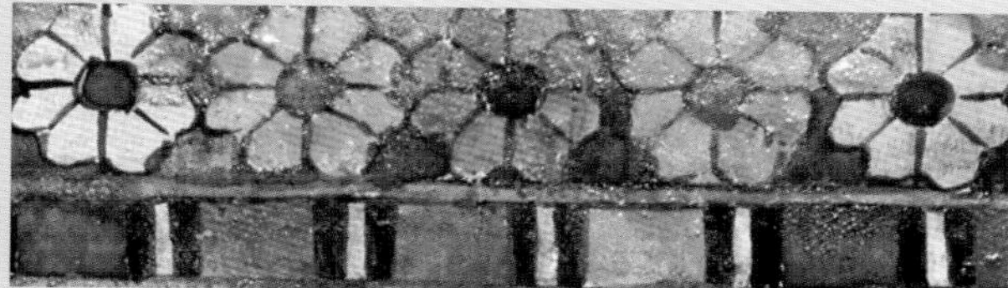

Striped banding
Of the two edging patterns – the rosette and striped ribbon – the latter was a more common decorative feature. The irregularly striped band, with wider bands of colour separated by a black-white-black divider (or white-black-white) was used to frame sacred shrines, jewellery, tomb painting panels and on sarcophagi. The rosette was a less common motif but was sometimes used with interlinked patterns for tomb ceiling decorations.

Wooden sarcophagus, 950–900 BCE
The painted sarcophagus interior shows a figure, probably Ankh-ef-en-khonsu, a high-ranking official from Thebes, dressed in the panther skin of a priest. He is presenting gifts and food to Osiris, who is seated with the symbols of the goddess Wadjet – the cobra and sun, and the Uraeus, the winged rearing cobra – who was the protectress of all Egypt. The scene encompasses characteristic patterns – such as the chevron pattern at the bottom of the panel which was often used to represent the Nile in life or after death – and symbols of the rituals of death and the passage to the afterlife.

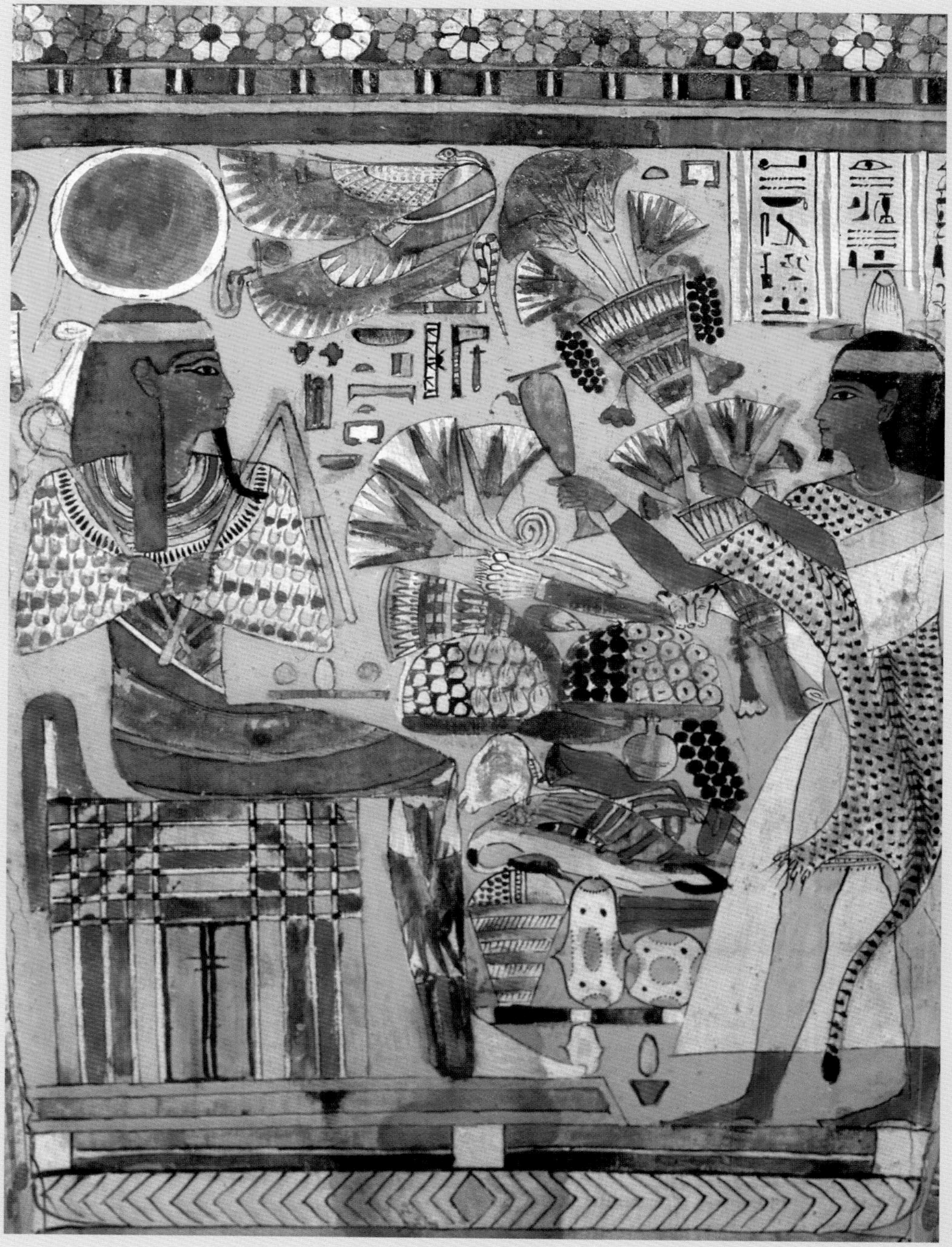

Sacred Fruits & Flowers 934–330 BCE

'Sacred trees' and motifs in neo-Assyria and ancient Persia

The patterns of the neo-Assyrian Empire (934–609 BCE), centred on the Upper Tigris River (in modern Iraq), were symbolic of their divine motif – the 'sacred tree'. Reproduced in imperial palaces, on jewellery or textiles, the 'sacred tree' could include palmette, pine cone or pomegranate motifs, each contributing a powerful symbolism – fertility, unity, regeneration and self-renewal. The ancient Persian Achaemenid Empire (550–330 BCE), centred on the southern Tigris and Euphrates, took on many designs from Assyria – the lotus, palmette, rosette and guilloche (interwoven wavy lines) – and emulated their costumes and textiles.

Carved pavement slab, 704 BCE,
Central Palace, Koyunjik, Nineveh, neo-Assyria
The palace of Koyunjik was built by Sennacherib (704–681 BCE) and this carved pavement slab contains all the pattern elements of neo-Assyrian decoration and symbolism. The outer band contains open lotus flowers, which take many elements from the Egyptian motif, alternating with the lotus bud; the next contains linked palmettes flanked by rows of rosettes; the central square contains a combined pattern of lotus and pine-cone motifs.

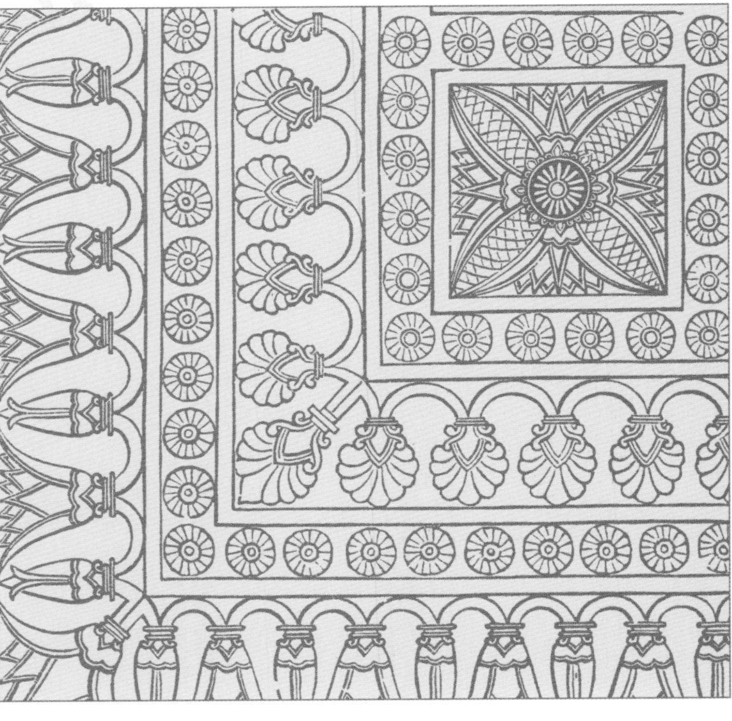

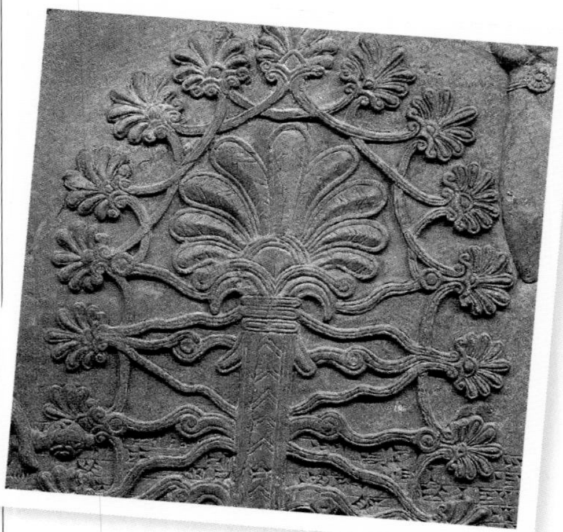

'Sacred tree' carved relief, c. 865 BCE,
Nimrud (Calah), neo-Assyria
The 'sacred tree' from Ashurnasirpal's throne room has a central trunk topped by a large palmette. The surrounding smaller palmettes are linked by ribbons that run between them and the trunk, resembling streams of water. Although the meaning of the 'sacred tree' is unclear, it may play a role in the Assyrian divine world-order and could contain palmettes, pine cones or pomegranates.

> **'The sacred tree was an extremely important symbol ... it may have represented both the king and Ashur, the chief god of Assyria ...'**
>
> METROPOLITAN MUSEUM WEBSITE, NEW YORK, 2010

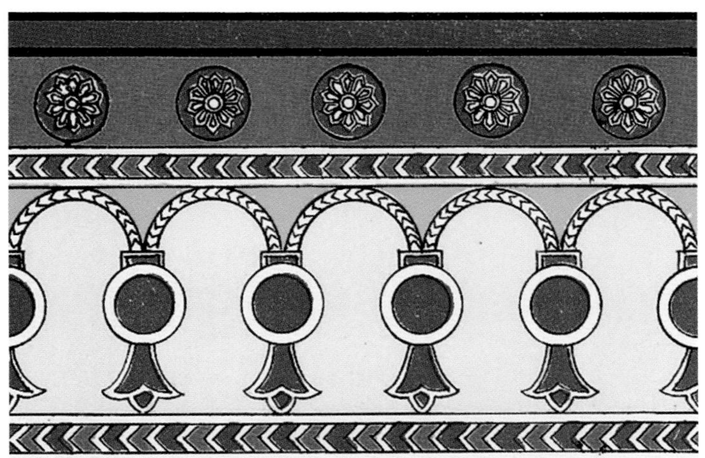

Painted ornaments, 9th–8th century BCE, *Nimrud (Calah)*
The main element of this frieze is another important motif in Assyrian patterns – the immature developing pomegranate (*Punica granatum*) represented by the circular seed casing with a tri-petal flower. The complex rosette in the upper band matching the pomegranate is a circle containing a flower – possibly a representation of the open lotus – sometimes called the *patera*. The bi-colour separating chevron ribbons add movement and flow.

Archers, Palace of Darius I, 522–486 BCE, *Susa, Persia*
This painted tile panel shows the decorated costumes of the Persian Royal Guard with patterned textiles hinting at intricate weaving techniques. These two archers have rosettes and squares on their robes, which have the long form similar to Assyrian costume. The fabric border of each robe is patterned with a circle and zigzag (right) and what might be a pomegranate design (left).

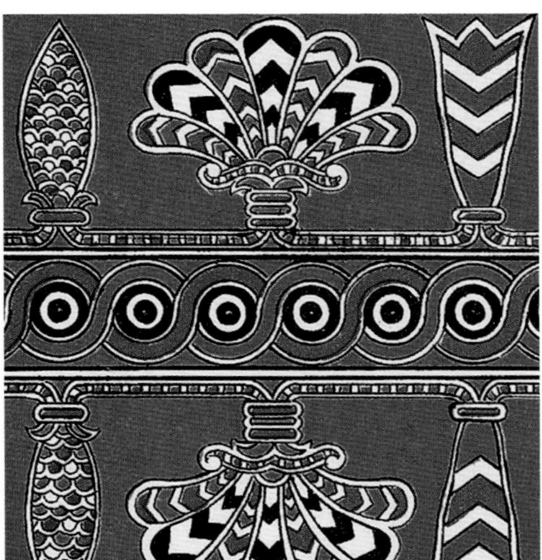

Painted ornaments, 9th–8th century BCE
Drawn during Henry Layard's excavation of the palace of Ashurnasirpal II (884–859 BCE) in Nimrud in 1849, the linked frieze of palmettes, pine cones and opening lotus bud with a central twisted core (guilloche) is comparable to the 'sacred tree'. The blue background colour may have emulated the valuable lapis lazuli or the lighter Egyptian blue pigment found on some neo-Assyrian reliefs.

ELEMENTS OF PATTERN

- *lotus flower and bud frieze*
- *simple rosettes and complex* patera
- *palmettes linked by ribbons*
- *decorated palmettes large and small*
- *pine cones*
- *pomegranate*
- *twist or guilloche*

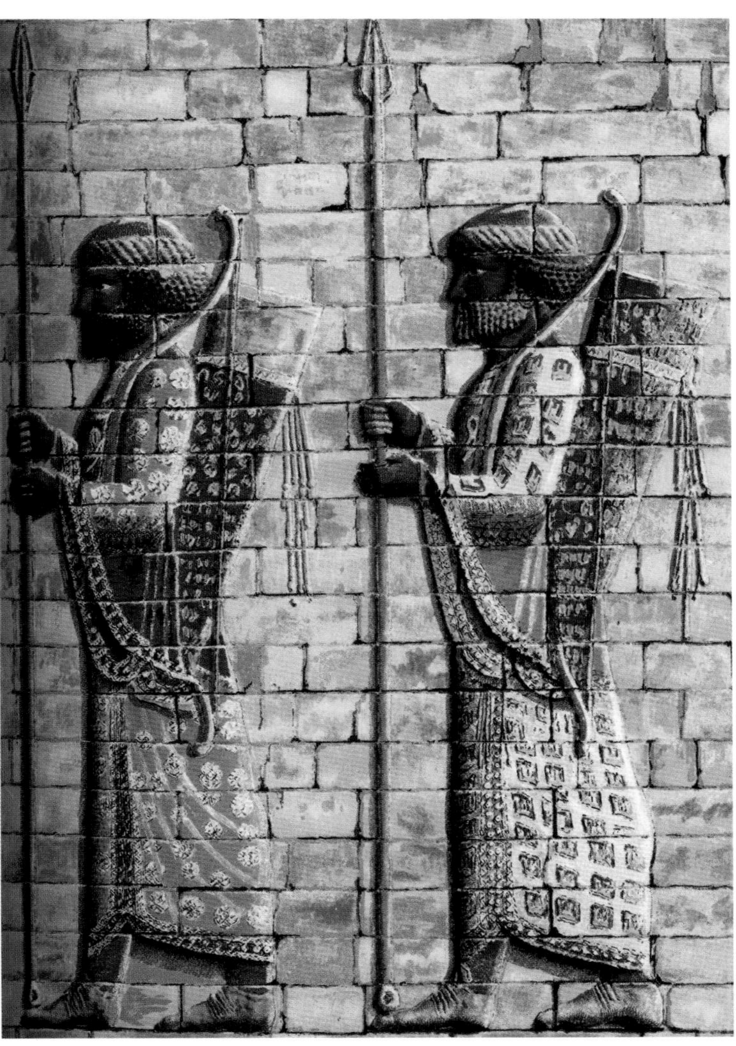

Versatile Monsters & Dragons 1100 BCE–100 CE

Chinese patterns and rituals of death

Patterns decorated vessels found in graves and their form and symbolism were associated with the rituals of death. The stylised face of a fierce imaginary monster – the *taotie* – was used extensively on ritual vessels during the Shang (c. 1500-1050 BCE) and Zhou (1050–221 BCE) dynasties. The *taotie* pattern was incorporated into the design of the vessels, which were themselves designed for specific ritual purposes. In legend, the *taotie* was associated with courage and bravery but also with greediness. In later designs, patterns were drawn from the forms of dragons or snakes, which dwelt in the spirit world between earth and the heavens.

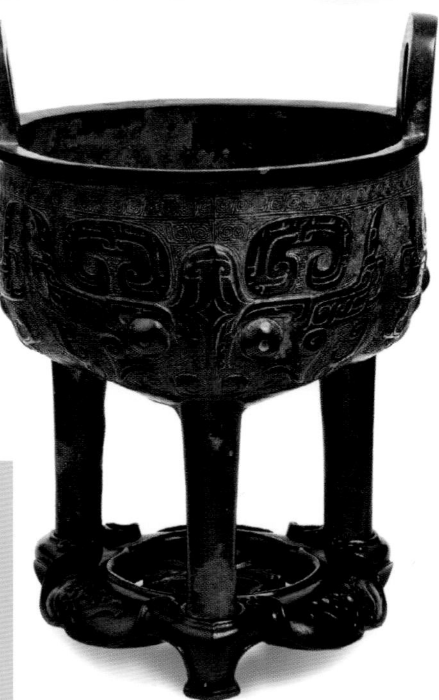

Cast-bronze three-legged vessel (*ding*), 1100–1000 BCE
The *taotie* face is orientated above the legs of the *ding* vessel, which contained food used for ancestors' rites. The eyes are bosses on either side of a stylised nose with prominent nostrils at the top of the leg shaft. Curves and scrolls create and decorate the forehead, eyebrows, horns, beard and mouth. The *taotie* could sometimes resemble a dragon, tiger, deer, sheep, phoenix or human.

ELEMENTS OF PATTERN

- taotie *meaning 'courage' or 'the glutton'*
- *dragon and snake motifs*
- *twisted, writhing two-headed beasts*
- *animals of the spirit world*
- *scrolls, swirls, curls and cusps*

Cast-bronze vessel (*jue*), Shang-Zhou dynasties, 1100–1000 BCE
The decorative patterning of the *taotie* became more complex and intricate as it developed. The different elements of the face merged into a relief of swirls and curves. Here, two *taotie* faces decorate a *jue* vessel with the eyes of one face on either side of the handle. The elaborately patterned horns and mouth are bordered by rows of circles and inlaid with blue pigment.

'Eyes are extremely compelling ... Scrolls and cusps surrounded the eyes, making a symmetrical motif to fill a ... horizontal border.'

JESSICA RAWSON, *The British Museum Book of Chinese Art*, 1992

Unglazed earthenware jar, 2nd–1st century BCE
The central decorated band contains two dragons fighting over a flaming pearl – a symbol of wealth and good fortune. The scaly, sinuous, prancing bodies of the dragons provide a contrast to the stylised *taotie* mask but the dragons' eyes, beards, horns, nostrils and tongues still capture the monster of the spirit world. The jar is also decorated with painted zigzag and vandyke (V-shaped) patterns on the neck.

Cast-bronze wine vessel (*fang hu*), 8th century BCE
Intricately interwoven two-headed snakes or dragons cover this vessel. Overlapping double Z-shaped snakes decorate the top and base alternating with linked, interlaced and twisting forms of snakes. The snake or dragon in Chinese symbolism represented supernatural spiritual power and the complex swirling patterns of their writhing forms were popular during the Eastern Zhou dynasty.

Carved nephrite jade pendant, 4th century BCE
The simplified dragon body carved in jade, without legs, is decorated with curls and swirls to represent scales. The curved shape and detail of the stylised head are reminiscent of the patterning detail of the *taotie*. Jade and bronze were highly valued materials in the 1st millennium BCE, and many of this type of ornament, representing birds, fish or other animals, survive from the period.

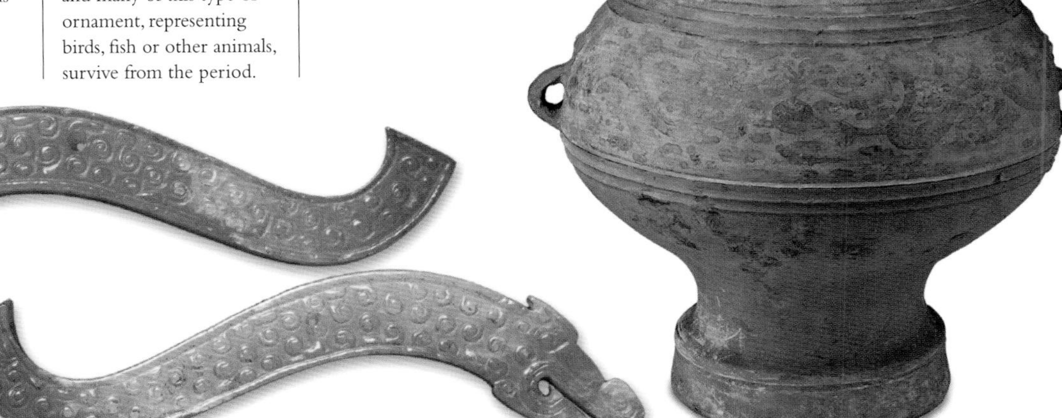

PATTERN IN DETAIL

Patterns of Life & Death 750–700 BCE

Stylised human figures and horses in Athens

Strong geometric patterns in pot decoration reached their peak with the designs produced in the second half of the 8th century BCE in Athens. The sharply angled repeating motifs contrasted with the earlier scroll and swirl designs but most prominent were the stylised human and horse figures used as pattern elements. The human form was reduced to a torso of two triangles, a circular head with a dot and two long, spindly legs, while horses or animals were also composed of simple triangular forms.

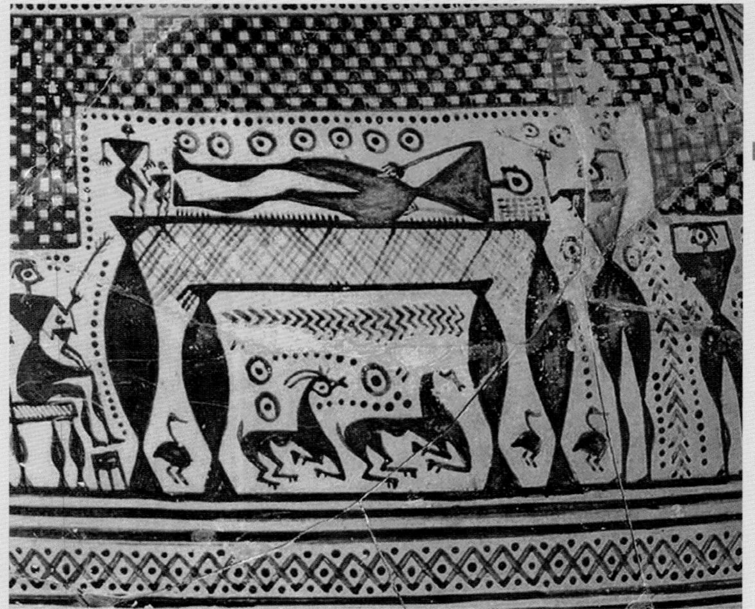

Diamonds and circles
The lower horizontal scenes on the pot show a continuous procession of warriors and chariots. The interspersed dotted circles fill the spaces, as in the funerary scene above, and patterns are formed by the broken circular shields of the warriors. Incidental pattern elements in the frieze include tiers of squares and chevrons which match the pattern banding of diamonds and dots that separate the registers.

Key pattern
The double-interlocking key pattern on the pot's rim, created by the meander of a continuous band, provides the visual language and anchor for the scenes below. The flow of the pattern draws the eye around the decoration following the scenes in a continuous procession. The sharp angles that form the pattern are a development from the circular and curved meanders and swirls used in earlier styles of decoration.

Checks and triangles
The funeral scene of a warrior is encompassed by a chequer-board shroud. Dots, circles and chevrons create a pattern between the stylised mourners and animals surrounding the bier. The lozenge, triangular and circular shapes of the human figures, animals and birds are echoed in the legs of the funerary furniture creating a pattern of their own. The unity of pattern and subject balance the decorative with the emotive.

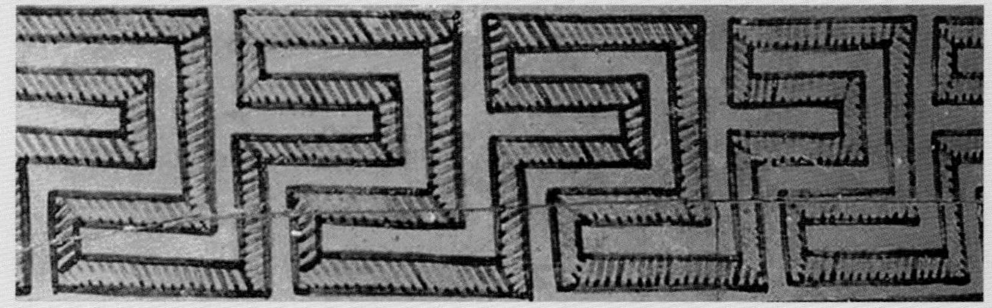

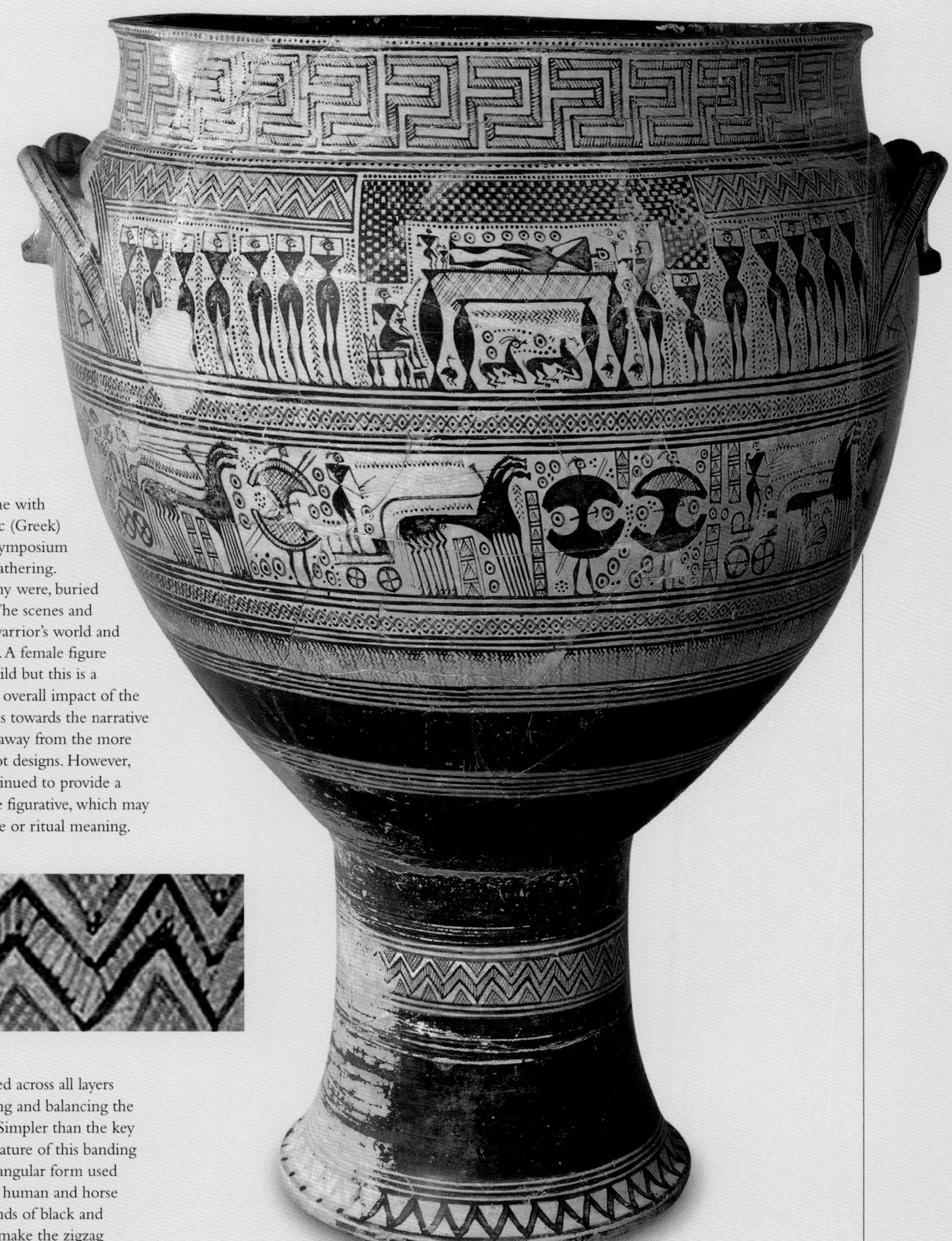

Athenian late geometric *krater*, c. 750 BCE
A *krater* was used to mix wine with water in the ancient Hellenic (Greek) world at events such as the symposium – a male intellectual social gathering. This *krater* was found, as many were, buried with the corpse in a grave. The scenes and patterns illustrate the dead warrior's world and his journey in life and death. A female figure sits beside the bier with a child but this is a male-dominated world. The overall impact of the decoration of this vessel leans towards the narrative scenes of life and death and away from the more patterned forms of earlier pot designs. However, the patterns themselves continued to provide a structure and context for the figurative, which may have had symbolic, protective or ritual meaning.

Zigzag
The zigzag pattern is repeated across all layers of the pot decoration, framing and balancing the visual impact of the design. Simpler than the key pattern, the strong angular nature of this banding nevertheless provides the triangular form used across the pot in the stylised human and horse figures. The tri-coloured bands of black and white against the terracotta make the zigzag visually resonate, strengthening its impact.

Flowers, Leaves & the Labyrinth
480–323 BCE

Architectural and painted patterns in classical Greece

Stylistic experimentation with lotus buds and flowers linked by curving stems led to patterns of alternating lotus with palmettes and motifs with darts. From the mid-6th century BCE, the egg-and-dart and the leaf-and-dart patterns were developed for the capitals of Ionic columns.

In the early 5th century BCE, curling acanthus leaves were added to volutes, or scrolls, on Ionic capitals, giving the aspect of a lush, growing plant. Acanthus leaves were also added to a lotus or palmette to create the *anthemion* ('honeysuckle') motif. Geometric meanders or key patterns developed as important decorative devices. In 5th-century BCE pottery painting they represent the legendary Labyrinth.

'Many patterns belonged to woodwork, but have become more familiar translated and enlarged on to stone architecture.'

SIMON PRICE, *Greece and the Hellenistic World,* 1988

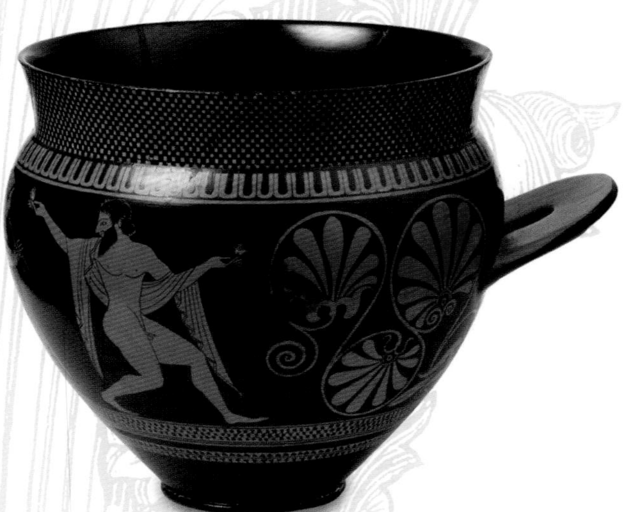

Cup, 520 BCE,
Athens, Greece
A pattern of palmettes is rhythmically linked and enclosed by a curling tendril terminating in a tight scroll that complements the procession of dancing revellers, all depicted in the red-figure technique on earthenware.

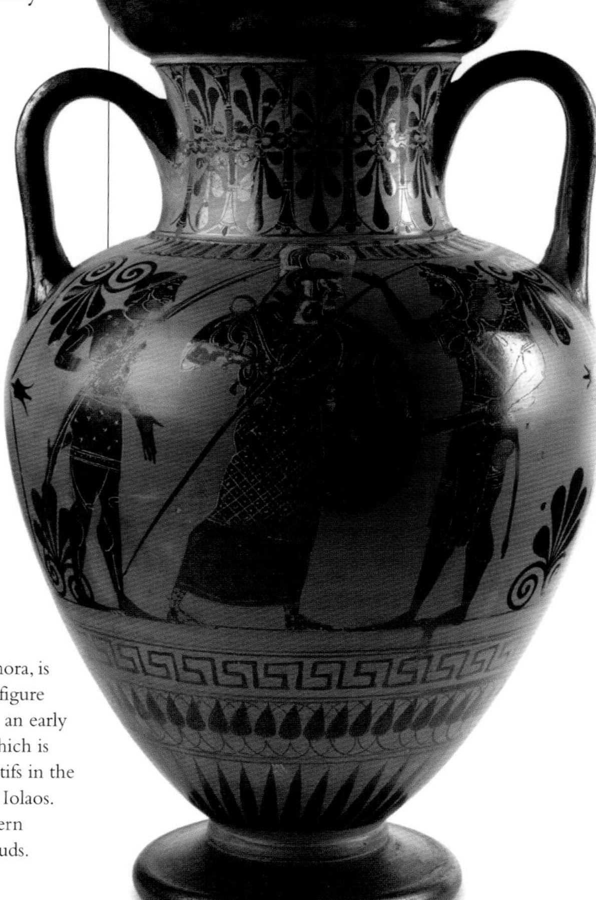

Storage jar, 520–500 BCE,
Athens, Greece
This earthenware storage jar, or amphora, is decorated with patterns in the black-figure technique. On the neck of the vase is an early type of lotus and palmette pattern, which is echoed in the palmette and scroll motifs in the scene below, of Herakles, Athene and Iolaos. Below these figures a simple key pattern surmounts a pattern of linked lotus buds.

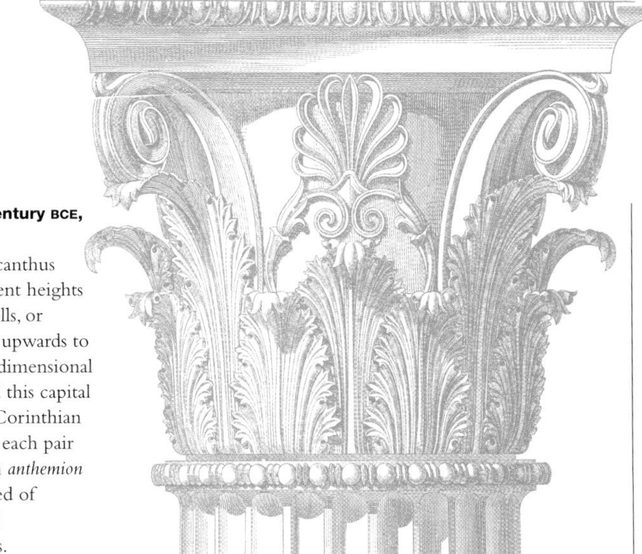

Capital, 4th century BCE, *Greece*
Overlapping acanthus leaves of different heights in front of scrolls, or volutes, spring upwards to create a three-dimensional pattern around this capital carved in the Corinthian style. Between each pair of volutes is an *anthemion* motif composed of a palmette and acanthus leaves.

ELEMENTS OF PATTERN

- *lotus bud and flower*
- *palmette leaves linked by tendrils*
- *acanthus leaves in curling natural shapes animate stone*
- *palmette and acanthus leaves combine to form the* anthemion
- *geometric meander or key borders*
- *swastika meanders*
- *egg-and-dart pattern*

Cup, 440–430 BCE, *Athens, Greece*
A circular band decorated with key patterns and checked motifs encloses the central scene on this red-figure cup. The complexity of the Labyrinth, from which Theseus drags the Minotaur, is further symbolised and emphasised by a pattern on the entrance panel. Swastika meanders, signifying dynamic creative forces around a cosmic centre, alternate with check motifs. Viewed psychoanalytically, this myth portrays overcoming deepest fears and suppressed emotions; depicted on this cup, it perhaps reflects the mind-changing effects of drinking wine.

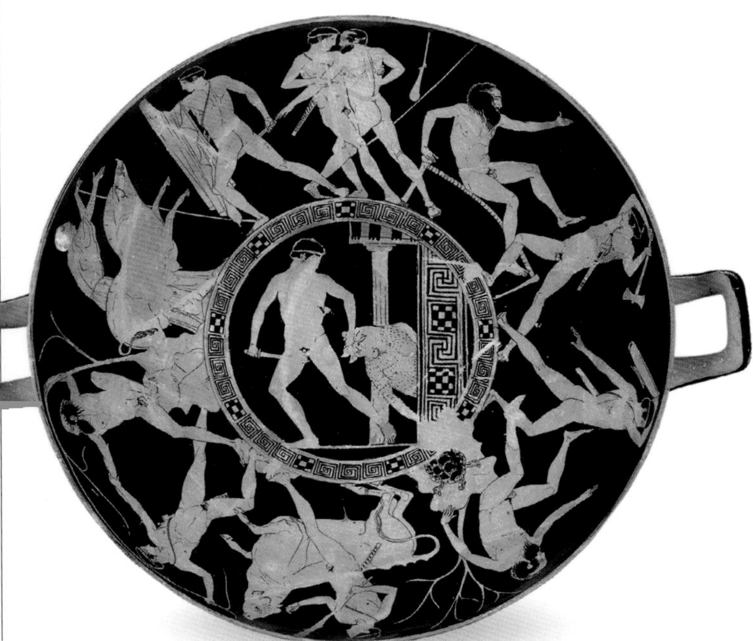

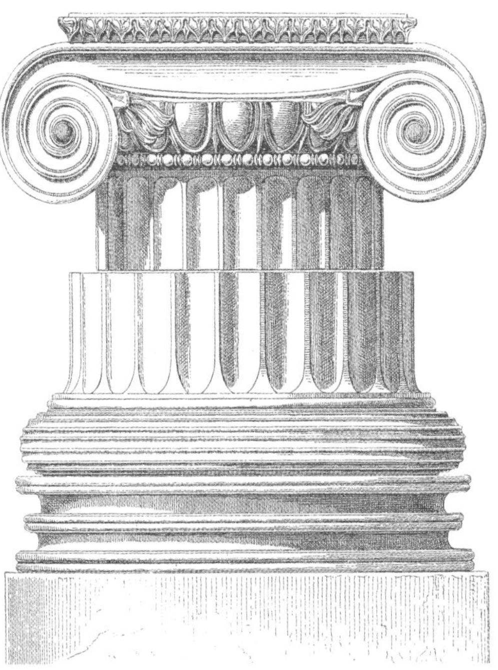

Capital, 334 BCE, Temple of Athene, *Priene, Ionia, Turkey*
The egg-and-dart pattern decorates the convex moulding, called the *ovolo* or *echinus*, between the scrolled volutes of this Ionic capital. This pattern developed from Near Eastern designs of lotus-and-bud motifs in the mid-6th century BCE.

Mirror Patterns 300 BCE–50 CE

Iron-Age mirror art

From around 200 BCE, a network of land and sea routes known as the 'Silk Road' developed through the action of diplomacy and trade to link China to the Mediterranean, extending across the Alps to ports in Europe. Merchants exchanged art and technologies from China, India, Tibet and ancient Persia over a distance of 6,500 km (4,000 miles).

Decorated Iron-Age mirrors from 150 BCE to 50 CE were placed in graves, mostly in southern England where they were made. The patterns of interlocking curvilinear shapes inscribed on their backs may have signified the permeability between worlds glimpsed in the distorted mirror face. Whoever possessed the mirror was perhaps endowed with the insight of a seer.

'The decorated and reflective faces of the mirror plate possess a kind of "inner logic": they metaphorically refer to one another and act to reinforce meaning.'

JODI JOY, *Rethinking Celtic Art*, 2008

Vase (*fanghu*), 300–100 BCE, *China*
This bronze vessel is inlaid with thin shapes of gold and silver. The three strongly contrasting colours of the bronze, silver and gold create an illusion of three dimensions – each can be seen as areas of different emphasis within the design or as a separate pattern woven together with the others. Such containers were put on display to reveal the wealth and prestige of their owners, and were often buried with them.

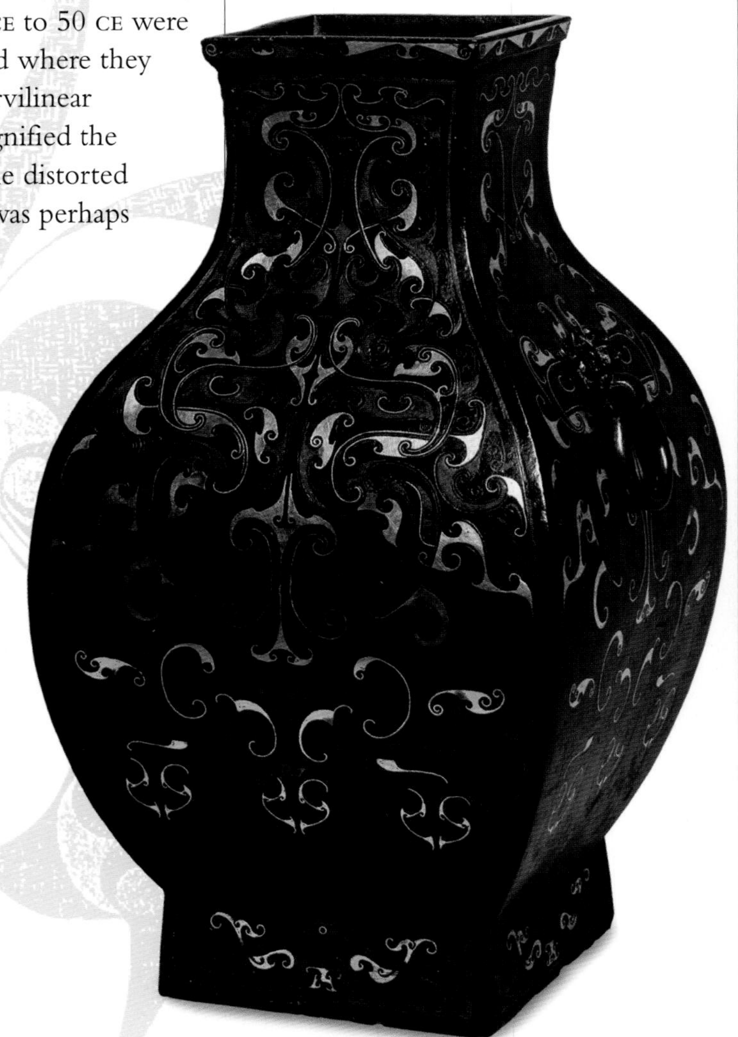

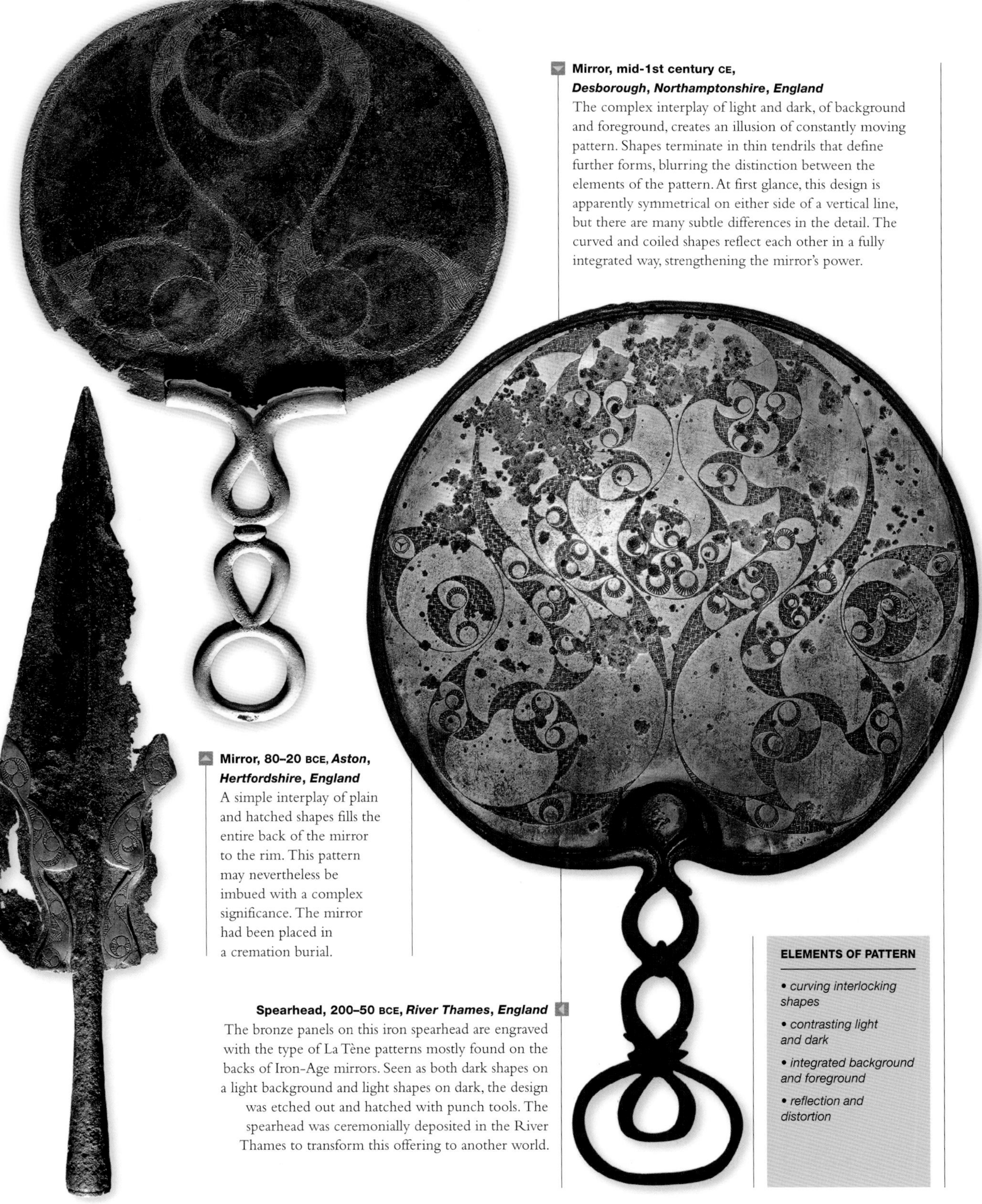

Mirror, mid-1st century CE,
Desborough, Northamptonshire, England
The complex interplay of light and dark, of background and foreground, creates an illusion of constantly moving pattern. Shapes terminate in thin tendrils that define further forms, blurring the distinction between the elements of the pattern. At first glance, this design is apparently symmetrical on either side of a vertical line, but there are many subtle differences in the detail. The curved and coiled shapes reflect each other in a fully integrated way, strengthening the mirror's power.

Mirror, 80–20 BCE, *Aston, Hertfordshire, England*
A simple interplay of plain and hatched shapes fills the entire back of the mirror to the rim. This pattern may nevertheless be imbued with a complex significance. The mirror had been placed in a cremation burial.

Spearhead, 200–50 BCE, *River Thames, England*
The bronze panels on this iron spearhead are engraved with the type of La Tène patterns mostly found on the backs of Iron-Age mirrors. Seen as both dark shapes on a light background and light shapes on dark, the design was etched out and hatched with punch tools. The spearhead was ceremonially deposited in the River Thames to transform this offering to another world.

ELEMENTS OF PATTERN

- *curving interlocking shapes*
- *contrasting light and dark*
- *integrated background and foreground*
- *reflection and distortion*

Scrolls & Intricate Meanders 13 BCE–79 CE

Early Roman Empire mosaics, sculpture and wall painting

Patterns adorned all types of Roman buildings from temples to baths, from imperial palaces to seaside villas. The acanthus and other vegetal forms were symbolic of fertility and immortality, while elaborate scrolls, meanders and geometric puzzles were formed from intersecting and overlapping circles, triangles, squares and hexagons. The wall paintings and mosaics of Pompeii and Herculaneum, preserved for nearly 2,000 years under the volcanic ash of Vesuvius, provide an idea of the importance of pattern to Roman culture and daily life. Intricate geometric designs contrast with fine vegetal, floral and animal patterns in vibrant colours.

House of the Vettii, 62–79 CE, watercolour by Luigi Bazzani (1897), *Pompeii, Italy*

These fine wall paintings combine delicate vegetal scrolls with fantastic sculptural and architectural details. The Vitruvian, or running-wave scrolls (after Vitruvius, the 1st-century-CE Roman author of the book *Architecture*) border the upper edge, and patterns of tracery plants, scrolls, arches with palmettes, beading and grotesques decorate the imaginary structure. This design was classified as the 'Fourth or Intricate style' of Roman wall painting by the art historian August Mau (1840–1909).

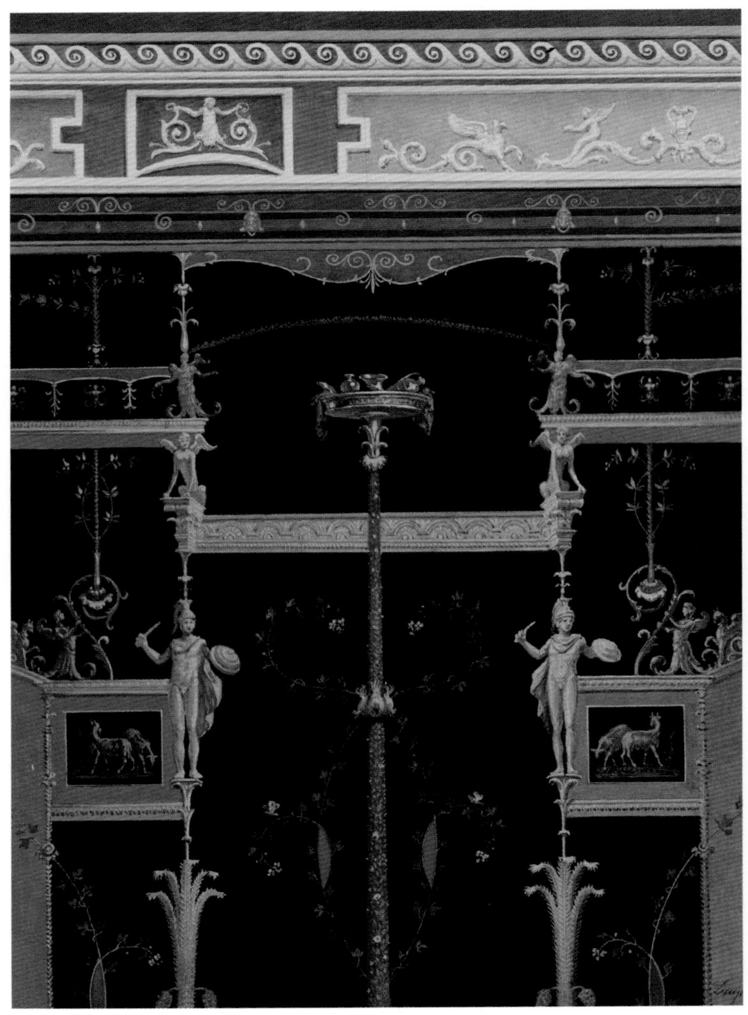

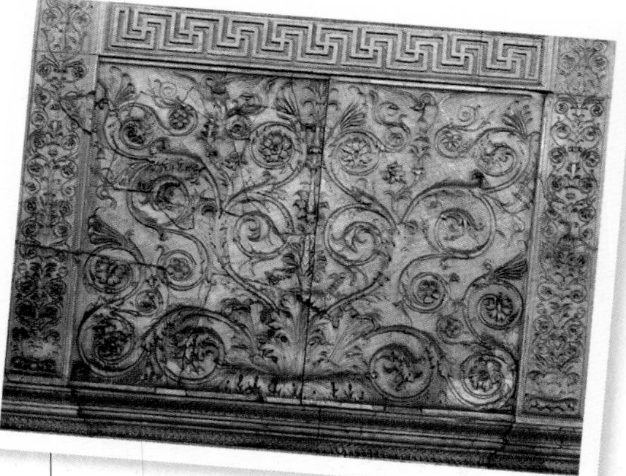

Ara Pacis Augustae (Altar of Augustan Peace), 13–9 BCE, *Rome, Italy*

In the central panel and pilasters, scrolling tendrils issue from a base of acanthus leaves in mirror-image patterns, each tendril ending with a different plant, fruit or flower. Animals appear in the vegetation, for example, the swans at the top on each side of the plant. Built to commemorate the Augustan Peace after Augustus's military victories, the decorative scheme signifies divine blessing on the Augustan order.

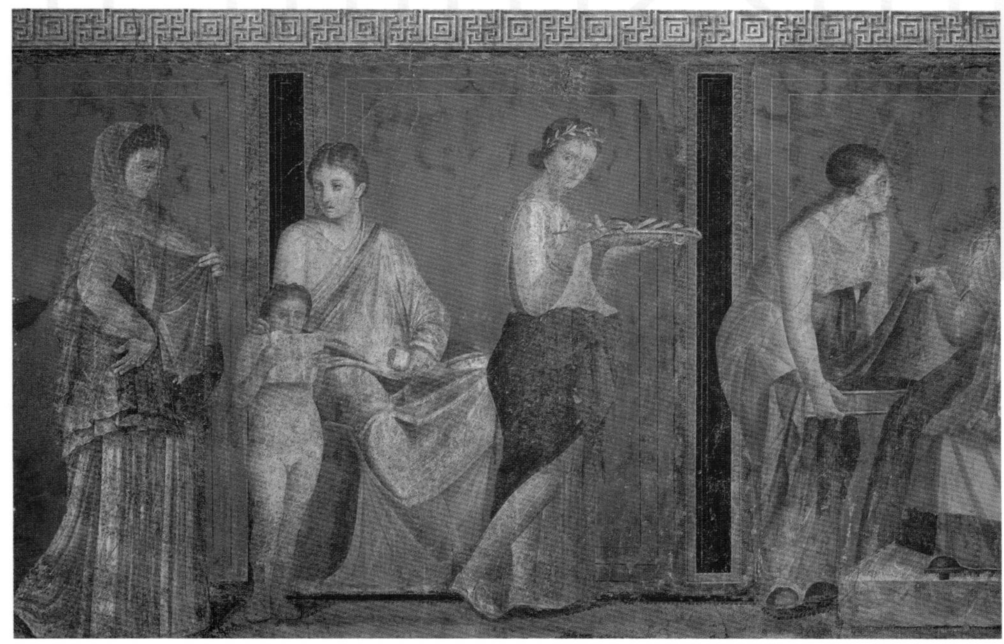

Villa of Mysteries, 62–79 CE, *Pompeii, Italy*
Even in this narrative scene, showing a boy reading to a matron and a girl carrying a tray, part of a full frieze covering all the walls in the room, the image is bordered with a complex key pattern of combined meander, swastika and squares. The matron on the left wears a striped robe and the background is repeating rectangles in red, green, gold and brown – colours used throughout Pompeii.

'Pompeian painters produced ... elegantly restrained two-colour designs to multi-coloured virtuoso displays of illusionism.'

MARY BEARD AND JOHN HENDERSON,
Classical Art From Greece to Rome, 2001

ELEMENTS OF PATTERN

- *Vitruvian scrolls, running spirals, wave or running dog*
- *key pattern and meander*
- *swastikas*
- *triangles, squares and hexagons*
- *lily and palmettes*
- *twist or guilloche*
- *acanthus and vegetal scrolls*
- *grotesques*

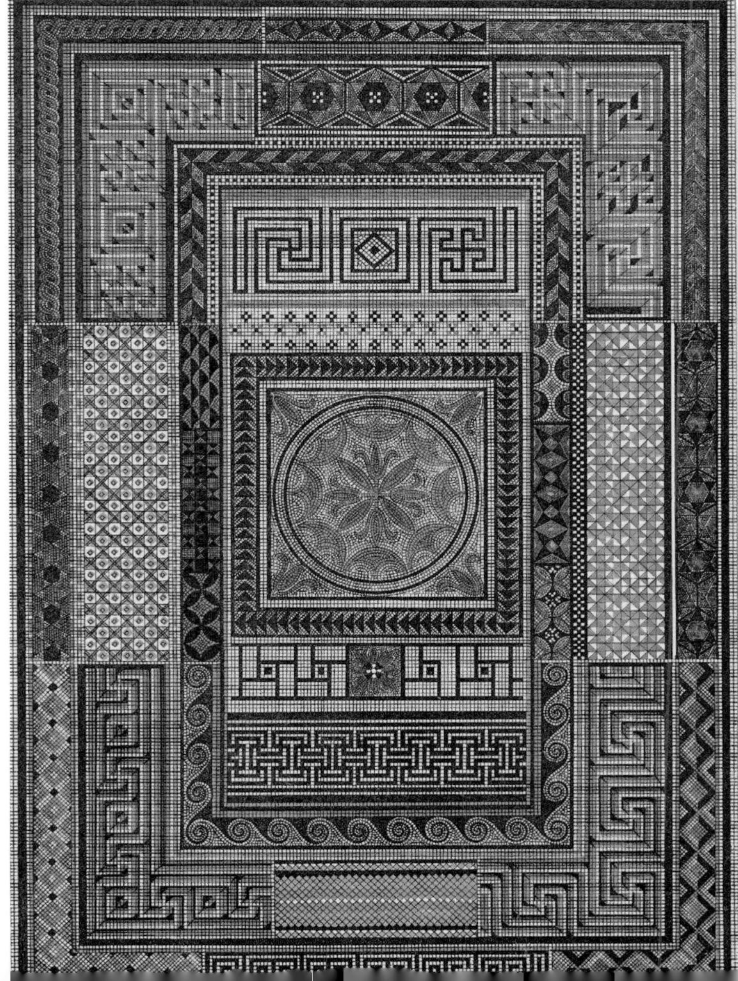

Mosaics, before 79 CE, *Pompeii, Italy*
This collage illustrates a wide range of geometric patterns used in Roman design. This includes forms of chequer-boards and squares; key patterns with meanders, swastikas and squares, some subdivided into triangles or simulating a 3D effect; bi-coloured running patterns with triangles and rhomboids; the running wave or Vitruvian scrolls; triangles and hexagons; intersecting circles; and in the centre, an intricate pattern of lilies and peltae.

PATTERN IN DETAIL

Intriguing Borders 100–400 CE

Roman mosaics

The complex, distracting and visually absorbing patterns surrounding pictorial scenes in Roman mosaic floors engaged the viewer who was crossing into a particular interior space. They incorporated protective devices associated with the idea of boundaries and the threshold – that stepping through a doorway and into a room involved averting the 'evil eye' through the intricacy of design. Chosen to be complementary to the narrative scenes they enclosed, these patterns conveyed ideas about inclusion and exclusion in Roman society.

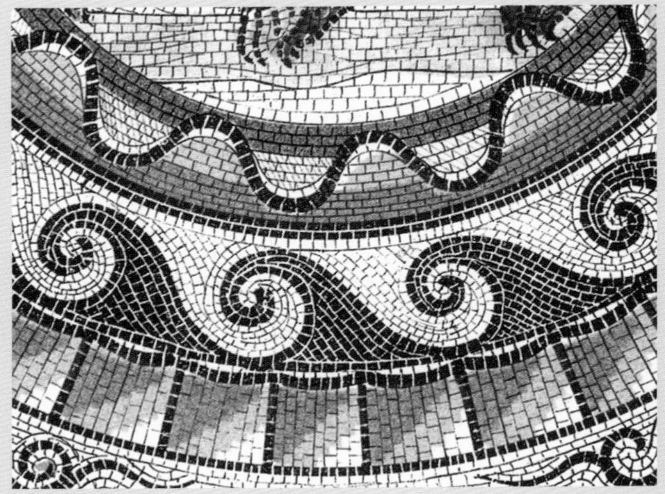

Lozenge and peltae

The shield-shaped motifs of lozenge and pelta have protective qualities, which are magnified when they are combined with central guilloche-link devices. The repetition of highly apotropaic (intended to ward off evil) composite forms is common in 3rd-century mosaics from Germany, and particularly Trier.

Awning, waves, undulating band

Encircling the central scene of Bacchus reclining upon a tigress are three concentric bands of ornament. A shaded 'awning' pattern encircles a series of interlocking dark grey and white waves with scrolled ends. They enclose an undulating line running through rings of different colours that change to either side of the curve.

Guilloche

This rippling round-tongued, double-strand guilloche is shaded to provide a three-dimensional effect. This rippling pattern directs the eye of the viewer in a single direction.

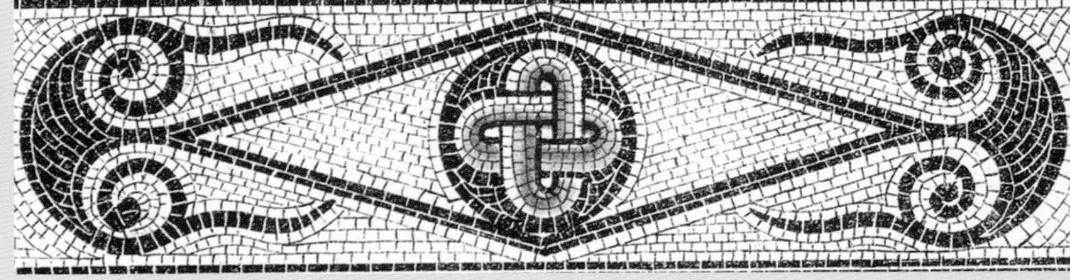

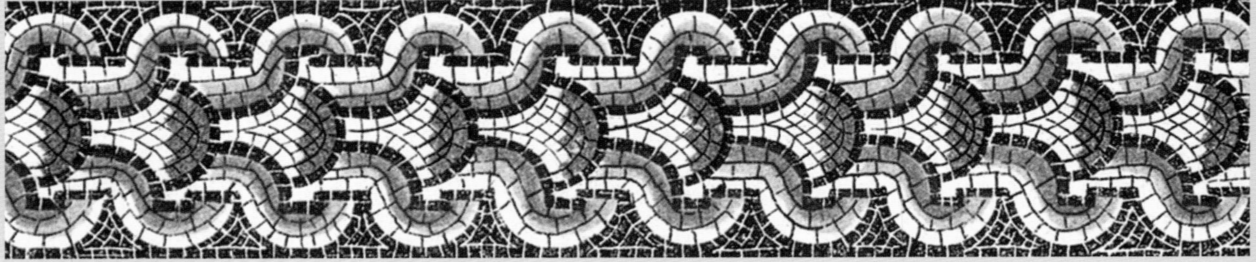

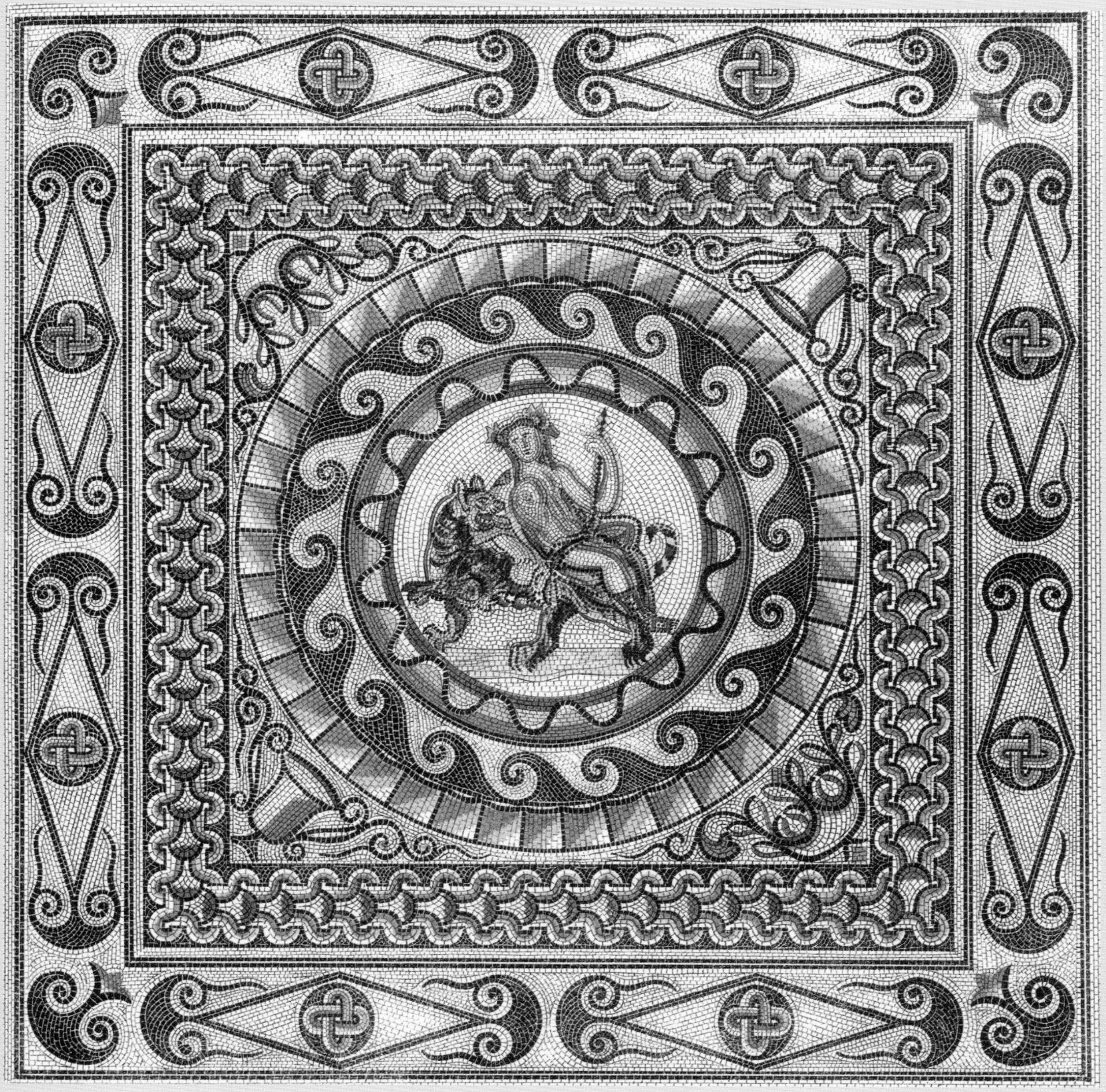

Guilloche-link
Forming the visual illusion of a knot, this motif is composed of two separate loops. Creating the visual centre of the composite lozenge-peltae pattern, it is imbued with symbolic force.

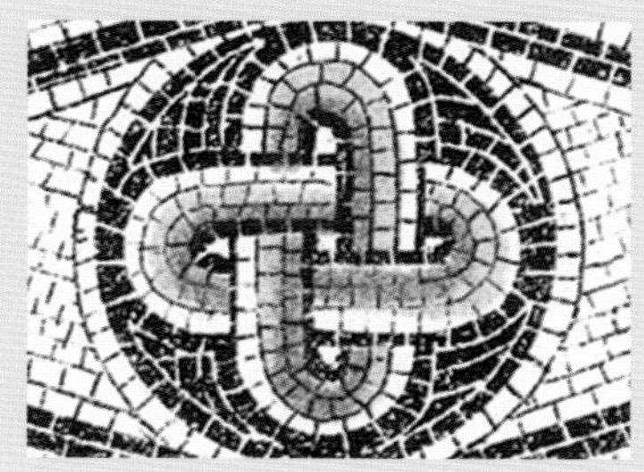

Town-house mosaic, 3rd century CE,
Leadenhall Street, London
Elaborate borders of lozenge-peltae motifs and guilloche interlace and circling patterns of 'awning', waves and undulating bands enclose the central scene of an intoxicated Bacchus reclining on a tigress. The floor of a formal reception room used for entertaining and dining, this mosaic was commissioned by a wealthy official or merchant for a substantial town house. The design, or the mosaicist who produced it, may have been commissioned from a source in Germany.

300
700

Early Medieval

Introduction

The dissemination and exchange of design elements in contexts of rich patronage helped to increase the interaction and recycling of motifs across cultural territories and through time. Patterns were closely integrated with both the forms of objects for which they were designed and also the media in which they were created.

At the end of the 4th century, the animal motifs on Roman bronze metalwork, such as military buckle-plates, were reworked by Germanic craftworkers into a new artistic concepts and identities. The late Roman animal forms were broken up into body parts and recomposed in a stylised way that allowed them to be integrated as new patterns. During the 5th and 6th centuries, under the rule of Childeric and his descendants, the Merovingian Franks became the main successors to the Romans in western Europe. During the 6th century, interlace was incorporated into Germanic animal design from Mediterranean art, resulting in patterns of complex dynamic convolutions.

Early Christian church decoration included pattern elements with pre-Christian origins, such as vegetal scrolls and key patterns. The acanthus or plant scroll 'tree of life' developed

Daoist imagery involved the complex mixing of animals, script and circular forms that reflected concepts of cosmic order. The patterns were used as decorative filling or to support the main religious themes.

from both Near Eastern and Roman concepts of the 'sacred tree'. Other symbols were reinvested with specifically Christian meanings, such as the cross and tripartite motifs, the latter symbolising the Holy Trinity. The association of the Byzantine imperial motif of bands of simulated jewels and pearls with Christian imagery linked the emperor closely to Christ. In 768 Charlemagne became king of the Franks, under whose rule the arts and education flourished. Elements of classical, Germanic and Christian design were combined during this 'Carolingian Renaissance' to create new types of designs for a wide range of artforms and media.

The Near Eastern, perhaps Sasanian, metalworking skill of inlaying semi-precious stones and glass into cells of flattened wire fused to a metal sheet was widespread in the Roman Empire. Known as *cloisonné* work, the technique was brought westwards by Germanic peoples crossing the Rhine during the 5th century, and was used to decorate jewellery, buckles, chalices and prestigious weapons. Patterns of the Sasanian Empire drew on decorative forms from earlier cultures in the region, including Assyrian, and spread into Europe and Asia. Complex unified motifs created decorative models that were imitated in the Byzantine Empire, Merovingian France, Central Asia and China. Simple circular pattern forms were closely linked to the rich materials used, such as carved crystal, precious metalwork and glass. The designs are linked to ancient Persian and Assyrian motifs but also to those in the Byzantine cultural sphere.

The prominent Asian religions of Buddhism and Daoism both sought, in different ways, a form of personal development towards salvation or enlightenment. Buddhist art often exploited the lotus, which was significant for its symbolic meaning of purity and enlightenment. In Buddhist art the lotus flower was represented with a more bulbous form than the Egyptian motif and rounded petals.

Vibrant interlace style was expressed by Germanic craftworkers throughout western and central Europe, in Scandinavia (Danes, Swedes and Norse), England (Anglo-Saxons), France and Belgium (Merovingian Franks, Visigoths and Burgundians), the Netherlands (Frisians), Germany (Alemanni, Thuringians and Saxons) and Italy (Ostrogoths).

Patterns of Cosmic Design 100–700

Pattern elements in Buddhist and Daoist Asian art

The religions of Asia and China used pattern features in different ways to decorate their deities and symbolise cosmic ideals and the search for enlightenment. For Daoism (Taoism) – one of the indigenous religions in China, *dao* meaning 'the way' to personal salvation and immortality – patterns surround and encompass the linked elements of the cosmos. The highly decorated cave paintings of Dunhuang, discovered around 1900, are some of the only surviving evidence of the true nature of the elaborate patterning of Buddhist art in China. A key element included the lotus flower, symbolising purity and enlightenment.

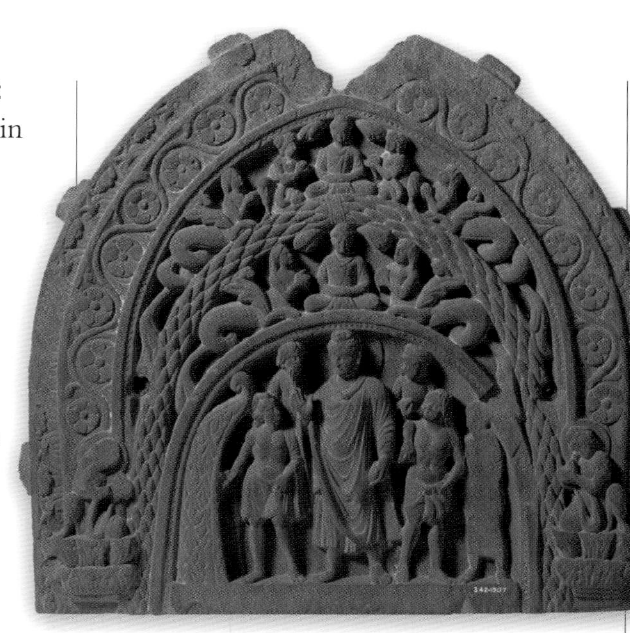

Bronze mirror with black patina, 1st–2nd century (Late Han Dynasty), *China*

Vegetal scrolls, zigzags, ridging and Chinese text surround decorated bosses and fabulous animals of Daoist mythology. These possibly include the Daoist Four Divinities – Azure Dragon of the East, White Tiger of the South, Vermilion Bird of the West and Dark Warrior of the North. Mirrors were important in Daoist mysticism, offering a light source for the journey to the afterlife, with the circular imagery representing the cosmological order.

Relief panel, grey schist, 3rd century, *Gandhara, Pakistan*

The relief panel of scenes from the life of Buddha is edged with bands of leaf and rosette scroll patterns. There are three registers – the upper two separated by a raised torus (semicircular convex moulding) decorated with overlapping lotus petals. The scenes of Buddha show him with his worshippers and an ascetic, while in the lowest register he is seen rejecting orthodox Brahmanical teaching.

> **'The elaborate scenes ... include solar and lunar heavens, narratives of the life of the historical Buddha, and scenes of the Western Paradise, the Pure Land in which Buddhist devotees could hope to be reborn.'**
>
> CRAIG CLUNAS, *Art in China,* 1997

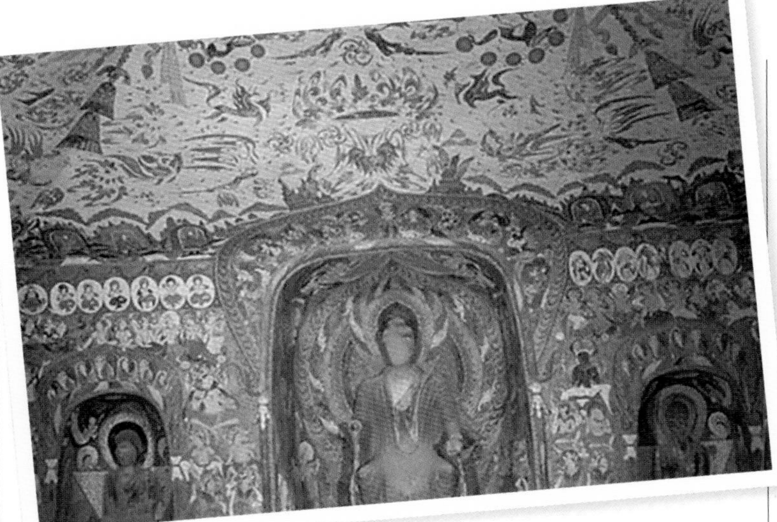

Sculpture and mural paintings, Tang dynasty, c. 538–39, Cave 285, *Dunhuang, China*
The colouring and patterning of this shrine illustrates the vibrancy of Buddhist murals. One of hundreds of decorated cave temples in Dunhuang, the patterns include flames, lotus, scrolls and swirls around the Buddha with rows of medallions and niches containing other Buddha figures. On the ceiling, deities are seen among plants, wheels and bells while every surface is filled with shapes and patterns in 11 colours including blues, greens and reds.

ELEMENTS OF PATTERN

- *zigzags, diamonds and hatching*
- *vegetal scrolls, leaves and flowers*
- *the lotus*
- *animals, birds and deities*

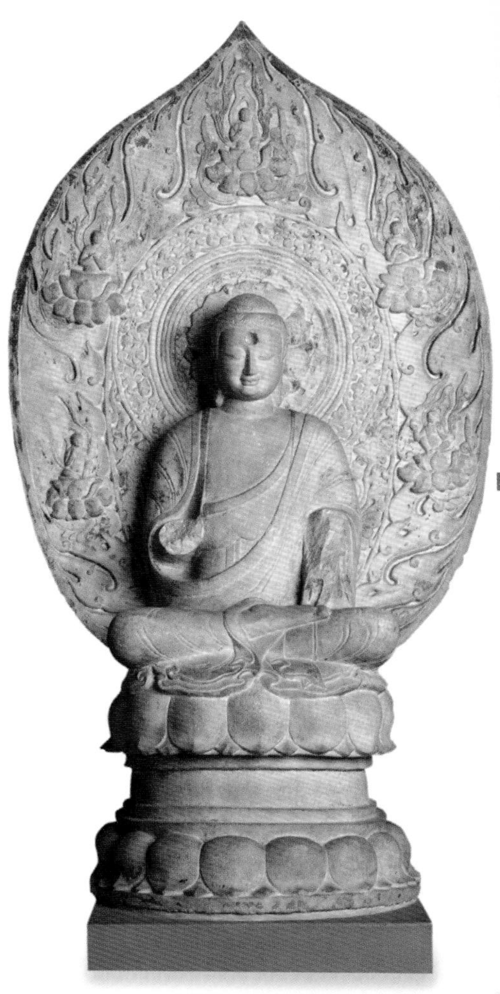

Seated Buddha, 550–77, *Quyang, China*
Buddha's halo has a floral and leaf-scroll pattern band with an inner circle of lotus petals. This is set against a panel of swirling flames containing smaller floating Buddhas. Each Buddha is sitting on a lotus flower throne represented by two tiers of petals. The sculpture would have been vibrantly coloured, including red and green elements, which would have emphasised the pattern detail.

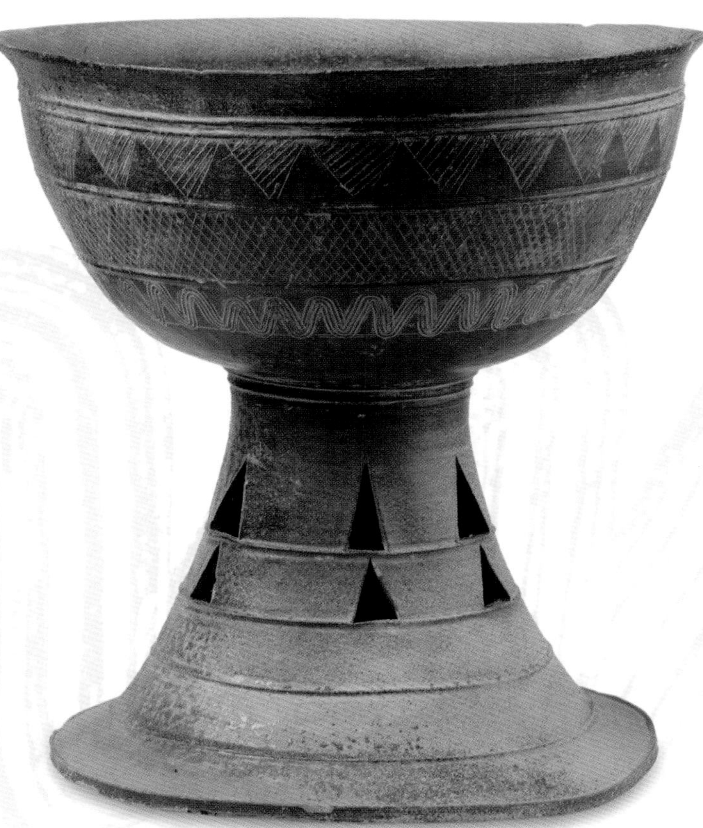

Pedestal vessel, 400–600, *Korea*
The potter's wheel and high-firing kilns arrived in Korea around 300, leading to the development of fine and complex stoneware, such as this pedestal vessel, and allowing for delicate incised, pierced and raised patterning. The zigzag, hatched, wave and cut patterns on this vessel provide a simple but elegant decoration for a tomb vessel, which is possibly from the states of Kaya or Silla, in the southeast.

Symbols of Power & Wealth 224–651

Patterns of the Sasanian Empire

The patterns of the Sasanian (Achaemenid) Empire drew on decorative forms from earlier cultures in the region including the Assyrian Empire (934–609 BCE). Materials such as silver, gold, bronze, semi-precious and precious stones provided rich surfaces for decoration, and patterns reproduced on glass and textiles later spread into Europe and Asia. Patterns drawn from plants and animals provided the foundational forms but complex unified motifs created decorative models that were imitated in the Byzantine Empire (330–1453), Merovingian France (c. 457–751), Central Asia and China.

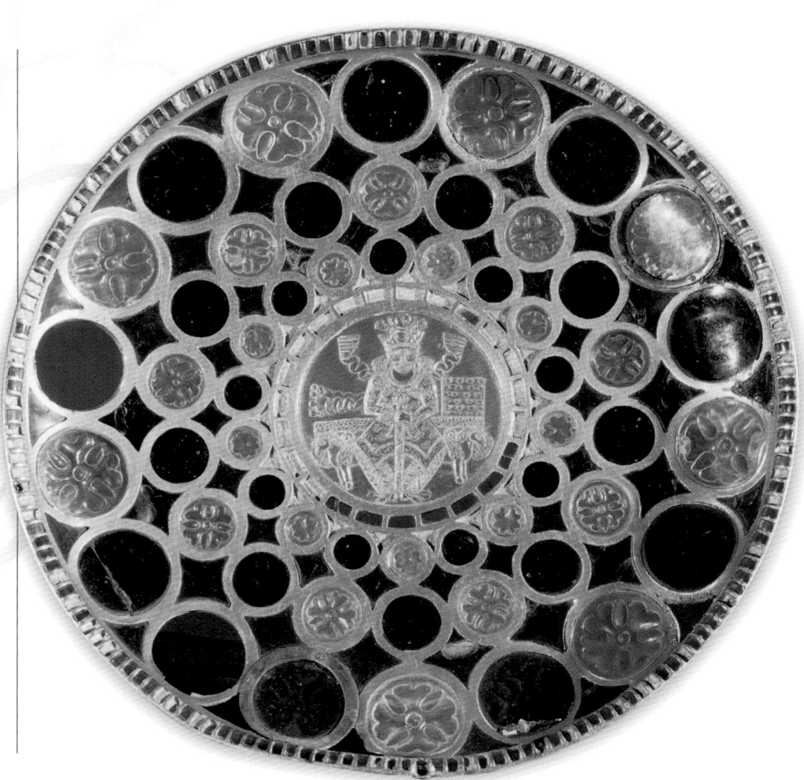

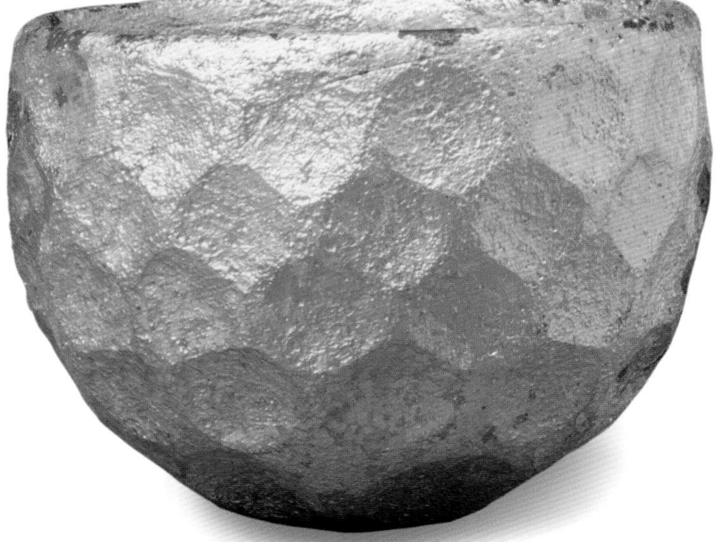

Glass bowl, 6th century, *Iran*
This glass bowl is a faceted hemisphere with the outer glass surface cut into hollow circles forming a honeycomb pattern. The cutting technique used on precious and semi-precious stones was commonly applied to glass in this way in pre-Islamic Iran. The iridescent patina was caused by changes resulting from burial but the original bowl would have had the reflective and sparkling qualities of a faceted jewel.

The Khosrau dish, 531–79, *Iran*
Made of crystal and garnet discs set in gold circles and cut with rosettes so they would glitter in the light, this dish would have been highly prized and possibly used at royal banquets. The alternating colours and circles form interlocking star patterns surrounding the central image of the Sasanian king, Khosrau I (531–79), enthroned and richly decorated with trefoil, swirl and diamond patterns.

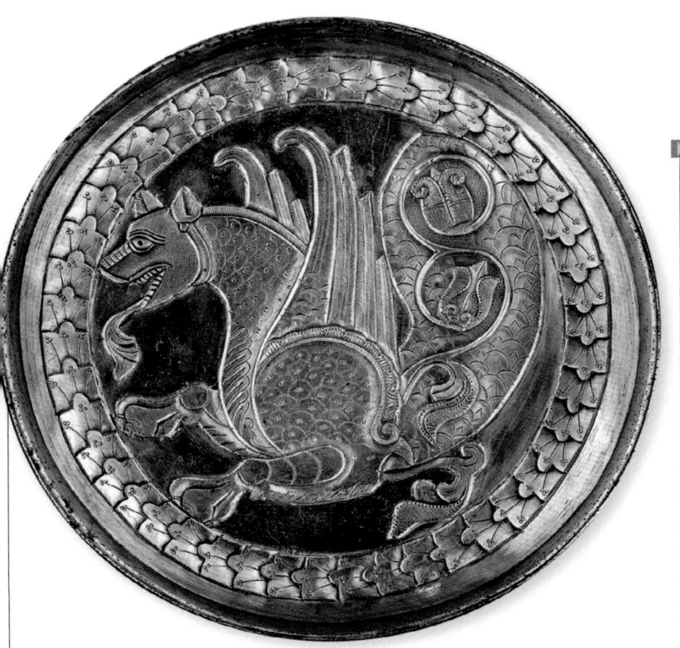

Cast-bronze ewer, 7th century, *Iran*

The simple teardrop pattern used to decorate the main body of this ewer emulates the textured forms created on Sasanian glassware. Together with the notched and ridged base, neck and lip of the ewer, the pattern creates a raised surface decoration that would have enriched the look and feel of the jug. Its handle, typically, takes the form of a rampant animal with its mouth and front paws clasping the rim.

Gilded silver plate, 7th century, *Iran*

The plate's leaf-pattern edging is decorated with three stems ending in three small balls. The central animal is an ancient mythical dog-headed bird commonly called the *senmurv* or *simurgh*. This circular motif appears from the Late Sasanian period (6th century) and was used extensively as a roundel pattern in textiles. Symbolic of royal power, purity or fertility, the *simurgh*'s scaly tail is decorated with a vegetal scroll.

'Sasanian art exported its forms and motifs eastward into India, Turkestan and China, westward into Syria, Asia Minor, Constantinople, the Balkans, Egypt and Spain.'

WILL DURANT, *The Story of Civilisation Volume 4: The Age of Faith*, 1950

ELEMENTS OF PATTERN

- *rosettes and circles*
- *stars and diamonds*
- *trefoils, overlapping leaves and palmettes*
- *swirls and vegetal scrolls*
- *arches*
- see also *Magnificent Medallions*, pages 60–1

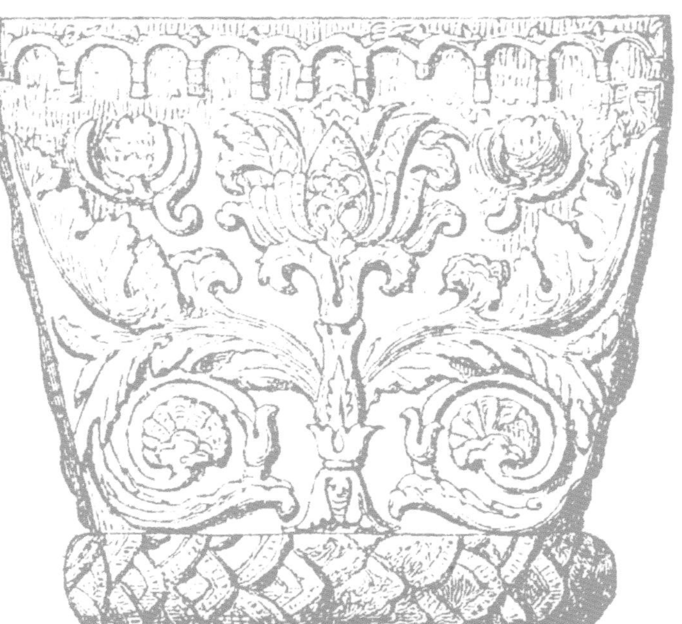

Sasanian capital *Isfahan, Iran*

Decorated with a form of acanthus scroll culminating in vegetal, pine-cone and palmette features, this form of elaborate capital design was found in ancient Isfahan (Esfahān, Iran), one of the main cities in the Sasanian Empire. Drawing on motifs from the Assyrian 'sacred tree,' the capital sits on a cushion with an overlapping leaf pattern and has an upper border of arches.

Cross-Cultural Designs 500–800

Merovingians and Carolingians

Ribbon animal interlace patterns in the Germanic tradition, the late Roman technique of chip-carving metal with angled tools to create glittering surfaces, and influences ultimately from the Near East were all combined in Merovingian Frankish art. In the later 8th century, Charlemagne's patronage encouraged the development of lavish styles and patterns for metalwork, manuscript painting and for carving in ivory, wood and stone. The acanthus leaf motif was introduced to Germanic art during this 'Carolingian' period from classical sources, creating important designs and patterns for manuscripts and ivory carving. These lush curling plant designs strongly influenced Anglo-Saxon style in the 10th century, particularly in English manuscript painting.

'The Franks had so quickly adopted a Mediterranean Romance role and language that by about 800 they had become in effect an extension of the Mediterranean world.'

DAVID M. WILSON,
The Northern World, 1980

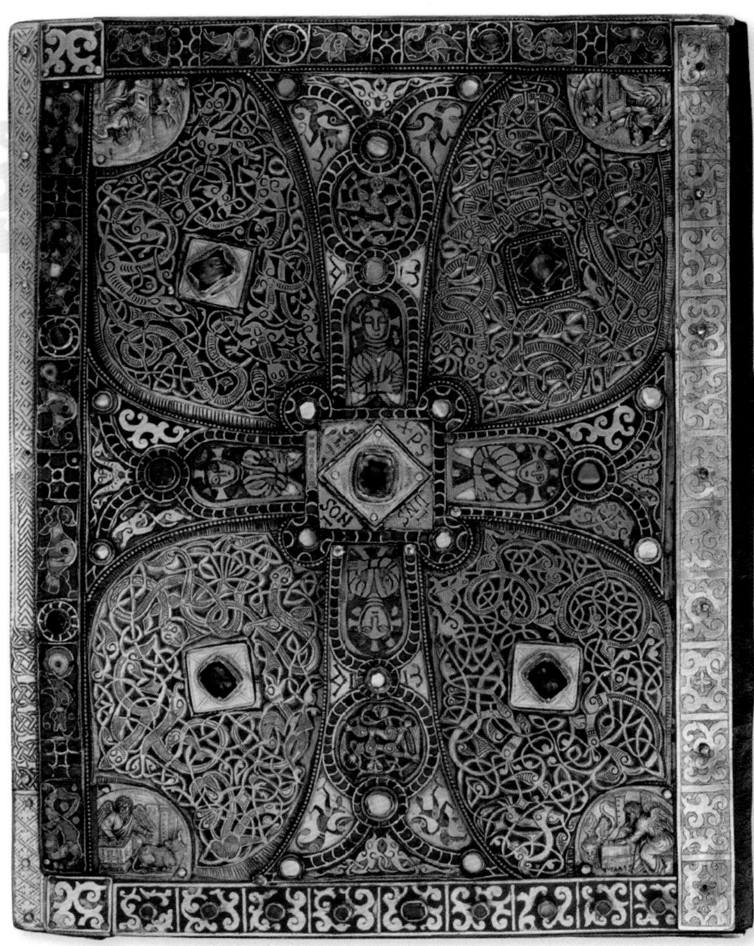

Gospel cover, 750–800, *Salzburg, Austria*
The design of the silver-gilt back cover of the Lindau Gospels is dominated by a cruciform derived from Byzantine prototypes. The complex and varied animal interlace patterns between the arms of the cross are carved in silver with black niello burnished into the background. The spirals at the animals' hip joints and the extension of their legs into ribbons, triangular and leaf shapes are comparable to metalwork and manuscript patterns in England and Ireland.

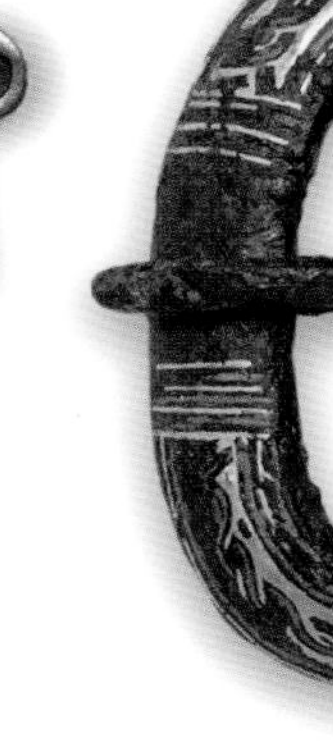

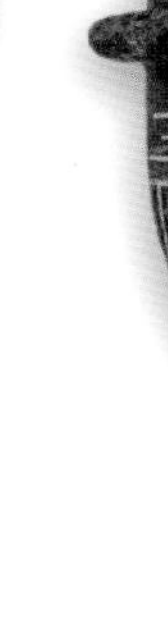

ELEMENTS OF PATTERN

- *chip-carving, a late Roman metalwork technique*
- *running scrolls and bead-and-reel from classical sources*
- *birds of prey*
- *ribbon animal interlace (see Sutton Hoo buckle, page 48)*
- *extended animal interlace*
- *Byzantine cross*

Belt buckle, late 6th to 7th century, *France*
The plate of this iron buckle is ornamented with an interlace pattern of ribbon-like animals curving round to bite their own bodies with elongated mouthparts, one element of which is developed into narrower interlace. They are defined with brass wire inlaid against a silver background. The buckle, which may originally have had a matching decorated counter-plate, was probably buried with its owner.

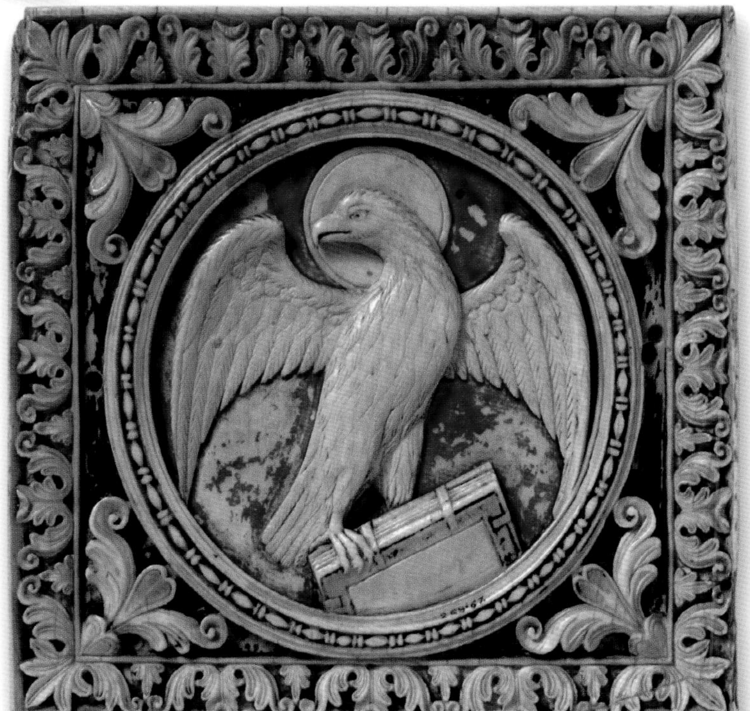

Brooch, 500–50, *Herpes, Charente, France*
Chip-carved patterns gilded in gold decorate this silver brooch set with garnets. The scrolling patterns are influenced by late Roman designs, and the birds of prey heads with garnet eyes around the head-plate are probably of south Russian origin. A zigzag pattern in silver niello runs around the edges and across the bowed part of the brooch. One of a pair, it was worn by a wealthy woman as a dress fastener.

Plaque, 800–10, *Germany*
This Carolingian ivory carving depicts the eagle, the symbol of St John the Evangelist. The acanthus leaf pattern in the outer border, the ring of bead-and-reel and the overall three-dimensional style are influenced by classical designs. The plaque formed part of a triptych. It was made by artists closely associated with Charlemagne's court at Aachen.

PATTERN IN DETAIL

Patterns for Salvation & Paradise 530s–547

Decorative programmes in Early Christian and Byzantine churches

The mosaic decoration in the church of San Vitale, Ravenna, encompasses the theme of salvation through Christ in its patterned ornament and religious narratives. Imagery and symbolism of Heaven, salvation and Christ's sacrifice surround the place in which the Christian liturgy and sacrament was enacted. A complex range of patterns, as much as the mosaics of Christ, the Old Testament and the imperial panels, embody the message and soaring symbolism of the promise of Heaven.

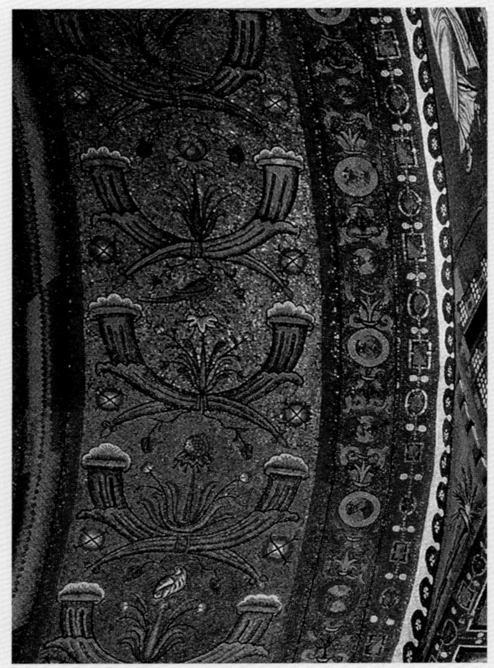

Bountiful cornucopia
The patterned arch links the presbytery and apse, which contains an image of Christ enthroned in Paradise with angels, San Vitale and the church's founding bishop, Ecclesius. The paired cornucopias, or horns of plenty, echo the shape of the dolphins in the opposite arch and have plants and birds issuing from their base. With the edging of stylised vegetation and segmented circles, these motifs may symbolise the heavenly bounty of Christ's promised salvation.

The Apostles' message of Christian redemption
A patterned band of medallions containing the Apostles in decorative roundels are surrounded by elaborate details – including intertwined dolphins symbolising Christ as the bearer of souls, a simplified egg-and-dart pattern and a jewelled band of precious stones and pearls – used extensively as ornamentation in imperial and divine Byzantine art. The band is bordered by coloured circles and segments decorated with trident or three-petal lily forms.

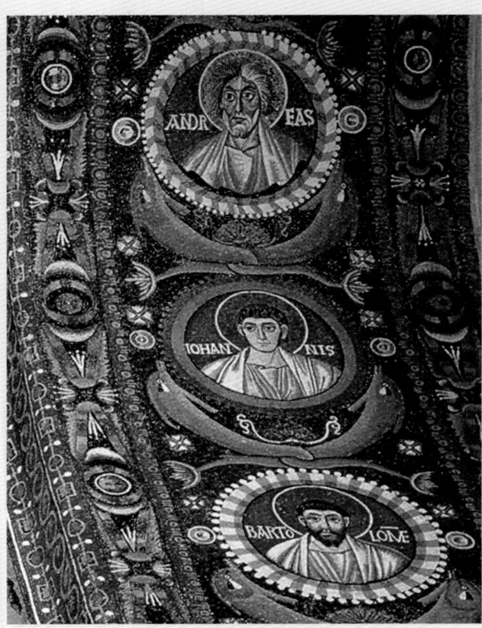

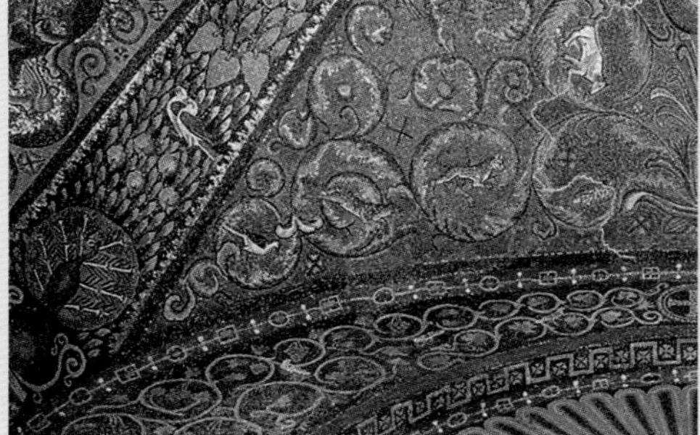

Motifs of heavenly salvation
The presbytery vault is divided by a cross containing abundant fruits issuing from peacocks standing on an orb, above paired dolphins, which together symbolise resurrection in Heaven. Each segment contains stylised plant scrolls with an acanthus base, symbolising the 'tree of life', inhabited with animals and angels supporting Christ the Lamb. Edging the vault are vines referencing Christ's message of salvation: 'I am the true vine' (John 15:1).

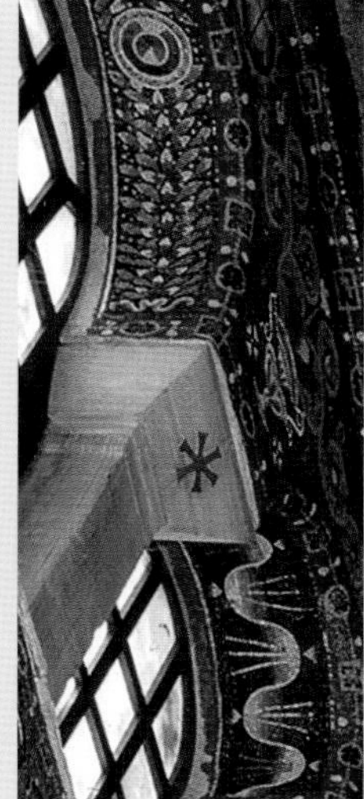

Swags and waves
The east window arches above the sanctuary are patterned with a simple swag of leaves centred on a multi-coloured circle and a subtly toned waving ribbon pierced with three shafts of golden light, a symbolic reference to the Trinity.

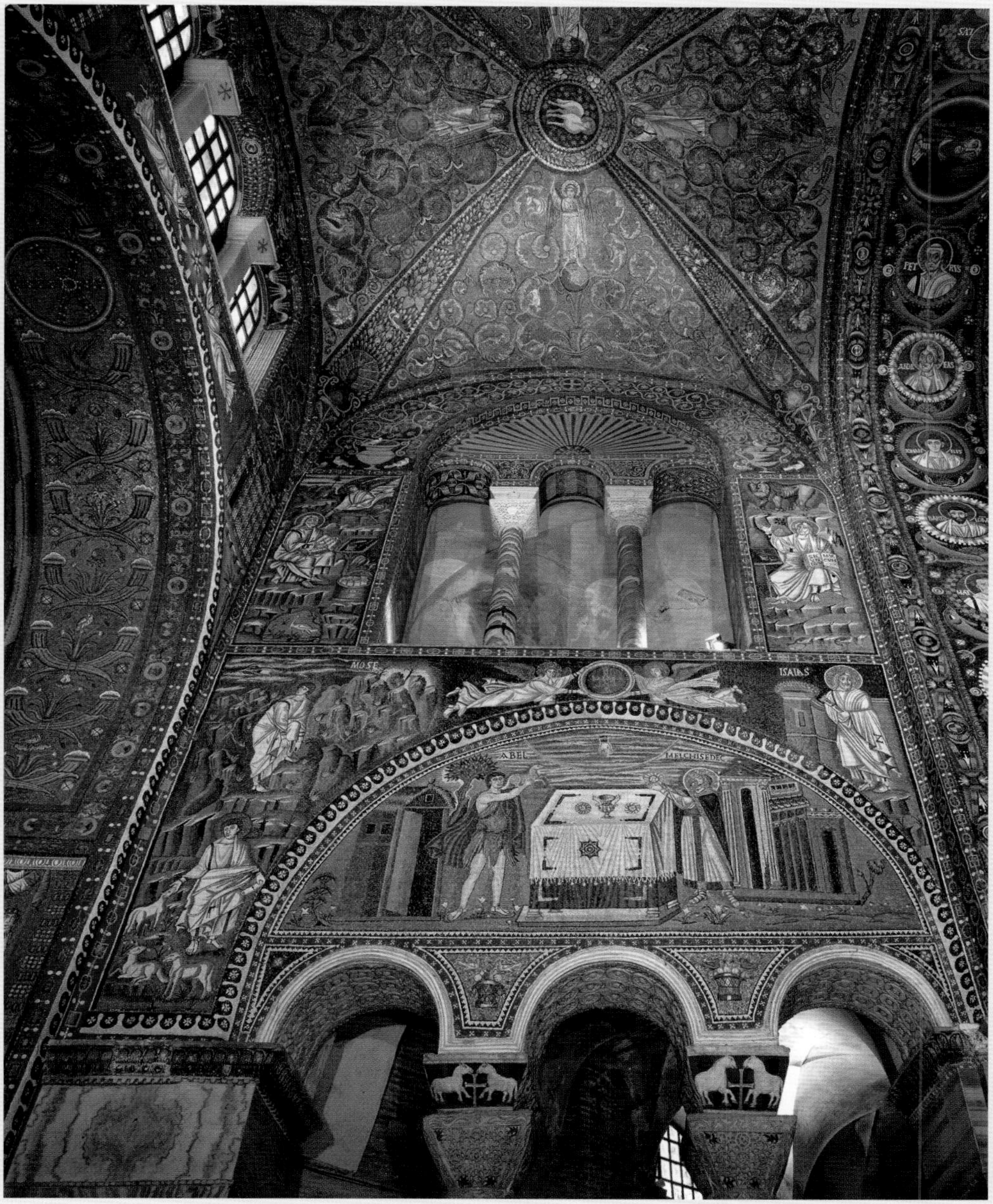

Ribbons and scales
The arches in the pillared opening below the heavenly vault are each decorated with different motifs – a blue and red three-dimensional double spiralling ribbon, a geometrically folded ribbon in greens and gold, and a stylised three-petal lily within overlapping lunettes forming coloured scales.

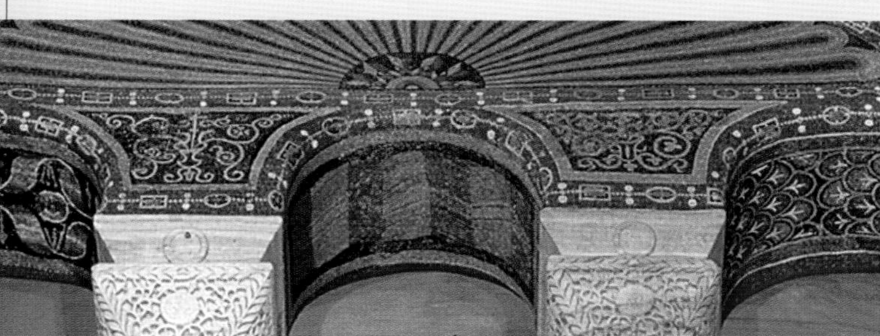

The presbytery, San Vitale, *Ravenna, Italy*
The variety of decorative patterning on the south wall of the presbytery, the area in front of the altar and apse of the church, represents salvation, the predominant theme of Early Christian and Byzantine imagery. The frequent use of tri-form motifs symbolised the Trinity – Father, Son and Holy Ghost – while the decorative patterning was as intrinsic to creating the awe-inspiring heavenly context of the Church on Earth.

Glittering Insignia
400–650

Early Anglo-Saxon metalwork patterns

The rich visual experience of Anglo-Saxon metalwork patterns was further elaborated by using other materials – cuprite glass paste heated and pressed into settings, interlace enhanced with black niello paste, inlaid micro-patterns of *millefiori* cut from fused rods of different coloured glass, and *cloisonné* work of garnets and glass set into raised interlocking cells. Colour and light were crucial qualities in the patterns of the Anglo-Saxons. Their literature constantly demonstrates their love of colour, light and glitter. In their poetry, surfaces are often described as bright, glowing or shining; precious stones were considered to be sources of light, and surface reflection is often elaborately described.

Belt buckle, early 7th century,
Sutton Hoo, Suffolk, England
The buckle plate is filled with patterns of interlacing ribbon animals with nielloed lines and punched dots. A pair of intercutting animals arch their backs along each side and intertwine their back legs between the pair of studs. Between them, a pair of animals form an asymmetrical pattern of their own. The circular tongue plate has a pattern of two animals interlacing through each other, while the buckle loop is decorated with two single knotted animals.

ELEMENTS OF PATTERN

- *running spiral*
- millefiori *glass micro-pattern inlay*
- cloisonné *patterns of shaped garnets in raised cells*
- *niello black metallic paste ribbed into carved lines and punch marks*
- see *illuminated manuscripts (spiral,* cloisonné*), pages 56–7*

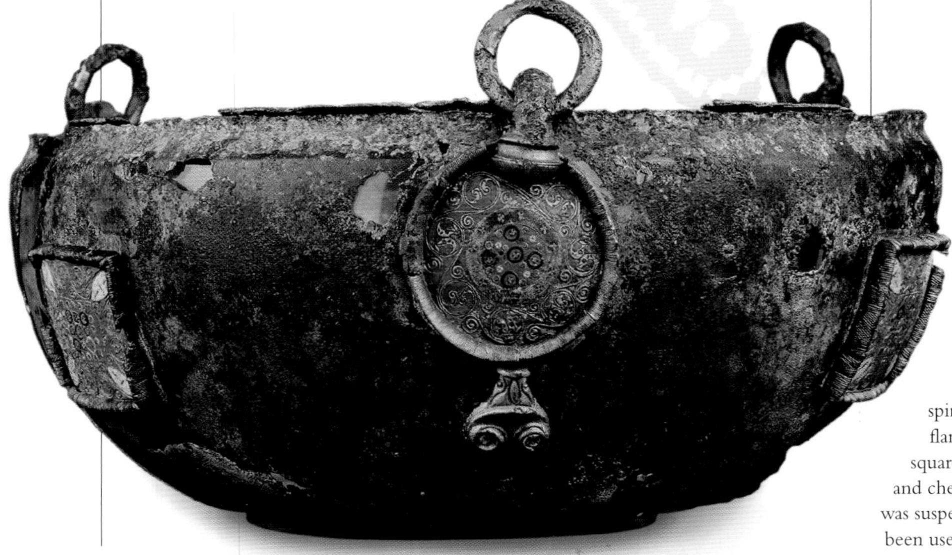

Hanging bowl, late 6th to early 7th century
Sutton Hoo, Suffolk, England
The mounts on this bronze bowl are decorated with raised patterns of polished spirals filled with red, blue and pale green cuprite glass paste. The spirals interlock tightly with each other, their terminals flaring into perhaps bird heads and leaf forms. *Millefiori* squares of checks or crosses and circles filled with flowers and checks are inlaid in blue, white and red glass. The bowl was suspended from the rim by the three rings and may have been used to mix alcoholic drinks during a ceremonial feast.

‘The origins of much Anglo-Saxon art of the Christian period are clearly seen in pagan Anglo-Saxon grave goods.’

DAVID M. WILSON,
Anglo-Saxon Art, 1984

Helmet cheek guard, 7th century, *England*
This gilt bronze cheek guard is decorated with two bands of the same pattern of interlocking animals, divided by a band of animal interlace. The interlocking animals turn their heads backwards to grip their own bodies with elongated jaws, their feet pressing against the frame. The bodies of the interlacing animals give the effect of a two-strand plait, their heads and feet filling the edges of the pattern space. The guard was part of a large hoard of items removed from weapons and armour, perhaps ritually buried in a ceremony of war.

Purse lid mounts, 620–55, *Sutton Hoo, Suffolk, England*
Originally decorating the whalebone lid of a leather pouch, these gold mounts are inlaid with patterns of red garnet *cloisonné* and blue and white checks of *millefiori* glass. The purse was fastened with a gold buckle and suspended from a waist belt by the three gold hinges.

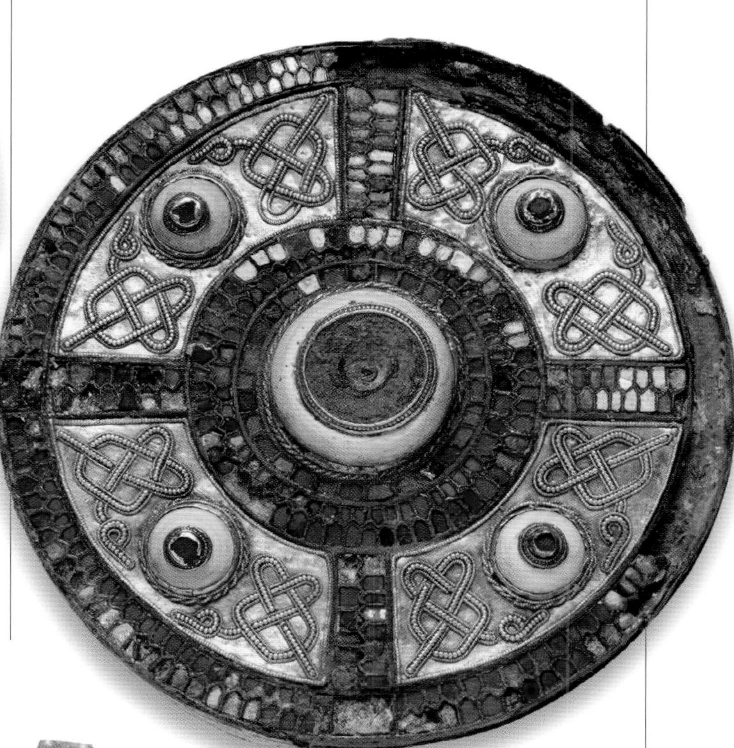

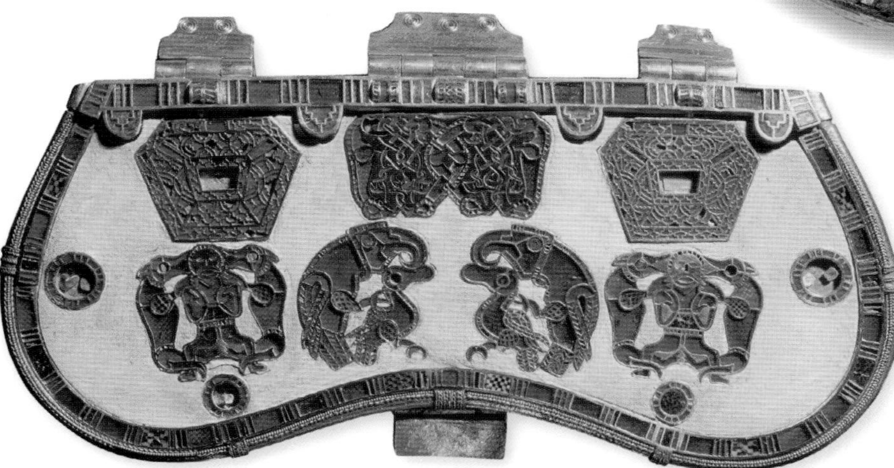

Brooch, 7th century, *Oxfordshire, England*
Gold plaques, each decorated with a pattern of animals in filigree knotwork and a boss of Mediterranean shell, are separated and framed with garnets. Probably from Sri Lanka, these have been cut and set in the *cloisonné* technique in a pattern of interlocking cells. Originally made in Kent, this brooch was buried in the grave of a woman of high status.

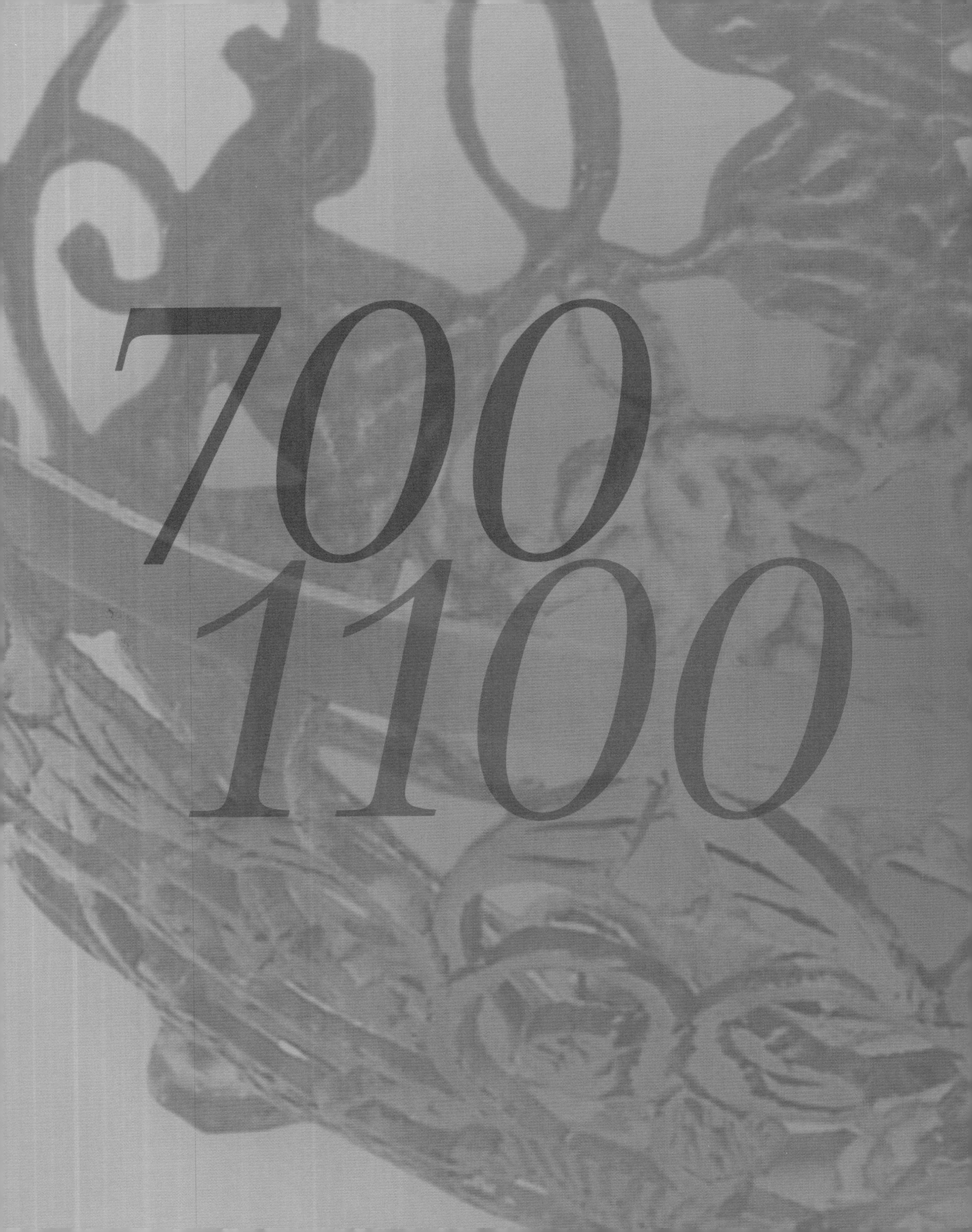

700
1100

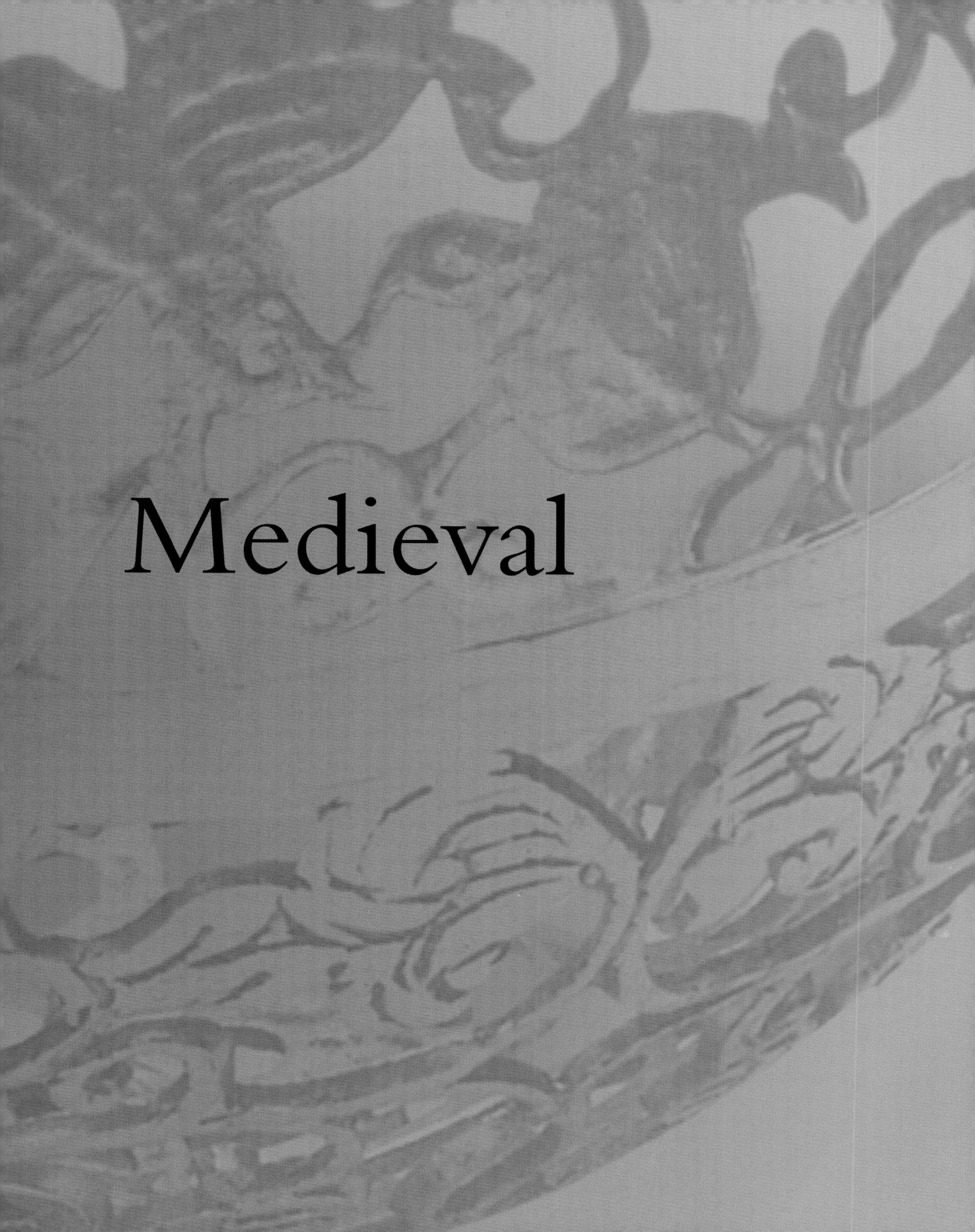

Medieval

Introduction

Patterns became increasingly inventive in their expression of the transcendent and the divine, integrating figurative motifs into patterns of spirituality and devotion. In the East, the significant pattern element of the delicate vegetal scroll began to emerge.

During the Christian Anglo-Saxon period (650–1050), patterns and motifs were derived from Roman, Gaulish, Scottish, Irish, German, Scandinavian, Italian, Byzantine and Arab sources. Missionaries from Italy and Gaul brought Bibles and service books to Britain from continental religious foundations. These illuminated manuscripts inspired artists working in the scriptoria of the great monasteries such as Lindisfarne, and secular metalworkers added new eclectic designs to their work. During the 9th century, Carolingian patterns inspired Anglo-Saxon artists to adopt the acanthus leaf motif, leading to the creation of the luxuriantly patterned ecclesiastical manuscripts that were fashioned in the 10th century.

While Germanic peoples such as the Anglo-Saxons and Franks established themselves in Europe, during the late 8th and early 9th centuries the Scandinavian 'Vikings' sailed to England, Ireland, northern France, Iceland, Greenland, the Baltic, Russia and America, initially as raiders but later becoming traders and settlers. In their Scandinavian homelands, designs of animal bodies abstracted into parts had been elongated and intertwined to create interlace patterns for metalwork. In Britain, Vikings adapted stone-carving traditions to produce sculpture with their own designs. Anglo-Saxon sculptors, metalworkers and wood carvers were, in turn, inspired by

In China, ceramics were initially decorated with simple motifs, representing and imitating fish, birds, flowers and dragons, emphasised by the way the glaze pooled into the incised forms. Buddhism continued to be influential in the use of motifs and the natural forms of lotus and bamboo inspired a profusion of patterns and decoration.

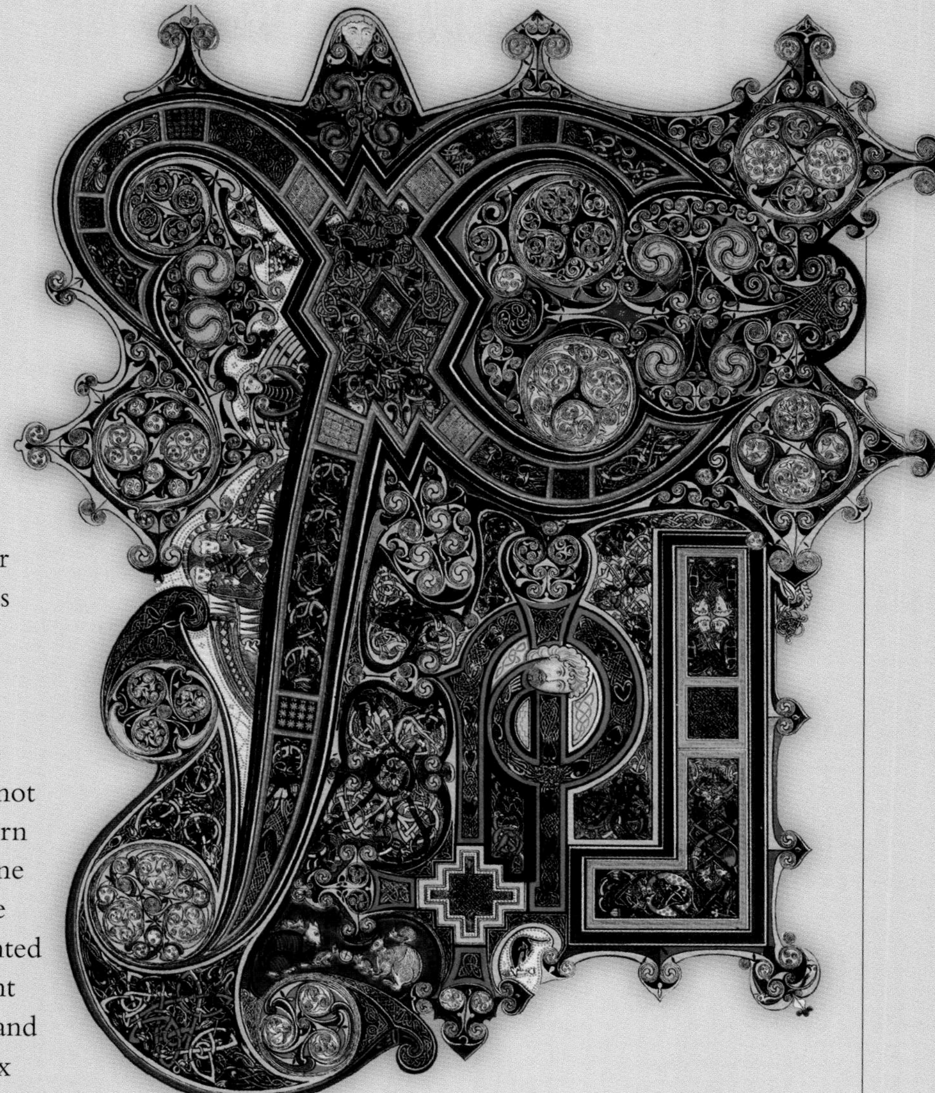

In Britain, dynamic spiral patterns developed before the 7th century were incorporated into the new art forms of manuscript painting and sculpture. Pre-Christian Germanic animal ornament still inspired artists and craftworkers to fill every surface with colourful patterns.

these new interlace patterns. In Iceland, the Viking craftworker Margaret carved a valuable walrus ivory crozier with such skill that it was considered to be the finest in the country.

Early Islamic imagery from the 690s was strongly decorative but not always non-figurative. Some pattern imagery can be traced to Byzantine origins but it seems likely that the choices made specifically represented Islamic interests. The scrolled plant form continued to be important and was developed into more complex twists, but also into simpler vegetative elements. Interspersed with the patterns were Qur'anic calligraphy, which itself became a form of patterning. Brilliant blue, silver and gold decorations alluded to Paradise, the desired goal of the devout Muslim. Under the Tang dynasty (618–1127) in China, new materials including silver and ceramics became highly sought after, expanding the range of desirable materials beyond the earlier preference for bronze, jade and gold. Some delicate vegetal patterns and the technical skills to execute them were transferred from the Middle East to China.

Medallion patterns of motifs enclosed by rings were developed in Byzantium but they also feature on some early textiles which may be Sasanian, with elements such as the fantastic animal-bird *simurgh* motif. The technology of the draw-loom allowed textiles to be woven with a wide variety of repeated pattern forms, including mythical animals, imperial or status figurative imagery, Christian subjects and non-figurative motifs. The medallion style spread throughout western Europe to Asia and was adopted by craftworkers in other media such as ivory.

The Encompassing Vine
700–1050

Inhabited plant scrolls

As a signifier of Christ, the vine became a widespread element in the design of Christian patterns in many media, including metalwork and carving in stone, bone and ivory. It was developed into many different forms as plant scrolls with different leaves, flowers and fruits. Patterns of scrolling vegetation including animals and birds were symbolic of God and Creation or of Christ and the Church. These inhabited plant scrolls were also shown as growing from a basal point as a 'tree of life', the tree element derived from the Middle Eastern concept of the 'sacred tree'. Plant and animal elements were also combined in patterns to represent a duality between God and the created world.

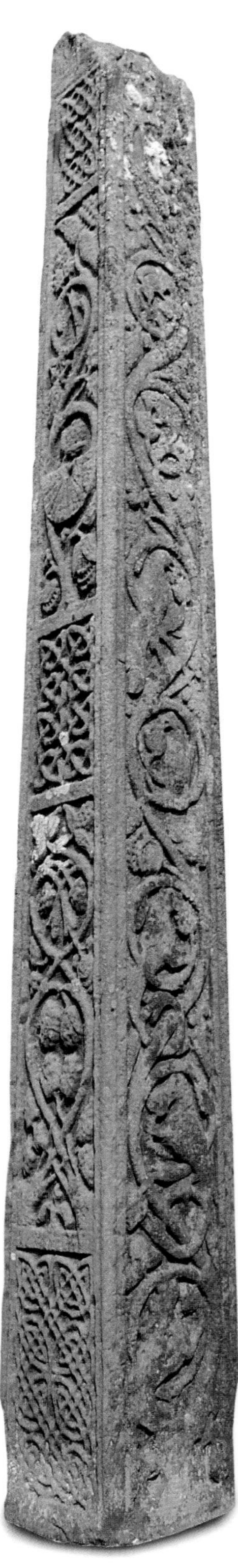

Cross-shaft, 750–850,
Bewcastle, Cumbria, England
An inhabited plant-scroll pattern has been carved along the entire length of one side of this freestanding stone cross-shaft. A continuous main stem undulates from the base to the top of the shaft, where it terminates in a pair of flowers. The creatures inhabiting this 'tree of life' change in nature from terrestrial to aerial, from the quadruped standing on the ground with forepaws on the stem, through hybrid animals with sinuous bodies, to birds and squirrels in the upper tendrils – all consuming the tree's flowers and fruits.

ELEMENTS OF PATTERN

- *'tree of life'*
- *real and fantastical animals*
- *flowers and fruits*
- *scrolling and looping interlace*

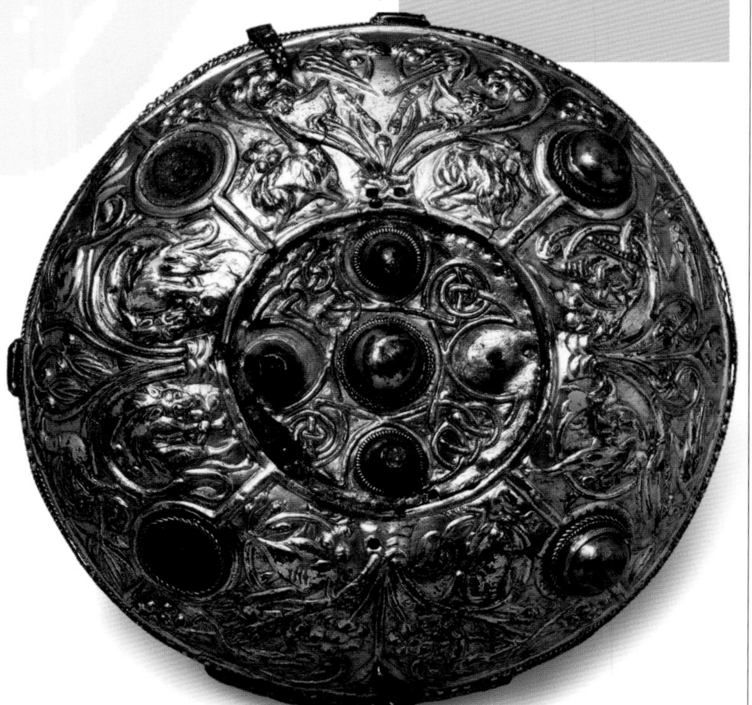

Bowl, 700–50,
Ormside, Cumbria, England
This embossed silver bowl is ornamented with panels containing patterns of 'sacred trees' developed into plant scrolls ending in bunches of grapes, berries and leaves. The fruits and leaves are being eaten by a variety of birds perching in the branches and fantastical quadrupeds that bite or step over them. The base of the bowl is decorated with plain interlace forming a series of loose knots.

Reliquary shrine, 750–800,
Gandersheim, Germany
The sides of this whalebone casket are carved with a pattern of panels containing animals with tails developed into a scrolling interlace, variously looping around their bodies, and wings and tongues, and sometimes gripped by forepaws. The lid is carved with animals caught up in tighter and more complex interlace. On the side panels the animals have become fully integrated into the plant scroll – interlacing branches sprouting from a central stem become animal bodies with forelimbs that in turn grip the curving tendrils around them. The casket may have been presented to Gandersheim Abbey as a reliquary shrine.

‘The vine scroll is a Christian motif with origins in the Mediterranean and perhaps Near Eastern Christianity ... it represents Christ – “I am the true vine” (John, 15, I).’

DAVID M. WILSON *Anglo-Saxon Art*, 1984

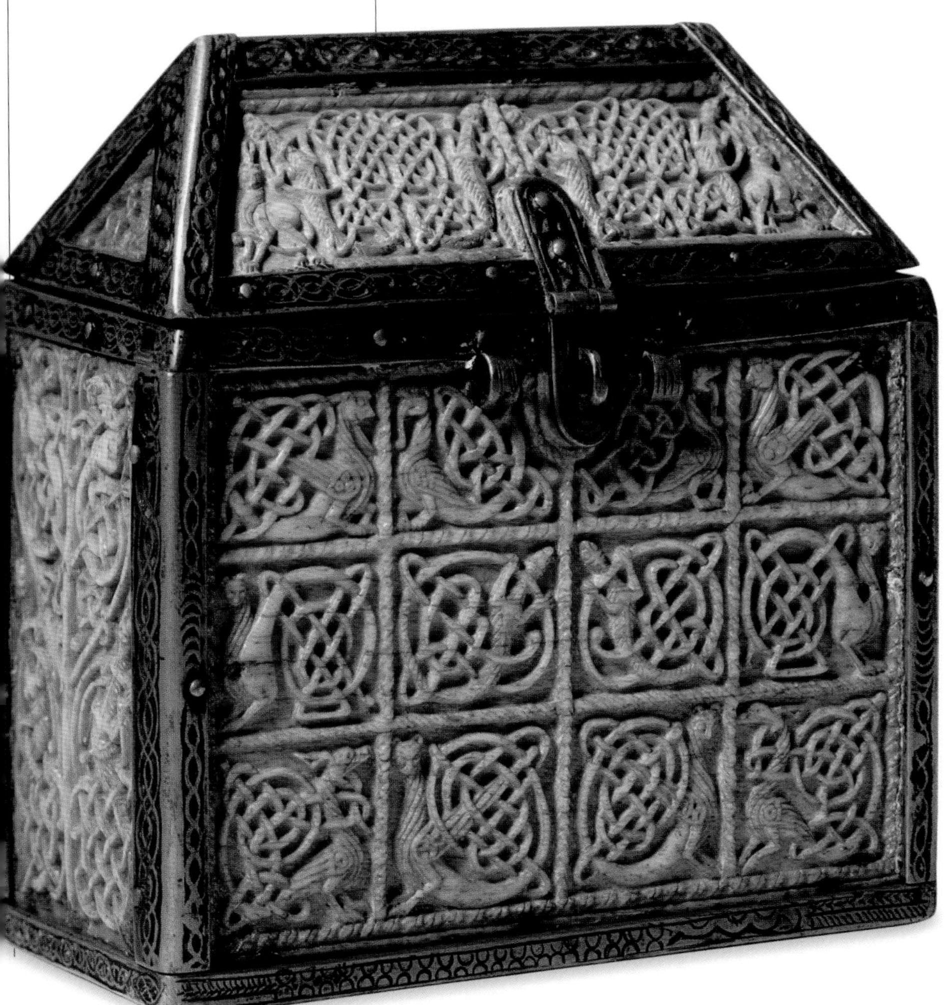

Reliquary, mid-11th century,
England
The base of this openwork walrus ivory box is carved with the Lamb of God in a central roundel and the four symbols of the evangelists at the ends of the arms of the cross. The spaces between these symbols are filled with a plant scroll closely integrated with animals and birds. On the sides, a plant scroll inhabited with quadrupeds and birds grows from the base as a single undulating stem with side shoots and sprouting leaves. Hung from a loop, this openwork casing was made to house a gold box that contained a holy relic, possibly a fragment of the True Cross.

Pages of Enchantment
650–1050

Illuminated manuscripts

Dynamic versatile patterns were created for the manuscript page from designs in metalwork. The forms and colours of pre-Roman Britain linked spirals in red glass paste, the *cloisonné* technique of inlaying crimson garnets into gold cells, and gold and silver animal or ribbon interlace were all adapted for two-dimensional art. The design of the manuscript page was underpinned by a grid laid out with compasses and rulers, a formal symmetrical composition of patterns contained within panels and borders. This was animated by the application of spiral scrolls and made more complex by the use of varied colours within interlace patterns to lead the gaze in different directions.

'There was continuous contact between the Church in England and the more established churches of Gaul and Italy and ... the eastern Church based on Byzantium.'

DAVID M. WILSON, *Anglo-Saxon Art*, 1984

Book of Durrow, 650–700,
Northumberland, England
Left The central roundel is filled with a pattern of plain spiral- and cross-interlace decorated roundels, the central one painted with a cross. Each side panel contains a row of animals with jaws, legs and tails extended into tendril interlace; the leading animal is similar to the motif at the end of the Sutton Hoo buckle. The end panels of the page have the same design of intertwined ribbon animals with tendril interlace limbs, except that red and yellow are reversed. *Right* The spiralling interlace patterns at the ends of the page are developed into knotted interlace patterns at the sides. These patterns protect and envelop the central cross.

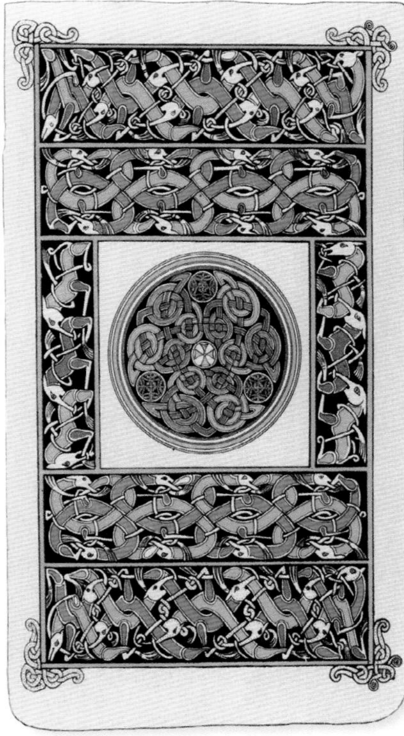

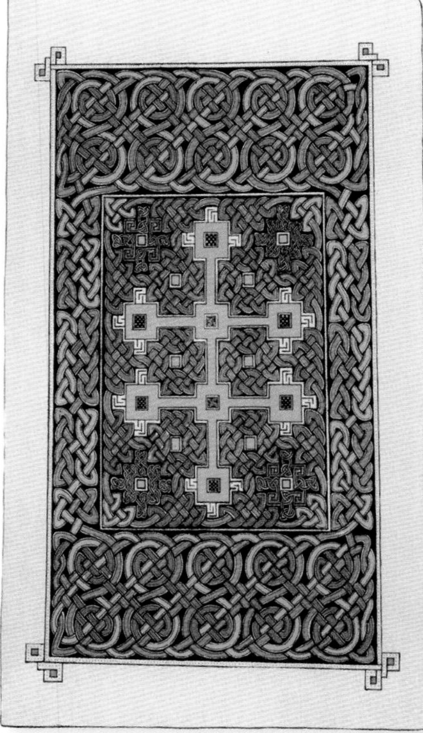

ELEMENTS OF PATTERN

- *plain spiral- and cross-interlace*
- *animals and birds with extended tendril interlace (see Sutton Hoo, pages 48–9)*
- *linked spiral scroll*
- *acanthus leaves in florid style*

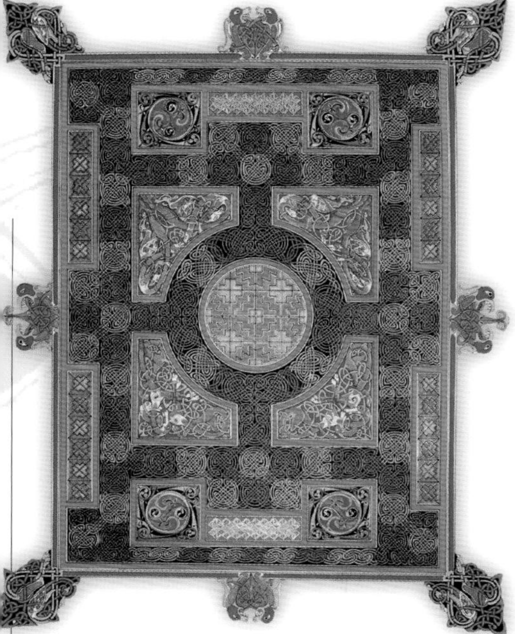

Lindisfarne Gospels, late 7th century, *Lindisfarne, Northumberland, England*
The square panels contain patterns of linked spiral scrolls varying in scales and tension, drawn out and developed to fit the quadrangular field. Geometric patterns, inspired by *cloisonné* work on metal objects, fill the central roundel and the rectangular panels. The panels around the centre are covered with interlacing animals and birds caught up in the tendril interlace of their ears, tails and crests.

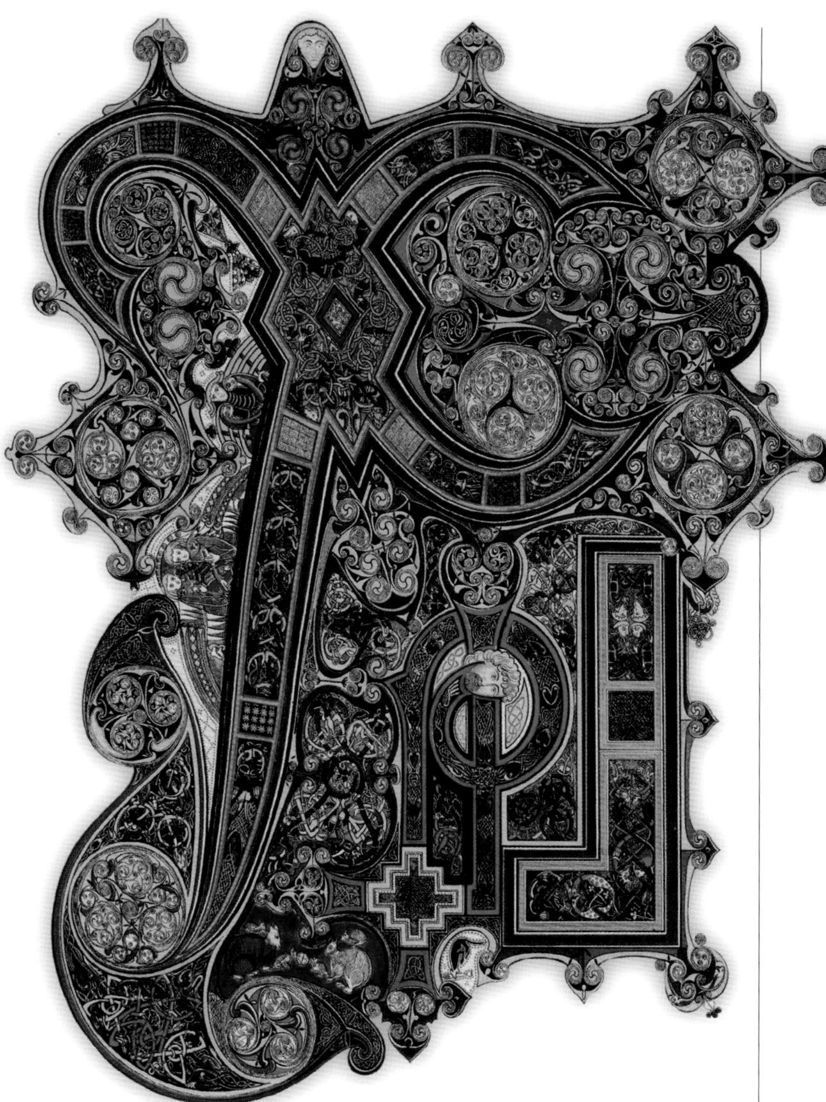

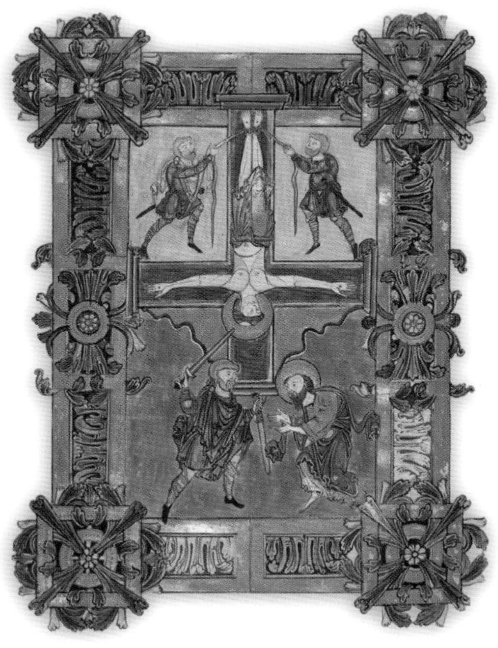

Benedictional of St Aethelwold 971–84, *Winchester, England*
The frames of the design are built up of layers of patterns. The heavy gold borders are filled with panels of rippling vegetation, while rosettes of acanthus leaves grow out through the frame and burst through the corners in a florid but constrained style. The rich tones of the acanthus patterns are overpainted to create a shaded three-dimensional effect. The Benedictional is a book of blessings used by Bishop Aethelwold of Winchester for Church feast days – this page commemorates St Peter.

Book of Kells, late 8th to early 9th century, *Iona, Scotland,* and *Kells, Ireland*
The Greek letters X (chi), P (rho) and I (iota) are the first three letters of 'Christos' or Christ. The chi or X has curling terminals filled with pattern; the rho or P is set below, the downstroke ending in a cross and its curling loop crossed by the letter I. The letters are surrounded by elaborate linked spirals, whirling disks with triskeles and complex interlace, the spaces between filled with yet smaller spirals and curling shapes. The letters are closely integrated with the patterns that fill and surround them, and no space on the page is left undecorated.

Animated Interlace
800–1170

Viking carving

In both the Scandinavian homelands and the Viking-settled territories, ornament was dominated by patterns of interlace. Animals, strands and plant-like elements such as leaves and tendrils were combined in powerful ways to decorate and add meaning to objects. Red, blue, black and white paints elaborated and emphasised patterns carved in stone and wood. Animal interlace patterns dominated Scandinavian art, but during the 8th and 9th centuries the Vikings adapted their styles to the tastes and media of their new homelands. Their patterns began to incorporate vegetal elements such as leaves, fronds and tendrils.

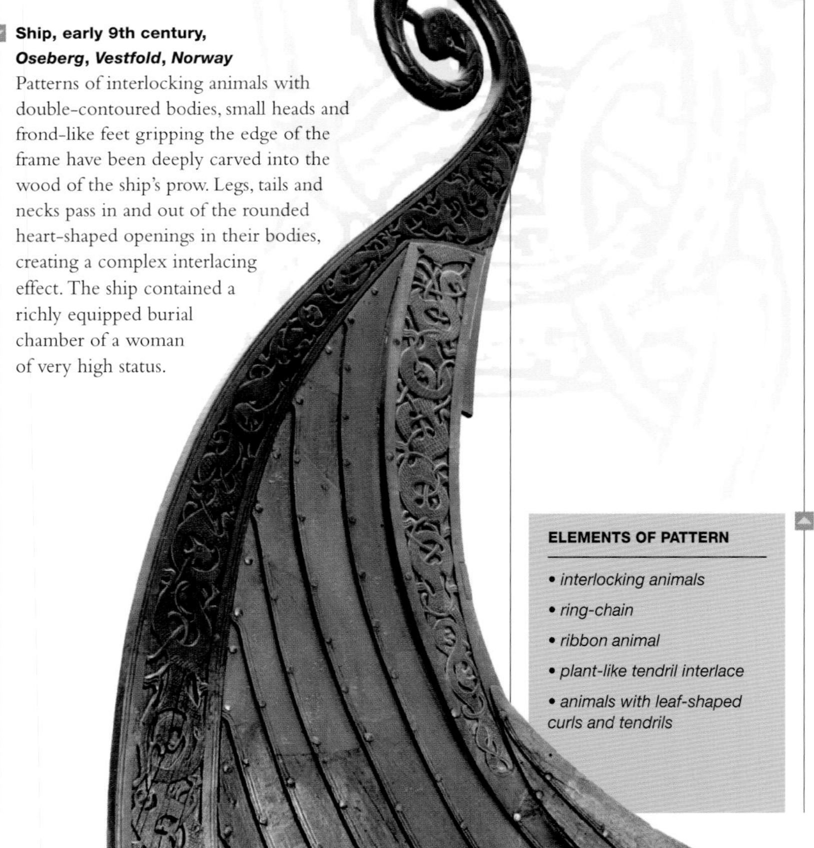

Ship, early 9th century,
Oseberg, Vestfold, Norway
Patterns of interlocking animals with double-contoured bodies, small heads and frond-like feet gripping the edge of the frame have been deeply carved into the wood of the ship's prow. Legs, tails and necks pass in and out of the rounded heart-shaped openings in their bodies, creating a complex interlacing effect. The ship contained a richly equipped burial chamber of a woman of very high status.

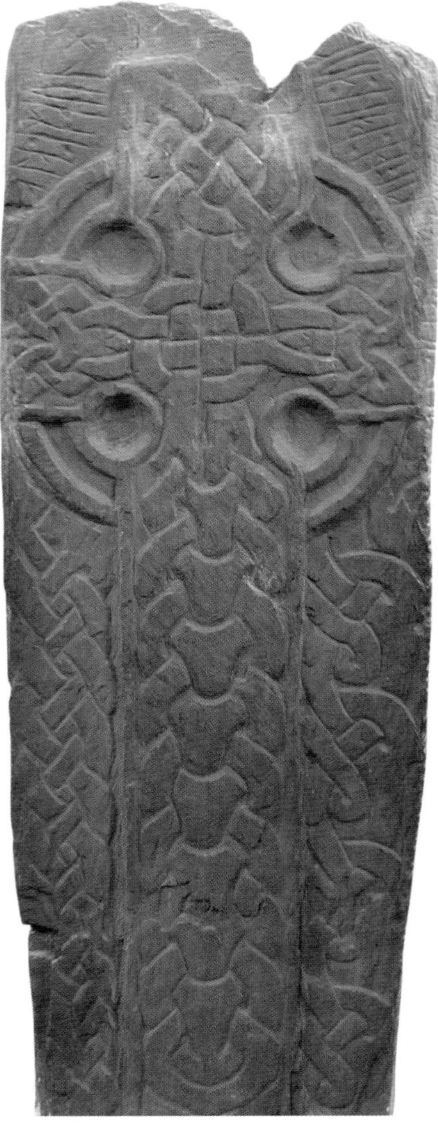

Memorial stone, 840–980,
Kirk Michael, Isle of Man
Bound by a ring at the centre and on the upper arm of the cross, the interlace pattern develops into a ring-chain running to the foot. The panels to either side each contain a different pattern of single-strand interlace. The runic inscription shows that the Christian descendants of the original Viking settlers were still using Scandinavian language and names. It states that the stone was carved by Gaut Bjornsson, a prominent sculptor whose work greatly influenced carving on the island.

ELEMENTS OF PATTERN

- *interlocking animals*
- *ring-chain*
- *ribbon animal*
- *plant-like tendril interlace*
- *animals with leaf-shaped curls and tendrils*

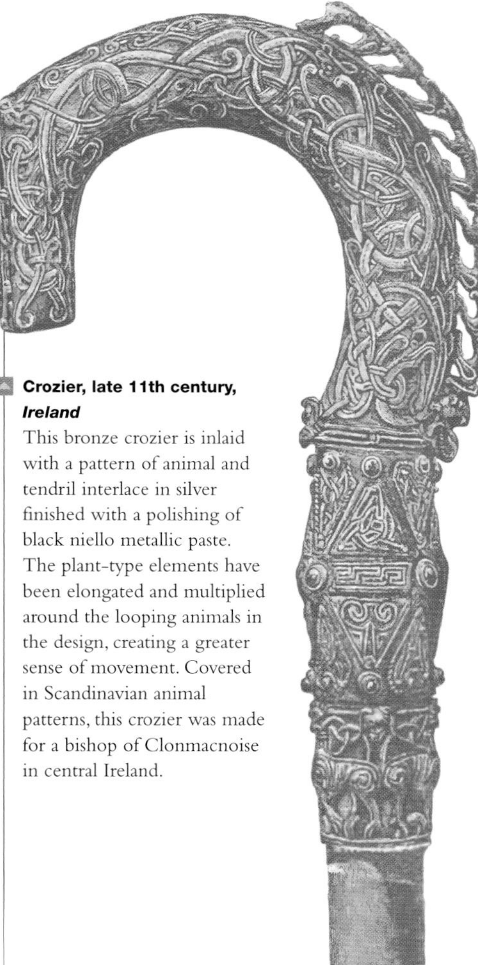

Crozier, late 11th century, *Ireland*
This bronze crozier is inlaid with a pattern of animal and tendril interlace in silver finished with a polishing of black niello metallic paste. The plant-type elements have been elongated and multiplied around the looping animals in the design, creating a greater sense of movement. Covered in Scandinavian animal patterns, this crozier was made for a bishop of Clonmacnoise in central Ireland.

‘Through their journeys, their conquests, their colonization and their opening up of trade routes, the Vikings more than any other people contrived to break down cultural barriers.’

DAVID M. WILSON, *The Northern World*, 1980

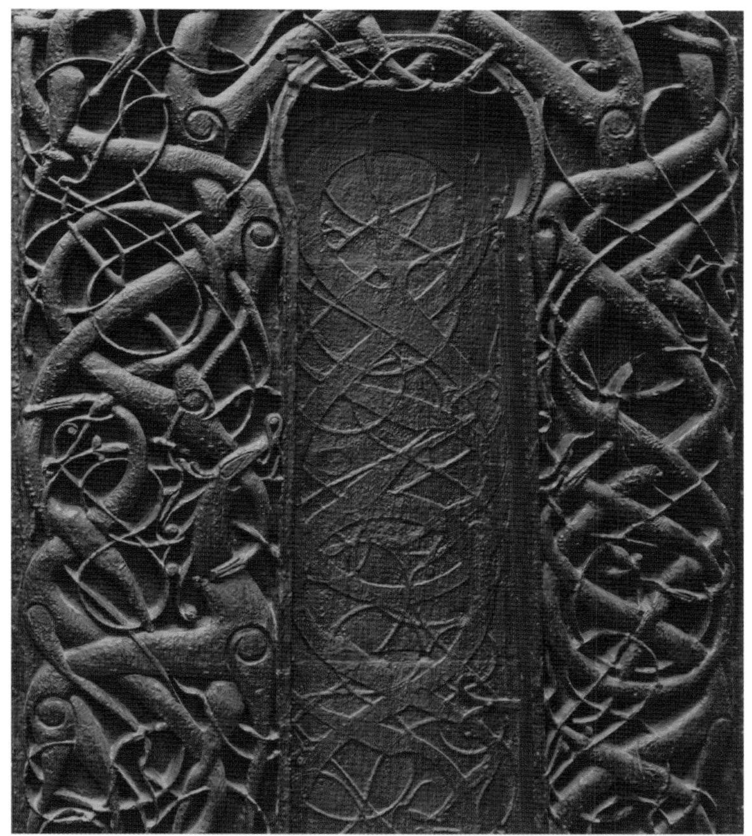

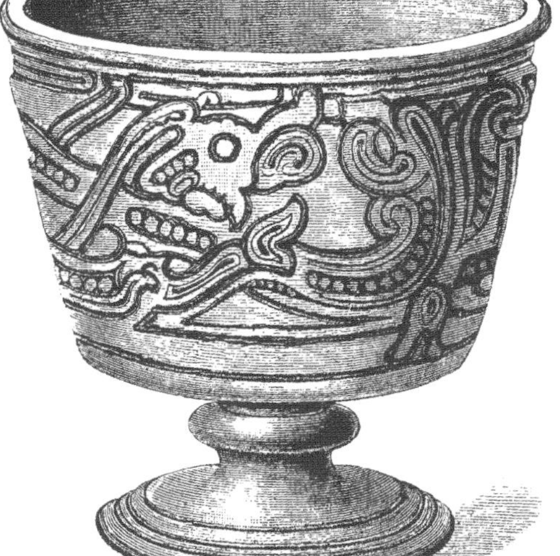

Cup, 870–1000, *Jelling, Jutland, Denmark*
This silver cup is incised with a ribbon-like animal whose elongated crest interlaces with a body defined by a double contour and filled with dots. Leaf-like curls springing from the animal's body create a more florid effect. The cup was found in a burial mound at the royal funerary site of Jelling.

Doorway, 1050–70, *Urnes, Sogn, Norway*
Sinuous quadrupeds and one-limbed serpent-like animals clasp each other in their jaws to create a delicate animal tendril interlace pattern. It is carved in rounded relief up to 4½ in (12 cm) deep into the wood. The four-legged animal's long eye shape, the filament curling from the end of its upper jaw and the spiral hip joints are all adapted from earlier Viking styles. This vibrant, skilfully executed pattern extends around the west portal of the timber-built church in a balanced asymmetrical design.

Magnificent Medallions 600–1100

Figurative patterns from Byzantium, Europe, the Middle East and beyond

The medallion style, in which figurative and non-figurative images were organised into repeating, often symmetrical, roundels, was ideal for patterning decorative silks woven using the draw-loom. Although probably originally developed in Byzantium, the pearled roundels have Sasanian origins. As the style developed, the roundels and motifs became more elaborate and were adapted for embroidery, tapestry and carved ivory. The figurative subjects might embody imperial, triumphal or religious iconography, including Christian scenes such as the Annunciation. The style became so popular that it spread along the Silk Road to China in the 7th/8th centuries.

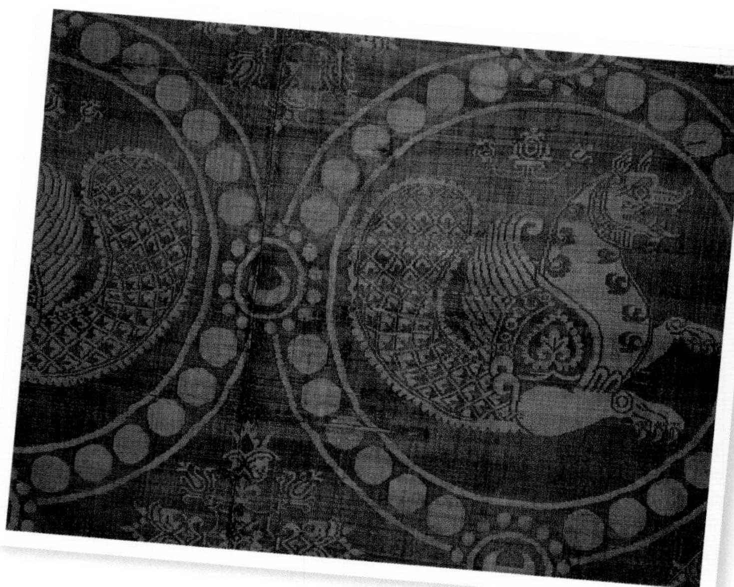

Dragon-peacock silk, 7th–9th century, ***Sasanian (Iranian) or Byzantine***
Taken from the motif of a *simurgh* in a roundel (see Sasanian decoration on pages 42–3) and incorporated into a figurative repetitive motif, this patterned silk may have come from Byzantium or the Middle East. The dog-bird, or dragon-peacock, surrounded by a pearled circle and interspersed with decorative floral diamonds and linked as if in a chain by smaller roundels, is repeated in a symmetrical mirror-image.

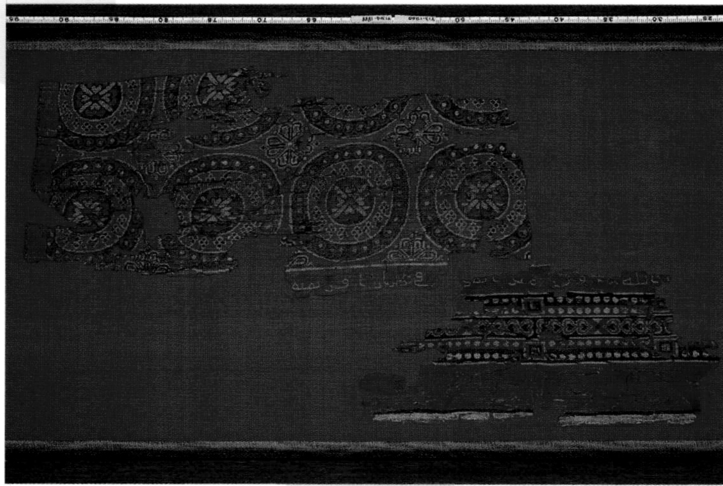

Silks, 684–750, ***North Africa***
Designed for an Islamic market (the Arabic text refers to 'Allah' and the name of an early Umayyad caliph), this medallion pattern contains non-figurative details but follows the principle of alternating bands of roundels and rosettes. The four colours of red, green, cream and yellow add complexity to the largely floral and circular motifs. The edging band is visually linked using the circles but also contains hearts and squares.

ELEMENTS OF PATTERN

- *repeating figurative motifs*
- *the quadriga – a four-horse chariot*
- *fabulous beasts and birds*
- *circles, diamonds and rosettes*
- *pearls and hearts*

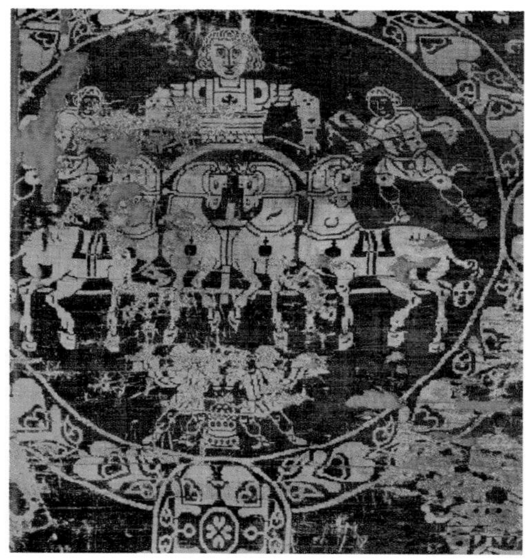

Silk, late 8th–early 9th century CE, *Constantinople*
The Roman quadriga (four-horse chariot), the central motif in this medallion pattern, is linked to the imperial ambitions of Charlemagne, in whose shrine in Aachen this silk fragment was found. Providing an ideal motif for a symmetrical design, the quadriga is surrounded by roundels of a linked vine, floral and heart pattern with small linking roundels of the same motif in quadrilateral symmetry. Between these are paired prancing beasts.

Silk (reconstruction), 8th century, *probably western Europe*
The roundels in this silk break with the band form by having the circular medallions made of interlocking scrolls and arches. The central figure is David enthroned with a cross or sceptre iconographically comparable to illuminations of King David in psalters (The Book of Psalms) of the same period. The intermediate lozenges comprise interlocking squares with a cross and foliate forms and are tipped with small birds.

‘Byzantine weavers ... [produced] ... the medallion style whose incorporation of detailed images into repetitive patterns made it one of the most influential innovations in the history of ornament.’

JAMES TRILLING, *The Language of Ornament*, 2001

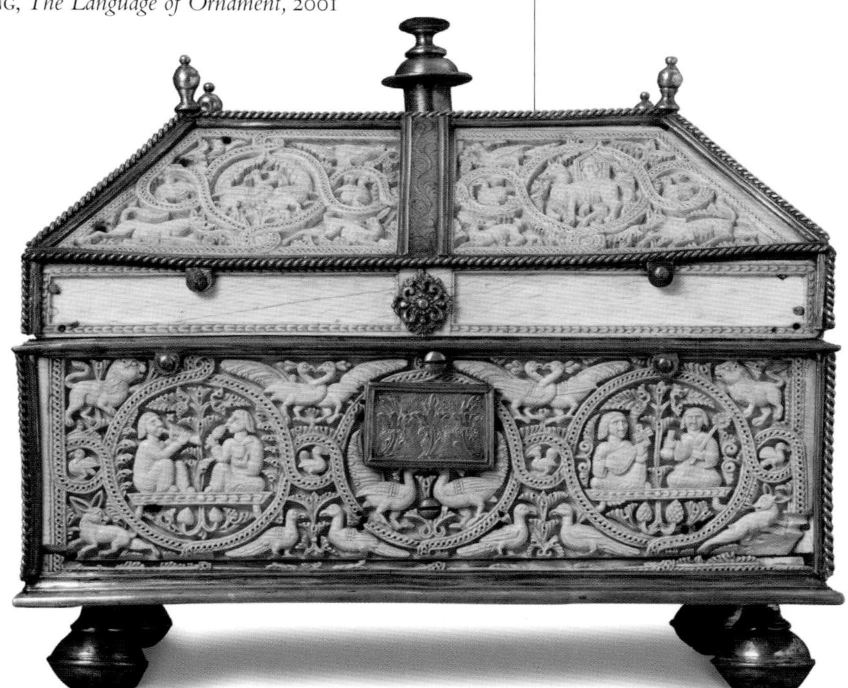

Ivory carved casket, early 11th century, *probably Cordoba, Spain*
The medallion style was adapted extensively for carved ivory objects and is here used to contain views of musicians (seen on this side) and drinkers surrounded by plants, beasts and birds. The roundels are created from a widened twist, itself carved with a fine twist. Although not constrained by the technical limits of weaving, the symmetrical and mirror-image effects are maintained both within and outside the roundels.

Creatures of Power
600–1100

European animal patterns

An important source for the medieval animal art of Christian Europe was the *Physiologos* ('Natural Philosopher'), a collection of writings by classical authors compiled from the 2nd century CE at Alexandria in Egypt. Real and imaginary animals, as well as some plants and precious stones, are described and accompanied by a story to show the moral and symbolic qualities of each. The text was translated into Latin and then into many other languages of the Middle East and Europe. It inspired the production of a large number of illuminated manuscripts and secular books, or 'bestiaries', and had a widespread influence on the design of patterns in other media.

'The beasts and the stories influenced not only popular thought and literature but all the decorative arts.'

EVA WILSON, *8000 Years of Ornament*, 1994

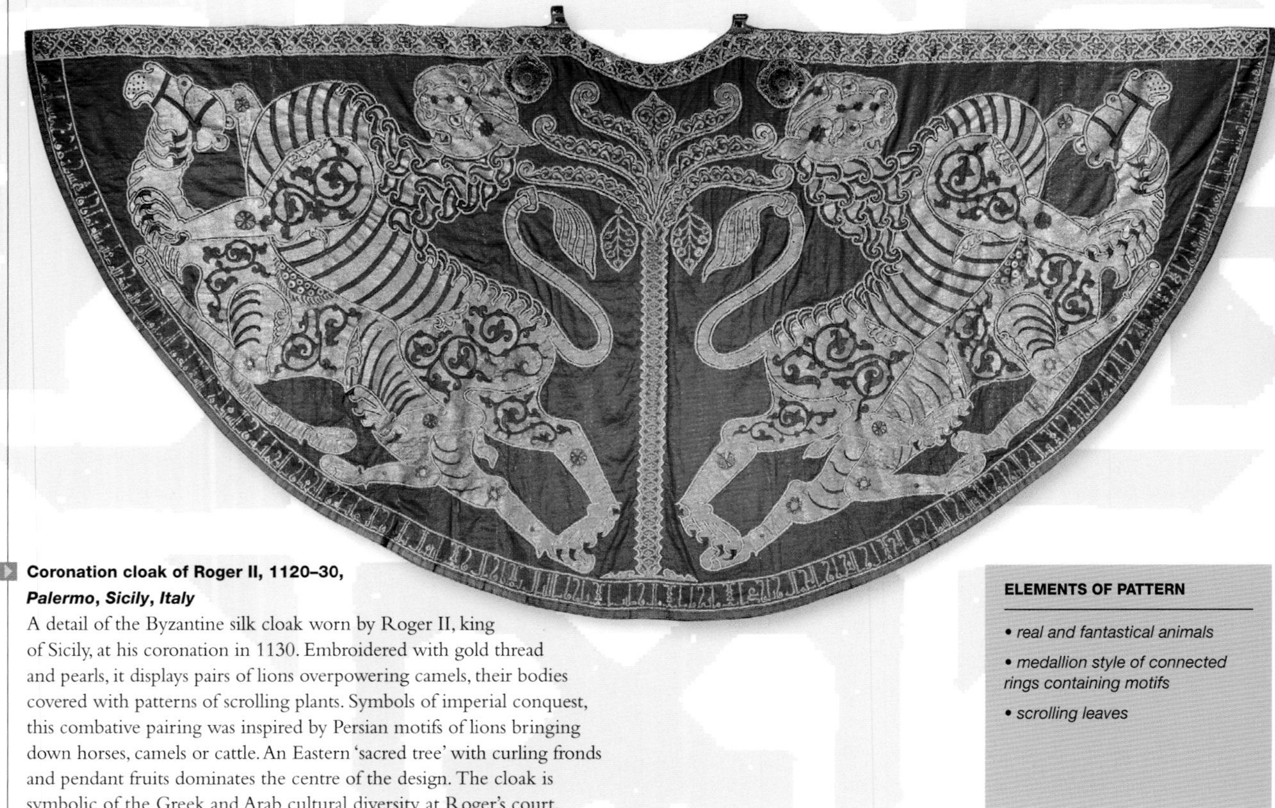

Coronation cloak of Roger II, 1120–30,
Palermo, Sicily, Italy
A detail of the Byzantine silk cloak worn by Roger II, king of Sicily, at his coronation in 1130. Embroidered with gold thread and pearls, it displays pairs of lions overpowering camels, their bodies covered with patterns of scrolling plants. Symbols of imperial conquest, this combative pairing was inspired by Persian motifs of lions bringing down horses, camels or cattle. An Eastern 'sacred tree' with curling fronds and pendant fruits dominates the centre of the design. The cloak is symbolic of the Greek and Arab cultural diversity at Roger's court.

ELEMENTS OF PATTERN

- *real and fantastical animals*
- *medallion style of connected rings containing motifs*
- *scrolling leaves*

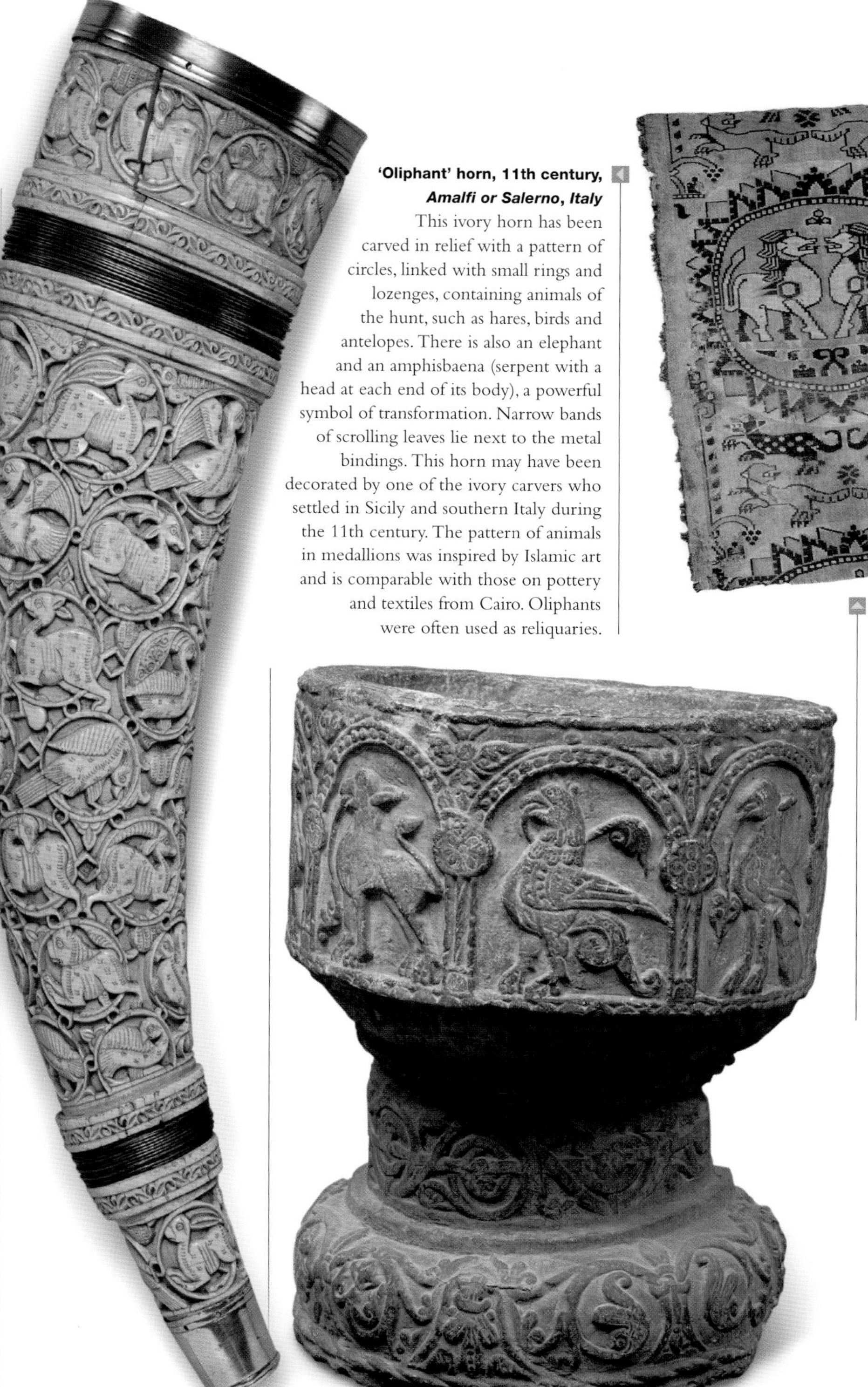

'Oliphant' horn, 11th century, *Amalfi or Salerno, Italy*
This ivory horn has been carved in relief with a pattern of circles, linked with small rings and lozenges, containing animals of the hunt, such as hares, birds and antelopes. There is also an elephant and an amphisbaena (serpent with a head at each end of its body), a powerful symbol of transformation. Narrow bands of scrolling leaves lie next to the metal bindings. This horn may have been decorated by one of the ivory carvers who settled in Sicily and southern Italy during the 11th century. The pattern of animals in medallions was inspired by Islamic art and is comparable with those on pottery and textiles from Cairo. Oliphants were often used as reliquaries.

Silk textile, c. 800–1000, *Zandaniji, Bukhara, Uzbekistan*
The pattern woven into this silk, in different coloured threads on an originally red background, shows the influence of Sasanian design from Iran. Opposing lions in medallions alternating with pairs of spotted and plain quadrupeds are set either side of 'tree of life' motifs sprouting leaves and lateral branches with bunches of fruit. The textile was perhaps part of a bishop's vestment from Verdun Cathedral in France.

Font, 12th century, *Sweden*
The bowl of the font is encircled with a pattern of processing lions and eagles, each enclosed by an arcade in an Eastern style. The scrolling and knotted tongues of the animals and the curling tails of the eagles are echoed in the leafy scroll patterns ornamenting other parts of the font. The stem has a pattern of spiralling vegetational fronds around a horizontal band, and the foot is decorated with vertical stems with scrolling branches sprouting curling and lobate leaves.

PATTERN IN DETAIL

Patterns of Paradise
692 and later

Interior mosaic of the Dome of the Rock

Early Islamic patterns drew on Roman and Byzantine forms, and the mosaics in the pilgrim shrine of the Dome of the Rock (Qubbat As-Sakhrah) in Jerusalem and the Great Umayyad Mosque in Damascus (707–15) were created by Byzantine mosaicists. However, the decorative scheme in the Dome of the Rock presents a unique imagery surely designed to create a new visual language. Possibly intended to challenge Christian and Jewish traditions, the vegetal patterns may link to themes of Paradise.

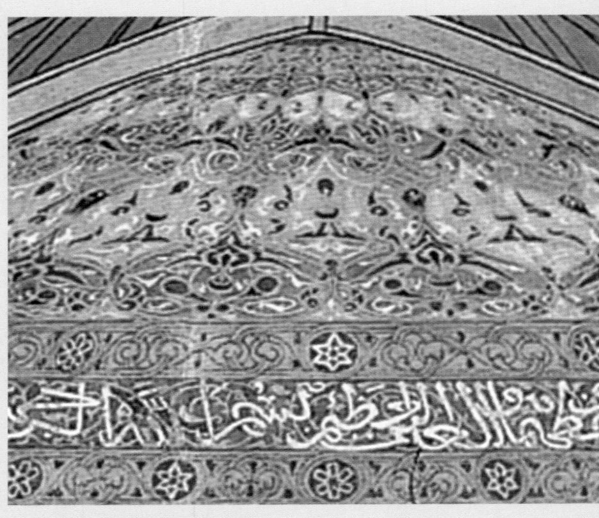

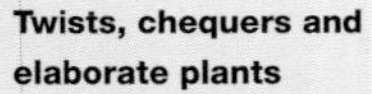

Twists, chequers and elaborate plants
The drum decoration includes a complex range of mosaic patterns around the windows. These include twisted lattice designs in varying colours, a decorative squared chequer-board with circles and small vegetal details, and a variety of elaborate scrolling plants in decorated pots. The windows are also decorated, surrounded by interwoven chain patterns and imitation jewelled banding, reminiscent of Byzantine patterns.

Calligraphy and scrolls
The pattern around the bottom of the dome contains calligraphic texts from the Qur'an (Koran) surrounded by an extended twisted band of vine scrolls. Used to frame and emphasise the words of Muhammad, this edges and unifies the dome decoration. The predominating colours of red, cream, pale blue, silver and gold in the dome, in reality create a delicately patterned golden surface climbing to a shining central motif.

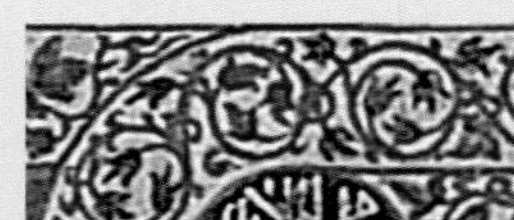

Stars and jewels
The dome's central decoration combines delicate scrolls on silver and gold coloured to imitate jewels, bands of rosettes, stars and swirls with more texts from the Qur'an. The architectural concept of the dome is thought to have been taken from contemporary Byzantine church design – the Dome of the Rock's diameter is within a centimetre of that of the dome of the Church of the Holy Sepulchre in Jerusalem.

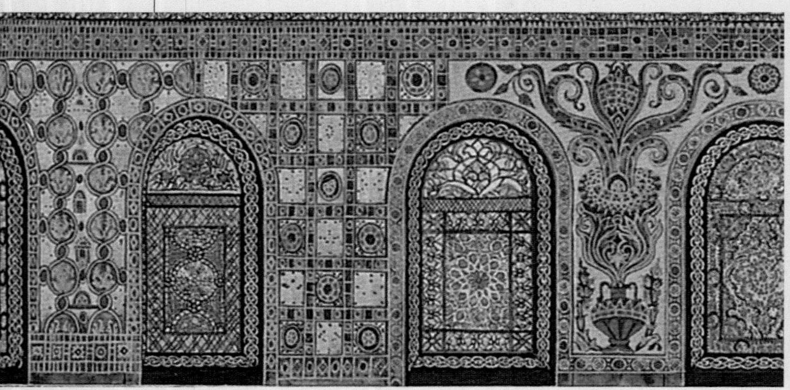

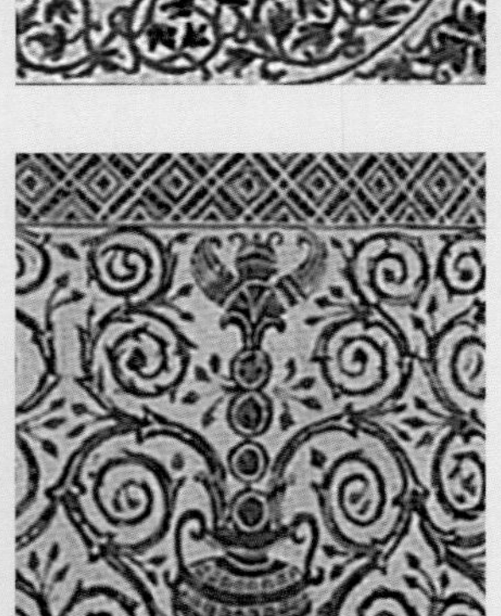

Plants of Paradise
The swirling tendrils of fantastical potted plants stretch across the drum's lower register. Drawn from Roman and Byzantine vegetal forms, seen on the *Ara Pacis*, 13–9 BCE (pages 32–3) and in San Vitale, 530s–547 (pages 46–7), these elaborate plants have associations with 'sacred trees', heavenly realms and Paradise. The patterning continues to develop in the edging of diamond hatching, arches and vine scrolls.

In the Gardens of Paradise

The patterning of the main area of the dome consists of sinuous tri-lobe wave forms, which flow evenly across the curved surface. Surrounding these, vegetal plant scrolls with red and green jewel-like leaf forms are set against pale blue and cream backgrounds. The symbolism of these forms is not recorded but they may represent the plants of the Gardens of Paradise, the destination for all devout Muslims.

Dome of the Rock, section looking south, William Harvey, 1909

This pen, ink and colour drawing of the Dome of the Rock captures the intense detail of the patterned interior of the shrine. In the main ambulatory below the dome, more decorative detail shows the architectural and ornamental links to Byzantine precursors in the coloured marble pillars, arches and revetment. The vegetal mosaic patterns continue through the lower levels while the marble provides additional naturally patterned elements.

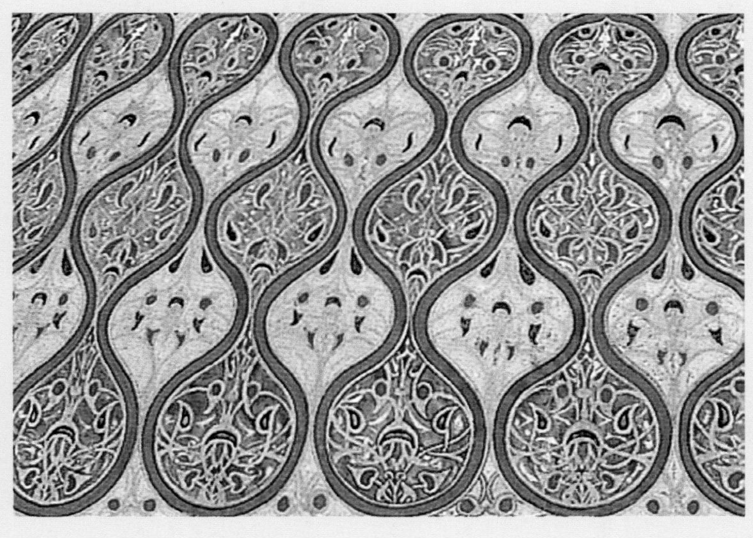

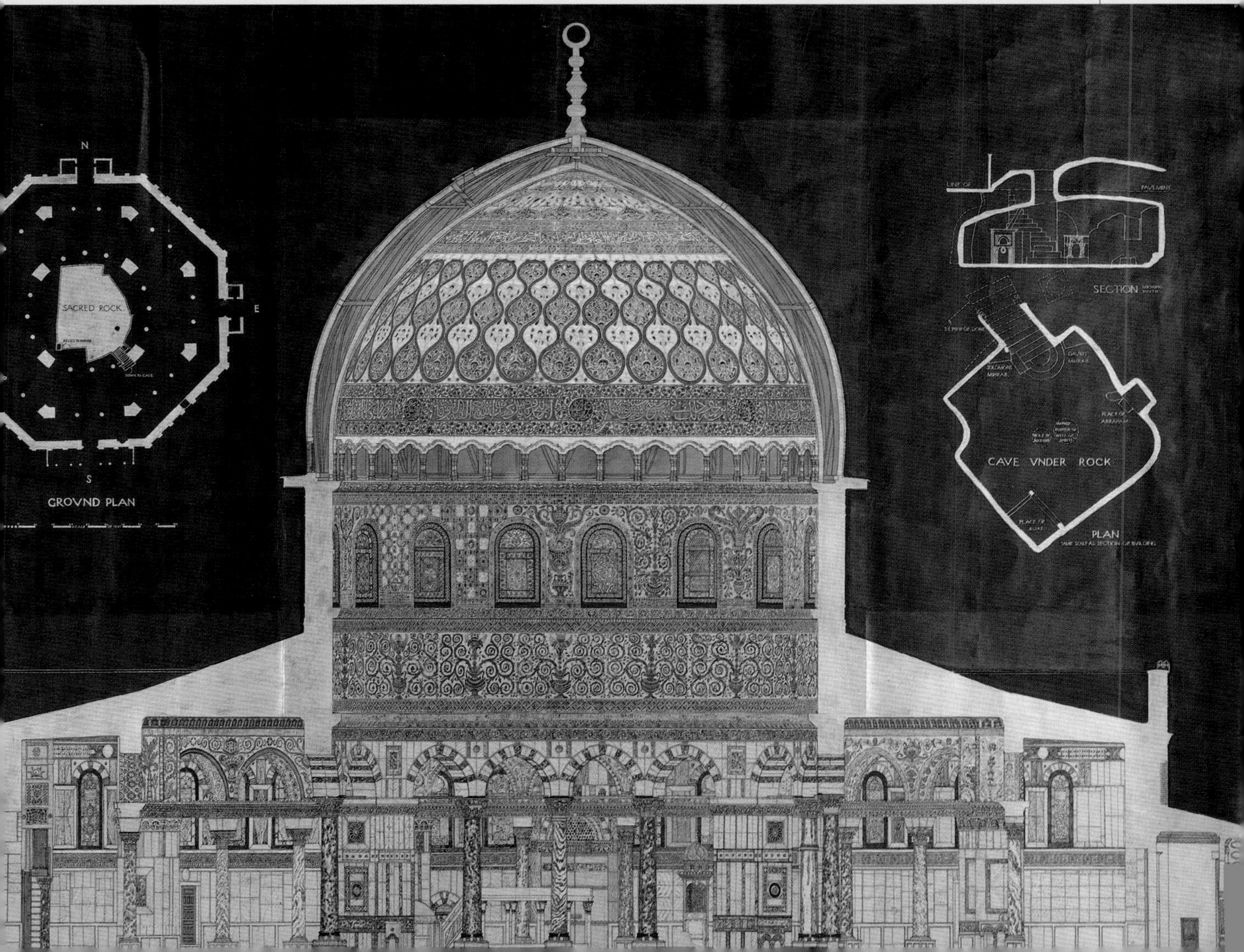

Flowers, Scrolls & Dragons
618–1127

Developing patterns in medieval China

The luxury items of the Tang (618–906) and Song (960–1279) dynasties were decorated with delicate patterns including floral and vegetal scrolls. The media of silver and stoneware enabled these fine patterning forms. Some of these luxury goods have been found in buried hoards. Many vessels from this period were used for rituals in Buddhist temples, and the multi-coloured decoration of the Buddhist shrines at Dunhuang demonstrates the vibrant patterns probably prevalent across China at this time. Silver and gold were highly valued and were also used to make images of the Buddha.

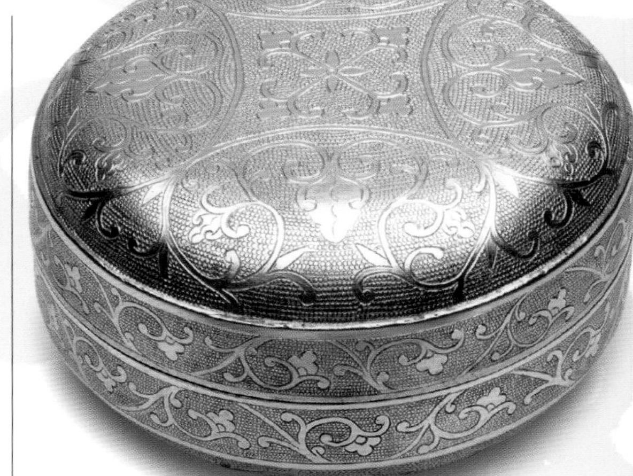

Silver lidded box, 618–907, *China*
Continuous floral scrolls decorate the sides of this finely patterned box. On the lid, a symmetrical arrangement of four scroll motifs with stylised flower heads surround a cross-form of similar flower scrolls. The background is textured with a fine weave-like pattern, which emphasises the smooth flowing lines of the scrolls. The box may have contained medicine or cosmetics and would have been a greatly prized possession.

Gold and chased silver censer, 618–960, *China*
The two halves of the censer are pierced and incised with a delicate scrolling pattern of single and tri-lobe leaves that surround the gimballed incense bowl. Silver was popular in the Tang dynasty and began to be imported for luxury items from Iran and Central Asia along the Silk Road from the 7th century. The fine vegetal patterning echoes scroll and leaf designs from the Middle East.

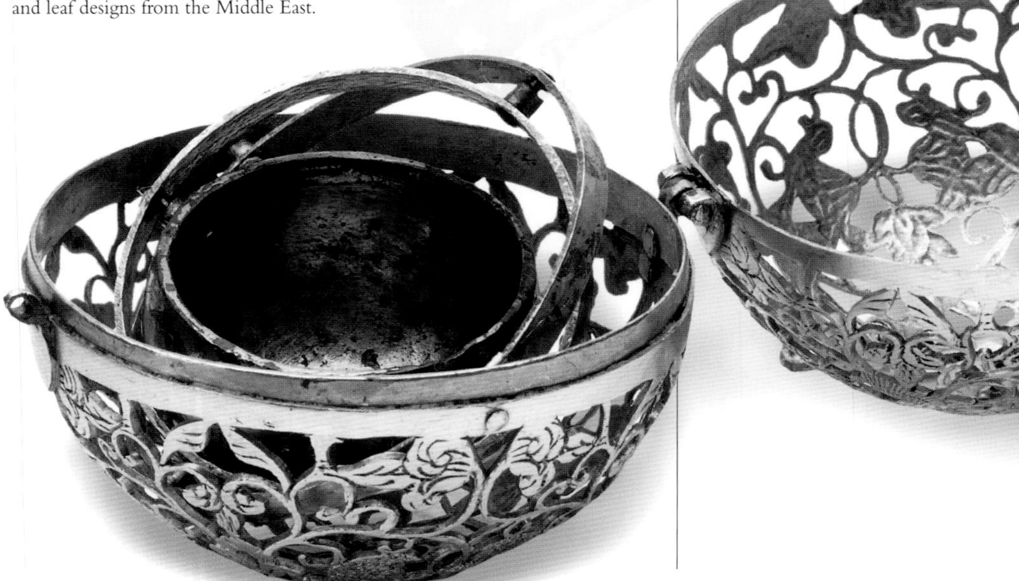

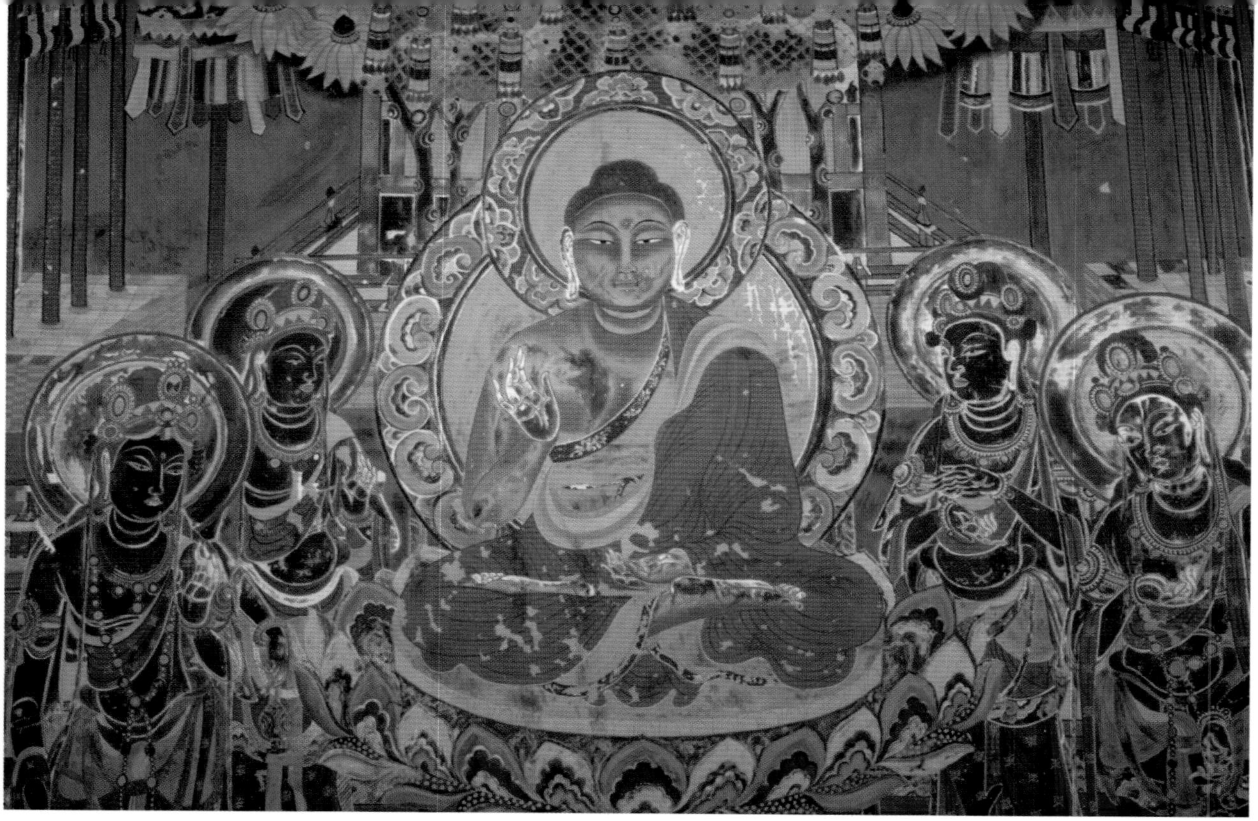

‘The artists and craftsmen of China were never closed to new ideas. At this period of ebullient experimentation … craftsmen evolved a whole canon of style.’

MARY TREGEAR,
Chinese Art, 1980

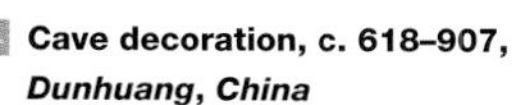

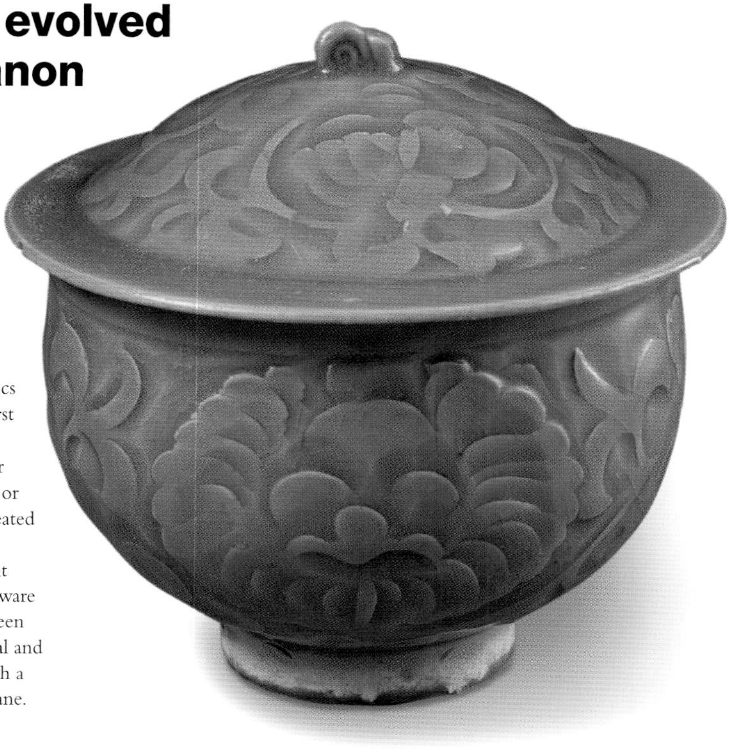

Cave decoration, c. 618–907,
Dunhuang, China
The Buddha Amitabha sits on a decorated lotus flower throne where each petal is patterned with multi-coloured ribbed bands. The halo and aura are edged with individual scrolls and multi-lobed patterns which continue the polychrome effect of the lotus. The Buddha is surrounded with bodhisattvas (figures on the way to acquiring Enlightenment) and sits within a palace with striped and checked detail under a canopy decorated with flowers.

Lidded bowl, 1000–1125,
Shaanxi, China
The earliest decorated ceramics in China, from early in the first millennium CE, had simple patterning often simulating or representing birds, fish, plants or flowers. These forms were created by carving into the clay and allowing the glaze to highlight the pattern. This lidded stoneware bowl, with a pale ‘celadon’ green glaze, is decorated with a floral and scroll pattern interspersed with a simplified dragon face and mane.

ELEMENTS OF PATTERN

- *single and tri-lobe leaf scrolls*
- *birds, fish and flowers*
- *the lotus flower*
- *multi-coloured stripes, ribs and scrolls*

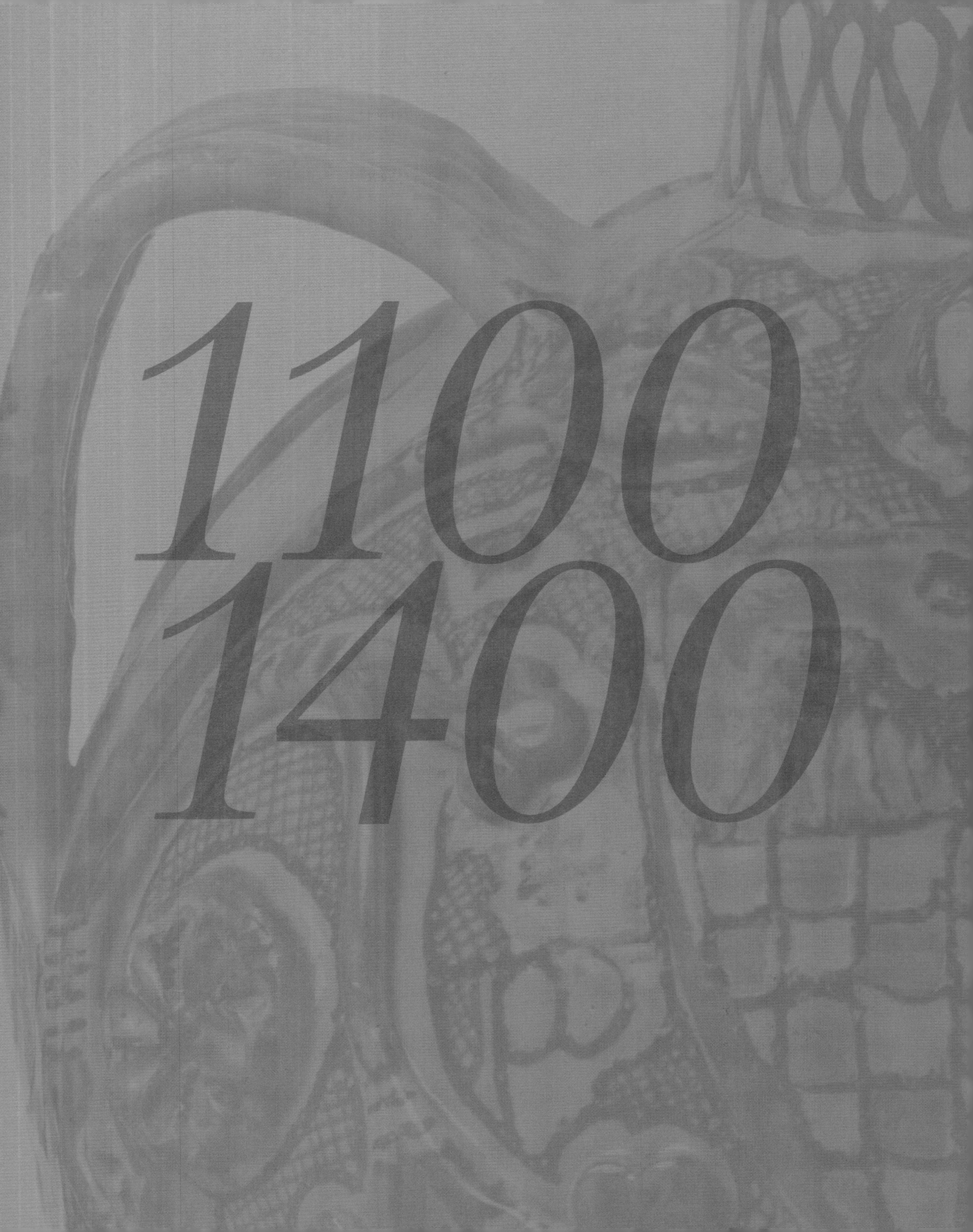

1100
1400

Late Medieval

Introduction

The supreme importance of colour, pattern, light and decoration in Christian contexts across all regions was articulated in many different ways to create heavenly effects on earth in order to express and celebrate Christianity. Motifs were formalised in specific contexts and for special purposes by agencies such as heraldry, Islamic design and the Cosmatesque tradition in Rome.

From the late 1120s, the new aesthetic principles and technological innovations of Gothic style were expressed in the rebuilt east end of the French royal abbey church of Saint-Denis, near Paris. By the mid-13th century, the Gothic building tradition was established throughout Europe and had deeply influenced design and pattern-making in all media. In Byzantium, *cloisonné* enamel, using wire cells filled with translucent enamel glass, created complex and finely made geometric and floral patterns on ecclesiastical objects, shining and twinkling in the candlelight of church interiors. The visual atmosphere of a Byzantine church was heightened by the effects of light on gold mosaics, recreating Heaven on earth and the appropriate context for the display of holy icons.

In Rome, especially in the 13th century, there were efforts to renovate and improve the status of the city through the redecoration of churches. Stoneworkers adorned pavements and church furniture with complex mosaic patterns drawn from designs executed in the Roman, and possibly Byzantine, *opus sectile* technique. These Cosmatesque patterns included the *quincunx*, a motif linked with the cross and symbolising heavenly order. Scrolls and the guilloche, patterned

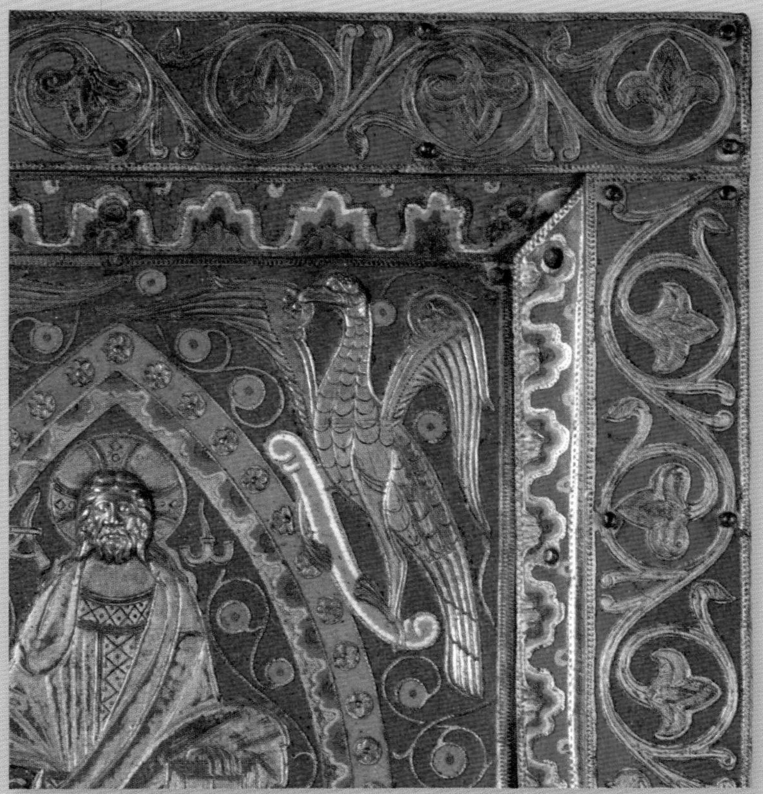

In northern Europe, the champlevé *technique of incising metal and filling it with coloured glass paste created subtle patterns on metal surfaces. This illuminated effect of heavenly imagery stimulated the making of strikingly rich visual objects for ecclesiastical use, such as reliquaries, book covers, panels, crosses and crosiers.*

inside and around twisting bands, also featured in these new designs. Strips decorated in gold and studded with multi-coloured stones created glittering effects with elaborate multi-layered interlocking designs.

The illuminated Luttrell Psalter was painted around 1320–40 for the private perusal of Sir Geoffrey Luttrell, an English nobleman owning lands at Irnham in Lincolnshire. The rich illustrations of the psalter are complex images of belief, imagination and reality that were derived from Sir Geoffrey's world. Ideals of chivalry and scenes from the agricultural year are combined with fantastical beasts and real animals in a complex expression of ideology in this document of late medieval society.

Designs for silk textiles comprising real and fantastical animals or birds in roundels were superseded by a new style featuring unenclosed animated creatures with foliage and flowers in a flowing composition. Woven in Italy, 'lampas' silks with exotic patterns based on Near Eastern designs were traded throughout Europe, and often exchanged as luxury gifts of secular and ecclesiastical clothing and furnishings. Pattern styles, motifs and craft techniques, such as silk weaving, were transferred along the Silk Road trading network, linking China with Iran, the Middle East and western Europe. In 13th-century Iran, patterns on religious and domestic objects began to show the emergence of the 'arabesque' style.

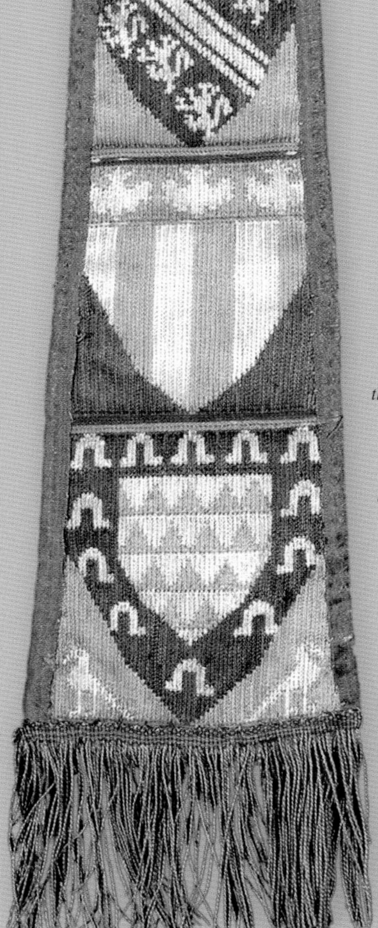

The 'occasional roll', a document recording the coats of arms of those present on a special occasion such as a military tournament or campaign, was first used in England during the late 13th century. It informed the layout of many designs for glazers and by the 14th century heraldry had become a common theme for stained-glass windows. The armorial roll inspired designs for other objects such as silk embroidered ecclesiastical vestments.

The arabesque featured fine floral scrolls with tendrils arranged within geometric or circular shapes overlapping as layered patterns.

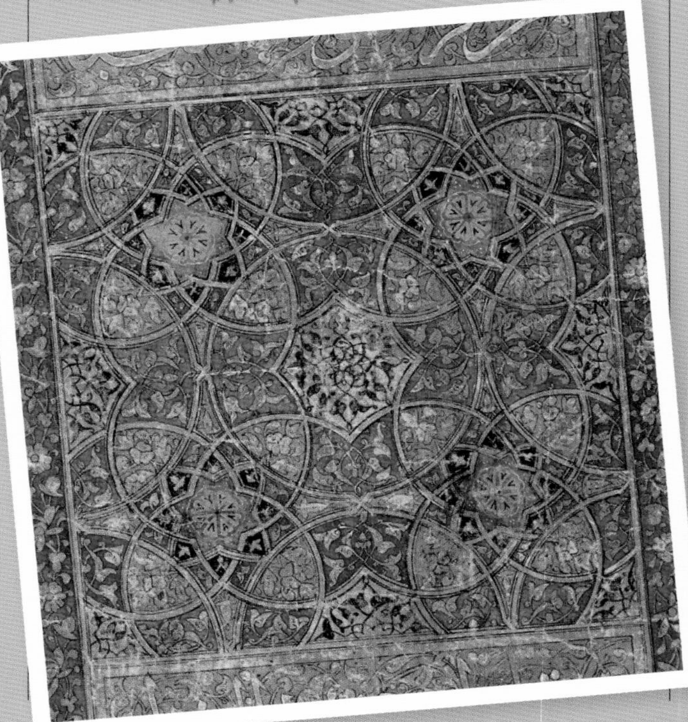

Patterning the Divine 1000–1200

Romanesque to Gothic

As tastes derived from the western Roman Empire combined with eastern Roman imperial style from Byzantine Christian art, a new European style emerged, known as 'Romanesque'. The first churches in stone were built with relatively simple plans, using round-headed arches above doors and windows, thick walls supporting semicircular barrel-vaulted ceilings and ornamental arcading. During the 12th century in France the Romanesque was developed into the 'Gothic' style. Ecclesiastical and civic buildings throughout Europe were built with complex plans, pointed arches, irregular internal spaces with rib-vaulted ceilings, and flying buttresses to support higher walls and towers. The emphasis on height and light was reinforced by windows with stone tracery patterns filled with multi-coloured glass.

Arcade, 1070–77, *Canterbury Cathedral, England*
The overlapping arches of the arcade form pointed shapes above rounded arches between the columns set into the exterior north wall of the cathedral. They are decorated with rows of cut-out rectangular motifs and pointed lozenges. Arcading in front of a wall ('blind' arcading) was frequently used in English Romanesque, or Norman, buildings. The Norman church at Canterbury was built by Archbishop Lanfranc in 1070–77 after the Anglo-Saxon church was destroyed by fire.

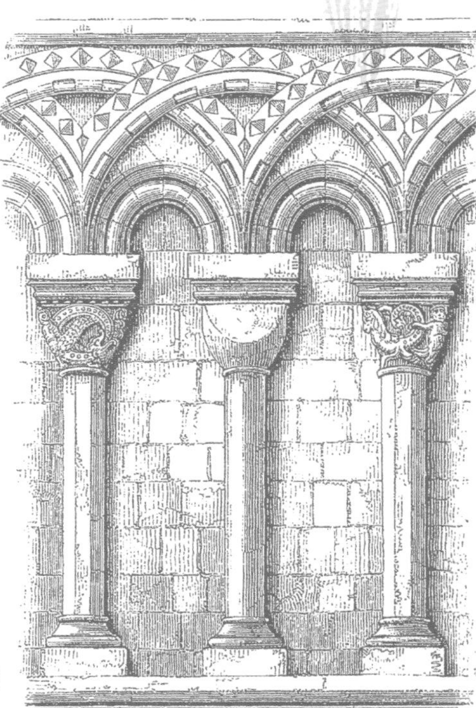

Column capital, c. 1100, *Moissac Abbey, France*
An arcade pattern of overlapping arches carved with pairs of acanthus leaves springs from small curling leaves around the upper part of this capital. The lower part is ornamented with a curving pattern infilled with rows of tripartite leaves, and three binding strips with small square pellets anchor the design. This capital is from one of the columns surrounding the cloister of Moissac Abbey.

'The medieval mind regarded light as a manifestation of the divine.'

BRIGITTE KERMANN-SCHWARZ, *Gothic*, 2004

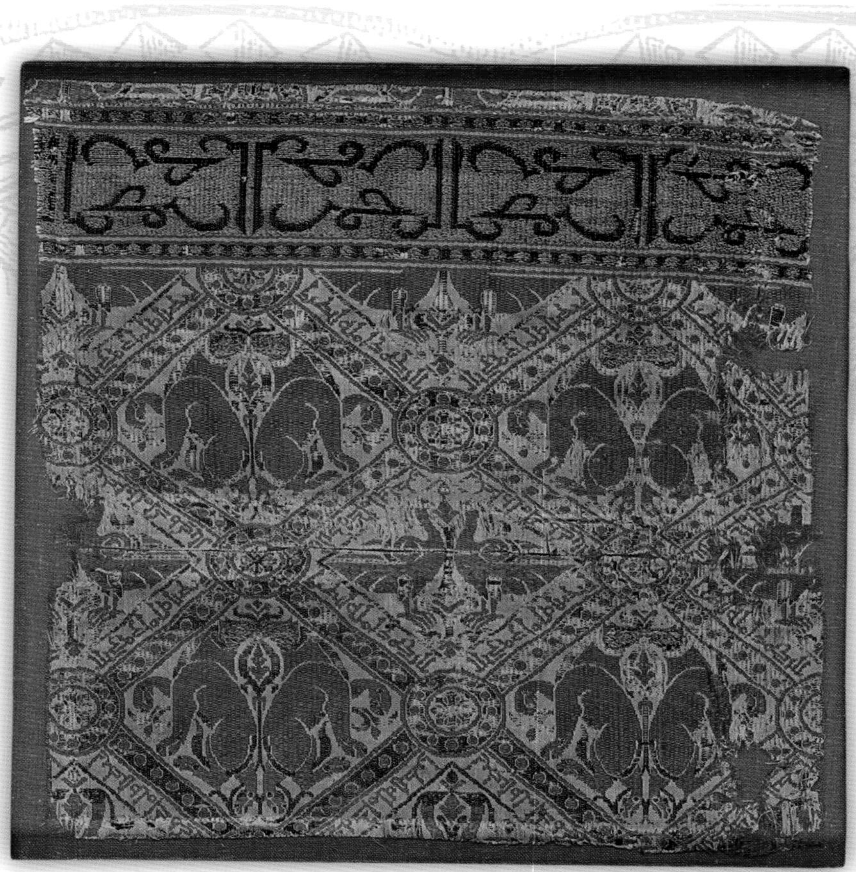

Silk textile, 1100–50,
Almeria, Andalucia, Spain
Symmetrically posed pairs of wingless gryphons and peacocks are arranged in lozenges with rings filled with small pellets at the intersections. An inscription in Islamic Kufic script runs around the inside of the lozenges containing the peacocks. The inscription in the border above, between two rows of lozenges, reads 'The merciful Kufic'. This woven lampas silk with gold thread was probably a royal or diplomatic gift.

Window glass, c. 1200,
Canterbury Cathedral, England
This painted glass panel contains a pattern of bunches of five acanthus leaves bound together with horizontal bands, set against a background alternately blue and red. The outer leaves of each bunch form the ends of an encircling ribbon around which two other longer leaves curl. The leaves and ribbons are shaded with darker paint to produce the illusion of movement.

ELEMENTS OF PATTERN

- *overlapping arcades*
- *acanthus petals and leaves with binding strips*
- *ribbons scrolling around other motifs*
- *rings as connecting devices*

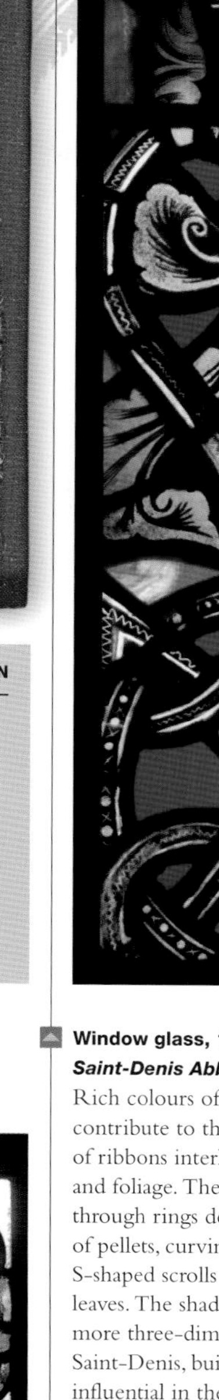

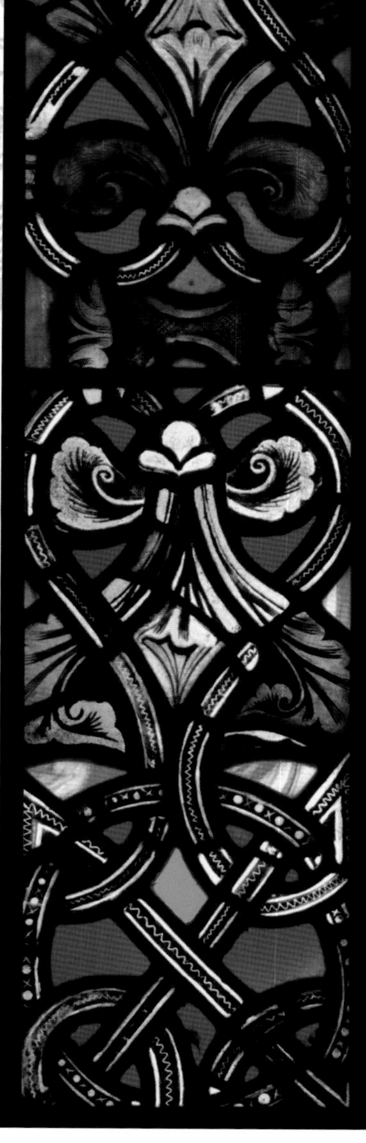

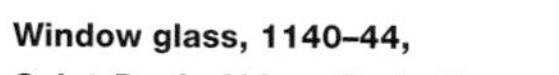

Window glass, 1140–44,
Saint-Denis Abbey, Paris, France
Rich colours of stained and painted glass contribute to the complexity of this pattern of ribbons interlacing with acanthus petals and foliage. The ribbons cross and loop through rings decorated with a pattern of pellets, curving away from the ring in S-shaped scrolls to end in pairs of acanthus leaves. The shading with black paint creates a more three-dimensional effect. The Abbey of Saint-Denis, built by Abbot Suger, was highly influential in the spread of the Gothic style.

PATTERN IN DETAIL

Heavenly Vines & Scrolls c. 1200

Decorative Limoges enamels

Early *champlevé* – 'raised field' – enamelling from Limoges in France (12th–13th centuries) included a range of patterns that employed both the variety of coloured glass and the worked metal surface. The objects that were produced in these workshops, and in the Mosan valley (of the Meuse River flowing through France, Belgium and the Netherlands), were largely religious – gospel covers, reliquaries, devotional panels and triptychs, crosses, crosiers, candlesticks and caskets – decorated with Christian subjects.

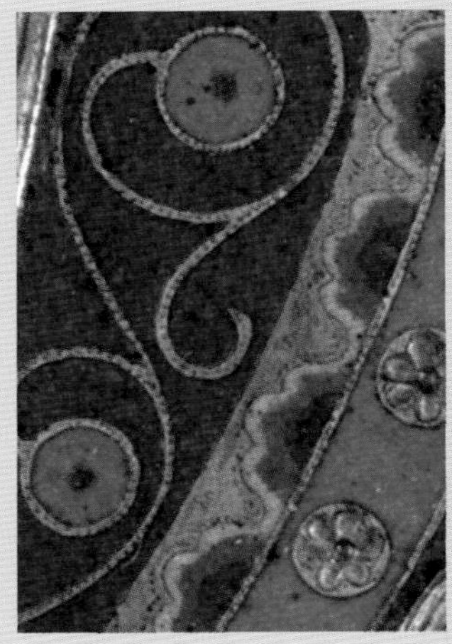

Scrolls and circles

The background of the main panel is decorated with a scroll ending in turquoise circles with red dots. *Champlevé* enamelling involved engraving or casting a metal panel with the design, leaving troughs for the enamel. These areas were then filled with coloured glass powder, fired to melting point and polished. The blue background emulated one of the most prized and expensive materials – lapis lazuli.

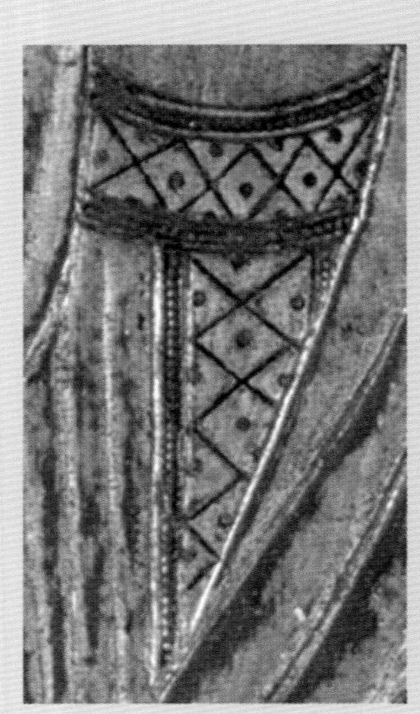

Diamonds and dots

Gilded copper alloy offered a practical and durable material for working and casting into figurative and decorative details. Christ's robe is mainly formed of metal worked into folds but underneath he wears a shift with decorative bands of diamonds and dots edged with beading. This simulates a jewelled or embroidered band of fabric often seen decorating the robes of Early Christian and medieval religious figures.

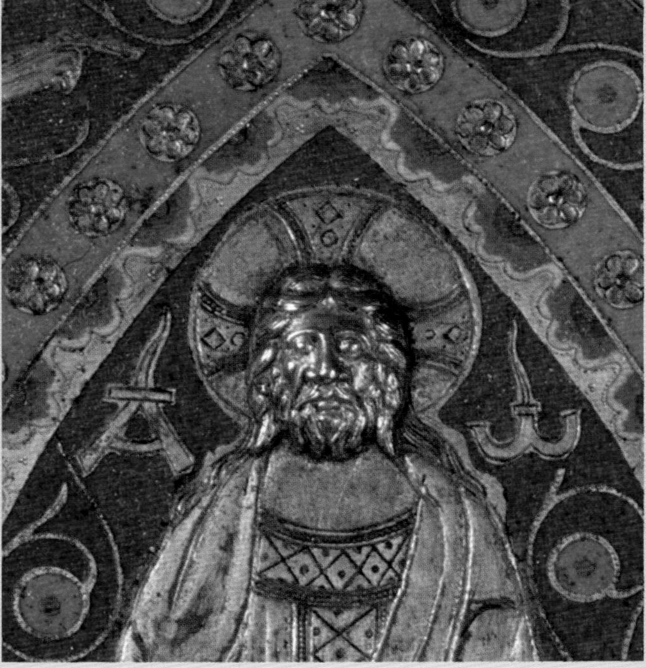

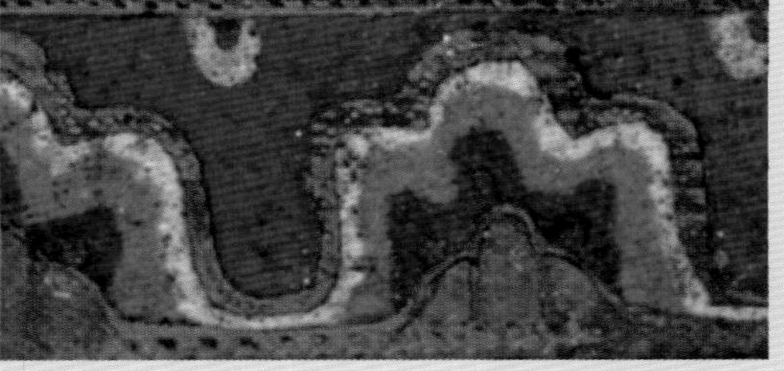

Coloured three-arched waves

The metal wave surrounded by coloured enamel is edged with a small scalloped metal strip over incised tri-lobed forms. The motif links to three red spines, which form the base for the royal blue, sky blue and white bands, and the three-arched beaded metal wave. Beyond the wave, lapis blue is interspersed with small yellow and red points.

Rainbow mandorla

Christ sits within a mandorla – an almond-shaped halo of light – edged with a rainbow. Echoing the frame's pattern, this coloured wave has a golden beaded scalloping with yellow, green, blue and red, completed by aligned raised rosettes in the outer turquoise band. The mandorla would originally have given the book cover a rich and sparkling centre.

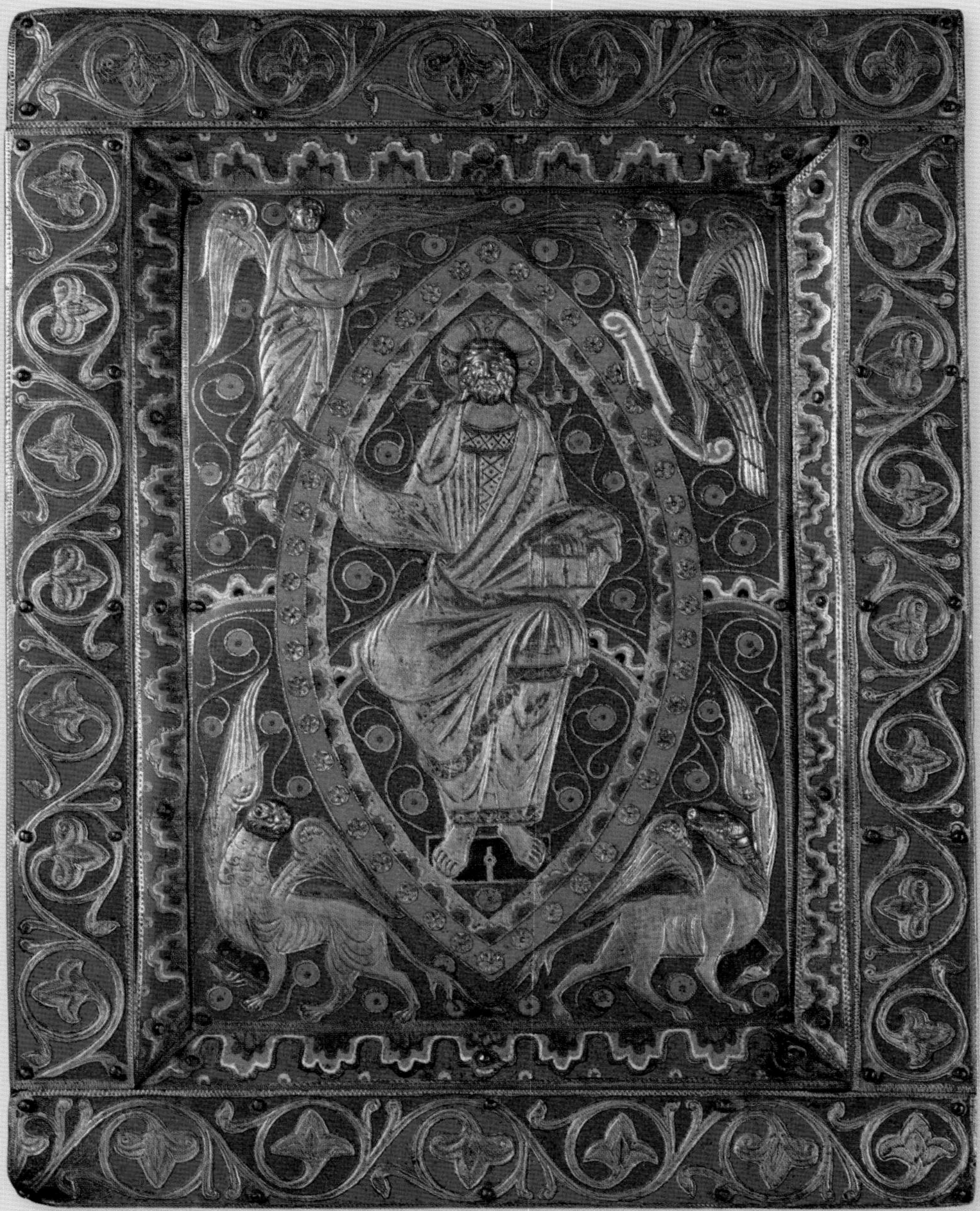

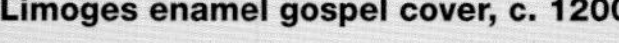

Limoges enamel gospel cover, c. 1200
The book cover represents Christ in majesty attended by the symbols of the winged Four Evangelists – Matthew (man/angel), Mark (lion), Luke (ox) and John (eagle). It is given depth and vibrancy by the subtle use of coloured enamels and gilded metal work. Different blues – royal, lapis, sky and turquoise – add light and form while fine beading and scalloping reflect the light. The frequent use of tri-formed motifs referenced the Holy Trinity.

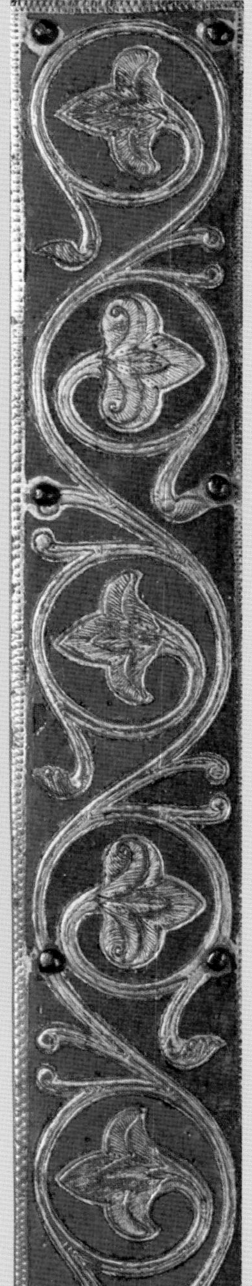

Vine scrolls
The outer panels of the frame are decorated with an intricately carved vine scroll arranged into a large wave. Each repeat contains a trident leaf on the end of a tendril and the whole vine is naturalistically engraved. The spaces created on alternating sides of the vine are filled on the outer with royal blue and on the inner with lapis blue.

PATTERN IN DETAIL

A Patterned Paradise Garden c. 1200

Patterns of Middle Byzantium

Middle Byzantine period (843–1204) patterns were often intricately worked in ivory, gold, precious and semi-precious stones, pearls and enamel. By the 12th century, enamels were designed to a very fine detail with the pattern created from tiny gold *cloisons* – partitions of translucent and opaque coloured glass enamel. Vegetal scrolling, fine medallions and rosettes contained details constructed at the micro-millimetre level, which were filled with powdered glass, fired and polished to create a rich glinting surface.

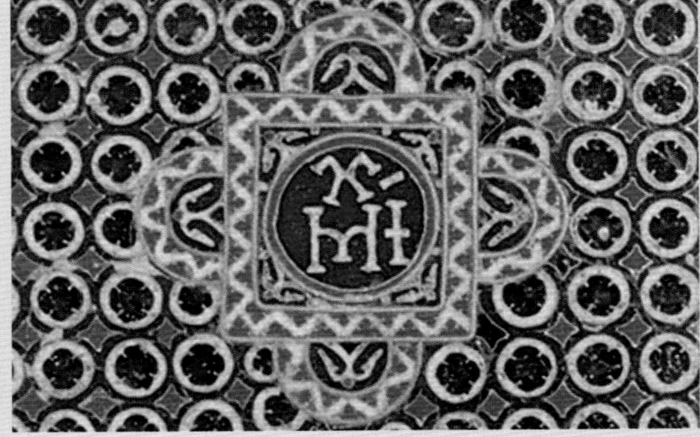

A carpet of rosettes
Behind Michael's head the surface is carpeted with translucent green rosettes set on white, blue and red. As is traditional on Byzantine icons, his name is inscribed beside his head – 'Archangel Michael'. This is set within a square and semicircular motif elaborately picked out with a minute scroll.

Jewelled banding
A universal pattern used in Byzantine imagery was a jewelled band, sometimes including pearls. It was reproduced extensively in representations of thrones and royal costumes. The jewels here are interspersed with vegetal motifs and interlocking scrolls, giving an idea of the rich decoration that existed in imperial circles.

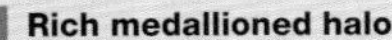

Rich medallioned halo

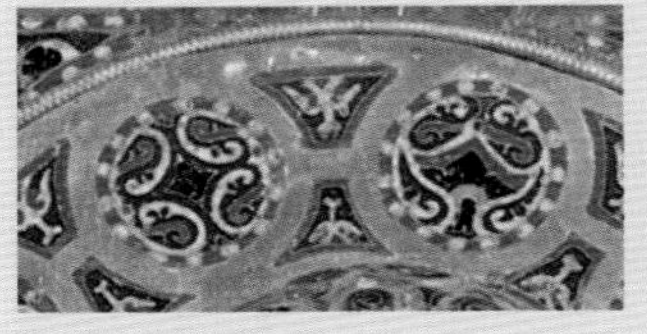

The Archangel Michael's halo is formed of medallions of two different patterns – an elaborate cross form turning into a vegetal scroll, and a schematic vase or plant form. In between, triangular motifs seem to contain stylised birds or plants. The teardrop or petal shape appears in both designs and was a popular motif, used in a larger form to emulate the cypress tree.

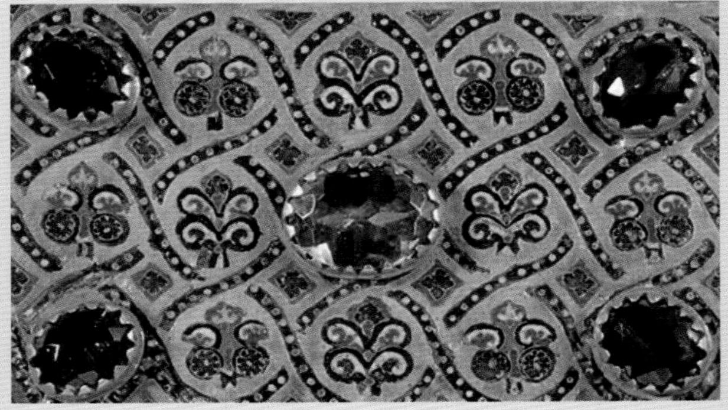

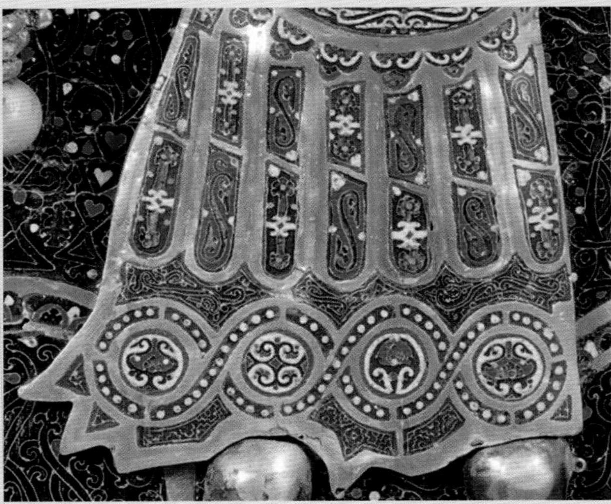

Enamelled armour
Soldier-saints and archangels were dressed as traditional Roman soldiers. The cuirass and skirt here are picked out with patterned details – little flowers and hexagons forming the armoured chest piece and coloured flower and scroll panels simulating stripes of leather. The roundels and scrolls at the edge of the skirt echo the halo pattern, and in between they are infilled with swirling blue and gold filigree.

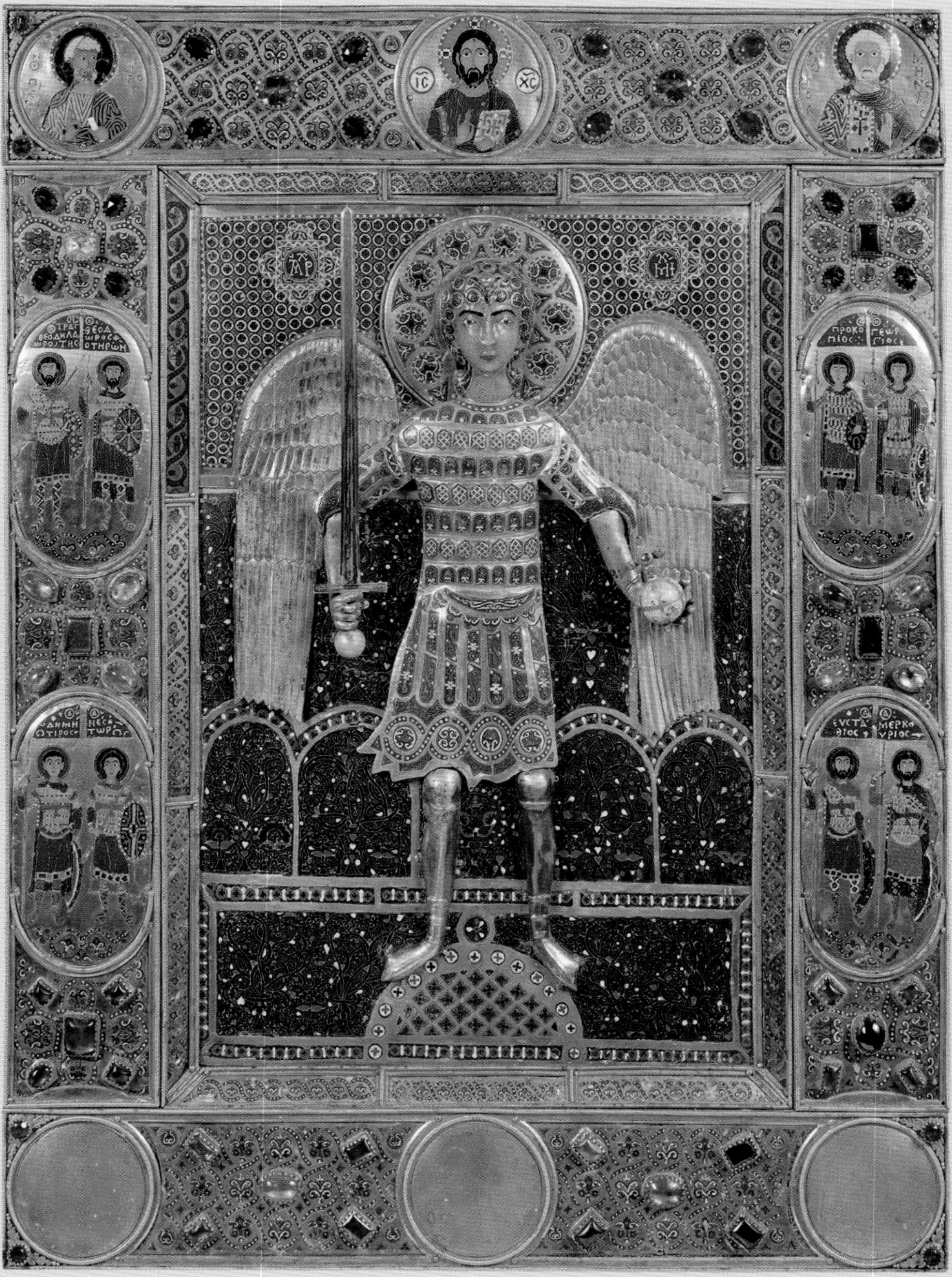

Icon of the Archangel Michael, *Constantinople*
The Archangel Michael protects a Paradise garden in this exquisite icon demonstrating the peak of achievement in Byzantine enamel work. The elaborately detailed pattern sets off the exceptionally enamelled embossed hair and three-dimensional face. The jewels and wings may have been replaced, but the complex, rich and unified patterns create a truly astounding impact.

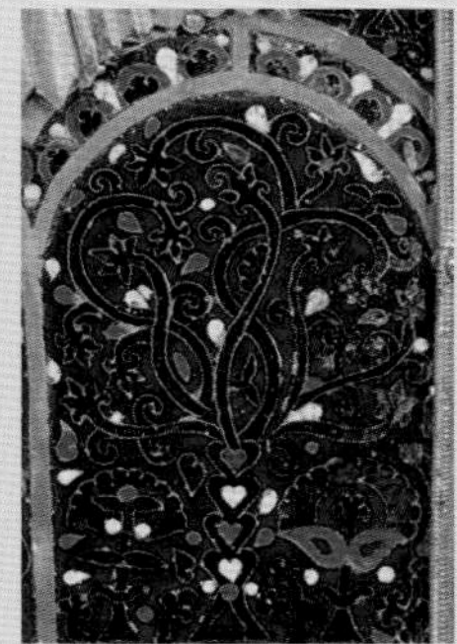

Plants in Paradise
The sinuous branches of exotic plants form the central motif of the lower panels behind Michael – the image of an imaginary Paradise. Reminiscent of the 'sacred tree', these plants contain scrolling tendrils, leaves, flowers and fruit issuing from a trunk of hearts. Beside these, other fantastical plants and flowers, including small cypress trees and colourful bushes, fill the spaces against a translucent heavenly blue.

Emblazoned Devices 1290–1450

Heraldry

During the 13th century, the art of heraldry and its language became formalised through a system of motifs and designs rendered in 'tinctures' (colours), metals and fur patterns. These marks of individual or family status were woven into textiles, painted on wood and applied to metal by glass enamelling, the only technique then available to permanently fix colours to metal. In the 14th century, plain areas in coloured glass window designs were often intricately 'diapered' (patterned) with foliage, scrolls or flourishes, painted in black or left in reserve in a black ground. Tiles and pottery were also decorated with heraldic designs as symbols of personal power.

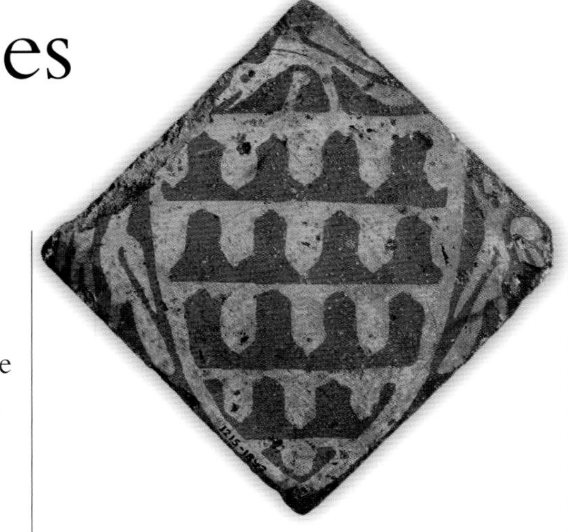

Tile, c. 1300, *Muchelney Abbey, Somerset, England*
This earthenware tile has been stamped and inlaid with a coat of arms in white clay. The shield has a pattern of interlocking light and dark shapes representing the fur 'vair'. The bird supporters around the shield may be eagles, in which case this is the coat of arms of Sir John Beauchamp of Hache, who died in 1301.

Variations of the field
Patterns used in heraldry on a 'field' (background colour or metal of a shield).

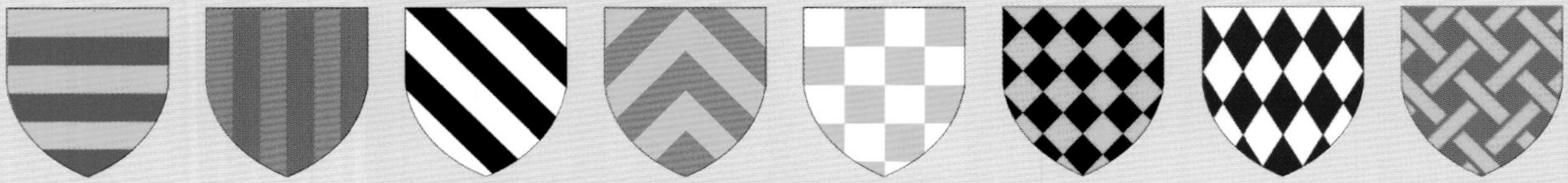

Barry
Or and *azure.*

Paly
Gules and *vert.*

Bendy
Argent and *sable.*

Chevrony
Or and *gules.*

Chequy
Argent and *or.*

Lozengy
Or and *sable.*

Fusily
Argent and *purpure.*

Fretty
Vert; fretty, or.

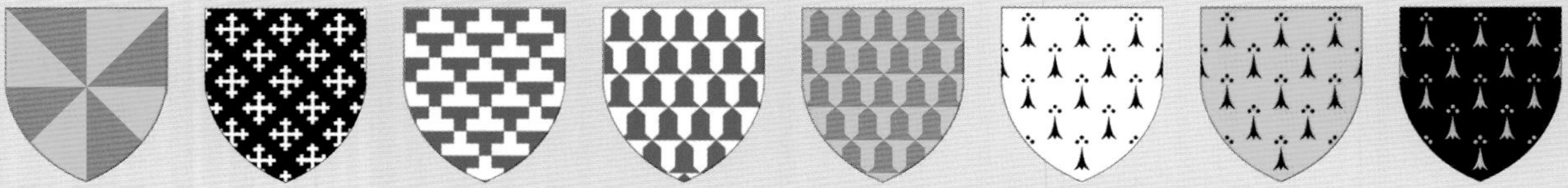

Gyronny
Gules and *or.*

Semy
Pattern of repeated devices, e.g. semy-crusilly; *sable*; cross-crosslets, *argent.*

Potent
Interlocking T-shaped 'potents' (crutches), *azure* and *argent.*

Vair
Fur of squirrel with grey-blue back and white front, *azure* and *argent.*

Vairy
Gules and *or.* Tinctures and metals other than *azure* and *argent.*

Ermine
Winter fur of stoat, white with black tail. Three studs attach the tufted stoat's tail or 'ermine spot'.

Erminois
Ermine with *or* background.

Pean
Erminois reversed.

KEY

Tinctures
gules
azure
vert
purpure
sable

Metals
or
argent

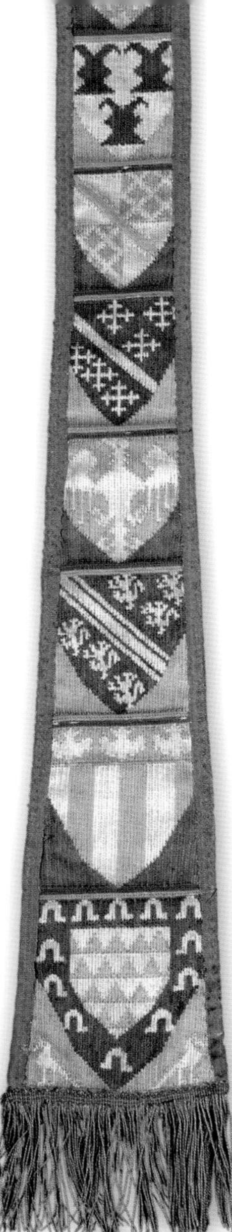

Stole, 1300–50, *England*
Made from linen embroidered with silk threads, this ecclesiastical stole displays a series of heraldic shields representing the arms of noble families – for example, the lowest shield is that of William de Ferrers. It displays an inner pattern of *vair* (fur) in *or* (gold) and *gules* (red) in a border of *azure* (blue) with 12 horseshoes in *argent* (silver), the latter a pun on the French *ferrier* (to shoe a horse).

Casket, 1290–1324, *France or England*
This copper casket is covered with a repeated pattern of lozenge shields displaying the royal arms of England (*gules*, three lions *or*) and the badges of five related families – Valence (Earls of Pembroke), Dreux (Brittany), Angoulême, Brabant and Lacy (Earls of Lincoln). All six badges are shown equally and in the same numbers, rendered in coloured glass enamel applied to engraved shapes in the *champlevé* technique.

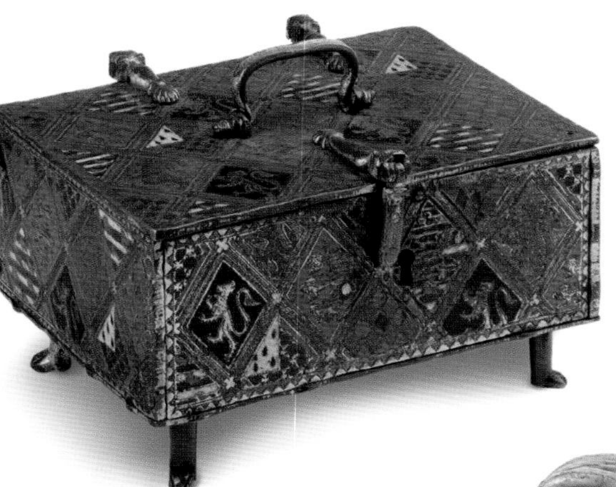

Panel, 1325–77, *England*
The red glass, against which the pattern of crosses is set, the yellow 'fess' (band) and clear glass shapes around the shield have been painted with leaf and flower patterns, or 'diapered'. This panel was perhaps made as part of a window to commemorate a tournament or military campaign. The shield shows the badge of Roger Beauchamp of Bletsoe, baron of Edward III, and Lord Chamberlain to the Royal Household from 1376 to 1377.

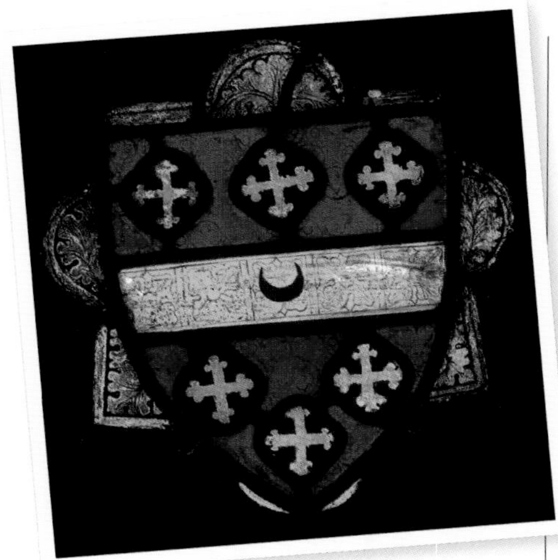

ELEMENTS OF PATTERN

- *multiple stripes, checks, chevrons and lozenges*
- *repeated individual 'charges' (devices) as semy patterns*
- *stylised furs*

'Heraldry ... the systematic hereditary use of an arrangement of charges or devices on a shield.'

THOMAS WOODCOCK & JOHN MARTIN ROBINSON, *The Oxford Guide to Heraldry*, 1990

Jar, 1395–1430, *Orvieto, Umbria, Italy*
This earthenware tin-glazed jar is decorated with a raised sinuous plant pattern growing from the base, with leafy shoots sometimes ending in flowers and faces, painted copper green. The background is crossed-hatched and painted in manganese brown, with flowers and lozenges with green centres. The heraldic shield shows a 'chequy' pattern of white and yellow. The jar was probably used to store dry medicines in the Ottoni family home.

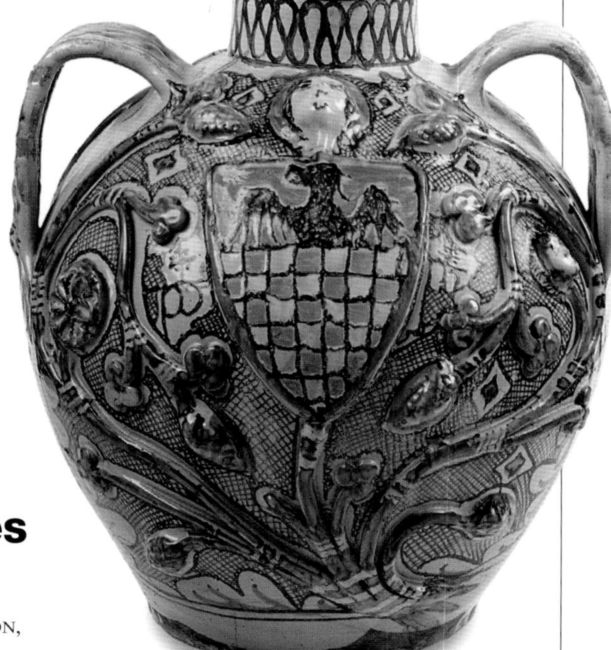

The Cosmati Family
Active 1190–1303

The Cosmati family worked in Rome in the 12th and 13th centuries and were skilled craftsmen of the decorative style of geometrically ornamented and coloured church furniture. The family was, perhaps, the most notable because the technique was named after them – Cosmatesque – but there were more than 60 craftsmen from five or six families working in this style in Rome during the 12th and 13th centuries. The style's popularity and magnificence spread across Europe, and it was used to decorate porticos, pavements, tombs and monuments, altars, *baldacchini*, choir-screens, column and paschal candlesticks, *ciboria*, *ambone*, pulpits and episcopal thrones in Rome, elsewhere in Italy, Sicily and as far afield as Westminster Abbey (1260s–90s).

The family of Cosma had two branches – the Tebaldo, who were active in the late 12th to mid-13th centuries, and the Mellini in the second half of the 13th century. Notably, inscriptions survive for Lorenzo, Jacopo, Cosma and his sons Luca and Jacopo (of the Tebaldo) and for Giovanni and Deodata, sons of Cosma II (of the Mellini). Cosmatesque ornament can be found in some of the most important medieval churches in Rome, including the chapel of the Sancta Sanctorum, the Lateran, Santa Maria in Cosmedin, San Clemente and Santa Maria Maggiore. The Mellini brothers Giovanni and Deodata executed commissions for the tombs of the papal chaplain Stefano Surdi (1295), Cardinal Guglielmo Durando (1300), and Cardinal Consalvo Garcia Gudiel (1299–1303), and the tabernacle of Santa Maria in Cosmedin for Francesco Caetani, nephew of Pope Boniface VIII (1295).

Born
Rome

Profession
Architects, sculptors and mosaicists

Manifesto
Intricate polychrome patterns of mathematical precision

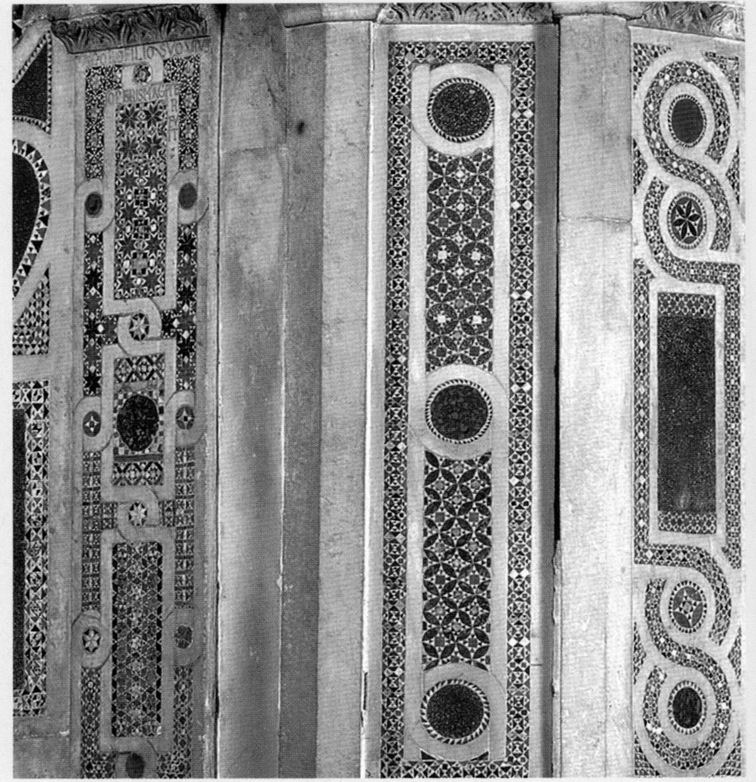

The technique practised by the Cosmati involved the creation of complex pattern matrices using cut and polished multi-coloured stones and sometimes coloured or gold glass, laid out in geometric designs calculated with mathematical precision. The method evolved from the traditions of Roman and Byzantine mosaics, especially the technique of *opus sectile*, which used larger and more irregularly shaped pieces of stone than the small square tesserae used in traditional mosaics. The Cosmati designs were elaborate interlocking compositions of twists and spirals contained by and containing circles, rosettes, hexagons and squares. The cut stones were selected for their range of colours – including purple and green porphyry, white and coloured marble, and serpentine – but an accurate analysis has been prevented by the amount of restoration that has taken place over the centuries as the stones wore away unevenly over time. The placement of the stones created contrasting patterns in red and yellow, pink and green, purple and white, which were built up into intricate shapes.

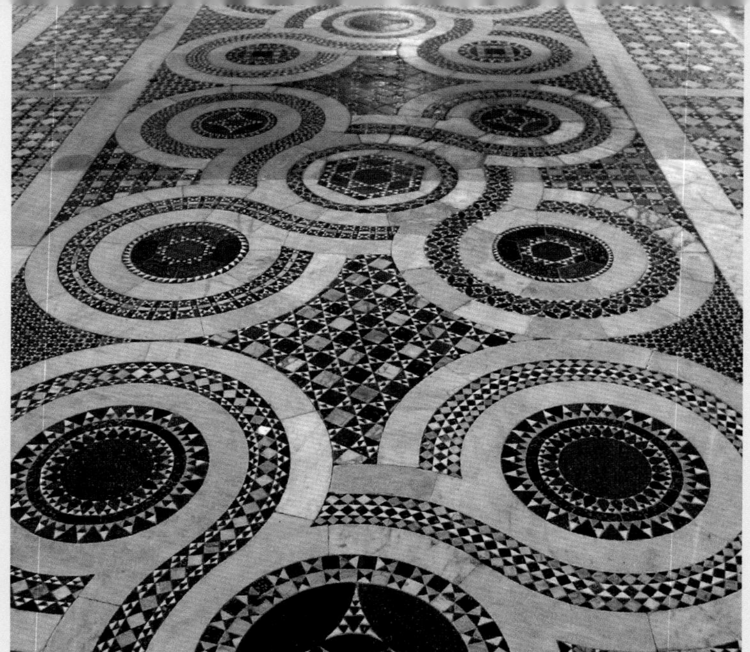

Cathedral pavement, 1231, Cosma and sons, *Anagni*
The continuous twisting patterned band on this pavement creates the components of the quincunx *with the placement and the arrangement of coloured cut stones of purple and green porphyry, and yellow and white marble.*

Ambo, c. 1200, Lorenzo and Jacopo, *Rome*
The Cosmatesque patterns provide edging and more intricate motifs to decorate the ambo in the Church of Santa Maria in Aracoeli in Rome; the finely patterned guilloche and twisted bands emphasise the area where the reader and speaker would stand.

The critical mathematical concept used by the Cosmati was the *quincunx*, a geometric motif consisting of five points – four forming a square or rectangle with the fifth point at the centre. This created complex visual operating on multiple levels – circles in squares; twisting bands and spirals enclosing circles; and hexagons and stars. These in turn were enhanced by a chequer-board of triangular- and square-cut stones – forming decorative backgrounds and inserts.

This popular style was re-introduced during the Renaissance and used to decorate the floors of the Sistine Chapel and the Stanza della Segnatura in Rome, adding to the rich settings of the painted works of Michelangelo and Raphael.

‘… inscriptions … accord them the high honour of *Magistri doctissimi*, an unusual acknowledgement of learning for medieval artists, but perhaps explicable by the mathematical intricacy of their abstract patterns.’

VERONICA SEKULES, *Medieval Art*, 2001

Fabulous Lampas Patterns 1270–1400

Lampas silks

Lampas weaves were probably developed for the production of silk textiles in order to highlight the contrast between the textures of pattern and background. During the weaving process, additional weft (horizontal) threads were brought to the front of the fabric to form the pattern and to emphasise the reflective quality of the silk threads. Lampas silks were often brocaded (patterned) with vibrant designs inspired by the art of different cultures – Chinese, Arab and western European. Animals such as leopards, elephants, swooping eagles, gryphons (eagle-headed winged lions) and wyverns (two-legged dragons) – often collared, chained or enclosed – were combined with flowering plants.

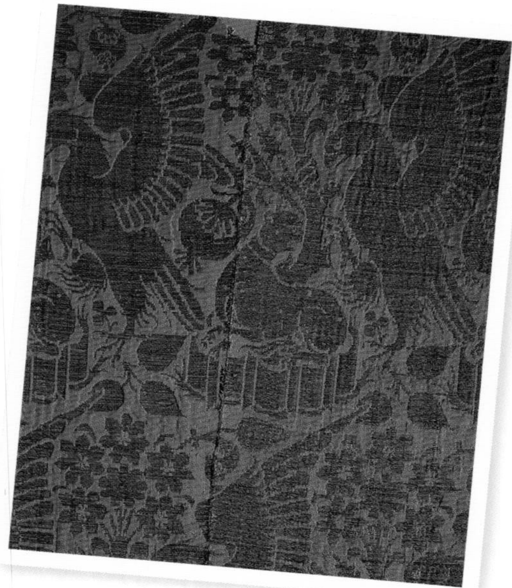

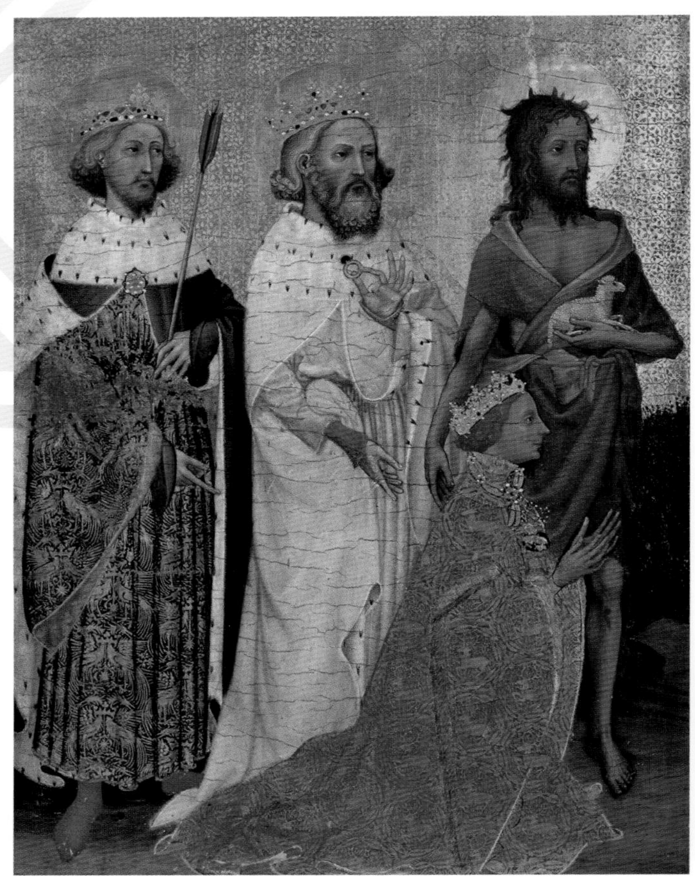

Silk textile, 14th century, *Italy*
This silk textile has been woven with a pattern of eagles swooping down over collared leopards lying in enclosures. A tree twists upwards from behind each leopard, with branches sprouting large flowers, pomegranates and leaves. Each group of motifs – leopard, tree and eagle – is linked into the overall pattern by a double sprig of a trefoil and three large leaves growing from a root curving around the base of the enclosure.

Wilton Diptych (left panel), 1395–99, *England or France*
Richard II, kneeling, is presented by his patron saints, Edmund the Martyr, Edward the Confessor and John the Baptist to Christ and Mary (surrounded by angels, on the right panel). The king's gown is a vermilion and gold textile patterned with his own heraldic device of the white hart, encircled by sprigs of rosemary, the badge of his wife Anne of Bohemia. St Edmund's gown is patterned with birds in pairs, confined by a crown encircling both their necks. This is the left-hand of two hinged oak panels that open to display the interior of the Wilton diptych, painted in egg tempura on a gold background.

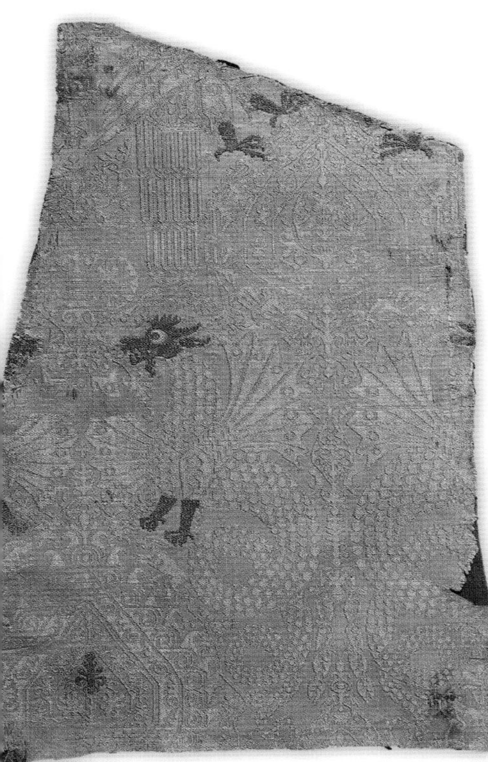

Silk textile, 1270–1330, *Italy or Spain*
The pattern of eagles and wyverns surrounded by complex palmettes, some with scrolled edges, is brocaded in silver and silver-gilt thread. The heads and feet of the animals are emphasised with the application of different colours. This textile may have been used for an ecclesiastical purpose, as most earlier lampas weaves survive from this type of context, but it may derive from the garment or furnishings of a wealthy person.

Hanging, 14th century, *Spain*
Four different motifs are repeated and interlinked by geometric interlace. They are infilled and surrounded by small, highly stylised plant elements of fleur-de-lis and curling leaves, double-links, lozenges and chevrons. The textile from which this was cut originally hung as a drapery behind a statue of the Virgin Mary in Florence. It was probably woven in the city of Granada, the capital of Islamic rule in Spain under the Nasrid kings from 1232 to 1492.

ELEMENTS OF PATTERN

- *real and fantastical animals*
- *restricted or confined beasts*
- *palmettes, leaves and trees*
- *geometric style*

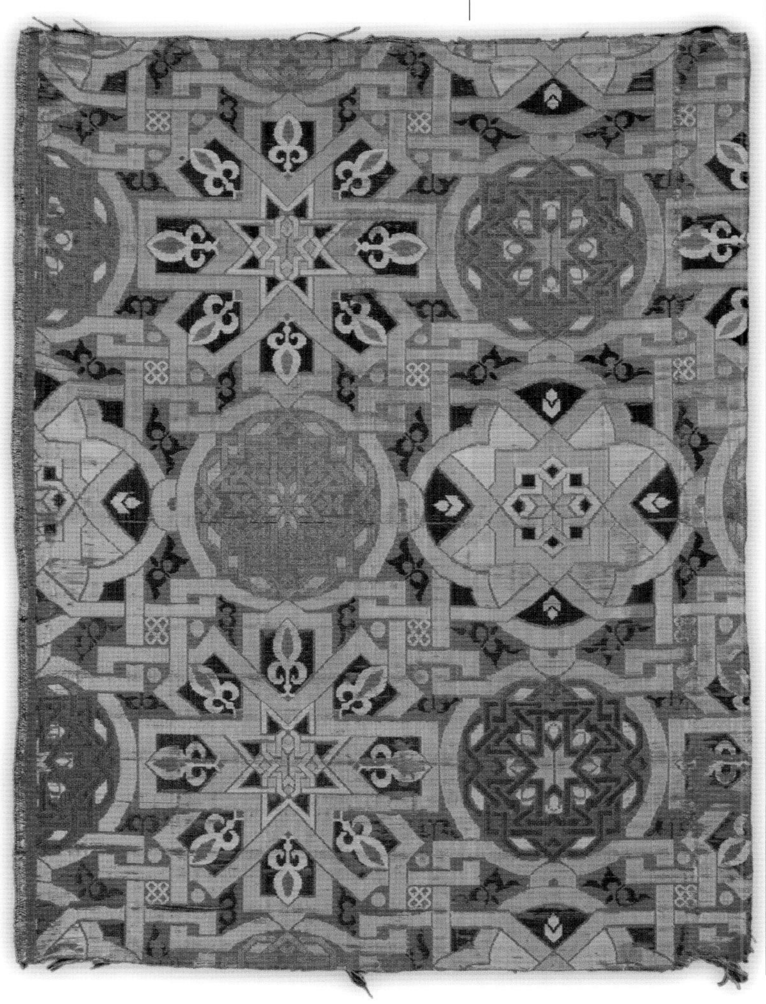

‘The new style, with its sinuous curves, proved especially congenial to European Gothic taste and was adapted and embellished by Italian designers with inexhaustible imagination and fantasy.’

DONALD KING, *European Textiles in the Keir Collection 400 BC to AD 1800,* 1990

PATTERN IN DETAIL

The Decorated Church

1297–1300

Fresco, Upper Church of St Francis, Assisi

The Upper Church of St Francis in Assisi is decorated with scenes from the life of the saint and attributed to Giotto di Bondone (1266/67–1337). Each scene is contained by ornamented bands simulating features of the real world in which the events took place with a *tromp l'oeil* of architectural details. The scenes are famous for the innovative and naturalistic representation of three-dimensional space but they also capture facets of contemporary Italian church decoration, including architecture, sculpture, furniture and hangings.

Sculptured spandrels

Between the pointed arches, the spandrels are decorated with a broken triangular motif that echoes elements of the tracery found in Gothic windows. The outer sections contain small Cosmati insets while a rosette occupies the central triangle. The arch is edged with a fine swag of oak leaves and acorns and behind the arches the blue vaulted ceiling is covered with numerous stars.

Patterned Papal throne

The technique of Cosmatesque decoration (see pages 80–1) was at the height of its popularity in churches in Rome at the end of the 13th century. The base of the Papal throne is decorated with a simple Cosmati square, circle and eight-pointed star motif made up of triangular- and square-cut pieces of stone. These are set into a marble base to form the plinth of the throne.

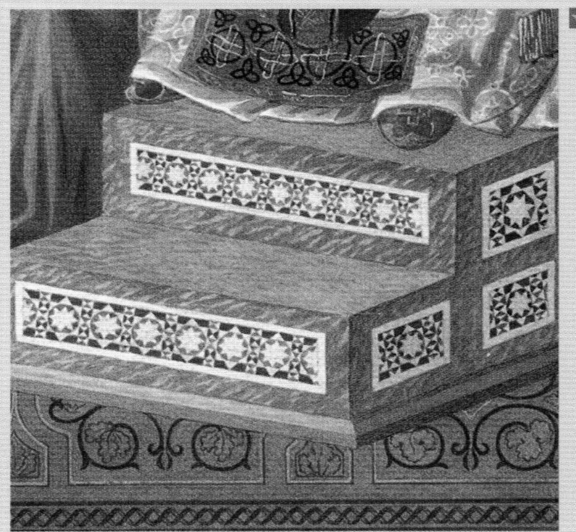

Decorative architrave

The upper frame of the scene simulates an architrave – the beam spanning two columns – as if the picture space was surrounded by real architecture. The front face of the beam is again decorated with a hexagonal Cosmati pattern while the underside represents coffering (recessed ceiling panels). The scene is further surrounded by a decorated band with a geometric twist inset with lozenges and swastikas.

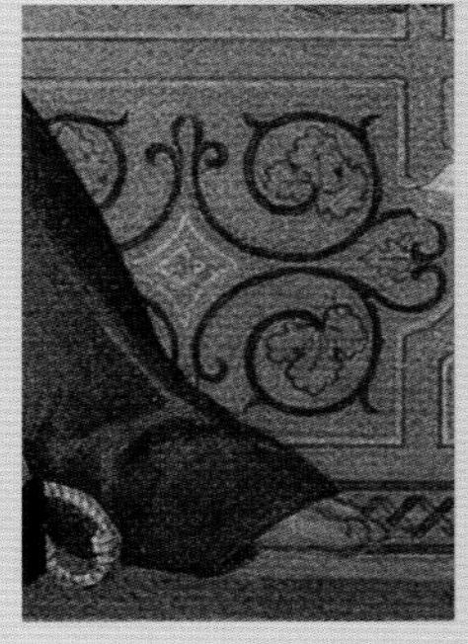

Vine scrolling tiles

The floor of the hall is covered with terracotta tiles patterned with a scroll motif arranged into a *quincunx* form. The outer four elements are the scroll tendrils ending in oak leaves with the central fifth element formed of nested lozenges. The squares are broken with a semicircle left and right and separated by a simple concave curved space containing more oak leaves.

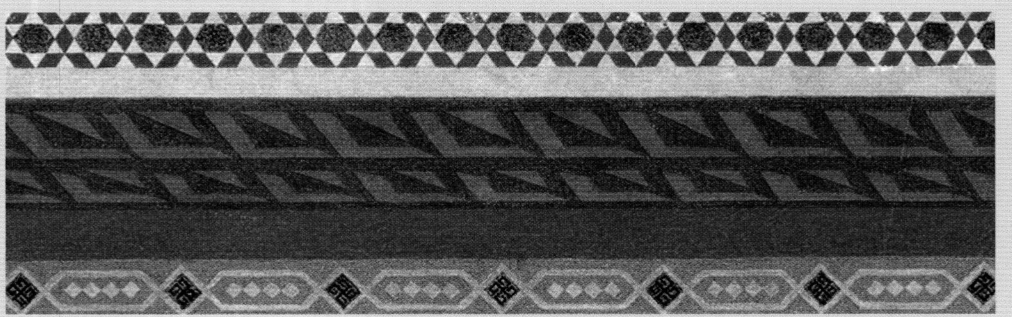

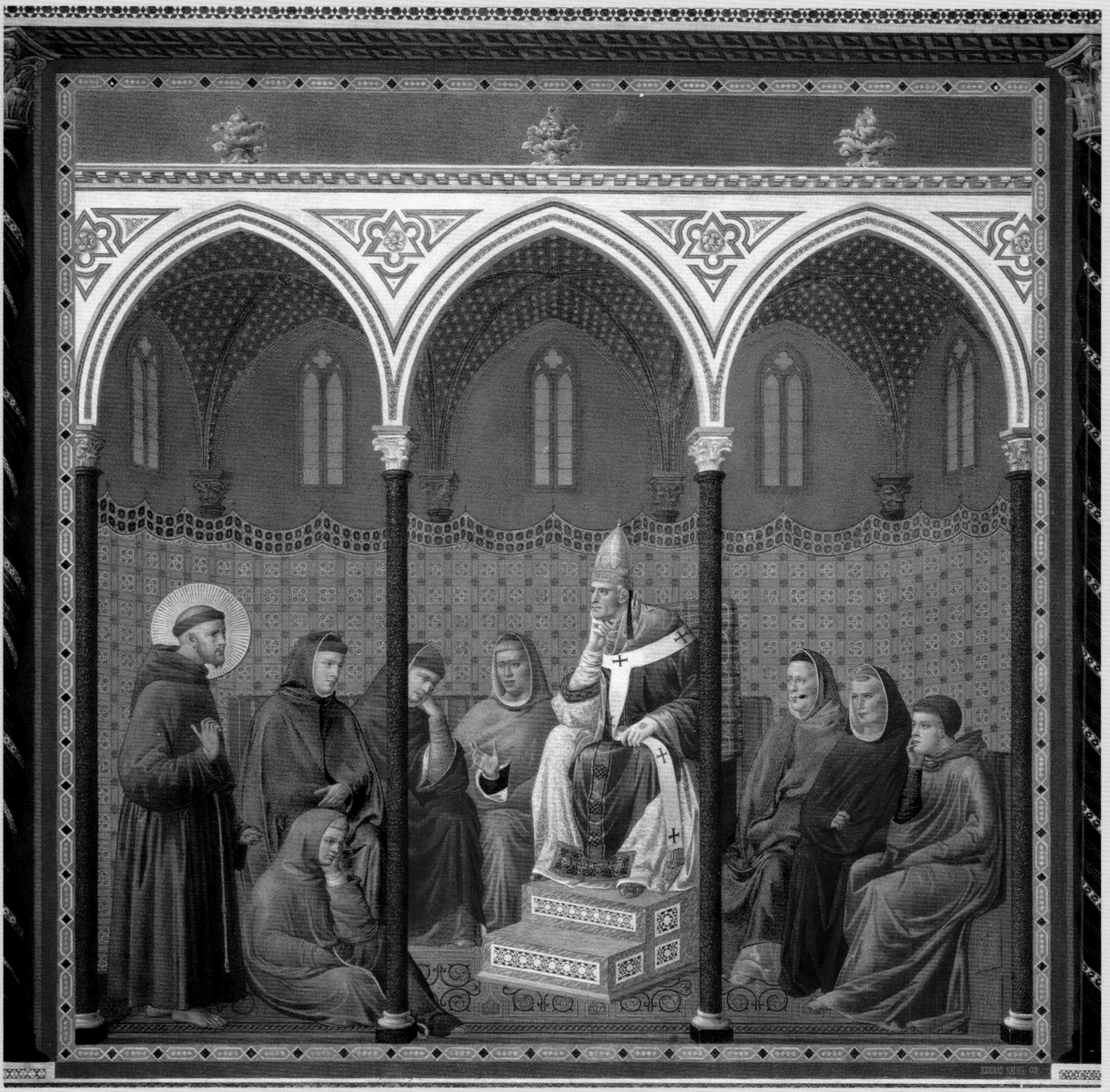

St Francis preaching before Pope Honorius

This late 19th-century watercolour copy by Eduard Kaiser of Giotto's 13th-century fresco shows St Francis of Assisi (1181/82–1226) preaching to Honorius III (Pope, 1216–27), who confirmed the Rule of the Franciscan Order in November 1223. Giotto has placed the event in an enclosed hall where Francis's audience sits enrapt by his eloquence. The scene is contained by porphyry pillars and bounded by twisted columns decorated with spiralling Cosmatesque patterns.

Woven checked hanging

Behind the seated figures is depicted a hanging with a chequered pattern edged with a band of a different check. Both patterns utilise the basic form of a square with corners occupied by smaller lozenges. The inner motif of the main textile again references the *quincunx* made by a continuous line forming a knot. The blue banding has a lozenge or cross motif within the squares.

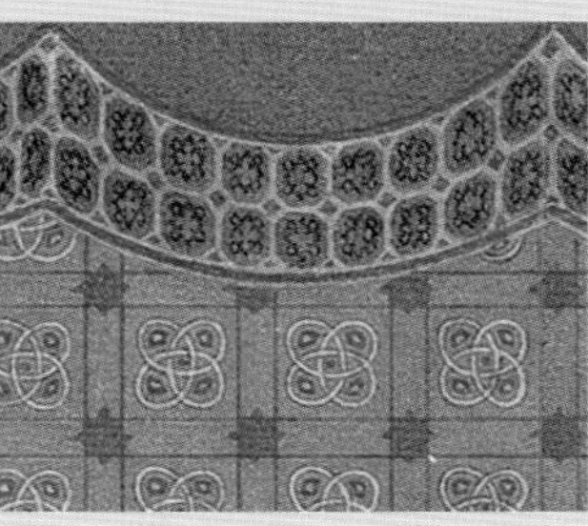

Emerging Islamic Patterns 1200–1400

Designs for all purposes in Islamic Iran

The patterns used in Iran in the 13th century reflect a range of motifs popular throughout the Middle East, Egypt and western Asia and point to future developments in Islamic design, which emerged in the 16th century. Central to this was the increasingly formalised scheme of repeating geometric shapes based on scrolling tendrils, flowers, leaves and vine motifs, which were formed into complex interlocking patterns often known as 'arabesque'. The developing styles of pattern were accompanied by an increasing virtuosity in many forms of craftsmanship – ceramics, painting, manuscript illumination, metalwork, calligraphy and textiles – for which the region was renowned.

'The arabesque, the distinctive decorative motif based on such natural forms as stems, leaves and tendrils, but rearranged in infinite geometric patterns, became a hallmark of Islamic art.'

JONATHAN BLOOM AND SHEILA BLAIR, *Islamic Arts,* 1997

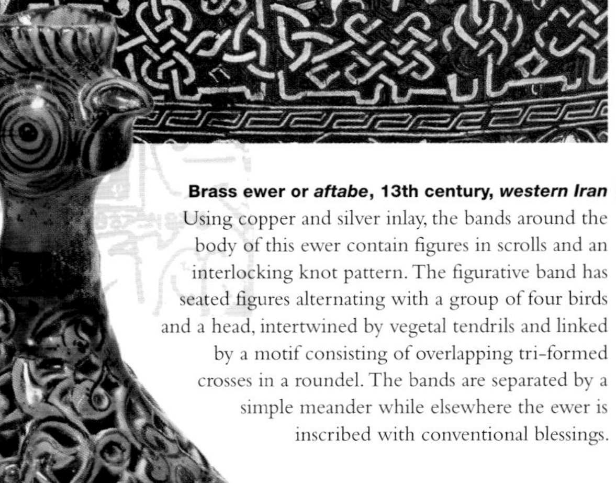

Brass ewer or *aftabe*, 13th century, *western Iran*
Using copper and silver inlay, the bands around the body of this ewer contain figures in scrolls and an interlocking knot pattern. The figurative band has seated figures alternating with a group of four birds and a head, intertwined by vegetal tendrils and linked by a motif consisting of overlapping tri-formed crosses in a roundel. The bands are separated by a simple meander while elsewhere the ewer is inscribed with conventional blessings.

Fritware jug, early 13th century, *Kashan, Iran*
The outer pierced layer of this fritware jug – ceramic material of finely ground sand and pebbles – forms a tangled pattern of scrolling tendrils and leaves. The ceramic material, introduced from China in the late 12th century, resulted in an explosion of creativity producing a wide range of incised, carved, glazed and decorated wares. The new material's versatility is apparent in the effect of the translucent glaze and the cock's moulded features.

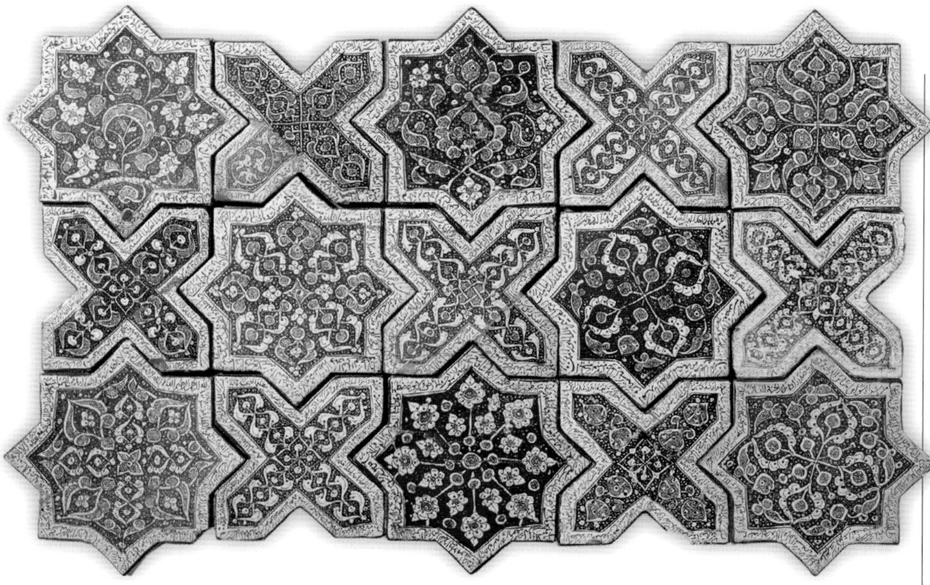

Tiles, 13th century, *Varamin, Iran*
The interlocking star and cross tiles are patterned with a variety of designs revolving around arrangements of leaves, plants and flowers from relatively straightforward floral stars to repeating and symmetrical waving and scrolling leaf forms. The designs are painted using a metallic lustre, developed in Iraq in the 9th century. The tiles are from a tomb of a descendent of Muhammad, and Qur'anic texts are written around the edge of each tile reversing the light on dark design.

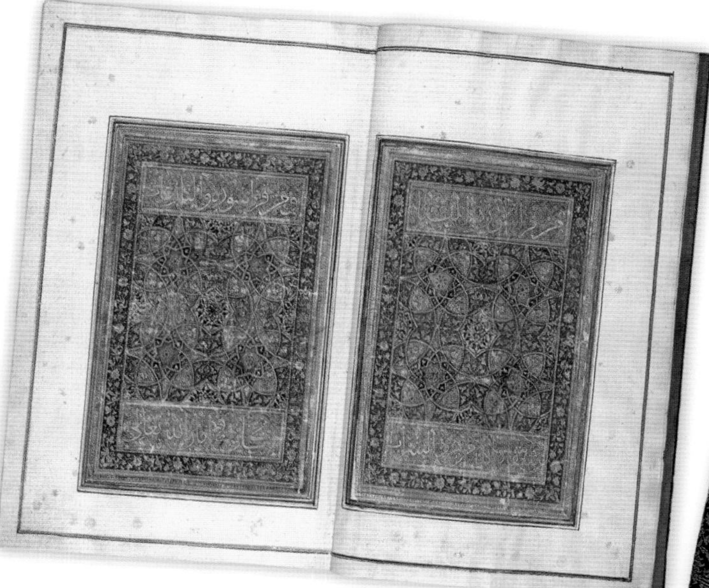

Illustrated pages of the Qur'an, c. 1370, *Iran*
The central panels of these carpet-like illuminations contain complex multi-faceted patterns. The main elements are overlapping circles of varying sizes, which overlay a background of leafy tendrils; the colours of blue, gold and black change depending on their position within the overall scheme. The circles break and change trajectory to form stars and curved polygons at their intersections so that a third layer of pattern emerges.

Ecclesiastical vestment, late 14th century, *Iran*
Woven using silk and metallic thread, the design on this vestment demonstrates the movement of patterns and goods between China, the Middle East and western Europe. Probably made in Mongol-ruled Iran, its motifs have varied sources – the bird may originate from Italy while the elaborate floral scroll has links to Chinese designs. These two elements are interspersed with stags, which also have a European feel. The robe itself is a dalmatic – a vestment of the Western Church.

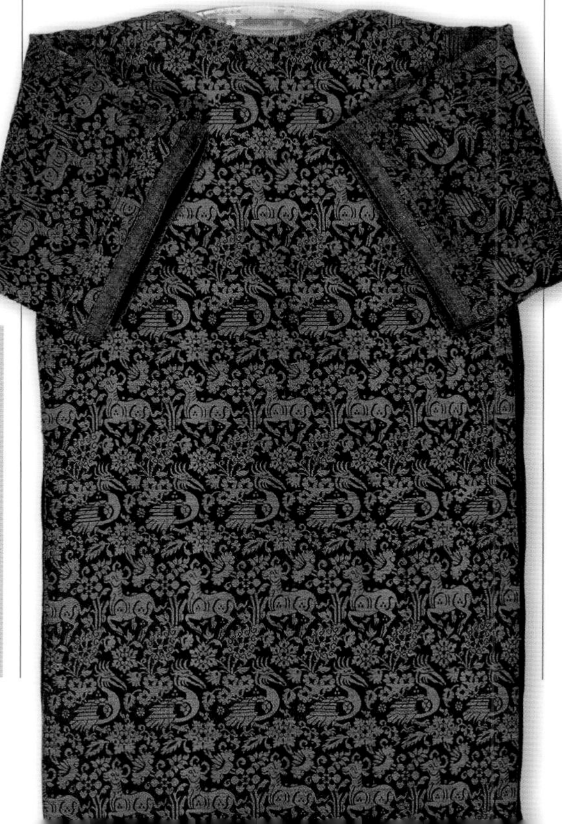

ELEMENTS OF PATTERN

- *knot pattern*
- *figurative vine scroll*
- *interlaced and overlapping vines*
- *vegetal twisted scrolls in stars and crosses*
- *birds and beasts with a floral stem*
- *interlocking circles forming star polygons*

PATTERN IN DETAIL

Patterns for a Noble Gaze c. 1320–1340

The Luttrell Psalter

Named after Sir Geoffrey Luttrell, who commissioned the psalter, this manuscript collection of Church feast days, psalms from the Bible and prayers is painted in vibrant colours and highlighted with gold and silver. Patterned with scrolling tendrils, tripartite leaves and heraldic motifs, the illustrations in the psalter depict aspects of working life and recreation on Geoffrey's estate at Irnham in Lincolnshire throughout the year, an idealised version of country life set out for his entertainment. The liturgies written at the back of the book were for Geoffrey to read during church services as well as for consultation during his private devotions.

Leaves and pellets

The initial capital letters of the lines in the psalm are painted against backgrounds patterned with branching leaves and pellets. The patterns alternate between those with stems ending in three-pointed leaves and those with trefoils, perhaps a reference to the Holy Trinity.

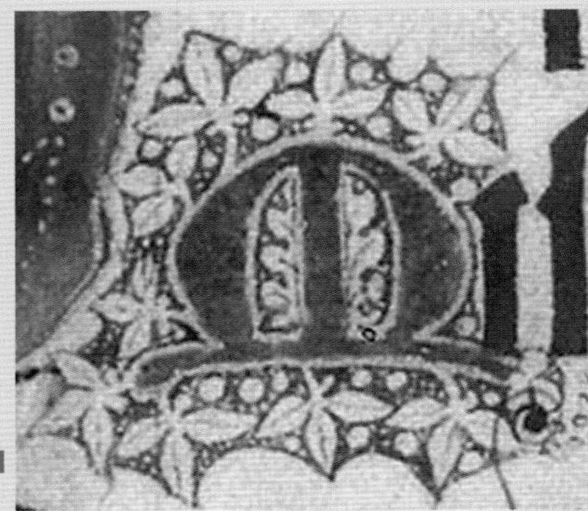

Plant scroll and eagles

The canopy of the royal coach is covered with a pattern of a rhythmical golden plant scroll that sprouts shoots with curling rounded ends. The side of the coach is painted with a panel of double-headed eagles, each framed by pillars and trefoil arcades. Each eagle is set against a background of fleur-de-lis.

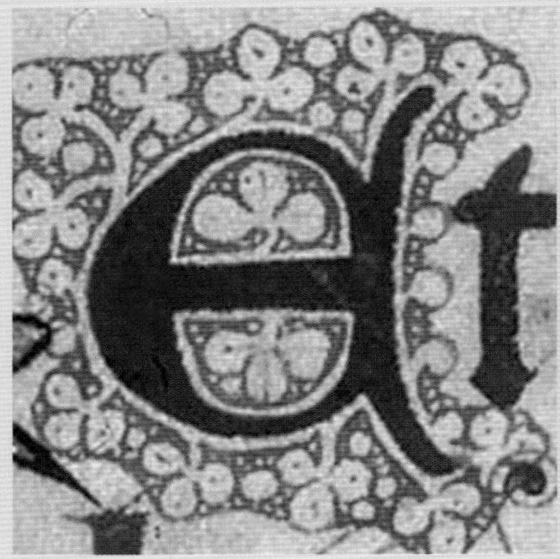

Crosses, squares and lozenges

These highly protective cruciform grid patterns of squares and lozenges enclosing crosses reflect the ubiquity of the sign of the cross made in daily life.

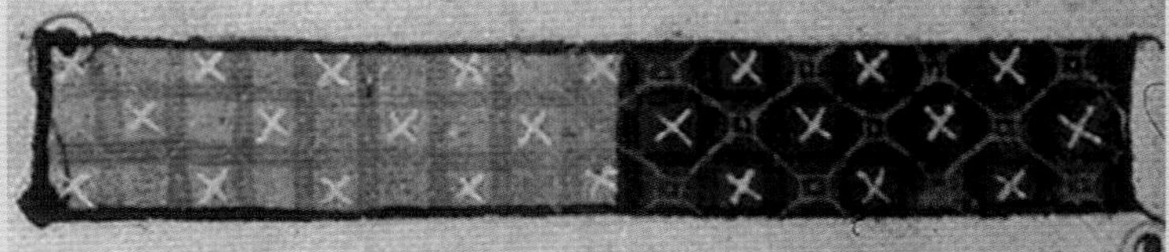

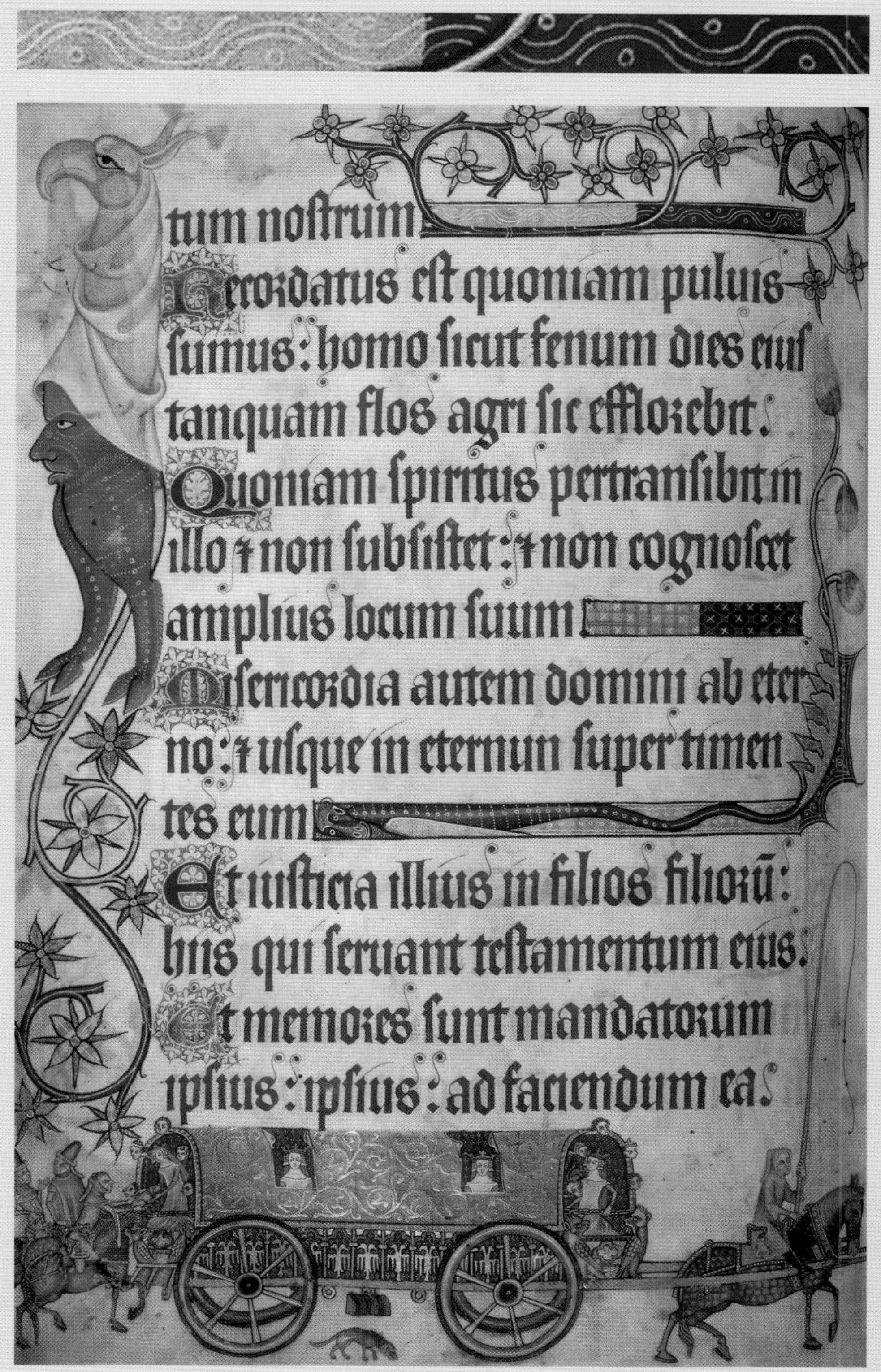

Wave and ring

This pattern of a triple wavy line interspersed with small circles suggests a watery concept, perhaps sustaining the visually entangling rose briar that is winding into the top of the page. Flowing water may also be a metaphor here for the passage of life.

Folio 181v

The Luttrell Psalter is not merely a picture book of medieval life, representing both rich and poor at labour, prayer and leisure. Elaborated with symbolic patterning, the complex scenes combine to project a medieval vision of the world where reality and imagination combine – where men, women and fantastical hybrid creatures all take part. The horse-drawn royal coach at the foot of this page of the psalter may be a metaphor for life and death, with portraits of the queens of the four kings who ruled during Geoffrey's lifetime – Eleanor, Margaret, Isabella and Philippa. The latter was the wife of Edward III, king when the manuscript was produced. Part of the text above reads, 'As for man, his days are as grass: as a flower of the field, so he flourishes. For the wind passes over it, and it is gone; and the place thereof shall know it no more.' (Psalm 103:15–16.)

1400
1500

Fifteenth Century

Introduction

The wealthy aristocracy commissioned rich textiles for clothes and furnishings, and luxurious vestments as patrons of the Church. From the late 14th century an international Gothic style of design spread throughout Europe, incorporating silk fabrics patterned with Eastern-style animals and flowers. In France and Italy, gold-decorated textiles displayed in the courts of kings and princes were patterned with royal motifs, such as the fleur-de-lis, or elaborate floral and foliate designs. Rich Italian silk brocade woven with gold or silver patterns was the most desirable, although sumptuary laws restricted displays of great extravagance. Nevertheless, the art of the period often portrayed wealthy individuals in these richly ornate textiles to signify their status and power.

The technique of producing pottery with a lustrous metallic surface originated in Iraq and spread to Moorish Spain by trade and the transfer of skills. Paterna and Manises in Valencia and Malaga in Granada were already famous for this type of pottery by the beginning of the 14th century. Exported throughout the Mediterranean, lustreware patterns included Islamic or Persian elements such as script, fish, curling foliage, the 'tree of life', pine cones, spurs, spirals, parallel lines, cross-hatched rings and lace patterns. Gothic motifs were also used – script, birds, animals, human figures, crowns, ribbons, thistles, chestnuts, ferns, bryony flowers, ivy and parsley leaves. After c. 1475, Plateresque ('silversmith's style') patterns of lacework, thistles, seeds, ivy leaves, four-lobed palmettes, small dots and stalks were developed for ceramics and architectural sculpture.

The patron's heraldic badge was often incorporated into the design as a personal statement of influence.

From the 14th century, the scholarly study of texts and art of ancient Greece and Rome led to a renewed interest in the designs, patterns and motifs of the classical world. The principles of classical architecture, drawn from Roman architectural ruins and treatises, changed building styles and stimulated artistic innovation in early 15th-century Florence. Leon Battista Alberti developed a visual harmony in the design of buildings, balancing patterns and re-introducing classical motifs such as scrolls, medallions and friezes. Artists such as Andrea Mantegna painted religious scenes in elaborately decorated porticos of classical architectural design. Decorative elements – such as egg-and-dart, bead-and-reel, wreaths, dentils and acanthus – emphasised the classical context, unifying both Christian and humanist ideals.

In China, the Ming dynasty (1368–1644) brought peace and stability to the region and innovation in the decorative arts. Collectors' fascination for ancient art inspired metalwork patterns such as the *taotie*, clouds and dragons, and the vessel shapes of the ancient Zhou and Shang dynasties.

Before the arrival of Europeans in the Americas following Columbus's landing of 1492, the visual languages of the Maya, Aztec and Inca cultures were closely related with animal and bird life. Subjects were highly stylised into geometric forms, sometimes to the point of complete abstraction. Tapestry, brocade, lace, embroidery and the extension of colour ranges using materials such as parrot feathers created highly significant and luxuriant textiles for ritual and ceremonial display.

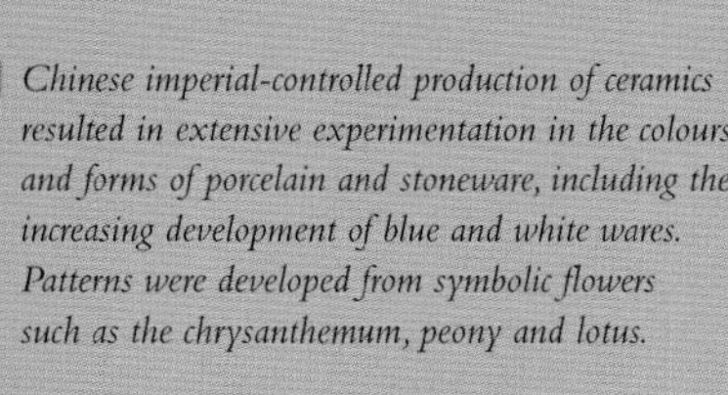

Chinese imperial-controlled production of ceramics resulted in extensive experimentation in the colours and forms of porcelain and stoneware, including the increasing development of blue and white wares. Patterns were developed from symbolic flowers such as the chrysanthemum, peony and lotus.

PATTERN IN DETAIL

Courtly Patterns
1413

Decoration at the Queen of France's court

The proto-feminist poet and scholar Christine de Pizan (1363–c. 1430) was highly influential on 15th-century poetry, exploring and critiquing the aristocratic and chivalric customs of the contemporary court. This illumination depicts the audience chamber of the Queen of France, Isabeau of Bavaria (c. 1370–1435), wife of Charles VI, with her ladies-in-waiting, in which Christine presents the manuscript of her works. The scene is richly decorated with courtly hangings featuring the royal heraldic patterns.

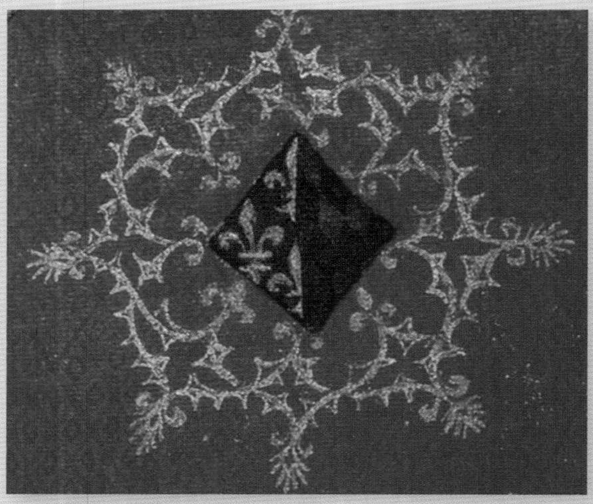

The fleur-de-lis, lozenge and rose
The bed hangings contain Isabeau's arms – golden fleur-de-lis and silver fusils on a blue lozenge (female shield) – set within a hexagonal floral motif. The spiny branches, possibly derived from a briar rose or thistle, are arranged to create trefoil and quatrefoil shapes reminiscent of Gothic tracery, and more golden three-petal lilies. The overall design unifies the blue heraldic hangings with the queen's dress and visually harmonises the scene.

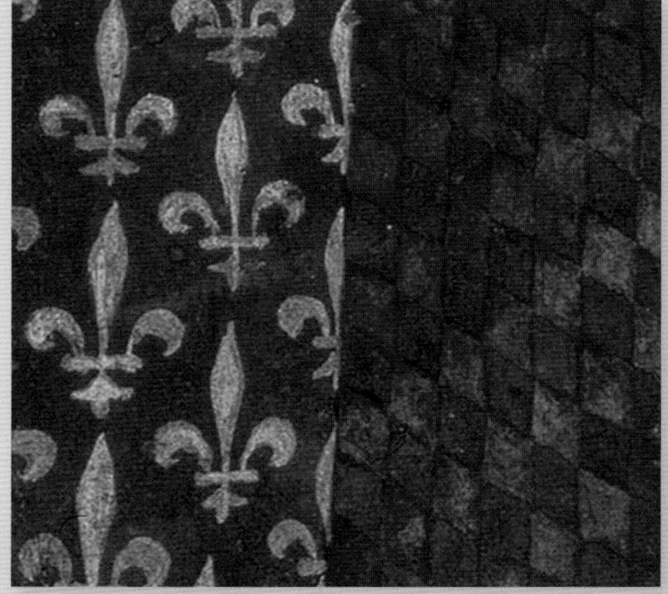

Royal heraldry
The blue wall hangings have two motifs – the gold fleur-de-lis of France and the pattern of slanted silver fusils ('fusily bendwise', see pages 78–9) of Wittelsbach, Isabeau's Bavarian royal family. Originally, the contrasting silver and gold motifs would have been more striking, as the silver has oxidised to a dull dark grey, and the lighter colour would have linked to other pale greys in the room.

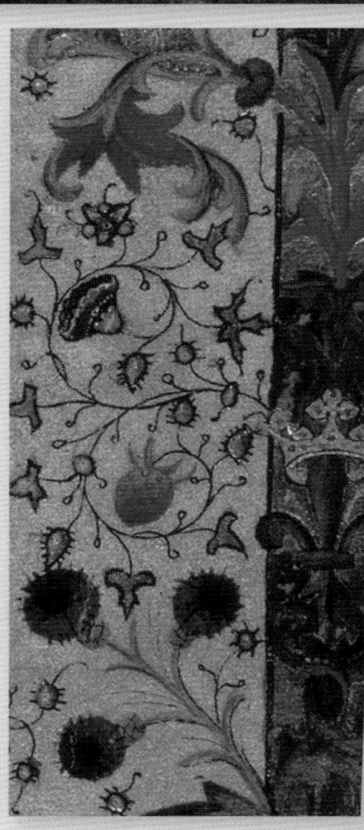

Acanthus and strawberries
The edge of the illumination contains a pattern of delicately painted flowers and leaves. The outer twisting vine of red and blue acanthus includes a crowned fleur-de-lis. The inner wider decoration contains naturalistic flowers interspersed with extended elaborate blue, gold, red and pink acanthus leaves. Cornflowers, strawberries, blue speedwell and carnations on fine gold vines are scattered with gold stars.

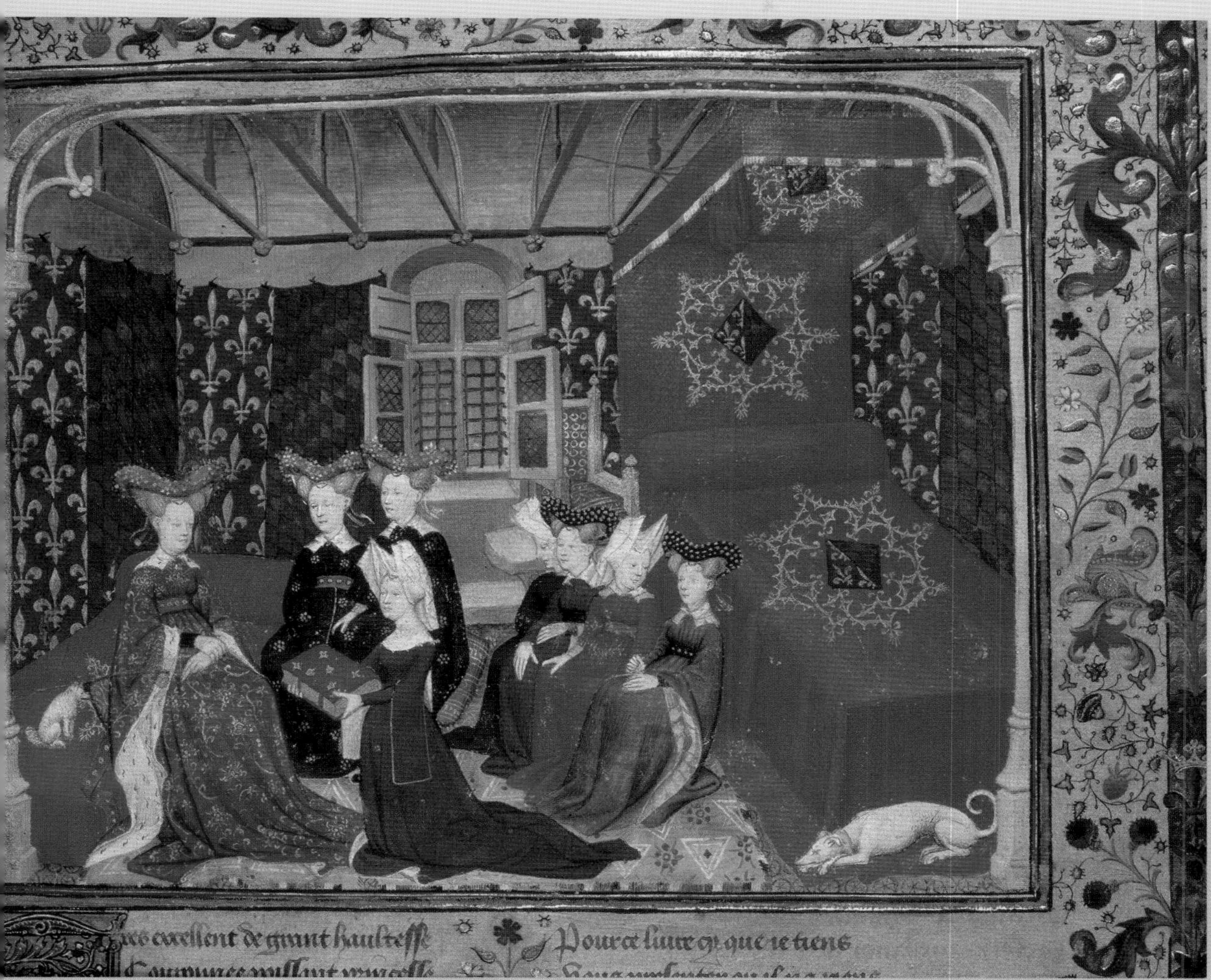

Miniature from works of Christine de Pizan (ms Harley 4431, fol 3r)
This illumination is at the front of the manuscript. The queen's ermine-trimmed and gold-embroidered gown differentiates her from the more simply attired attendants. The symbolic decorations of the chamber associate the queen's status and power with Christine's scholarship and with her commitment to celebrating the contributions of women.

Shield and rose
The chamber's floor is tiled with a pale green, segmented circle pattern. The figures sit on a pink carpet decorated with rosettes and white and yellow (silver and gold) hexagrams – possibly the protective motif of the 'Shield of David' (not an exclusively Jewish symbol at this time). Only royal courts placed valuable carpets on the floor, so the visible pile or fringe at the edge stresses the richness of the setting.

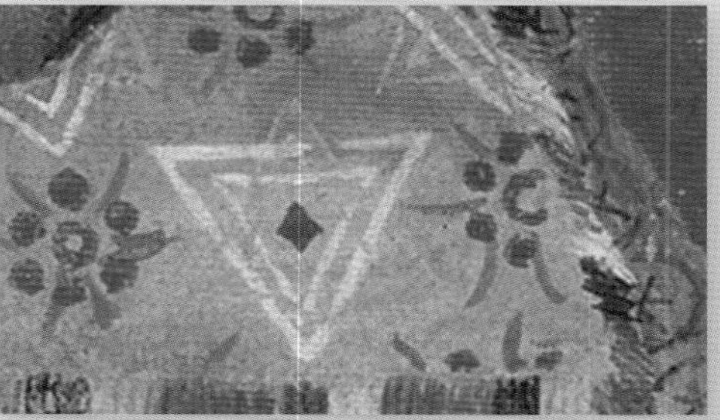

Designs of Luxury & Gold
1400–1490

Gold brocades in Late Gothic and Early Renaissance Italy
Gold brocades – silk fabrics, often velvet, woven and patterned with gold thread – were the most expensive textiles of the 15th century. They were used by the Church and for clothing and furnishings at the wealthiest courts of the Italian city-state rulers and aristocrats. Originating in China, velvets and brocades were made in Florence, Venice, Siena, Lucca and Genoa in the 14th and 15th centuries. Sumptuary laws restricted their use in clothing, for example, to the sleeves of women and only for men over a certain age, but they were nevertheless an accepted means of displaying social status, wealth and power – either real or aspirational.

‘The high value and visual attractiveness of gold-brocaded textiles secured an important role for them in Renaissance painting.’

REMBRANDT DUITS, ‘Figured Riches: The Value of Gold Brocades in Fifteenth-Century Florentine Painting’, 1999

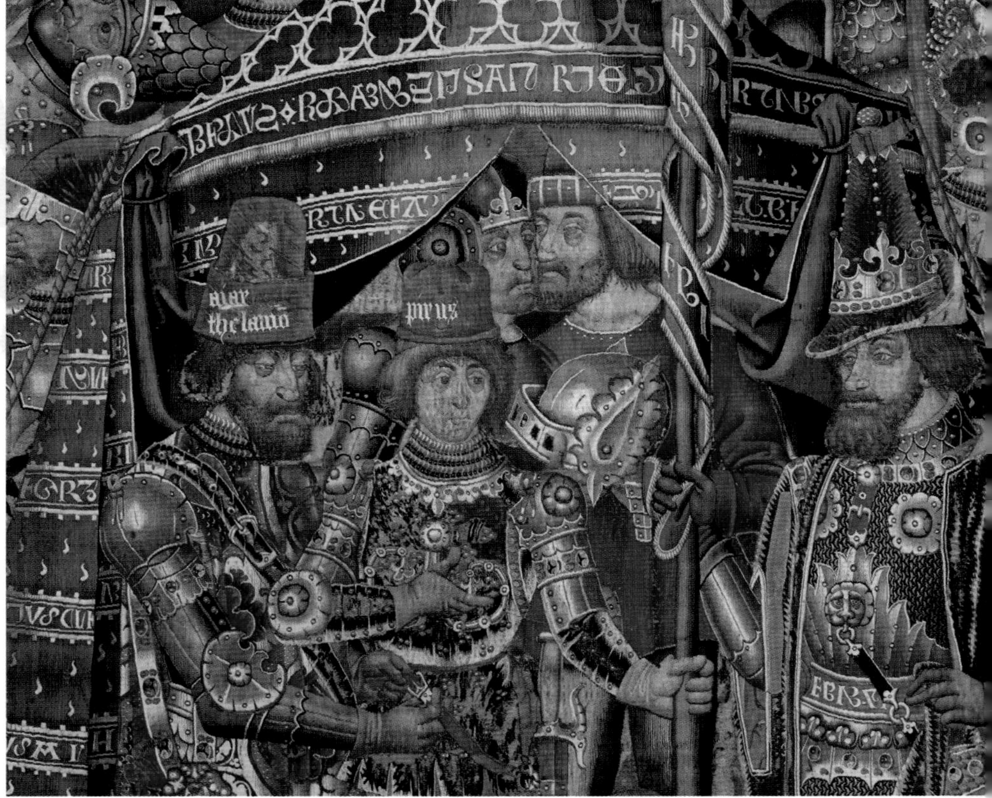

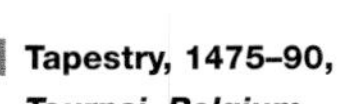

Tapestry, 1475–90,
Tournai, Belgium
Represented in contemporary costume, the story of the Sack of Troy originally consisted of 11 woven tapestries. Here the son of Achilles, Pyrrhus, who was to kill King Priam, is being armed for battle. Pyrrhus and his attendants wear sumptuous brocade robes with leaf and scroll patterns, decorative armour and fashionable hats. The tent is decorated with gold quatrefoils, *gouttes d'or* (drops of gold) and text banding.

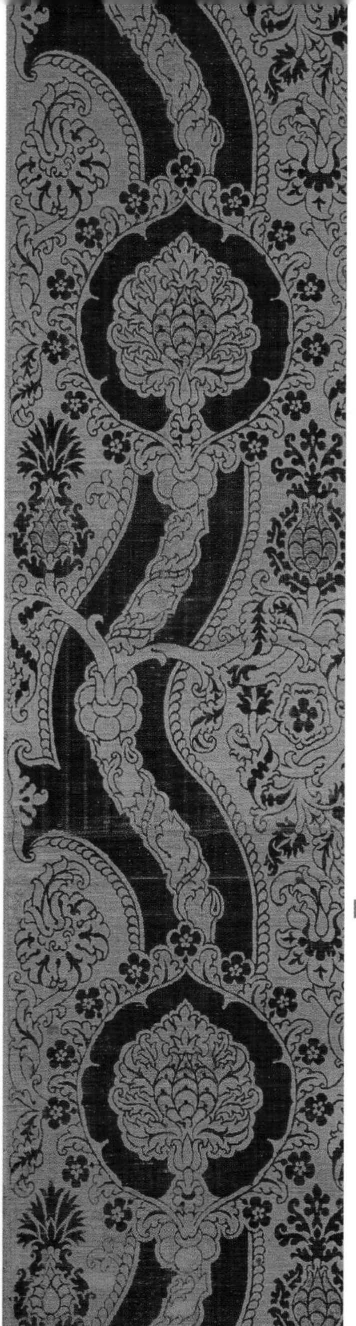

Brocade furnishing fabric, c. 1475, *Italy*
The central element of this scrolling design is the gold pomegranate – both in the main large floral ogee (double-curved) motif and on the secondary branches – symbolising unity and eternal life. The seed-casing's bulbous shape, surmounted with a small flower at its head, is encased in leaves and a scalloped surround with a floral edging. The sinuous and curved shapes continue in the main branch and in the subsidiary leaves and flowers.

The Procession of the Three Kings*, 1459–61, *Palazzo Medici-Riccardi, Florence
Although the overt public display of rich clothing was controlled in Florence, representations in paintings were permitted, and they could exaggerate impressions of wealth. The painting by Benozzo Gozzoli (c. 1421–97) shows King Balthasar in the guise of the Byzantine Emperor John VIII Palaiologos, who visited Florence in 1439. His exceedingly rich gold-brocade robe and the plain and silver brocades of his attendants' robes all carry elaborate pomegranate motifs.

ELEMENTS OF PATTERN

- *pomegranates*
- *elaborate floral and foliate scrolls*
- *gold and silver motifs*
- *acanthus*
- *quatrefoils and text bands*

Silk velvet brocade, 1400–29, *Italy*
This earlier example of silk brocade has been created with threads in three colours – a yellow ground with red and pale blue velvet cut to form a less elaborate floral and foliate scrolling pattern derived from the acanthus form. The skill in creating an interlinked pattern is apparent as the basic repeating of two curved leaves and one flower is linked across the fabric by connecting branches.

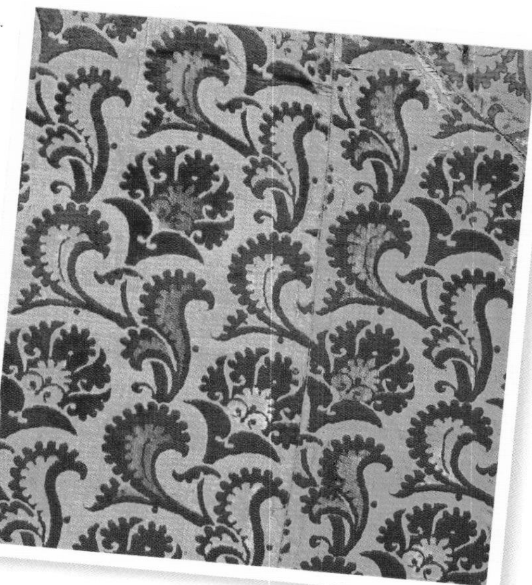

Flamboyant Gothic 1400–1500

European patterns of the 15th century

Luxurious patterns of animals, flowers and leaves were used to ornament textiles and glass for the Church and the nobility. Eastern textiles inspired new compositions of plants and animals, while enlarged leaves and flowers were used to create new designs. Flowers and leaves with serrated edges were arranged on strongly contrasting backgrounds and stylised floral motifs were surrounded by fine tendril patterns, often emphasised with metallic thread.

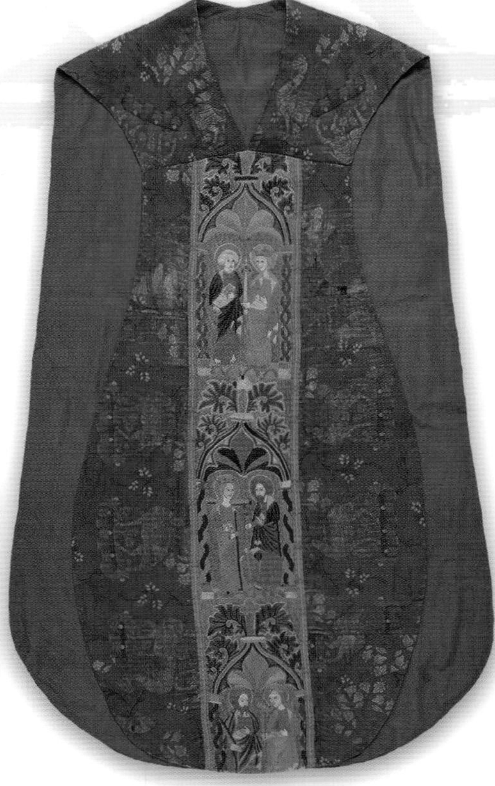

Chasuble, 1400–30, *Italy and England*
Woven in Italy and embroidered in England, this brocaded lampas silk has orphreys (decorated bands) embroidered in silk and silver-gilt thread. The Eastern-style pattern of the textile comprises bridled camels walking through a field of flowers and grass, with baskets strapped to their backs containing tall waving lilies. A pair of flowering leafy tendrils curve between each motif. The orphreys show a pattern of saints, each pair enclosed by an ogee (double-curved) arch on twisted columns surmounted by curling vegetation. Sir Thomas Erpingham commissioned the chasuble, perhaps for his personal chaplain.

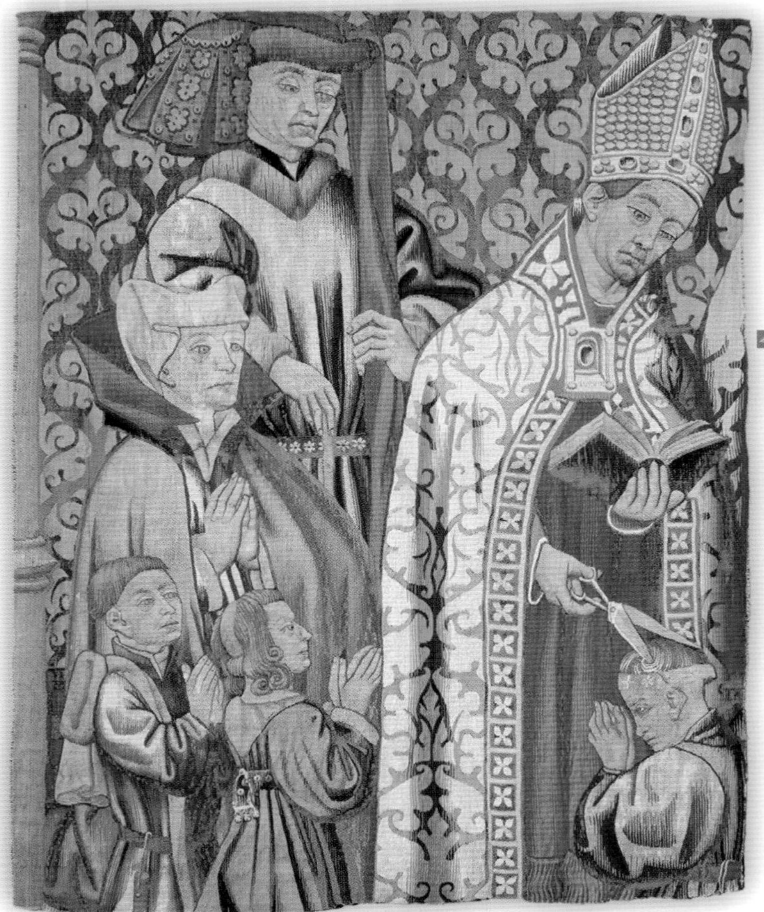

Tapestry, 1470–75, *Tournai, Belgium*
The bishop wears a cope (ceremonial mantle) woven with a stylised pattern of curling leaves, which is echoed by the similar pattern in the background to the figures. The cope is edged with bands of quatrefoils in squares, enlarged at the collar. Woven in wool and silk, the tapestry depicts the seven sacraments of ecclesiastical ceremonial – this detail shows the cutting of children's hair during their confirmation as members of the Church.

‘These patterns full of reversing curves, of serpentine and flame-like forms, seem imbued with the spirit of Flamboyant Gothic.’

MONIQUE AND DONALD KING,
European Textiles, 1990

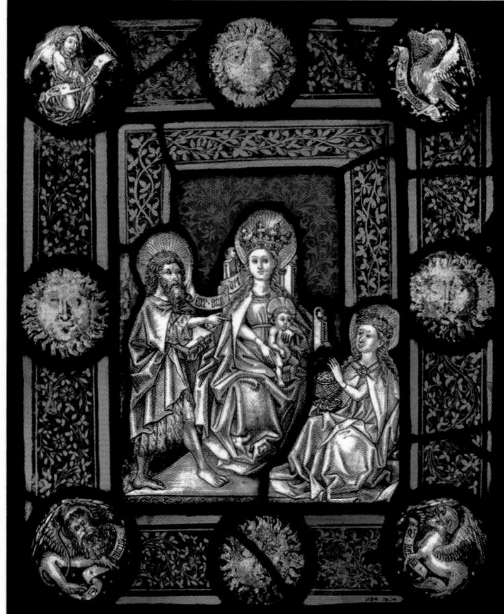

Glass panel, 1470–80, *Upper Rhineland, Germany*
The background to the central figures and the double frame surrounding them is delineated with elaborate diapers (patterns) of finely painted vegetation, all with tripartite leaves referencing the Holy Trinity. The Virgin and Child are flanked by St John the Baptist and St Dorothy, an early Christian martyr.

ELEMENTS OF PATTERN

- *animals and birds with flowering plants*
- *motifs contrasting with plain background*
- *formal plant motifs*
- *fine tendrils against background*

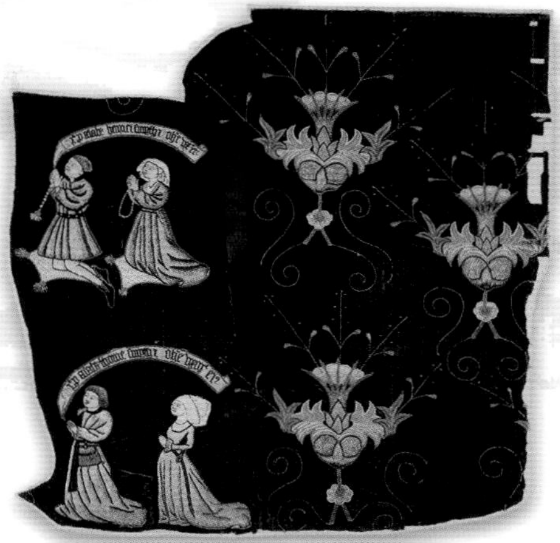

Altar hanging, 1470–1500, *Italy and England*
This Italian silk velvet was embroidered in England with a pattern of formalised florals in silver-gilt and silk threads linked with fine tripartite stamens and spirals. The donors are represented to the left, Henry and Thomas Smyth and their wives, both Johanna or Joan. This embroidered textile is possibly from an altar hanging.

Tapestry hanging, c. 1500, *Tournai, Belgium*
The borders of this hanging are filled with elaborate curving branches sprouting florid acanthus-type leaves that curl in different directions. They are inhabited by different kinds of birds, including water birds such as swans and cranes. This type of large scrolling leaf and bird pattern only occurs in commissions for German patrons. The tapestry is woven in wool and silk and the central scene depicts the Biblical story from the Book of Daniel of Susanna and the Elders. German nobles customarily bathed their feet before meals, and fountains and pools were often found in their gardens.

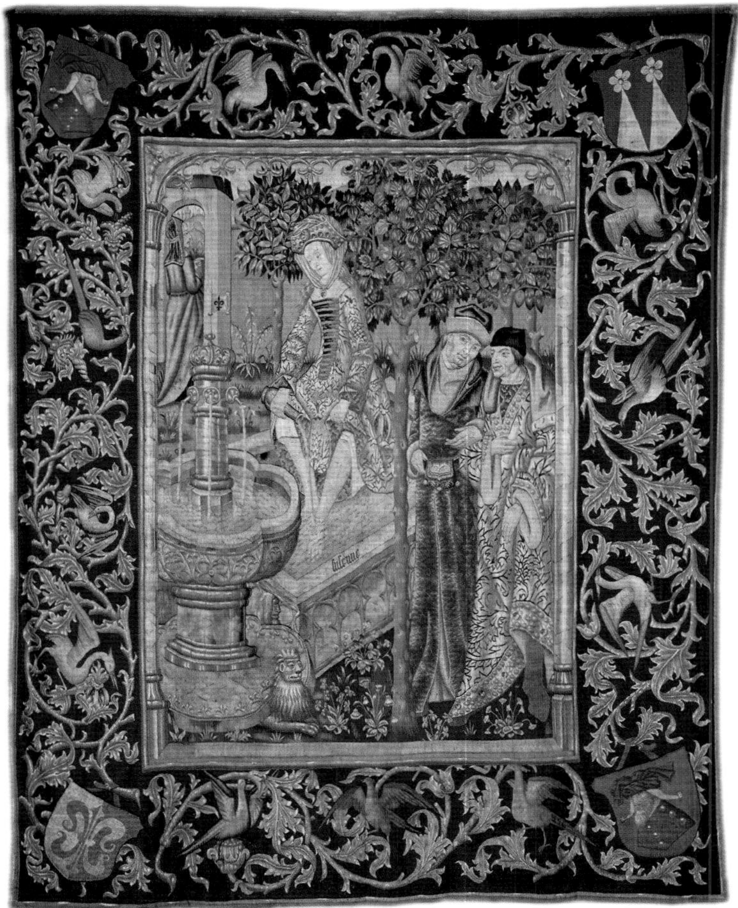

Lustrous Patterning
1430–1500

Lustreware ceramics

Manises in Valencia, Spain, was renowned for its lustrous pottery that was acquired for display by wealthy owners. As early as 1427, ceramics made for export to Italy were decorated with a pattern referred to in 15th-century Italian documents as *fioralixi* (fleur-de-lis), now known as 'bryony flowers'. Pottery painted with metallic colours (lustreware) was exported in large numbers to Tuscany in Italy. The Tuscan potters copied the designs from the Spanish pottery, initially using different colours to imitate the metallic effect.

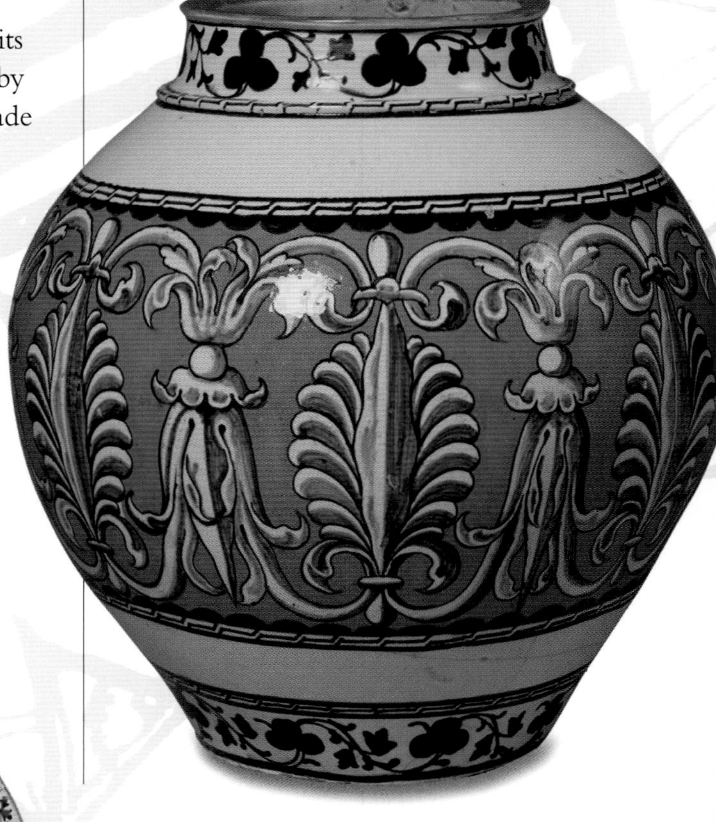

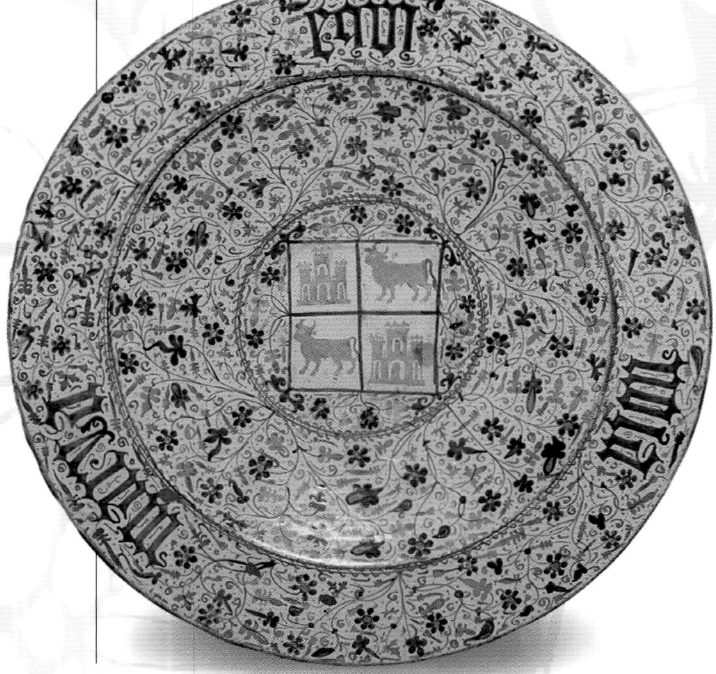

Dish, 1430–70, *Manises, Valencia, Spain*
This tin-glazed earthenware dish has been painted with a 'bryony flower' pattern. Waving tendrils sprout leaves and flowers painted in two colours, the yellow ones visually linked to the background by dots and curls in the same colour. The Catalan words in Gothic script – *equi noia marya* ('here is Maria') – may refer to King Alfonso of Aragon's queen. The heraldic badge represents the Buyl family of Manises. Made as part of a larger set, this dish was perhaps also used to cover another plate when meat was served at the table.

Vase, 1480–1500, *Pesaro, Marche, Italy*
The body of this vase is decorated with a pattern of alternating palmettes and downward-pointing lotus flowers copied from classical Roman architectural sculpture. The edges of the pattern band are finished with a scalloped 'awning' and geometric key patterns. The neck and foot of the vase, also edged with a key pattern towards the body of the pot, are painted with a running plant tendril sprouting trefoils and other tripartite leaves.

Drug storage jar, 1450–75, *Montelupo, Tuscany, Italy*
The body of this jar is painted with alternating blue and manganese purple ivy leaves, inspired by patterns on imported pottery from Valencia. Separated by vertical bands, the leaves are shown in a comparable way to a palmette frieze, but set vertically. The leaves are divided by a motif of curving lines bound together where the lotus flower would occur in a classical lotus and palmette pattern. The shoulder of the jar has a leafy tendril pattern with dots, as on the body, and the neck a diagonally cross-hatched or trellis pattern band.

Plate, 1476–90, *Pesaro, Marche, Italy*
Stylised flowers grow upright from between pairs of pointed spindles that touch at the tips. The flowers have scrolling stamens painted finely in black against the background. These motifs are linked by ribbons emerging from the base of the flower stem and forming a loop between each flower. A motif of three pine-cone seeds is repeated between the overlapping petals of the central rosette whose colouring and scrolling stamens provide a sense of rotational movement. The heraldic badges are those of King Matthias of Hungary and his wife, Beatrice of Aragon.

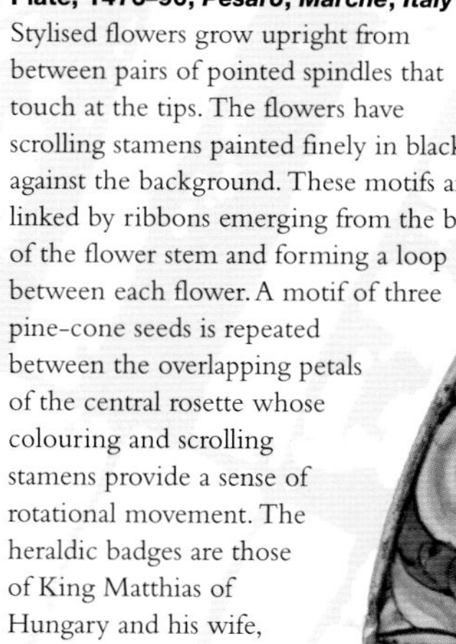

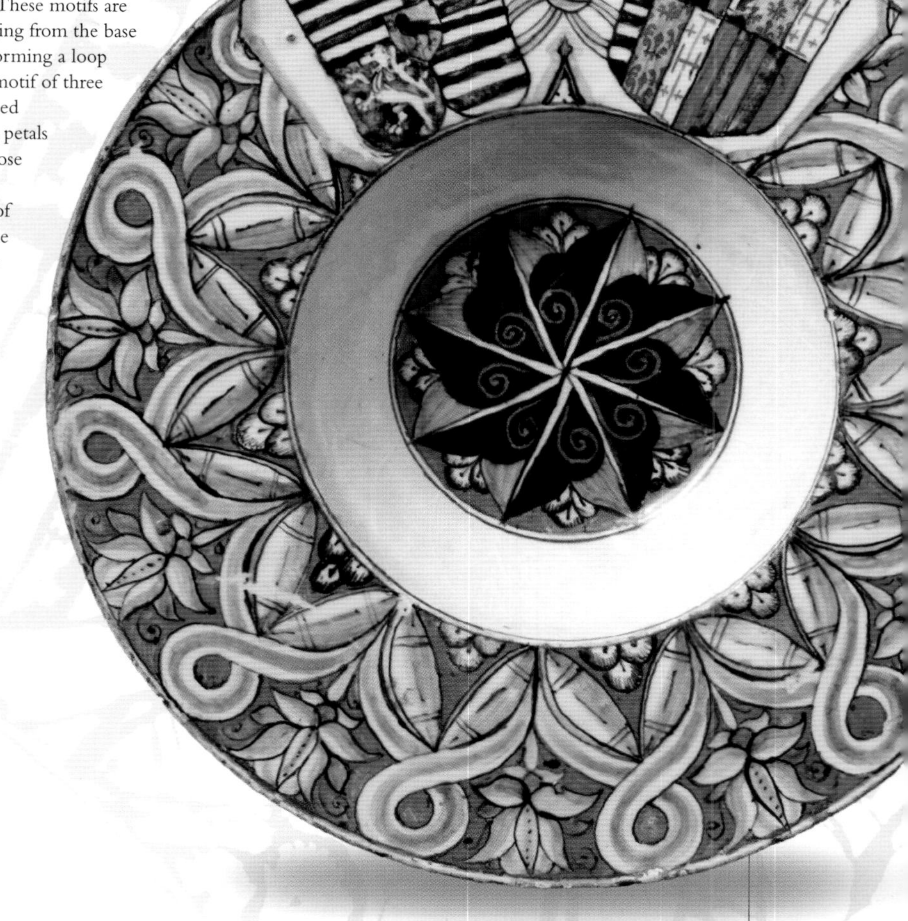

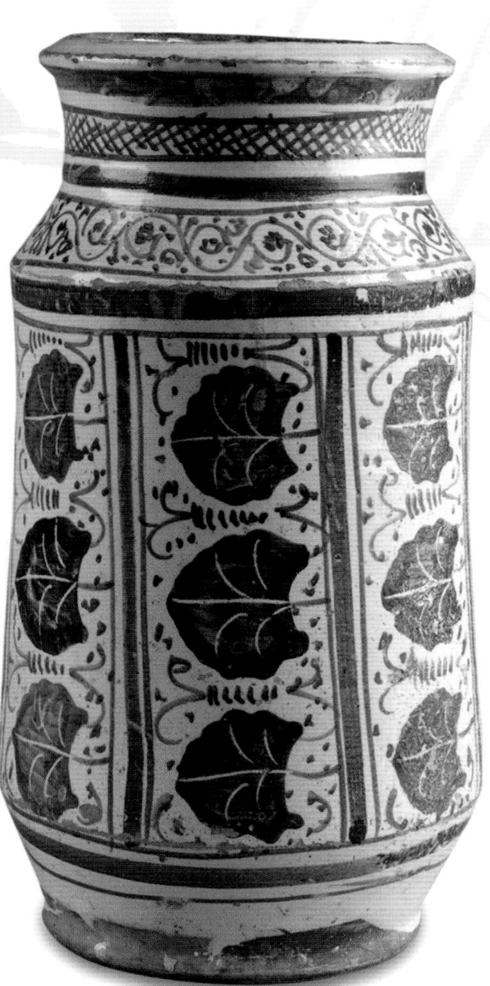

'The majority of lustred objects which reached Western Europe were manufactured in Spain.'

MARTA CAROSCIO,
Medieval Ceramics 28, 2004

ELEMENTS OF PATTERN

- *Islamic or Gothic script*
- *curling foliage*
- *flat leaf shapes*
- *complex small-scale florals*
- *stylised flowers*
- *ribbons*
- *classical lotus and palmette*

PATTERN IN DETAIL

Classical Cornucopia & Scrolls

1456–1459

Andrea Mantegna altarpiece, San Zeno, Verona

Andrea Mantegna (1430/31–1506) was born near Padua and became the painter at the Gonzaga court in Mantua, Italy, in 1459. As the revival of classical forms grew in importance, artists visited and learnt from the classical buildings and ruins that survived in Italy and Rome. Mantegna, like many of his contemporaries, often used elaborate decorative details taken from classical buildings to create sculptural and architectural forms that framed and contextualised his paintings. Classically derived decorative elements included scrolls, swags, acanthus and the detailed patterns associated with the orders of architecture – Doric, Ionic and Corinthian. The frieze running across the top of architectural structures also provided an ideal location for patterns, sometimes including heraldic or family motifs.

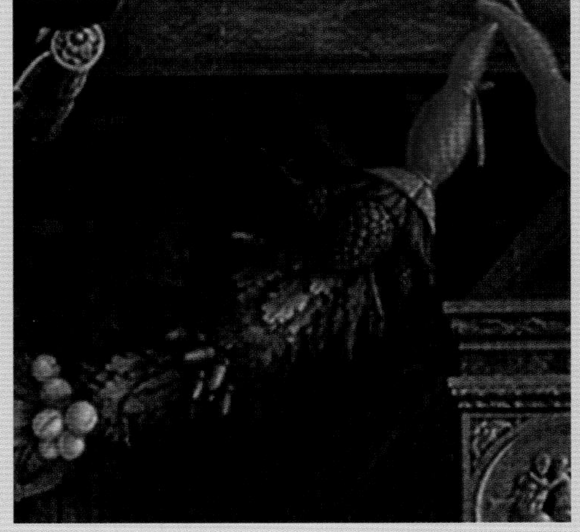

Cornucopia
Mantegna's works often included suspended cornucopia, which framed scenes with rich decoration. Here the red horns of plenty are filled with swags of leaves, fruits, nuts and vegetables. Symbolic of fertility and abundance, they were popular classical and Renaissance motifs sometimes used to signify rejoicing and celebration. Hung at the opening of the loggia above the seated Virgin, the ripe coloured fruits unify the scene.

Acanthus and flowers
The short pilasters that frame the painted predella panels (lower section) contain an exotic sheaf of acanthus leaf scrolls and flowers with a central arrangement of pine cones and rosettes. The thin capitals and bases have a threaded bead pattern with a band of leaves. Each of the elements has classical origins, although their juxtaposition has been developed to give visual impact rather than following ancient models precisely.

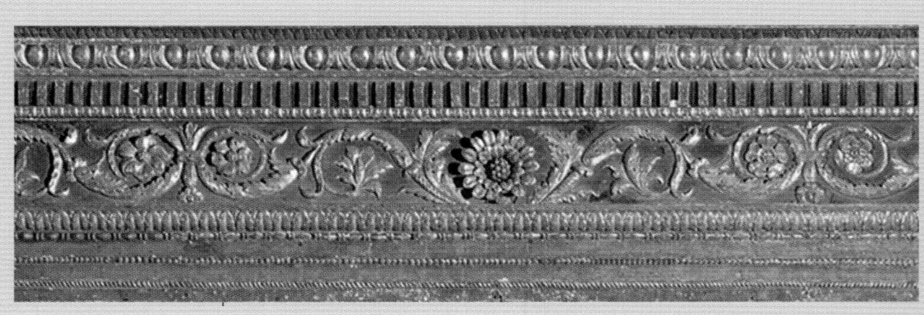

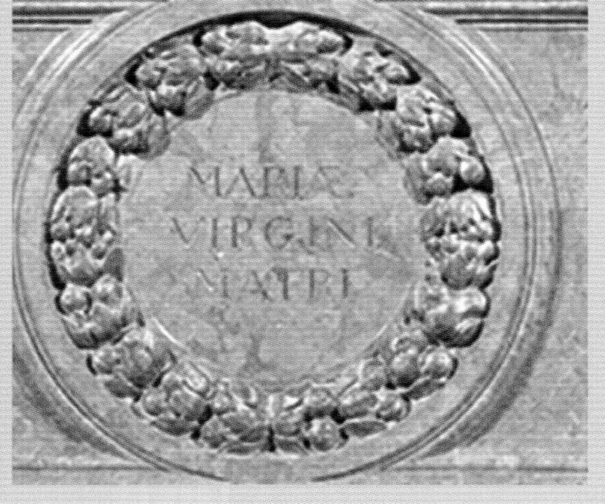

Fruitful wreaths
The marble plinth of the altarpiece also contains a swag of abundant leaves and fruits carved around the inscription *Mariae Virgini Matri* ('Virgin Mother Mary'). In antiquity, the wreathed medallion was used to commemorate the great emperors of Rome. Here the motif celebrates a Christian subject in a way that reflects how classical motifs and their symbolism were appropriated in the Renaissance.

The decorative entablature
Classical architecture featured pillars with architraves laid across their capitals, a frieze and a cornice above forming the roof edge. Each had its own pattern element – for example, Corinthian capitals were decorated with acanthus leaves. Here a number of the elements are present – the cornice with dentils and the patterned frieze – while other features are used decoratively, such as the lower cornice with bead-and-reel banding.

Vine scrolls

The classical orders of architecture in ancient Greece and Rome had pattern elements that were applied according to strict rules. Egg-and-dart, dentils, beading, acanthus and patterned frieze have been re-used here on an arched pediment in order to provide a decorative continuity with the rest of the frame. Ancient styles of architecture were used to meet contemporary taste rather than to emulate classical temple designs.

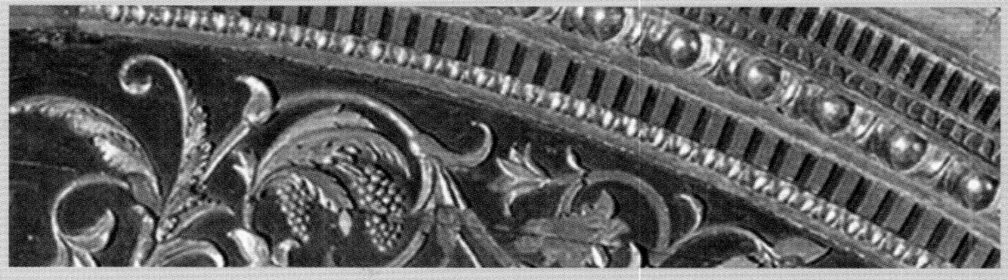

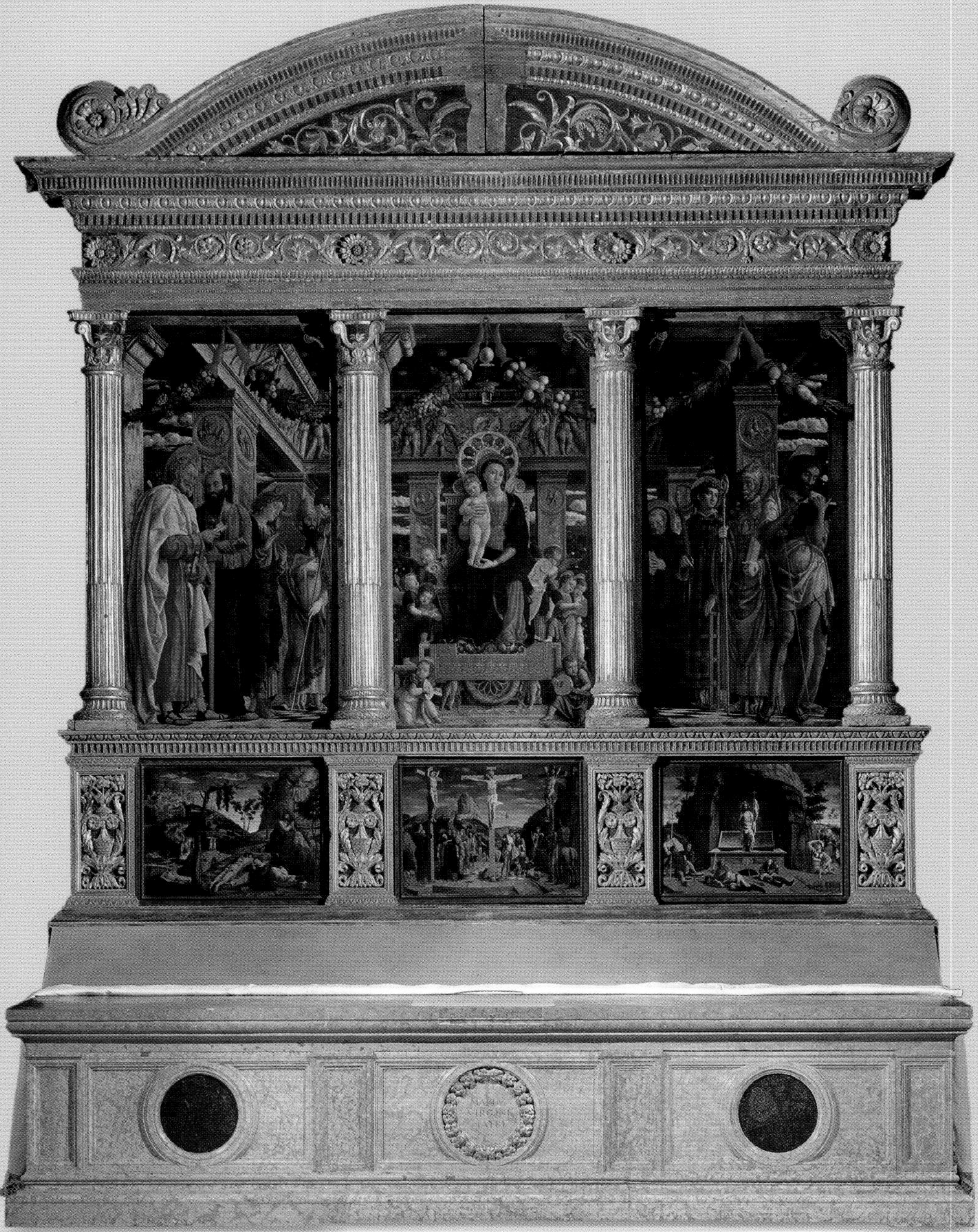

Enthroned Madonna and Child with saints

The scene of the enthroned Virgin with Christ standing on her lap, surrounded by saints, patrons and *putti* (cherub-like children) apparently in conversation or attending to their own concerns, was a popular composition in the 15th century called the *Sacra conversazione* (Holy conversation). Mantegna's decorative elaborations, classical motifs and complex faux architectural space embellish the scene with a rich and regal context appropriate for the Queen of Heaven.

Leon Battista Alberti
1404–1472

Born while his father was exiled from Florence, the young Alberti studied at the Universities of Padua and Bologna where he learned Latin and Greek. His studies led him to humanism and the study of classical manuscripts, which were being rediscovered in large numbers at the time. After completing his studies in 1427, he travelled widely in Italy, meeting other humanists of the period, and worked in the Papal Curia before being able to go to Florence when his family's exile was revoked in 1428. Innovations in styles of representation and architecture were developing in Florence through the work of Brunelleschi, Donatello, Ghiberti and Masaccio during the period known as the Early Renaissance.

Alberti continued to travel and spent time in Rome studying the classical ruins, seeking to discover the rules that governed the arts as they were used in the buildings of ancient Rome. He wrote three treatises, starting with *Della pittura* (*On Painting*, 1434–35), in which he provided a basis for single-point perspective, and a short pamphlet, *Della statua* (*On Sculpture*). He began his treatise on architecture, *De re aedificatoria* (*On Building*), in the 1450s, completing it in 1472. An inspiration for this work was the 1st-century CE *Ten Books on Architecture* of Vitruvius, which set out guidance and rules for a wide range of architectural and design matters. Vitruvius particularly advocated attention to 'perfect numbers', such as six and ten, and used the proportions of the human body in architecture. He stated that 'without symmetry and proportion no temple can have a regular plan; that is it must have an exact proportion worked out after the fashion of the members of a finely-shaped human figure' (in Benton, 2007). Alberti was concerned to provide a set of architectural rules in *On Building* which drew on such ancient sources, and to put these into practice in the buildings he himself designed and built.

For Alberti, the visual proportion and symmetry of a building would define its beauty, according to the ancient values he saw in the classical buildings of Rome. His first project was the unfinished façade of the Tempio Malatestiano in Rimini (1447), for which he drew on the structure and proportions of the triumphal arches of Rome. The façade of the Palazzo

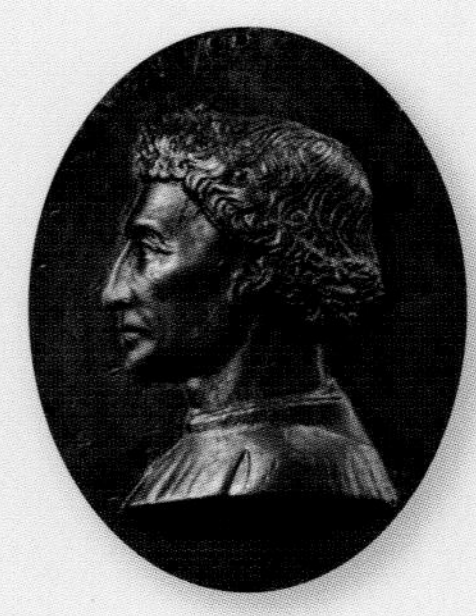

Born
Genoa, 1404

Profession
Artist, architect and scholar

Manifesto
'We must always take from nature [and] choose the most beautiful things.'

'A reasoned harmony of all parts within a body, so that nothing may be added, taken away or altered but for the worse.'

ALBERTI, *De re aedificatoria*, 1450–72

Rucellai (c. 1452–58) in Florence had a symmetrical arrangement of pilasters with differing patterns and designs across three floors. The general impact was of ordered harmony in the structure and ornament. The façade was designed to create a symmetrical and balanced pattern overall and in detail, which became one of the foundational principles of Renaissance architecture.

The proportions of the façade of Santa Maria Novella embody symmetry both in the height equalling the width and in the proportional squared sections on either side of and above the door, which follow the simple ratios of 1:1, 1:2 and 1:4. The classical features drawn from Roman models include the large scrolls on either side of the upper section and the triangular pediment that topped the structure. The detailed patterning uses sections of six and four to divide the squares, while rosettes and stars are structured by four and eight. A central frieze contains the decorative sail motif of the Rucellai family. As with Alberti's palazzo design, this façade would prove to be highly influential on the design of future Renaissance work, especially when applied to existing medieval churches.

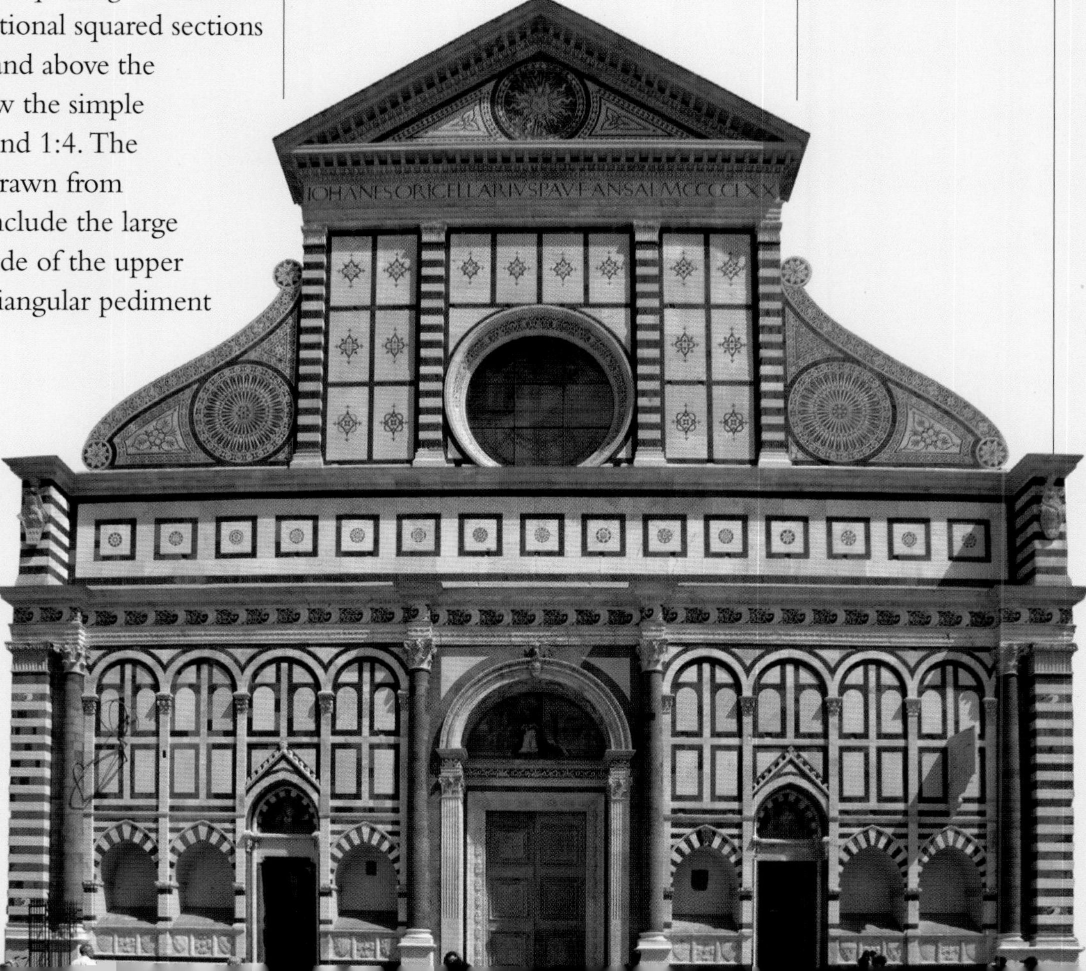

Santa Maria Novella, 1456–70, *Florence*
Alberti was commissioned by Giovanni di Paolo Rucellai to complete the façade of Santa Maria Novella, integrating it with the existing Gothic church and incorporating the dark green and white marble of Tuscany Romanesque.

Lotus, Chrysanthemum & Peony 1368–1644

Ming dynasty ceramics, lacquer and bronze

Established after the fall of the Mongol (Yuan) dynasty, the Ming dynasty brought political stability and great innovation and refinement to art in China. The Ming rulers started to build the Forbidden City in Beijing soon after founding their dynasty. Decorative art developed increasingly elaborate and complex forms, culminating in a refined connoisseurship in the late Ming period. Under imperial control, there was an expansion in the colours and techniques used for ceramics, while patterns often involved symbolic motifs such as the flowers of the four seasons – peony (spring), lotus (summer), chrysanthemum (autumn), and prunus blossom (winter) – and dragons, cloud and wave forms, bamboo, scrolls and foliate vines and tendrils.

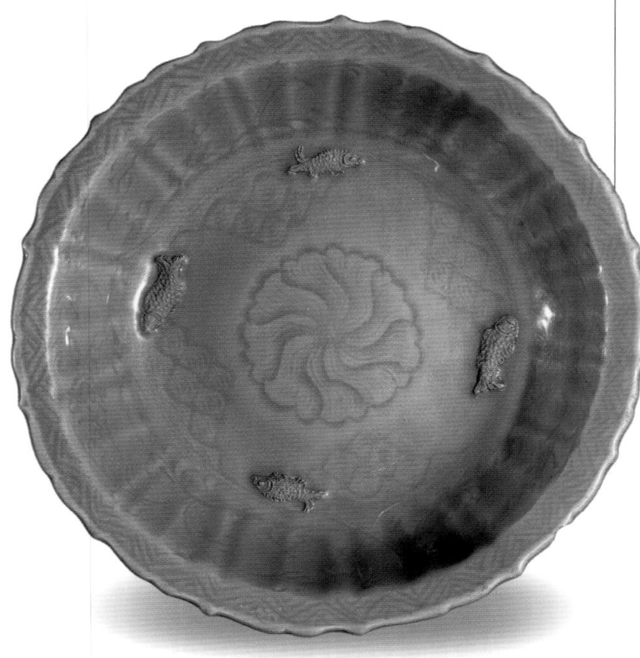

Longquan ware dish, 14th century, *Zhejiang, China*
The unfired earthenware surface of this dish was incised with a wavy chevron pattern on the rim, scrolling leaf fronds on the sides and a scaly motif forming waves arranged around a central stylised chrysanthemum. Before firing, the dish would have been covered with the celadon (jade green) glaze and the little moulded fish added. During the firing process, the glaze pooled in the pattern and the fish acquired a red colour.

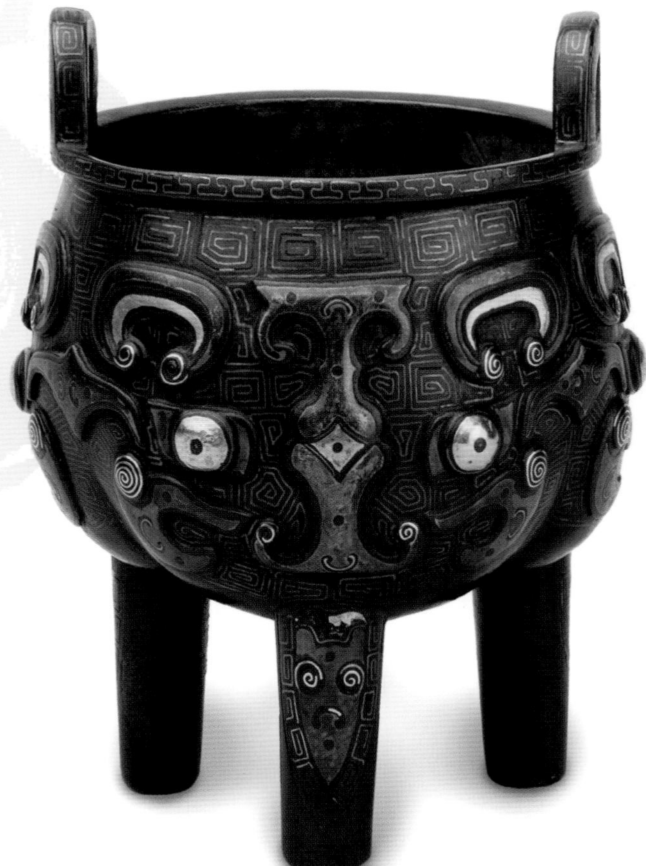

Bronze incense burner (*ding*), 1550–1640, *China*
The bronze vessels from the Shang and Zhou dynasties (see pages 24–5) provided important connections to ancestors and became models for contemporary objects, including incense burners. The *taotie* monster face is reproduced with gold inlaid features – boss eyes, curling nostrils and cheeks – orientated on the leg shafts of this traditional three-legged vessel. The silver inlaid meander background pattern and the face motif also occur on the legs.

‘Craftsmen working for the Ming court successfully blended decorative motifs from a great number of sources into a coherent visual language which was to carry associations of imperial power down to ... the twentieth century.’

CRAIG CLUNAS, *Art in China,* 1997

Porcelain vase, late 15th century, *China*
Cobalt blue and white glazed porcelain developed in China in the 14th century. This temple vase, one of a pair, includes many designs of the period – key pattern and plantain leaves at the neck, and a panel pattern of bamboo, lotus and scrolls on the base. The four-point *ruyi*-shaped (cloud or mushroom) cloud collar (*yun chien*) on the shoulder complements the elaborate dragon on the body.

ELEMENTS OF PATTERN

- *lotus, chrysanthemum, peony and prunus*
- *cloud collar*
- *scrolling leaves and tendrils*
- ruyi *motif – from a ceremonial sceptre with cloud- or mushroom-shaped head*
- *the* jian huan *motif – sword pommel rings*
- *ancestral symbolism*

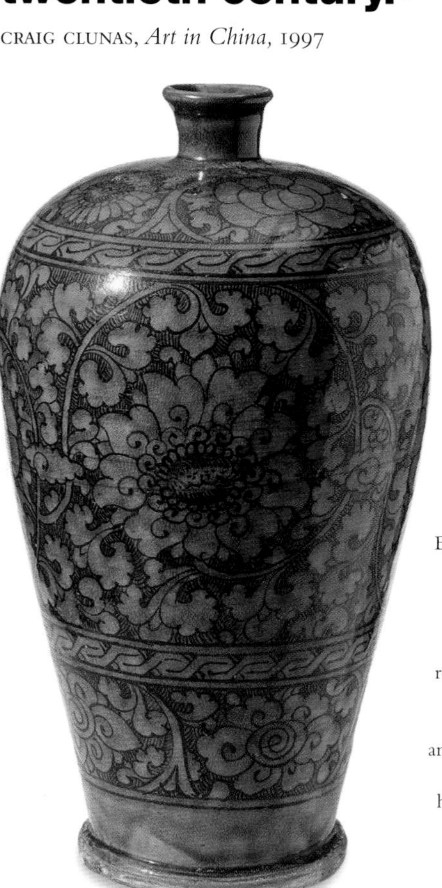

Stoneware vase, 1450–1550, *northern China*
Black painted flowers and scrolls cover this vase under a rich turquoise glaze. The stylised flowers on the neck, body and base have many forms representing the lotus, signifying purity and spiritual grace; the peony, bringing good fortune and love; and the chrysanthemum, symbolic of long life and happiness. These are surrounded by scrolling leaves and tendrils that stand out against a black hatched background.

Carved wooden food box, 15th century, *China*
During the Ming dynasty, carving was a popular medium for achieving high-quality surface effects. This box was carved through layers of black and red lacquer, giving it a smooth polished lustre. The *jian huan* (sword pommel rings) is a scrolling face-like or cloud motif. The box would have been used for gifts of food, elevating the contents above the ordinary.

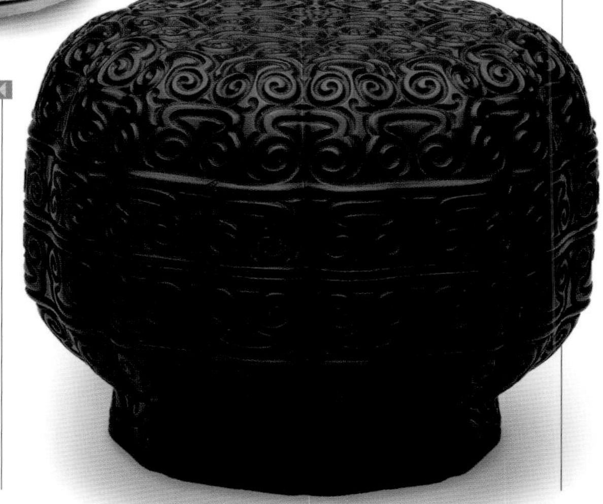

Birds & Triangles
before 1533

Patterns and designs from pre-Conquest Peru and Mexico

Textile technology in pre-Conquest Peru, including that of the Inca, involved almost every known technique – tapestry, brocade, lace and embroidery – demonstrating its rich cultural significance. Patterns used figurative models stylised into geometric forms, often far removed from the prototype. Known as the guano-bird, the stylised birds seen in the textiles may have been modelled on the Peruvian pelican, Peruvian booby or Guanay cormorant. In addition to birds and fish, patterns included the human figure and big cats – the puma, jaguar and panther. In Mesoamerica, geometric stylised patterns echoed the figurative art forms of the region, such as Mayan and Aztec design.

'An astonishing number of varied patterns, some easily recognizable ..., others carried so far into the domain of pure design.'

HORACE H. F. JAYNE, 'Peruvian Textiles', 1922

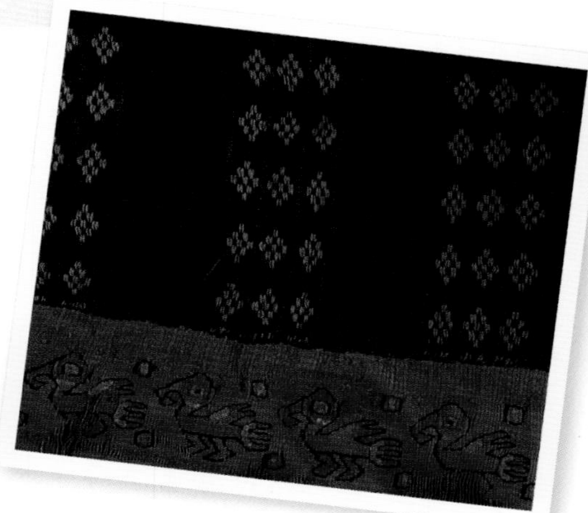

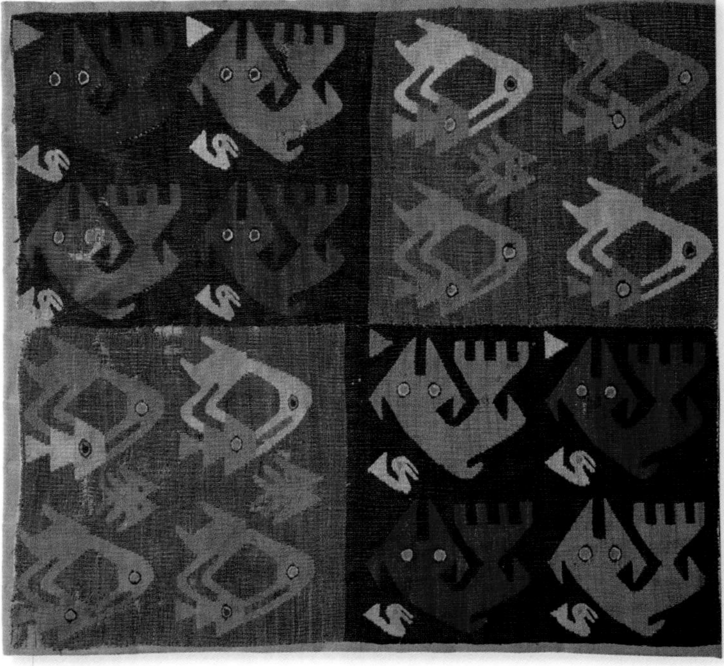

Cotton and wool tapestry, 14th century, *Peru*
The tapestry uses six colours – cream, three shades of green, grey and red – to create alternating patterned squares. One square shows large and small fish with prominent eyes, while in the other, birds eat fish. Triangles and lozenges are used to represent heads, fins, tails, bodies and mouths. The exceptional survival of ancient textiles (dating from 1200 to 1500) in Peru is due to their extensive use in burials.

Woven fabric, before 1533, *Peru*
The main pattern uses stripes and small lozenges to create a basic overall pattern for the fabric. The fringed border contains walking birds with hooked beaks and alternating black with brown eyes. Each bird also has white patches on its neck, wings and tail, suggesting that the motif might represent a specific bird, such as a condor, eagle or parrot.

Woven cotton fabric with feathers, 900–1476, *Peru*
South America has some of the most colourful birds in the world and their feathers provided colour and impact in ceremonial robes and headdresses. The blue and yellow feathers from a macaw create a wave pattern similar to the geometric forms of birds seen in the other textiles. This rich cloth may have belonged to a high-ranking individual or have been presented as a diplomatic gift.

ELEMENTS OF PATTERN

- *the human figure*
- *the puma, jaguar or panther*
- *guano-birds, condors and parrots*
- *fish*
- *triangles and geometric bands*

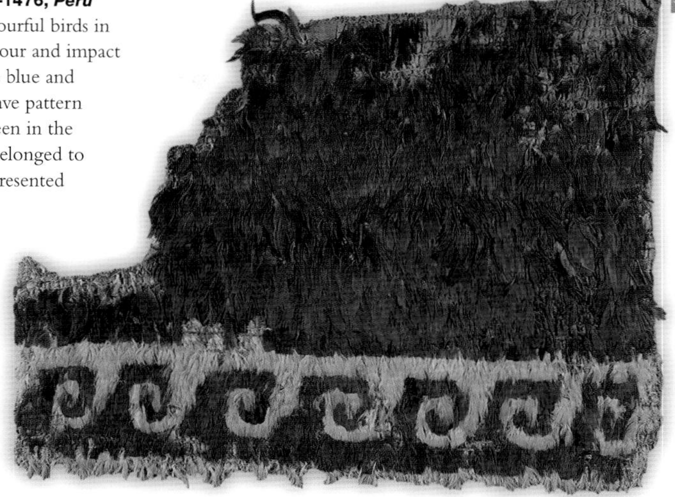

Jar with ritual scene, 15th century, *Mexico*
The patterns on the neck, shoulder and base of this jar use red, yellow, brown, black and white in interlocking angular patterns and circles. The geometric shapes form a triangle-and-hook bird-like motif that echoes the prancing gesticulating postures of the dancing figures on the body. This ritual scene includes a kneeling woman who may be symbolic of the mother of Quetzalcoátl (the feathered-serpent deity), who died in childbirth.

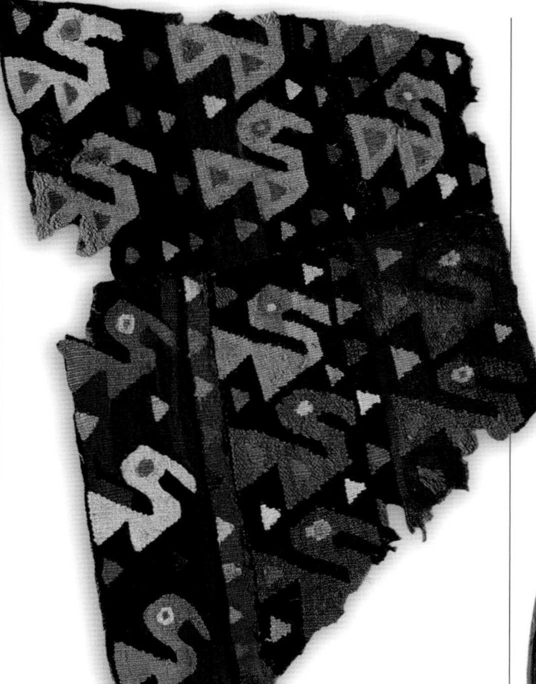

Tapestry, before 1533, *Peru*
The birds in this tapestry are so stylised that they have been reduced to two triangles, a neck and beak, almost forming a non-figurative design with the matching interspersed triangles. The use of blue and pink brightens the fabric, suggesting that this bird variety offered a desirable colourfulness. This composition of simple forms creates an overall design that is strikingly vivid.

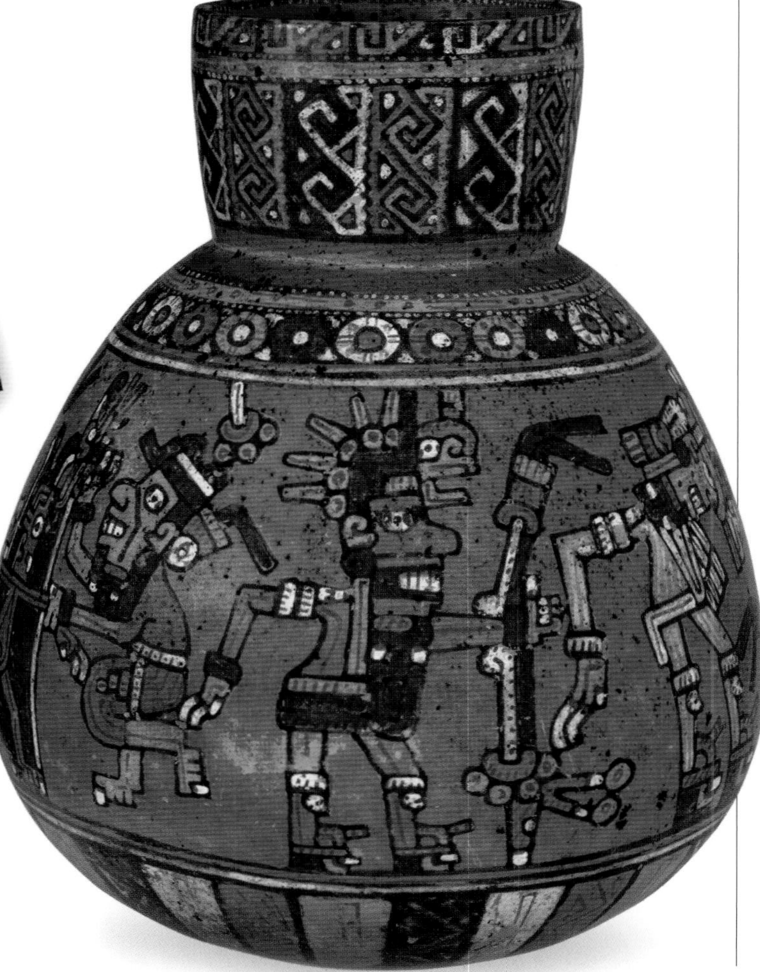

1500
1600

Sixteenth Century

Introduction

New luxuriantly patterned velvets from Italy and Spain were acquired by Dutch merchants to display their wealth and status in their own homes. Fashionable tin-glazed tiles were fitted to walls to display lustrous patterns. Wooden furniture inlaid with horn, bone and ivory was the height of luxury in European domestic settings. Delicately patterned accessories fastened around a gentleman's expensive clothing portrayed the wearer as a fashionable man-at-arms. In Italy, lustreware ceramics with a glowing tin glaze from Spain – called 'maiolica' – were copied by Umbrian workshops and by 1600 the term was applied to all tin-glazed pottery. Grotesque designs were combined with 'strapwork' bands imitating two- or three-dimensional leather or metalwork strips and used to decorate many objects.

Textiles embroidered with interlaced strapwork bands in metal thread became fashionable in France and were imitated throughout northern Europe by 1600. Additional textile dyes were sought out to colour the new patterns – expensive red cochineal was imported to Spain from the Spanish territories in central America. Linen openwork patterns were freed from the geometry of the woven grid by the Italian *reticella* lacemaking technique. Designs were stitched on to the fabric that was then removed to leave an openwork lace pattern. Cesar Ripa's book of allegorical emblems, *Iconologia* (1593), probably inspired John Davies's 1599 poem 'Hymnes of Astraea' in which Queen Elizabeth I was identified with Astraea, goddess of justice and purity. The 'Rainbow portrait' (1600–3) of the queen, allegorically costumed in symbolic patterns, may have been a prop for Astraea's shrine in a masque entertainment.

Luxury carpet-making in Iran developed detailed patterning in exotic floral and foliate arabesques, both for display at the royal court

The discovery of Emperor Nero's 1st-century-CE Domus Aurea *('Golden House') in Rome, with its frescoes of fantastical hybrid beings, inspired artists to design patterns of 'grotesques' for ceramics, textiles and architecture. The northern Italian engraver Nicoletto da Modena, who left his name on the wall of* Domus Aurea, *produced decorative 'grotesque' designs for ceramics.*

Ottoman tiles, vases, wall panels and textiles were decorated with arabesque and floral patterns with distinctive serrated leaves called saz style. Underglaze white slip-coated ceramics were first painted in blue, emulating blue-and-white Chinese porcelain, and further developed using other vibrant colours such as green and red.

and for export. Comprising millions of knots, carpets were woven with vibrant colours to emphasise and harmonise patterns that sometimes incorporated prancing animals. The popularity of carpets spread to Europe and Asia. At the Mughal court of India, Muslim rulers enjoyed strong artistic links with the Middle East but also encouraged the development of local designs for decorative pierced stonework, and intricate floral patterns in inlaid stone were applied to surfaces in palaces and on tombs.

Patterns and techniques circulated around the Mediterranean – patterned vessels and textiles from Mamluk Egypt drew on designs from the Islamic world and Africa. In sub-Saharan Africa, the kingdom of Benin produced decorated cast-bronze panels and sculptures. Patterns related to textiles and natural materials adorned images of kings and attendants commemorating court life and achievements. In the Ottoman Empire new decorative schemes developed in ceramics produced at Iznik in north-west Anatolia, and at Istanbul. The Ottoman imperial residence of Topkapı was covered with Iznik tiles in gorgeous complex floral designs of varied pattern and colour.

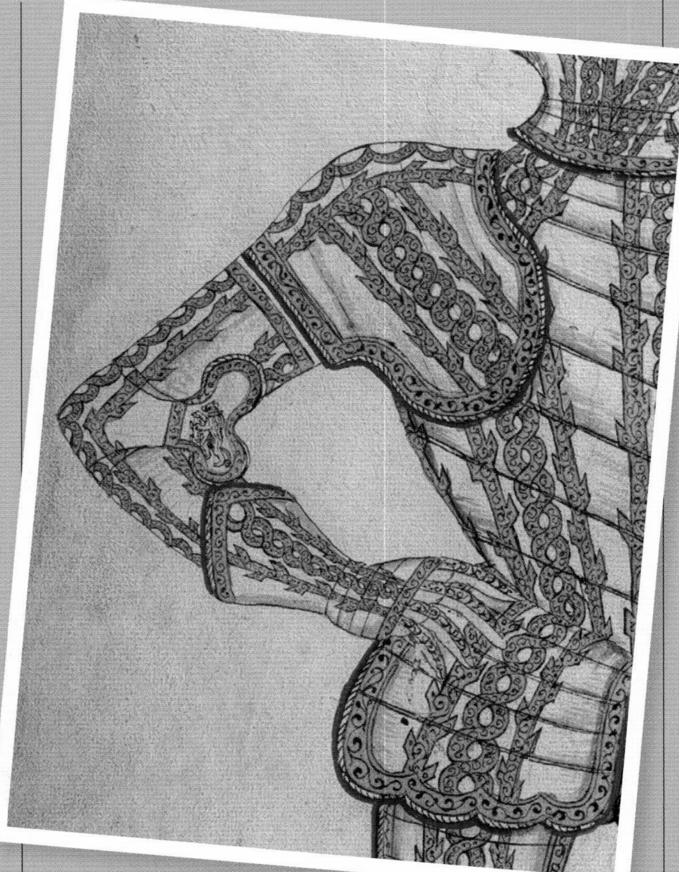

The Royal Almain Armoury, founded in 1525 by Henry VIII, employed master armourers from Germany. Jacob Halder was famous for his elaborate colourful designs that translated patterns from fashionable clothes to armour for prestigious nobles such as Robert Dudley, Earl of Leicester.

Ornamented Interiors 1500–1600

Domestic decoration

Merchants and traders making money from expanding trade in Europe elaborated the walls and floors of their houses with patterns in lustrous ceramic tiles and in luxurious hangings in the new velvet weaves. Rhythmical patterns of leaves, waves and flowers adorned furniture and fittings in richer domestic households to express the new wealth and social position of the owners and their families.

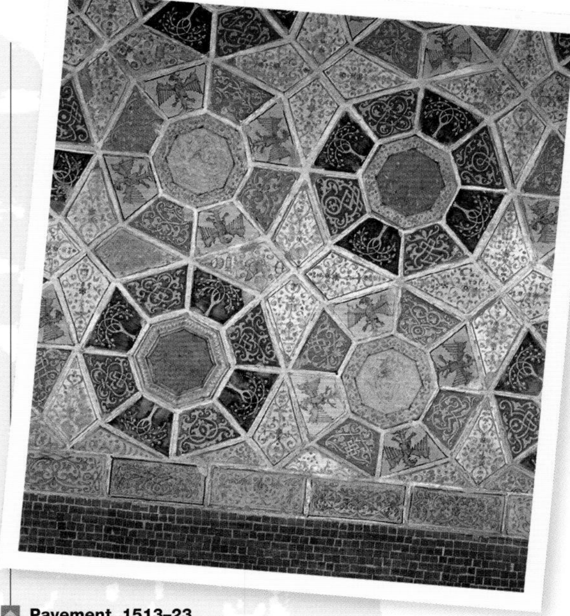

Pavement, 1513–23, *Forlì or Faenza, Emilia-Romagna, Italy*
Octagonal tiles, painted with classical heads, animals and compositions such as curved swords with trumpets and ribbons, are bordered with heraldic eagles blazoned with a fleur-de-lis or an oak tree (signifying the Della Rovere family) alternating with leafy tendril and strapwork designs. Between is a star shape of four tiles, each delicately patterned with subtly different arrangements of tendrils, curving leaves, flowers, acorns, open books, parchment scrolls, draped banners, pairs of wings, drums and torches. The pavement is from the chapel commissioned by physician Bartolomeo Lombadini for the church of San Francesco in Forlì.

‘For the wealthy and powerful, craftsmen developed artefacts of increasing variety and elegance to accommodate new tastes for luxury and artistic expression.’

JOHN PILE, *A History of Interior Design*, 2005

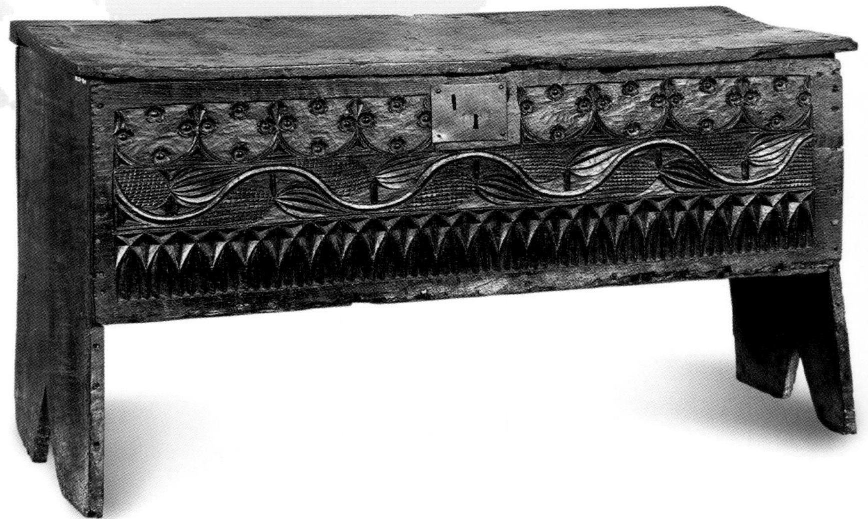

Chest, 1500–50, *Stamford, Lincolnshire, England*
The front of this oak chest is carved with three bands of pattern. The uppermost comprises a row of formal tripartite flowers on points of arcs, with metal studs incorporated into the design. An undulating tendril runs across the middle band, each curve filled with a pair of differently carved pointed leaves on a straight stem. The lowest band has interlocking arcading of pointed arches above vertical ribbing. Valuable clothes, metalwork, documents or money were locked inside this chest.

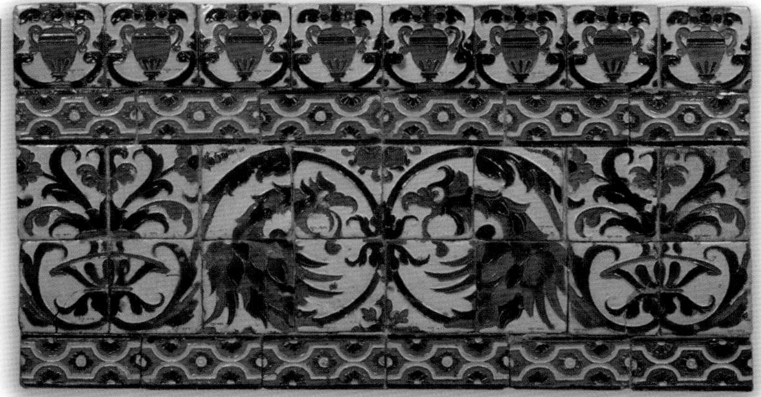

Tiles, 1550–1600, *Muel, Aragon, Spain*
The tails of opposing pairs of fantastical birds transform into leafy spiralling tendrils linked by a spray of leaves between them. The tendrils meet behind the birds with a formal arrangement of flowers and leaves curling upwards from a tiered base. Above and below are patterns of formal flowers arranged between strap-like bands. At the top is a running pattern of classical pedestal urns containing flowers and leaves, enclosed by scroll-ended arcs surmounted by a tripartite leaf at each juncture. These tin-glazed earthenware tiles were set into a wall.

Tiles, 1580–1600, *the Netherlands*
These tin-glazed earthenware tiles have been painted to make up a pattern of geometric eight-pointed stars with dark blue eight-pointed stars and yellow pointed crosses, each filled with a stylised leaf and flower design. These designs are reversed in white against a darker background in the style of earlier floor tiles. The tiles may have been set into a wall or laid into a floor, perhaps around a fireplace.

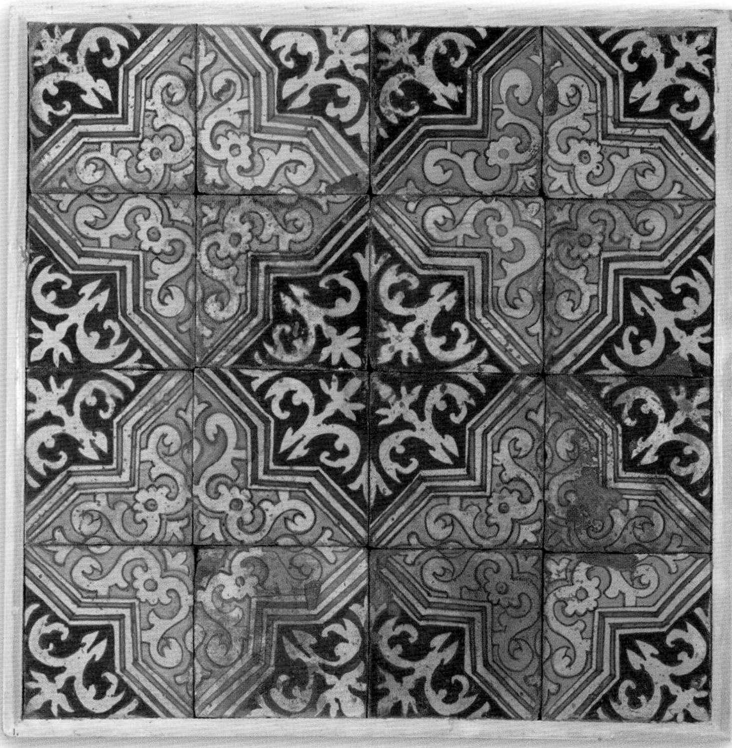

Wall hanging, 1570–1629, *Genoa, Florence or Venice, Italy*
The pattern on this textile woven in silk and metal thread is formed by a velvet weave – details, such as the leaf veins, have been created by cutting the pile short. Arranged symmetrically around a vertical line, the design comprises rich curving leaves, emphasised by the deep olive colour of the velvet, sprouting from scaled stems and encompassing large floral motifs and centrally placed suns shining with metallic thread. The foliage is both rhythmically bound by, and supports, central crowns with fleur-de-lis points.

ELEMENTS OF PATTERN

- *formalised leaves and flowers*
- *curling leaves*
- *strapwork*
- *personal motifs*

Patterns of Personal Delight 1500–1600

Portable items

Smaller items for personal use were often ornamented with patterns signifying their purpose and incorporating messages to the recipient or user. Heraldic devices were applied as open statements of authority, flowers and fruits as emblems of particular high-ranking individuals, and allegorical animals were integrated into patterns in a more covert way. Delicate floral patterns were also used in embroidery for domestic linens, while a wide range of personal items were ornamented with patterns inhabited by animals referring to their use. Such patterns were also applied to communicate ideas of sentiment and love.

Box, 1579, *England*
The pattern on this iron box has been made by 'damascening' (inlaying metals) in gold and silver and heating the iron to darken its colour. Fine scrolling branches with different types of leaves, buds and flowers, including Tudor roses and acorns, are grasped in each hand by a fantastical crowned figure. Perched among the foliage and florals are birds, including a cockerel, and serpents and snails. This small sweetmeats box was made as a New Year gift for Robert Dudley, Earl of Leicester, Queen Elizabeth I's favoured courtier, whom the acorn may here represent.

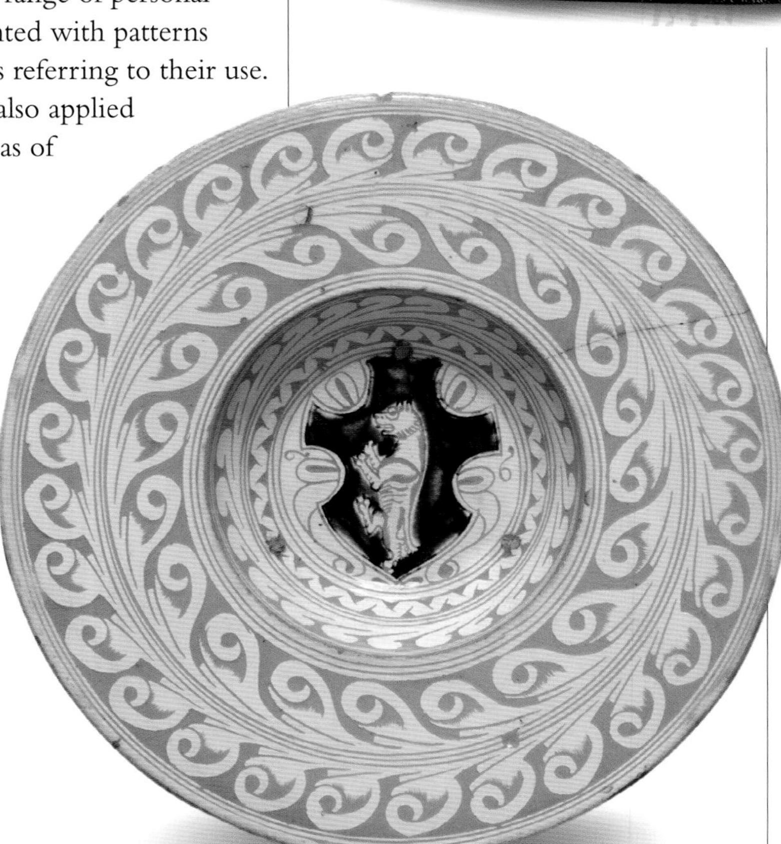

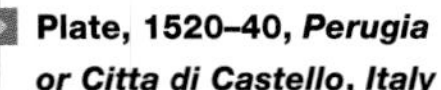

Plate, 1520–40, *Perugia or Citta di Castello, Italy*
Scrolling leaves sprouting from a central stem encircle the wide border of this earthenware plate. The pattern has been carved through the cream slip (outer layer coating) to expose the red background of the clay, a technique called *fondo ribasatto*. The central heraldic badge is encircled by a twisted ribbon pattern and another circle of sprouting leaves. This plate was probably part of a dining table set belonging to a noble family.

Powder flask, c. 1580, *south Germany*
The pattern on this walnut powder flask has been inlaid with carved stag horn. A lively hunting lion crouches between two sleeping birds of prey, perhaps owls, and a squirrel. Densely spiralling and interlocking branches sprouting tightly curled foliage and ending in open tripartite leaves surround them. Used to store fine-grained gunpowder, this flask would have been worn with a matching pistol by an aristocrat.

Comb, 16th century, *France*
The handle of this boxwood comb has five panels of openwork patterns of overlapping circles, spindle shapes and lozenge motifs. A central heart pierced by an arrow, surrounded by protective lozenges, is between the Old French words *vice* and *celle* in Gothic lettering – part of the sentiment *vice celle que jayme* ('may the one I love live'). Each edge of the handle has been carved with a wave pattern and the ends with patterns reminiscent of windows.

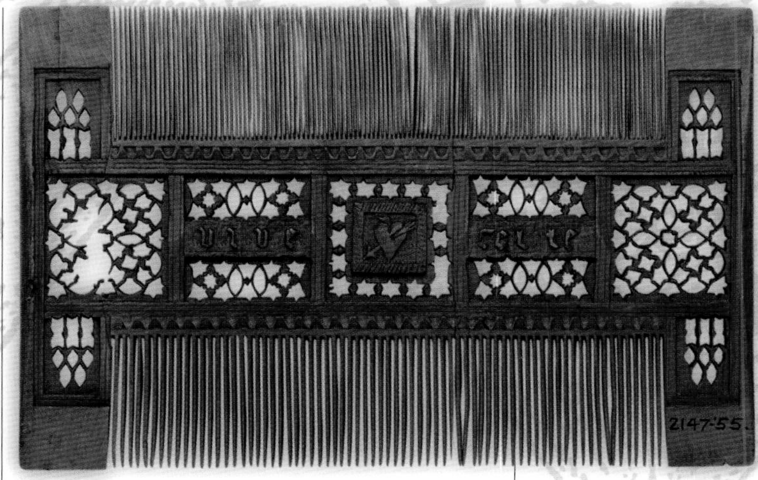

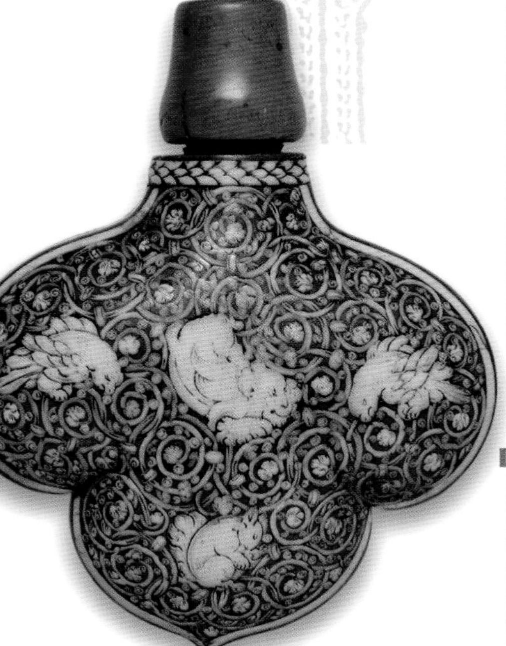

'Anything that could be worn to display status in society was turned into a beautiful object.'

MOIRA HOOK AND ARTHUR MACGREGOR, *Tudor England*, 2000

ELEMENTS OF PATTERN

- *fine spiralling tendrils with different types of leaves, flowers and fruits*
- *sprouting curling leaves*
- *animal signifiers*
- *personal devices*

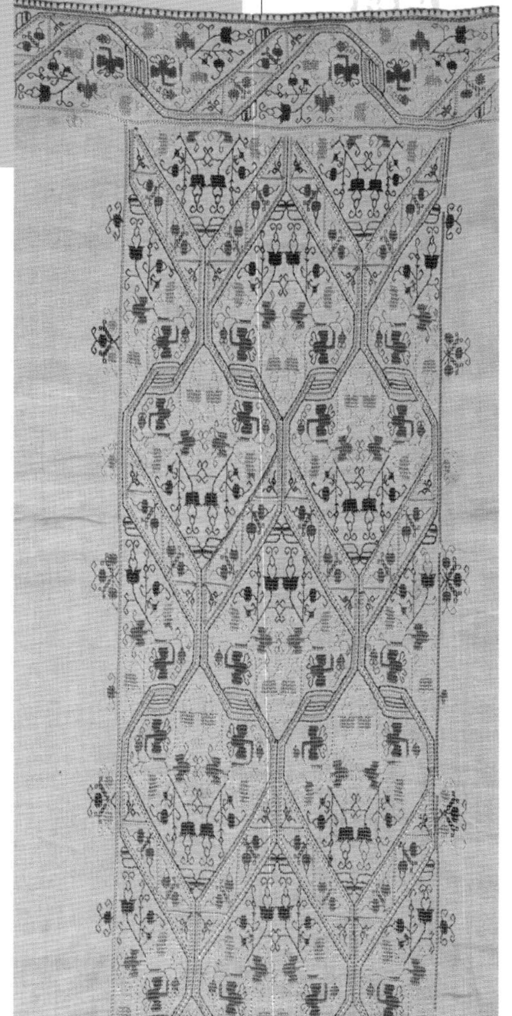

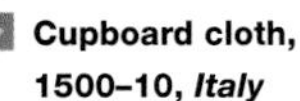

Cupboard cloth, 1500–10, *Italy*
Geometric leaf shapes formed by bands of contrasting width have been embroidered across the central part of the cloth, halved and repeated on the border. The pattern is filled with fine stems sprouting curling tendrils, leaves, flowers with stamens, and acorns. Embroidered with silk threads by a woman for her own household, this linen cloth may have been used to line the shelf of a cupboard on which pottery containers could be placed.

Glowing Grotesques 1490–1574

Italian maiolica

Italian workshops producing maiolica used their own colours, such as violet and overpainted blue with yellow, to produce a vivid green. Patterns painted in radially segmented borders, characteristic of plates made at Deruta in Umbria, and overlapping scales were copied from Spanish lustrewares derived from medieval Islamic ceramics. Patterns of 'grotesques' – small fantastical people, animals and plants, inspired by 1st-century Roman examples – became very fashionable and were highly influential among pattern-makers.

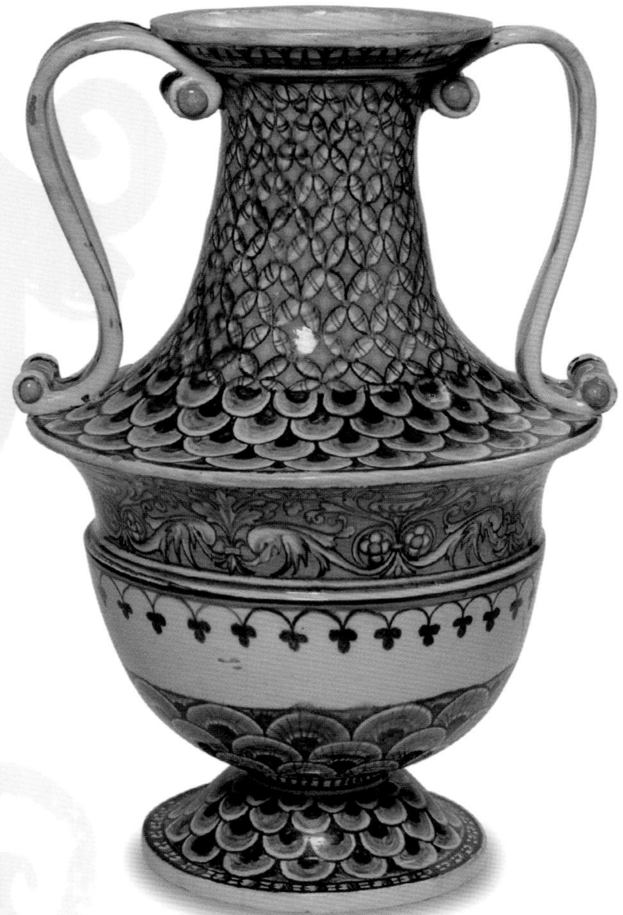

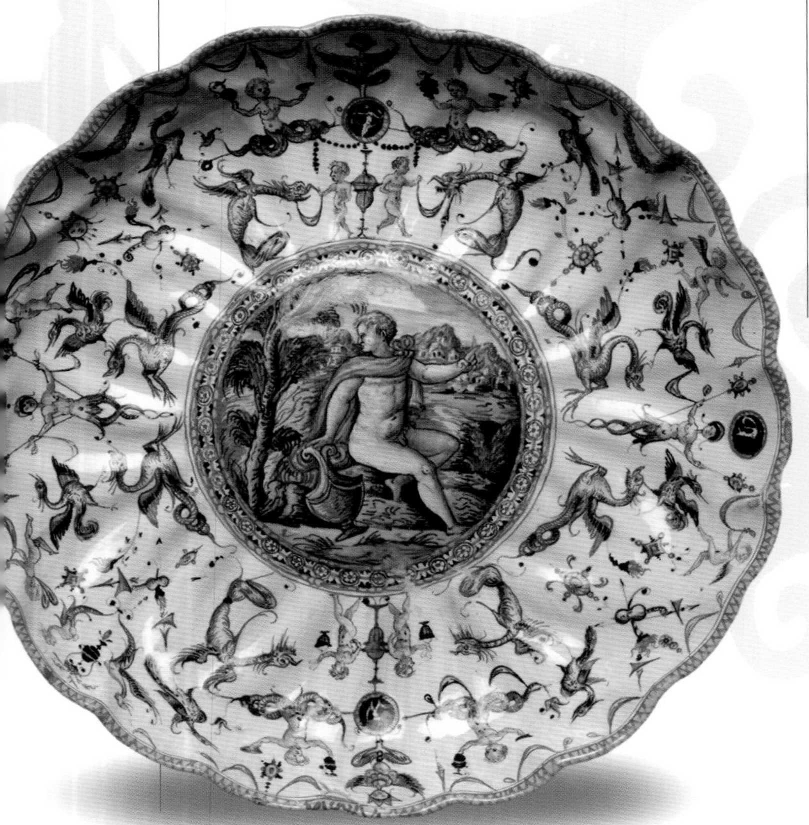

Dish, 1573–74,
Urbino, Marche, Italy
The ribbed surface of this fruit dish has a pattern built around urns between pairs of boys with an urn (above and below) and fantastical figures holding wands (left and right). The pattern is carefully balanced with subtly varied motifs – wyverns (two-legged dragons), bird-headed winged serpents, exotic birds, boys with serpent tails for legs, winged boys, medallions, garlands, swagged banners, violas with pike staffs, torches, a winged figure, a vase of flowers and a pendant-crowned human face. The dish was made in Flaminio Fontana's workshop.

Vase, 1490–1500,
Pesaro, Marche, Italy
The neck of this classically shaped vase has been painted with a lattice grid of overlapping ovals producing spindle shapes and curved-sided lozenges. The shoulder and foot are decorated with a scale pattern. The body has a band of flowing and curling leaf ornament with stylised flowers, bound at regular points by short horizontal bands. Underneath is a pattern of arcs with trefoils at the points, with large overlapping scallops in banded colours below.

Plate, 1525–35, *Gubbio, Umbria, Italy*
The vibrant finely painted pattern around the border of this plate is composed of upright wands bound to a pair of scrolling tendrils on either side. The tendrils sprout curling leaves and end in the centre of the spiral with round orange fruits. Each lower tendril curls upwards to form a broader middle leaf and is met by a similar motif curving downwards from the rim, between which are smaller round fruits. This plate, which depicts the god of love Cupid, was made in the workshop of Maestro Giorgio.

Dish, mid-16th century, *Deruta, Umbria, Italy*
An overlapping scale or feather pattern alternates with a plant design on the border of this dish. Half-bunches of leaves and yellow fruits are bound together with a scrolling tendril sprouting curling leaves, fine shoots, and flowers with three petals. The central figure wears fantasy Roman armour, the helmet ornamented with a bearded face reflecting the wearer's own and a scrolling tripartite leaf pattern. The breastplate is decorated with a human face, wings and long curling leaves bound together, with a row of rosettes towards the shoulder.

'Immediate sources of inspiration must have been contemporary Italian books and prints and popular imported Islamic metalwork.'

ROSAMOND E. MACK,
Bazaar to Piazza: Islamic Trade and Italian Art, 1300–1600, 2002

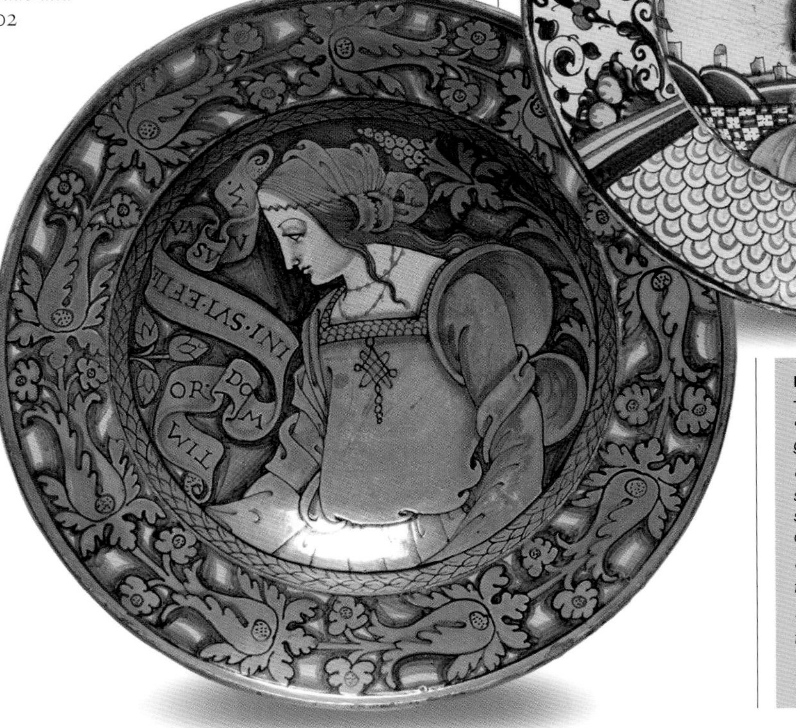

Dish, c. 1520, *Deruta, Umbria, Italy*
The border of this dish is decorated with a pattern of continuously sprouting acanthus-like leaves and flowers. There is a band patterned with overlapping pointed scales encircling the central portrait and repeated in the neckband of the woman's gown. She contemplates a curling banner inscribed with a medieval Latin phrase that translates as, 'Fear the Lord God and His Son'.

ELEMENTS OF PATTERN

- *circle- or oval-based grid*
- *overlapping scallop shapes, reminiscent of scales, feathers or pine cones*
- *scrolling tendrils with fruits and flowers*
- *'grotesques' of fantastical figures*

Nicoletto da Modena
Active c. 1500–c. 1520

The life of Nicoletto (Rosex, Rossi or Rosa) da Modena, a northern Italian engraver, is not known in detail, but it is possible to develop an idea of his works and design interests. In the early 16th century, fascination with the arts of the classical world was encouraged by discoveries of important antique works in Rome. Along with significant pieces of classical sculpture – such as the Belvedere Apollo (2nd-century BCE copy of 4th-century BCE bronze original, rediscovered c. 1489), which provided stimuli for 16th-century artists such as Michelangelo and Dürer – the discovery of the astonishing *Domus Aurea* ('Golden House') of the Emperor Nero created a new language of ornament and pattern. Built in 64 CE on the Esquiline Hill after the fire that destroyed Rome, the *Domus Aurea* was an extensive villa complex filled with ornate and finely painted rooms. Artists flocked to see it and among the graffiti is the signature of Nicoletto da Modena Ferrara, dated 1507.

The wall designs of the *Domus Aurea*, classified as the 'Fourth Style' of Roman wall painting (see pages 32–3), became one of the most highly desirable models for 16th-century artists and architects – the artists Raphael and Giovanni da Udine used the style to decorate the Vatican *Loggetta* (c. 1519). The decorative elements involved delicately painted swags, vegetal and vine scrolls, running spirals, geometric banding, birds, animals and, most notably, 'grotesques' (see also pages 118–19).

The work of Nicoletto da Modena includes engravings of mythical and religious figures in ruined classical settings with decorative architectural details; architectural drawings; possibly designs for furniture and theatrical productions; and patterns of 'grotesques', probably used by goldsmiths and by

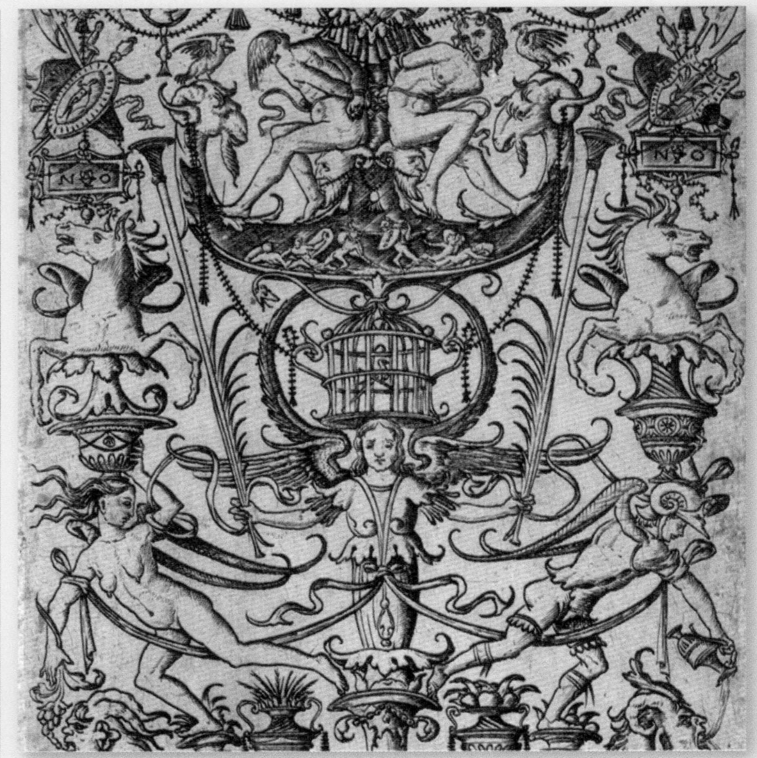

Born
Modena, probably c. 1470s–80s

Profession
Engraver and designer

Manifesto
Ornamentation and decoration of a classical setting

Engraving, c. 1500–12
Using the human body as a design or structural feature had a long tradition in classical art. 'Grotesque' human and animal bodies and limbs metamorphosed into other shapes and objects – here Nicoletto has copied some from the Domus Aurea.

‘Nicoletto provided both figural and ornamental compositions for ceramic work ...’

M. M. LICHT, ‘A Book of Drawings by Nicoletto da Modena’, *Master Drawings,* WINTER 1970

decorators of maiolica ceramics. Although full details of Nicoletto’s life are sketchy, his early work follows that of Andrea Mantegna (see pages 102–3) and he appears to have studied Dürer around 1500. It is possible that he worked at the court of Ercole I d’Este (1431–1505) in Ferrara and was involved with the ceramic factories and workshops of Padua. Nicoletto was first identified as a 16th-century designer and engraver in a biography written by the Modenese Lodovico Vedriani, which cites his works as collected beside engravings by Dürer and Lucas van Leyden. More recently, a range of works signed with a variety of signatures and personal devices have been attributed to Nicoletto by Arthur M. Hind (1923).

The elaborate patterns drawn by Nicoletto appeared in almost all of his works, either as incidental decorative ornamentation on the architecture in his figurative engravings or as fully worked design drawings. These contained complex continuous mirror-image constructions, involving fantastical human or animal figures linked by decorated imaginary pillars, cages and vases, vegetal scrolls, masks, ribbons, festoons, elongated limbs and heraldic devices. The naked human figure, as an adult or a *putto* (cherub-like child), often winged, contorted or stretched into impossible forms, provided the principal motif. The vibrant colouring used in the decoration of ceramics at this time helped to emphasise and contrast the fantastical elements of the designs.

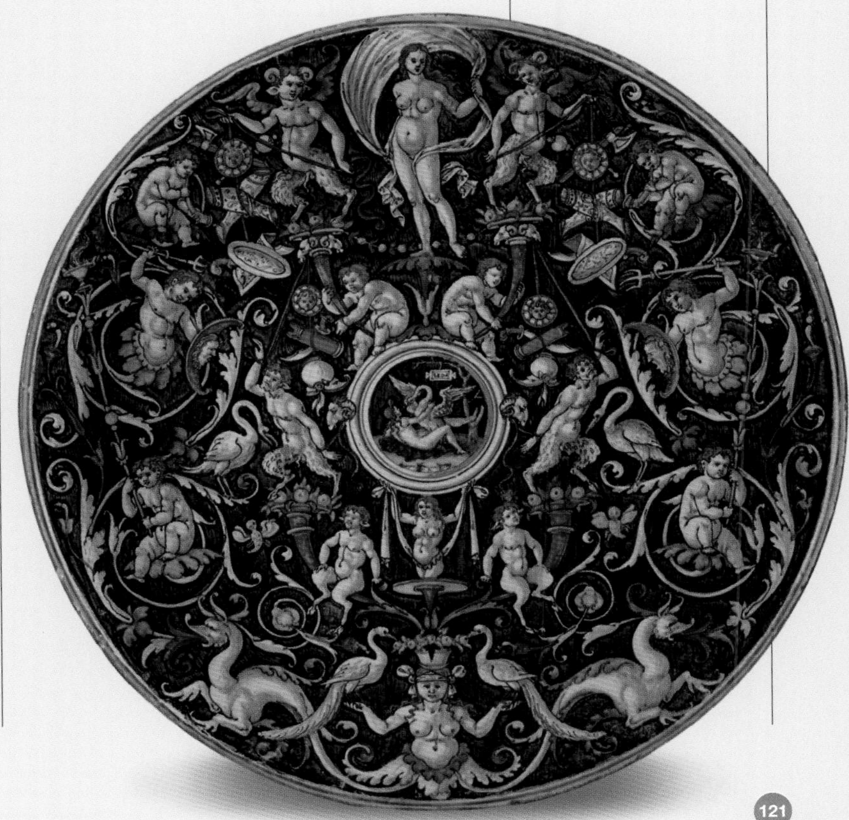

Dish, c. 1515, probably by Maestro Jacopo
The pattern represents the myth of Leda seduced by Zeus disguised as a swan, a popular contemporary narrative from Ovid’s Metamorphoses, *surrounded by satyrs (fauns) and* putti. *The figure of Fortuna at the bottom is taken from Nicoletto’s drawings, and many of the elements closely follow the designs of his grotesques.*

PATTERN IN DETAIL

The Floral Arabesque 1539–1540

Carpet production in Safavid Iran

Carpet-making developed in Iran through the 14th and 15th centuries but it became a national industry during the 16th, producing luxury carpets for royal use, gifts and export. The designs shifted from the earlier geometric forms to floral arabesque patterns as the technology for tying knots allowed for more detail and complexity. The popularity of the intricate and enormously varied floral designs ensured the huge success of the carpet industry, which became an important source of state revenue.

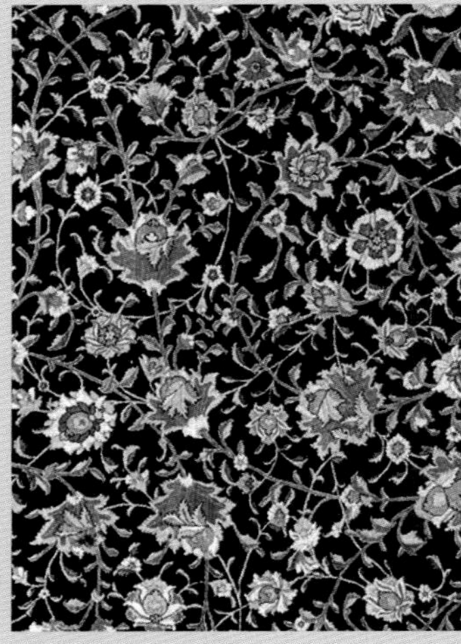

Blue heaven of arabesque
The pattern in the main background is symmetrically organised with mirrored designs on either side of the central long axis. The curving tendrils, stylised flowers and small leaves appear to be random but, as the viewer's gaze follows the sweeping branch, overlapping circles and curls appear. The flowers are multi-layered but always set within their own space, ensuring clarity and impact.

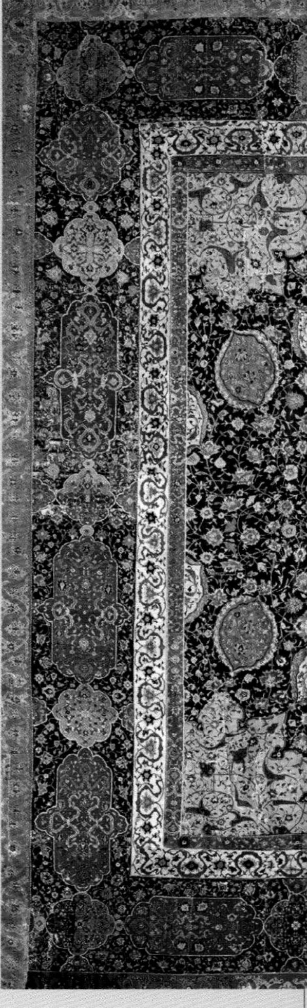

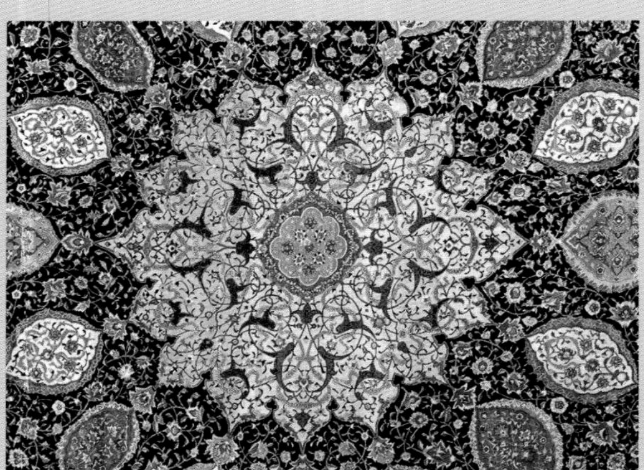

Golden starburst
Set on a golden yellow background, the central starburst (repeated as quadrants in the corners) contains several elements – twisting Chinese cloud-like scrolls in white and turquoise, and spiky leaves and flowers in light brown and deep turquoise, all linked together with curling tendrils interspersed with a variety of pale flowers. The coordinated colours and intersecting forms are contained within an elegantly flowing edging linked to alternating coloured ogee (double-curved) pendants.

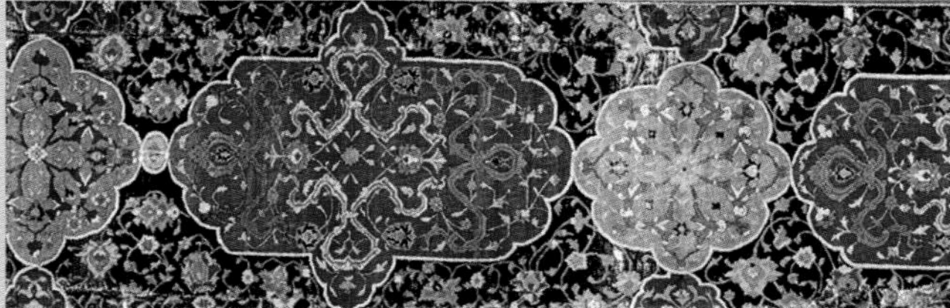

Twisting borders
The main border colours of red-brown and green provide a firm contrast to the blues and yellows in the central panel. A cream twisted edging contains areas which are filled with small, ordered arabesque tendrils and coloured ribbons. The subtle juxtaposition of colours – often following the principles of complementary rules (red and green, blue and orange) – even at the level of the smallest leaf and flower, reinforces the harmony of the design.

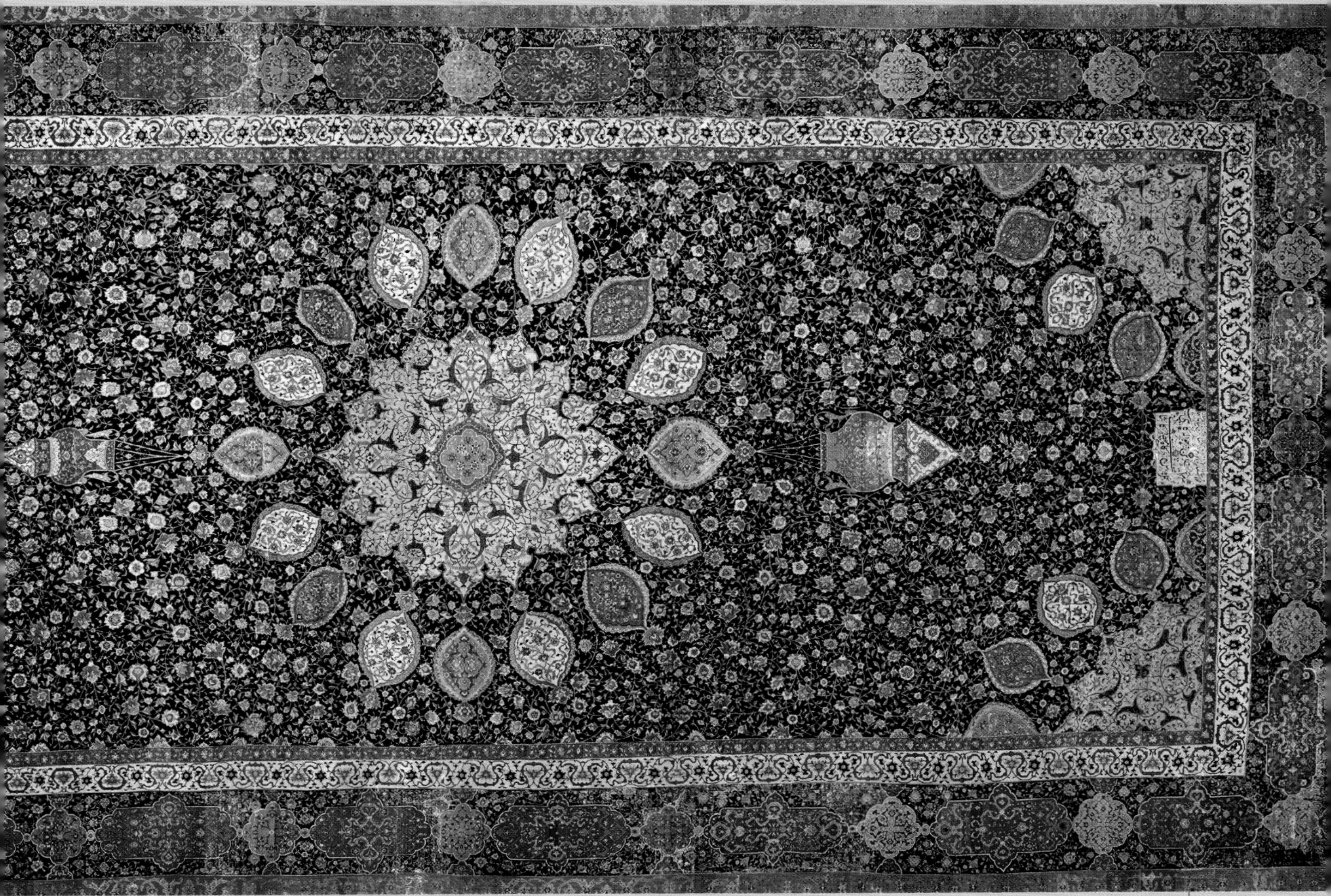

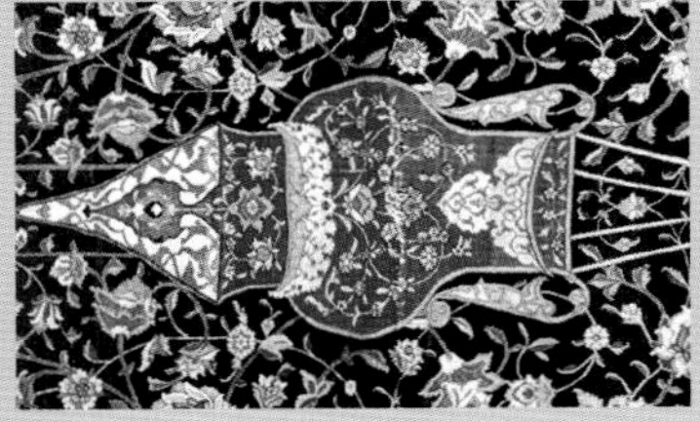

Decorative mosque lamps

To emphasise the Islamic context of the carpet, two mosque lamps hang from the pendants along the central axis. Such lamps could be made of glass and were heavily decorated. The arabesque theme continues in the delicate symmetrical flowers and tendrils covering this lamp, using red-brown, yellow and pale blue to ensure that it stands out against the darker background.

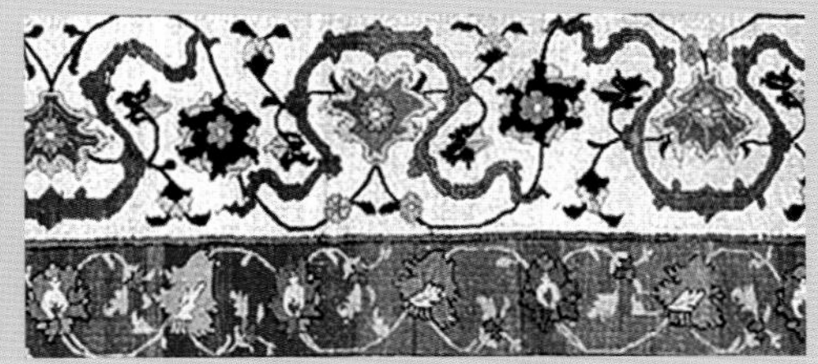

Scrolling branches and flowers

On the small inner borders, the key elements of the main design are used to create a simple scrolling floral band, and ribbon and flower pattern. Here, only a limited range of colours are used – blue and green on red-brown for the smaller border, and red-brown, yellow and black, with little rosettes of green on cream, in the larger. Again, subtle colour coordination unifies and differentiates the design features.

The Ardabil carpet

The Ardabil carpet (10.51 x 5.35 m/ 34 ft 6 in x 17 ft 7 in) is one of a pair with the same design, demonstrating that paper-pattern cartoons were used for the layout of the decorative scheme. The carpet is made of ten colours of wool on silk warps (vertical threads) and wefts (horizontal threads) and contains 25 million knots. It is the earliest dated carpet from Iran, identified from the inscription knotted into the small cream panel at the right-hand end. The carpet is thought to have come from Ardabil, the city that contained the shrine of the founder of the Safavid dynasty, Sheikh Safi (1252–1334).

Twists, Textures & Textiles c. 1300–1600

Patterns of Egypt and Benin

Islamic North Africa had many links with Europe in terms of the appropriation of designs and in the trading of goods, and consequently patterns and objects had connections to many locations around the Mediterranean. Thousands of bronze and brass plaques and figures made in Benin in the 16th century, which were brought to Europe in 19th century, closely reflect a rich hierarchical society in sub-Saharan Africa. The patterns appear to imitate natural materials and textiles decorated with flowers and geometric bands and motifs. Some of the plaques depict Portuguese traders who travelled to and exchanged goods with the people of Benin from the later 15th century.

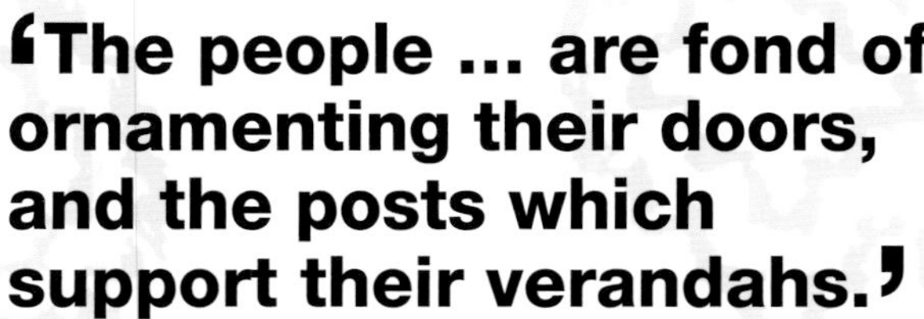

'The people ... are fond of ornamenting their doors, and the posts which support their verandahs.'

HUGH CLAPPERTON,
1826, IN FRANK WILLETT, *African Art,* 1993

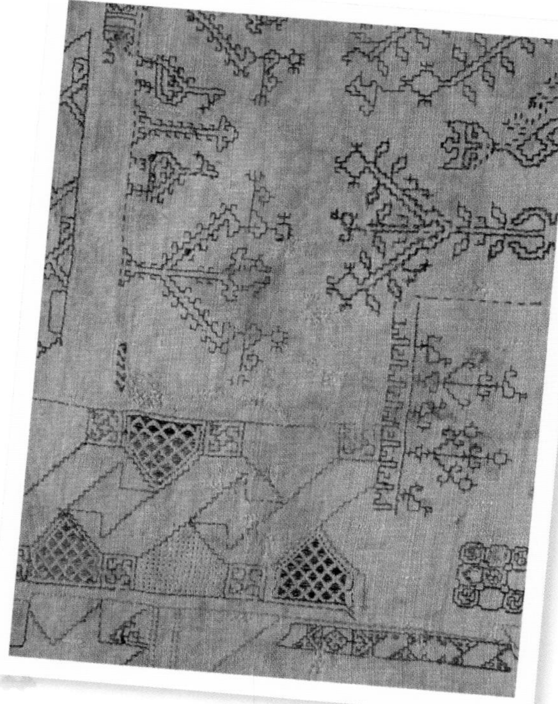

Sampler, 14th–16th century, *Egypt*
Textile production was an important industry in Africa. This sampler, found in an Egyptian burial ground, captures a small selection of patterns found in carpets and textiles. The patterns, worked in silk on linen, include geometric vegetal forms, a complex twisting ribbon band with square and chequered details and various interlocking border designs. These designs were reproduced and embroidered in vibrant colours.

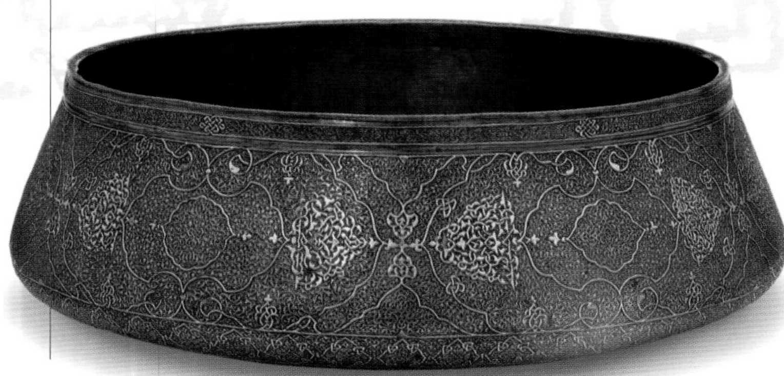

Basin, 1450–1500, *Mameluke Egypt or Syria*
Although the origin of this water vessel is uncertain, its shape and decoration link it closely to Mameluke Egypt (1250–1517). The damascening (metal inlay) of brass and silver uses fine arabesque tendril, foliate and floral patterns divided by silver twisting bands. Known as 'Veneto-Saracenic', because such metalwork is linked to the trading spheres of Venice, Egypt and Syria, it was most probably made in Cairo.

ELEMENTS OF PATTERN

- *geometric and floral bands*
- *twisted ropes and beads*
- *floral and foliate tendrils in arabesque forms*
- *textured details*

Bronze plaque, 16th century, *Benin, Nigeria*
Benin bronze plaques including the king, attendants, the Portuguese, soldiers and hunters probably represented court life, government activities, events and achievements. On this plaque, the king, his attendants and musicians are attired in decorated clothing, headdresses and armour covered in twisting bands, flowers and masks, stippling and textured details. Some of these patterns emulate natural materials such as rope or animal skins, woven decorated textiles and metalwork.

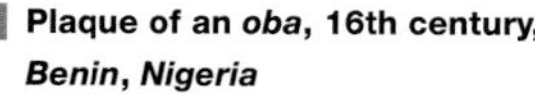

Plaque of an *oba*, 16th century, *Benin, Nigeria*
Plaques were made using lost wax casting. A detailed wax model was covered in clay, heated to melt out the wax to leave a cavity, and then the intricate carved design would be filled with molten metal. The figure of an *oba* (king of Benin) is depicted dressed in a bead or rope robe, surrounded by twisting rope motifs on the background frame. The plaques were hung on the front of the palace.

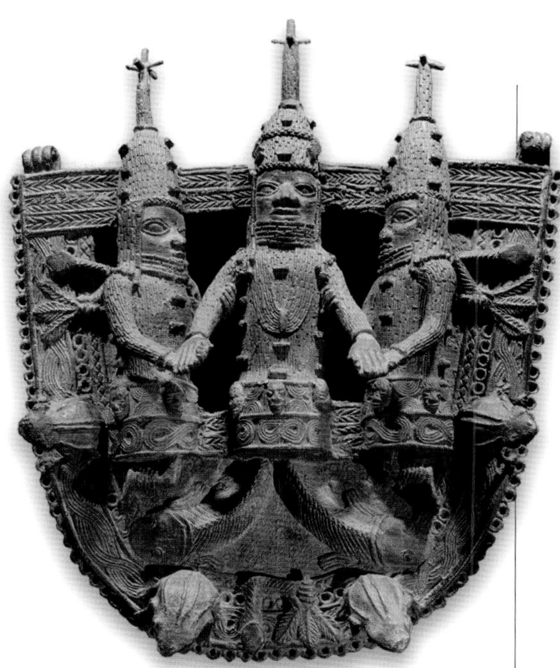

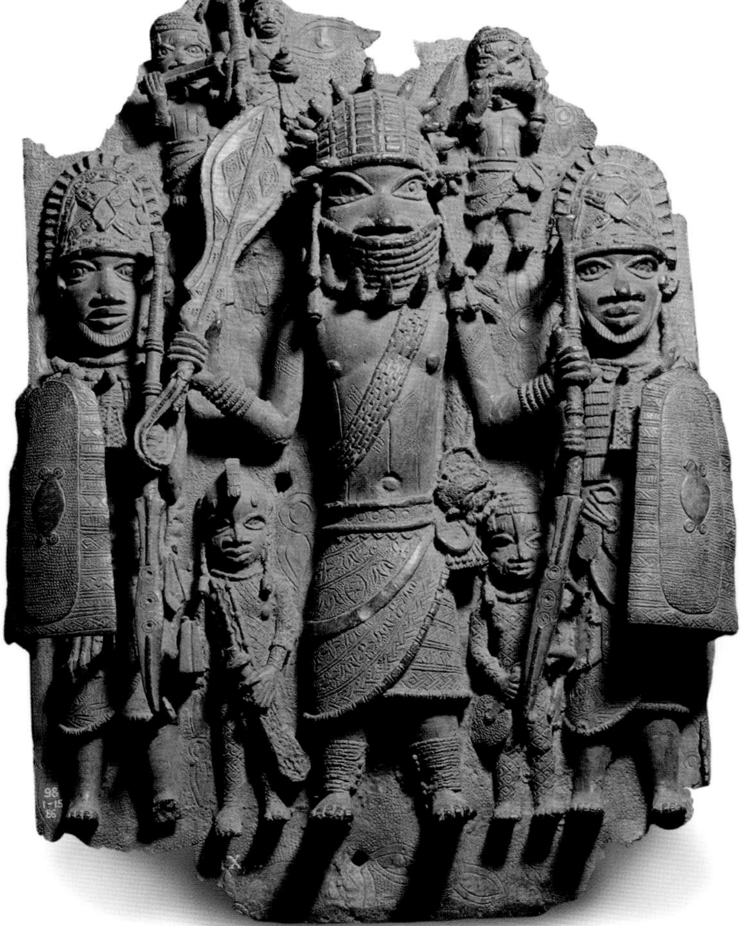

Breast or hip mask, 16th century, *Benin, Nigeria*
The twisted and textured collar of the animal's head is decorated with rope-like patterns filled with ring-and-dots. The edge appears to be a motif shaped like a seed with further rings at the edge. The ram's head may have been worn as a sign of status or to signify a particular role or ceremony at court to which the symbolism of the design may have been linked.

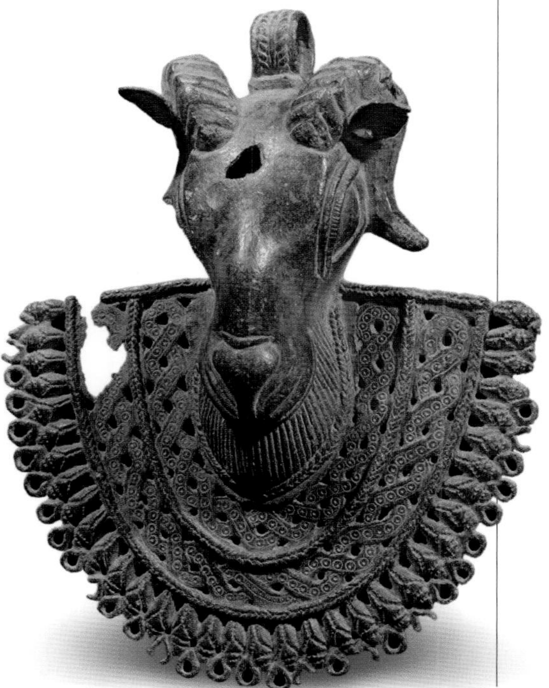

Foliate & Floral *Saz* Designs
c.1545–c.1590

Iznik ceramics and designs in the Ottoman Empire`

Blue-and-white porcelain imported from China from the 14th century stimulated local ceramic industries to produce white slip fritware (see pages 86–7) with underglaze cobalt blue painted designs. Ottoman ceramic production at Iznik (north-west Anatolia) and Istanbul flourished in the 16th century. The *saz* (serrated leaf motif) design and exotic floral arabesques were developed into many variations and became the highly prized court style, differentiated from contemporary Iranian design by its lack of human or animal figures. Topkapı Palace (begun 1459), the residence of the Ottoman sultan, was covered in decorative tile panels, while sumptuous palace furniture, dishes, bowls and vases incorporated similar designs.

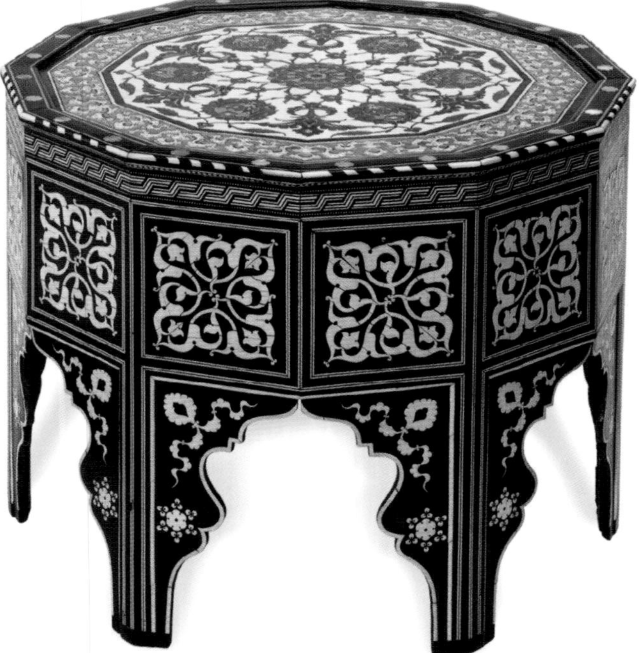

Table, c. 1560, *Iznik, Turkey*
This inlaid wood, ebony and mother-of-pearl table has a single polygonal tile top. The inlay patterns on the ogee-arched legs, spandrels and drum emulate the top's ribbon and arabesque motifs. The tile's border contains tied ribbons incorporating Chinese wave-and-foam motifs, surrounding a circular repeating design of fantastic flowers and *saz* motifs. Such a table would have been used to serve drinks and food in the palace.

Basin, c. 1545, *Iznik, Turkey*
Dark green concentric scrolls cover the basin in ever-decreasing spirals, known as the 'Golden Horn style' after the sea inlet along the north shore of Istanbul where it was first discovered. The tendril circles of leaves, flowers and crescents are linked by blue motifs. The basin's base has an arabesque band between a small line of leaves and serrated lobes, which is repeated on the curving base of the stand.

ELEMENTS OF PATTERN

- saz design – *serrated leaves*
- *Chinese wave-and-foam ribbons*
- *tulips, carnations, bluebells and pomegranates*
- *ogival lattice – interlocking ogee-shaped bands*
- hatayi – *fantastic blossoms*
- rumi – *symmetrical arabesque scrollwork*

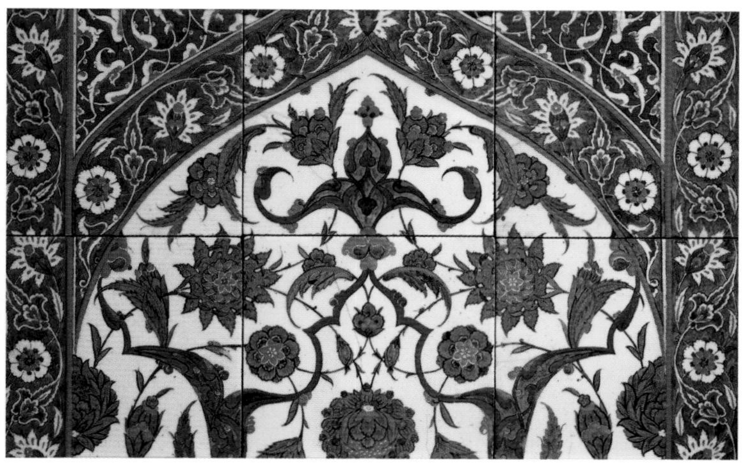

Tile panel, 1570–74, *Iznik (probably), Turkey*
Part of a larger panel from the palace at Edirne, these tiles integrate different patterned sections in red, blues and green in a typical form of imperial wall decoration. Arabesque tendrils are built up with *saz* and flowers: the blue upper section with *saz* scrolls; the green banding in a twisting flower-leaf motif; and the main area with elaborate flowers and leaves, decorated branches and ogee curves.

Woven silk, late 16th century, *Turkey*
This silk and metal thread fabric, made using the lampas technique (see pages 82–3), incorporates arabesque and *saz* designs. The ogival lattice, after the ogee-shaped ovals, has serrated edgings with *rumi* (symmetrical arabesque scrollwork) infill and a *hatayi* (fantastic floral) and pomegranate border. The *kemha* silk (a type of fabric) was used to make kaftans or silk coats for the Ottoman imperial court.

Vase, c. 1575, *Iznik (probably), Turkey*
The colours and clarity of design were developed through the 16th century, leading to floral and foliate designs in cobalt blue (from Kashan), turquoise, green, black and purple and, eventually, a vibrant red. The swaying flowers that hug this vase's curves include carnations, bluebells and tulips – a flower from the region that would become an obsession in Europe in the 17th century – painted in cobalt, green and red.

'The heyday of Ottoman ceramics took place in the second half of the 16th century when potters produced thousands of tiles for imperial Ottoman buildings [and] private residences.'

JONATHAN BLOOM AND SHEILA BLAIR, *Islamic Arts,* 1997

Public & Private Patterns
1570–1600

Clothing and armour

Fashionable outer garments were decorated with patterns of flowers, leaves and fruits caught up in curling tendrils, based on lattice grids or combined with strapwork. A richly coloured cloak was the most expensive item of male clothing, and could be finely decorated with applied patterns. A suit of armour and its 'garniture' (extra pieces for horse and rider) was always made for a specific individual, the shaping of the curved plate steel and its ornamentation imitating the cut and decoration of his clothes. Women's undergarments of smocks and petticoats were decorated with private patterns close to the wearer's body and personality, to be partly displayed at the wearer's discretion.

ELEMENTS OF PATTERN

- *tendrils with flowers, fruits and leaves*
- *lattice grid base*
- *strapwork imitating leather*
- *symbolic flowers, fruits and animals*

Petticoat, 1570–75, *Coromandel coast, India and Alsace*
Around the hem, a wave pattern filled with ring-and-dots is underscored by a looping tendril sprouting leaves and flowers. Above, exotic flowers and fern-like leaves on fine stems are bound together by spindle-shaped motifs, alternating with smaller unbound arrangements linked by curling fronds. A garland of leafy rosettes zigzags around the middle, above which are flowers and leaves loosely connected by looping tendrils. The painted cotton chintz was imported from India to Alsace and made up into this petticoat for mourning wear.

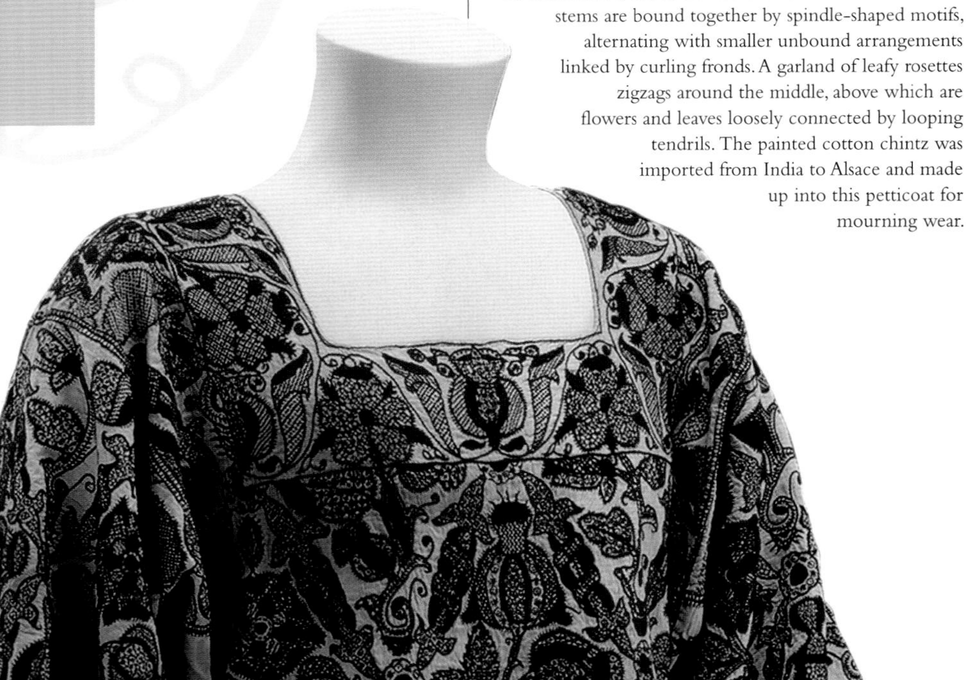

Smock, 1575–85, *England*
This long linen undergarment is embroidered in black Spanish silk with lozenges formed by double-ended fleur-de-lis linked by small rosettes. Exotic composite motifs of leaves, flowers and fruits with curling roots alternate with Tudor roses and pomegranates. The neckline and cuffs are embroidered with a running pattern of roses and pomegranates linked by a fine undulating leafy tendril. Made for a wealthy woman in her own household, the smock was worn partly revealed in a layered style.

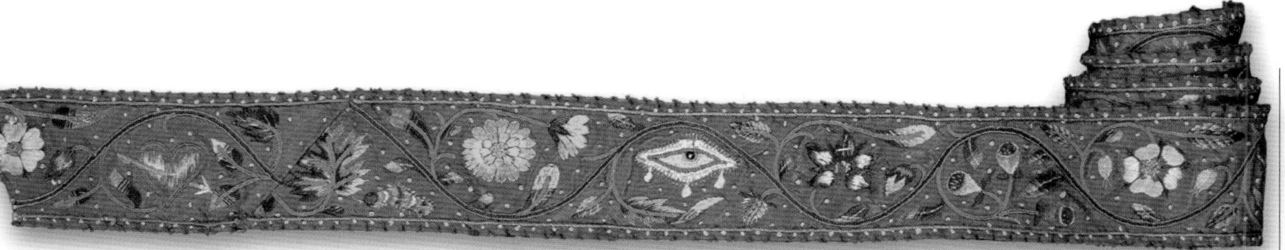

Silk band, c. 1600, *England*

This silk band, originally purple in colour, has been embroidered with a repeating pattern of an undulating tendril that sprouts eglantine roses and rosehips, marigolds, borage flowers, strawberries and their leaves. Other motifs are incorporated into the rhythm of the curving tendril include a heart pierced by an arrow, a caterpillar and an eye weeping three tears. The ribbon was perhaps sewn to a garment as a fastening or to cover a seam.

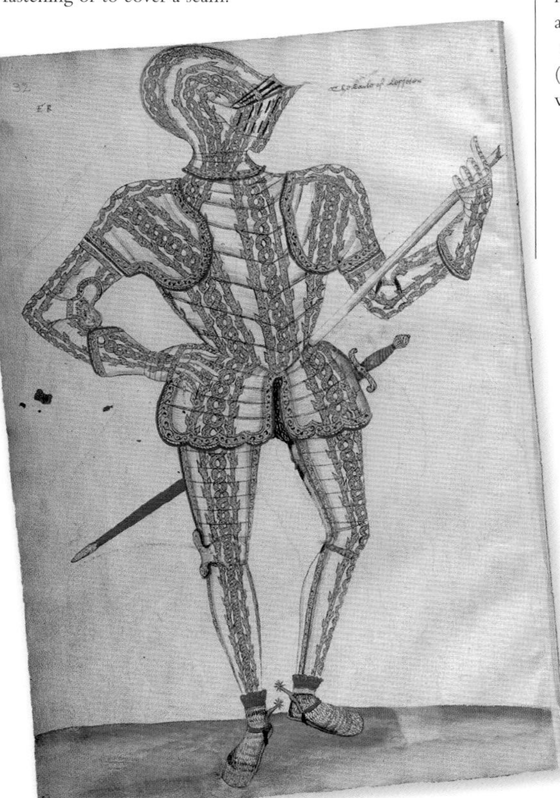

Armour, 1586–1590, *England*

Designed by Jacob Halder for Robert Dudley, Earl of Leicester, this suit of armour is ornamented with gilded patterns indicating the wearer's identity. The bright polished steel has been inlaid with etched gilded strips imitating embroidered bands on fashionable clothes. Interlace and jagged stems, derived from Dudley's heraldic badge of the bear and ragged staff – shown on the wing of the couter (elbow piece) – are filled with scrolling tendrils.

'Fashionable costume [became] a canvas or panel for the loaded plant, animal and architectural forms...'

CHRISTOPHER BREWARD, *The Culture of Fashion,* 1995

Cloak, 1580–1600, *France*

The front panels of this satin-weave silk cloak are embroidered with a pattern imitating pierced and curling leather straps in silver, silver-gilt and coloured silk threads. The alternating flowers at the centres of the rectangular spaces are combined in a motif that alternates with a dagged (cut into points or scallops) banner looped through the lateral rings. The owner of this expensive cloak wore it to display his status and wealth.

PATTERN IN DETAIL

Indian Court Designs 1590–1596

The *Akbarnama* (Book of Akbar), India or Pakistan

Descended from the Mongols and Genghis Khan, the Mughal emperors (1526–1858) united India and supported flourishing artistic and architectural developments. The third emperor, Akbar 'the Great' (1556–1605), commissioned huge illustration projects including the fantasy life of Hamza (uncle to the Prophet Muhammad), the *Hamzanama*, which included 1,400 paintings. The *Akbarnama*, the official chronicle of Akbar's life by Abul Fazi, was extensively illustrated with a detailed record of the buildings, designs and patterns at court.

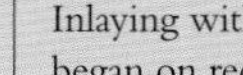

Inlaid throne
Inlaying with marble and coloured stones began on red sandstone. The throne base is inlaid with white marble, green, grey and cream stones in a square and six-point star design. This technique developed further on Akbar's tomb (c. 1610) with intricate geometric and floral patterns, symbolising Paradise, and reached its zenith in the magnificent white marble tomb of Shah Jahan – the Taj Mahal (1631–43).

Decorated canopy
Buildings commissioned by Akbar were made of red sandstone and marble, for example at the town of Fatehpur Sikri (c. 1571–76) and the tomb of his father Humayun in Delhi (1571). The red sandstone canopy in this scene is decorated with carving, piercing and a floral inlay of coloured stones, possibly illustrating the work of temple carvers from western India.

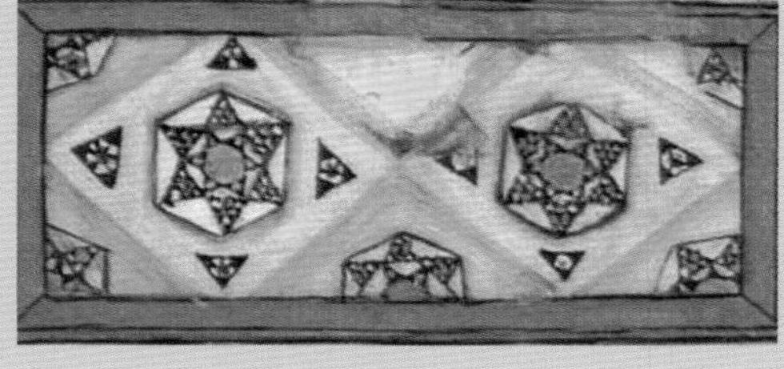

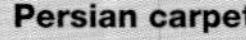

Persian carpet
The artistic links to Safavid Iran are apparent in the presence of a Persian carpet in the canopied dais, which is delicately patterned with contemporary arabesque designs (see pages 122–3). The fine curving tendrils with exotic flowers are precisely recorded, both in the dark blue background and in the central golden sunburst. The design appears again on Akbar's throne, on the canopy and in a large ogee fan behind.

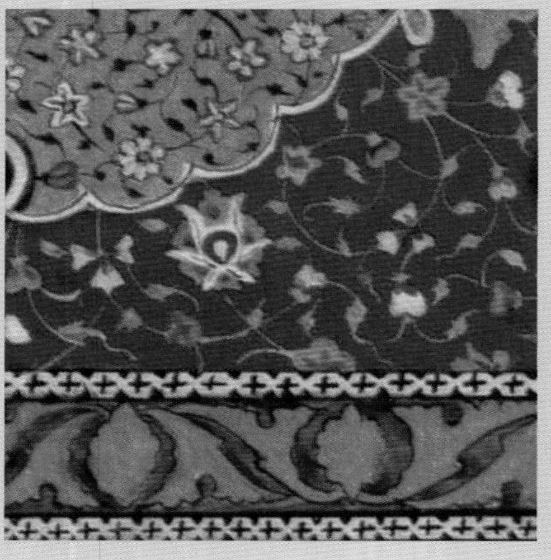

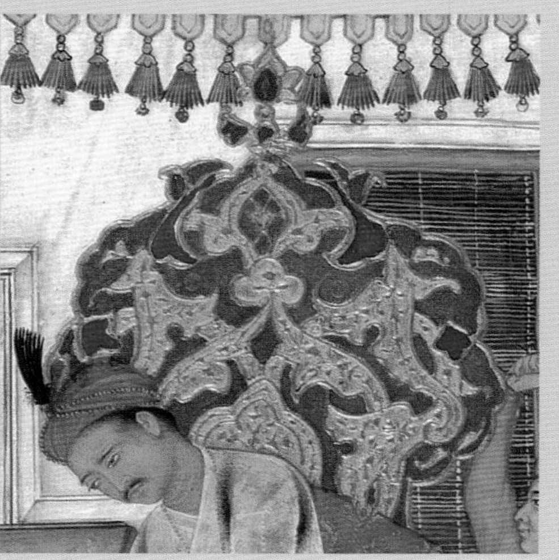

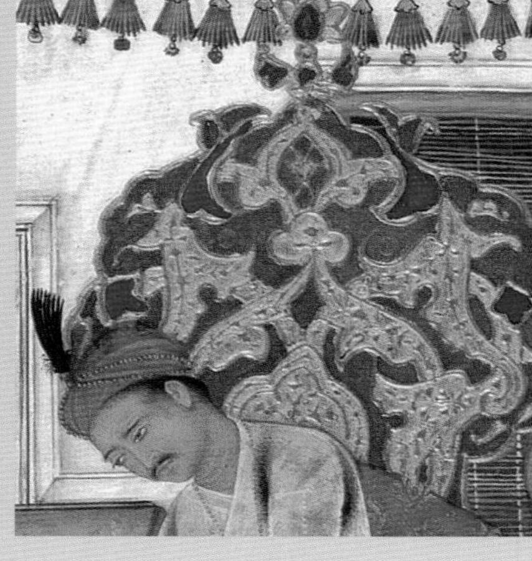

Golden screen
Behind the Emperor Akbar hangs an inlaid metal panel, probably symbolising his status and power, shaped with an elegantly curved edge comparable to the sunburst in the carpet. It is also decorated with an enlarged floral and foliate arabesque pattern in gold and blue lapis lazuli. After the Islamic expansion into India, local art forms often looked to the Middle East and Iran for inspiration.

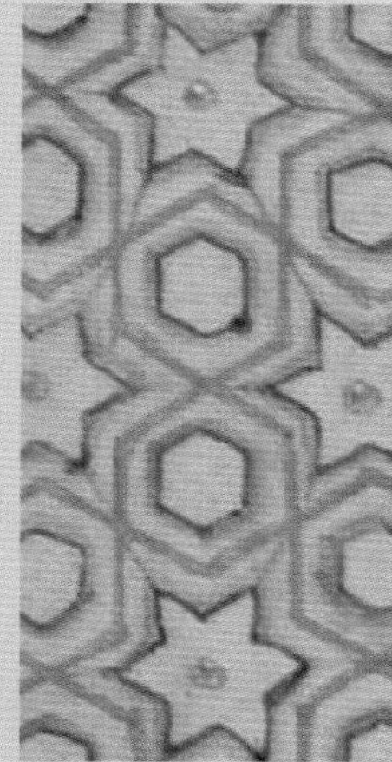

Tiled floor

Again, the tiled pattern on the floor of the enclosed audience area has links to tile designs of the Islamic Middle East (see pages 86–7). The pattern of interlocking six-pointed stars and hexagons, possibly in glazed green tiles, appears as the flooring of the palace precinct throughout the illustrations in the *Akbarnama*, differentiating the imperial space from the outer courtyard areas.

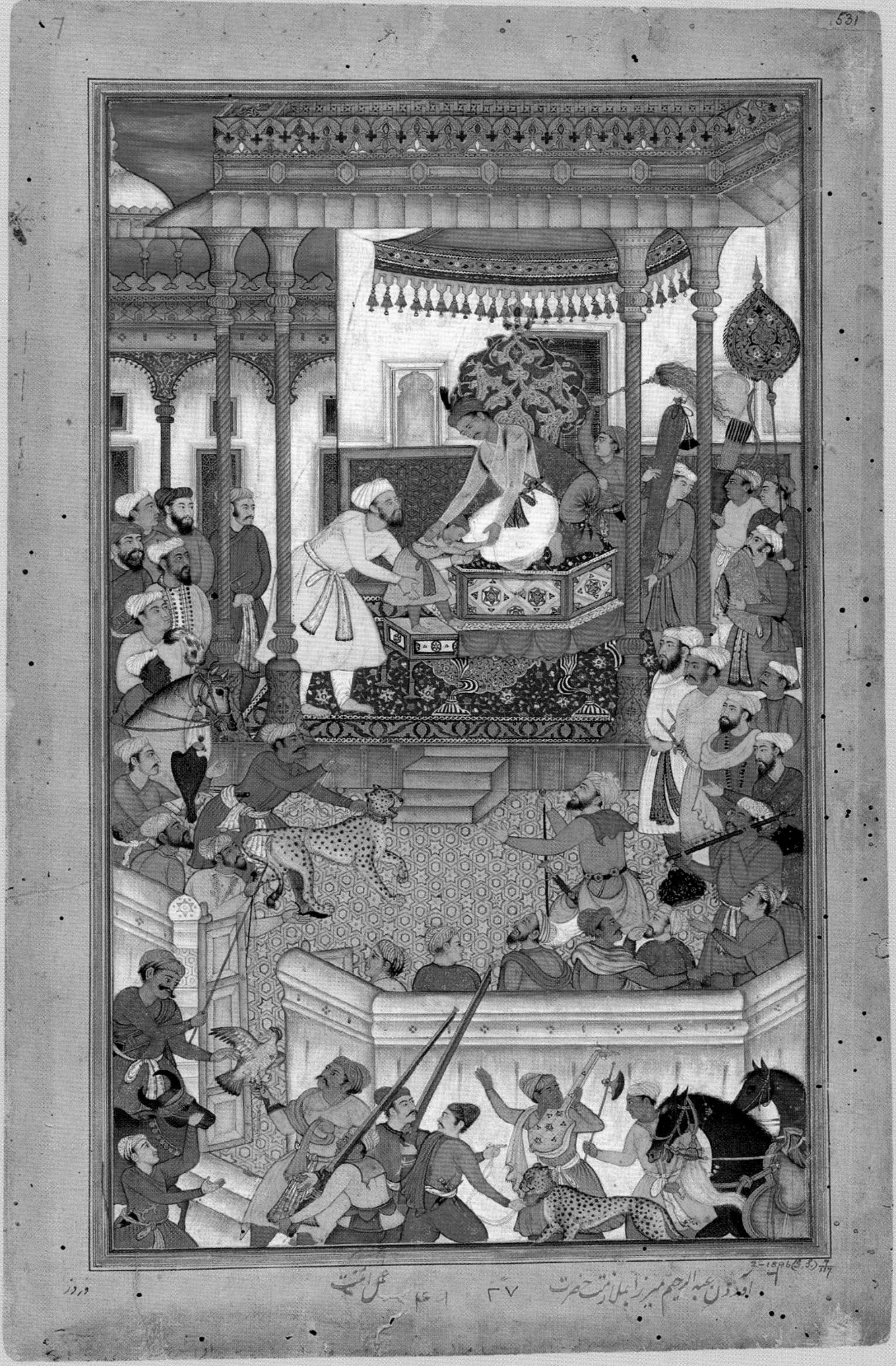

Akbar receives the child Abdu'r Rahim at court

The court space depicting Akbar receiving Abdu'r Rahim, son of the assassinated Bairam Khan, is highly decorated. Some attendants' robes, Akbar's cushions, the carved red sandstone canopy pillars, the screen behind the emperor, the arches and the pierced screens in the palace buildings in the background, all demonstrate intricate patterns – geometric, floral and arabesque – and the craftworker's skill.

PATTERN IN DETAIL

The Dramatic & the Divine 1600–1603

The 'Rainbow Portrait' of Elizabeth I

Richly attired in glowing silks, translucent lace and shining jewels, Elizabeth is portrayed as dressed for a masque entertainment in patterns of complex symbolic significance. The queen's costume transforms her into the virgin goddess of justice, Astraea, with gossamer wings and grasping the rainbow of peace. Elizabeth exploited the drama of costume in the pursuit of her image as Gloriana, appointing tailors to design fabulous creations in Italian, Spanish and French styles for which she acquired laces from Spain, Genoa and Venice.

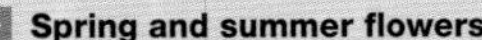

Spring and summer flowers
The pattern of mixed floral sprigs embroidered on the bodice and sleeves of Elizabeth's gown symbolises the perpetual spring and summer she brings as Astraea, the virgin goddess of the Golden Age. The carnation symbolises purity and the betrothal of the queen to her country, the pansy signifies that her subjects are always in her mind, the cowslip her thoughtfulness for her subjects and the honeysuckle flower her devotion.

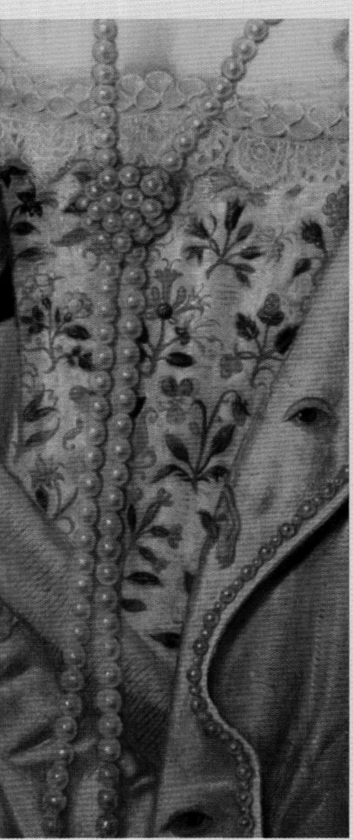

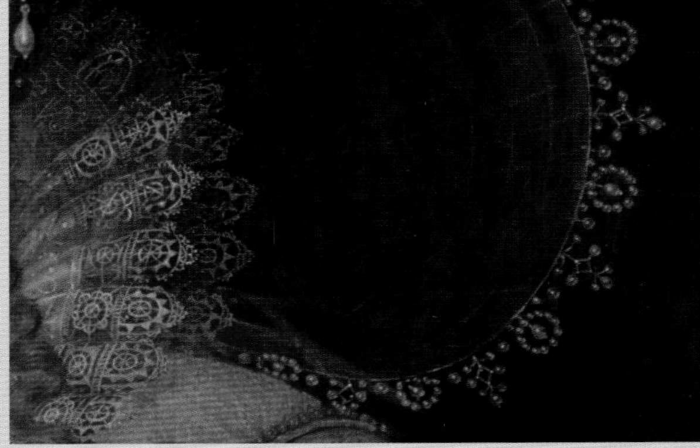

Lace and pearls
The floral-patterned linen of the outer ruff has been worked into a design of *reticella* lace. Two rows of formal floral motifs, probably roses, are divided by fine bands, the outer row forming the scalloped edge of the collar and finished with fine points. Behind, a pair of wired gauzy wings is edged with pearls, signifying purity, in a pattern of alternating rounded and pointed motifs that imitate the lace design.

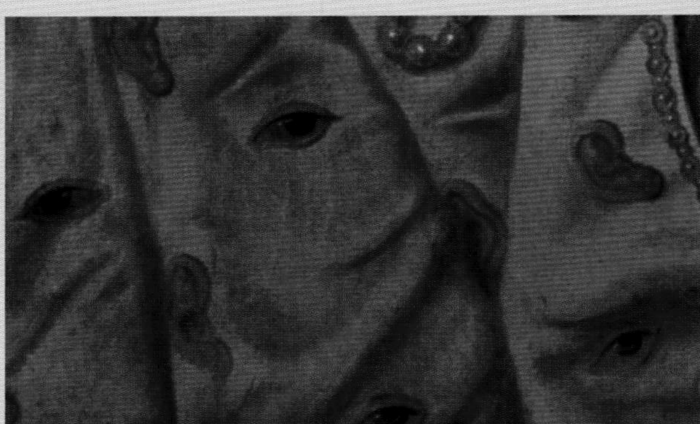

Eyes and ears
The outside of Elizabeth's mantle is covered with a pattern of human eyes – dark, like hers – and ears. The contemporary Italian iconographer Cesare Ripa portrays Fame with wings, 'having as many eyes and ears as she has feathers, also many mouths and ears.' Elizabeth's universal fame makes her ever-present, like a goddess, but she is also open to scrutiny as well as self-criticism: 'We princes, I tell you, are set on stages in the sight and view of all the world duly observed. The eyes of many behold our actions; a spot is soon spied in our garments; a blemish quickly noted in our doings.' This pattern may also refer to Elizabeth's extremely efficient intelligence service that was overseen by her chief spymaster, Robert Cecil.

No rainbow without a sun

On the left of this portrait by Isaac Oliver is written 'NON SINE SOLE IRIS' ('no rainbow without a sun'), meaning that Elizabeth brings serenity after the stormy troubled times. The queen grasps the rainbow of peace – she is the pattern-clothed sun at the centre of her world. The rainbow refers to Elizabeth's relationship with England, modelled on God's covenant with Noah after the Flood: 'I do set my bow in a cloud, and it shall be for a token of a covenant between me and the earth' (Genesis 9:13).

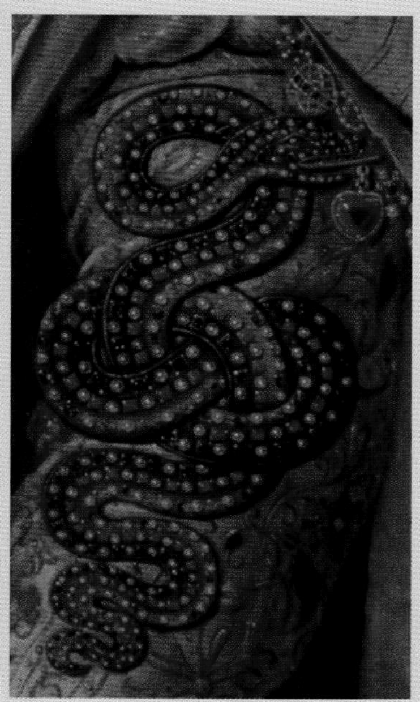

Heavenly wisdom

The tightly curled serpent embroidered on the queen's left sleeve is dotted with pearls and red stones, its body looped into a knot. From its mouth hangs a heart-shaped ruby on a gold chain and there is a small celestial sphere above its head. The serpent represents wisdom, here in command of the heart as well as the affairs of the world. In Ripa's *Iconologia*, Intelligence balances a celestial sphere on her right hand and grasps a serpent in her left.

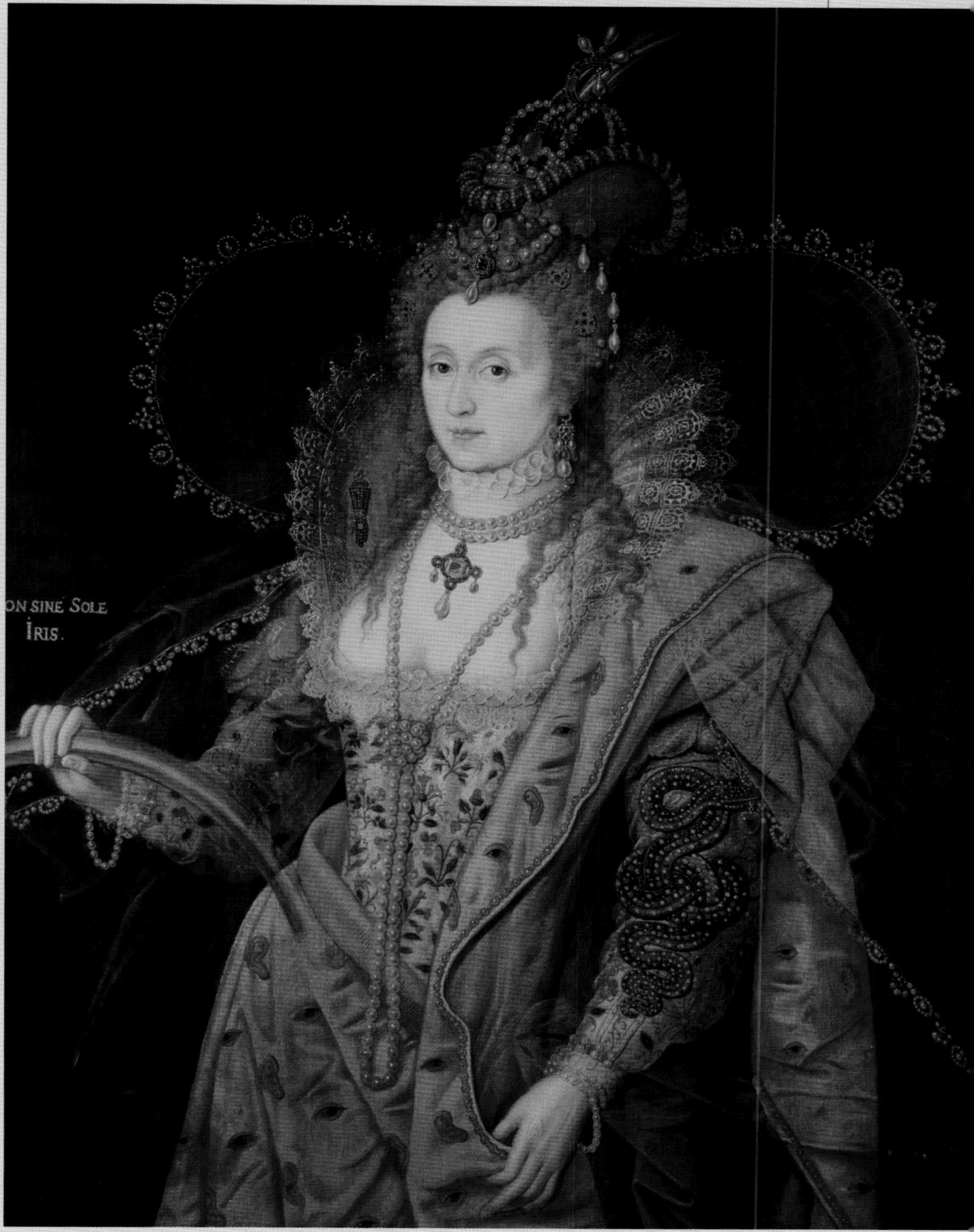

1600
1700

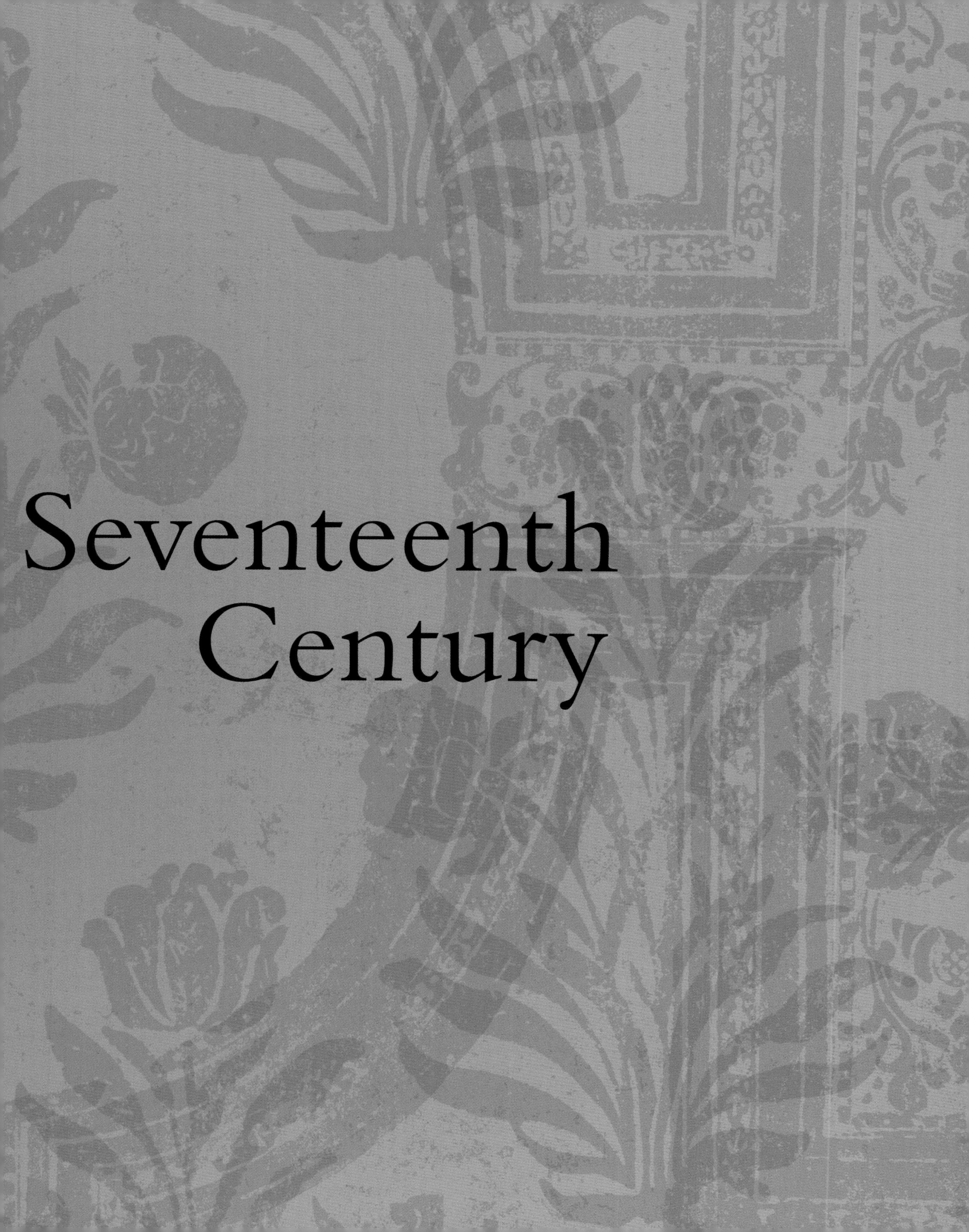

Seventeenth Century

Introduction

The Dutch East India Company, formed in 1602, was the largest commercial enterprise in Europe. In the Dutch Republic, wealthy merchants invested in fashionable luxuries for domestic interiors. Among commodity-conscious Protestants, flamboyant dress was often thought inappropriate but they dressed for their portraits in expensive clothes with discretely displayed patterns. Linen cutwork, the earliest form of needle lace, was fashionable until the 1620s, but Italian *punto in aria* ('stitch in air') lace made with needles enabled lacemakers to design patterns without the geometric constraints of woven fabric.

The huge Grand Bazaar founded by Shah Abbas I in his newly founded city of Isfahan in Iran attracted merchants and wealth from across the world. The new city was adorned with complex decorative tile-panel work on mosques and palaces.

In India, richly decorated textiles, embroidered clothes, jewellery and inlaid furniture were covered with exotic and symbolic flowers. The shining white marble garden tomb built by the Mughal emperor Shah Jahan for his beloved wife, Mumtaz Mahal – the Taj Mahal – was covered in delicately formed floral designs of inlaid coloured stones.

In England, Inigo Jones designed buildings drawing on Italian Renaissance architecture to create a new visual language of order. His designs applied the principles of proportion and symmetry developed by Andrea Palladio, laying the foundations for an architectural style that would persist in Britain and its colonies until the 19th century. In Europe, perceptions of the natural world changed through the experience of exploration and colonisation. The desire for order and control was reflected in grand domestic landscape designs, the enthusiastic collecting of Asian and American flowering plants for gardens and the display of antiques and other rare objects in 'cabinets of curiosities'. In China, collecting continued to be an important pastime and records of collections were created on scrolls and lacquer screens, capturing the range of patterns from centuries past. Patterns continued to be linked closely to the symbolism of Chinese mythology.

In early 17th-century Europe, the tulip, imported from Turkey from the mid-16th century, became a coveted, obsessively valued item. Even after the price of tulips fell in 1637, this flower remained a popular pattern motif. Compact Dutch schemes of floral planting, especially tulips, and topiary forms, influenced English garden designs with parterres of grass or gravel patterns filled with new varieties of flowers and fruit trees. Botanical books with illustrations informed by scientific enquiry were a rich source for European pattern designers. Previously exclusive to expensive brocaded silks, floral patterns on calico, chintz, percale and muslin enabled the wider appreciation of natural forms and colours. The idea of display was changing and spreading, as flowers, leaves, fruits, birds and insects became inventive motifs for embroidered and painted patterned clothing. Flowers became closely integrated with European secular and religious traditions in the form of wreaths, nosegays and decorative cut plants.

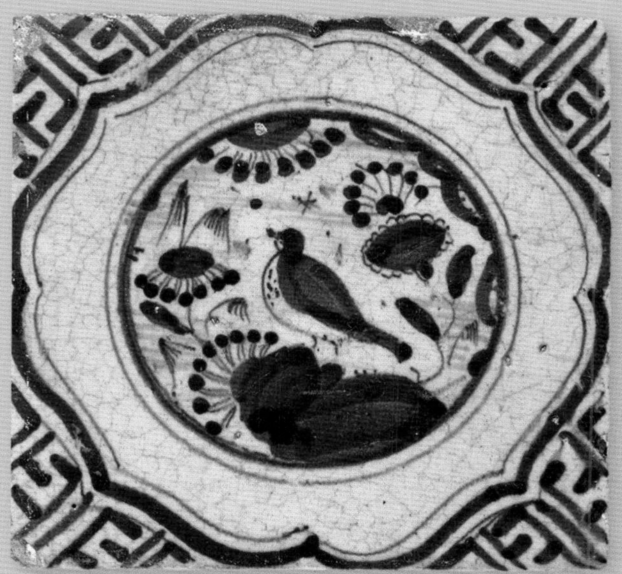

The Dutch capture of Portuguese ships carrying Chinese Ming porcelain in 1602 and 1604 instigated a new fashion in ceramic patterning, and blue-and-white designs became synonymous with Dutch style, notably on ceramics manufactured in Delft. Tiles covered walls and floors; plates, dishes and jugs were displayed singly, perhaps filled with cut flowers, or in sets above fireplaces and doorways.

European interior and decorative design often followed the curving, dynamic and complex forms of Baroque style. Wallpaper was an increasingly popular means of decorating interiors, emulating expensive plaster mouldings or exotic painted papers from China. In France, at the court of King Louis XIV (1638–1715), ornate patterns and extravagant decorative programmes were commissioned for the palace and gardens of Versailles. Baroque style spread into European colonial territories, including Mexico, where new expressive patterns were developed.

Patterned Interiors 1600–1700

Domestic wealth in the Netherlands

New luxury goods displaying the owner's wealth and prosperity were ornamented with patterns reflecting places far distant from the domestic rooms they furnished. Patterns in gilded leather derived from Spanish Islamic designs, and Chinese blue-and-white schemes for pottery and tiles were in great demand in the Netherlands and copied in Dutch workshops. The investment in and fascination with interiors led to a desire for personal items such as decorated caskets and mirrors in intricately patterned frames. In the later 17th century, luxury items for grand household interiors were made of more expensive materials and were more intricately patterned.

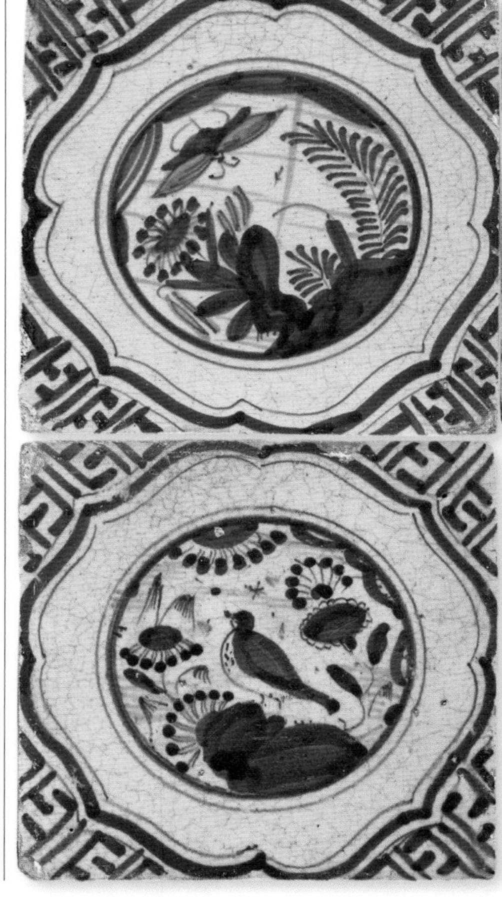

Tiles, 1620–40,
the Netherlands
The corners of each tile are decorated with an interlocking linear pattern based on a diagonal grid, forming undulating lozenge shapes when the tiles are assembled on a wall surface. These tin-glazed earthenware tiles are painted in cobalt blue on a white background in the Chinese style, and the butterfly, bird, flowers and rounded rocks are motifs inspired by Chinese art.

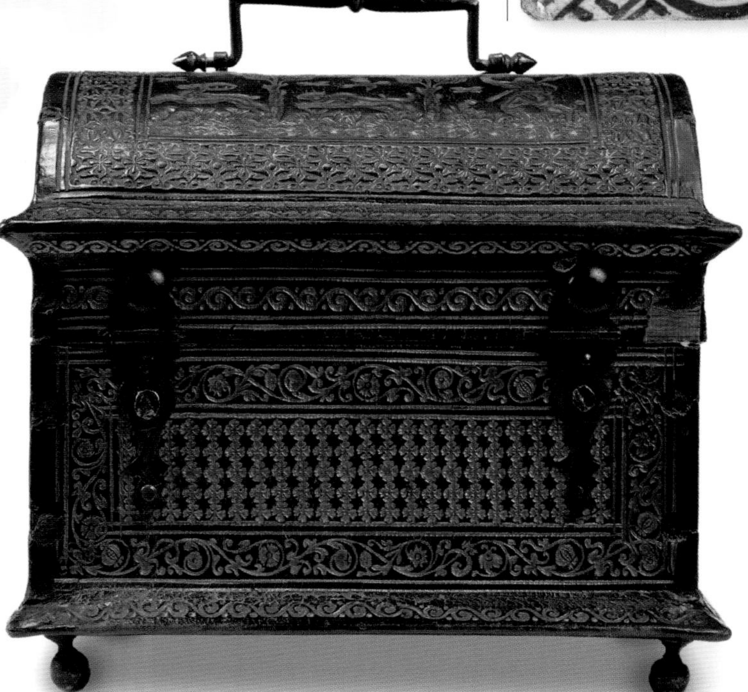

Casket, c. 1600,
Friesland, the Netherlands
The leather covering of this wooden casket has been tooled with gilded patterns. The panels are framed with a running tendril of spiralling shoots with curling leaves, flowers and fruits. The carnations signify pure love, borage flowers fidelity and split-open pomegranates fertility. The frame is filled with a stamped pattern of flowers with four petals, and the lid is bordered with a band of similar motifs with cross-shaped stamens, set between dots and edged with curling shoots. Running around the casket above and below the frames are tendril patterns with simple curling lobed leaves and dots.

Dish, 1640–70, *Delft or Haarlem, the Netherlands*
This tin-glazed earthenware dish has been painted with a Nativity scene surrounded by a pattern of leafy flowering tendrils and birds on a white background. Either singly or opposed in pairs around the central scene, birds alternate with fantastical 'grotesques' that also inhabit the border – woman-birds with wings, long-feathered tails and horns, or bearded faces with horns and tendril necks on bird bodies. They are integrated into the pattern by perching on stems, and leafy curls develop from arms and extend from tail feathers.

ELEMENTS OF PATTERN

- *gilding*
- *Chinese motifs in blue and white*
- *flowers, fruits and birds*
- *fantastical 'grotesques'*

'Much attention was now paid to achieving a high degree of comfort and convenience.'

PETER THORNTON, *Authentic Décor*, 1993

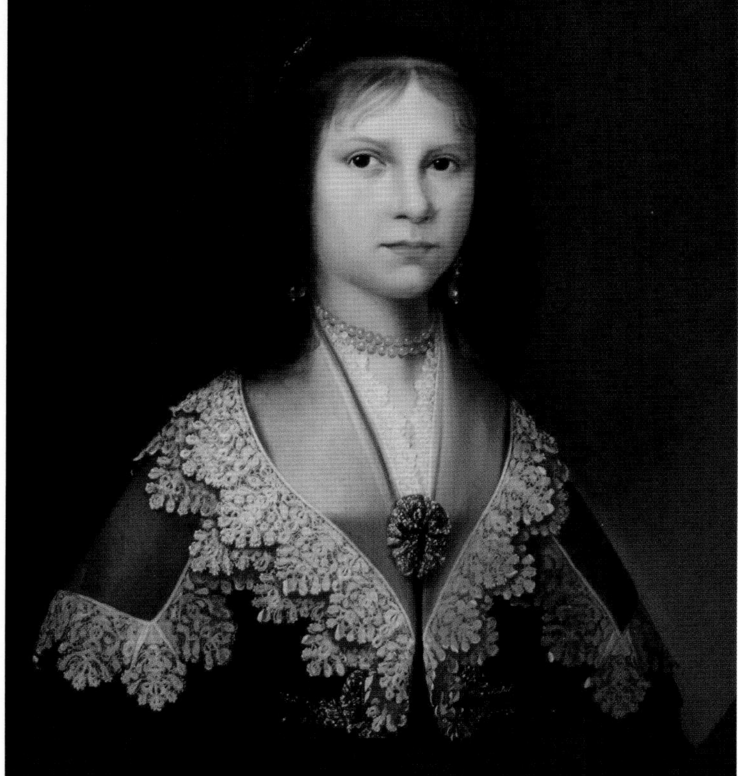

Portrait, c. 1635, *Utrecht, the Netherlands*
The linen lace bordering a folded shawl and shoulder cape has been created in the Italian *punto de aria* technique. The pattern creates a complex leafy effect, which is exaggerated by the overlapping border of the collar. This portrait in oils of an unknown girl, by Gerrit van Honhorst, would have been displayed in the household of a wealthy family.

Mirror frame, c. 1700, *the Netherlands*
The pattern in this silver frame is made up of curling tendrils sprouting lush acanthus leaves and flowers. Roses for purity, sunflowers for devotion and fertility, and carnations for pure love are displayed at the middle of the leafy curves. Central to each side of the frame is a small mask – a veiled female face to each side of the viewer and a satyr above and below, perhaps to deter evil influence.

Inigo Jones
1573–1652

Inigo Jones was the first architect to bring Italianate Renaissance architecture to England. He travelled twice to Italy, first in c. 1605 and then again in 1613–15 with Thomas Howard, Earl of Arundel (1585–1646). In the late 16th century, Italian architecture was dominated by the work of Andrea Palladio (1508–80), who designed buildings in Venice and the Veneto, including the Palazzo Chiericati (1550–57), the churches of San Giorgio Maggiore (1565) and Il Redentore (1577), and the Teatro Olimpico in Vicenza (1580–85). Palladio influenced architecture for centuries, primarily through his treatise *I Quattro Libri dell'Architettura* (*The Four Books of Architecture*, 1570), his own copy of which he heavily annotated. Palladio's principles of architectural design were based on balance, purity and symmetry drawn from classical

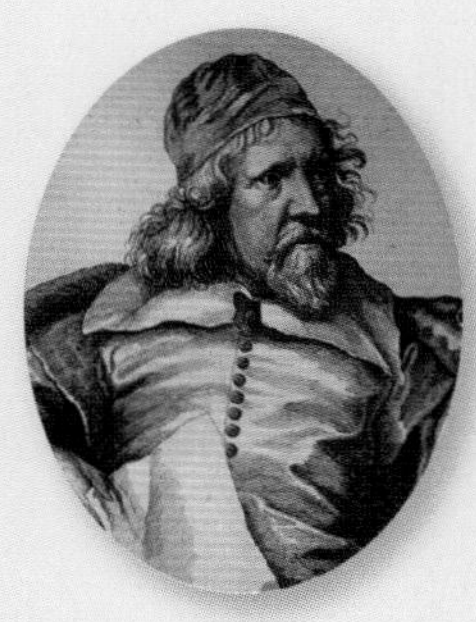

Born
Smithfield, London, 1573

Profession
Architect and theatrical designer

Manifesto
Symmetry, proportion and the harmonious application of classical ornament

Roman buildings. Inigo Jones applied these to both the structure and the design of his buildings – in other words, their construction and appearance.

Initially a painter, set and costume designer for masques performed at the court of Anne of Denmark (1574–1619), queen consort to James I of England, Jones returned from Italy in 1615 with an extensive knowledge of Roman antiquities, the major architectural monuments in Rome and northern Italy, and of Palladio's villas in Vicenza. Jones became the Surveyor of the King's Works, overseeing the construction of royal castles and residences. Jones's first two major building projects, which survive, were the Queen's House in Greenwich (1616/18–29/38) and the Banqueting House in Whitehall (1619–22). Jones carried out many projects for both James I and Charles I, including chapels at St James's Palace and Somerset House (since demolished), a remodelling of the Old St Paul's Cathedral, various works at the Palace of Whitehall and designs for other more extensive projects. His plan for the residential square at Covent Garden, commissioned by the Earl of Bedford to emulate an Italian piazza, provided a model for future squares in London.

‘In architecture ye outward ornaments oft [ought] to be sollid, proporsionable according to the rulles, masculine and unaffected.’

INIGO JONES, 1615, IN ANN SUTHERLAND HARRIS, *Seventeenth Century Art and Architecture,* 2005

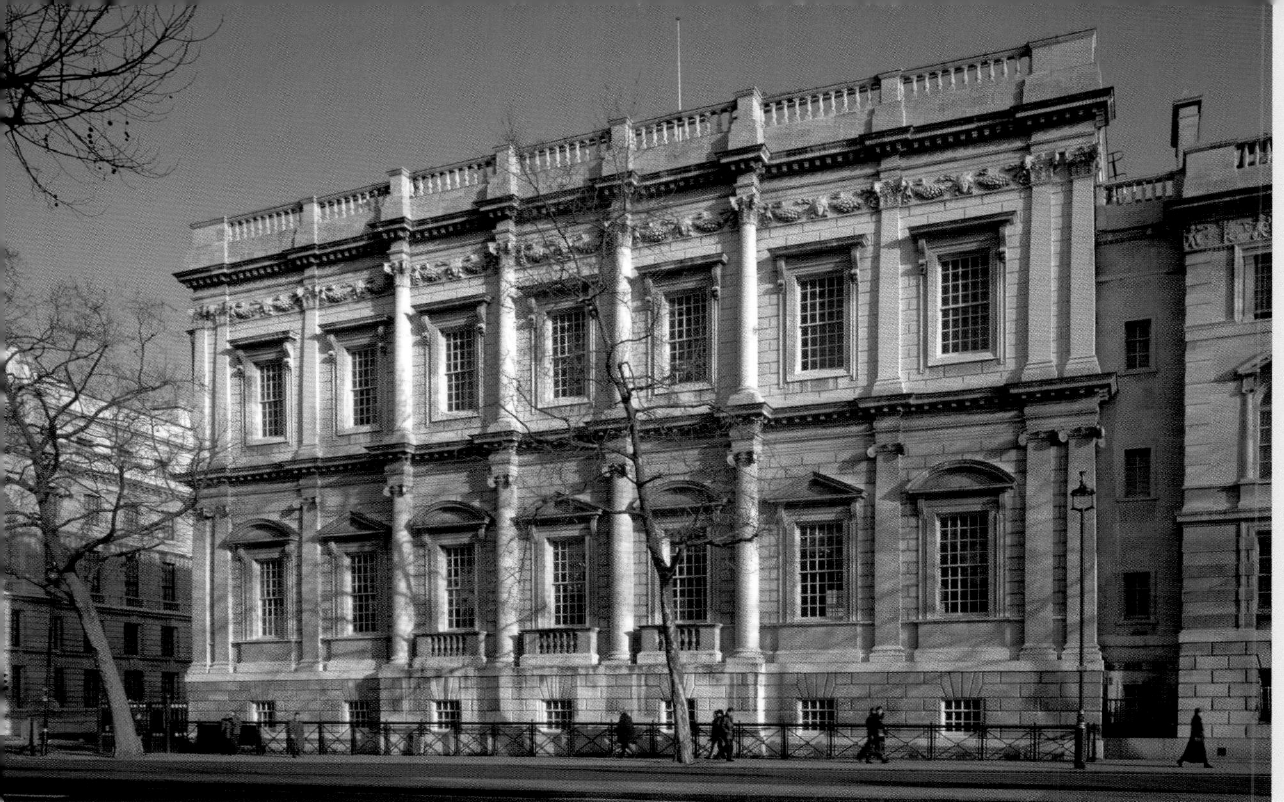

Jones's two surviving buildings clearly demonstrate his ideals in creating a new form of architecture in England. He followed Palladio's principles of balanced proportions and the rational application of classical structural and ornamental forms. As with many of Palladio's villas, the Queen's House was designed on a symmetrical plan. The main house was a 12-m (40-ft) cube with an interior plan formed of regular proportional mirror-image spaces and outer walls divided by seven ordered windows on two floors.

The Banqueting House has the same symmetry, following the proportions of a double cube. The symmetrical façade design echoes Palladio's villas with the three central sections emphasised by columns. The façade is divided into equal areas, with pilasters, cornices and windows decorated according to the principles of classical Roman architectural orders. The lower floor follows the simpler Ionic order, with scrolling volute capitals, and the upper floor uses the more complex Composite order, with acanthus and volute capitals and a garlanded frieze. The alternating curved segment and triangular pediment windows of the lower floor provide visual strength, whereas the decorative frieze offsets the simpler upper window pediments. Inside, the ceiling is covered by nine canvases painted by Peter Paul Rubens celebrating the life of James I of England.

With the advent of the Civil War in 1642, Inigo Jones's association with the king meant that his career was cut short, but the symmetrical classical forms that he introduced would influence architectural design in England and America for the next two centuries.

Banqueting House, 1619–22, *London, England*
The Banqueting House, which replaced an earlier building destroyed by fire, was built close to the King's Palace of Whitehall. In the 17th century, it would have dominated the smaller brick-built buildings that surrounded it.

Geometry, Arabesques & Floral Motifs 1600–1700

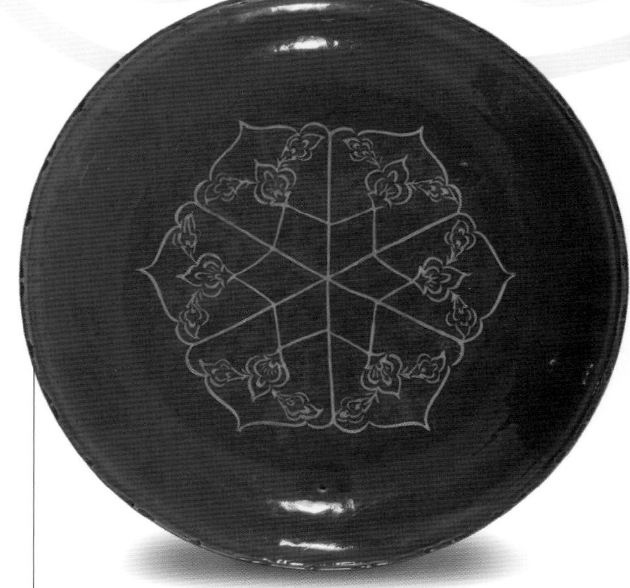

Glazed fritware dish, 17th century, *Iran*
The delicate curves and geometric shapes of the arabesque form are reduced to their basic elements on this incised dish. The arabesque hexagonal and six-pointed star motif creates a perfect flower with elegant simplicity. Luxury pottery and tile production expanded in the early 17th century, possibly as a result of the economic and commercial growth that led to technical and stylistic development under Shah Abbas.

Patterns of Safavid Iran following Shah Abbas I

Shah Abbas I (reigned 1588–1629) promoted trade, resulting in many artistic, design and technological developments in 17th-century Iran. He moved the capital to Isfahan at the country's centre in the 1590s to avoid his threatening neighbours. An Iranian proverb says 'Isfahan is half the world', alluding to its critical location on the trade routes from East to West. The new city's centre was a Grand Bazaar – a *maidān* half a kilometre long – where merchants from all over the world came to trade, including the British and the Dutch. It was surrounded by mosques and palaces, where rich and flamboyant decorative arts with their elegant floral and arabesque patterns were on display.

'The Shah Mosque is also remarkable for its colourful decoration ... all vertical surfaces, both inside and out, are clad in polychrome glazed tiles.'

JONATHAN BLOOM AND SHEILA BLAIR, *Islamic Arts*, 1997

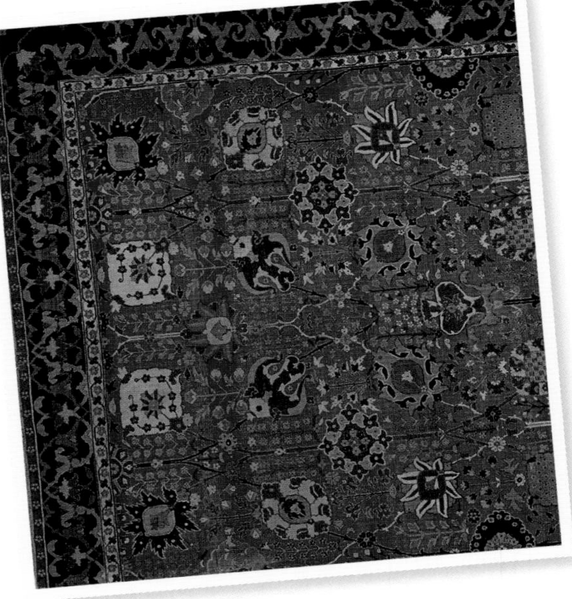

Silk and cotton carpet, 17th century, *Iran*
The flamboyant fantastical flowers and arabesque motifs are arranged in an orderly way on a dark pink background, mirrored along the long axis and centred on a blue vase. The main border contains meanders in pink and light blue, interspersed with fringed blossom on a deep midnight blue. The contrast of small and large flower motifs in such a wide range of colours gives the carpet a rich vibrancy.

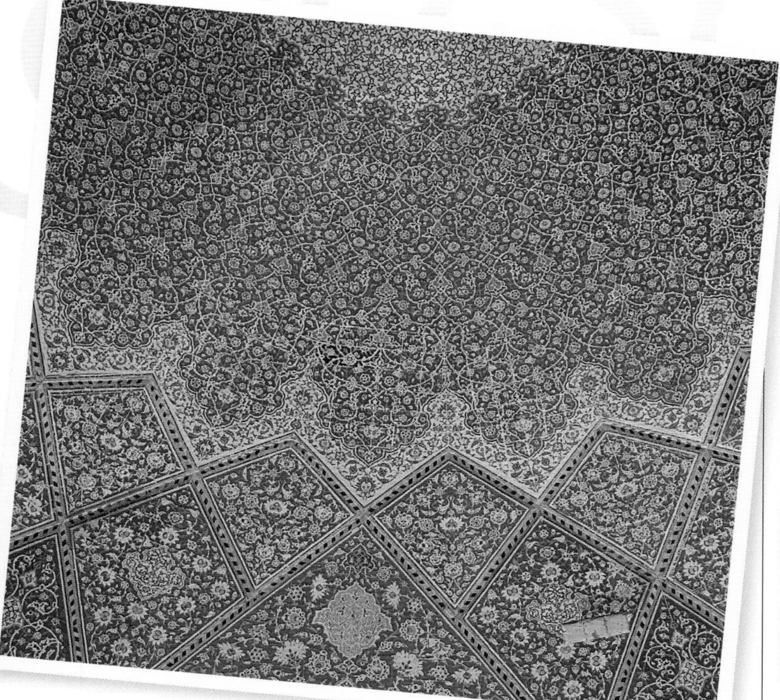

Shah Mosque (Masjed-e Shah), 1611–66, *Isfahan, Iran*
One of the masterpieces of Iranian architecture, the Shah Mosque commissioned by Shah Abbas contains some of the most fabulous patterned decoration in Islamic art. Covered with ethereal blue, cool turquoise and golden yellow patterned tiles, the decorative design creates a Paradise on earth. The stylised curvilinear floral arabesque designs set on honeycomb vaults – *muqarnas* – soar above the devout.

ELEMENTS OF PATTERN

- *fantastical flowers*
- *arabesque motifs*
- *floral textiles*
- *honeycomb vaulting*
- *motifs and forms from China*

Fritware tile panel, 17th century, *Isfahan* (?), *Iran*
The scene on this tile panel depicts figures clothed with delicate floral patterns within an arabesque and Chinese cloud meander border. Probably placed on a palace wall in Shah Abbas's new capital, Isfahan, the scene represents a picnic or outdoor entertainment, possibly a poetry reading. The ceramics in the scene are decorated with Chinese designs, but they may be Iranian copies.

Fritware dish, 17th century, *Iran*
The central quadripartite motif builds from a lozenge to a star, finishing with sweeping arabesque curves to form a geometric floral motif. This dynamic design is infilled with floral and foliate patterns and surrounded by small clouds. Iranian designs drew on Chinese motifs, such as the cloud, and also had links with Ottoman design, but by the 17th century they had a distinctive and flourishing character of their own.

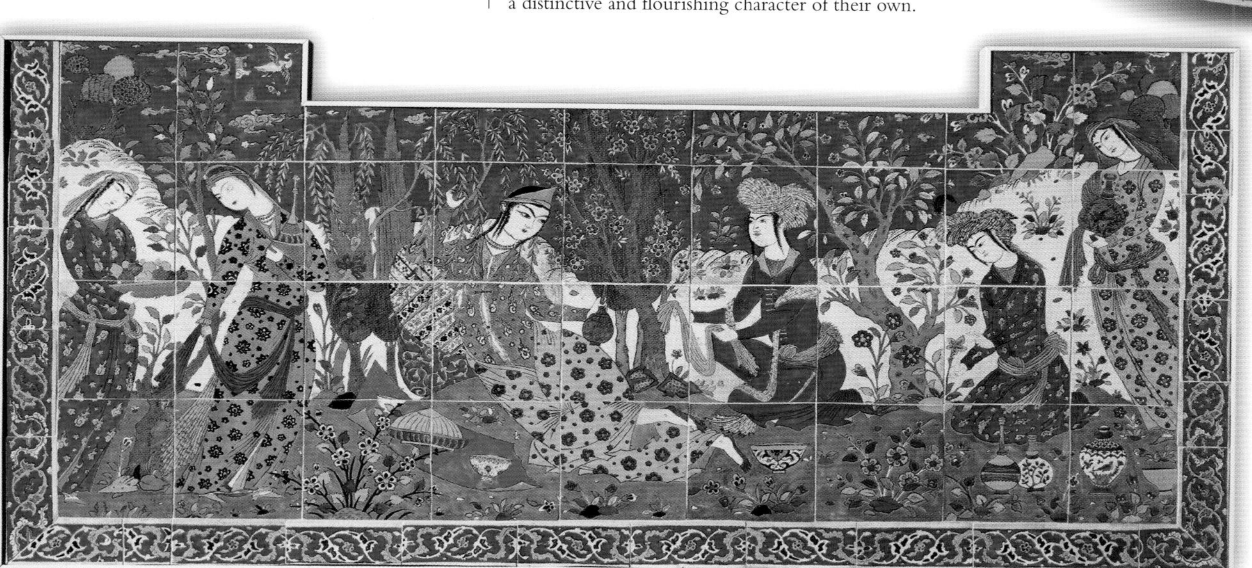

Stylised & Scattered Flora & Fauna 1600–1650

European clothing

The clothes of fashionable men and women were patterned with a wide range of plants and animals, varying from stylised flowers with strapwork to a scattered effect of more naturalistically rendered motifs. Garments specifically for indoor wear, either on formal occasions such as receiving visitors or during more relaxed hours at home, were colourfully patterned in embroidered and knitted linen and silk fabrics. Indoor shoes for men and women, such as the low-heeled, backless mule slipper of the earlier 17th century, were ornamented with popular designs such as botanical patterns.

‘Repeating patterns of scattered motifs, generally flowers and animals, were very popular in secular needlework ... as indeed they were in woven fabrics.’

MONIQUE AND DONALD KING, *European Textiles*, 1990

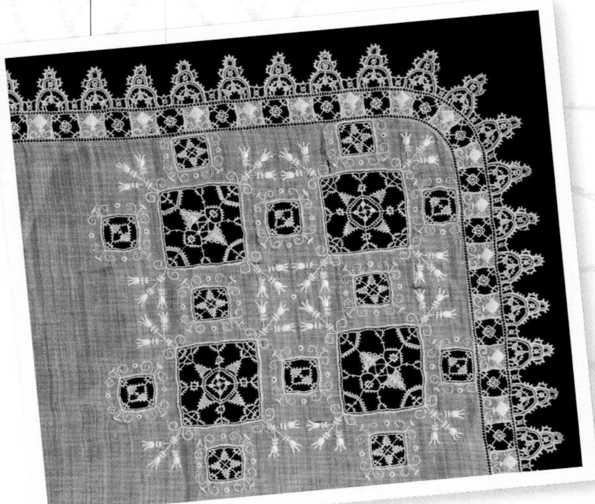

Handkerchief, c. 1600, *Italy*
This linen handkerchief has been worked with patterns in embroidery, in cutwork and *reticella* needle lace. Openwork squares filled with delicate designs of stylised flowers, leaves and small crosses are laid out as a cross. Pomegranates are represented by the three-stemmed motif at the corners of each openwork square and within the embroidered squares of the border.

Smock, 1600–20, *England*
The linen in this detail from woman's smock is embroidered with silk in an outline pattern of strapwork in a lozenge grid, the angles formed by interconnecting loops as the strands progress horizontally across the pattern. Each lozenge encloses a stylised flower head on a straight stem with a pair of leaves and curling roots, including roses and carnations representing purity, love and devotion.

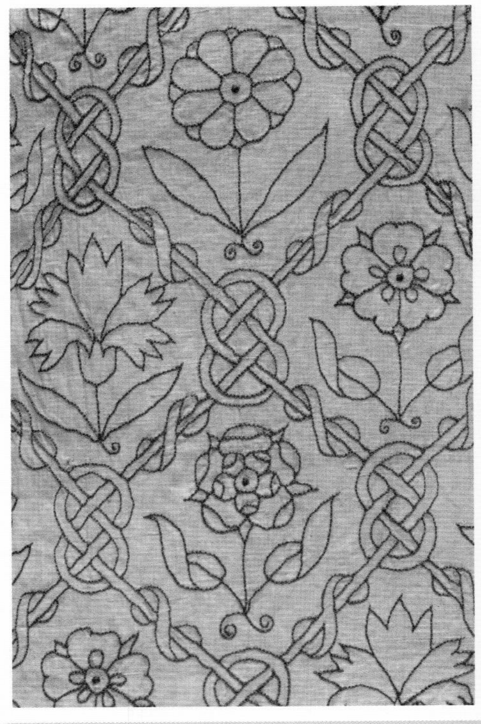

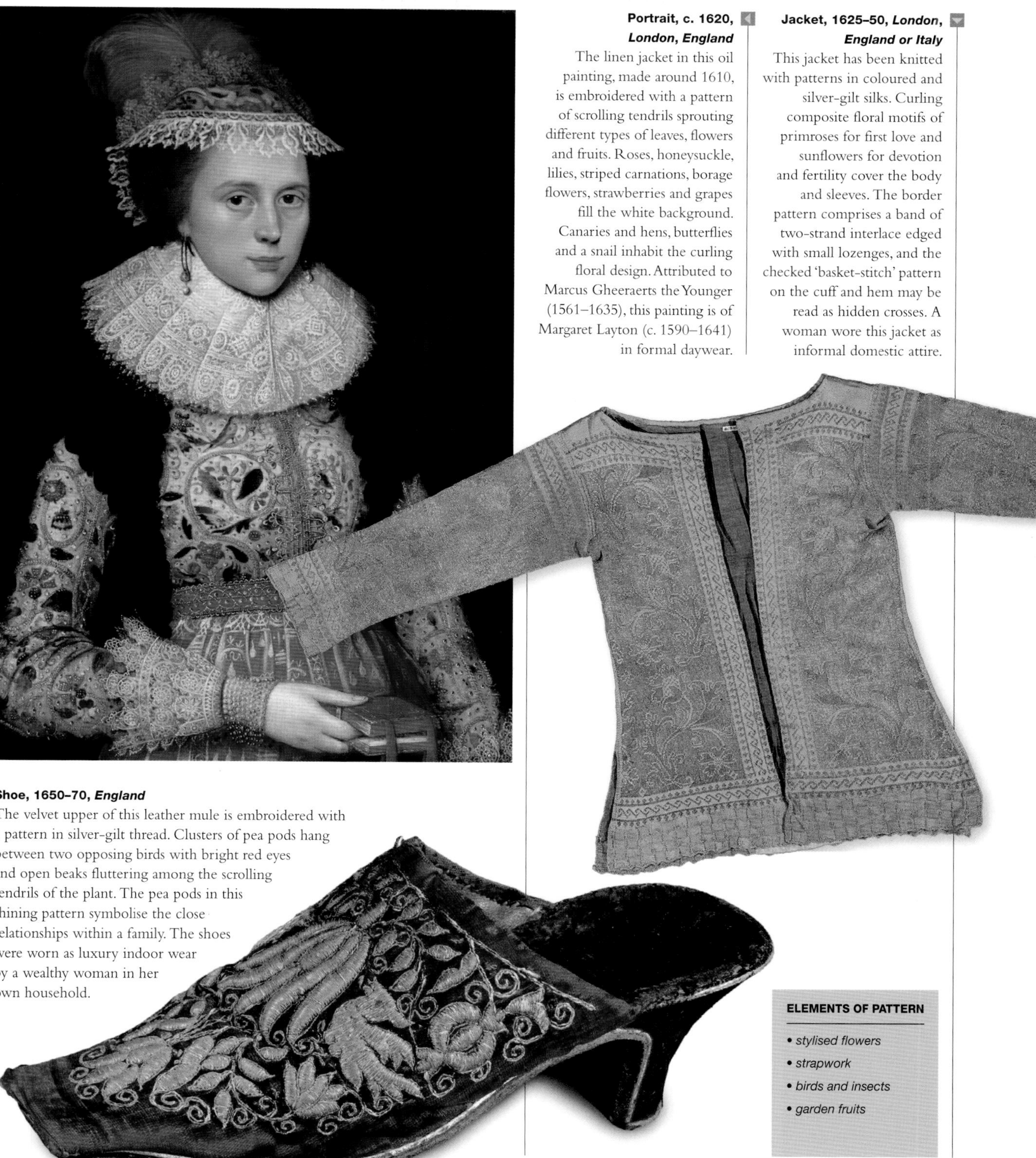

Portrait, c. 1620, *London, England*
The linen jacket in this oil painting, made around 1610, is embroidered with a pattern of scrolling tendrils sprouting different types of leaves, flowers and fruits. Roses, honeysuckle, lilies, striped carnations, borage flowers, strawberries and grapes fill the white background. Canaries and hens, butterflies and a snail inhabit the curling floral design. Attributed to Marcus Gheeraerts the Younger (1561–1635), this painting is of Margaret Layton (c. 1590–1641) in formal daywear.

Jacket, 1625–50, *London, England or Italy*
This jacket has been knitted with patterns in coloured and silver-gilt silks. Curling composite floral motifs of primroses for first love and sunflowers for devotion and fertility cover the body and sleeves. The border pattern comprises a band of two-strand interlace edged with small lozenges, and the checked 'basket-stitch' pattern on the cuff and hem may be read as hidden crosses. A woman wore this jacket as informal domestic attire.

Shoe, 1650–70, *England*
The velvet upper of this leather mule is embroidered with a pattern in silver-gilt thread. Clusters of pea pods hang between two opposing birds with bright red eyes and open beaks fluttering among the scrolling tendrils of the plant. The pea pods in this shining pattern symbolise the close relationships within a family. The shoes were worn as luxury indoor wear by a wealthy woman in her own household.

ELEMENTS OF PATTERN

- *stylised flowers*
- *strapwork*
- *birds and insects*
- *garden fruits*

Floral Perfection c. 1610–c. 1650

Exotic decoration at the time of Shah Jahan

The Mughal emperor Shah Jahan ('World Ruler', reigned 1628–58) grandson of Akbar (see pages 130–1), is famous for the garden tomb, the Taj Mahal (1632–43). Built in white marble for his beloved wife Mumtaz Mahal, it is inlaid with thin sections of precious and semi-precious stones, using the *pietra dura* technique, forming flowers of Paradise. Flowers were also grown in the garden in front – carnations, iris, tulips, hyacinth, jasmine, lotus, marigolds, narcissus, zinnia. These flowers, and the precisely designed floral forms standing out against the background, can also be seen on jewellery, embroidery, furniture and tiles of the period.

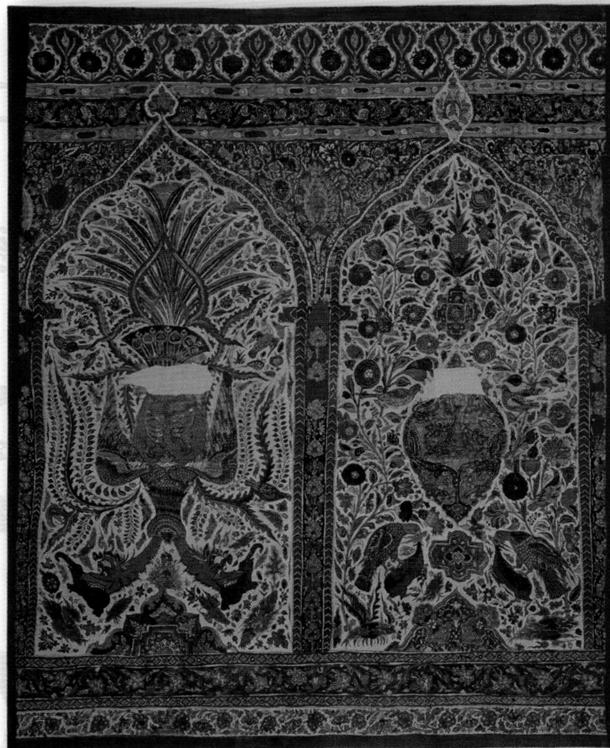

Cotton tent hanging, mid-17th century, *south-east India*
The two ogee (double-curved) arches are filled with elaborate floral backgrounds – the left-hand one containing a mythical double-headed bird, the *bherunda*, with elephants in its jaws and claws, a popular decorative subject in south India. Surrounding the niches are more floral and ogival motifs with elaborate floral scroll borders. This double-niched, mordant- and resist-dyed hanging probably lined the inside of a tent or divided an interior space.

Satin, silk-embroidered riding coat, c. 1620–30, *India*
Made for a man at the Mughal court, this coat is sewn in a chain stitch associated with Gujarati embroiderers. The borders are decorated with a floral arabesque design suggesting links to Safavid Iran (see pages 122–3). Symbolic of its possible use for hunting, the coat is covered with lions, tigers, deer and birds inhabiting a fabulous floral landscape in pale pink, beige, blue, grey, green and yellow.

ELEMENTS OF PATTERN

- *flowers of paradise*
- *the two-headed bird* – bherunda
- *ogival motifs*
- *floral scrolls and arabesques*

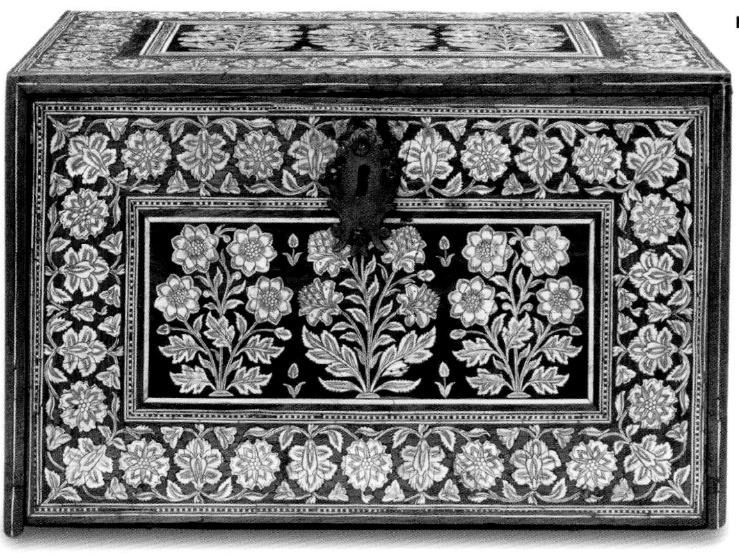

Inlaid ivory cabinet, mid-17th century, *Gujarat or Sindh*
The floral patterns on this cabinet were popular in India and the West, to which many such decorated objects were exported. The edging bands of stylised flowers have some degree of geometric regularity with serrated leaves reminiscent of Middle Eastern forms. The plants in the central panels perhaps link to popular 17th-century Western floral motifs. The cabinet was designed to store documents and valuables.

Pendant (*Ta'viz*), early 17th century, *India*
The flowers and birds are made up of rubies and emeralds set in white nephrite jade using fine gold strips – a technique called *kundan*. The cabochon stones (polished rather that faceted) are shaped into delicate details such as petals and bird's eyes. The gold settings are also shaped to add serrations and lobing. This amuletic pendant (*ta'viz*), with Qur'anic text on the back, was for a Muslim.

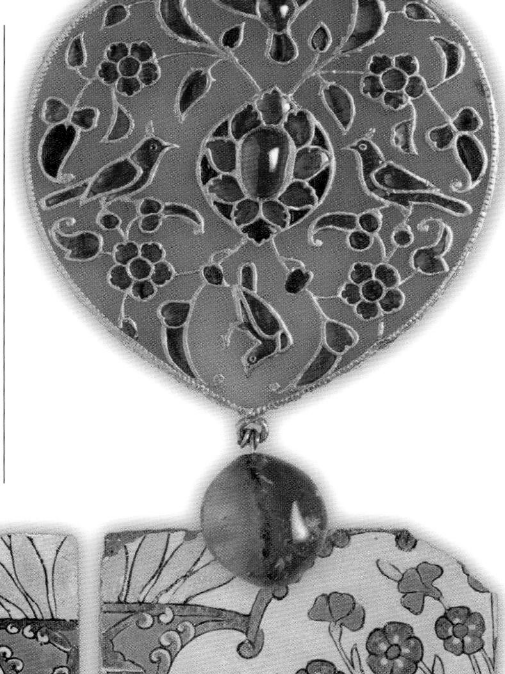

'This Islamic monument [the Taj Mahal] has become a national symbol of beauty and excellence for all Indians regardless of religion or sectarian affiliation.'

VIDYA DEHEJIA, *Indian Art*, 1997

Glazed earthenware tiles, c. 1650, *Lahore or Kashmir*
Tile patterns consisting of vases containing a variety of exotic flowers were especially popular during the reign of Shah Jahan and may have decorated any of his monuments in Lahore or Kashmir. The vibrant colours of yellow, blue and orange, the elegant shapes which define the vases, and the linking scrolls which frame the flowers would have created a dramatic design of the finest quality.

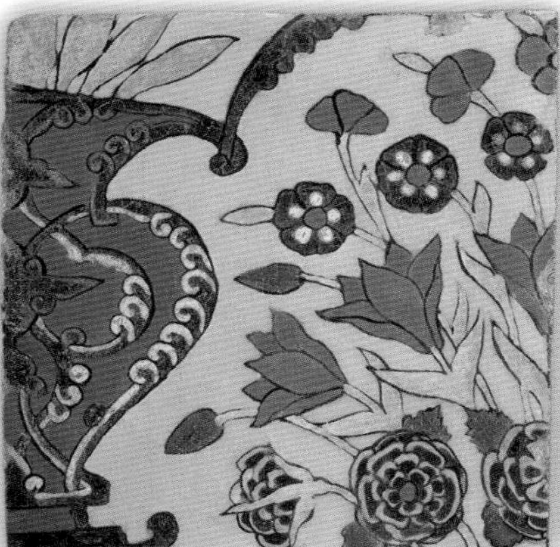

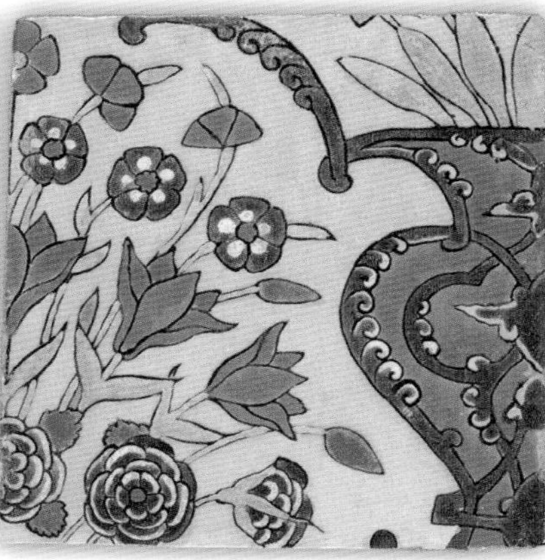

PATTERN IN DETAIL

Symbols of Happiness & Long Life 1670–1690

Qing dynasty, decorative lacquer screen

The 17th century saw a move towards a more affluent and diverse cultural life in China, which meant that merchants had increasing independence from imperial control. The advent of the Manchu Qing dynasty, which overthrew the Ming in 1644, would stimulate innovation in crafts. Although decorative arts and painting were focused on figurative scenes, patterns and designs were important adjuncts to ornamentation and the fundamental elements and motifs remained as expressively powerful as ever.

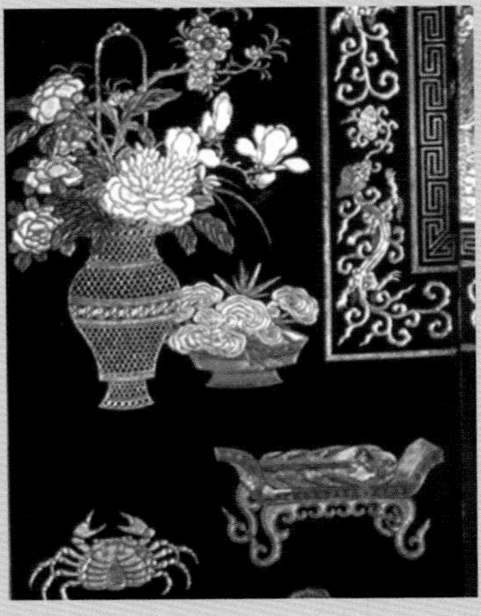

Four seasons

A wire-work hanging vase contains an arrangement of symbolic flowers – the magnolia is a flower of spring, meaning self-esteem, feminine charm and beauty; the chrysanthemum represents autumn, retirement, ease, wealth and longevity; and the camellia symbolises health, and physical and mental strength. In the bowl beside the vase is possibly a dish of oysters, which signify cosmic life, the *yin* power and fertility.

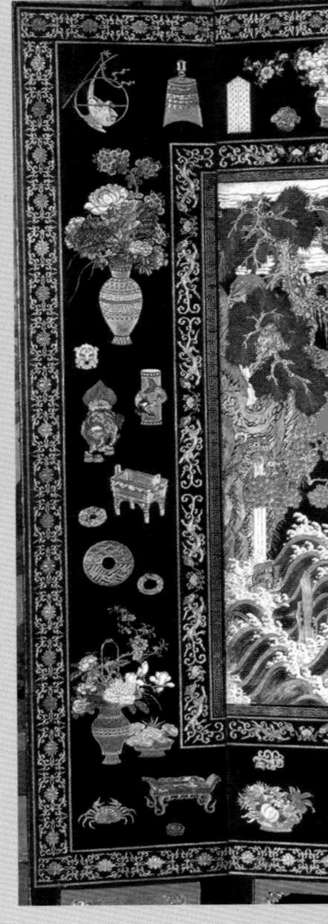

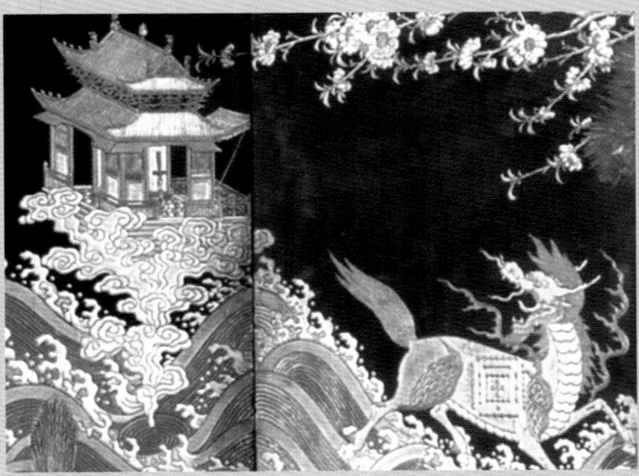

Clouds and waves

The wave form design, here depicting a river, was an important pattern, which represented the water's swell and foam. Above the river floats a small temple and a dragon-horse – a *longma* – walking on the water. This mythical creature, with a dragon's head and scaled body of a horse with a map on its back, constitutes the vital spirit (*qi*) of Heaven and earth.

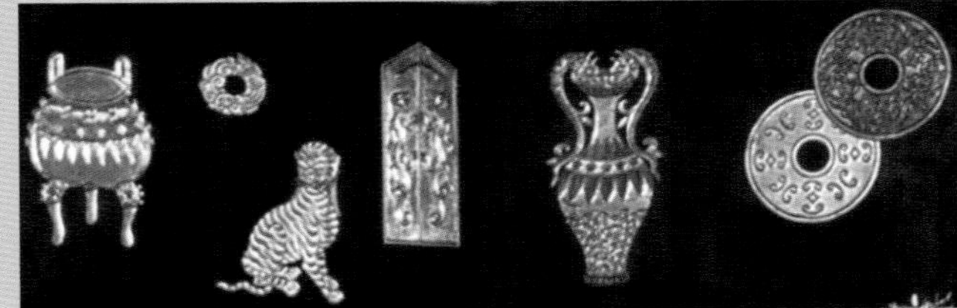

Decorative collectables

In Chinese society, the cult veneration of ancestors was an important part of continuity between the living and the dead, while collecting ancient and antique vessels, objects and forms – antiquarianism – provided a tangible link to an illustrious past. Scrolls were painted with a record of each object in a collection and the border of this screen – called the 'hundred antiques' design – may have served a similar purpose.

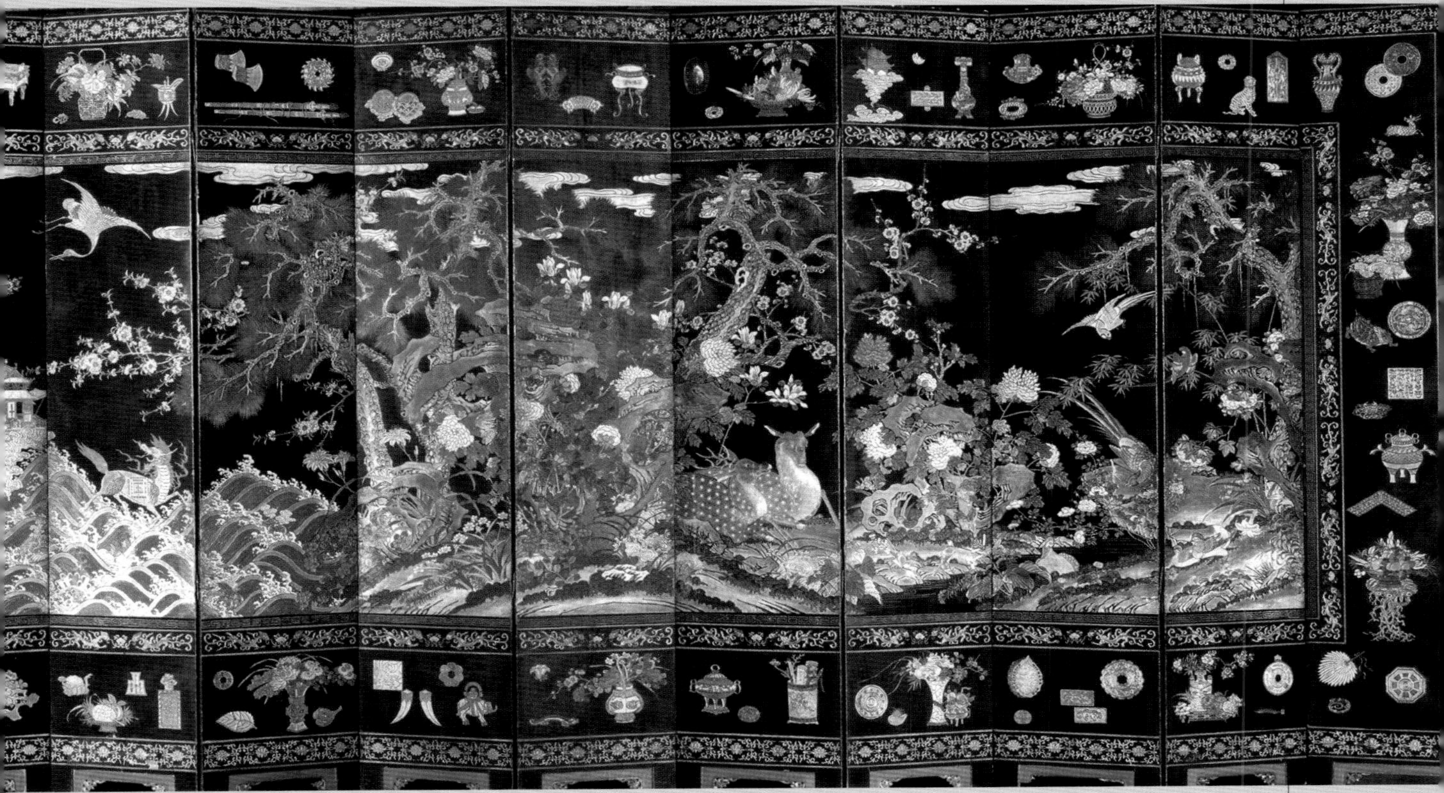

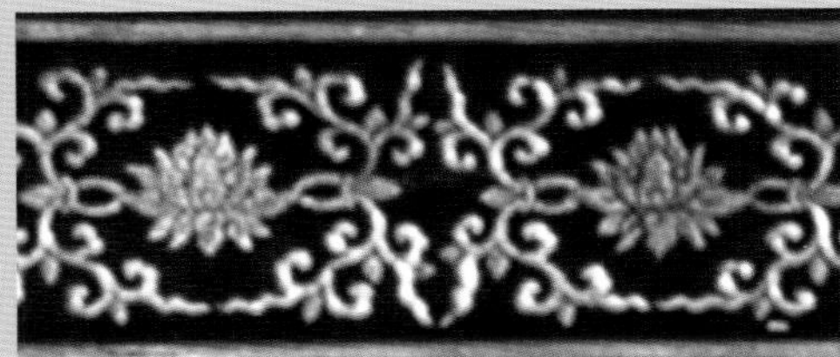

Chrysanthemum banding
A band of chrysanthemums surrounded by a scroll motif in gold emphasises the powerful symbolism of this screen. Along with many of the motifs and objects represented in the landscape and the 'hundred antiques' border, the chrysanthemum radiates a positive symbolic spiritual force. Yellow, blue, green and red flowers alternate in sequence, highlighting the chrysanthemum's powerful *yang* energy and symbolic good luck.

Dragons and flowers
In the inner border, paired dragons hold the green tendrils of a flower or cloud in their mouths. The golden scrolling shape forms the body of the dragon with its clawed legs splayed out on either side, and curled tendrils turn the figure into a popular motif. The dragon was a central symbolic character in Chinese mythology, its many forms and types embodying the highest spiritual power.

Landscape of animals and birds, 12-panel screen
Possibly an expensive elite gift, this decorative screen may have divided the luxurious rooms of a Chinese mansion or have been exported to an equally aristocratic setting in England. The rolling landscape presents a panorama to be enjoyed from a distance and details for close viewing. The screen was made using the specialist lacquer technique of *kuan cai* or 'incised polychrome', unique to the Kangxi period in China.

Patterns of Private Enclosure 1600–1670

Garden design

The love of geometry and order expressed in grand Iranian gardens by the use of geometrical shapes, interconnecting water channels and formally planted beds was very influential on European design. The Age of Reason concept of rationality and the pursuit of scientific enquiry, particularly in the area of botany, inspired new patterns for gardens and textiles. Flowering plants, shrubs and trees were arranged to full effect in a desire to display newly acquired botanical knowledge and taste. Flowering plants and their woven and embroidered forms were displayed in patterns of order and control that embodied the new aristocratic taste for restrained beauty.

Carpet, 1670–1750, *Iran*

Woven in wool with the design of a Persian garden, plants and trees are shown from different angles. Water ripples from an eight-pointed star-shaped bed on the central island in patterns of stepped lines, with spotted fish, bordered by plants and leaves. In each corner six plots reflect each other with subtle colour variations. White plots patterned with a chenar tree (oriental plane) form a *quincunx* with the yellow island. Star-shaped beds or chenar tree motifs pattern the other plots. The border has flowering plants and shrubs between cypress trees.

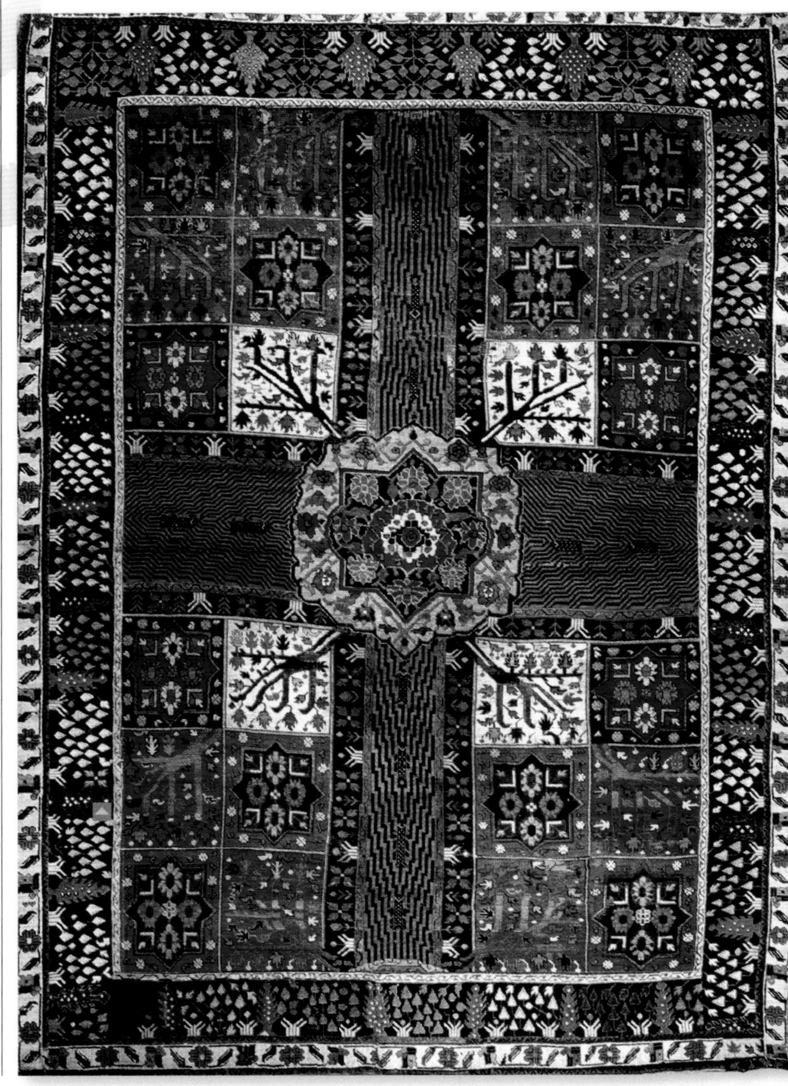

ELEMENTS OF PATTERN

- *geometric grids*
- *flowers and trees enclosed with other plants*
- *new exotic plants displayed as valued objects and symbols of influence*
- *luxury constrained*

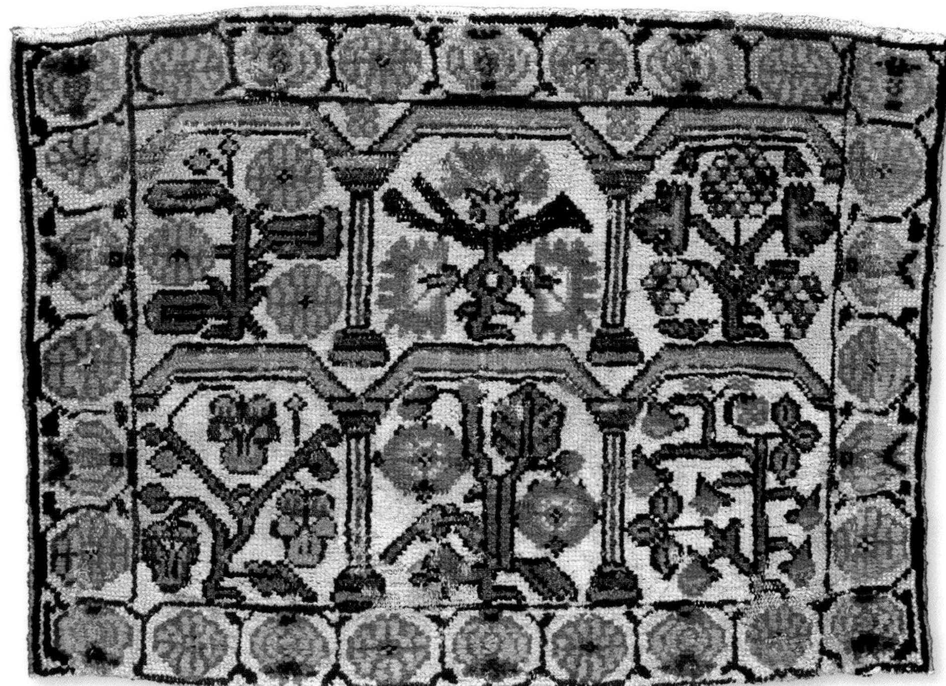

Furnishing panel, 1600–20, *England*
This panel, probably for a chair seat, is woven in wool with a pattern of plant motifs beneath arcades supported by columns with plain capitals. From the top-left corner clockwise, marigolds, carnations, a grape vine, a strawberry plant, roses and pansies are shown growing from curling roots, the types of plants usually cultivated in English gardens of the period. The border has a pattern of alternating marigolds and pomegranates.

'Collecting a wide range of exotic plants in gardens of the 17th century was part of a larger cultural and economic shift that was indeed new.'

CHANDRA MUKERJI, *Consumption and the World of Goods*, 1993

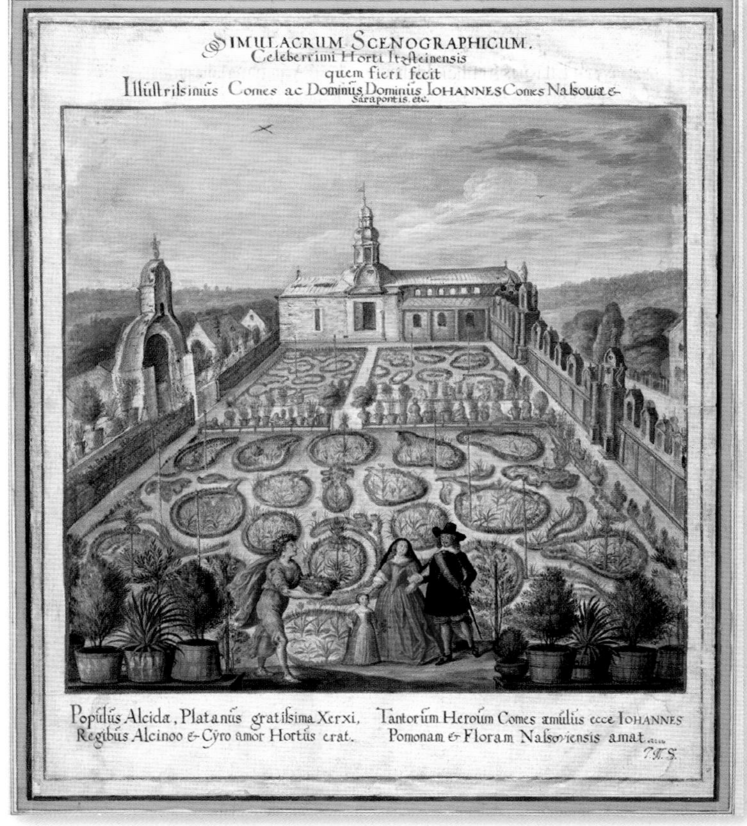

Painting, c. 1645–72, *Idstein, Germany*
Flower beds shaped as oranges, pears, a pineapple and other fruits interplay like a pattern on a luxurious textile. The beds are planted with highly desirable expensive tulips and the tall orange fritillary (*Fritillaria imperialis* 'Rubra Maxima'), which was like the orange, an emblem of William of Orange), carnations and columbine. This watercolour and gouache painting on vellum is from Count Johann of Nassau's plant collection album, *Simulacrum Scenographicum Celeberrimi Horti Itzsteinensis*, by Johann Jakob Walter. The classically dressed goddess Flora presents Johann and his family with a basket of many-coloured flowers of the exotic *Mirabilis jalapa* (Marvel of Peru), a plant newly imported to Europe from the Americas.

Designs in Royal Taste 1660–1700

English Restoration

From the mid-17th century, the development of the wood-turning lathe allowed spiralling forms inspired by interlace design to be made for furniture and fitted woodwork. Fashionable men and women who followed royal taste sought out luxurious designs for their domestic interiors to increase their comfort and convenience. Patterns in relief created with inlaid materials were integral with the new curving forms of furniture, creating a sense of flowing movement that was constrained by the overall design.

‘Here I saw the new fabrique of French Tapissry, for designe, tendernesse of worke, & incomparable imitation of the best paintings; beyond any thing, I had ever beheld.’

JOHN EVELYN, *Diary*, 4TH OCTOBER 1683

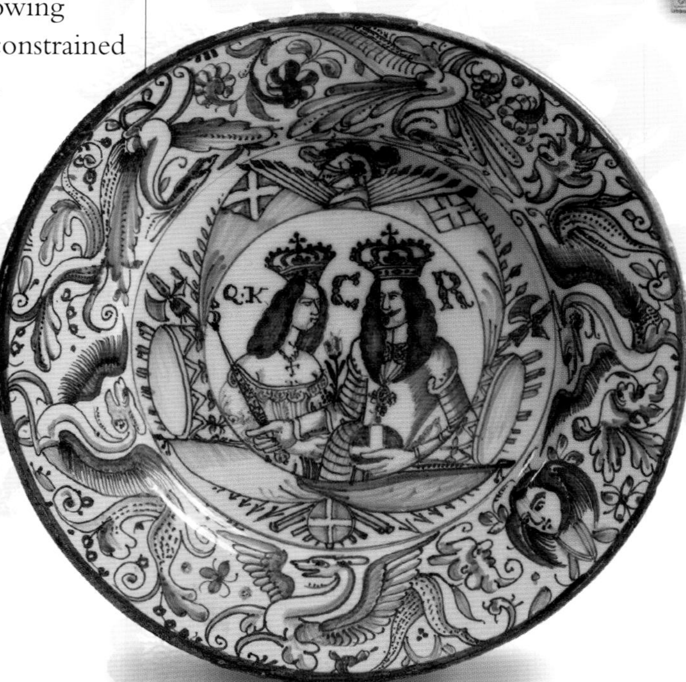

Dish, 1662–1685, *Brislington, England or the Netherlands*
This delftware dish commemorates the marriage of Charles II and Catherine of Braganza in 1662. Their portraits, surrounded by banners, drums, pikestaffs, spears, and surmounted by a helmet, are encompassed by a pattern of parading ‘grotesques’ punctuated by a face framed with wings. With long sinuous necks and wings displayed, their forelegs and hind limbs metamorphose into scrolling plant tendrils and flowers, integrating them with florid masks in profile and scattered plant elements in the background.

Sampler, 1660, *England*
The uppermost pattern in drawn threadwork shows scrolling plant elements bound together like a fleur-de-lis, a unicorn, acorn and small florals, followed by a band of lozenges. The motifs are embroidered in silk and linen thread. They include the alphabet dated ‘1660’ with the embroiderer’s initials ‘MD’; geometric tendrils enclosing pansies, carnations and strawberries; men carrying plants divided by a multi-coloured column, with rose-acorn motifs; roses and acorns formally arranged with delicate florals around a multi-coloured tendril; and roses, gentian-acorn motifs and honeysuckle around a tendril with interlace columns. This sampler demonstrates patterns for household linen textiles and clothing.

Curtain, 1660–1700, *England*
A pattern of different leaves is embroidered in crewel wool on a linen and cotton fabric. The heavy shaded outlines and delicately veined surfaces unite the varying forms in a rich design. Many of the leaves curl at the tips to display both sides. This contrasting pattern of dark leaves on a pale background was inspired by contemporary painted, printed and embroidered textiles imported from India.

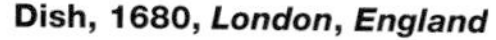

ELEMENTS OF PATTERN

- *curling leaves*
- *flowers and fruits contained by geometric tendrils*
- *fantastical figures*
- *columns of interlace*

Dish, 1680, *London, England*
The border of this deltware dish is patterned with panels of designs with an undulating edge in the Chinese fashion. Above and below are the heraldic arms of the Feltmakers' Company, with other panels containing an artemesia leaf surrounded by scrolls of undulating lines, stylised fruits and flowers, and a male figure in a landscape, all painted in Chinese style. The central image is of General George Monck, an influential figure in the Restoration in 1660 of the monarchy under Charles II, who became a popular hero. The dish commemorates the marriage of Benjamin Taylor and Anne Aldridge at Shoreditch in London.

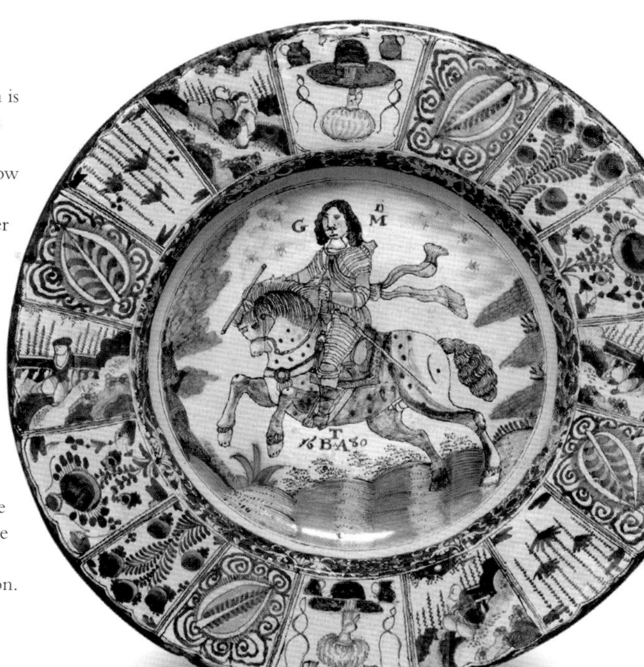

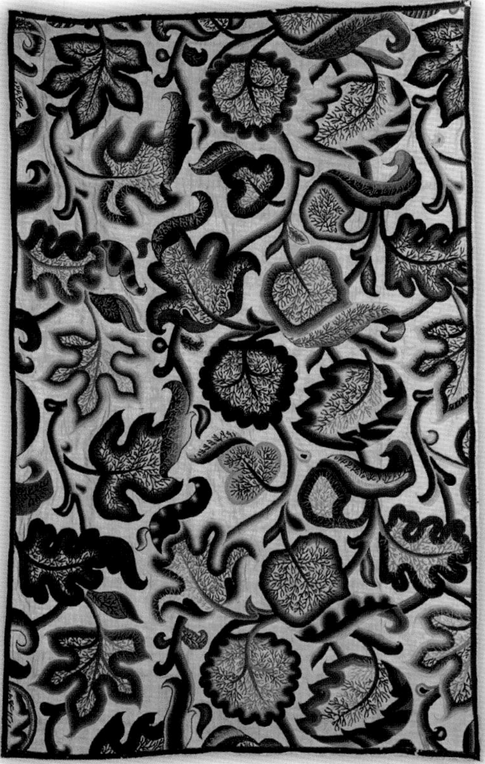

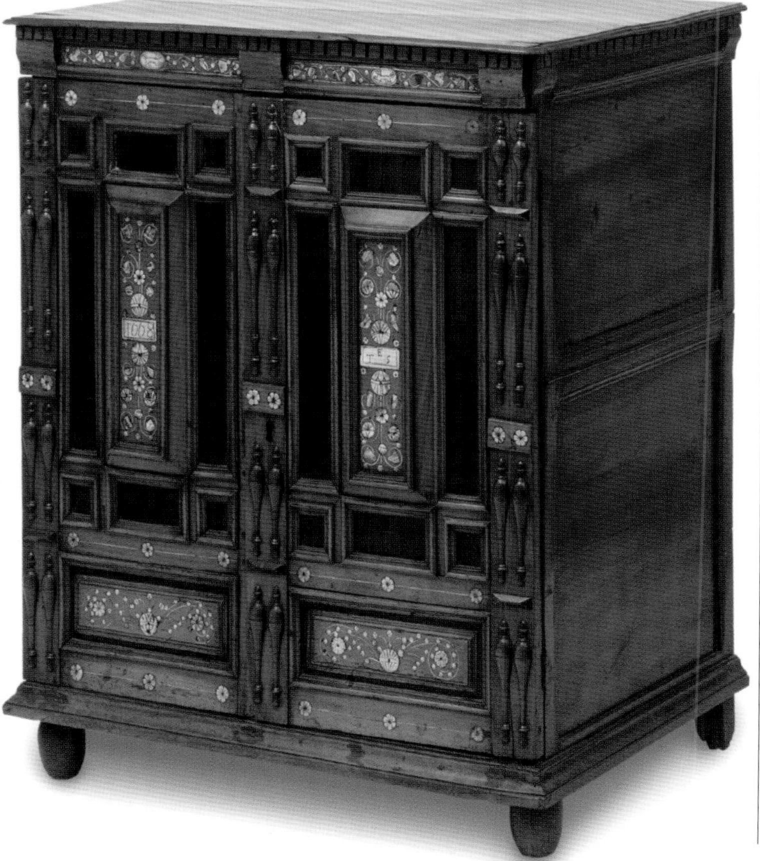

Cabinet, 1688, *England*
This walnut-panelled cabinet is inlaid with ivory, incised in lines filled with black paste and mother-of-pearl. The uppermost panels are ornamented with a running tendril sprouting flowers and small leaves, with a central motif of a running dog enclosed by an oval. The doors are decorated with flower heads punctuating a fine horizontal band. Floral motifs with curling tendrils and small leaves spring from Chinese-type vases, the central patterns including plaques inscribed '1668' and 'TES'. Spindle-shaped motifs inspired by classical pilasters have been applied vertically in pairs. This Anglo-Dutch style was popular in England after 1650.

Patterns of Aspiration 1675–1705

Wallpaper designs in England

During medieval and Renaissance times, expensive tapestries and other fabric hangings, only affordable by the wealthy, covered interior walls. When access to foreign tapestry supplies was disrupted by war, wallpaper became an alternative. Banned in England during the Puritan period (c. 1646–60) for its frivolity, the fashion for wallpaper flourished in the late 17th century, to the extent that a wallpaper tax was introduced in 1712. Patterns followed the floral styles of ornamentation in interior design and also emulated plasterwork. In the early 18th century, painted wallpapers from China began to appear in England, shifting the taste to more exotic designs.

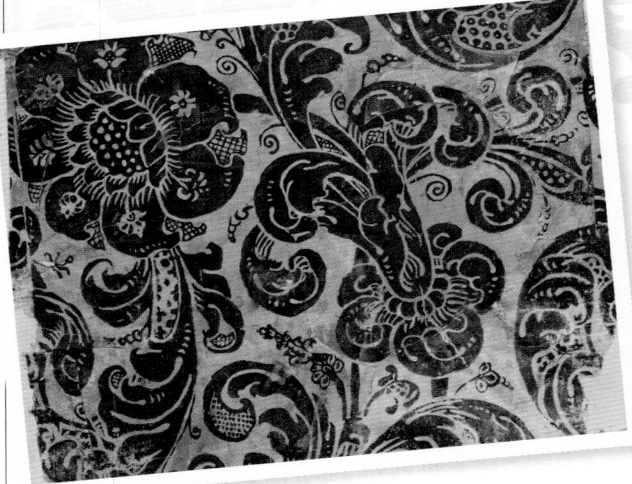

Woodblock print wallpaper, c. 1705, *England*
The woodblock print technique provided the ideal means of creating a pattern repeat. A block of wood carved in the relief method – where the area left raised after the cutting forms the design – is repeatedly coated in dye and pressed on to the paper. Patterns, like this scrolling leaf and floral motif, would be designed to align across each repeat so that the final effect would be continuous.

Print wallpaper, c. 1700, Ord House, *Northumberland, England*
This wallpaper was influenced by Chinese designs of floral trees with exotic birds, animals and figures. The continuous weaving branch – with fruits, flowers, squirrels, peacocks, parrots and 'oriental' figures – was printed with a woodblock. At least five colours were then added with stencil cutouts. The paper was painted with a black background and varnished to give it a glossy sheen.

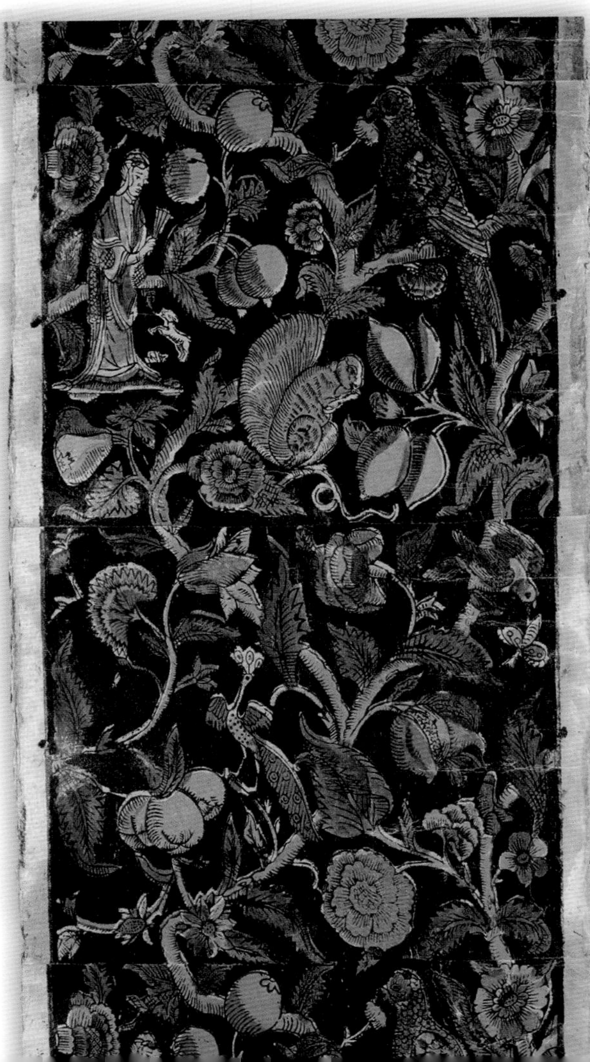

ELEMENTS OF PATTERN

- *exotic flowers and leaves*
- *Chinese figures and designs*
- *mouldings and strapwork*
- *structural and architectural*
- *the tulip*
- *figurative scenes*

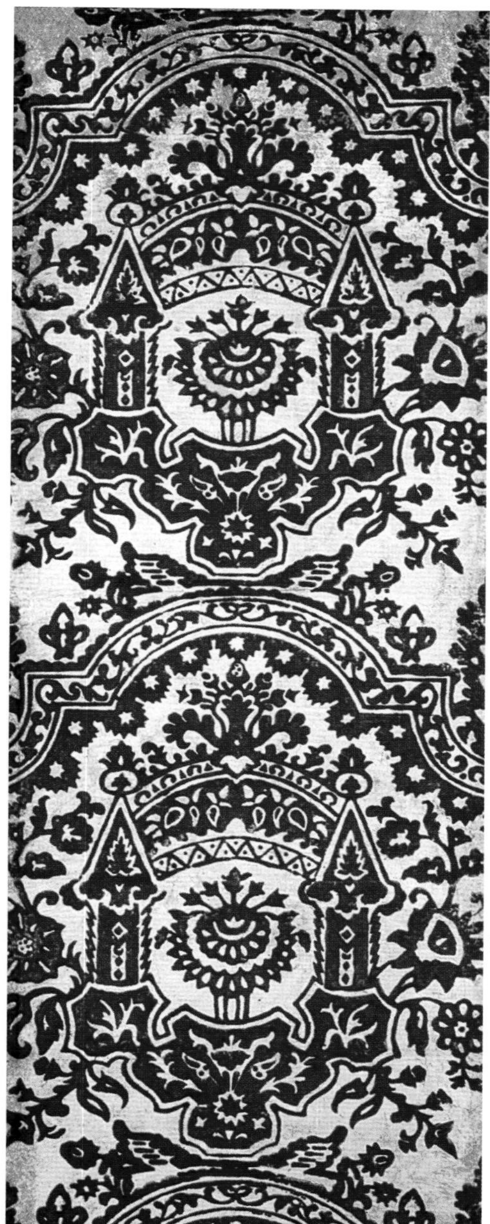

Flock wallpaper panel, c. 1680, *Worcester, made in England or the Netherlands*
'Flock' was expensive wallpaper with a fine layer of powdered wool glued to its surface to create a velvet effect. This architecturally themed crimson flock pattern comprises a small castle separated by bands with various floral and foliate scrolls. This early flock panel was hung, possibly in a dining room, with a companion panel made of embossed leather decorated with a quatrefoil of *putti* (cherub-like children) and swags.

'Wallpaper is reflective of both popular and elite aesthetic tastes. [It] dramatically reflects trends in fine art, popular culture and technological innovation.'

JOANNE KOSUDA-WARNER, *Landscape Wallcoverings*, 2001

Woodblock wallpaper, late 17th century, *England*
This pattern seems to adapt a plasterwork design, more usually found in the houses of the wealthy. The geometric enclosures are formed of strapwork borders decorated with floral scrolls and simple oval rosettes. The central motif of flowers contains the expensive and wildly popular tulip. Found in a merchant's house, it may reflect a middle-class desire to use wallpaper to emulate more expensive fashionable interiors.

Engraving print wallpaper, 1675–99, *England*
The figurative pattern on this wallpaper was made using engraving – an intaglio method where an incised pattern is filled with dye for printing, which allowed for a more detailed style. The fashion for figurative designs was growing by the late 17th century and here the pattern represents a range of mythical scenes – Diana and Actaeon, Venus and satyrs – interspersed with naturalistic but exotic flower stems.

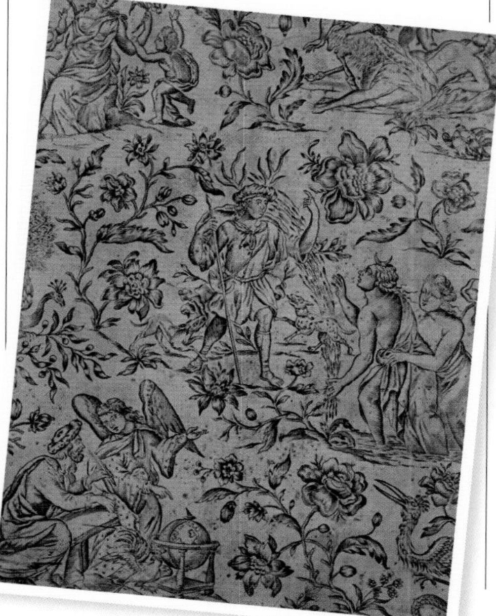

PATTERN IN DETAIL

Marriage Lines c. 1700

Thorbjörg Magnúsdóttir's bedcover

Worked in patterns of wool yarn, this woollen textile bedcover was stitched by the reputed Icelandic embroiderer Thorbjörg Magnúsdóttir. It was probably finished after her marriage in 1696, when the text border was added. The script was written by Thorbjörg's husband, the magistrate Páll Vídalín, and is integrated into the overall design by the use of different colours. The text is bordered with a repeating S-shaped scroll pattern.

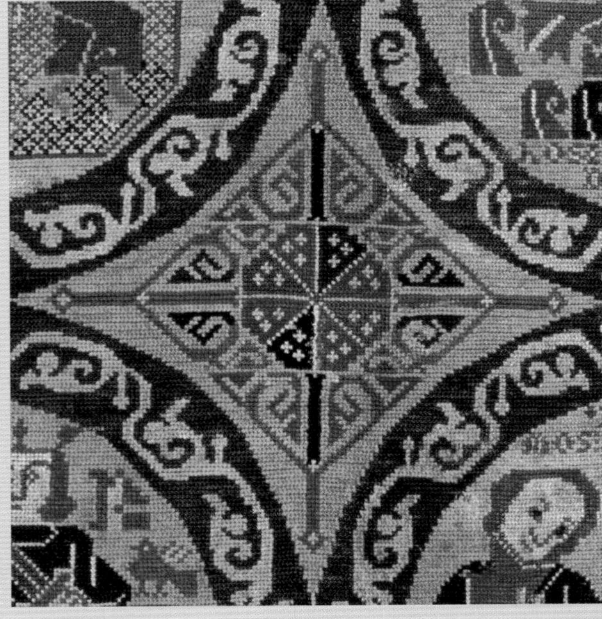

Eight-pointed star

The upper wide border has a pattern of eight-pointed stars, geometric motifs of triangles containing three lozenges, angled lines and dots. The stars are filled with stylised flowering plants, either as four motifs arranged around a central lozenge or as a single upright plant with a duck to either side, symbolic of faithfulness.

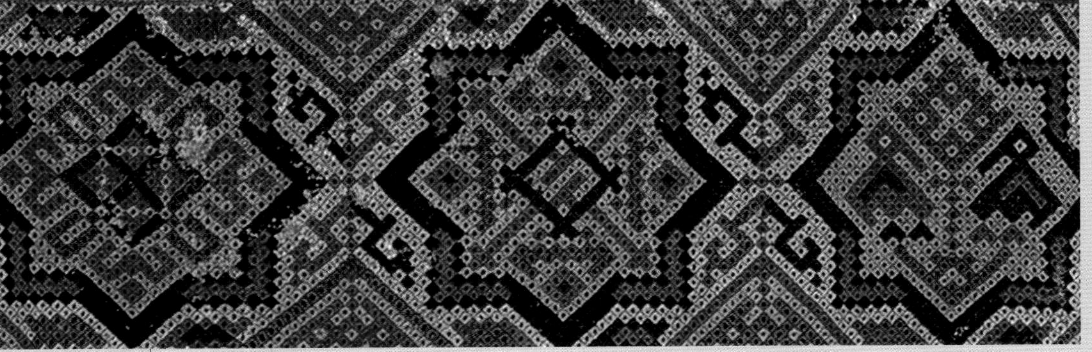

Cross, octagon and lozenge

A cruciform motif terminating in small lozenges forms the basis for this pattern full of protective devices. In the centre, a varicoloured and segmented eight-sided motif filled with small crosses includes a red cruciform shape. This octagon is surrounded by four stylised and pointed leaves arranged as a lozenge. A small cross lies at the point where the angles of the lozenge meet the arm of the cruciform.

Medallions, plants and birds

A row of medallions, framed with bands of alternating leaf and flower elements, runs along the lower wide border. They enclose double-headed eagles, opposing pairs of birds perched on a plant and reindeer with long curling tongues. The medallions alternate with upright stylised plant forms, each alternate motif with a pair of facing birds at the base. Above is a running leaf scroll with alternating colours every two leaves.

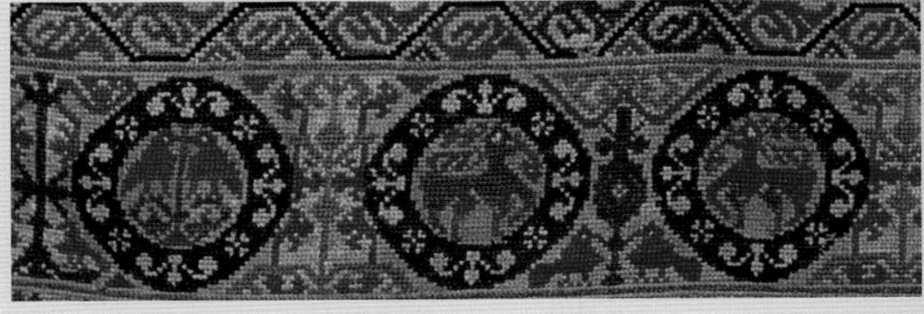

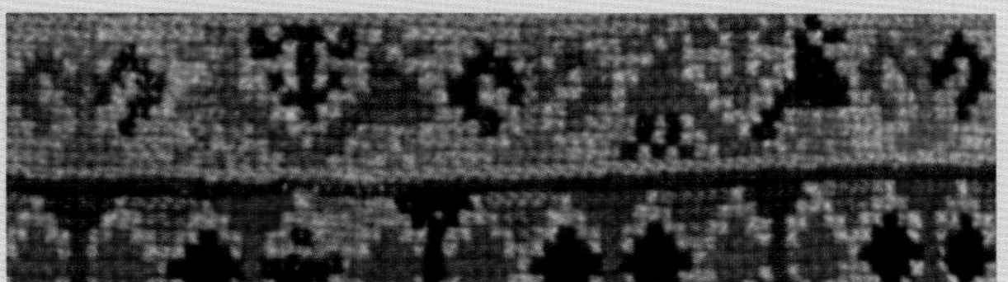

Birds, flowering plants and lozenges
The two patterned bands along the short sides of the bedcover are embroidered with rows of small motifs. The innermost band is embroidered with pairs of opposing birds facing an upright flowering plant and divided by a reversed plant motif. The pattern is made visually more complex by the alternating colours of the birds. The outermost band is decorated with a row of triangles alternating with cruciforms of stems with three lozenges.

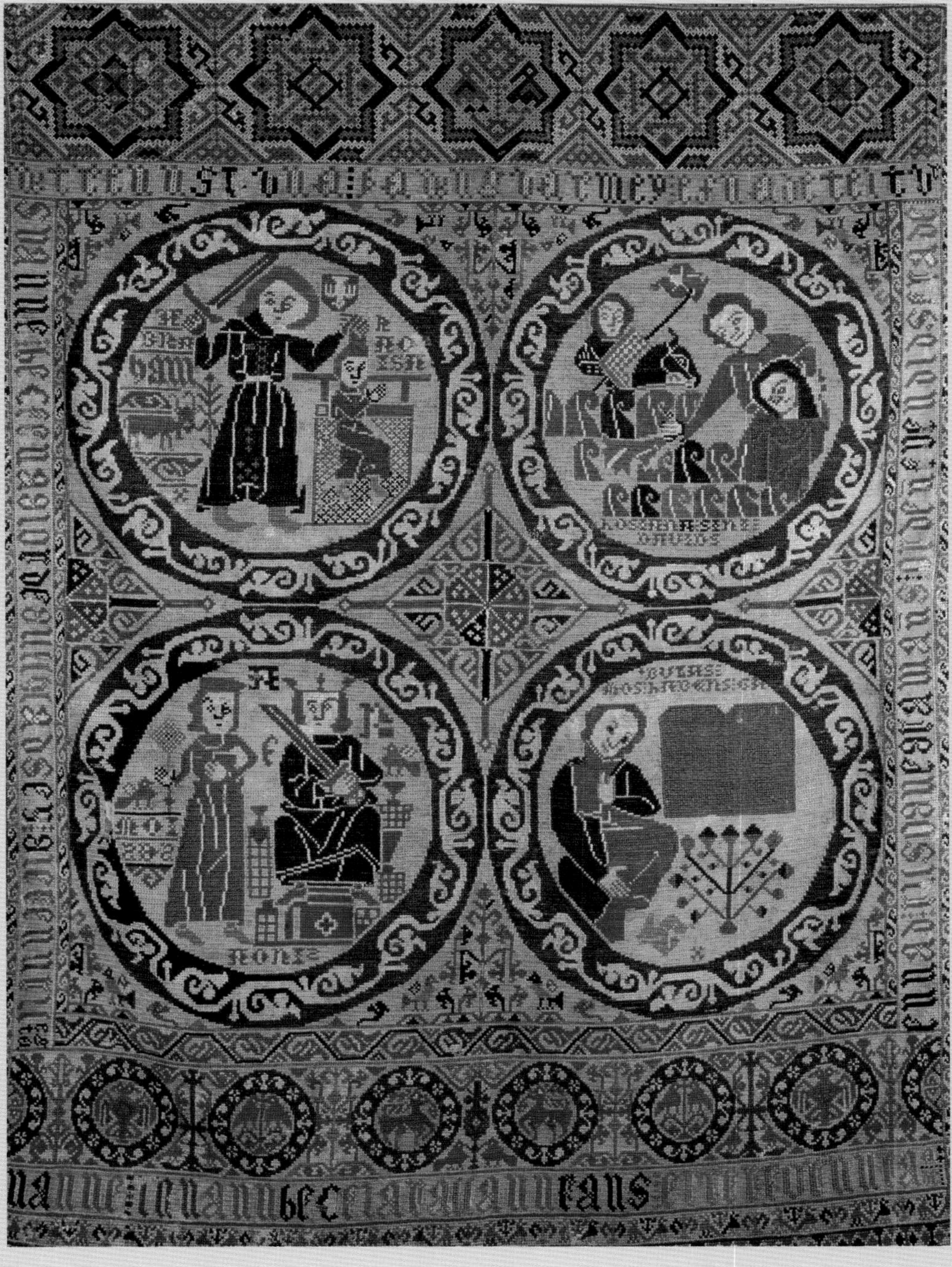

Bedcover, *Iceland*
Four large medallions framed with a running leaf scroll portray, clockwise from top left, Abraham and Isaac, Christ riding into Jerusalem, Moses and the Law tablets, and Moses before Pharaoh. Between the medallions and the inner frame is a pattern of opposing birds and leaves around a central flowering plant, half repeated in the corners.

Opulent Baroque
1650–1700

Patterns of the aristocracy and the Church

The patterns of the so-called Baroque style built on those of the Renaissance and the 16th century, creating elaborate, dynamic and complex effects of shape, colour and light with curving forms derived from nature. Originating in Italy in the early 17th century, the style spread throughout Europe and beyond, and was used to design churches and palaces and decorate their interiors with rich awe-inspiring grandeur. The term 'Baroque' – thought to originate as a description of distorted pearls from Portugal – has sometimes been used derogatorily because of the style's perceived over-ornamentation, but its flamboyant forms satisfied a demand for the emotional and the sensuous.

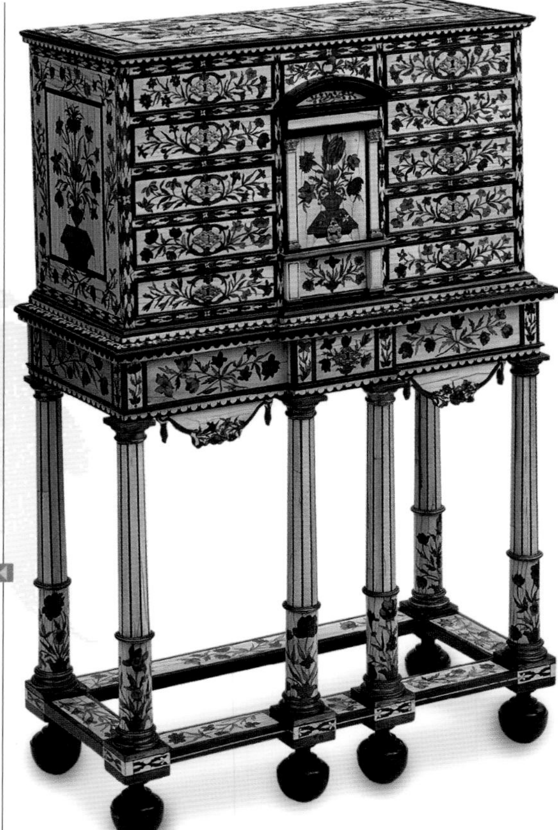

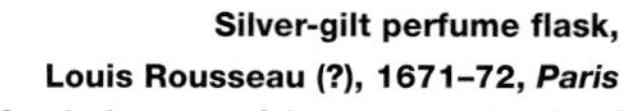

Silver-gilt perfume flask, Louis Rousseau (?), 1671–72, *Paris*
The floral plant motif decorates each side of this flask, echoing earlier forms of acanthus pattern. Elaborate leaves and an exotic flower sprout from a single stem – a motif often used to decorate pillars and pilasters. Botanical patterns were a popular form of the Baroque style and this flask, possibly for perfume as part of a toilet set, also has a delicate scrolling pattern on the stopper.

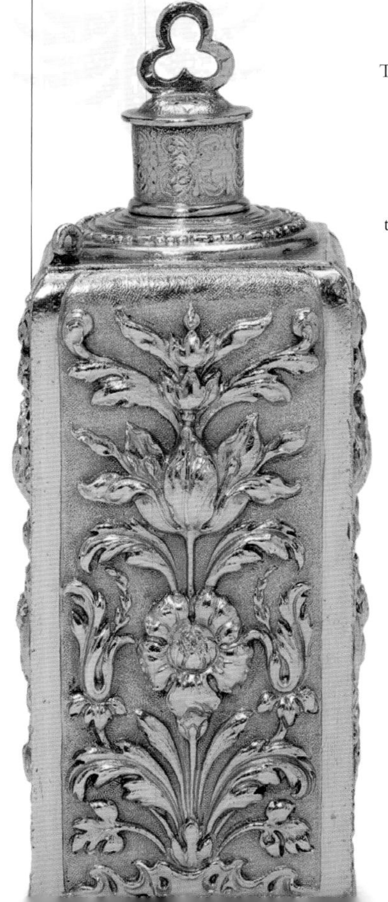

'A new appreciation ... has emerged ... with an understanding that the Baroque emphasis on spatial complexity relates to modern concepts of design.'

JOHN PILE, *A History of Interior Design,* 2005

Cabinet-on-stand, Pierre Gole (attributed), 1661–65, *Paris*
This small veneered marquetry cabinet is extensively patterned with floral bouquets and vases made using ivory, tortoiseshell, various woods and green-stained bone. The ebullient floral stems include many popular flowers of the period – the exotic two-coloured tulip, carnations and anemones – supported by scrolling brass fittings. A piece of exceptional delicacy, it was probably made for the Duc d'Orléans, brother of King Louis XIV of France.

Silk valance, 1685–1700, *Lyons or Spitalfields*

This damask panel would have appeared as rich and elegant with the textured weave in pale blue, yellow and white creating a three-dimensional effect. Hung with other panels, the simulated fringing and tassels would have formed a swag, possibly hanging on a wall or covering a bed. The detailed elements of the floral and foliate pattern are complex – ferns and scrolls, delicate tendrils and flowers, waves and three-leaf motifs.

ELEMENTS OF PATTERN

- *floral and botanical motifs*
- *stems of exotic leaves and flowers*
- *swags and tassels*
- *gilt, enamel and painted patterns*
- *three-dimensional forms*

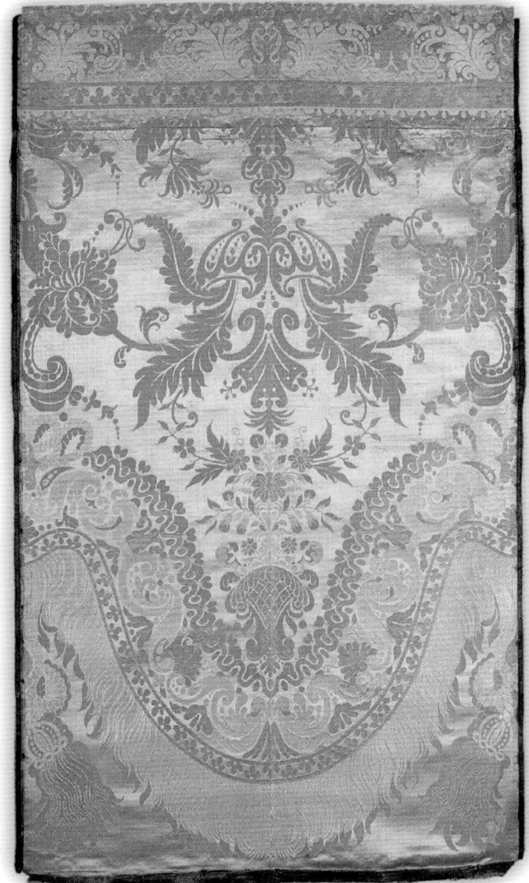

Shrine pendant, c. 1650, *Trapani, Sicily*

This shrine pendant decorated with gilt metal, white enamel and coral was a speciality of western Sicily. The frame consists of scrolling leaf motifs containing carved coral flowers and cherub heads. Typical of Baroque floral designs, the delicate scrolling leaves curve and twist in three-dimensions, alternating between tied bouquets and open palmettes with shells. The shrine probably commemorates St Rosalia, the patron saint of Palermo.

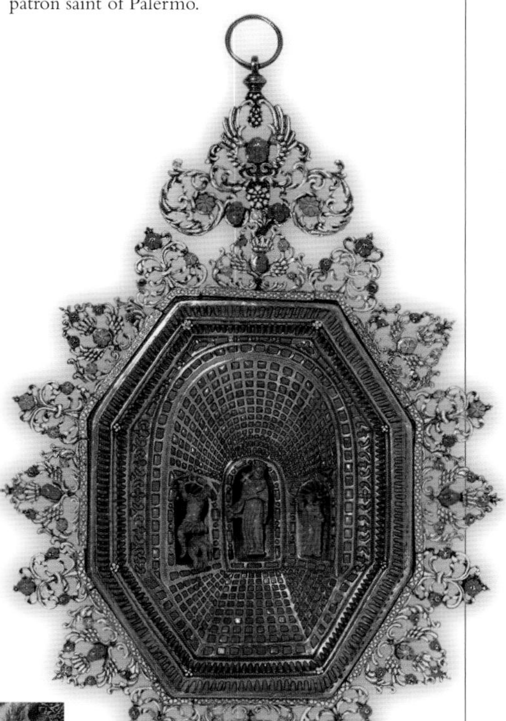

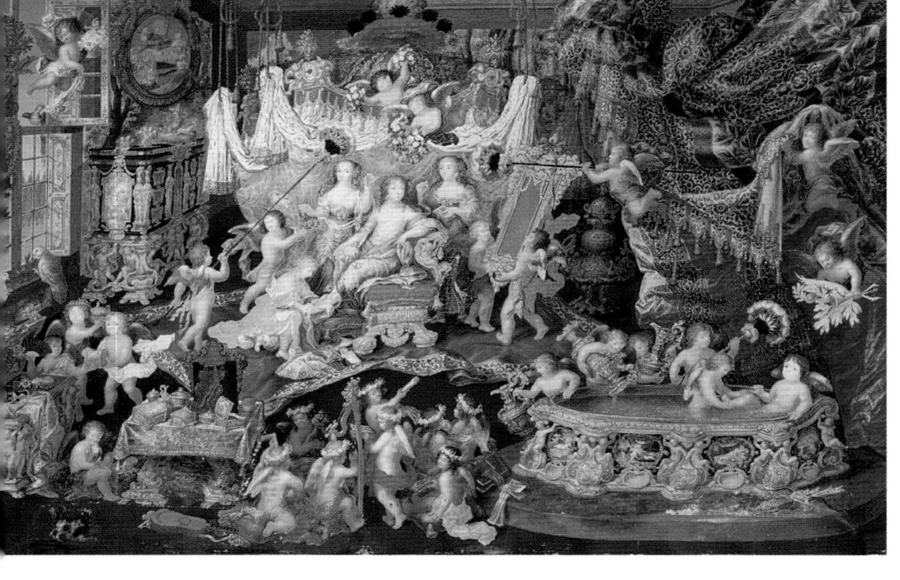

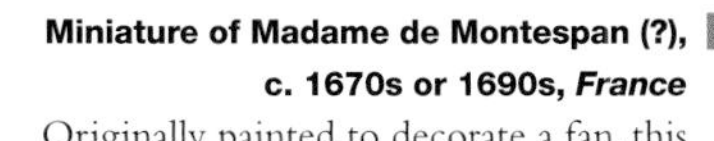

Miniature of Madame de Montespan (?), c. 1670s or 1690s, *France*

Originally painted to decorate a fan, this miniature probably represents the *Trianon de Porcelaine*, a tea-house built by Louis XIV for his principal mistress, and it reflects the extravagance of the Baroque style. Furniture, mirrors, silverware and pictures are heavily decorated in gilt and painted scrolls, swags, mythical figures and floral designs. Fabrics are damasks, silks and embroidery with valances and tassels. The heart motif in some patterning suggests that this painting depicts a celebration of love.

PATTERN IN DETAIL

Spectacular Scrolls

Late 17th Century

Templo de Santo Domingo de Guzmán, San Cristobal de las Casas, Chiapas, Mexico

Baroque architecture embellished restrained Renaissance classicism to create an emotional and theatrical intensity. Prompted by the Counter-Reformation's need for an accessible visual language, architects used classical features such as pilasters and acanthus to create opulent decoration. In Spain ornamentation became increasingly elaborate, and in Spanish colonial America Baroque ornamentation melded with local art forms. The style of Mexican *churrigueresque*, named after the Spanish architect José Benito Churriguera (1665–1725), covered buildings with extravagant, finely sculptured stucco patterns and ornament.

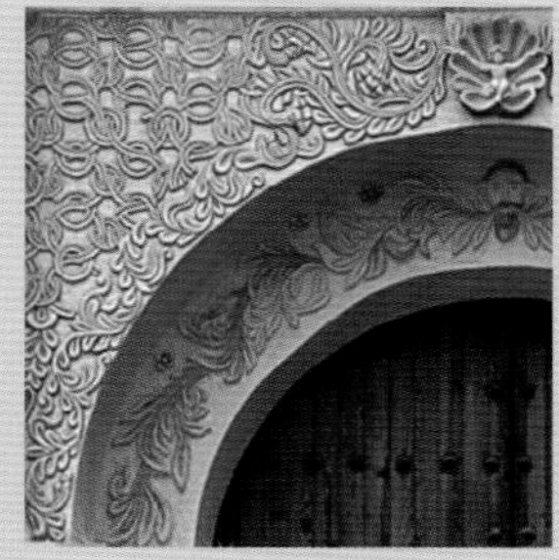
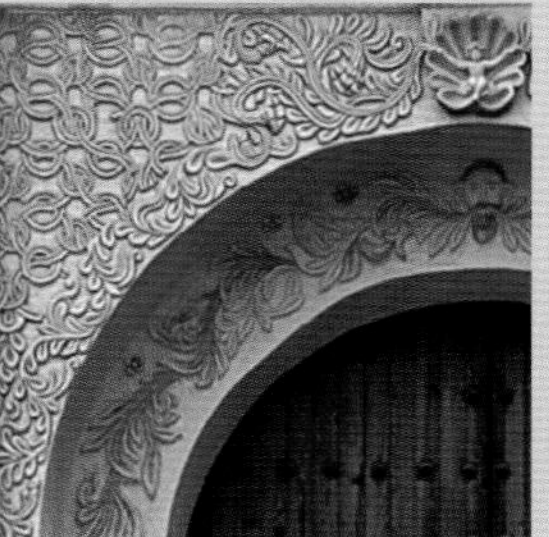

Links and vines
The spandrels over the door are edged with acanthus-like leaves and filled with sinuous vines and links. The frenetic twists recall the coils and rings of the Mayan snake god, replacing the head with a flamboyant foliate and floral motif. Around the inner arch, scrolling leafy branches issue from the mouth of a Christ face at the keystone, perhaps symbolising the 'tree of life'.

Foliate scrolls
The church façade is heavily decorated with a scrolling acanthus-like leaf pattern. Where two weaving scrolls meet, they mirror each other, creating a tight leafy trellis. On the right, a geometric zigzag or diamond pattern contrasts with the organic scrolls. The central motif of the double-headed eagle was the heraldic symbol of the Habsburg rulers of the Spanish Empire in the 16th and 17th centuries.

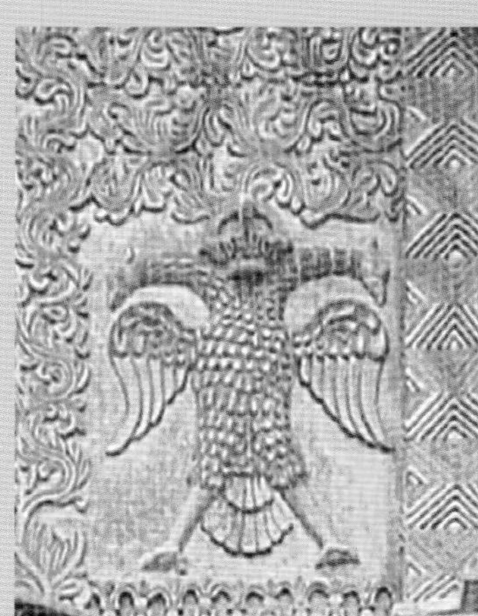

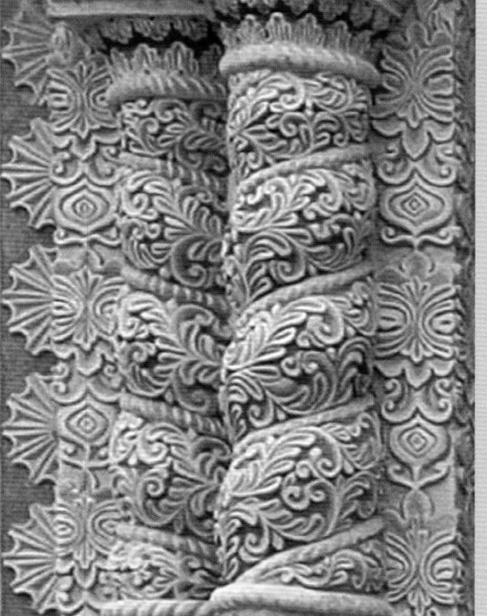

Twisting acanthus spirals
Acanthus leaves are rendered very differently from the classical or Renaissance forms on these twisted 'Solomonic' columns (also known as 'barley-sugar' or helical). Carved in rosy stucco – a mortar applied wet, which can be shaped into sculptural forms – the prominent characteristic is the raised snaking outline of the shapes. On the walls each side, the starburst and diamond shapes may be more reminiscent of Mayan sculpture than European Baroque.

Scrolls, rosettes and palmettes
On the frieze along the top tier of the church façade, curved enclosures formed by four scrolls contain rosettes. Between these shapes, elongated palmettes fill the triangular spaces. The scroll was an important motif of the Baroque in Europe, used both structurally to provide pseudo-buttresses, for example, for pediments, as ornamentation on exterior and interior walls, and as a key decorative element in furniture and interior design.

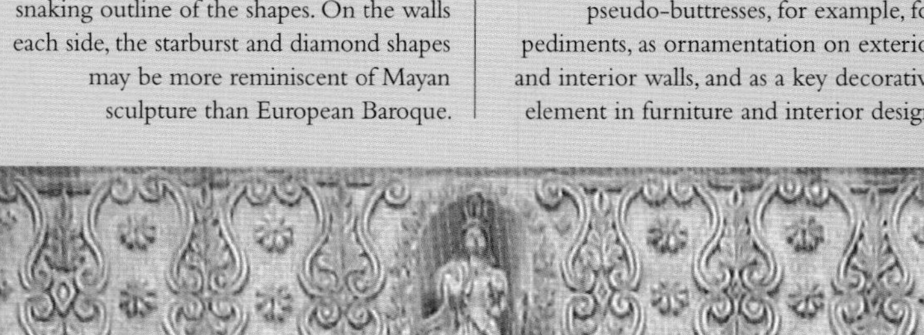

Templo de Santo Domingo, façade
San Cristobal de las Casas was founded in 1528 by the Spanish conquistadors as the new colonial capital of Chiapas province in southern Mexico. The Templo de Santo Domingo, possibly the city's most impressive church, was built in 1547 by the Dominicans, and the filigree stucco façade was added in the 17th century. The interior is equally spectacular, with gold and white stucco covering the walls and dome.

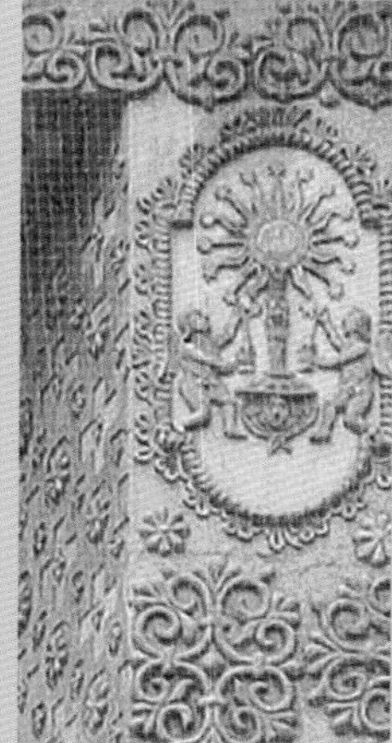

Crosses and stars
The window opening is decorated with crosses and rosettes, which contrast with the linked scroll motif on the neighbouring wall. The four-part design of scrolls and tri-leaf shapes is comparable to European quatropartite textile decorations of earlier centuries, given definition by the raised lines of the design. The central panel displays two *putti* with a sunburst monstrance (a stand for displaying the Eucharist), which rests on the figure of a cherub.

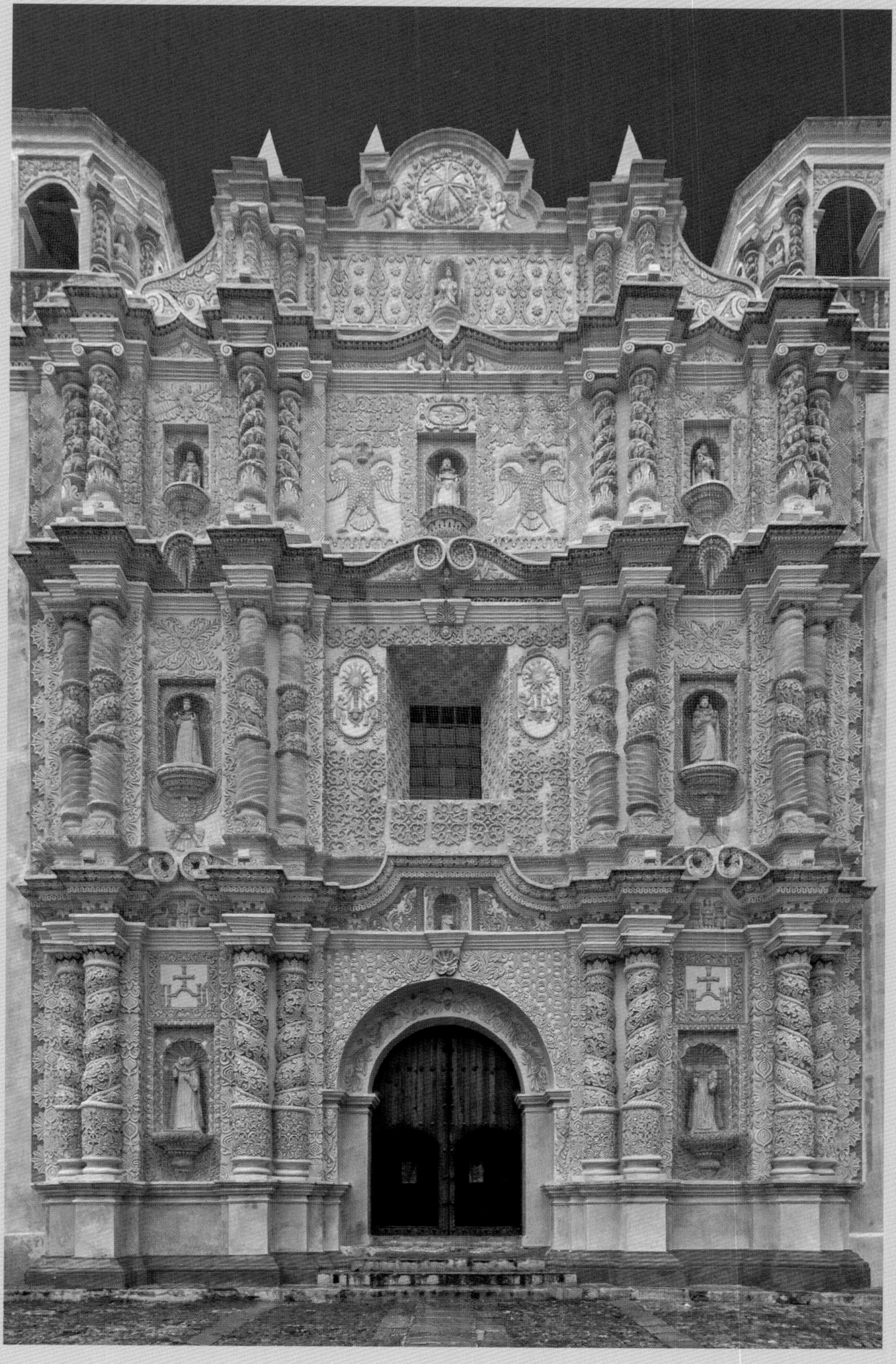

1700
1800

Eighteenth Century

Introduction

After the death of Louis XIV in 1715, French nobles freed from court obligations at Versailles built elegant town houses in Paris. Architects indulged their clients' individual tastes for more intimate decoration, removed from court classicism. French designers created a style inspired by Italian garden grottoes with shells and stones – the 'Rococo', from *rocaille* ('pebble') and *coquille* ('shell'). Decorators, dealers and collectors catered for demanding aristocratic tastes, designing comprehensive interior schemes that met their passionate desire for the new. Textiles of rich floral designs in silk were developed to create naturalistic representations. In France, Jean Revel played a key role in developing the new technique, which was then adopted by Anna Maria Garthwaite (1688–1763) for textiles manufactured at Spitalfields, London.

Japanese lacquer had been enthusiastically collected by European princes and aristocrats since the 17th century. By the 1750s, cabinetmakers in Paris could reshape lacquer panels for fashionable furniture. Dealers, for example François-Charles Darnault, traded in lacquerware, porcelain, clocks and gilt-bronzes, bringing in the expensive materials required by cabinetmakers such as Joseph Baumhauer. Chinese lacquerwork, silks, porcelain, screens, fans and painted silks and wallpaper increased wealthy European taste for private rooms and intimate settings. The demand for all things Chinese led European manufacturers to develop their own popular Chinoiserie designs.

Colourful Japanese *Arita-yaki* porcelain reinterpreted Chinese designs to attract European customers. In England, it was copied in soft-paste wares at the porcelain factory established in 1751 at Worcester.

The Rococo style informed wealthy taste throughout mainland Europe, becoming fashionable in Britain around 1730–70. Rooms with rounded corners had an organic appearance, the fanciful detail of their decorative wallpaper and their gilded marine-inspired ornament subtly illuminated by candlelight and casting soft shadows, with large wall-hung plate-glass mirrors infinitely reflecting the opulent scene.

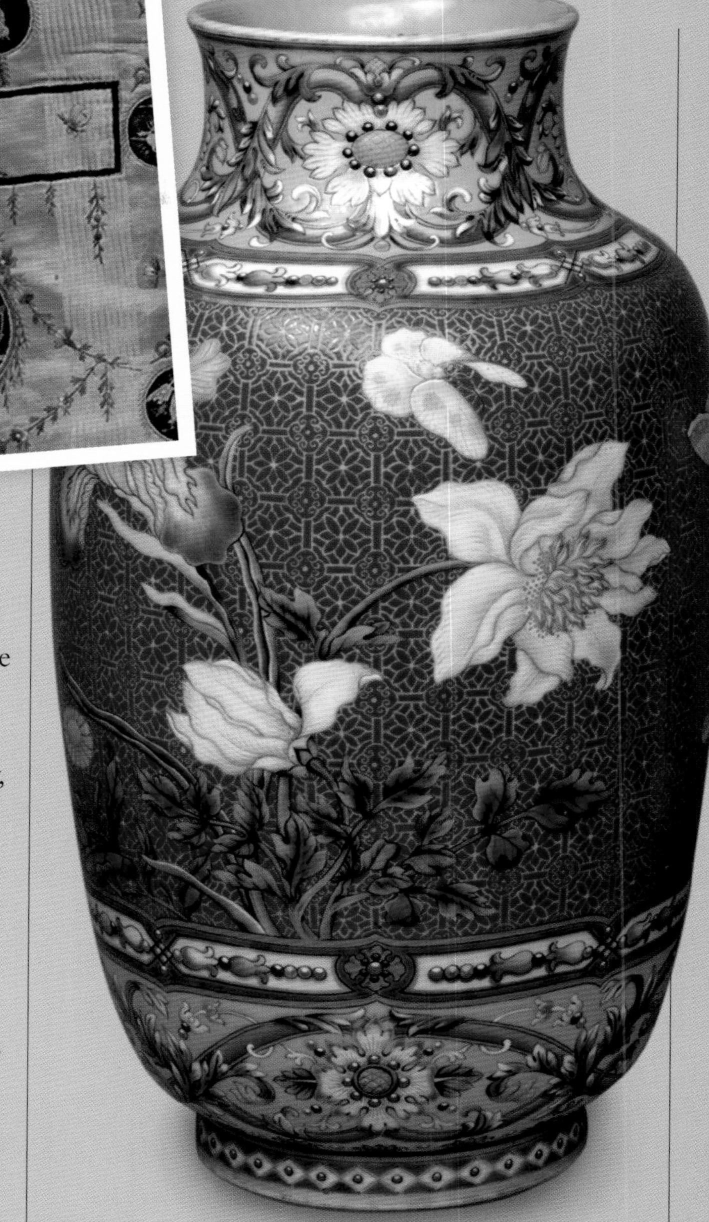

Aristocratic, literary and artistic individuals regarded fashionable clothing and interiors as essential to their social standing. In 1772 the famous actor David Garrick purchased a townhouse in the new Adelphi riverside development by the Thames, designed by the fashionable architects, Adam Brothers, and filled it with a new silver service and Chinoiserie furniture by Thomas Chippendale. Paper printed with textile and architectural patterns had been used to decorate walls in Britain since the 16th century, imitating more expensive wall coverings such as tapestry silks and velvets. Newly fashionable and more affordable paper sheets printed with picture frames, garlands and ornaments could be cut out and pasted on to walls.

The wall paintings at Herculaneum and Pompeii greatly influenced European artistic tastes and provided an entirely new source of motifs to inspire architects and designers. Wealthy Grand Tourists travelled to Italy to see the masterpieces of the ancient world and artists such as Giovanni Battista Piranesi met the demand for mementoes with atmospheric views and imaginary restored vases and candelabra with opulent classical motifs. The painted 'grotesque' style, termed 'arabesque' by the French, derived from ancient Roman grottoes and named after Italian *grotteschi*, comprised vertically aligned medallions and rectangular panels surrounded by scrollwork and classical motifs.

The Enlightenment concepts of liberation, sensation and individualism were also expressed in styles of clothing. Smaller rooms in townhouses and apartments were furnished with comfortable seating, encouraging informality of dress. In Europe in the 1780s wealthy fashionable men and women wore more comfortable styles, influenced by English sporting dress and a pastoral fantasy of rural living and classically derived patterns and motifs.

The Three Emperors of the Qing dynasty (1644–1911) took artistic forms to new heights of refinement and elaboration. Technical, aesthetic and artistic advances brought sophisticated designs and naturalistic styles into ceramic decoration, while skilled artisans were employed by the emperor in court workshops within the Forbidden City.

Fantasy Compositions 1740–1766

Rococo patterns

The vivacious fantasies of Rococo patterns expressed a culture of aristocratic taste independent of royal influence. Shells and flowers, and hybrid forms, were painted and woven in softer colours. They were carved in subtly moulded forms in relief to catch the rippling effects of light from candle sconces, reflected in large wall mirrors. Chinese-style flower forms and animal heads were incorporated into new eclectic fantasies that blended the worlds of nature and mythology in fine and inventive detail. The first original system of ornament for interiors, Rococo design comprised imaginative interpretations of Chinese, Turkish and Indian style, classical figures and highly elaborate scrollwork.

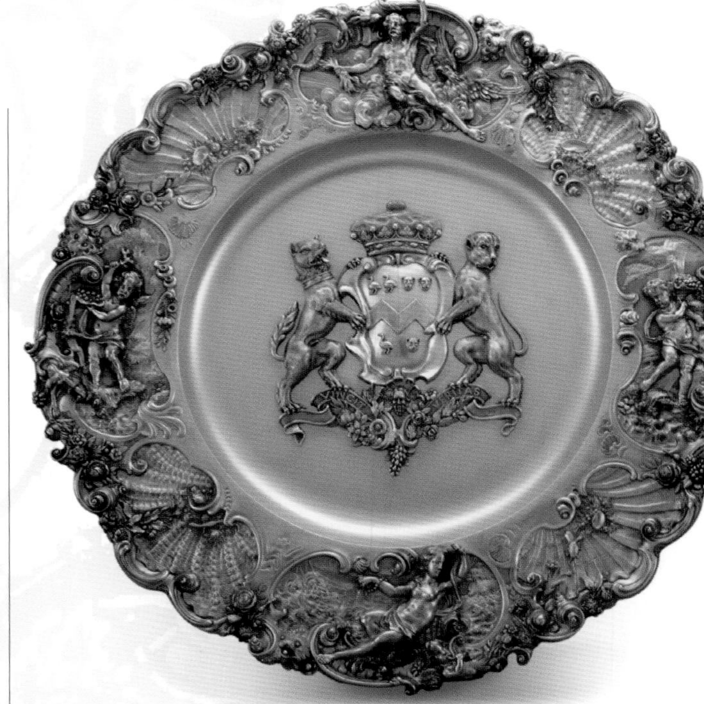

Dish, 1742–43, *London, England*
The border of this silver dish is carved in high relief with mythological figures alternating with scallop-shell motifs. Jupiter above, Amphitryte below and a *putto* on each side are divided by scallop shells containing smaller shells, seaweed and pearls. The scallop shells are edged with curling scrolls, floral garlands and lion masks. Shells and leaves in low relief delicately fill the spaces between. The dish was made by the celebrated French silversmith Paul de Lamarie for the Sixth Earl of Mountrath, a patron who allowed him to express his creativity to fashionable extremes.

ELEMENTS OF PATTERN

- *curving scroll-ended forms*
- *hybrids of shells, flowers and leaves*
- *naturalistic florals*
- *twisting ribbons*
- *pastel colours*
- *backgrounds of shapes with fine lines*
- *contrasting high and low relief*

Furnishing flounce, c. 1740, *Brussels, Belgium*
This bobbin lace in linen thread has been worked with a pattern of alternating motifs – a fantastical vase of composite shell forms containing flowers, leaves and seedheads inspired by marine forms, and flower-shells arranged with seaweed-like leaves. The fine mesh background complements the segmented and dotted forms of the curves and double-curves inspired by crustaceans, sea-molluscs and ammonites.

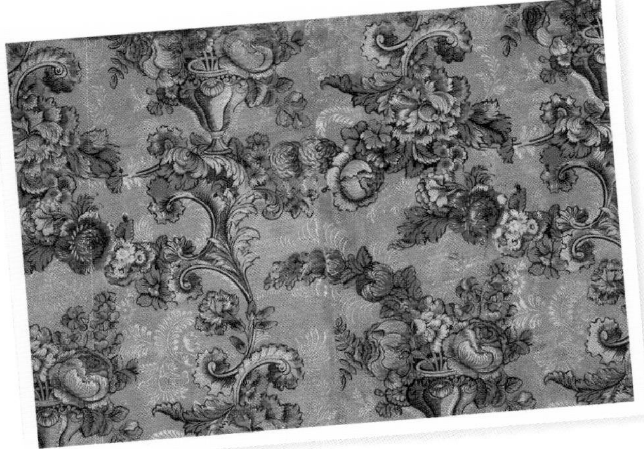

‘With the decors representing/reflecting the people who inhabited them ... mirrors were often placed so as to reflect people in the room ... reflections of reflections.’

MELISSA LEE HYDE AND FRANCOIS BOUCHER, *Making Up the Rococo*, 2006

Wallpaper, c. 1755–60, *England*
Patterned with regularly spaced fruit-shaped vases of full-blown flowers, this wallpaper has been printed with woodblock designs and stencils to emulate silk damask textiles. Curling hybrid leaf-shell elements link the vases with garlands of flowers, including roses, anemones, carnations and chrysanthemums, against a background of lace-like florals, leaves and shells. The wallpaper was hung in a house in the High Street, Brentford, Middlesex.

Commode, 1755–58, *Paris, France*
Gilt-bronze mounts framing the Far Eastern landscape scenes on the panels of this commode comprise sinuous vegetal lines sprouting flowers and leaves that curl over each other in high relief. The commode was made by master-cabinetmaker Joseph Baumhauer. The admiration for natural forms is emphasised by the natural patterning of the lid of French marble. This oak commode is veneered with fruitwood finished with *hiramakie* (low relief) and *takamakie* (high relief) Japanese lacquer and ‘vernis Martin’, a varnish created to imitate the lacquer of furniture imported from the Far East.

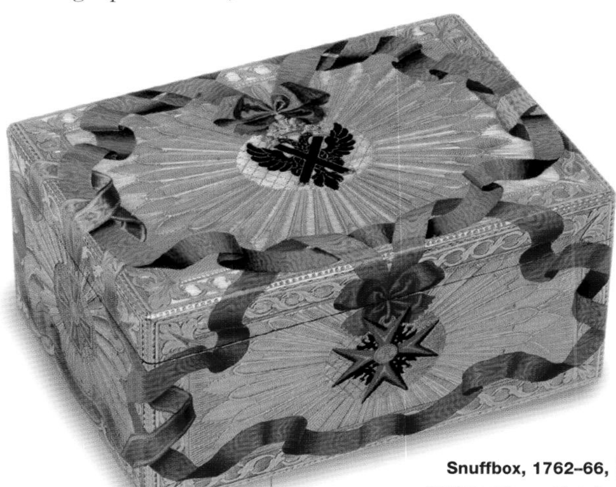

Snuffbox, 1762–66, *St Petersburg, Russia*
This gold snuffbox is engraved on each side with an enamelled medal hung from a twisted ribbon, each interlocked with those on the adjacent sides of the box. The background is engraved with a sunburst, framed by a double-strand leaf interlace border. The snuffbox was made by Jean-Pierre Ador, the noted Swiss craftsman who emigrated to Russia in 1760, for Baron Nicolaus von Korff (1710–66), a distinguished soldier and official. The medals represent the five chivalric orders received by the baron.

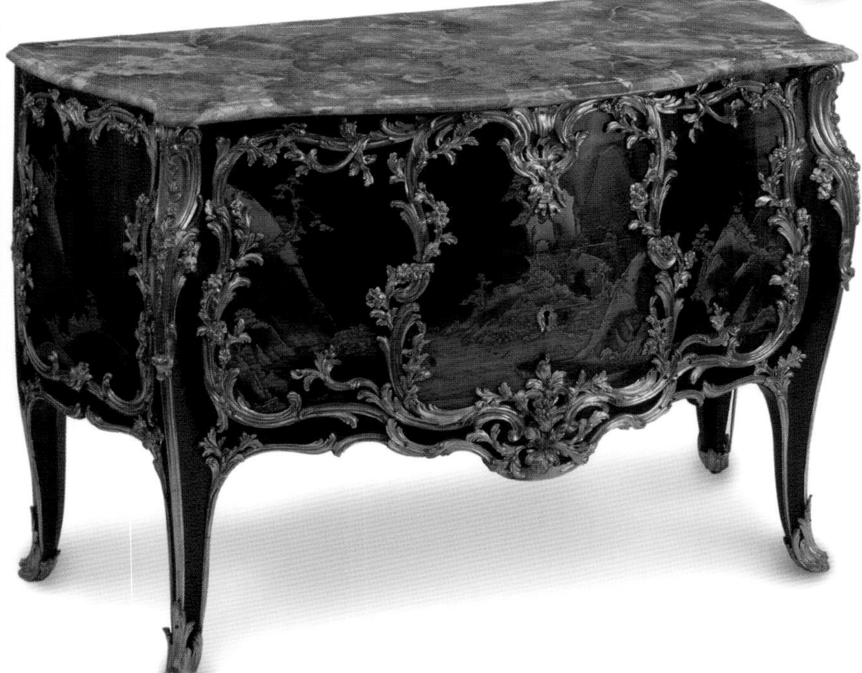

Jean Revel
1684–1751

In the first half of the 18th century in France, silk brocade manufacturing was a thriving industry producing extravagant silver- and gold-patterned fabrics both for the court and for export. Lyons was an expanding centre of silk textile production with all the associated weavers, designers, suppliers, merchants and entrepreneurs. Accounts of major figures in Lyonnais history written later in the century, including *The Designers for the Manufacture of Gold, Silver and Silk Cloth* (1765) by N. Joubert de l'Hiberderie, describe Jean Revel as a key figure in the development of silk design throughout the early 18th century. In particular, he is credited with introducing the technique for creating naturalistic designs with three-dimensional shading and relief effects, called *points rentrés*, in the 1730s. This technique dovetailed colours together to integrate the tones more naturally to create subtle shading, possibly inspired by tapestry work. The increasing demand for sophisticated naturalistic floral and figurative designs in textiles contributed to the growing status of the Lyonnais silk industry and to a successful career for Revel.

‘His triumph ... lay in his ability to analyse and involve himself in a product which depended upon its appearance for its appeal.’

LESLEY ELLIS MILLER, ‘Jean Revel: Silk Designer, Fine Artist or Entrepreneur?’ IN *Journal of Design History,* 1995

Born
Paris, France, 1684

Profession
Silk and textile merchant, businessman and designer

Manifesto
Paintings in silk

The role that Revel played in the development of this new technique, which was effectively a stylistic change – a new way to organise warp and weft threads rather than a technological advance – has recently been explored in archival sources in Lyons and Paris. He was the son of the painter Gabriel

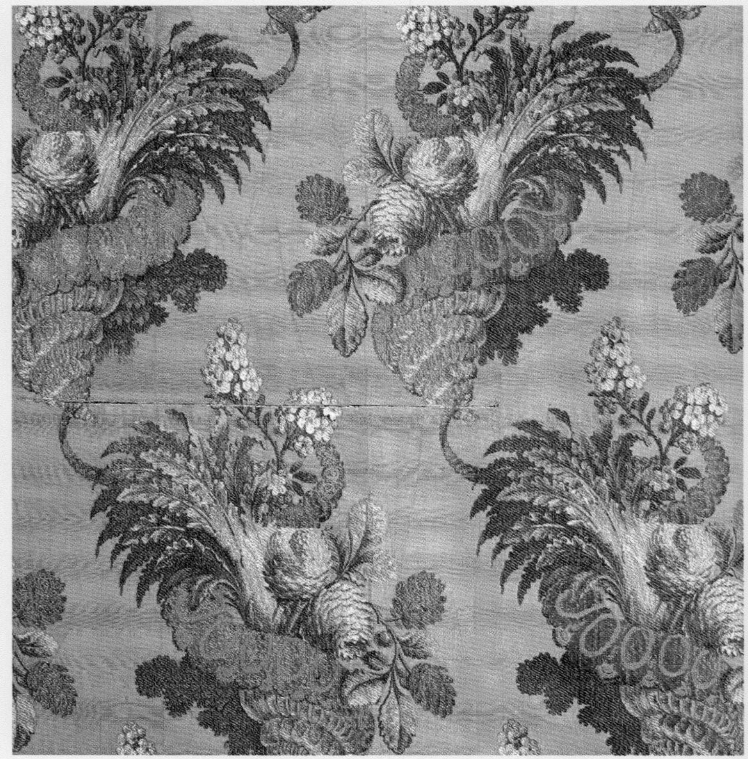

Brocaded silk textile, 1735–40, *Lyons (?), France*
The new way of arranging the different colours of silk thread meant that shadows and tones created shape and volume in this opulent horn of plenty.

Revel (1643–1712) and, although he may have had artistic training, there is no evidence he was a textile designer as such. He moved to Lyons in 1710 where he worked initially as a barrister but was soon closely involved in the silk industry. His business interests included the production of metallic – using real silver and gold – and silk thread. Some paper designs survive marked with his name, such as a leafy tree with forest flowers that illustrates the visual impact of the rich shading.

Designs had developed from the simple stylised two-dimensional floral patterns that predominated in the 17th century to become complex naturalistic, sometimes fantastical, motifs. Abundant floral cornucopia, luxuriant swags, wreaths and scrolls were popular but the new technique also allowed for more figurative creations. These were a response to the demand for the curved shell surfaces of Rococo motifs (see pages 166–7) and the pictorial and architectural details of Chinoiserie designs (see pages 174–5). Set against plain silk backgrounds, the large bold motifs appear to be raised above the surface. The introduction of areas of subtly coloured silk threads imitated flowers and fruits while brighter colours presented rich combinations of exotic flowers and fantasy landscapes.

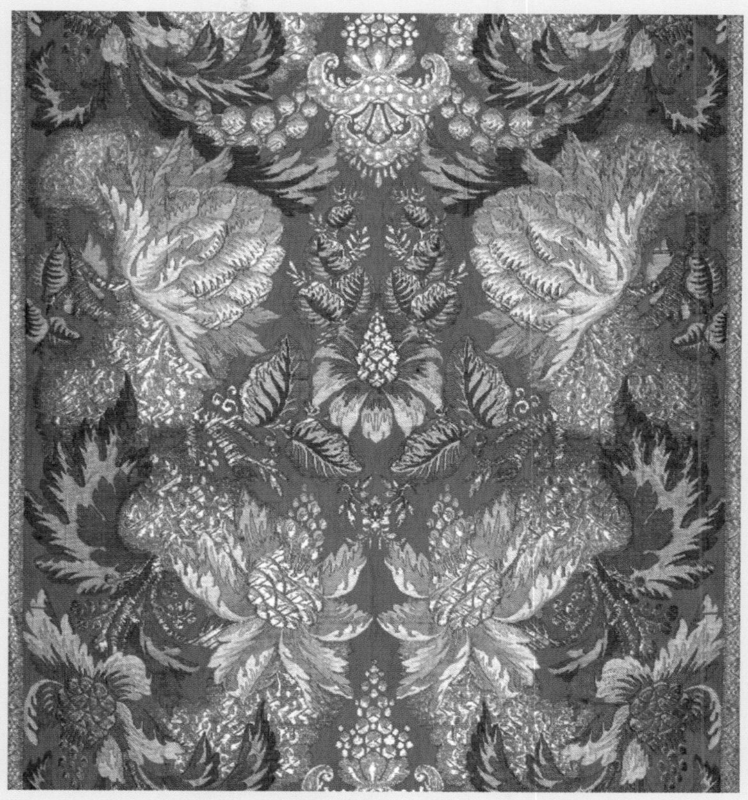

Jean Revel's role in the development of *points rentrés* may have been as an entrepreneur who saw its potential. He came from a family of painters and it seems feasible that he was a skilful draughtsman who could have developed the idea for more naturalistic representations. The dowries of his daughters and his will show that he was an extremely successful and wealthy businessman who had exploited the new style of brocade to make his name in the history of textile design.

Brocaded silk textile, 1730–35, *Lyon (?), France*
The richness of the fabric is accentuated with subtle colours and highlights of silver thread, the production of such extravagant fabrics contributed to Jean Revel's business success.

Patterns for Patriotism
1700–1800

Spanish taste

After years of war, the revival of Spain's prestige and economy under the enlightened policies of the Bourbon kings Charles II and Charles IV produced a new merchant class that equated profit with patriotism. Catholic identity was integrated with allegiance to the Spanish Crown and the purchase of fashionable luxury goods such as lace and leather gloves was promoted as beneficial to Spain. Potters from the Talavera de la Reina area made blue-and-white ceramics patterned with spiralling foliage and motifs, influenced by designs on Chinese wares imported by the Dutch and acquired by the Spanish royal court. Designs produced in Spain for ceramics and leather comprised patterns made up of motifs from naturalistic plants and animals, classical mythology, the popular plays and contemporary rural life.

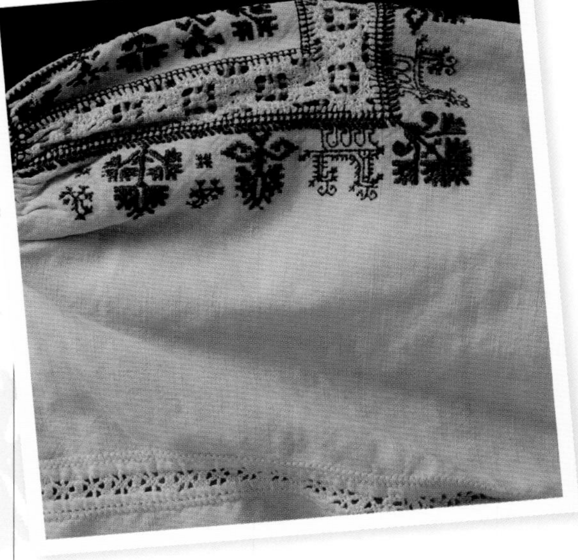

Blouse, 18th century, *Murcia, Spain*
This child's linen blouse is embroidered with patterns in silk thread in imitation of lace. Over the shoulders, a panel of black floral and leaf motifs is bordered by an openwork pattern of squares and dots formed by linen threads drawn together with brown and white silk. Symmetrical floral motifs alternating with stylised quadrupeds or small sprigs and flowers edge the border. Delicate openwork flowerheads pattern the linen inserts at the seams.

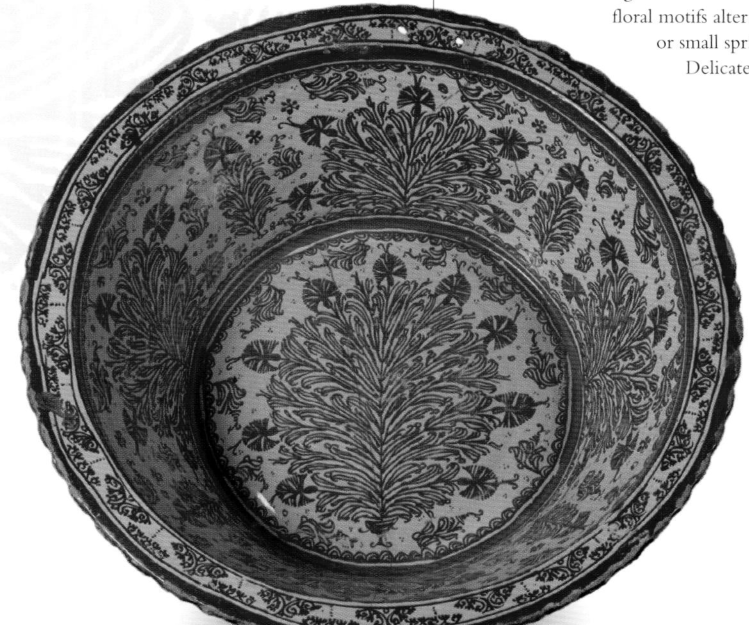

Bowl (*bazzeño*), c. 1700–50, *Manises, Spain*
The base of this tin-glazed earthenware bowl is decorated with a spray of lilies with fan-shaped flowers contained in a small pedestal vase, with a background of small dots and a scalloped border from which wave leafy buds. The sides of the bowl are patterned with the same motifs, larger lily sprays alternating with smaller, against a background of leafy buds, small flowerheads, rings and dots. The rim is patterned with scrolling plant motifs alternately on dotted stems.

ELEMENTS OF PATTERN

- *floral plants and their parts*
- *human figures, birds and flowers*
- *curling acanthus leaves*
- *Chinese-style growing plants*

Dish, 1782, *Talavera de la Reina or Puente del Arzobispo, Spain*
This dish of tin-glazed earthenware is painted with an exotic flower-and-bud motif with fern-like leaves in a Chinese style, surrounded by small stylised flowerheads and sprouting leaves. The yellow band is patterned with an undulating tendril with a small stylised leaf in each curve.

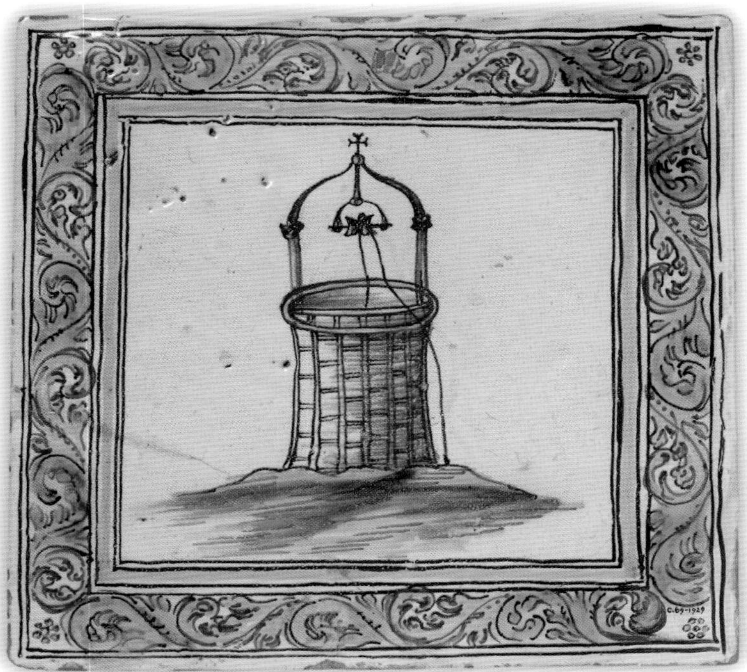

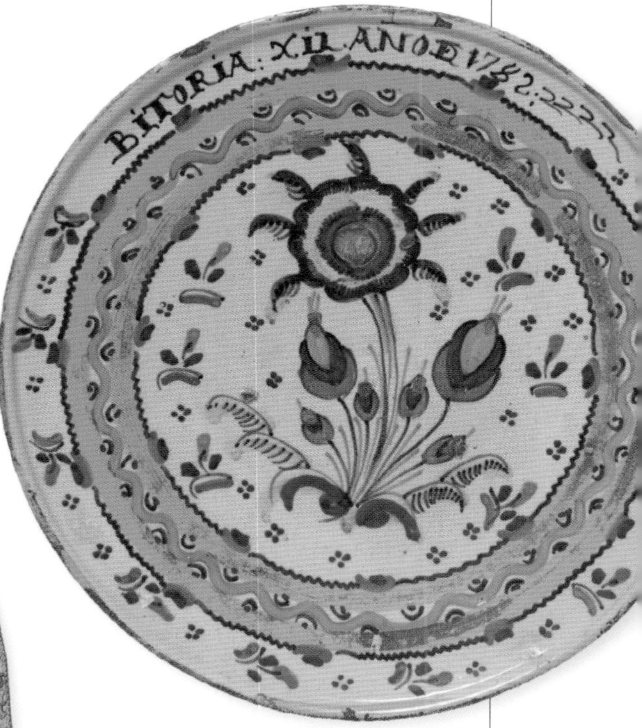

Tile, 18th century, *Talavera de la Reina, Spain*
Painted with the design of a well, this tin-glazed earthenware tile has been framed with a pattern of running acanthus scrolls. The leaves are differentiated by alternating colours and opposite directions of curl. The pattern is articulated at each corner by a small stylised flowerhead.

'By the 1780s, the expansion of the Spanish calico industry and other state-sponsored measures had given those arguing the virtues of fashion and luxury the upper hand.'

ULRICH L. LEHNER AND MICHAEL O'NEILL PRINTY, *A Companion to the Catholic Enlightenment in Europe*, 2010

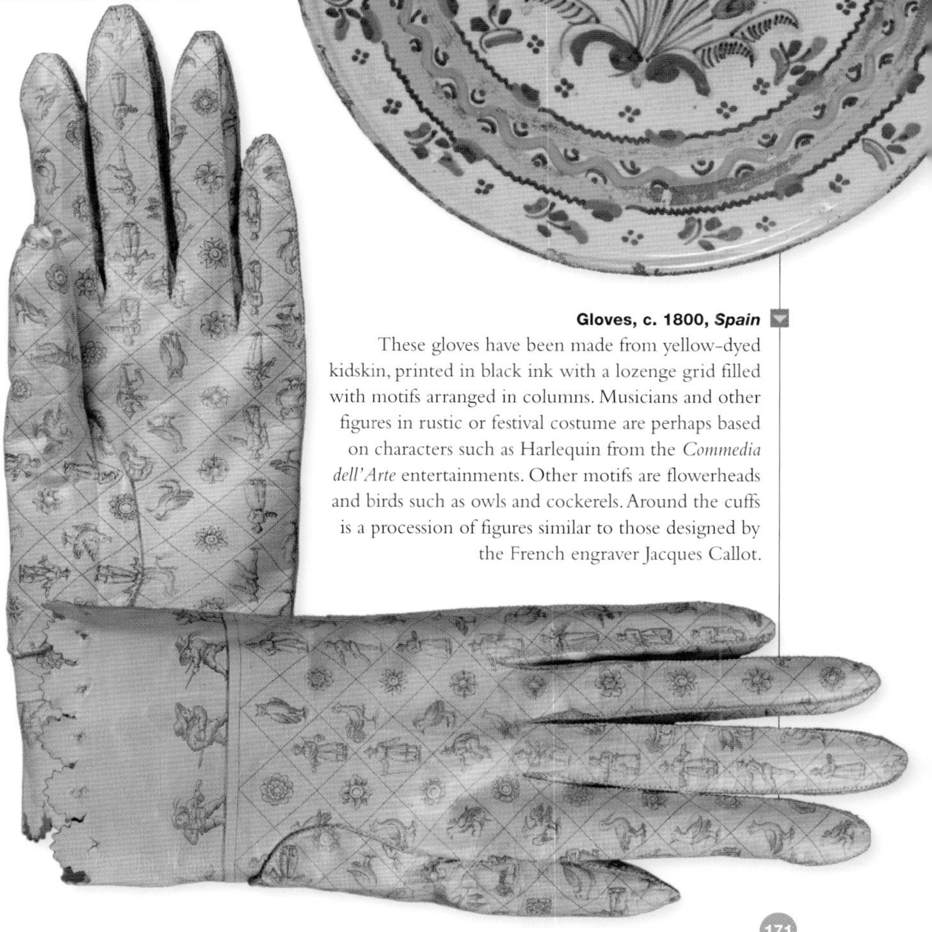

Gloves, c. 1800, *Spain*
These gloves have been made from yellow-dyed kidskin, printed in black ink with a lozenge grid filled with motifs arranged in columns. Musicians and other figures in rustic or festival costume are perhaps based on characters such as Harlequin from the *Commedia dell'Arte* entertainments. Other motifs are flowerheads and birds such as owls and cockerels. Around the cuffs is a procession of figures similar to those designed by the French engraver Jacques Callot.

Compositions of Refinement 1662–1795

Artistic achievements of the Three Qing Emperors in China

Three reigns of the Manchu Qing dynasty – Kangxi (1662–1722), Yongzheng (1722–35) and Qianlong (1736–95) – instigated exceptional artistic innovation through the personal patronage of the emperor. Each brought his own special interests to bear, especially in porcelain design where technical, aesthetic and artistic refinement led to unprecedented advances. Economic and political power brought wealth to the imperial court in the Forbidden City, Beijing, with its manifestations of dominance, state ceremony and temple ritual. Refined decoration was apparent everywhere – *objets d'art* carved in rich and exotic materials, woven silk court robes, bronze religious objects, ritual porcelain vessels and lacquer furnishings. Patterns followed traditional forms, such as dragons, clouds, scrolling and symbolic flowers, but technical and aesthetic elaborations deepened and extended the styles of representation.

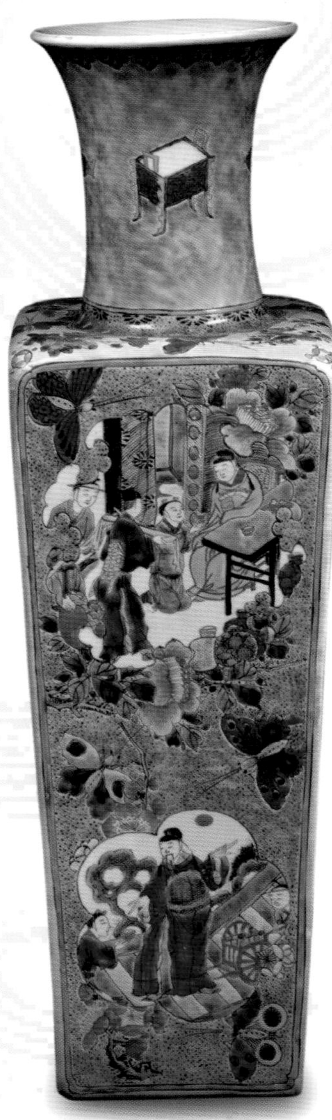

Painted porcelain vase, Kangxi period, 1662–1722, *Jingdezhen*
Scrolling and floral bands edge the rim and neck of this vase. The main motifs of soft orange cherry blossoms and blue butterflies that decorate the pale yellow shoulders are repeated and interspersed through the domestic scene on the body. The mottled and dotted pale green background of the *famille verte* palette is painted with overglaze enamels and gilding to create a vibrant coordinated design.

Enamel and gilt porcelain vase, Yongzheng period, 1722–35, *Jingdezhen*
This exaggerated design reflects technical and aesthetic developments. Enamel pigments painted on to glazed fired porcelain were fused to the surface during additional firings, the latter stages often taking place in the Forbidden City where the emperor oversaw innovations. Curves and corners are patterned with bold floral scrolls and birds in orange, blue and green on pale yellow, and a Buddhist wheel and Ming vase fill the side panels.

ELEMENTS OF PATTERN

- *floral and foliage scrolls and motifs*
- *butterflies*
- *Buddhist symbolic wheel*
- *patterned backgrounds*
- *clouds and dramatic dragons*

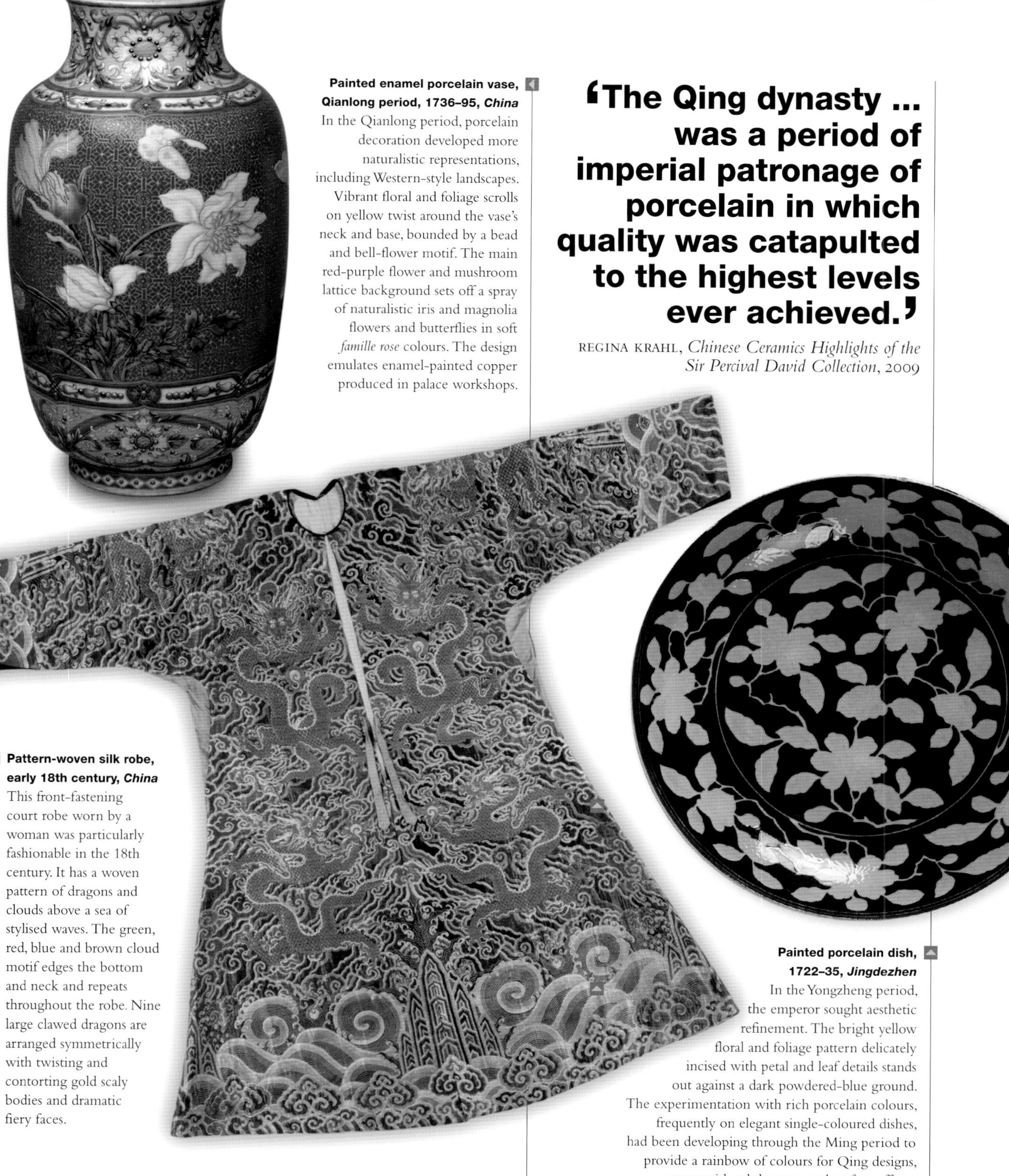

Painted enamel porcelain vase, Qianlong period, 1736–95, *China*
In the Qianlong period, porcelain decoration developed more naturalistic representations, including Western-style landscapes. Vibrant floral and foliage scrolls on yellow twist around the vase's neck and base, bounded by a bead and bell-flower motif. The main red-purple flower and mushroom lattice background sets off a spray of naturalistic iris and magnolia flowers and butterflies in soft *famille rose* colours. The design emulates enamel-painted copper produced in palace workshops.

'The Qing dynasty ... was a period of imperial patronage of porcelain in which quality was catapulted to the highest levels ever achieved.'

REGINA KRAHL, *Chinese Ceramics Highlights of the Sir Percival David Collection*, 2009

Pattern-woven silk robe, early 18th century, *China*
This front-fastening court robe worn by a woman was particularly fashionable in the 18th century. It has a woven pattern of dragons and clouds above a sea of stylised waves. The green, red, blue and brown cloud motif edges the bottom and neck and repeats throughout the robe. Nine large clawed dragons are arranged symmetrically with twisting and contorting gold scaly bodies and dramatic fiery faces.

Painted porcelain dish, 1722–35, *Jingdezhen*
In the Yongzheng period, the emperor sought aesthetic refinement. The bright yellow floral and foliage pattern delicately incised with petal and leaf details stands out against a dark powdered-blue ground. The experimentation with rich porcelain colours, frequently on elegant single-coloured dishes, had been developing through the Ming period to provide a rainbow of colours for Qing designs, some with subtle tones and surface effects.

Chinoiserie
1725–1778

European fascination with Chinese patterns and designs

Long before Marco Polo's *Travels*, published in the early 14th century, western Europeans had been fascinated by the distant land of Cathay – the old name for China. Silks had been imported since Roman times but, by the late 17th century, the passion for all things Chinese – porcelain, lacquer, silks and tea – was fuelled by accounts and images brought back by travellers and merchants. Imports from China were still expensive in the 18th century so European manufacturers met this new demand with their own designs of exotic and fantastical views and patterns drawn from prints and an imagined Chinese world – a style known as Chinoiserie.

'True Chinoiseries are not pallid or incomplete imitations of Chinese objects. They are tangible and solid realizations of a land of the imagination.'

DAWN JACOBSON, *Chinoiserie*, 1993

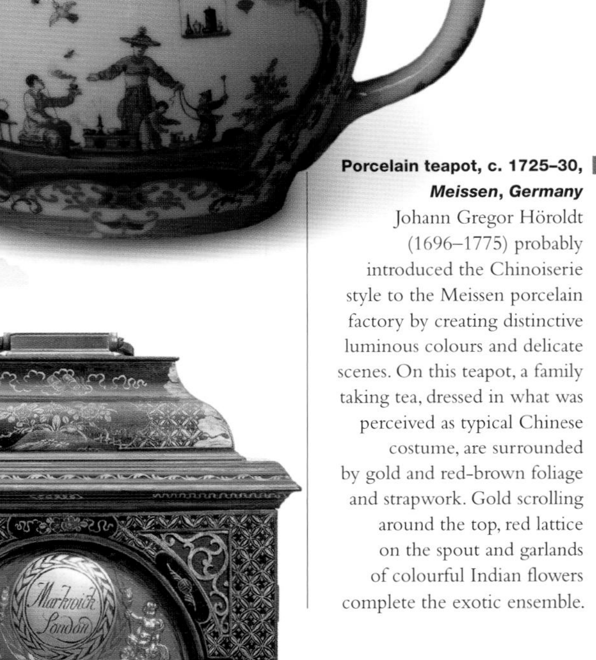

Porcelain teapot, c. 1725–30, *Meissen, Germany*
Johann Gregor Höroldt (1696–1775) probably introduced the Chinoiserie style to the Meissen porcelain factory by creating distinctive luminous colours and delicate scenes. On this teapot, a family taking tea, dressed in what was perceived as typical Chinese costume, are surrounded by gold and red-brown foliage and strapwork. Gold scrolling around the top, red lattice on the spout and garlands of colourful Indian flowers complete the exotic ensemble.

Bracket clock, c. 1730, James Markwick (the Younger), *London*
This clock has several motifs that were typical of Chinoiserie. Cloud-bands – distinctive rippling ribbons – decorate the top and base; and the flowers, and rocks and dragonfly motifs run up the sides. By contrast, the cherubs, brass scrollwork and gold diaper pattern on the case are European motifs. English clocks such as this were traded with Turkey and Spain throughout the first half of the 18th century.

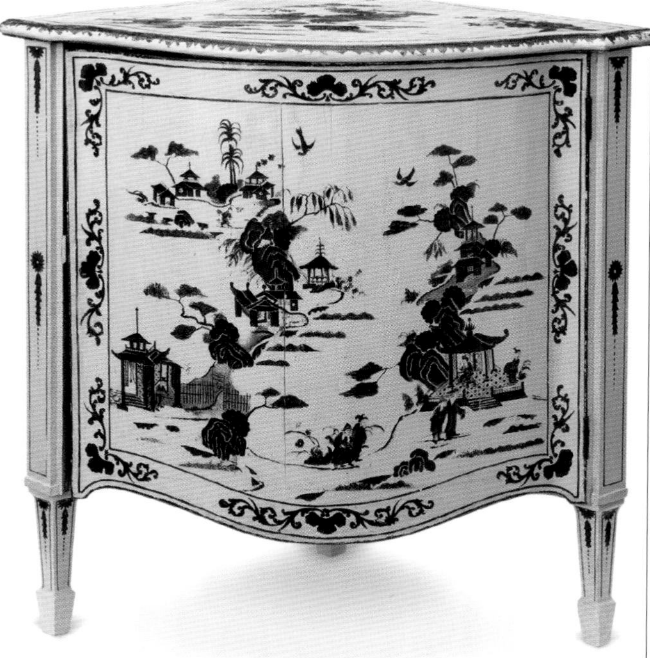

Painted cupboard, 1768–78, *London, England*
The central scene of this bow-fronted corner cabinet is a typical Chinoiserie subject, including pagodas, Chinese bridges, bamboo and other exotic trees, rocks and birds linked in landscape motifs. The border pattern is an adaptation of Chinese ribbon and cloud motifs. The cabinet was supplied by Thomas Chippendale (1718–79) as part of the furniture for the Hampton villa of his friend, the renowned actor David Garrick (1717–79).

ELEMENTS OF PATTERN

- *imaginary Chinese motifs*
- *Chinese pagodas, costumes and flowers*
- *scrolling, ribbons and clouds*
- *exotic trees and rock landscapes*
- *delicate Eastern flowers and foliage*

Mahogany carved settee, c. 1760–70, *England*
This settee's back is carved with an open fretwork Chinoiserie design of pagodas with characteristic wide fans or bell-like roofs, scrolls, and diagonal cross forms on the low screening at the base. 'C' scrolls form the leg brackets, echoing the lattice design on the back, and open fretwork struts span the legs. Initially associated with Thomas Chippendale, Chinoiserie designs were developed by a great many furniture manufacturers in 18th-century England.

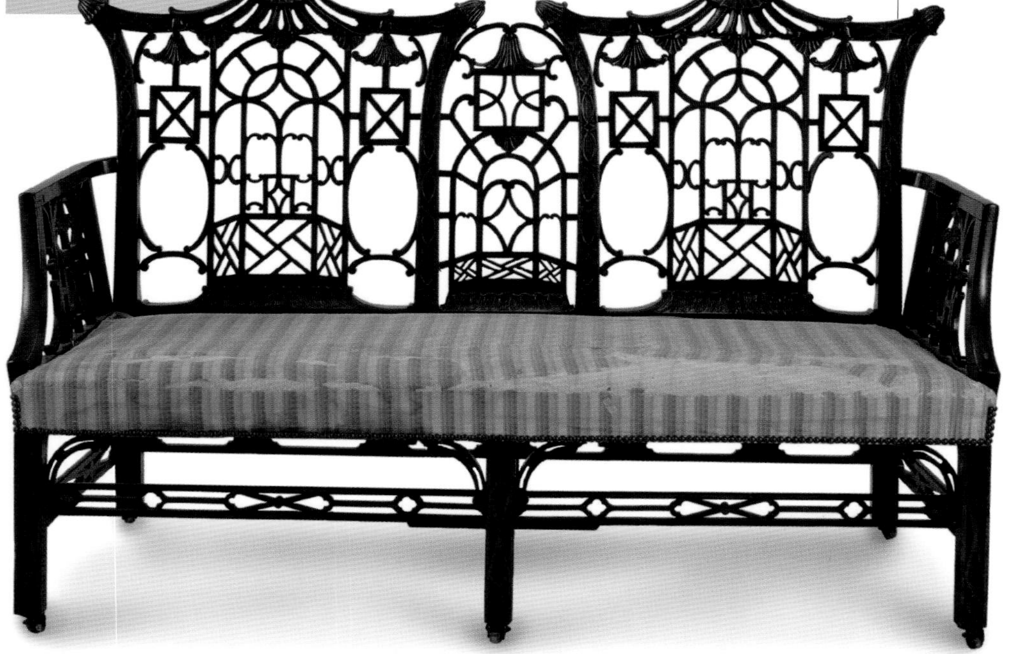

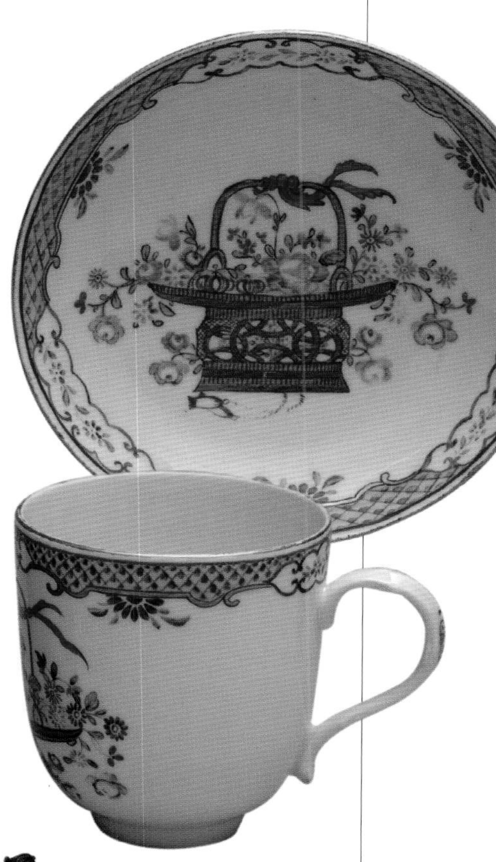

Cup and saucer, c. 1775, *England*
A Chinoiserie basket with roses and lilies edged with pink and gold diaper, scrolls and delicate floral sprigs decorates the cup and saucer in *famille rose* style. This was a popular style – in Chinese, *fencai* or *ruancai* meaning 'soft colours', mainly pinks and purples – decorated with overglaze enamels that allowed delicate patterning and design. European porcelain factories including Delft, Meissen, Sèvres, Worcester, Chelsea and Bristol emulated *famille rose*.

PATTERN IN DETAIL

Courtly Florals 1740–1745

Court costume

Aristocracy invited to the royal courts of England and France dressed exclusively for the occasion. Women wore a heavy silk costume with a *pannier* ('hooped') skirt extending up to 2 m (6 ft) wide and requiring the wearer to walk sideways through doorways. Versailles courtiers were carried up staircases in sedan chairs. The skirt displayed the elaborate patterning of silk textiles and emphasised the two-dimensional effect of the costume.

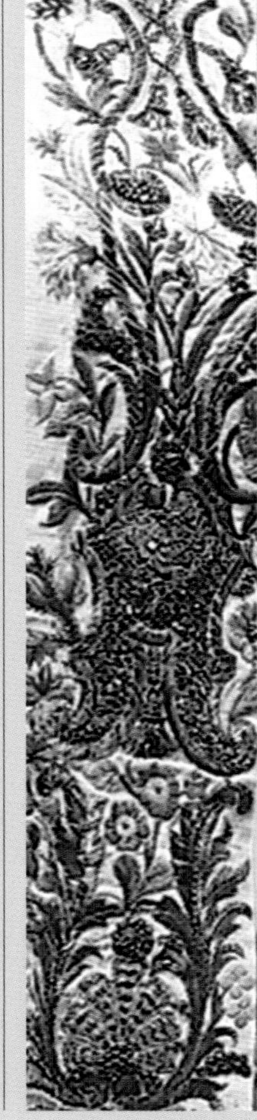

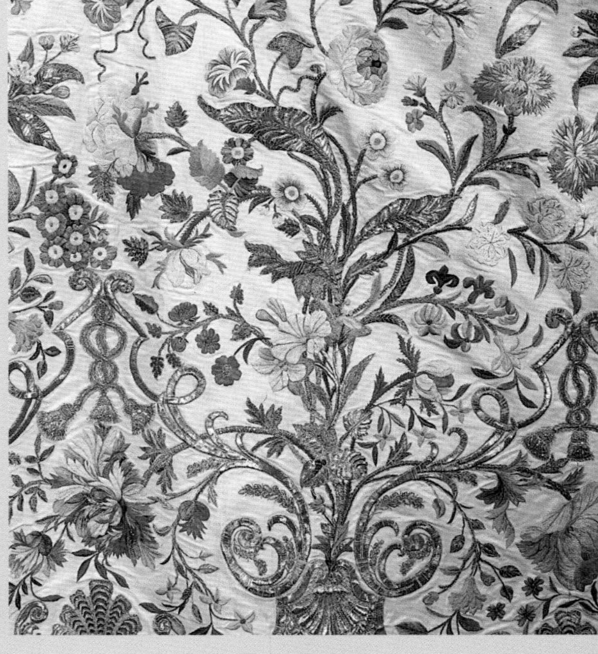

Bodice front

The prominent silver motifs on the skirt hem of shells, leaves, scale-patterned shapes, strapwork and tassels have been reworked into a vertical pattern for the fronts of the bodice. Smaller sprays of multi-coloured flowers and green and silver leaves are also incorporated into the bodice design.

Flower sprays

Scrolling leafy stems curl away from each pair and transform into looping and angled strapwork, ending in a curl above tassels. Large sprays of naturalistic flowers stemming from the scaled motifs at the hem include jasmine, morning glory, honeysuckle, peonies, roses, poppies, anemones, auriculas, hyacinths, carnations and cornflowers. The stems are embroidered in silver thread and the leaves in green or silver. The silver leaves, which have been padded to different thicknesses, endow the overall pattern with a rippling light, adding to the subtle sheen of the white silk background.

Marine elements

Ribbed scallop shells between curling seeded fern leaves alternate with composite motifs of fan-shells with pairs of curving shapes patterned with scales or lozenges. The bases of the shells have been thickly padded to make them appear more prominent.

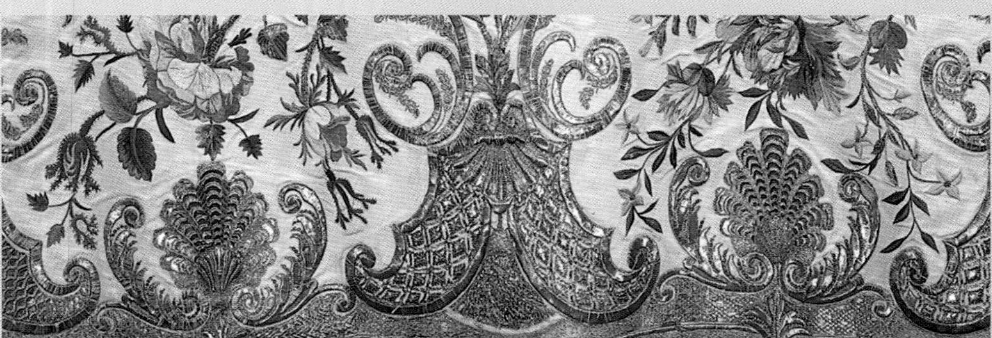

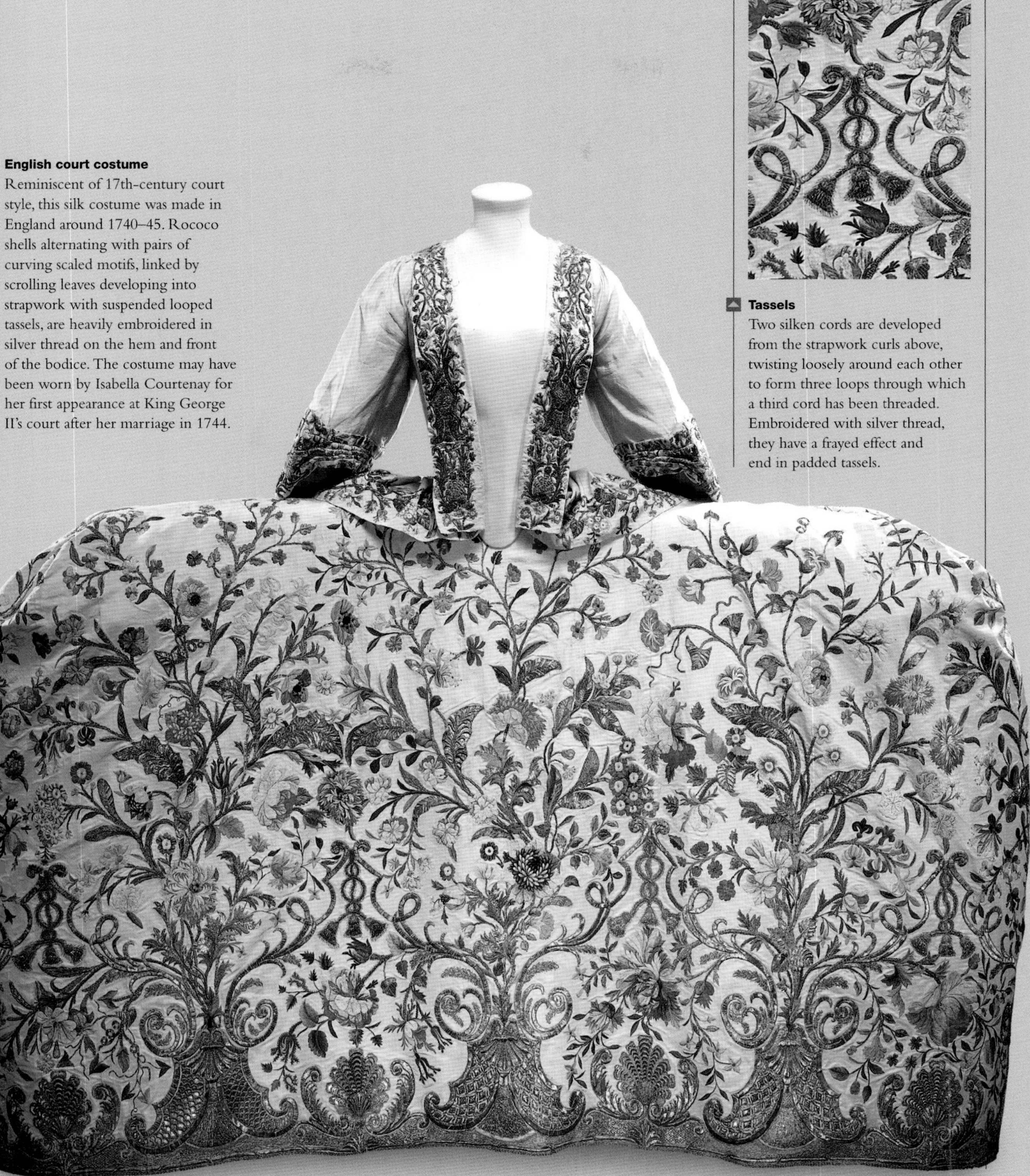

English court costume
Reminiscent of 17th-century court style, this silk costume was made in England around 1740–45. Rococo shells alternating with pairs of curving scaled motifs, linked by scrolling leaves developing into strapwork with suspended looped tassels, are heavily embroidered in silver thread on the hem and front of the bodice. The costume may have been worn by Isabella Courtenay for her first appearance at King George II's court after her marriage in 1744.

Tassels
Two silken cords are developed from the strapwork curls above, twisting loosely around each other to form three loops through which a third cord has been threaded. Embroidered with silver thread, they have a frayed effect and end in padded tassels.

Georgian Antiquarianism
1760–1792

Georgian design

Fashions of Georgian taste changed through early Roman 'Palladian' style, the 'Gothick' English version of the French Rococo and a renewed interest in Chinese style, to a neoclassicism inspired by the art of Classical Greece and Rome. This eclectic elegance was expressed through pattern designs for the new wallpapers, furnishing textiles, porcelain and silverware, and in high-fashion garments embroidered in silk with ribbons, medallions, garlands and naturalistic wild flowers. The increasing fashion for private and intimate rooms and collections of antiques encouraged new individual taste in designing schemes of patterns for all aspects of interiors for the wealthy client.

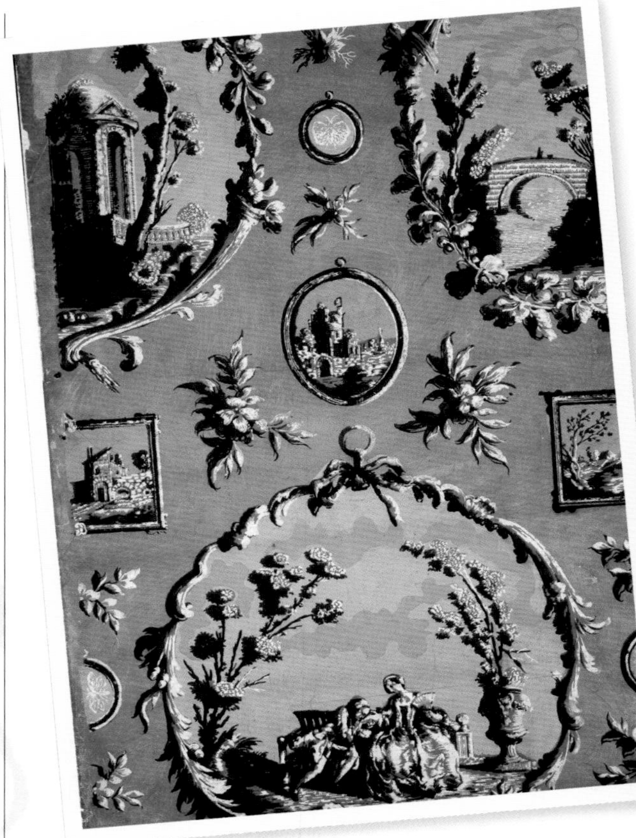

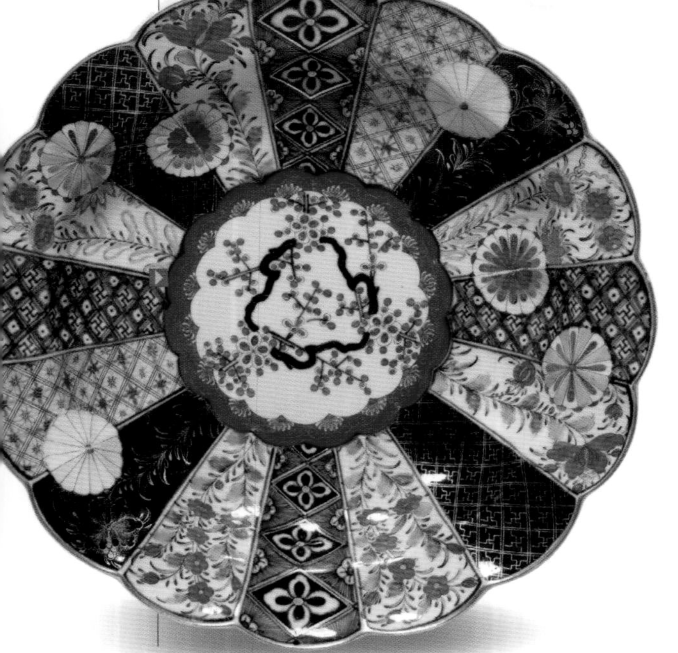

Dish, 1765, *Worcester, England*
The sections of the moulded scalloped-edged form of this porcelain dish are decorated with 16 patterns in pairs, painted in blue paint, coloured enamels and gilding, imitating Japanese *Arita-yaki* ware. Most of the patterns comprise protective lozenges of good fortune containing flowerheads and bent cross symbols of creative force. Other patterns imitate Chinese flower designs, and stylised flowerhead motifs are scattered over the patterns in an apparently random way. The centre of the dish is bordered with a band of 16 scallops, reflecting the outer edge, with half-florals linked by fine gilded tendrils. The centre is painted with a rotating pattern of stylised cherry blossom growing from rocky ground.

Wallpaper, c. 1760, *England*
Large medallions edged with curling leaves, acorns and topped with a ribbon bow are formally arranged with smaller medallions of landscapes and butterflies, framed prints and flower sprays on a plain background. This pattern was designed to imitate 'print room' decoration, a fashionable pastime in the 1760s and 1770s of pasting printed images and frames to walls to give the impression of a room hung with pictures. Printed with woodblocks in a high-contrast effect, this wallpaper was hung at Doddington Hall in Lincolnshire as part of Sir John Hussey Delaval's new decorative scheme.

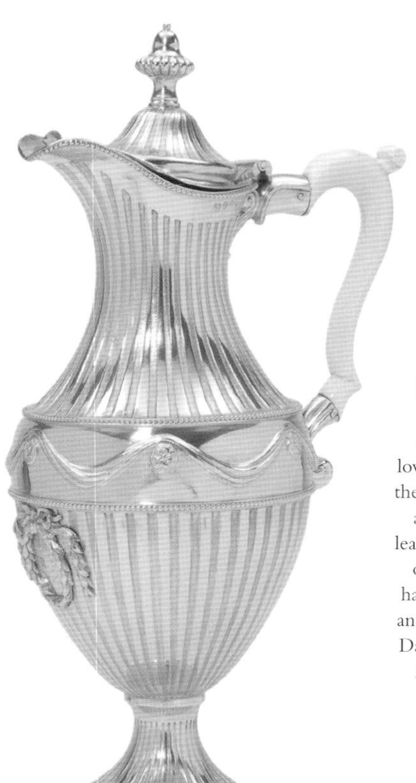

Coffee pot, 1774–45,
London, England
This silver coffee pot has been decorated with fluted lines, and a middle band edged with beads and carved with a flowing swagged banner over floral medallions. An applied laurel wreath tied up with a rippling ribbon has been applied to the fluting of the lower front. The fluted foot of the pot is edged with a ring of alternating lotus flowers and leaves. The coffee pot was part of a silver service with ivory handles made by James Young and Orlando Jackson for actor David Garrick's new house in Adelphi Buildings, designed by the Adam brothers.

'Georgian style was never static ... veering between elegant restraint and exuberant ornamentation but always retaining its ... attention to detail.'

HENRIETTA SPENCER-CHURCHILL,
Classic Georgian Style, 1997

Waistcoat, 1780–90,
England
The standing collar and front of this man's waistcoat are cut from ivory silk woven with satin stripes. Silk medallions painted like cameos with classical images derived from newly discovered Roman frescoes at Pompeii and Herculaneum, are regularly applied to the stripes. Two larger medallions below the pockets show a woman selling Cupids – a classical Roman image from the Villa Arianna in Stabiae, near Pompeii. Finely embroidered ribbons, leaf trails and garlands decorate the cameos and festoon the hem of this high-fashion garment.

ELEMENTS OF PATTERN

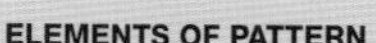

- *floral garlands*
- *naturalistic flowers*
- *ribbons*
- *swags and wreaths*
- *fluting and stripes*
- *medallions*
- *classical images*
- *Chinese style*

Textile design,
c. 1788–92, *England*
Seemingly randomly scattered naturalistic bunches of English wild flowers – including roses, cornflowers, strawberry, borage, vetch and birdsfoot trefoil – are loosely linked with trailing leafy flowering stems. The natural pale brown colour of the background delicately displays the soft tones of the finely drawn and realistic flowers. This pattern for cotton fabric is from an album of watercolour designs for printed textiles painted by William Kilburn.

Josiah Wedgwood
1730–1795

Josiah was the youngest son of Thomas Wedgwood, the potter-owner of a workshop at Burslem in Staffordshire. From the time he was apprenticed to his father, the intellectually curious, aesthetically sensitive and commercially aware Josiah sought to exploit the opportunities presented by scientific endeavour and expanding commercial markets. He was attracted by analytical experimental procedure, politics, literature, philosophy and botany.

In 1754 Wedgwood went into partnership with Thomas Whieldon, an experienced potter who owned a large prosperous workshop at Fenton Low. Working extensively with colours and glazes, he began to write his 'experiment books', recording his own endeavours and realising that innovation was needed to reverse the declining trade in earthenware. Wedgwood continued to keep logbooks throughout his career, entering his formulae in code, applying scientific method to the manufacture of pottery.

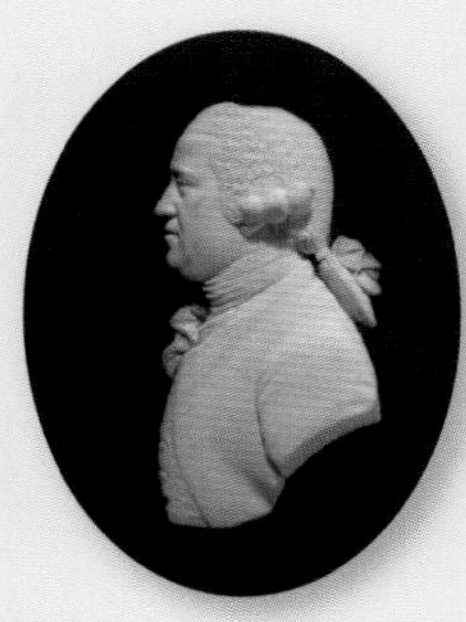

Born
Burslem, Staffordshire, 1730

Profession
Potter and industrialist

Manifesto
'Beautiful forms and compositions are not made by chance.'

'Wedgwood was the greatest man who ever, in any age, or in any country ... applied himself to the important work of uniting art and industry.'

WILLIAM EWART GLADSTONE, 1863

In 1759 he set up as an independent potter. He had perfected some new green and yellow glazes while working for Whieldon, which he now applied to creamware teapots and plates moulded in the shapes of fruit and vegetables, ornate novel pieces that were instantly popular. By 1765, Wedgwood's sales of household wares had grown significantly and he realised that there was a market for ornamental patterned wares.

Wedgwood understood that purchases were often made to imitate the nobility who dictated fashionable taste. In 1765 he presented Queen Charlotte, the wife of George III, with a fine creamware tea set. He was appointed 'Potter to Her Majesty' and creamware was subsequently known as Queensware. Wedgwood placed advertisements in London newspapers to capitalise on his royal patronage and pursued high-status commissions, naming particular ceramic pieces after members of the aristocracy. The attributes of quality and fashion were stressed in advertising to wealthier customers, but the company catalogues advertised sophisticated style at a reasonable price to a wider market.

In 1766 Wedgwood bought an extensive site at Stoke-on-Trent on the path of the planned Trent–Mersey Canal for the 'Etruria' factory and estate, named after the classical pottery then being excavated in Etruria in central Italy. After thousands of experiments with colour-firing with accurate kiln temperatures, he produced jasperware with its first colour, Poland Blue, and black basaltware, both with white classical figures and patterns applied in low relief. Envisioning a new way of selling ceramics, he opened showrooms at Portland Place in London, Bath and Dublin. Complete china services were arranged on tables, and vases displayed on shelves were changed often to attract and amuse customers.

In 1769 Wedgwood set up a formal partnership with Thomas Bentley in the manufacturing and selling of ornamental china. The Etruria factory, now complete, was organised into separate workshops for household and ornamental wares and fitted out with the latest technology, including an engine-turned lathe to make uniform vertical fluting and other patterns in clay. Prior to firing, Wedgwood had his own name impressed into pieces to authenticate and advertise them.

By 1771 production at Etruria was so efficient that Wedgwood began to target the foreign market. He sent parcels of china, costing £20 each, to one thousand German aristocrats with a promotional letter and an invoice; they could pay, or return the goods at no extra cost. It was a significant financial risk, but most of the solicited customers bought the pottery. Large amounts of china were subsequently despatched to Ireland, Germany, Holland, Russia, Spain, the East Indies and America, with some of the finer wares exported to France. By 1783, almost 80 per cent of Etruria's production of household and ornamental wares was being exported, and in 1790 the business was officially incorporated as Josiah Wedgwood & Sons.

Josiah Wedgwood changed the way earthenware was perceived, raising its image above the everyday and expanding its markets at home and abroad. His name has maintained loyal markets for household wares and giftware around the world.

This blue jasperware vase is decorated in applied relief. Topped with the winged horse Pegasus, the lid is decorated with a pattern of overlapping vine and bay leaves. The neck is ringed with leaves and white beads and the shoulder with an elongated egg-and-dart pattern. Figures of the god Apollo and the Muses parade around the body of the pot, representing the arts. Below is a band of bunched acanthus leaves alternating with groups of musical instruments – lyre, trumpets, flutes and violas – and a bearded mask. The foot is decorated with fluted tongues ringed with white beads and the plinth with an anthemion *pattern.*

PATTERN IN DETAIL

Roman Designs Reborn 1778

Capturing Rome on the Grand Tour

From the mid-18th century, the Grand Tour brought aristocrats, writers and artists to Italy to see the classical world. Hungry to examine the sites of ancient Rome, tourists hired local guides and purchased artistic mementoes. Giovanni Battista Piranesi (1720–78) was the greatest artist, producing views and prints of classical monuments. An archaeologist, designer and writer, he created picturesque views for the tourists as well as accurate records of classical Rome and imaginatively restored antiquities.

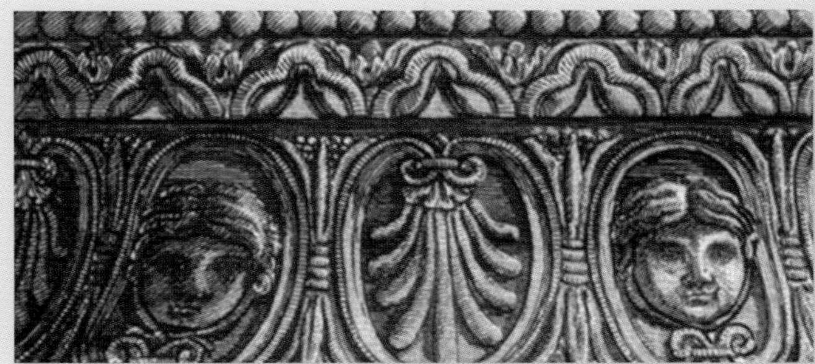

Palmettes, faces and beading
The central design on the ornate lid of the vase comprises an open oval scroll containing alternating *anthemion* palmettes and faces interspersed with thin three-petal floral or lily motifs. Above are a complex water-leaf-and-dart band and beading. The naturalistic faces link to the grotesque Bacchus head on the body of the vase, stressing its probable function as a wine vessel.

Egg-and-dart, key and swags
On the vase stand, a profusion of patterns creates an opulent decadent effect. Egg-and-dart, swags with rosettes and pot motifs, simple acanthus-leaf capitals with tridents and a key pattern edged with twisted ropes are all present within a relatively narrow band across the upper register of the stand. Usually these elements would be applied in different architectural orders but appear together here in exuberant profusion.

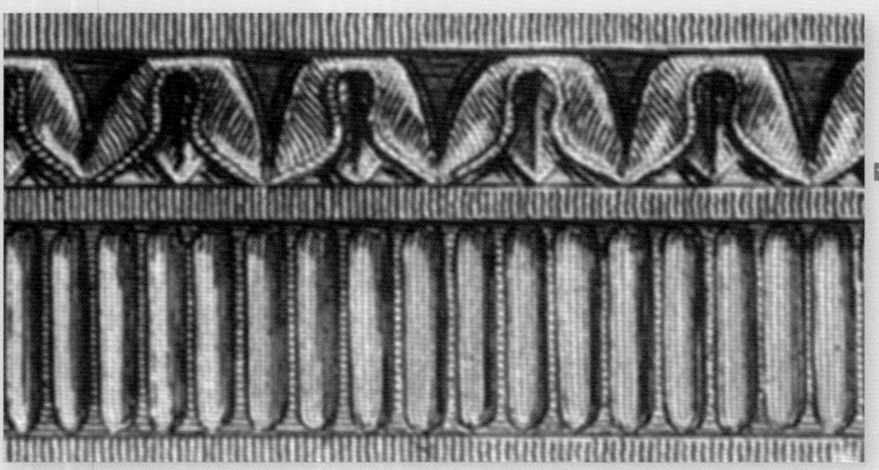

Leaf and flute
The design around the broadest area of the vase has a trifoliate pattern that seems to be a development of the egg-and-dart or leaf-and-dart motif usually associated with the Ionic order. Below is a fluted band that balances the design on the handles. Motifs such as these will have been drawn from actual sculpture or vases excavated in Rome but may have been restored in an imaginary design.

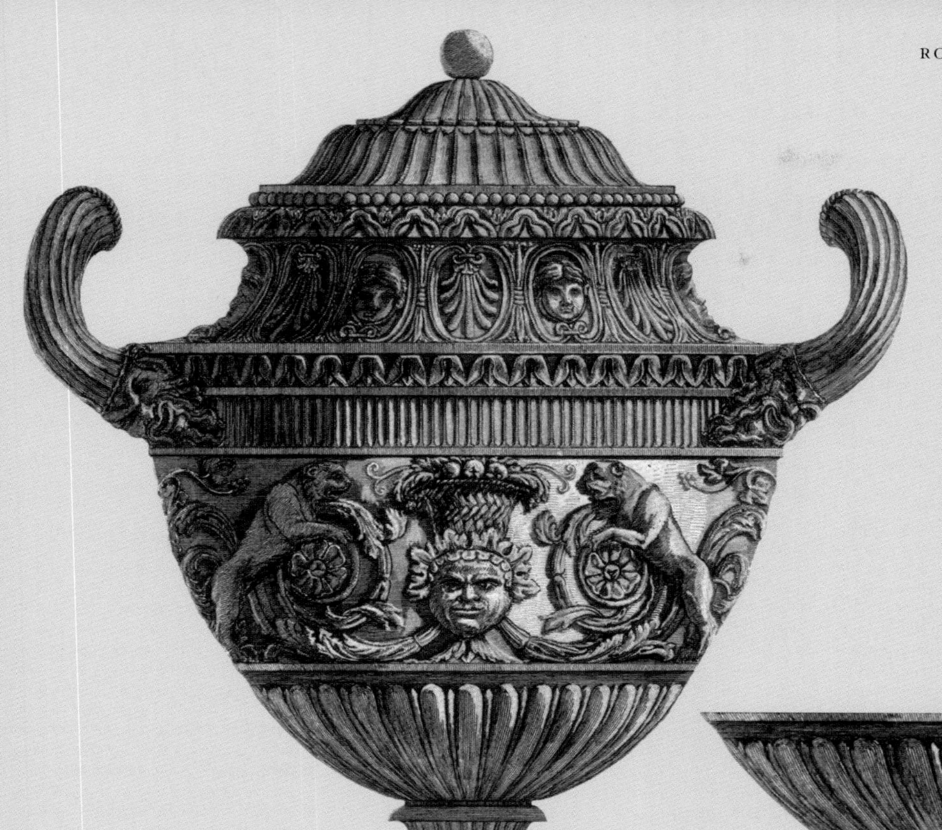

Print of a vase supported by a tripod, 1778, *Rome*
Piranesi used etching and engraving to produce this print. Both techniques involved incising the surface of a plate so that ink would fill the grooves for printing. They produced the differing textures in the print and allowed Piranesi to give the final image greater three-dimensional volume to imitate sculptured stone. He used to produce these prints for aristocratic Grand Tourists and they were eventually collected together in one publication.

Ribs
Both the lower body of the vase and the hemispherical section of the base are ribbed with a pattern that combines elongated lobes and darts similar in composition to the egg-and-dart border. A very traditional formulation of vase bases, these could be carved or hammered in metal. The pattern could easily follow the curved shape of the base without losing its integrity.

Vitruvian wave scroll or 'running dog'
The Vitruvian wave scroll or 'running dog' is bi-coloured with both light and dark matching scrolling waves. The tonal contrast here is created by imitating a carved band of a raised lighter and a recessed darker wave. The pattern is named after the 1st-century-CE Roman architect Vitruvius who wrote *The Ten Books on Architecture* in which he described and defined the classical forms of architecture.

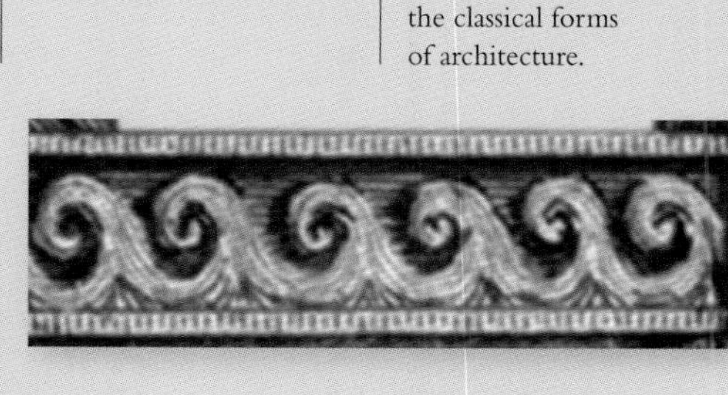

Robert Adam
1728–1792

Robert Adam was trained as an architect by his father William, who was Master Mason to the Board of Ordnance. In 1748 Robert's brother John inherited the family business, taking over his father's position and forming a partnership with Robert and, later, with their younger brother James.

In 1754 Adam travelled to Italy to be instructed by two of the most influential designers of architectural images in Europe, Giovanni Battista Piranesi (see pages 182–3) and the French artist Charles-Louis Clérisseau, whose paintings of ruined classical Roman buildings inspired the 'picturesque' tradition of describing beauty in architectural decay. Robert studied buildings of all periods, but particularly the classical Roman painted and stuccoed domestic interiors recorded by Renaissance artists such as Raphael and Vasari.

Adam began his journey back to Britain in 1757, visiting Split in Dalmatia with Clérisseau to make drawings of the remains of Diocletian's palace, which he published in 1764. In Italy Adam had found 'the true, the simple, the grand', qualities he sought to reattribute to British architecture with imposing dimensions and ordered niches, columns and colonnades.

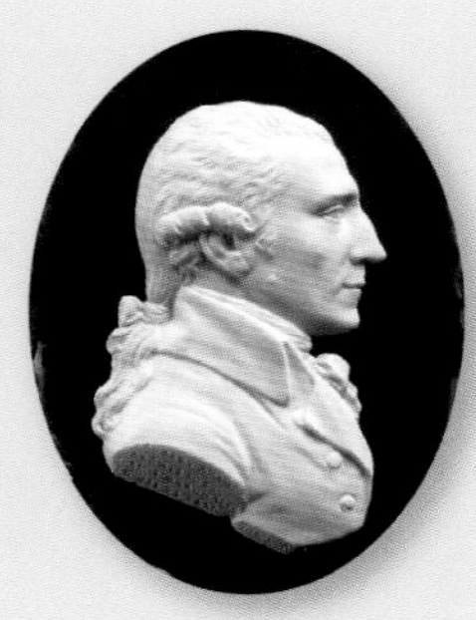

Born
Kirckaldy, Fife, Scotland
1728

Profession
Architect designer

Manifesto
'*Movement* is meant to express, the rise and fall, the advance and recess, with other diversity of form, in the different parts of the building, so as to add greatly to the picturesque of the composition.'

In 1758 Robert and James set up their own architectural practice, Adam Brothers, concentrating on the design of unified detailed decorative schemes for domestic interiors. Their new style was informed by classical Roman design with Greek, Byzantine and Baroque influences. Their own principle of 'movement' depended on contrast and diversity of form that drew on the complex aesthetic of the 'picturesque', derived from Pliny the Younger's concept of elite country life in late 1st- to 2nd-century Italy – a retreat from city life for hunting, collecting books and art, and improving farming methods and workers' conditions. The brothers established a reputation for a distinctive style and their ability to organise large comprehensive schemes for architectural design, construction, interior design and decoration. The publication of their designs in *The Works in Architecture of Robert and James Adam* increased their fame in England and later in America. In 1761, Robert was appointed Architect of the King's Works.

'Adam's recreation of antique Roman splendour for modern domestic purposes was an achievement unequalled since the days of Raphael.'

DAVID WATKIN, *A History of Western Architecture*, 2005

In the 1760s, the Adam brothers completed a house at Kedleston in Derbyshire for Sir Nathaniel Curzon, one of the wealthy Whig landowners who kept pace with changing visual and social fashions. A formal house, it was surrounded by informal gardens and open countryside. The Adam brothers conceptualised these changing visual textures as 'movement' to apply to design. The great hall was decorated in imperial Roman style, with wall niches for casts of classical sculpture and panels that were painted using the shaded monochrome grisaille technique imitating stone carving, and lined with Corinthian columns.

Many Adam Brothers projects had involved the renovation of existing buildings or their interior design and decoration, but during the 1770s they were commissioned to design new townhouses with complex layouts for long narrow sites in London. The rooms were designed with contrasting shapes, often with oval plans and column screens. At Derby House in Grosvenor Square, Robert Adam described three interconnecting drawing rooms and an anteroom on the first floor as 'an attempt to arrange the apartments in the French style, which … is best calculated for the convenience and elegance of life'.

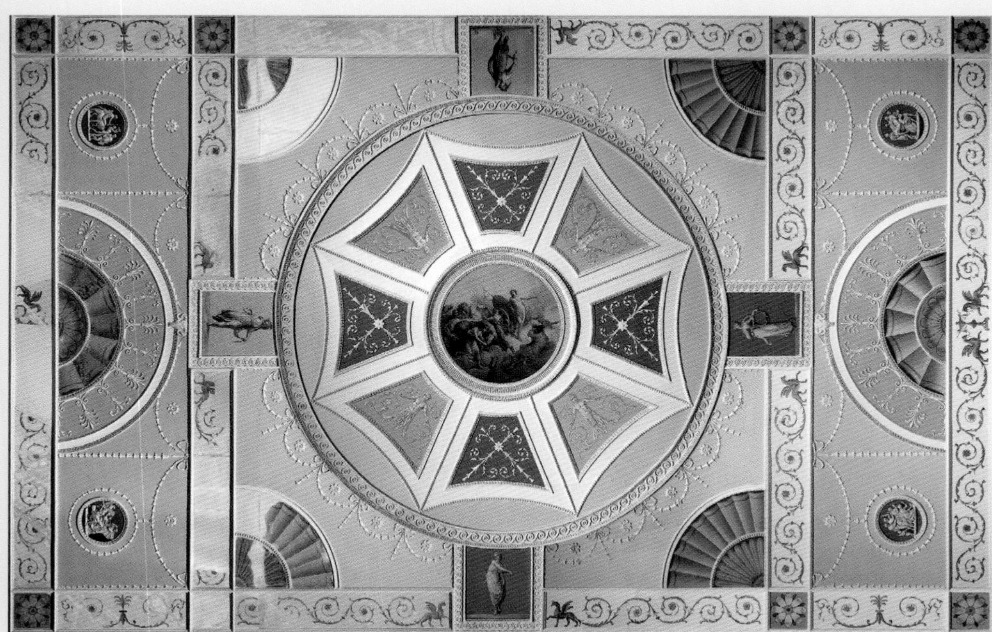

Ceiling, c. 1771, 5 Royal Terrace, *Adelphi, London*
Borders of gryphons with tails transforming into running leaf scrolls are linked to formal roses by symmetrical palmette and leaf scrolls. A painting of Apollo and the Four Seasons is surrounded by panels of 'grotesque' male figures transforming into leafy flowering scrolls alternating with crossed foliate wands. They are encompassed by a running scroll and individual portraits of the Four Seasons. At each end a semicircle half-floral 'awning' and delicate lotus-palmette is flanked by medallions, and lines of bell-flowers swag and trail from ribbon bows. The Adams' Adelphi housing development was named from the Greek word for 'brothers'. Number 5 was bought by the famous actor David Garrick, the first-floor drawing room of which was decorated with this plasterwork ceiling. Designed by Robert Adam, it was installed by David Adamson and painted in oils by the Italian decorator Antonio Zucchi.

1800
1900

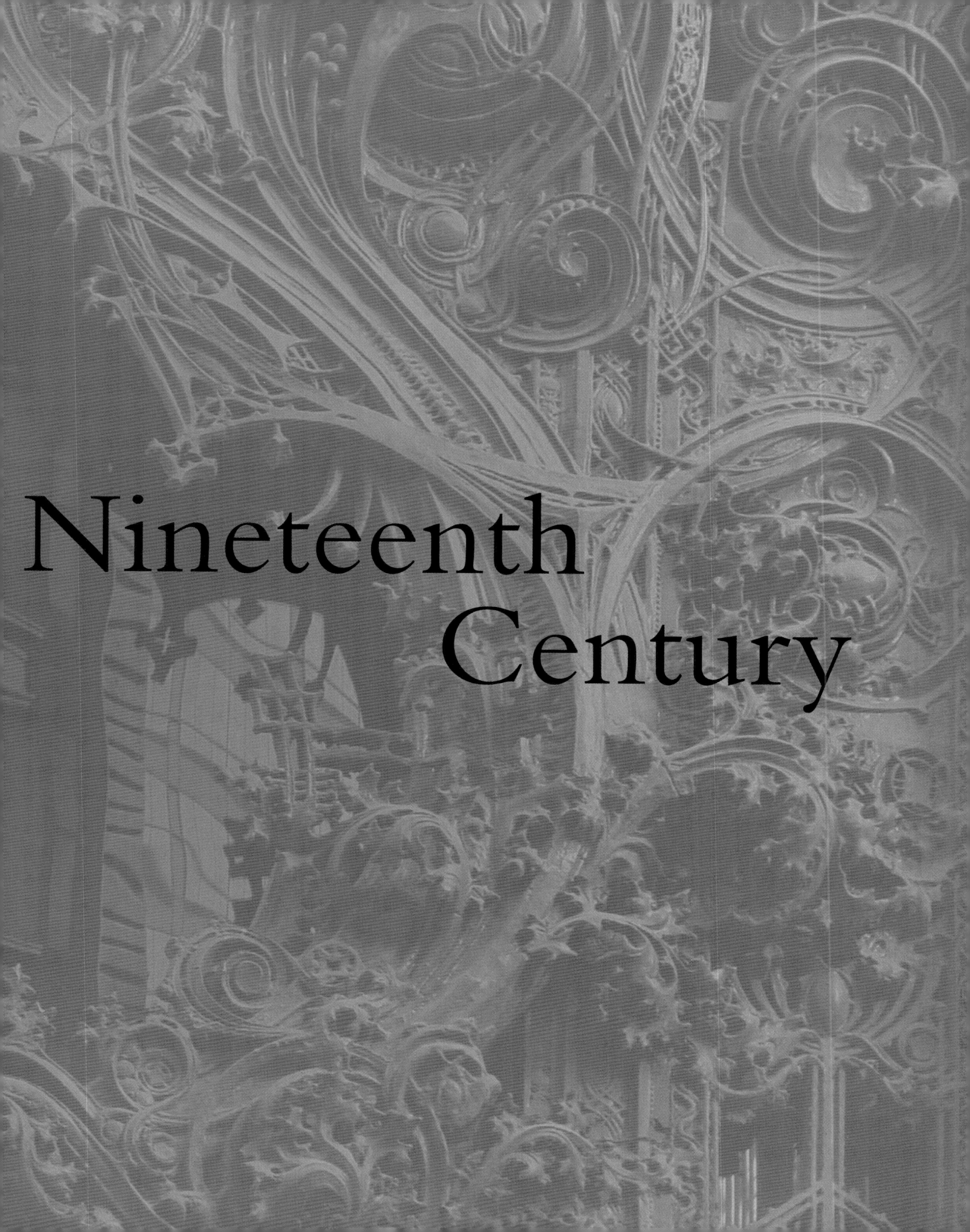

Nineteenth Century

Introduction

The revival of Gothic style was a reaction to the formality of neoclassicism and a perceived lack of authentic forms and patterns in art and architecture. In England, Augustus Pugin designed new clearly defined, richly coloured neo-Gothic motifs for interiors, including patterned tiles, wallpapers and furnishing textiles. The bold colour effects in paint or block-printed wallpaper were used in the main rooms of the New Palace of Westminster. The art and social theorist John Ruskin initiated a campaign for aesthetic reform with *The Stones of Venice* (1851–53), advocating that artists and architects revive the creative honesty and discipline of the medieval period. In 1856 architect-designer Owen Jones's *The Grammar of Ornament*, with decorative motifs from world historical sources, enabled designers to see the wider potential of pattern design. Other revivals included a renewed interest in Baroque and Renaissance styles, and later in the century a resurgence of neoclassicism and Byzantine styles.

A revolution in arts led by William Morris returned to the fundamental concepts of design and traditional production techniques. His firm of artist-designers revitalised pattern-making in all the applied arts with highly inventive plant forms in rhythmically exuberant compositions. Morris's aesthetic reforms were realised in foundations such as the Art Workers' Guild in 1884 and the Arts and Crafts Exhibition Society in 1888, and by links between artist-designers and production. From the late 1860s these new

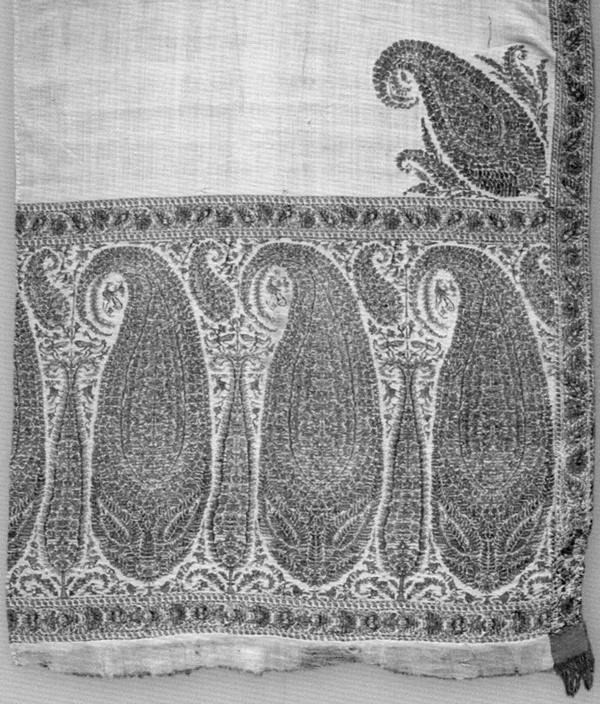

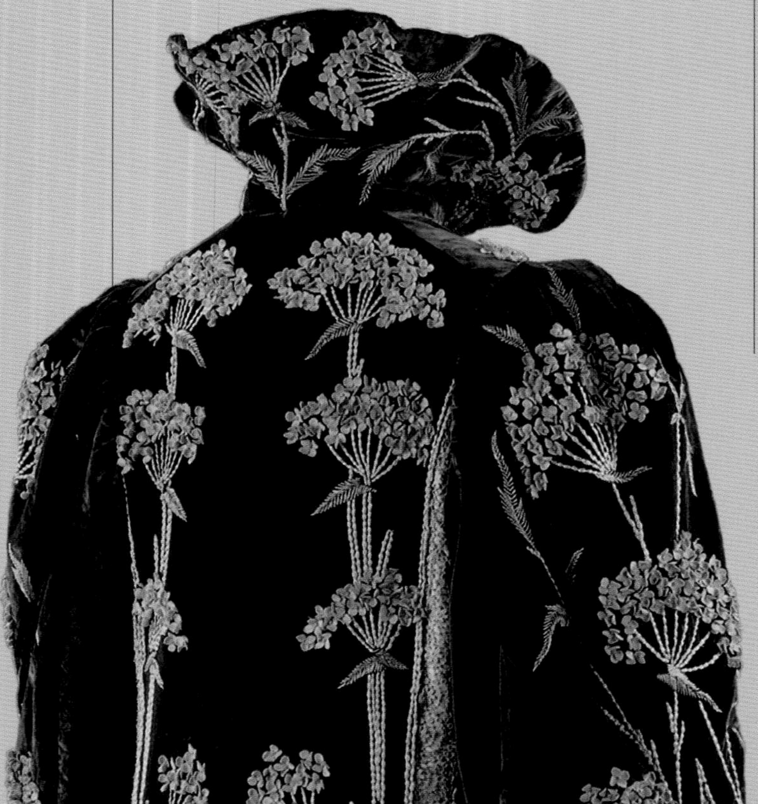

From extensive European, Middle Eastern and Asian historical sources, William Morris created very English, yet exotic, hybrid patterns of wild plants and birds with fluidity and rhythm. These designs, and the writings of the influential critic and art historian John Ruskin, inspired the Arts and Crafts movement throughout Europe and in North America.

In Iran and India, patterns and designs continued to employ styles and forms established in earlier centuries. Increasing contact with Europe, especially the establishment of the British Raj in 1858, gave rise to an increasing popularity for Asian designs in Europe. Kashmir shawls with their boteh *(paisley) motifs were highly sought after.*

artistic concepts were publicised in England and America by Charles Locke Eastlake's highly popular book, *Hints on Household Taste*.

In London, the Great Exhibition of 1851 and the 1862 International Exhibition of Japanese Art brought world arts and cultures to Britain, inspiring many designers to innovate by drawing on Iranian, Japanese and Indian styles. In America, architectural developments were stimulated by economic growth and social change, which gave rise to the innovation of skyscrapers. Louis Sullivan conceived the idea of 'form follows function' and his steel-framed buildings set a new trend. Emphasising the verticality of the buildings, they were also ornately decorated with designs drawn from European sources. At the centre of the fashion world in Paris, machine-made clothing and rich new colours brought patterned and vibrant designs to a wider range of female clients.

From 1883, architect Charles Voysey created designs that reduced motifs to their basic shapes in flat, sinuous forms with strong outlines and few details, a style particularly suited to block-printing and carpet-weaving. The painter and illustrator Walter Crane designed patterns with a new fluidity for stained glass, metalwork, tiles, pottery, wallpapers and textiles. In Scotland, decorative artists such as Jessie Newbery and Anne Macbeth at the Glasgow School of Art produced embroidered designs with patterns in the new abstract formula of the Glasgow style.

Siegfried Bing's gallery shop, 'L'Art Nouveau' ('New Art'), for contemporary art opened in Paris in 1895 and its name was taken for the new stylistic movement in France and England. In Germany and Austria it was named *Jugendstil* ('Young Style'), and in Italy '*Stile Liberty*' after the London shop Liberty that favoured suitable materials and colours for these designs. The new-wave Arts and Crafts movement and Art Nouveau were transitional developments between historically derived and modernist design.

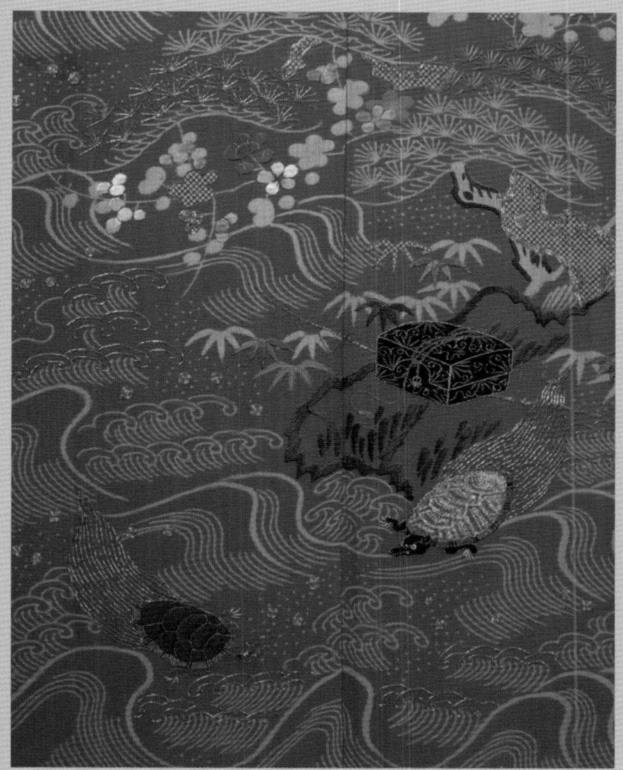

Traditional Japanese designs and styles of representation incorporated symbolic natural and mythical subjects such as cranes, tortoises, pine, bamboo and blossom. The opening of Japan to trade with the rest of the world in the mid-19th century brought Japanese arts and designs to Europe. Christopher Dresser in England and Emile Gallé in France reinterpreted Japanese style in influential new ways.

Neo-Gothic Patterns 1811–1851

A celebration of natural forms

The new value placed by designers on high-quality craftworking as a creative force involved a renewed interest in the function, purpose and inherent beauty of the materials used. This integrity of thought in design also characterised decorative style, comprising patterns of motifs translated from naturally created organic forms. The new approach to constructing elements of pattern in two dimensions opened up a comprehensive range of applications for the neo-Gothic style. All kinds of hard and soft media could be decorated in new, rich, clear colours that reflected the self-confidence of the age.

'The Gothic revival had paved the way, paradoxically, to the most creative and original interior architecture of the last decades of the century.'

PETER THORNTON, *Authentic Décor*, 1993

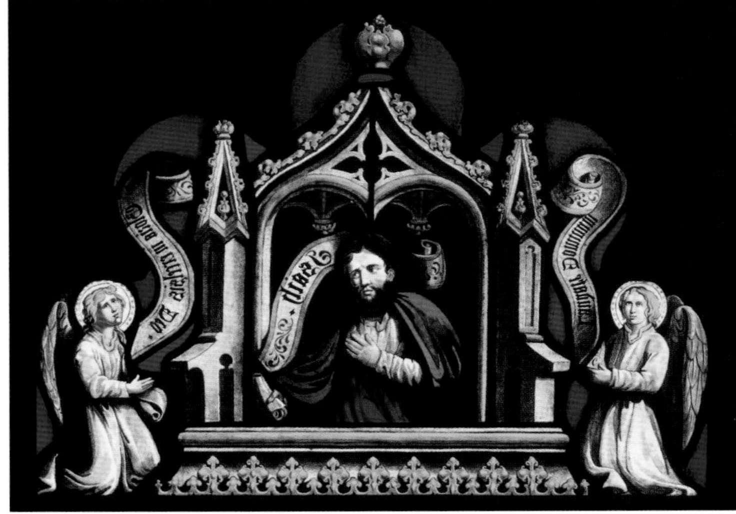

Glass panel, 1811–31, *London, England*
The curving arch of the central niche over a quatrefoil motif and flanking pinnacles is edged with a running pattern of curving ivy leaves. The prophet Isaiah holds a banner inscribed with his name between two leaf scrolls. Below, alternating larger and smaller ivy leaves anchor the design. Possibly made by Joseph Hale Miller, in clear glass painted with brown enamel, green stained glass, and 'flashed' clear glass coated with red and blue layers, this panel was fitted into the tracery at the top of the chapel window at Ashridge Park in Hertfordshire.

ELEMENTS OF PATTERN

- *leaf motifs: trefoils, quatrefoils, cinquefoils*
- *flower forms: rosettes*
- *architectural forms derived from nature: arches, niches*
- *natural leaf forms: acanthus, ivy*
- *heraldic devices*
- *clear rich colours*

Earrings, c. 1820–30, *Germany*
These earrings are delicately cast from iron. The tripartite lanceolate style of the pendants is formed of pointed arch tongues filled with openwork Gothic tracery, including quatrefoil motifs taken from architectural details, and modelled ivy leaves. The attachment comprises a six-pointed flower with trefoils in the petals, superimposed by a rosette above a tripartite arrangement of ruffling acanthus leaves. This type of cast-iron jewellery was very fashionable in Germany, Austria and France in the 1830s.

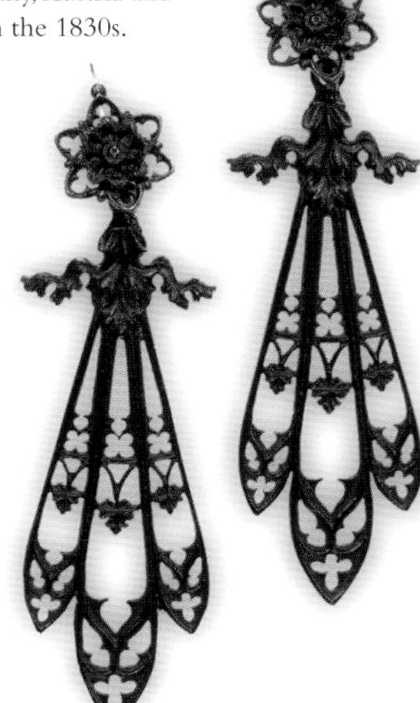

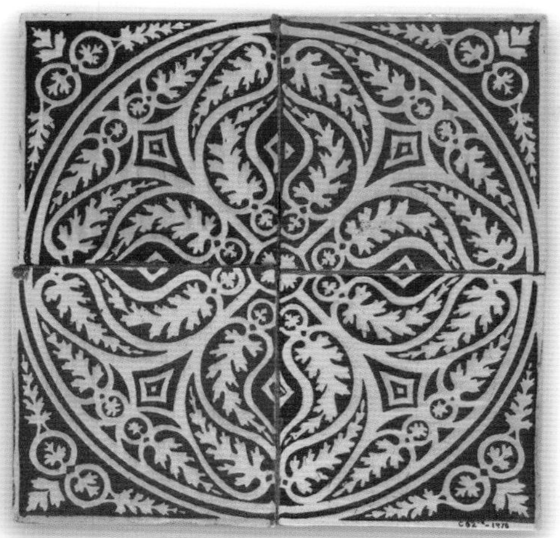

Tile, c. 1846, *Worcester, England*
This earthenware encaustic tile is inlaid with a quatrefoil design enclosed by a circle. Serrated leaves are enclosed by stems of varying thicknesses that rhythmically curve around lozenges to describe the shape of the quatrefoil. On the diagonal axes, stems loop to form pairs of circles, echoed in the encircled trefoil leaves and serrated leaf motifs that fill the corners. This tile was made as one of a set of four by the Worcester firm of Chamberlain & Co., from a medieval mid-15th-century design in Great Malvern Priory in Worcestershire.

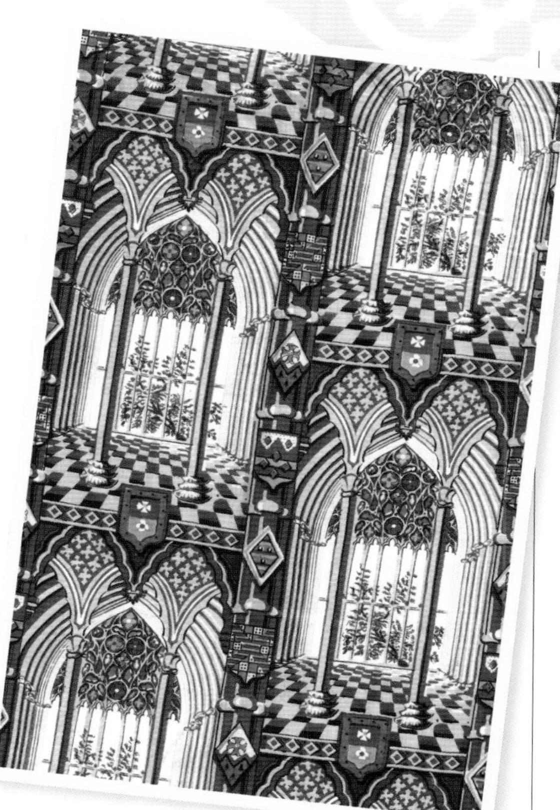

Furnishing textile, c. 1830–40, *London*
This block-printed pattern has been given the effect of movement with a Gothic-style interior scene repeated in an offset layout. A pair of columns standing on a checked floor support an arcaded screen, patterned with quatrefoils, behind pendant arches in the same shape. Beyond the columns a floor-to-ceiling tracery window, bejewelled with stained-glass quatrefoils above clear trefoil-headed panes, overlooks the tree outside. The scenes are divided vertically by bands of heraldic shields (male) and lozenges (female) and horizontally by a band of mascles (hollow lozenges).

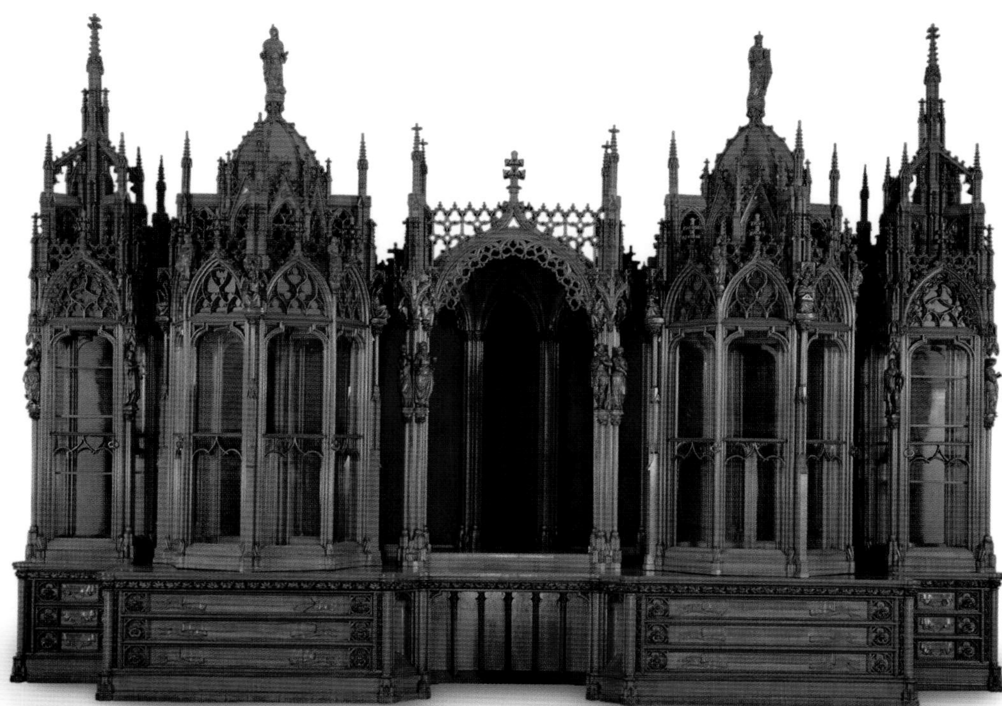

Bookcase, 1850–51, *Vienna, Austria*
The compartment doors of this flamboyantly Gothic bookcase, designed to resemble the windows in a medieval architectural façade, are patterned with curving and cusped tracery. The central compartment has a pinnacled arch surmounted by tracery of trefoils and curving shapes, below which is a pattern of suspended arcaded trefoils. The bookcase was designed by Bernado di Bernardis and sculpted by Anton Dominik Fernkorn. The makers Carl Leistler & Son included it in their display at the 1851 Great Exhibition in London, and it was presented to Queen Victoria by the Austrian Emperor Franz Josef.

PATTERN IN DETAIL

American Quilted Compositions 1830–1839

'Pineapple log cabin' motif

The advent of commercial fabric production in the early 19th century led to a surge in quilt-making in the United States, where traditional sewing and homemaking skills had been used to create bedcovers in the 18th century. A wide range of designs existed to show off fine stitching and elegant patterning. Some quilts were complex and beautiful works of art that might only be used for guests but would, in time, become heirlooms.

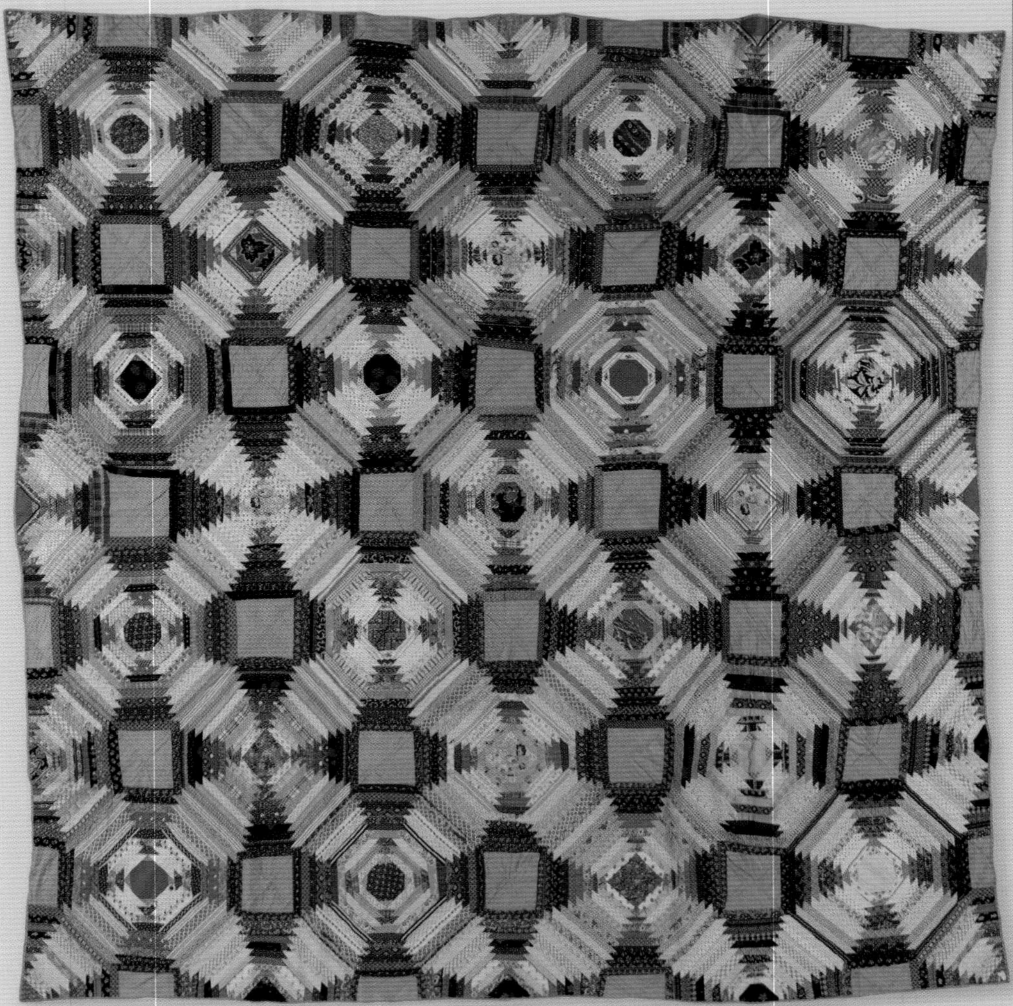

Stripes, small checks and leaves

The central area of each section, arranged around the octagonal panel, is usually made up of lighter fabrics to provide a visual hub. This is pronounced in this section, where a soft peach and cream patterned fabric twinned with a beige and cream check create a larger octagon. Within this hub, small patterns provide the background for bold blue and brown stripes and a distinctive orange floral.

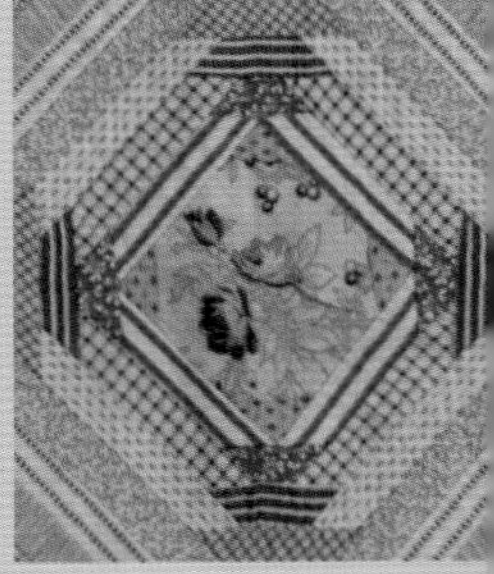

Bed cover, 1830–69, *United States*

The choices of fabrics – their designs and colours, their juxtaposition and fine symmetry – create a vibrant and dynamic design. Known as the 'pineapple' or 'pineapple log cabin' motif, the zigzagging of the interlacing strips forms bold contrasting-coloured sections that radiate across the quilt. Overall, the soft pink square panels offset the bright colours scattered throughout the design – powder blue, red and rich browns.

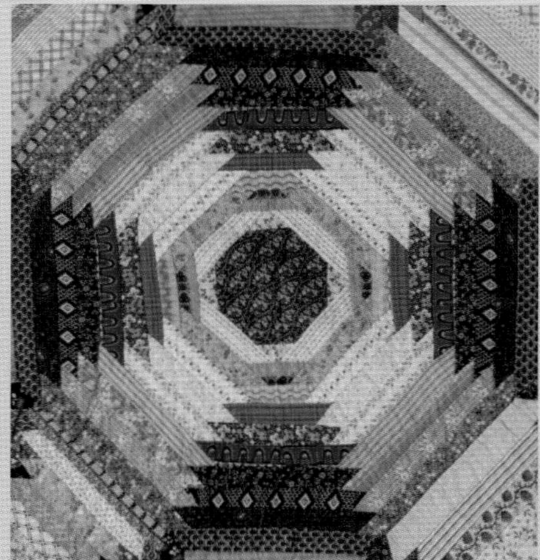

Contrasting red, white and blue

This design's fundamental elements are the bold contrasting light and dark sections arranged around octagonal and square panels. The zigzag created by the narrow tapered rectangles adds vibrancy and symmetry but the mirrored fabric selections make each section of the pattern unique. In this section the soft blues, greys and small sprig-patterned fabrics contrast with the bolder, carefully cut geometrics in browns and reds.

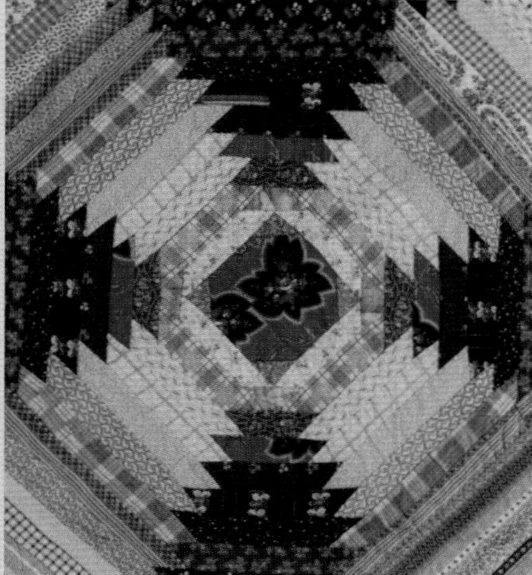

Flowers, checks and paisley

The relationship between the fabrics in each section is imaginatively arranged. In this section, pale chequered fabrics, similar to shirting, and light, fine all-over designs are contrasted with bold dark florals, including a striking dark blue, linked to the exotic leaf motif in the central octagon. The designer has skilfully linked one section to the next at the largest light strip using coordinating colour details.

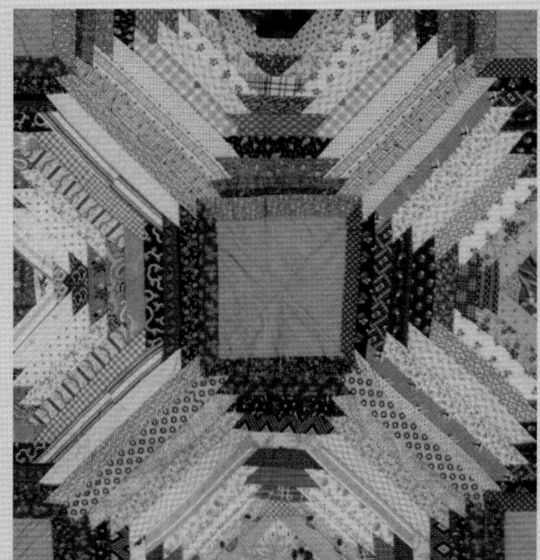

Vibrant stars

If you focus on the sections created by the darker fabrics arranged around the pink squares, a four-point star appears in which each point is made of different fabrics. In some cases the points are broken by incidental lighter stripes such as the powder blue on the left point. Within the star the muted brown fabrics are shot through with vibrant oranges and more subtle greys.

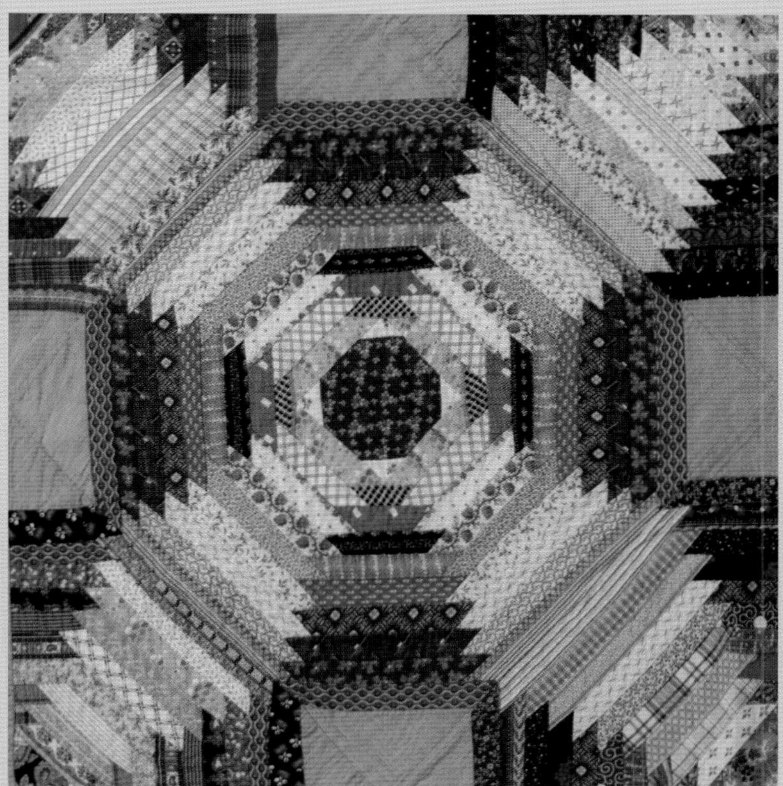

Selective banding

A close look at the narrow stripes of fabric shows the care taken in selecting pattern details to enhance the overall design. In this section, a brown lozenge pattern is cut to create a band of motifs which link around the middle of the section. In the centre, checks, spots and dots form an ordered pattern, which is edged by a small foliate wave fabric.

Augustus Pugin
1812–1852

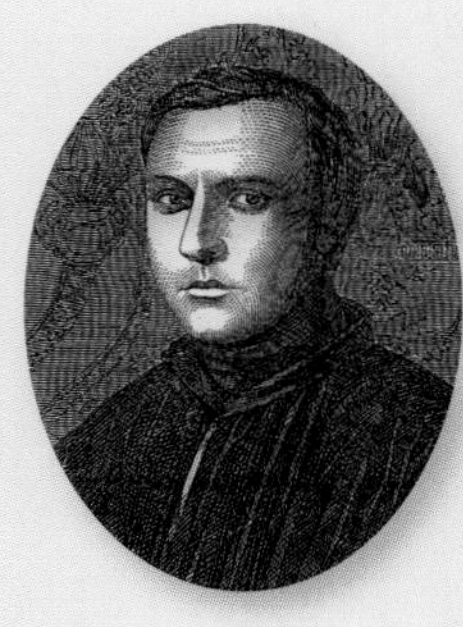

Born
London, England, 1812

Profession
Architect, designer and antiquarian

Manifesto
'The smallest detail should have a meaning or serve a purpose; and even the construction itself should vary with the material employed, and the designs should be adapted to the material in which they are executed.'

Augustus Northmoor Welby Pugin was the son of a French Catholic, Auguste Charles Pugin, and an English Protestant, Catherine Welby. His father, an expert on medieval buildings, who published books on Gothic architecture, furniture and ornament, was a draughtsman for the royal architect John Nash. He owned a large collection of medieval objects and frequently took Augustus to study Gothic buildings. Like his father, Augustus collected antiquarian objects, an important source of inspiration for his work. By the age of 15, he was designing Gothic-style furniture for George IV's restored Windsor Castle.

In 1834, on the death of his mother, Pugin converted to Catholicism. The recent introduction of full legal rights of worship for Catholics was creating a demand for new churches and Pugin received several commissions. He saw architecture as integral to the Roman Catholic Church.

From 1835 Pugin collaborated with Charles Barry in building the New Palace of Westminster after the destruction of the old building by fire. In charge of the interiors, he designed every feature in 15th-century Perpendicular Gothic style – stained glass, wallpapers, textiles, metalwork, light fittings, ceiling ornament, carpets, floor tiles, and carved oak woodwork and furniture. He provided drawings for his team of craftsmen and manufacturers, who interpreted them as designs and taught their apprentices medieval arts and techniques.

In 1836 he gained public attention by publishing *Contrasts: or, A Parallel between the Noble Edifices of the Fourteenth and Fifteenth Centuries, and Similar Buildings of the Present Day; Shewing the Present-Day Decay of Taste*. He compared medieval and modern towns, showing how Protestant classical-style chapels had replaced Catholic churches. He denounced the neoclassical style as 'degraded and pagan', stating that it was a religious and moral necessity to return to the principles of medieval Gothic architecture and decoration.

In 1841, Pugin set out his basic rules of design in *The True Principles of Pointed or Christian Architecture*. He stated 'that there should be no features about a building which are not necessary for convenience, construction, and propriety' and 'that all ornament should consist of the enrichment of the essential construction of the building'. Pugin equated faith and design, in that each should be equally sincere.

‘[Pugin] has marvellously fulfilled his own intention of demonstrating the applicability of Medieval art in all its richness and variety to the uses of the present day.’

Illustrated London News, 1851

A building’s structural form should be clear and express its function, unlike the symmetrical façades of neoclassical buildings that concealed their form.

In 1849, Pugin called for a return to two-dimensional patterns with stylised natural forms in his book *Floriated Ornament*, stating that it was how plants were adapted and arranged that created a design style.

At the Great Exhibition at Crystal Palace in London’s Hyde Park in 1851, Pugin and his colleagues, John Hardman, Herbert Minton, J. G. Crace and George Myers, created a display called the ‘Medieval Court’ that represented all the decorative arts they had designed. It was acclaimed by the *Illustrated London News* as ‘the most unique and best harmonised display of art and skill’.

Pugin designed more than 20 churches, chapels and cathedrals but, apart from two houses for himself, he undertook only a few domestic projects for wealthy Catholic clients. In 1837 he remodelled Scarisbrick Hall in Lancashire, providing the great hall with two-storey woodwork screens carved with many Flemish designs from the 15th–17th centuries, bay windows and a patterned mosaic floor.

In a period of increasing mass production, Pugin’s emphasis on the work of the individual craftworker and his desire for an honest return to two-dimensional pattern-making deeply influenced all aspects of interior design, and especially the designers who formed the Arts and Crafts movement. Pugin’s advocacy of Gothic as the only true style for public and domestic buildings, and of the revival of traditional medieval skills, gave architecture a new moral position. He promoted a ‘muscular’ Gothic style and denounced patterns that used colours not seen in medieval decoration. Pugin’s work inspired John Ruskin’s theory of honesty in architecture and design and influenced British architects.

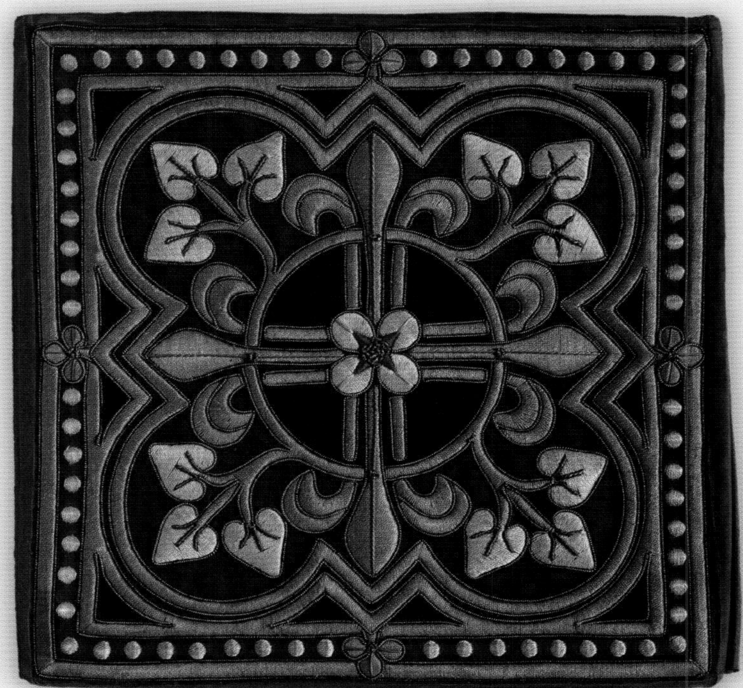

Burse, 1848–50, *London, England*
This silk velvet burse (a flat cloth case used for carrying bread wafers during Mass) is embroidered with raised patterns in silver-gilt and silk threads. A cross design of fleur-de-lis centred with a four-petalled rose is interlaced by a ring sprouting three leaves on each diagonal. The elements are enclosed by a double-banded quatrefoil with points from which small trefoils link the design to the pelleted frame. Designed by Pugin for his own use in his local church of St Augustine’s at Ramsgate in Kent, this burse was made in the workshops of Lonsdale & Tyler, Covent Garden in London.

Nineteenth-Century Revivals 1857–1874

The renewed popularity of Classicism, Baroque and Renaissance design

Throughout the 19th and early 20th century, design styles from previous centuries were revived in architecture and interior design – Renaissance, Baroque, Palladianism, Classicism and Byzantine styles were all recreated. The reconstruction of the centre of Paris in the 1860s by Baron Haussmann (1809–91) in the Beaux-Arts style recalled the Baroque and Renaissance periods. Neo-Baroque was reproduced across the world in Britain, the USA, Japan, Hungary, Sri Lanka, Russia and Cuba. Neoclassicism was also popular in the late 19th century, echoing the elegant forms of Robert Adam – the 'Adams style' seen in the cabinet. Palladianism (see pages 140–1), with its balanced and symmetrical forms, continued to be popular and was often used for civic buildings. These styles were rivalled by the neo-Gothic, discussed in the previous pages.

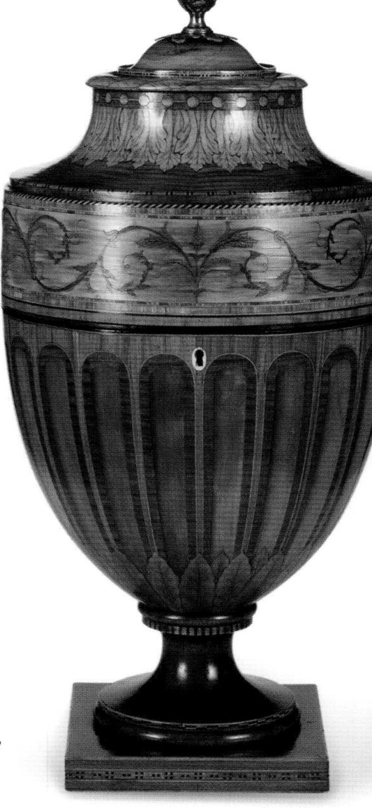

Marquetry knife box, 1860–70
This vase-shaped knife box copied an 18th-century neoclassical design, popular again in the 1860s and 1870s. Classical motifs decorate the surface with overlapping acanthus and laurel leaves on the lid and base; a foliate scroll with pine cones winds around the top and simulated tapered fluting adorns the body. Woods, including holly, harewood, elm, oak and mahogany, create the design.

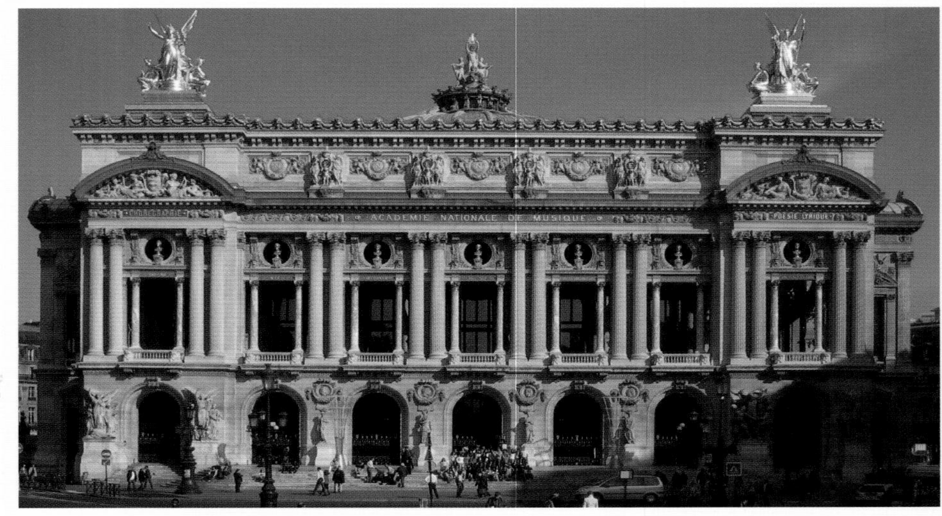

Paris Opera House, Charles Garnier, 1861–75
Neo-Baroque – part of the Beaux-Arts style used in the Second Empire reconstruction of Paris – rejected neoclassical austerity to revive the flamboyant ornamentation and decorative opulence of the 17th century. The multi-coloured and gilded façade has swags and medallions, Corinthian columns with acanthus capitals, classical architectural elements such as dentils, and symmetrically organised sculptures of Greek gods, great composers and representations of the arts.

'Nineteenth-century culture, especially its architecture, decked out with quilting made up of fragments drawn from the great styles of the past.'

KARSTEN HARRIES, 'Theatricality and Re-presentation' IN *Perspecta*, 1990

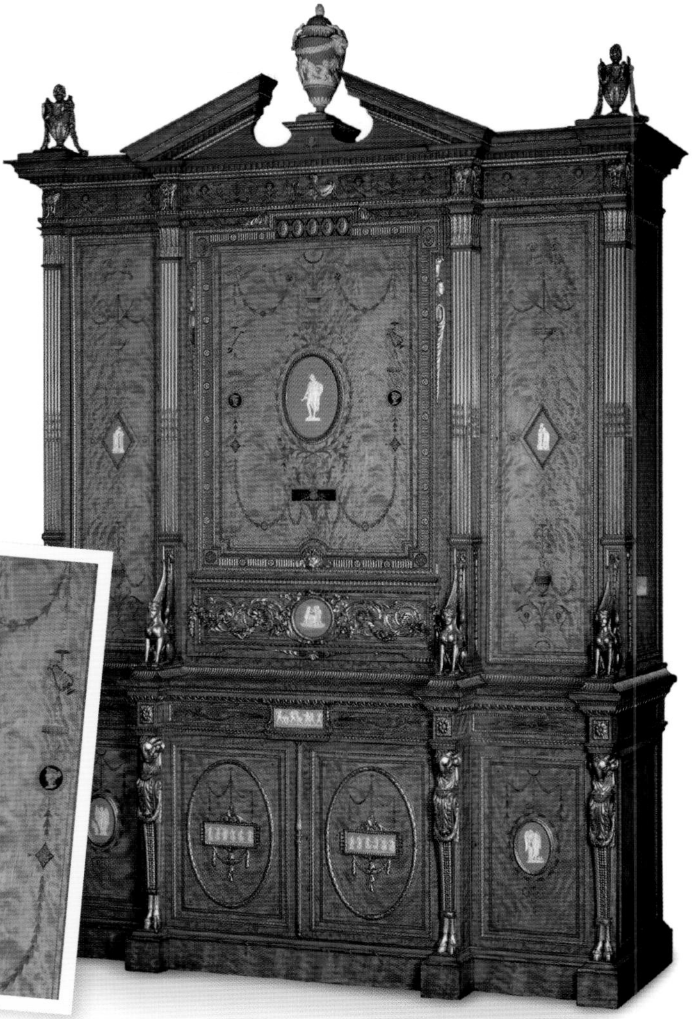

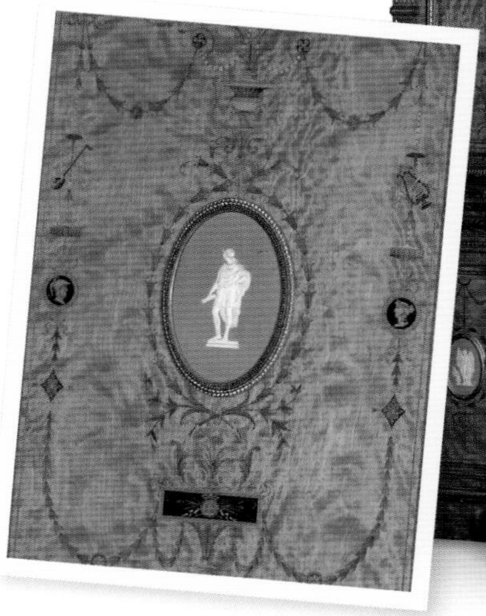

Marquetry cabinet, Crosse for Wright and Mansfield, 1867, *London*
This imposing cabinet combines decorative features of 18th-century neoclassicism with Wedgwood plaques of traditional classical subjects. The classical features include the fluted pilasters (although the elongated capitals are more reminiscent of Egyptian design), a broken pediment, egg-and-dart edging, fluting, rosettes, elements of grotesques from Roman 1st-century-CE painting with fine floral swags, flamboyant gilded acanthus scrolls, and rams' heads and urns.

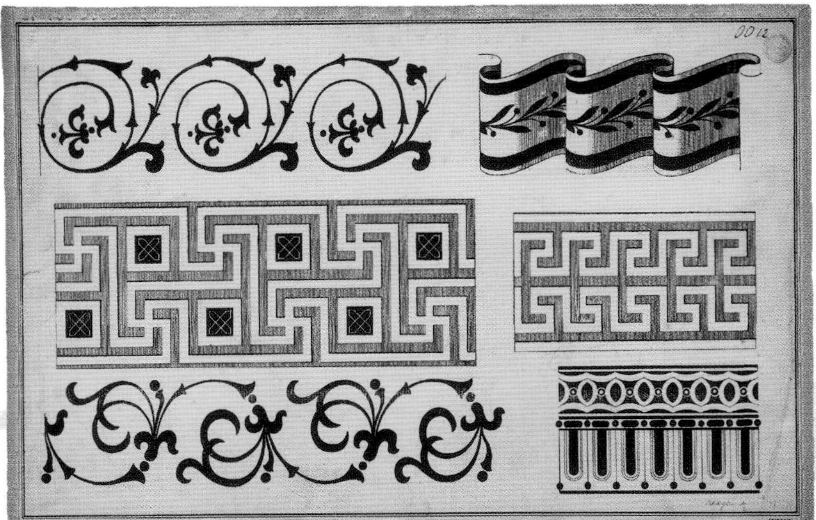

ELEMENTS OF PATTERN

- *flamboyant swags*
- *multi-coloured and gilded patterns*
- *grotesques*
- *classical architectural features*

Motif diagram, Carl August Menzel, printed c. 1872–73, *Berlin, Germany*
These decorative motifs, originally created by Carl August Menzel (1794–1853?) in around 1832, were probably used to teach design students as part of the later 19th-century neoclassical revival. The designs, drawn from classical Greek and Roman architecture, include floral and leaf scrolls, an intricate key with a small quincunx motif, a geometric meander and a ribbon design with olive tendrils.

Fine Fashions of Paris 1855–1893

Changing patterns in women's dress design and decoration

Through the second half of the 19th century, European fashion, centred on Paris, was affected by many changes in design, often involving elaborate patterning in the fabrics themselves and in the additional ornamentation. The wide crinoline skirts of the 1850s and 1860s provided expansive areas for striking decorative elements – bold geometric borders and delicate floral and embroidered details. Patterns were created with ribbon, lace, scalloping and ruching (folded and frilled fabric), especially with the advent of the bustle in the early 1870s. Stripes and lace were particularly popular in the 1880s. These were combined with bold contrasting textures, fabrics and colours, which were used to edge and decorate skirts and bodices.

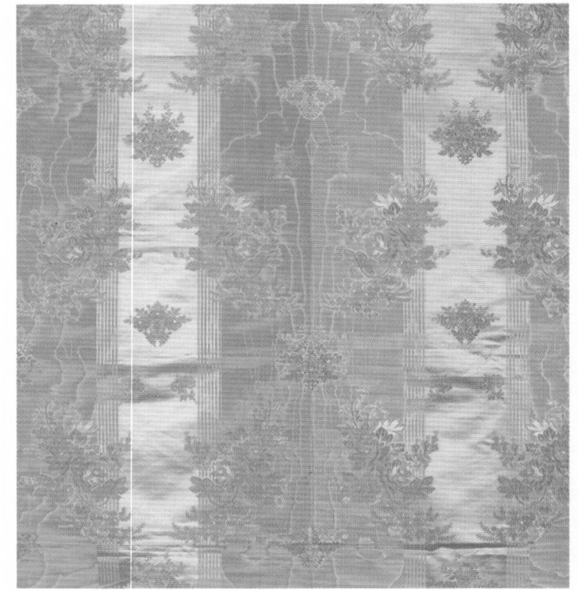

Silk dress fabric, Tholozan et Cie, 1855, *Lyons*
Since the 18th century, Lyons had produced fashionable silks for the pre-eminent Paris couturiers (see pages 168–9). This jacquard moiré satin silk, patterned with abundant yellow and white floral bouquets on stripes, combined the key features of popular fashion in the mid-19th century. The rich textures of broad and fine stripes would have shimmered on the rustling skirts of an elegant gown.

Silk and satin trimmed dress, Madame Vignon, 1869–70, *Paris*
Synthetic dyes appeared in the late 1850s, providing new vibrant colours. This astonishing magenta was very popular and is emphasised with textures and shapes on the skirt and collar. Contrasting satin geometric forms and organic scalloping and frills create complex three-dimensional patterns. This elaborate gown was made by one of the eminent Paris couturiers to the Empress Eugénie, wife of Napoleon III.

ELEMENTS OF PATTERN

- *stripes and geometrics*
- *textured flowers and stripes*
- *self-coloured ribbons and scallops*
- *lace, chiffon and embroidered leaves and flowers*

Fashion plate, Goubaud, 1864, *Paris*
From 1860, the wide availability of the sewing machine and the advent of machine-made clothing led to greater accessibility to fashion. Paris fashion appealed to English taste. *The Englishwoman's Domestic Magazine*, published by Samuel Beeton (husband of the cookery writer Mrs Isabella Beeton), included plates and paper patterns. The black, possibly velvet, geometric border and the fine embroidery and tassels on these day dresses would have been highly popular at the time.

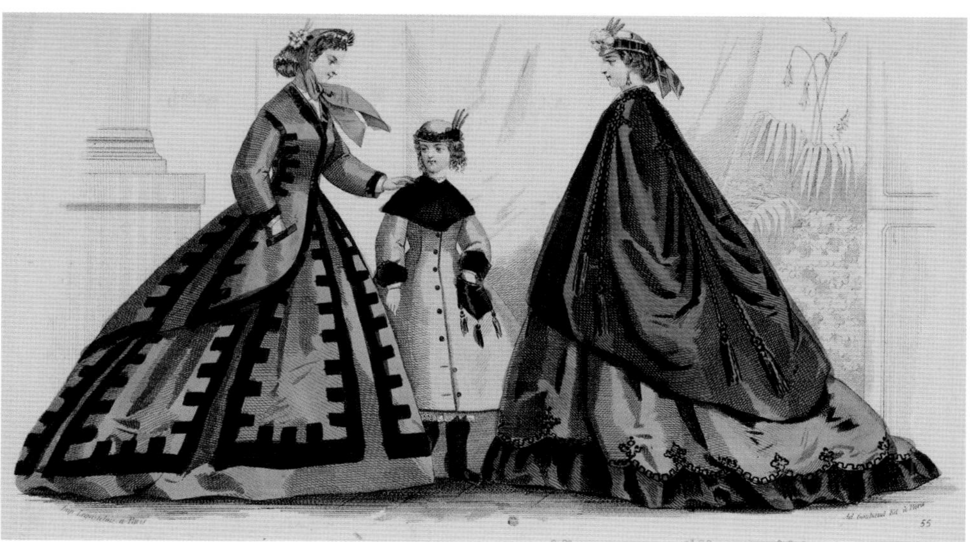

'It was the fashion ... to cut the dress out of two different materials, one patterned and one plain.'

JAMES LAVER, *A Concise History of Costume*, 1969

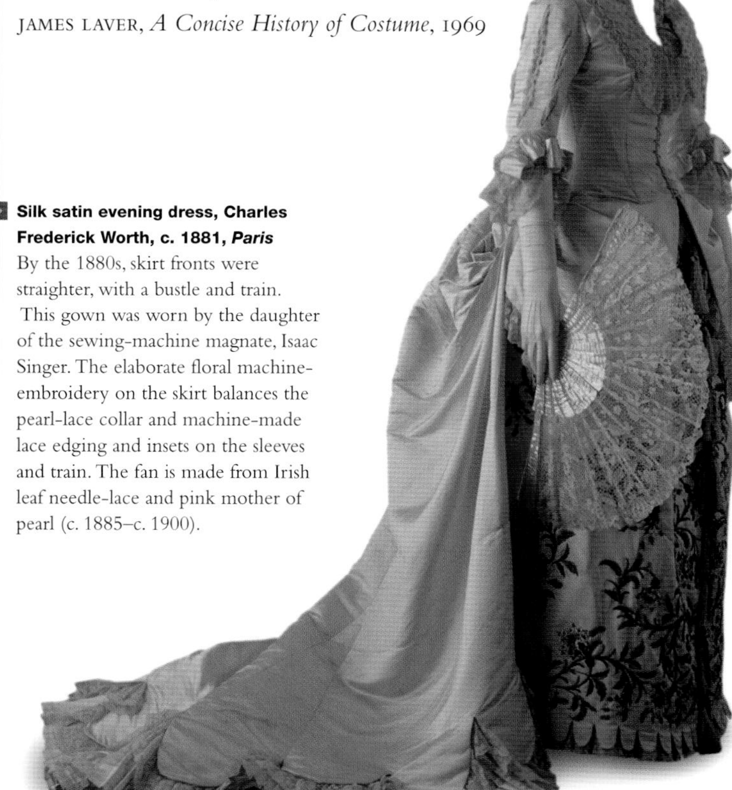

Silk satin evening dress, Charles Frederick Worth, c. 1881, *Paris*
By the 1880s, skirt fronts were straighter, with a bustle and train. This gown was worn by the daughter of the sewing-machine magnate, Isaac Singer. The elaborate floral machine-embroidery on the skirt balances the pearl-lace collar and machine-made lace edging and insets on the sleeves and train. The fan is made from Irish leaf needle-lace and pink mother of pearl (c. 1885–c. 1900).

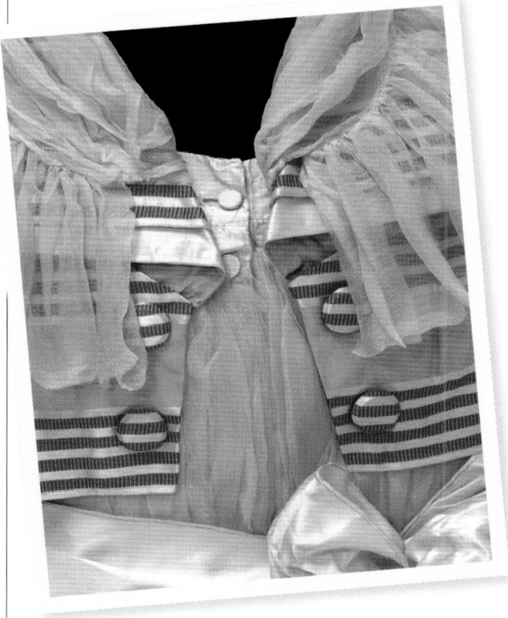

Dress bodice, Maison Worth, 1890–93, *Paris*
The bodice updates a late 18th-century 'riding coat' design with vibrant pink silk stripes and chiffon. Charles Frederick Worth (1825–95) drew on historical designs, especially as seen in the famous paintings of artists such as Titian and Gainsborough. The open-jacket style reveals soft clouds of chiffon and the bold strips contrast with the rich textures of satin and tulle.

William Morris
1834–1896

The eldest son of wealthy parents, Morris was an avid reader of medieval romance and folktales. He attended Marlborough College and explored the ruins and churches of the Wiltshire countryside, acquiring his love of landscape and medieval architecture. In 1853 he went to study Literature and Classics at Exeter College, Oxford, with a view to a career in the Church; there he met the artists Edward Burne-Jones and Dante Gabriel Rossetti, and his future wife Jane Burden. Deeply inspired by the writings of John Ruskin, Morris became fascinated with illuminated manuscripts, whose patterns seemed to express a harmony between the illuminators and the contemplative world in which they lived and worked.

Morris reacted against mass-production for social reasons, the use of machines to produce profit by exploiting others and the negative consequences of repetitive labour.

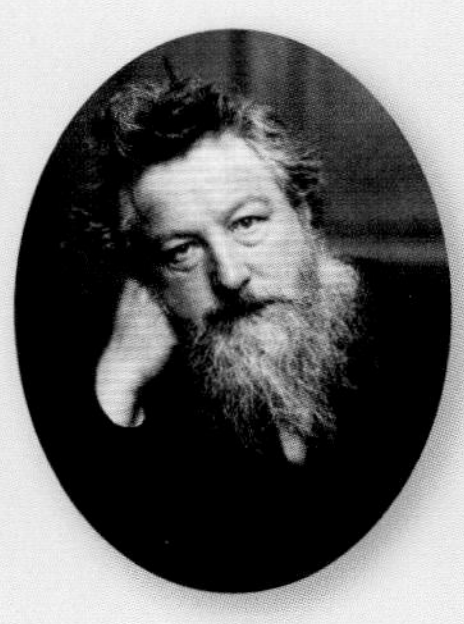

Born
Walthamstow, Essex, England, 1834

Profession
Artist, craftsman, poet, pioneer

Manifesto
'The past is not dead, it is living in us, and will be alive in the future we are now helping to make.'

'Poet, painter, designer, typographer, polemicist, manufacturer and socialist, Morris leapt from one enthusiasm to another, living his life with a restless energy that continually led him to seek and solve new challenges.'

ROSALIND ORMISTON AND NICHOLAS WELLS,
William Morris: Artist, Craftsman, Pioneer, 2010

On his visit to the Great Exhibition in London of 1851 he commented on the 'wonderful ugliness' of the machine-made products on display.

In 1855 Morris travelled to northern France with Burne-Jones and discovered the soaring cathedrals of Rouen, Chartres, Amiens and Beauvais and the transcendent beauty of the flowering countryside, he perceived the cathedrals as a powerful link with the past and as structures ageing amid nature. In Paris, he came across an inspirational exhibition of Pre-Raphaelite paintings in the Louvre. Morris decided to become an architect, and trained under the Gothic revivalist George Street but, increasingly interested in the paintings of Rossetti, he opted to devote himself to art. He collaborated with architect Philip Webb in the design of his own home, Red House at Bexleyheath in Kent, and in 1861 founded 'The Firm' of 'Morris, Marshall, Faulkner, Fine Art Workmen in Painting, Carving, Furniture, and the Metals' to provide suitable furnishings.

Skilled at creating flowing patterns based on natural and medieval forms, Morris designed the wallpapers, tapestries and textiles that stimulated the Arts and Crafts movement. He wrote poetry, inspired by the Viking sagas and his journeys to Iceland. Morris was involved in politics, conservation and social reform. He founded the Society for the Preservation of Ancient Buildings in 1877, the Hammersmith Socialist League in 1884 and set up the Kelmscott Press to spearhead the revival of Renaissance printing techniques.

Morris's earlier designs were lighter and more delicately stylised, influenced by Owen Jones's theory in *The Grammar of Ornament* (1856) that the natural geometry of plants was present in formal patterns, although Morris preferred less precision and softer colours.

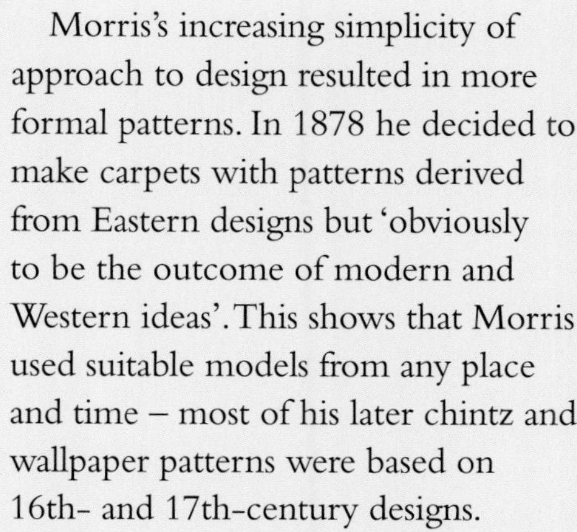

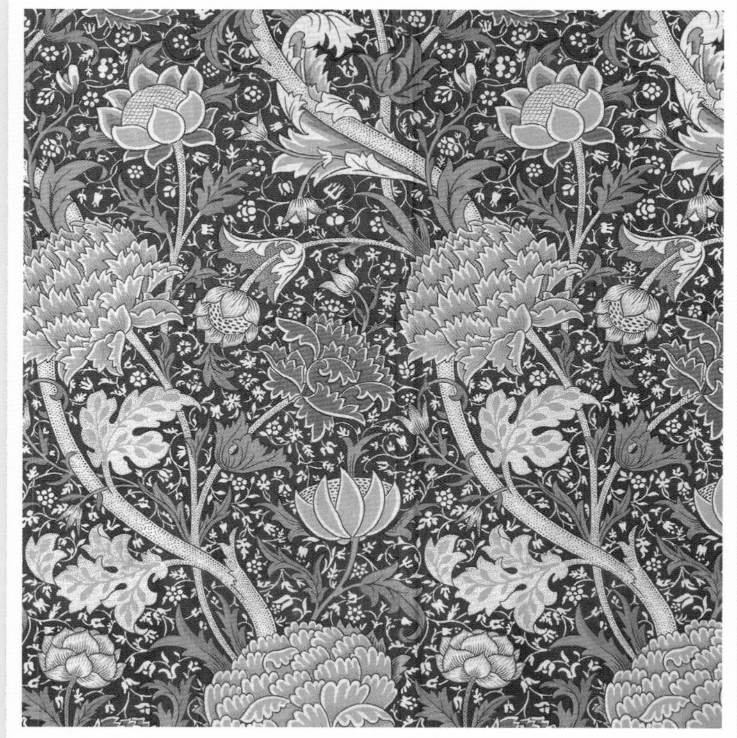

'Cray' furnishing fabric, 1884–85, *Surrey, England*
In this layered design that reflects its block-printing, a pale winding stem sprouts serrated leaves and florals, including carnations, against a background patterned with delicate curling flowering plants. Red and blue was a favourite combination of Morris. After moving to new dyeworks and workshops at Merton, Morris designed flowing patterns for printed cotton textiles. With undulating flowering tendrils and leafy shoots, he named the series after southern English rivers, such as the Cray in Kent.

Morris's increasing simplicity of approach to design resulted in more formal patterns. In 1878 he decided to make carpets with patterns derived from Eastern designs but 'obviously to be the outcome of modern and Western ideas'. This shows that Morris used suitable models from any place and time – most of his later chintz and wallpaper patterns were based on 16th- and 17th-century designs.

Morris gave equal value to philosophy, writing, politics and art, advocating that abilities and materials should be used where they were most suitable to reflect the fluidity of the natural world. For him, designing patterns was a pleasurable process, from the research of natural and historical sources to the selection, mixing and application of colour. He felt strongly that labour should be fulfilling and worthwhile in the tradition of individual craft skills. He campaigned against the lack of unity in building design and laid the foundations of modern architectural style. His revival of decorative honesty was deeply significant for the Modern movement as it inspired others, such as artist-designer Walter Crane and potter William de Morgan, to reinstate craftworking as a serious occupation and led to the foundation of craft guilds and associations.

Beautiful Patterns of Necessity

1880–1900

Arts and Crafts

The concept of choosing materials suitable to the purpose of an object was part of the Arts and Crafts quest for authentic forms and patterns. Native plants and animals were incorporated into stylised rhythmical designs for textiles and wallpapers, composed in harmonious elegant ways, in reaction to the over-worked designs produced by machines. The significance attached by the movement to craftworking traditions and the revival of medieval techniques of colour mixing and dyeing resulted in patterns designed with natural colours, in contrast to those derived from the chemicals used for factory-made products.

'The Arts and Crafts Movement had a lasting effect on British, European and American design, contributing to the great revival of the decorative arts.'

BRENDA M. KING, *Silk and Empire*, 2005

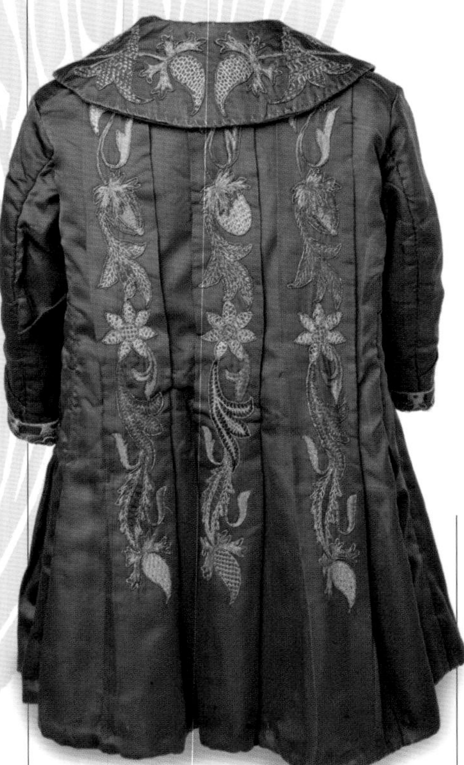

Coat, 1880–95, *Britain*
The collar, cuffs and box-pleats of this child's silk coat are richly embroidered in coloured silk thread with flowers, fruit and leaves, and outlined with couched gold thread; some are embellished with beadwork. The back of the garment is decorated with three flowing patterns of linked stylised fruits, flowers and leaves, each terminating with a tear-shaped motif. This motif is also embroidered on the collar back in an opposing pair at the ends of the patterns.

ELEMENTS OF PATTERN

- *native plants and animals*
- *stylised flower, fruit and leaf forms*
- *flowing rhythms from nature*
- *natural colours*

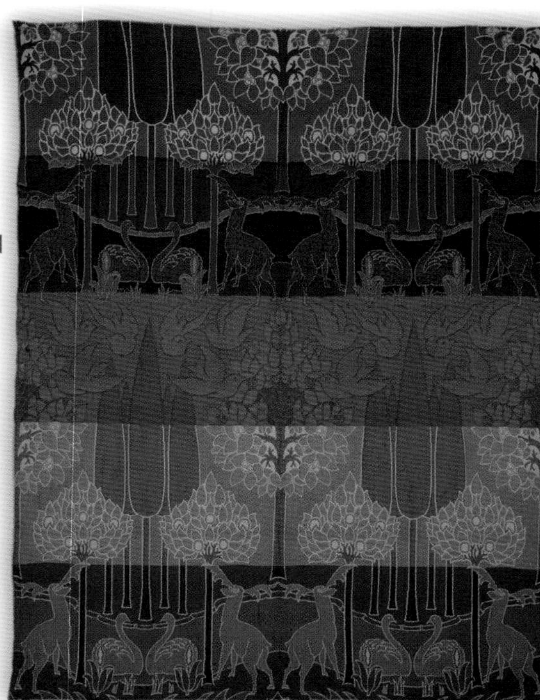

Hanging, 1899, *Britain*
This woven wool hanging designed by Charles Voysey is subtly varied with bands of different colour through the vertical pattern repeat. Stands of poplars alternate with flowering trees and rows of fruit trees, divided by a winding river with pairs of swans swimming and pairs of stags standing on the banks. Around the tops of the trees flocks of birds flutter. The shapes of the poplars, stags and birds are flat areas of colour with clear outlines and minimal line detail.

Coat, 1895–1900, *London, England*
The medieval-style collar of this hand-embroidered coat shows the influence of Arts and Crafts design in its cut and decoration. The shape is inspired by the simple flowing lines of the 'aesthetic' dress of the 1870s and it has a medieval-style collar. The velvet and lace over satin panels are patterned with large drifting sprays of the English wildflower sweet cicely, the lace patterned with delicate flowerheads in a mesh background. This bespoke coat was made at the exclusive department store Marshall and Snelgrove in London.

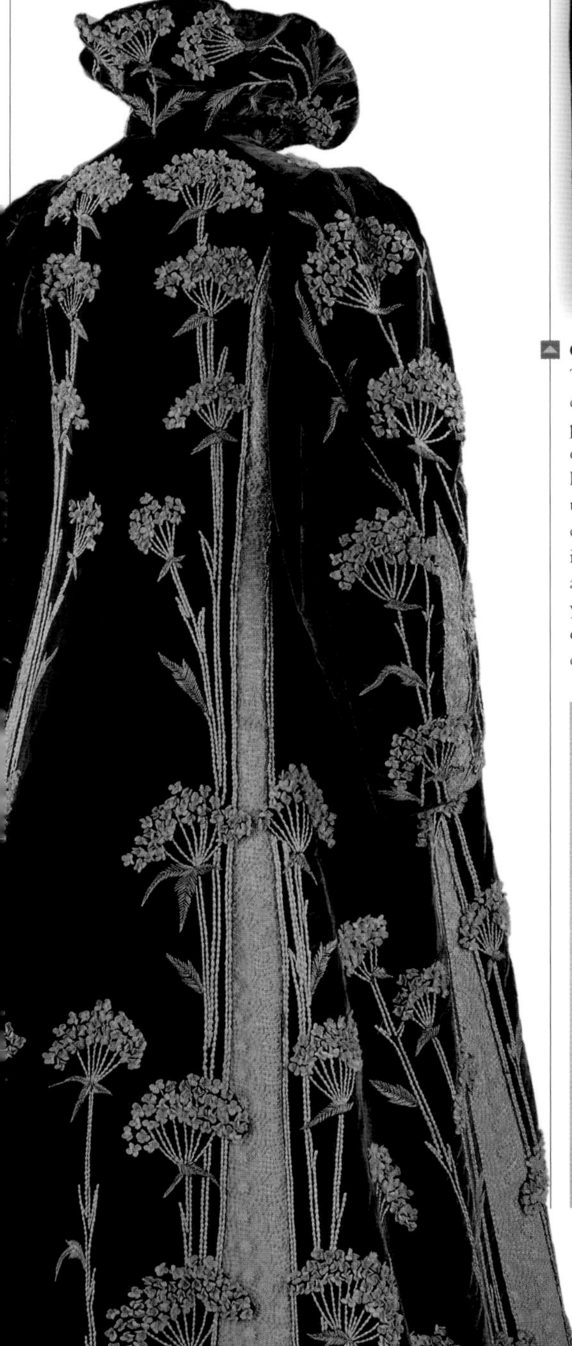

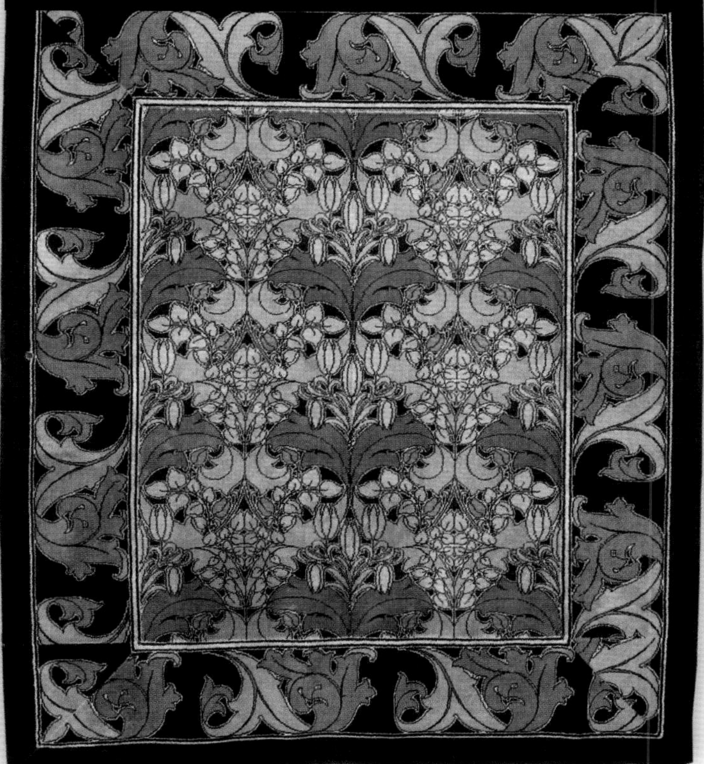

Carpet, 1896, *Kidderminster, England*
This machine-woven wool carpet designed by Charles Voysey is centrally patterned with vertical lines of clusters of small orange tulips with stems of heart-shaped leaves, alternating with upright and pendant yellow tulips with curving leaves. The lines of motifs are integrated with opposed pairs of acanthus-like leaves that curl to show yellow and olive green sides. A pattern of similar two-coloured bifurcated leaves curls around the border.

Wallpaper or textile design, c. 1882, *England*
The shape of the coral-like sea lily is rhythmically repeated in groups in this charcoal and watercolour design by Arthur Mackmurdo. Pointed bunches of sea lilies with pairs of leaves on a diagonal grid wave above fanned sprays of single repeated flowers set in an oblique line. Mackmurdo was inspired by Edward Burne-Jones's swirling designs for stained glass and his patterns were often derived from unusual natural forms.

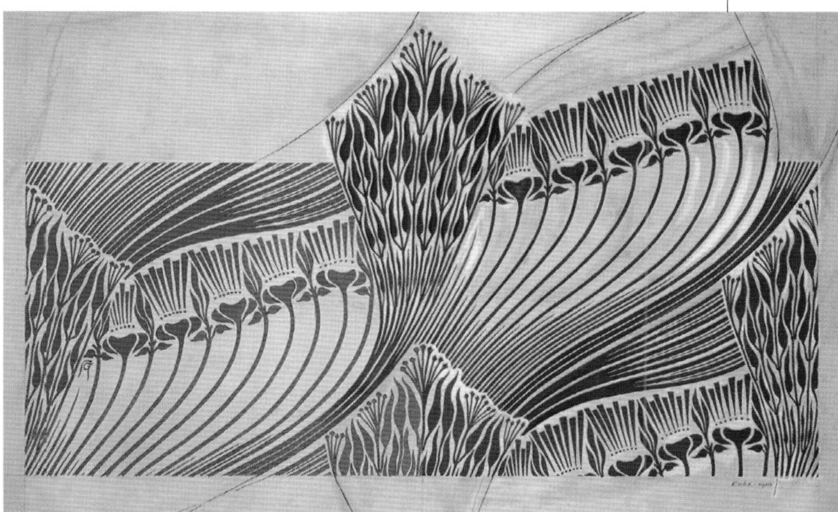

Patterns of Richness c. 1820–c. 1880s

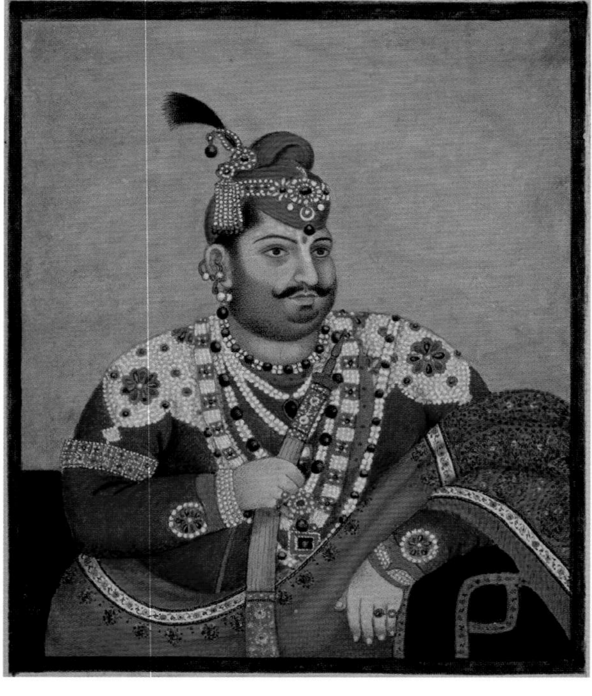

The Raj in British colonial India

The appointment of a viceroy in 1858 brought direct British rule to India, exiling the last Mughal emperor and establishing the British Raj. In India, Western styles of representation developed, and in Britain, Indian textiles and designs were popular. Elite art of the Raj encompassed traditional themes, subjects and patterns including Hindu gods, legends, elephants and tigers. The paisley design – the *boteh*, pine cone or mango motif, renamed after the Scottish town where shawls were made – had a long Iranian and Indian heritage and was gaining popularity in Europe through the 18th century. In the 19th century original Kashmir paisley shawls were highly valued in preference to the cheaper European imitations.

'A shawl was a required fashion accessory ... hand woven in India with *boteh* (pine-cone) or paisley patterned end panels, [they] were coveted.'

ALICE ZREBIEC, 'European 16th–19th Centuries' IN *The Metropolitan Museum of Art Bulletin*, 1995–96.

Gold elephant goad (*ankus*), c. 1870, *Jaipur*
This ceremonial elephant goad, an attribute of the elephant-god Ganesha, is decorated with enamel and colourless precious stones. Used to handle elephants, the sharp end has an elephant head decoration with other animal heads apparent on the spikes. The shaft is covered in jewelled flowers and the grip has hunting scenes including a horse and rider, rabbits, peacocks, tigers, birds and flowers.

Portrait of Ishwari Sen of Mandi, c. 1825, *Delhi*
This portrait shows Ishwari Sen (1784–1826), Raja of Mandi, dressed in rich robes. This is a 'Company Painting' produced by a Western artist associated with the East India Company in a Western style of representation. The robe is patterned with pearls and jewels arranged in rosettes and bands. The Kashmir shawl has a delicate floral scroll band edging the paisley design.

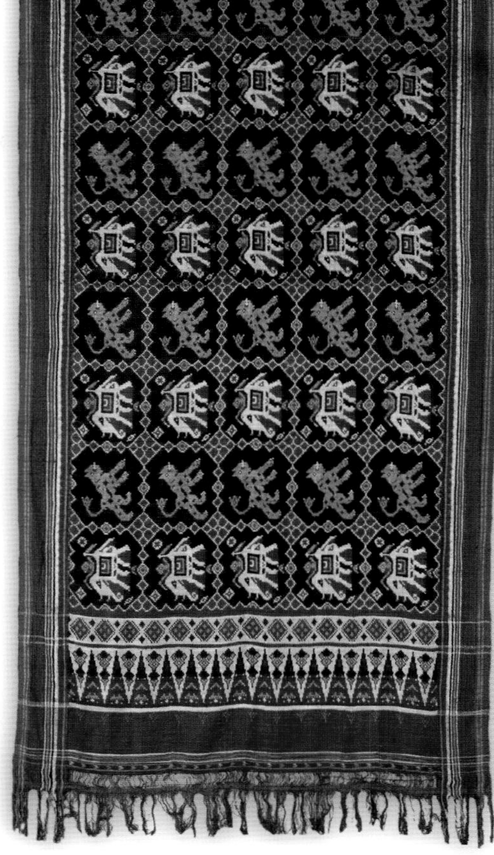

Silk ceremonial cloth, late 19th century, *Gujarat*
The weaving process for this ceremonial silk cloth (*patolu*) was complex, producing a pattern on both sides of the fabric. The 'double ikat' technique – where the threads are resist-dyed before weaving – produces a rich design. Elephants and tigers alternate within a grid of small lozenges and a striking zigzag decorates the border. The cloth was made for an elite Indonesian individual.

ELEMENTS OF PATTERN

- *paisley* (boteh) *motifs*
- *elephants and tigers*
- *flowers, scrolls and leaves*
- *gold, pearl and jewelled patterns*

Woven cashmere shawl (*doshala*), c. 1820–c. 1840, *Kashmir*
Woven by hand into complex designs, Kashmir shawls were prized in Europe. On this shawl, the paisley pattern (or *boteh*) of a floral cone with a curved tip is made up of interwoven blue and red threads. The shape encompasses small paisley forms and is interspersed with tree-like forms of a similar design, birds and floral swirls. The borders contain smaller floral and leaf patterns.

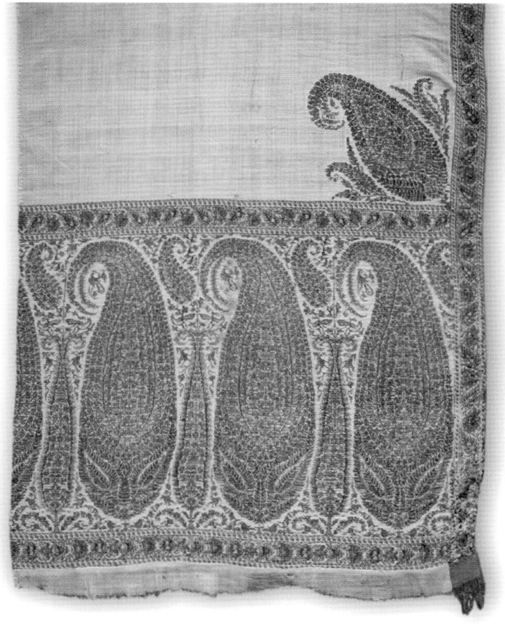

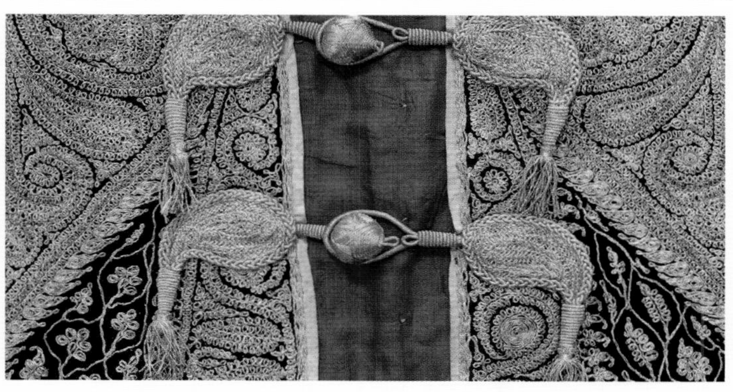

Robe (*choga*), mid-19th century, *Amritsar*, *Punjab* (or *Panjab*)
The embroidery and couching on the front of this robe is patterned with swirling scrolls and paisley motifs. The curling forms edge the opening, fill in around the rich rosettes and form the shape of the fasteners. Delicate gold-embroidered leaf chains stand out against the black background. This type of decorative loose robe originated in Central Asia, and was usually worn open to show its colourful lining.

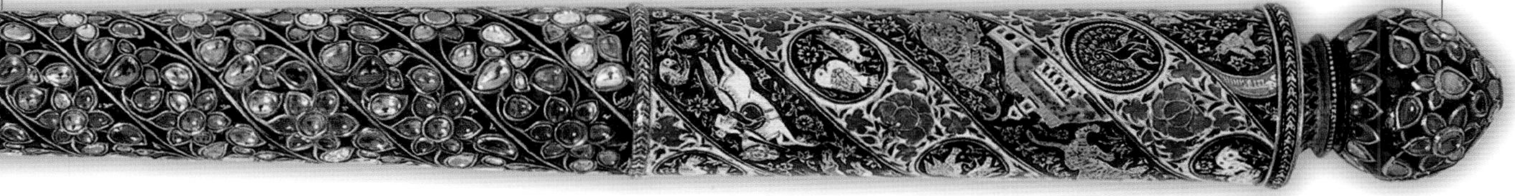

Flowers, Birds & Weaves c. 1800–1876

Carpet, clothes and panel designs in Iran

The Qajar dynasty (1794–1925) brought stability to Iran although the country was also affected by various political, military and economic interference in the region from Britain and Russia. Innovations from Europe brought modernisation, but conversely there were revivals of ancient poetic traditions and art forms of earlier Iranian dynasties. The arabesque remained a major pattern. Iranian carpets continued to be an important export and were displayed at the Great Exhibition in London (1851) that stimulated the Arts and Crafts movement (see pages 202–3). Floral motifs predominated; some were drawn from Chinese or Indian origins but others, such as the carnation, continued the strong traditions of earlier Islamic designs (see pages 126–7 and 142–3).

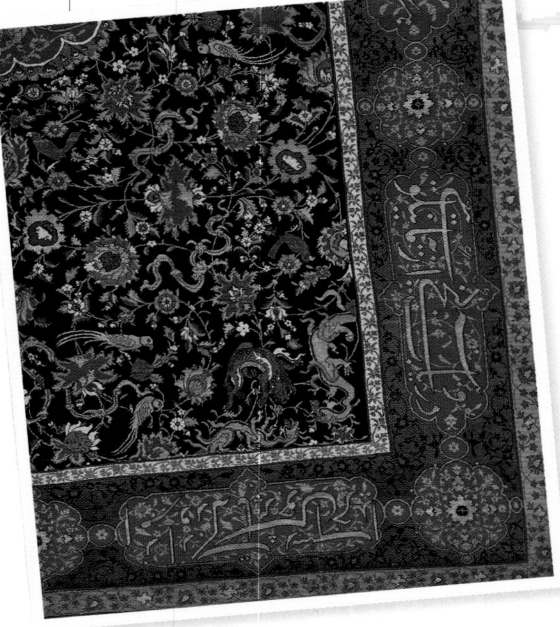

The Salting Carpet, 1850–80, *Iran or Turkey*
The four quarters of this carpet mirror each other with colourful arabesques, animals and birds. Metal thread is used for the grey calligraphy – verses by Hafiz, a 14th-century poet – in the border and to highlight aspects of the pattern, including sinuous Chinese dragons. The fantastical flowers reflect earlier Iranian arabesque designs but the dragons, tigers and clouds come from China.

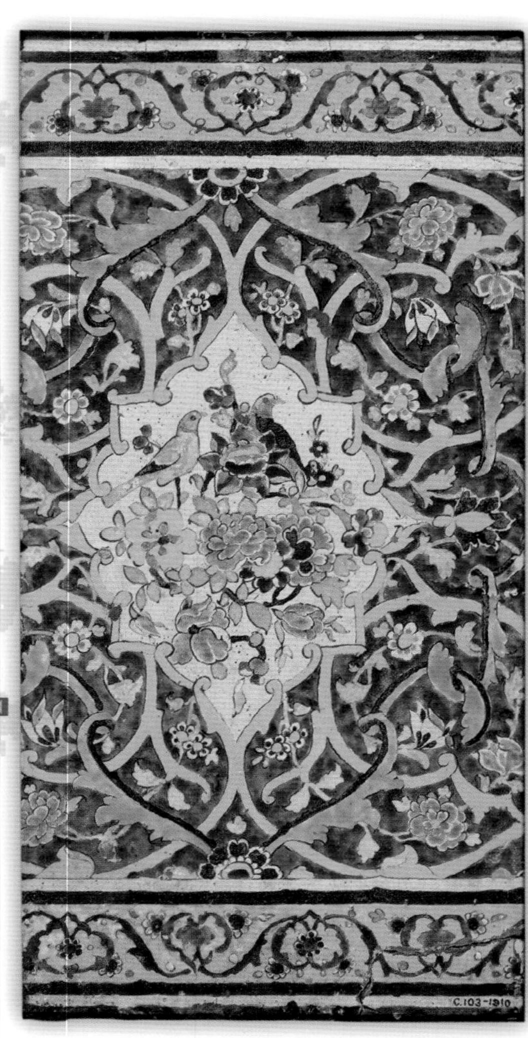

Tile panel, late 18th–early 19th century, *Iran*
This tile would probably have been part of a frieze with the scroll-edge lozenge of birds and flowers repeated against the vibrant background of blue, yellow, turquoise and pale green arabesques. In the border the colours are switched for the floral meander. The flowers in the central panel have similarities to popular Chinese blooms such as chrysanthemum and *Prunus* blossom.

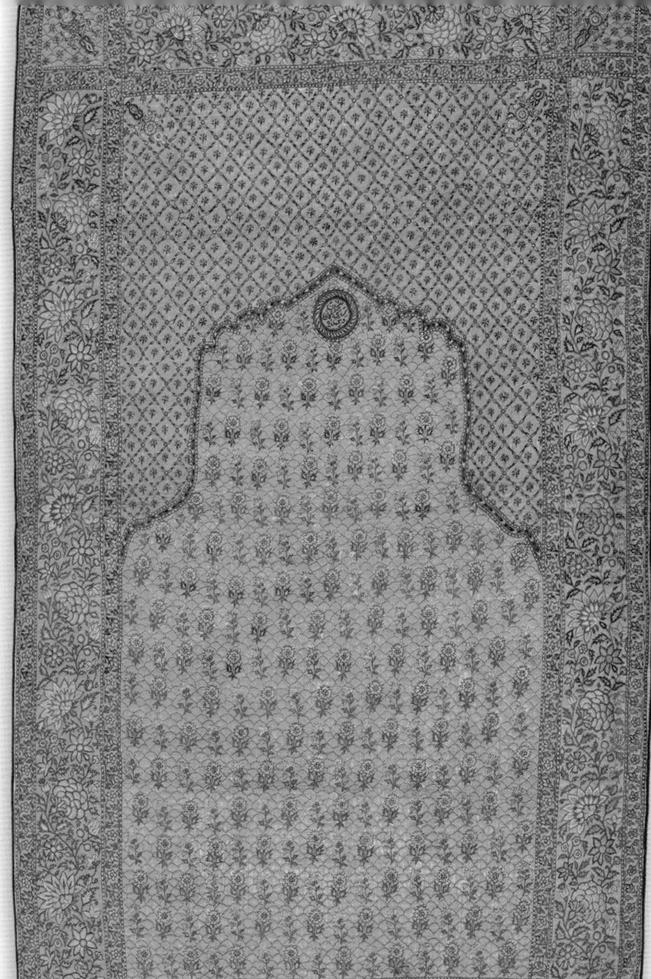

ELEMENTS OF PATTERN

- *carnations, birds and flowers*
- *Chinese dragons, tigers and clouds*
- *arabesques and floral scrolls*
- *zigzag, lozenges and V-shapes*

Silk and cotton satin prayer mat, 1830–70, *Iran*
This prayer mat has the small embroidered and inscribed circle where holy earth would be placed and touched to the forehead during prayers. It represents a heavenly golden profusion of flowers and features a large *saz* (serrated leaf motif) and flower border reminiscent of ceramic designs edged by small scrolling bands. Tiny carnation blooms in lozenges cover the upper area and larger flowers (similar to Indian forms) fill the quilted kneeling section.

Silk robe (*abba*) with metal thread, 1876, *Iran*
This type of robe – the *abba* – was versatile and used for ordinary activities such as sleeping. Made from two fabric lengths sewn across the shoulders and around the middle, it could be draped or pulled back as required. The rich blue-purple fabric is patterned with fine white metallic, silver and gold threads forming zigzags, decorated 'tongues', V-shaped panels and lozenges.

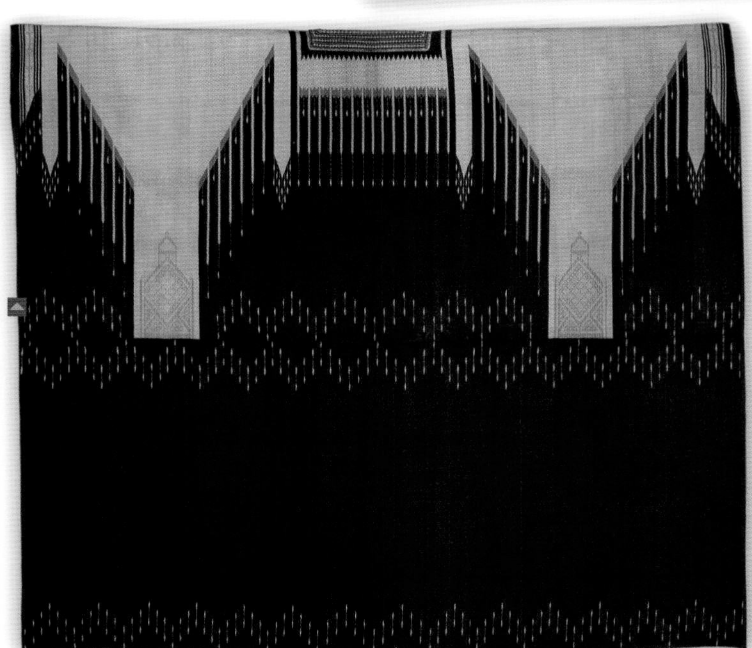

'The interior of the saloon was profusely decorated with carving, gilding, arabesque painting, and looking glass ... interwoven with all the other wreathing ornaments, gleaming and glittering in every part.'

SIR FRANCIS HOPKINS OF ATHBOY, 1835
(ON THE COURT OF THE SHAH OF PERSIA)

Pine, Blossom, Bamboo & Carp 1800–1900

Japanese patterns and designs, and their imitators

The feudal Edo period (1600–1868) was a stable and prosperous period in Japan during which literary and artistic refinements were associated with the tea ceremony. Contact with China brought cultural interaction with the Ming (see pages 106–7). The Meiji Restoration (1868) opened the country to Western trade, which had a significant impact on artistic developments in Europe and also triggered modernisation in Japan. Traditional motifs in Japanese art were associated with the court, the *Samurai* (warrior class) and the religions of Shinto, meaning 'the way of the gods' (*kami*) and Buddhism. They included the powerful spirituality of nature, earth and Heaven symbolised by flowers, fish, trees, water, animals and mythical beasts.

ELEMENTS OF PATTERN

- *swimming carp*
- *pine and bamboo for longevity*
- *cranes and tortoises for happiness and good luck*
- *peonies, convolvulus and blossom*

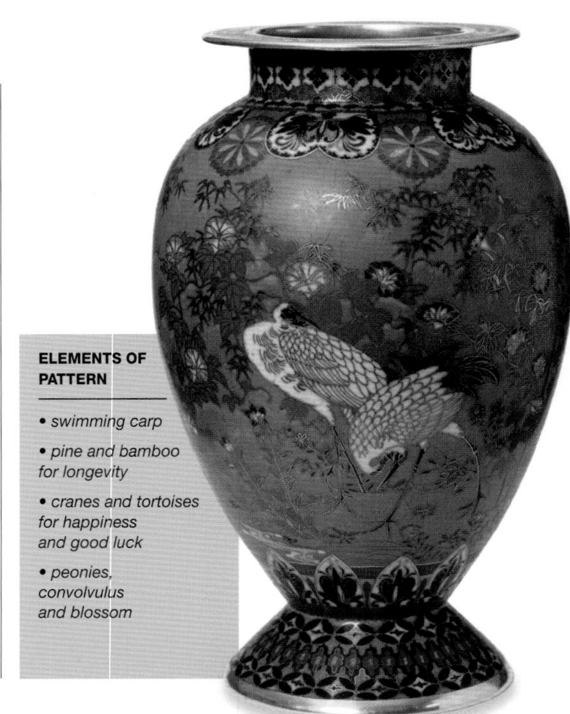

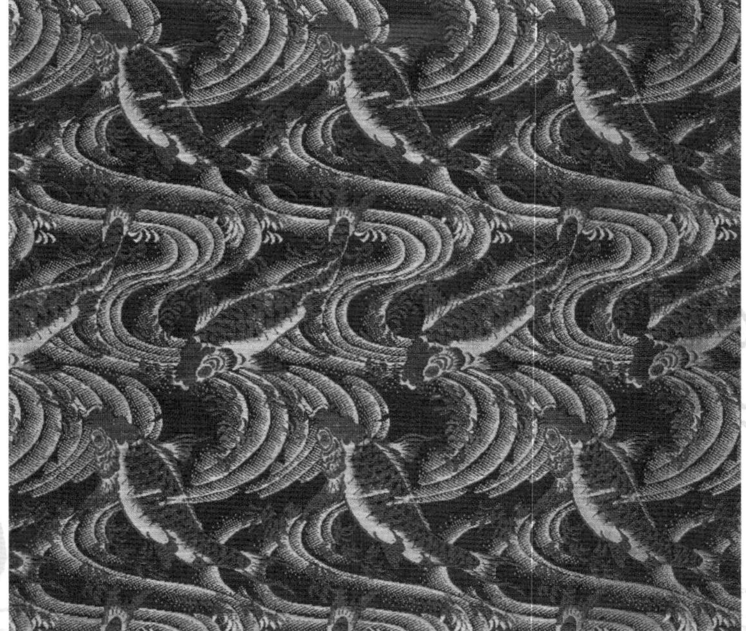

Obi (length of silk), 1860–1920, *possibly Kyoto*
This *obi* sash, used to secure a kimono, is a woven *nishiki* textile – sometimes described as brocade – with popular colourful patterning. The *koi* carp swimming through the waves symbolise perseverance and strength of purpose. In legend the *koi* swim upstream into the mists of a waterfall to become water dragons. Rich and ornamented kimonos developed in association with the *Noh* theatre.

Enamel *cloisonné* vase, 1860–80, *Nagoya*
Large-scale enamel works, such as this vase, were based on Chinese styles – here the decorative patterned border motifs also follow Chinese models. The naturalistic pattern around the body contains elegant red-crowned cranes – symbolising happiness, eternal youth and immortality – in a bamboo grove covered in convolvulus. Bamboo was often used to ward off evil and can signify strength of character or longevity.

> **'The taste for realistic pictorial ornament, like the taste for ever more richly and confusingly decorated *obi*, is an aspect of the late Edo style.'**
>
> OLIVER IMPEY & WILLIAM WATSON, 'Textiles' IN *The Great Japan Exhibition. Art of the Edo Period, 1600–1868*, 1981

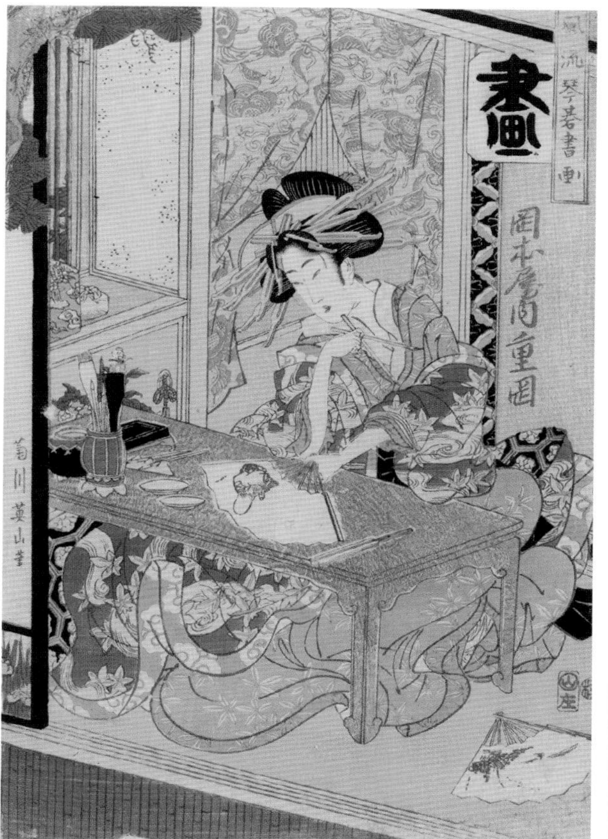

Woodblock print, 19th century, *Eisan*
The woodblock print was a major art form in Japan and its flat, structured style was highly influential on European artists such as Monet and van Gogh. This print of the courtesan Shigeoka of Okamoto-ya shows a patterned screen of exotic scrolling plants. She wears a kimono with patterned fabrics covered in maple leaves, rocks, bamboo leaves and flowers.

Silk kimono, 1850–1900, *Japan*
This kimono is patterned with a moment in the love story of Urashima Taro, a fisherman, and Otomine, a tortoise princess at the court of the Dragon King of the Sea. The pattern shows the eternal lives of the two tortoise lovers, swimming in the waves, maintained by the magical box. The scene is surrounded by auspicious pines, bamboo and blossoms.

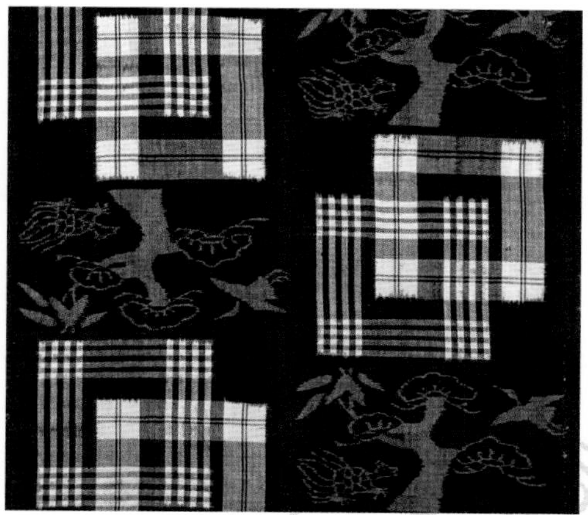

Futon cover, 1850–1900, *Fukuoka*
This cover for a traditional form of Japanese bedding combines geometric and natural motifs, a popular form of design. The chequered double square offsets a motif containing the auspicious elements of the pine tree, crane and tortoise to bring good luck and long life. The design was created by the *kasuri* technique where skeins of yarn are bound in order to reserve areas during dyeing.

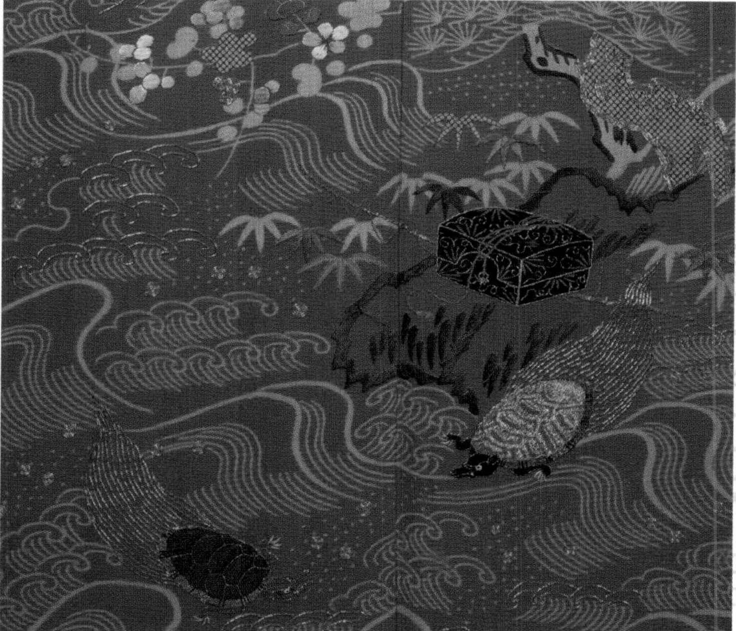

Louis Henry Sullivan
1856–1924

Economic growth, urbanisation and social change in the United States in the late 19th century fuelled the demand for bigger and taller buildings. Louis Sullivan has been called the 'father of the skyscraper' and the 'father of modernism' as his new approach to design changed architecture forever.

Sullivan studied architecture initially at the Massachusetts Institute of Technology in Boston before moving to pursue an apprenticeship in Philadelphia. Following the great Chicago Fire in 1871 and the economic depression of 1873, he moved to Chicago to take advantage of the resulting building boom. For a while he studied at the École des Beaux-Arts in Paris where he developed an interest in Michelangelo and the Renaissance with its classical principles of creativity. After he returned to Chicago, he became a partner with the German Dankmar Adler (1844–1900) and his most productive years began. The young Frank Lloyd Wright joined the Adler Sullivan firm as a draughtsman in 1887 and was heavily influenced by Sullivan's design ethos (see pages 222-3).

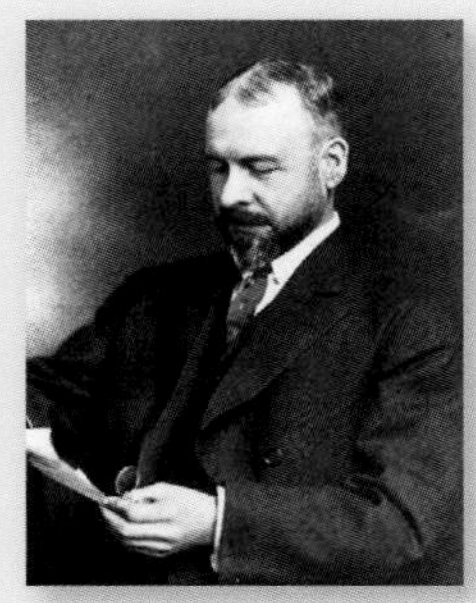

Born
Wakefield, Massachusetts, USA, 1856

Profession
Architect

Manifesto
Form follows function

Traditional styles of architecture in the second half of the 19th century in America were dependent on masonry structures that needed massive lower-level load-bearing walls to take the weight of taller building designs. The development of steel offered a cheaper, versatile and strong option that would create lighter, taller buildings. These buildings could be constructed with steel frames on which walls, floors and ceilings were hung – called the 'column-frame' construction. The frame system could have bigger windows allowing more light into the building and lighter interior walls giving more usable floor space.

Louis Sullivan's critical contribution to the development of steel-frame buildings was to create a new set of principles that rejected traditional architectural constraints. He developed the concept of 'form following function' – a foundational principle of

'Sullivan accentuated the individual layers with ornamented bands under the windows, as well as throughout the attic story, and crowned the building with a projecting cornice that brings the structure back to the horizontal.'

H. H. ARNASON, *History of Modern Art. Painting, Sculpture, Architecture, Photography*, 2004

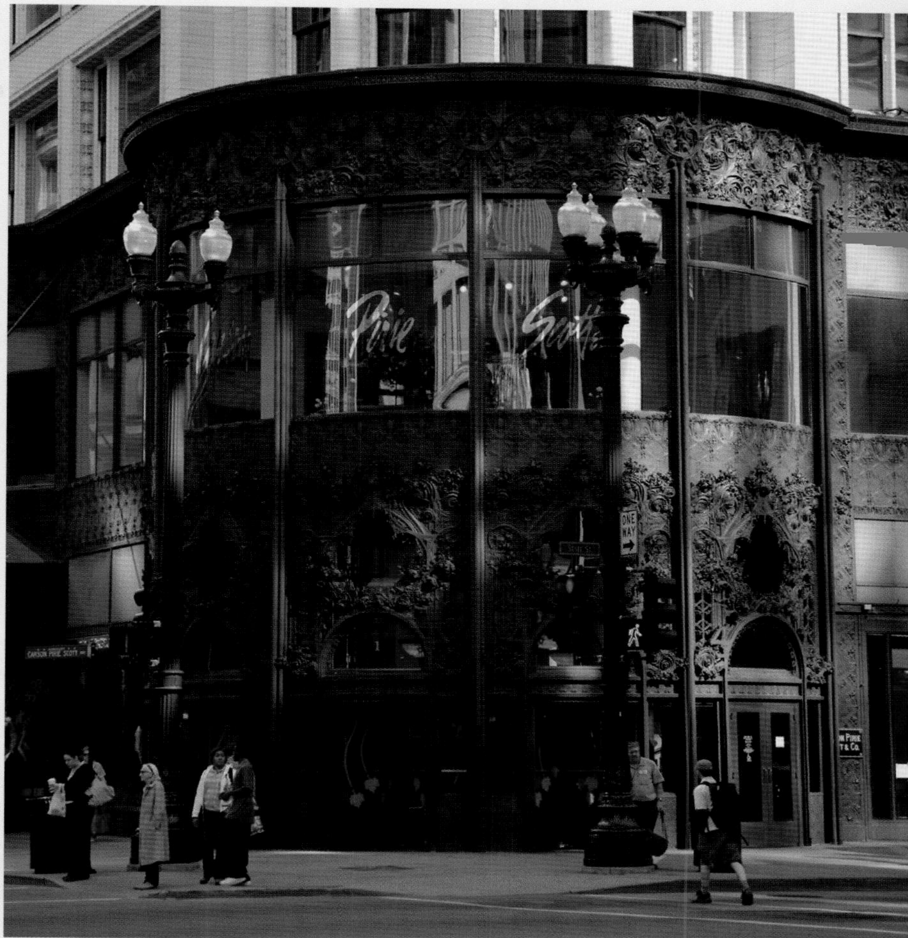

modernism which would drive design and architecture for the next century. Aesthetics would be subordinated to function; form would be driven by the practical needs of the function. The basic design for buildings would involve three elements – the base, piers and attic – which emphasised its vertical form and introduced an 'honest' and commercially successful simplicity.

An important exemplar of Sullivan's style is the office skyscraper, the Guaranty Building in Buffalo, New York, opened in 1895. Its base spans two floors with a large arched entrance – a signature element in much of Sullivan's work. Above, 11 floors stretch up, defined by tall façade arches and large windows; on the top floor circular windows run along under an overhanging pediment. The façade is elaborately decorated with organic patterns on all surfaces, weaving up the arches and on each floor below the windows, developing into exuberant twisting vines and leaves around the top floor windows.

The lush forms of decorative foliage were inherited from one of Sullivan's first influences, Frank Furness (1839–1912), and were rooted in earlier European aesthetic ideals and especially the interlacing scrolling forms of Anglo-Saxon designs.

The base and entrance level of the building are covered with a variety of patterns, including interacting geometric and organic forms. The complex pierced foliate capitals with ornate scrolling monograms on the ground-floor pillars are reminiscent of Byzantine capitals from the 6th century. In addition to the patterned surface of the façade, the overall building design has the clear lines and simple grid form which would become characteristics of modernist architecture in the 20th century.

Carson Pirie Scott Store, 1899, *Chicago*
The ornamentation of the corner entrance was designed to attract customers to the new store. The elaborate decorative metal scrollwork, probably designed by Sullivan's chief draughtsman George Grant Elmslie, echoed Anglo-Saxon forms. The ornate decoration is confined to the base formed by the lowest two floors. The broad grid structure of the rest of the building is not ornamented but was formed by the clean lines that frame the windows.

Surfaces Form Mythic Animals 1800–1900

Decorative patterns of the Pacific North-west of America

The powerful art and visual culture of the First Peoples of the Pacific North-west – who occupied the coastal regions of Washington State, British Columbia and Alaska – followed distinctive principles in representing animals. The composition of patterns involved primary formlines filled in with colours according to rules – red for features, blue for infill. Everyday tools, clothes and objects of display, such as totem poles, were covered in stylised patterns representing humans, salmon, animals, bears, whales and birds, revealing the natural and supernatural worlds. The Tlingit peoples lived along the northern coast of British Columbia; their kinship was matrilineal and their art had strong visual and symbolic impact.

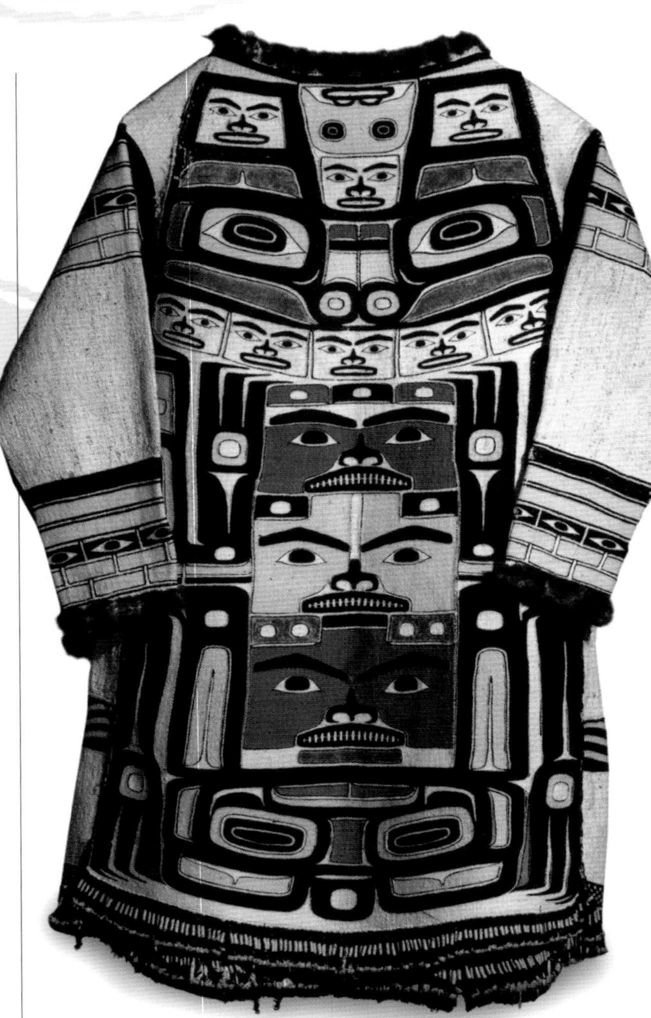

Chilkat tunic, Tlingit, *Pacific North-west coast of America*

Made of mountain-goat wool, this Chilkat tunic is covered with faces in a range of sizes but the central motif is the stylised animal head at the bottom of the tunic. To each side of the main part of the tunic are limbs with claws, which together with the face comprise a representation of the brown bear – an animal which was hunted by the Tlingit.

ELEMENTS OF PATTERN

- *black formlines in different thicknesses*
- *the natural and supernatural worlds*
- *brown bears, salmon and eagles*
- *geometric designs*
- *ovals, claws and eyes*

'Even the most utilitarian objects such as spoons, fish clubs, and paddles were decorated. The two-dimensional art is founded on rules which order design organisation.'

PETER L. MACNAIR, Introduction to *The Legacy*, ROYAL BRITISH COLUMBIA MUSEUM, 1984

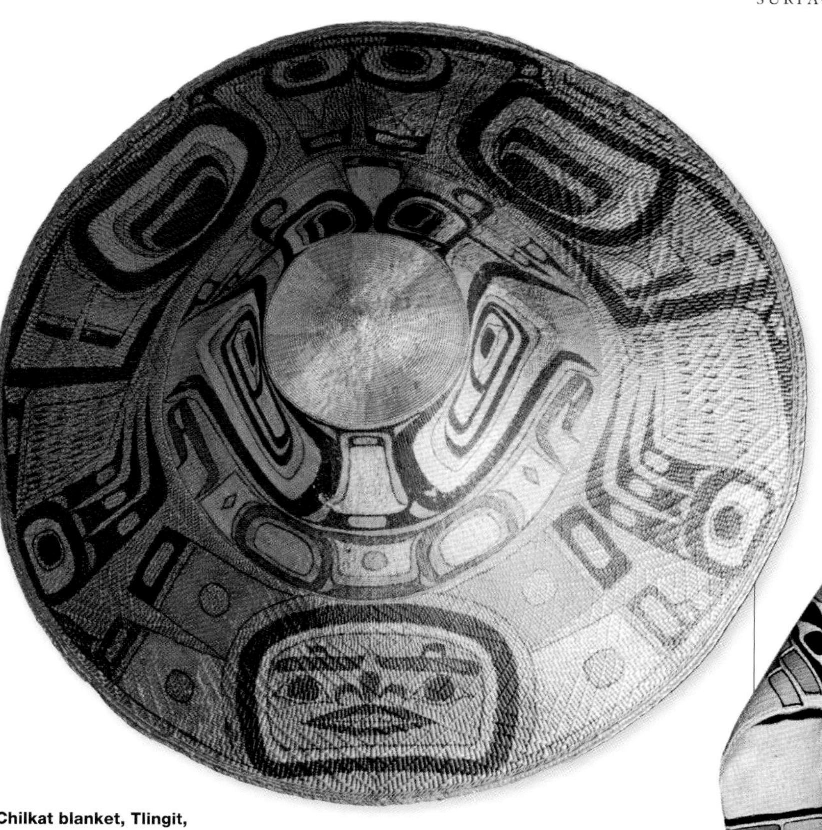

Tlingit hat, *Pacific North-west coast of America*
The patterns on this woven hat follow the colour principles of Tlingit design. The brown bear on the brim has a face at the top with two clawed limbs and fur. On the crown, two stylised eye-like forms represent the salmon's head. The salmon was a main diet item of the peoples of the Pacific North-west and its form featured regularly in this indigenous art.

Chilkat blanket, Tlingit, *Pacific North-west coast of America*
The pattern on this blanket shows a school of stylised killer whales, which frequent the waters along the Pacific North-west coast. In the winter, the Tlingit held ceremonies at which singing and dancing rituals would invoke the spirit world. The Chilkat blanket was a ceremonial cloak worn during dances. The movements of the dance would have been enhanced by the undulating of the long fringe.

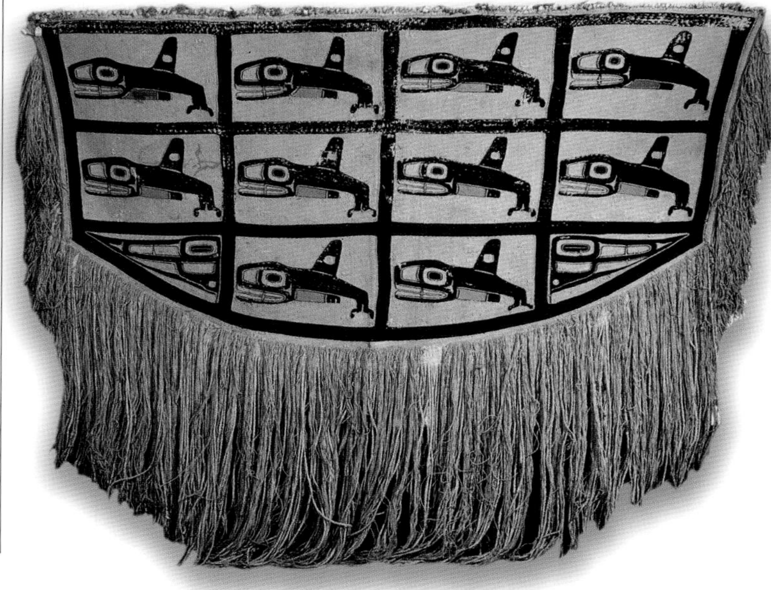

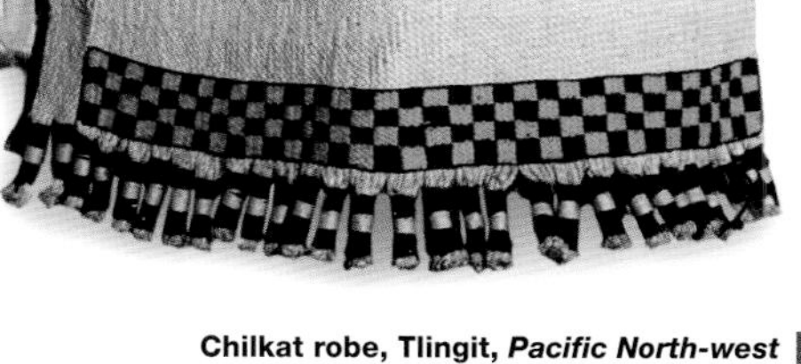

Chilkat robe, Tlingit, *Pacific North-west coast of America*
Decorative designs from the later 19th century began to break away from the traditional forms. This robe has simplified formline designs of a head and eyes but also has a colourful geometric zigzag pattern, checks and enclosed coloured rectangles. The arrival of Westerners decimated the First Peoples' population through smallpox and the arts declined, but recently they have been revived.

Antoni Gaudí
1852–1926

The son of a coppersmith in Reus, Catalonia, Gaudí studied architecture at Barcelona University, and worked in local architects' offices to earn money. He studied the neo-Gothic style of French architects such as Viollet-le-Duc, who wrote on 11th–13th-century architecture.

The Gothic revival was highly significant for Catalans and became the political signifier of their nationalist sentiment and regional independence in Spain. Gaudí deepened his knowledge of the history of Catalan architecture and analysed historic buildings for new insight that would allow him to design a new architectural style for Catalonia.

In 1883 Gaudí was commissioned to build Sagrada Familia (Holy Family). This Church-sponsored community project for a church surrounded by schools, meeting rooms and workshops was a protest against growing industrialisation and secularisation.

At the same time, Gaudí was commissioned to design houses for wealthy industrialists. In Barcelona, Casa Vicens was built with a façade influenced by the Islamic Spanish Mudejar style, with roof turrets reminiscent of mosque minarets and decorated tiles arranged in contrasting check patterns emulating Islamic latticework. El Capricho in Comillas was built with brick walls banded with coloured tiles decorated with European sunflower heads and leaves but repeated in the Moorish tradition, contrasting with lower levels of undressed stone.

Gaudí had first met the wealthy industrialist and patron of the arts Eusebi Güell i Bacigalupi at the Paris World Fair in 1878. Gaudí may have discovered the works of John Ruskin and William Morris, and the Pre-Raphaelite ideals of medieval art and elaborate ornamentation, in Güell's library. From 1884 Gaudí redesigned Güell's estate and residence in Barcelona, including turrets and introducing neo-Gothic pointed arches and Art Nouveau ornamentation.

During 1888–89 Gaudí designed the upper halls of the School of the Order of St Theresa in Barcelona, with his own interpretation of a strict neo-Gothic form, soaring parabolic arches with slanted pillars instead of Gothic flying buttresses. Apart from

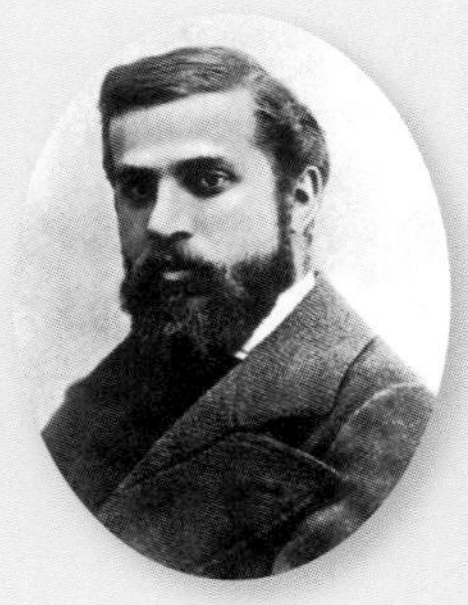

Born
Reus, Catalonia, Spain, 1852

Profession
Architect and designer

Manifesto
'Those who look for the laws of Nature as a support for their new works collaborate with the creator.'

> **'Gaudí's works could never have been designed solely on the drawing board ... not only because of the organic-looking spatial design, but also Gaudí's specific feel for space.'**
>
> RAINER ZERBST, *Antoni Gaudí*, 2002

using Art Nouveau style occasionally for ornament, Gaudí no longer imitated past styles.

During 1906–10 Gaudí designed two Barcelona houses that were completely innovative. Casa Batlló had a greenish-blue façade with window frames like sea-rounded stone, undulating between neighbouring necoclassical-style houses, and roofs shaped like sea monsters' backs rose and fell amid fantastical chimneys. Casa Milá, a huge corner house, was designed without colour to emphasise its rippling sculptural form, with windows set like honeycomb and an undulating roof-line.

Güell had planned to create an ideal colony of houses and gardens in Barcelona based on English models, and during 1900–14 this became Parc Güell. Radical organic shapes and spaces, such as the large central terrace, combined with the unrestrained patterning of surfaces in vibrant colours.

The Sagrada Familia project increasingly occupied Gaudí – his model for this building was the tree, designing a forest of pillars with high curving branches. His discipline and creativity were synthesised in high parabolic arches and towers topped with multi-coloured spires. Gaudí believed that nature should not be expressed in monochrome and applied vivid colours to surfaces in the medieval tradition.

He felt that surfaces should express the forces beneath, as they would in nature. He used everyday materials such as brick, rather than concrete, and decoration taken from Catalan ceramic and metalwork traditions. His architecture was not concerned with static structures and became increasingly organic in form.

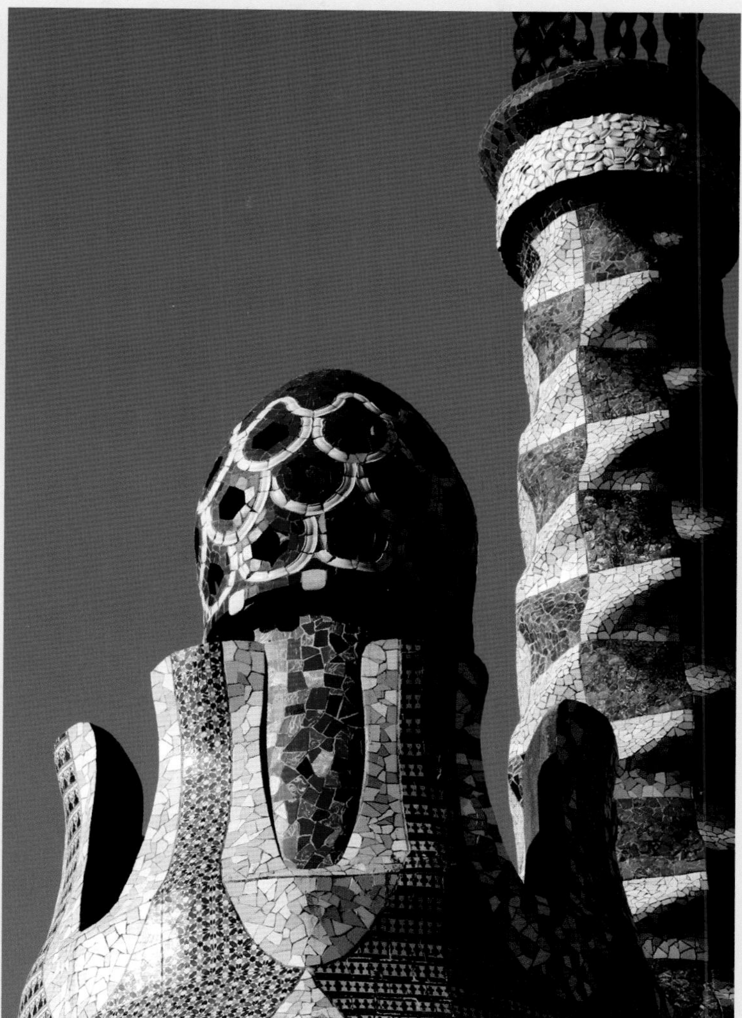

Pavilion, 1900–14, *Parc Güell, Barcelona*
The office pavilion was roofed with crenellated forms derived from an elephant's howdah. The projections are ornamented with patterns borrowed from Islamic and Gothic designs such as rippling arcades, formal florals and quatrefoil bands. Within is a chimney capped with the overlapping scale pattern of a fly agaric toadstool. Another chimney is patterned in blue and white checks, its form twisted like palm-tree bark.

Fluidity & Abstraction
1897–1906

Art Nouveau

British patterns were influential across Europe, where aspects of Arts and Crafts style were taken to new extremes. Art Nouveau designers in France, Belgium, Germany and Austria created patterns of high contrast tension with 'whiplash' curves. The new geometric architecture, pioneered by Charles Rennie Mackintosh in Glasgow and Josef Hoffman in Vienna, was associated with patterns produced by the Vienna Secession group of architects and artists working in a new spirit of enlightenment.

'So by sheer chance, liberty, youth and novelty appear together in the names given to this remarkable, if brief and transitory, movement.'

NIKOLAUS PEVSNER,
Pioneers of Modern Design, 2004

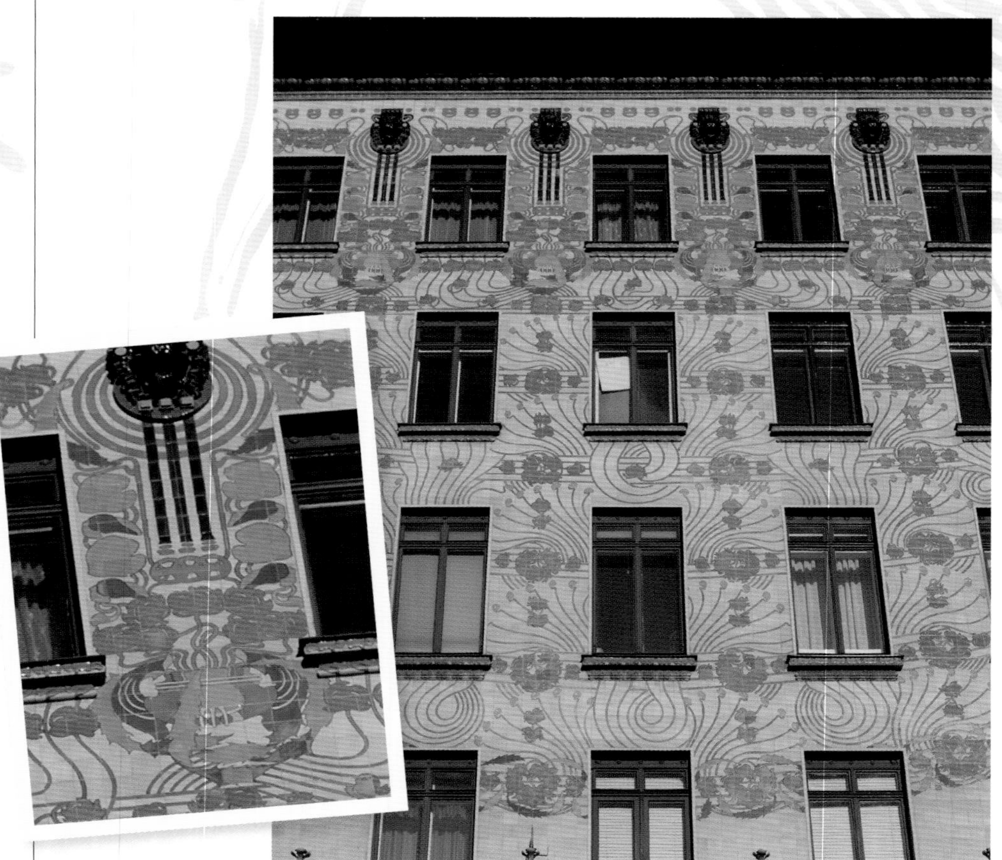

Majolikahaus, 1898,
Vienna, Austria
The tiled façade of this apartment block is patterned with blue waterlily flowers and leaves between the upper windows. Bunches of full ragged-edged pink flowers are arranged in a grid pattern between the windows below, each on horizontal trellis lines that increasingly curve towards the lower edge of the pattern, where the garlands are caught up with circling serrated leaves that curl to show sides in different greens. Blue-tipped shoots swirl and flare behind the bunches and single flowers. This *Jugendstil* building was designed by Otto Wagner.

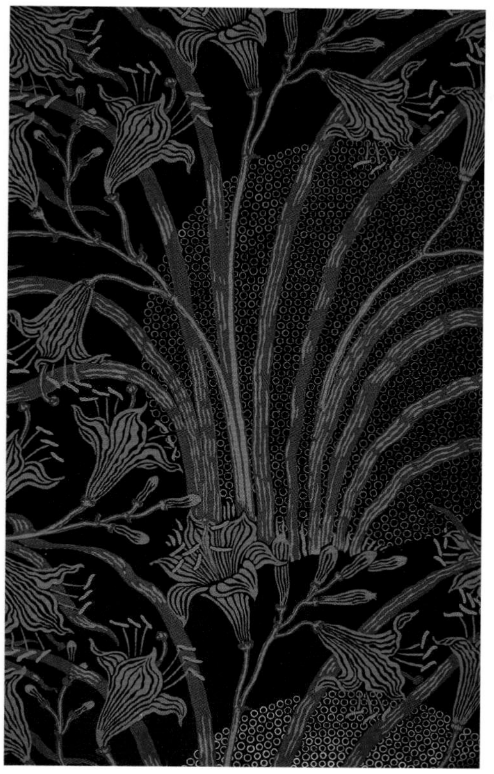

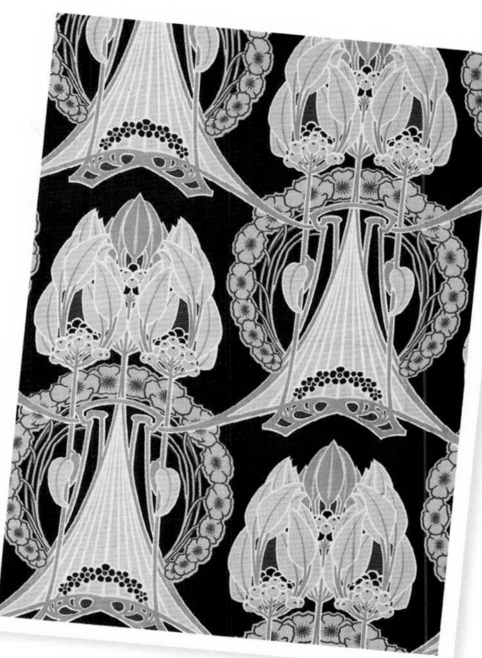

Furnishing textile, 1906, *Lancashire, England*
The pattern of this cotton sateen textile comprises groups of three stems with laurel leaves and berries. The central stem with colour-differentiated leaves bifurcates and returns to link with the roots, forming a curved triangular area fluted with pale lines. A garland of small formal flowerheads grows from the curling roots and a wreath of stemmed flowerheads of gradated size circles behind the group. Each composite motif of laurel stems, roots, garland and wreath is intricately linked to the next by tendril stems. The textile was roller-printed by the Lancashire firm of Frederick Steiner & Co.

Wallpaper, 1897–98, *London, England*
Printed with woodblocks, this 'day lily' wallpaper design is composed of spread bunches of flaring lily flowers on curving stems and with slender rippling leaves, highlighted with flowing lines. Each group is emphasised by a fan-shaped mesh of small gleaming gold rings in the background. The varied angles of the flowerheads and their delicate anthers give a swaying effect. The wallpaper was designed by Walter Crane and made by Jeffrey & Co.

ELEMENTS OF PATTERN

- *fluid variations of rhythm*
- *sensibility of Japanese-style linear fluidity and tension*
- *shorthand formulae for motifs*
- *cross-media application*

Collar, c. 1900, *Glasgow, Scotland*
Applied and embroidered with coloured silk, this detachable collar for a woman's dress is derived from a Renaissance shape. It is patterned with rose flowers, stems and pairs of leaves on trellis lines in the highly stylised formula of the Glasgow School of Art. The colours are delicate, to suit the silk material, and the rose leaves vary subtly in colour. The collar, and a matching belt, were designed, made and embroidered by Jessie Newbery.

1900
2000

Twentieth Century

Introduction

At the beginning of the 20th century, the organic and curvilinear forms of Art Nouveau were juxtaposed with early developments in modernist design. Designers still inspired by nature, such as Charles Rennie Mackintosh in Glasgow and Frank Lloyd Wright, produced new geometric patterns moving towards abstraction. Late 19th-century avant-garde art forms from France, promoted by Roger Fry and Clive Bell, accelerated the development of abstract designs at the Omega Workshops of the Bloomsbury Group.

In Russia, the radicalisation of art following the Revolution produced Constructivism, in which highly stylised geometric designs were created for industrial production in support of the new order. By the mid-1920s new designs developed rejecting historicism and embracing bold and colourful patterns modelled on natural geometry and more ancient and distant artforms. The Bauhaus, founded at Weimar in Germany in 1919 by Walter Gropius, sought to define and teach new modernist principles for architecture and design. Gunta Stölzl, who ran the weaving workshop from 1925, led the way from craft to industrial design.

In the 1920s and 1930s, the futuristic effect of the Art Deco style in Europe was adopted in the USA for fashionable houses in New York, Los Angeles and Miami Beach. Designers used

The avant-garde developments in art and design in Europe were paralleled in Russia as artists and designers looked to traditional Russian visual forms for inspiration. Central to the innovation of the early 20th century was Serge Diaghilev and the Ballets Russes in which bold colours and patterns were incorporated into costume design.

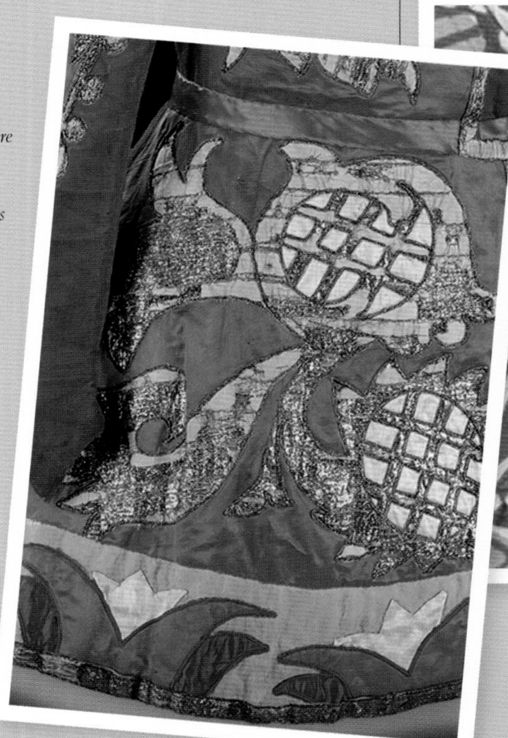

The founding of the Biba store in 1964 by Barbara Hulanicki and Steven Fitz-Simon created a new paradigm for design. Biba produced designs simultaneously looking back to the colourful and elegant styles of the late 19th century and Art Deco periods and forwards with futuristic psychedelic geometric patterns.

reflective modern materials such as chromed steel and glass with natural materials such as jade and marble to produce buildings and objects for the modern machine age. Art Deco permeated fashion, transport and graphic design, incorporating concepts from ancient Egypt, Mesoamerica, Africa and the Far East, and inspired by the flamboyance and abstraction of the rhythms of jazz music and Expressionist painting.

The austerity policy of Second World War Britain demanded good-quality clothing made with minimum material wastage for a fair price. In the USA, guidelines were issued for the design of household goods made from scarce resources such as timber for furniture, and textiles for clothing were printed with small patterns.

After 1945, colourful and joyful designs replaced the drab clothes of the war years. At the Festival of Britain in 1951 Lucienne Day won great praise for her vivid, striking modern patterns. In the 1960s, renewed economic strength shifted the fashion world's hub to London, where Biba opened its first boutique in 1964. This new showcase for young London fashion, inspired by the eclectic design of the 1890s and by 1930s Hollywood glamour, reflected Biba's carefree spirit. In the late 1970s, Zandra Rhodes was named the 'princess of punk' for her innovative, flamboyant designs.

Banned after the defeat of the 1745 Jacobite uprising, tartan became a pattern of fashion and opposition. These grids of infinite colour combinations inspired new directions in fashion and architectural theory, transforming tartan's socio-historical meanings. Designers such as Bill Gibb in the 1970s and Vivienne Westwood in the 1990s used tartan to create stylish and subversive fashion, referencing both tradition and sedition to create a 'nostalgia for the future' for clothes that parodied the past as personal propaganda.

During the late 20th century, fringe designers created highly eclectic 'neo-Baroque' aesthetics. An oppositional style, its theatrical approach pirated high fashion, into which it was then swiftly incorporated. Designers such as Gianni Versace drew on the historic Baroque of the late 16th to early 18th century with flamboyant, confident, dynamic forms and vibrant colours for fashion clothing and the lifestyles market.

In Japan, traditional styles of robe, used for Japanese theatre, continued to represent the important and symbolic flowers, such as the peony. The rich textured effects and glowing satin flower motif is created by using the jacquard loom.

New Geometry
1903–1955

Transitions of interior design

After the radical reassessment from first principles made by the Arts and Crafts movement, Art Nouveau's exploration of the dynamics of linear form and coded visual language inspired designers to develop geometric patterns that analysed and transformed natural shapes in new ways. A novel rigour and geometry of straight lines and angles began to emerge and was articulated and expressed in patterns for interior decoration, applied to furnishing textiles, wallpaper and glass.

ELEMENTS OF PATTERN

- *stylised identity of plant parts coded and recomposed*
- *geometric shapes: circles, squares and triangles*
- *engaging visual puzzles*

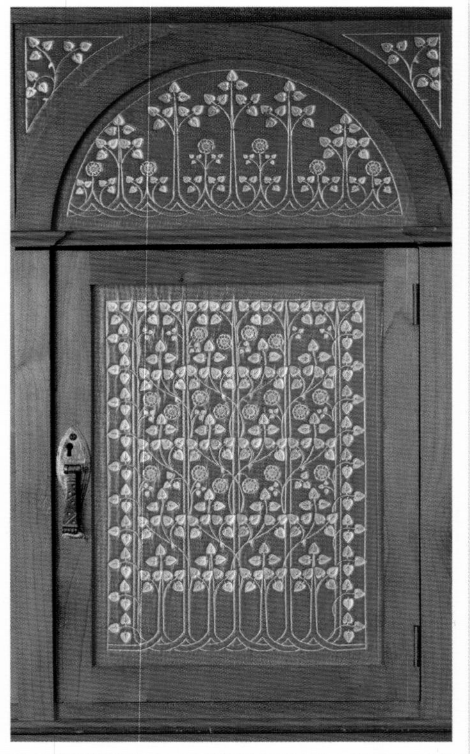

Cabinet, c. 1905, *Chipping Camden, Gloucestershire, England*

This cabinet with walnut stand, sycamore frame and cedar drawers is panelled in morocco leather with patterns tooled in gold foil, inspired by Spanish *vargueno* writing cabinets with plain exteriors and elaborately tooled leather interiors. Trios of heart-shaped leaves and formal flowerheads on fine curling tendrils sprout from simple outline stems interlinked at the roots. This cabinet was displayed at a 1906 exhibition of the Arts and Crafts Exhibition Society, to which the designer, Charles Ashbee, belonged. It furnished Ashbee's mother's house at 37 Cheyne Walk, Chelsea, London.

Window, 1904, *Chicago, Illinois, USA*

The 'tree of life' leaded window was fitted in the upstairs rooms and reception area of the house designed by Frank Lloyd Wright for Darwin D. Martin, the vice-president of Larkin Soap Company in Buffalo, New York. The pattern was based on the sumac tree, each three-lined stem branching into seven pairs of leaves stylised as chevrons. Large square panels of yellow glass anchor the complex upper part of the design and small amber and green squares and triangles glitter with the light source. The window was made by the Linden Glass Company, Chicago, which was in business from 1882 to 1934.

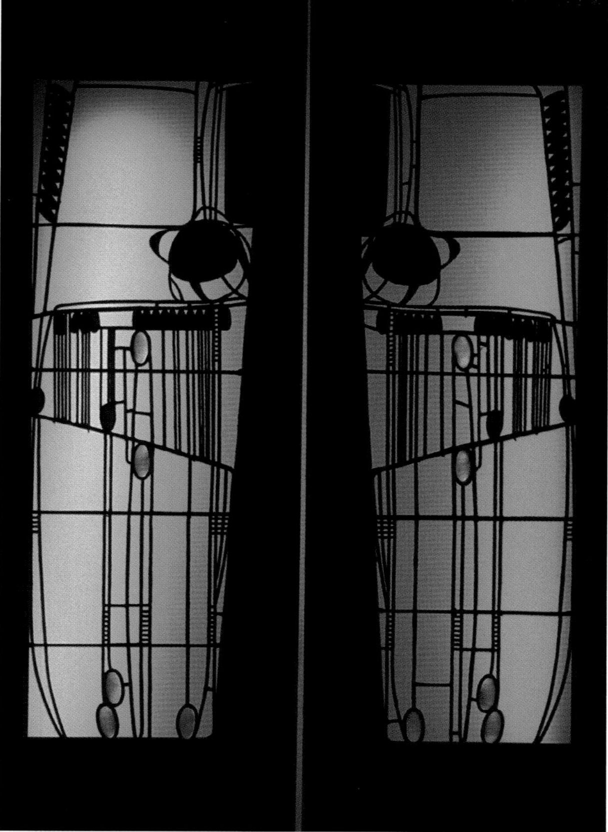

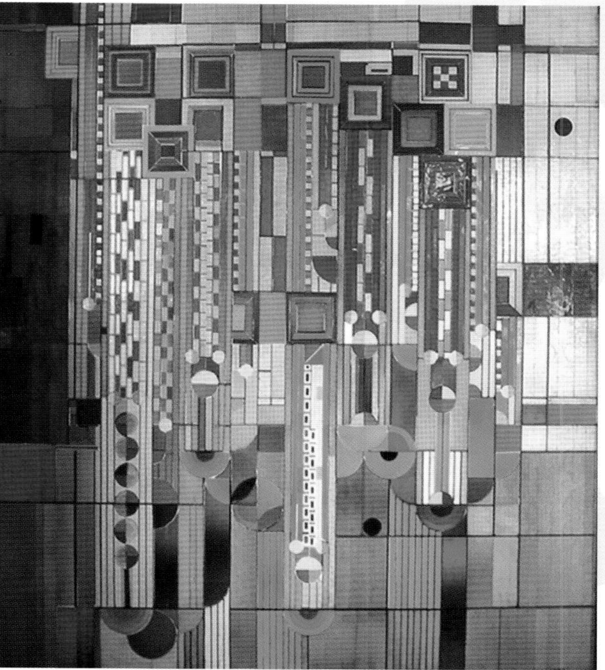

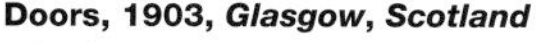

Doors, 1903, *Glasgow, Scotland*
Charles Rennie Mackintosh designed these double doors for Kate Cranston's Willow Tea Rooms in Sauchiehall Street, Glasgow. Fitted at the entrance to the Salon de Luxe, a fantasy room for afternoon tea, this decoration of the leaded glass and bronze panels comprised a pattern based on the natural forms of the willow tree and the rose, clearly showing Mackintosh's fascination with rhythmic tension of line. The oval shapes and rose motifs were characteristic of the Glasgow style.

Glass screen, 1928, *Biltmore Hotel, Phoenix, Arizona, USA*
Frank Lloyd Wright was inspired by the sculptural upright branching form of the ribbed saguaro cactus of the Arizona Desert landscape, adapting its shape to patterns for different media. The green saguaro stems and semicircular branching points are transformed into columns of plain and patterned colours capped with composite inset squares. This exuberantly colourful design combines formal geometric elements in a grid matrix for a complex and balanced composition.

'Ideas about ornament evolved from advanced design theories that began during the eighteenth-century Enlightenment and that were developed during the nineteenth century.'

DAVID A. HANKS, *The Decorative Designs of Frank Lloyd Wright*, 1979

Design for furnishing textile and wallpaper, 1955, *New York, USA*
Designed by Frank Lloyd Wright for the interiors firm Schumacher & Co., this pattern of triangles arranged as half- and quarter-lozenges, has a shifting optical effect of interplaying zigzags and different-scale geometric motifs. 'Design 706' of the 'Taliesin Line' range was recommended for a single wall in a room. It was screen-printed on both white furnishing cotton and wallpaper.

The Patterns of Mother Russia c. 1870–1917

Artistic and design developments in pre-revolutionary Russia

During the 19th century, the traditional cultural forms of Russia were renewed, in opposition to the French-orientated imperial academy arts of St Petersburg. Movements arose such as the Wanderers, who brought arts to rural communities, and the community at Abramtsevo, set up by Savva Mamontov (1841–1918) to revive traditional crafts. In the early 20th century, traditional art forms, including *lubki* (block-printed news and folk sheets), colourful and spiritual Orthodox Byzantine imagery and Russian historical themes were drawn into the innovative theatrical productions of the *Mir iskusstva* ('World Art Movement') and the dance productions of Serge Diaghilev (1872–1929). Further innovations followed, influenced by avant-garde developments in Europe.

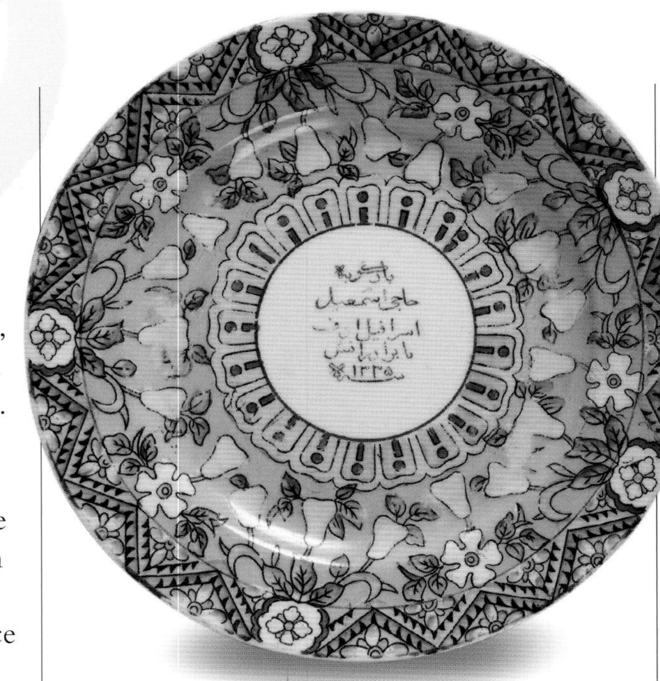

Porcelain plate, Gardner Porcelain Factory, c. 1870–c. 1917, *Moscow*
The designs from the imperial porcelain factory in Moscow tended to follow the styles of Europe. This plate, over-painted with enamels, has a zigzag and floral-patterned rim and a flower and pear design, reflecting a taste for the colourful and decorative. The contemporary imperial court also demanded more exotic and richly ornamented works such as those produced by the Fabergé factory in St Petersburg.

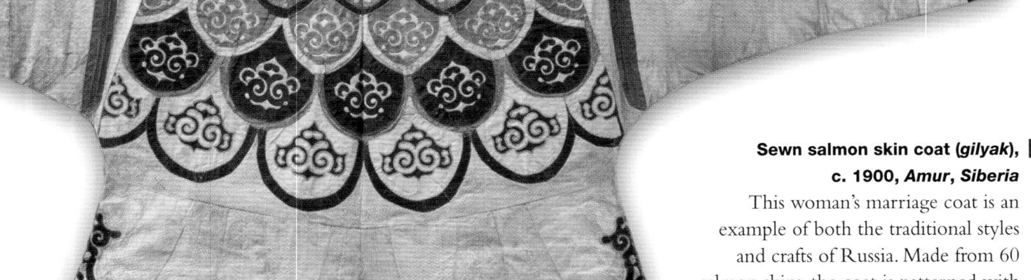

Sewn salmon skin coat (*gilyak*), c. 1900, *Amur, Siberia*
This woman's marriage coat is an example of both the traditional styles and crafts of Russia. Made from 60 salmon skins, the coat is patterned with painted appliqué in red, black and blue, cut into a scrolling design reminiscent of Chinese *taotie* faces or cloud motifs. The sides of the coat are painted with black wavy designs ending with a scrolling finial containing a beast's face.

ELEMENTS OF PATTERN

- *decorative florals and fruits of Imperial taste*
- *bold scrolls and foliates*
- *vibrant colours and forms of Russian and Asian tradition*
- *geometric and abstract forms of the avant-garde*

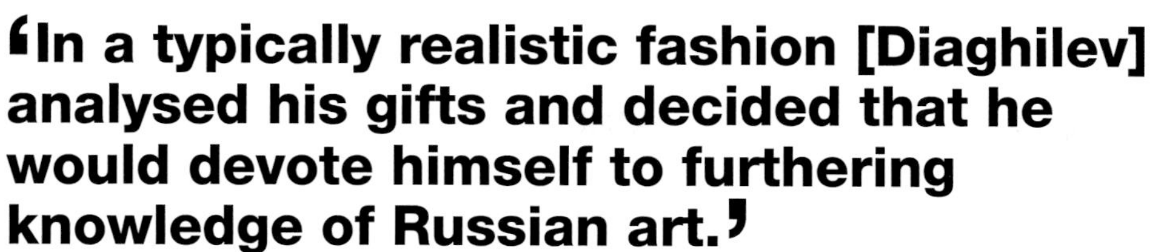

'In a typically realistic fashion [Diaghilev] analysed his gifts and decided that he would devote himself to furthering knowledge of Russian art.'

CAMILLA GRAY, *The Russian Experiment in Art 1863–1922*, 1962 AND 1986

Dance costume, Léon Bakst, Diaghilev Ballet, 1912, *Russia*
In the late 19th century, the painter and designer Léon Bakst (1866–1924) became associated with the 'World Art Movement' and the theatre and ballet choreographer Diaghilev. His set and costume designs epitomised the movement's ideals. This bold costume with both geometric patterns and construction was a precursor to the later innovations that were influenced by moves to abstraction and the search for new elevating forms of visual expression.

Dance costume, Diaghilev Ballet, 1916, *Russia*
In the years before the Russian Revolution, art and design were radically innovative and the artist Natalia Goncharova (1881–1962) was at the forefront of these changes. Her costume designs reflect her interest in peasants and traditional cultural forms. The striking gold scrolling foliate pattern on scarlet includes geometric elements unifying the strong simple lines of traditional design with avant-garde abstraction.

Boris Godunov opera costume, Alexander Golovin, c. 1910, *Russia*
The famous 16th-century Russian tsar Boris Godunov was immortalised in a play of the same name by Alexander Pushkin (1799–1837). Diaghilev staged an opera by Modest Mussorgsky (1839–81) based on the play, in Paris in 1909 and in London in 1913. This Coronation costume – covered in gold scrolling, jewels, pearls, and floral motifs, including the pomegranate and religious symbols – recreates the forms of Byzantine imperial robes.

Bold Colours & Abstracts 1902–c. 1925

European avant-garde textile designs

Early 20th-century designs in Europe were rooted in the contrasting imperatives of Art Nouveau and the accelerating changes associated with modernism. Florals and organic motifs continued to be popular, but more abstract and geometric patterns emerged from avant-garde design movements in England, the Netherlands, Germany and Russia. In London in 1910, Roger Fry (1866–1934) organised the Manet and the Post-Impressionists exhibition, introducing the innovative developments from France. With other members of the Bloomsbury Group, including Clive Bell (1881–1964), Fry set up the Omega Workshops, producing household items in avant-garde designs. As more radical abstract and surrealist ideas developed after the First World War, designs became increasingly stylised.

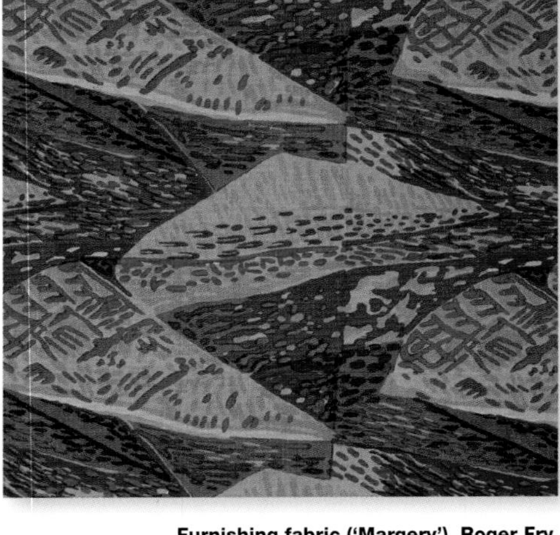

Furnishing fabric ('Margery'), Roger Fry, Omega Workshops, 1913, *London*
The ideal of a visual aesthetic independent of subject was articulated by Clive Bell in 1914. At the Omega Workshops, involving artists Vanessa Bell (1879–1961) and Duncan Grant (1885–1978), these principles were implemented. The soft purple, blue and green of this abstract design exemplify the ideals of a harmonious aesthetic. The workshops produced furniture, fabrics and ceramics until 1919.

Furnishing fabric, Steiner & Co., 1902, *Lancashire*
The legacy of the Arts and Crafts movement is apparent in this colourful pattern of an exotic floral landscape, although the curved and sweeping forms were also central to Art Nouveau styles in Europe. The two-tone green gives it depth, complementing the pinks and oranges. Lancashire textile factories had dominated fabric manufacture since the 19th century and Steiner maintained an independent and innovative approach to design.

ELEMENTS OF PATTERN

- *sweeping organic and floral designs*
- *abstracts in soft colours*
- *energetic and bold abstracts*
- *simple and colourful flowers and butterflies*

Dress fabric, Paul Poiret, Atelier Martine, 1919, *Paris*
After 1918, female fashion changed with a preference for new looser designs. Paul Poiret (1879–1944) favoured vibrant colours and bold patterns, influenced by the Ballet Russes (see pages 224–5) and the designs of the Wiener Werkstätte (Vienna Workshop) associated with the *Jugendstil* movement. The simple, fresh designs were produced in his studio by untutored apprentices. This fabric has two different colour-ways – blue and orange, yellow and coral.

‘The Viennese decorative style of the early ... twentieth century had many affinities with the style which has come to be known as Art Deco.’

STUART DURANT, *Ornament: A Survey of Decoration since 1830*, 1986

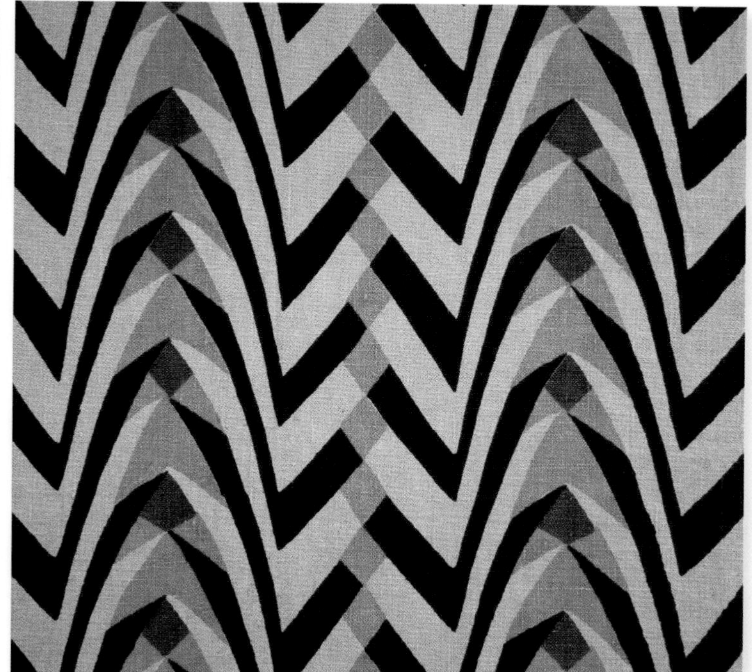

Furnishing fabric, F. Gregory Brown, 1922, *England*
In 1914, the Vorticist art movement emerged in England. Influenced by the dynamic art of the Italian Futurists, the work conveyed the geometric angular energy of a vortex. This design captures elements of Vorticism with its strident receding arches created by subtle greys and black. It was one of the most contemporary patterns displayed at the Paris Exhibition of Decorative Arts of 1925.

Dress fabric, Wiener Werkstätte, c. 1925, *Vienna*
The Wiener Werkstätte was founded in 1897 to implement the Art Nouveau ideals of the Vienna Secession (see pages 216–17). Textiles were produced with vibrant colours and simple patterns for luxury furnishing and clothing that were influential on Art Deco design. This pattern uses the delicate shapes of insects, snails and butterflies in bold orange and brown stripes with the occasional blue to lift the design.

Patterns for the People
1923–1924

Russian Constructivist designs

In the years after the Russian Revolution, avant-garde artists enthusiastically applied their arts in support of the new political order. The abstraction developed before 1917 became a new visual language of constructed forms. Artists sought functional and utilitarian purposes for these forms, producing building designs, posters, clothing and ceramics. The Constructivist movement included Vladimir Tatlin (1885–1953), who made the first art constructions in 1913, Aleksandr Rodchenko (1891–1956), Liubov Popova (1889–1924) and Varvara Stepanova (1894–1958). For a short period, before the work of artists and designers came under tighter centralised control, influential and innovative designs were created based on Constructivist principles.

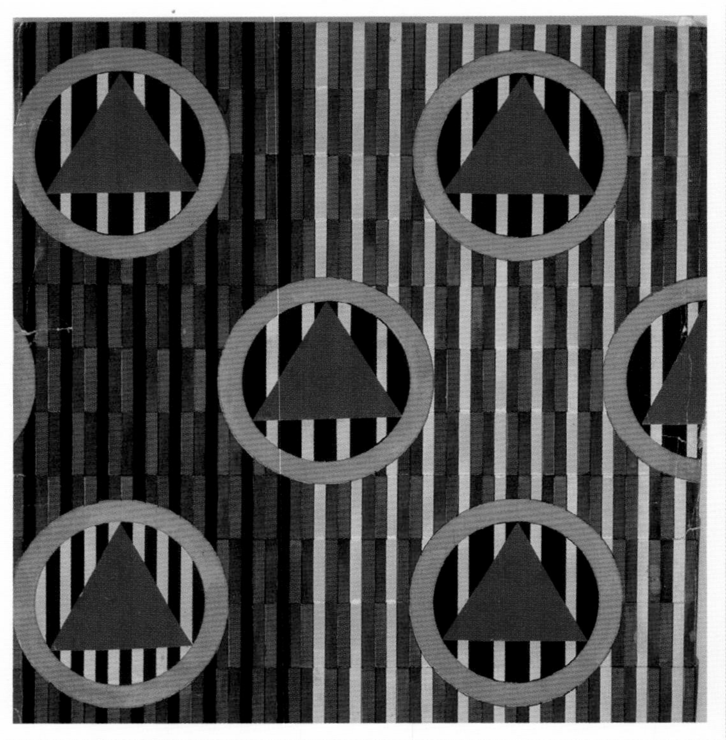

Drawing for a fabric, Liubov Popova, 1923–24, *Moscow*
Constructivism rejected elitist subject matter in favour of 'the communistic expression of material structures'. Following this principle, artist-constructors such as Liubov Popova developed new integrated designs for clothing and textiles constructed from geometric elements – lines, circles and triangles – in bold colours. Although production of Constructivist designs was very limited by a lack of resources, these patterns have resonated throughout the 20th century.

ELEMENTS OF PATTERN

- *lines, squares, circles and triangles*
- *bold colours and forms*
- *orange and blue; red and green*
- *constructed forms in support of Communist principles*

'Both Stepanova and Popova saw the replacement of traditional Russian ... patterns by geometrically based designs as an essential aspect of ... Constructivist principles.'

CHRISTINA LODDER, *Russian Constructivism*, 1983

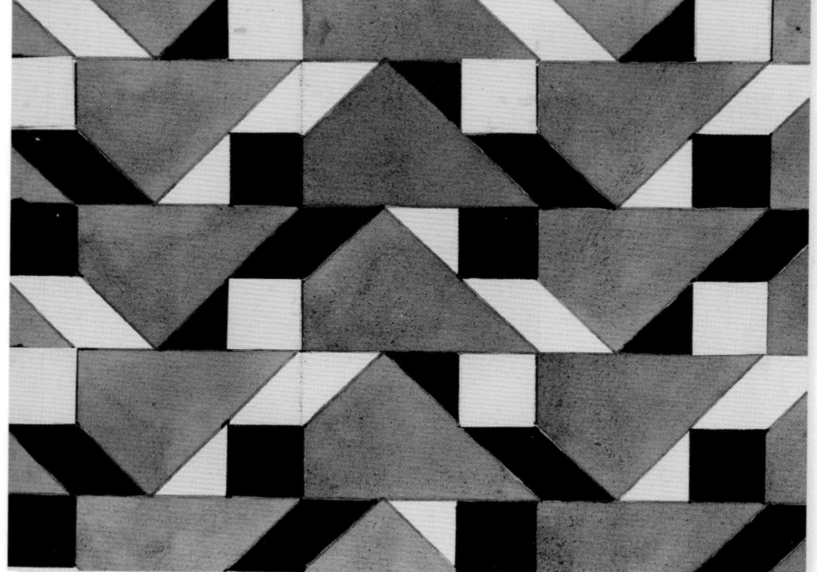

Textile design, Liubov Popova, 1923–24, *Moscow*
Colour theory, originating in 19th-century studies of colour and light, mapped out the relationship between primary colours – red, yellow and blue – and secondary colours – orange, green and purple – on a colour wheel. Complementary colours – blue with orange and red with green, seen here – produced the most harmonious combinations. Such principles would continue to be applied in Germany at the Bauhaus (see pages 232–3).

Sketch for fabric, Liubov Popova, 1923–24, *Moscow*
Constructivist designs using striking geometric forms developed through the early 1920s at art and design schools. These were established in the years after the Revolution, such as INKhUK – The Institute of Artistic Culture. The studying and teaching of the theory of colour and form, including the rejection of easel painting, led directly into the bold designs produced by Popova and others.

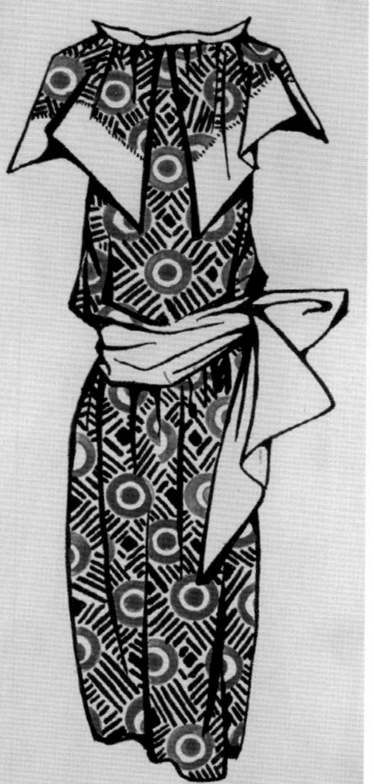

Design for a dress, Liubov Popova, 1923–24, *Moscow*
Basic pattern shapes, which could be readily reproduced, were used to design textiles and clothing with simple lines and uncomplicated forms. The desire to create functional clothing was sometimes subsumed within an urge for aesthetic impact and 'beauty'. Nevertheless, on the whole, the intention to design a new practical form of clothing was maintained, even if the outcomes were not implemented to any great degree.

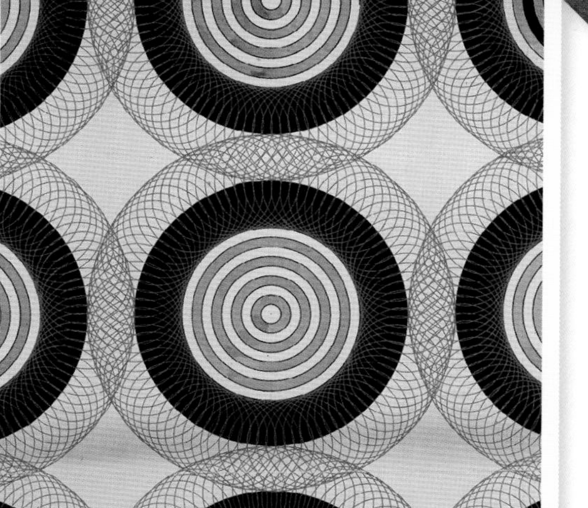

Textile design, Aleksandr Rodchenko, 1924, *Moscow*
Rodchenko's early art had been part of the radical abstract Suprematist style innovated by Kazimir Malevich (1878–1935) in the 1910s. Bold forms and colours were carried through into textile and other Constructivist designs, and easel painting was rejected. The spirals and circles of this pattern reflect Rodchenko's interest in form, which he later developed into photomontage designs in support of the Soviet Union.

Modern Schematics 1920–1930

Art Deco

The conscious rejection of historic styles as sources for design and the reordering of natural forms in abstract codes resulted in a collaboration of style among a wide range of designers and artists – architects, sculptors, jewellers, painters and bookbinders. This ubiquitous, systemically modernist style of fundamental patterns was deeply informed by natural geometry combined with influences from ancient and far-distant cultures. Rich jewel-like colours in polychrome mixes, as well as black-and-white schemes, were used in patterns of strongly definitive straight lines and arcs.

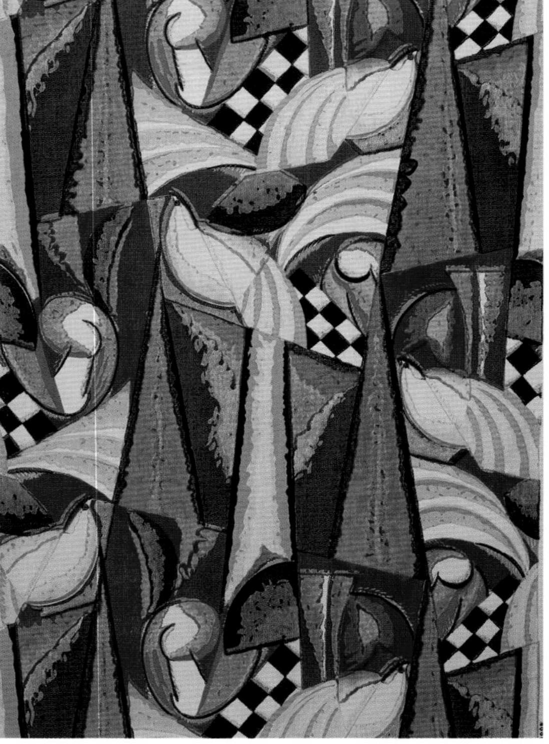

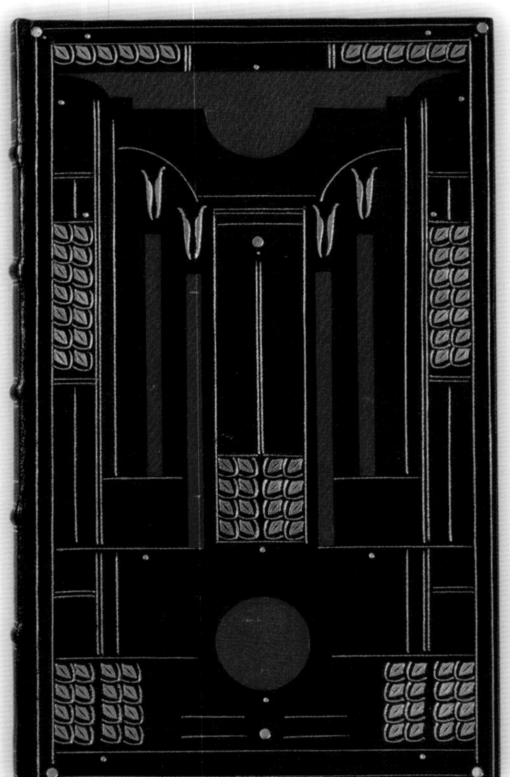

Book binding, 1927, *England*
This book binding was designed and hand-tooled by Sybil Pye for *The Marriage of Cupid and Psyche* by Lucius Apuleius. The geometric grid of the design contains patterns of overlapping feathers symbolising Cupid's wing plumage, in rows, rectangles and squares linked by fine gold lines and arcs. Pairs of vertical red bands represent candles with flickering gold flames, by the light of which Psyche gazed on Cupid while he was sleeping. The book was originally printed by the Vale Press in 1897.

Design for furnishing textile and wallpaper, 1925, *France*
Pendant triangular shapes like furling fabric contrast with a diagonal grid of checked patterns with red-and-white scrolling organic forms and fluted curving fans in shaded colours. Inspired by abstract painting and designed by Madame de Andrada, this pattern was block and screen printed in seven colours on to furnishing cotton and wallpaper.

'These gleaming streamlined forms celebrated the technological progress of the machine age.'

HSIAO-YUN CHU, *Material Culture in America*, 2003

Brooch, 1920–30, *France*
Composed of platinum and gold, the pattern of this brooch may have been inspired by a Native American or South American geometric textile design. The central part of the pattern is inlaid with mother-of-pearl and opal plates quartered in a stepped-edged lozenge with a gold angular motif, and triangular forms inlaid with the same materials. Complementary shapes to either side and the borders are set with diamonds, linked to reeded moonstone columns capped with sapphires.

Chrysler Building, 1926–30, *42nd Street, New York, USA*
Semicircular forms with radiating lines and triangular windows radiate in a progressively smaller scale towards the spire, with the effect that the building diminishes into the sky. Sheet steel, polished to a satiny gloss and reflecting the changing light, was an integral part of architect William van Alen's vision for the office of Walter P. Chrysler, and constituted the first extensive use of stainless steel in architecture.

ELEMENTS OF PATTERN

- *geometric forms*
- *stylised natural forms*
- *reeded surfaces*
- *symmetry*
- *exoticism*
- *highly reflective materials*

Jug, c. 1929–31, *Burslem, Staffordshire*
The patterns decorating this earthenware jug designed by Clarice Cliffe were inspired by the Persian lotus flower. Trios of petals with curling stamens and undulating tendril lines alternate between diagonal lines in a patterned band, both below the rim and at the shoulder. The neck and shoulder are decorated with large lotus-petal shapes pointing downwards and separated by curving forms with central petal trios. Rippling shapes between vertical scrolls and leaves pattern the body. The jug was made by the Newport Pottery Company.

Gunta Stölzl
1897–1983

Gunta Stölzl studied painting, ceramics and art history at the School of Arts & Crafts in Munich from 1913 to 1916, before breaking off her studies to served as a Red Cross nurse until the end of the First World War in 1918.

After the war she applied to be a student at the Bauhaus in Weimar, Germany, which had been founded by the architect Walter Gropius in 1919. Gropius had created the Bauhaus on the *Gesamtkunstwerk* ('total artwork') principle that combined aesthetics, design and technique. To transform craft into a fine art, he assigned painters to lead the workshops, articulating the main ethos of the Bauhaus to break with past concepts and to reassess the visual arts. This approach, called 'visual thinking' by the expressionist painter Paul Klee, resulted in the collaboration of students working in different artistic disciplines and the exchange of visual ideas. Students were attracted to the institution by the staff of inspirational designers, painters and theorists such as Paul Klee, Johannes Itten, Wassily Kandinsky and Josef Albers. In 1920 Stölzl enrolled in the preliminary course taught by Johannes Itten, and was later awarded a full scholarship.

She specialised in weaving and took her qualifying exam in 1922–23. Stölzl went to Krefeld in 1922 to study dyeing techniques with Benita Otte, another Bauhaus weaver, with whom she subsequently set up a dyeing facility at the Bauhaus. After graduating as a weaver, Stölzl assisted Itten in establishing the Ontos weaving workshops in Herrliberg, near Zürich in Switzerland, which she herself directed.

At the Weimar Bauhaus, Stölzl and her fellow weaving students began to perceive individual craft pieces, such as tapestries, curtains and tablecloths, as pretentious, and the rich colours as unsuitable for everyday living. They tried to simplify and further discipline their approach to weaving to create more straightforward and functional items for a room.

The Bauhaus moved premises to Dessau in 1925 to accommodate its shift from craft production to industrial design. Stölzl returned to become the technical director of the weaving workshop, and soon saw the possibilities for woven products.

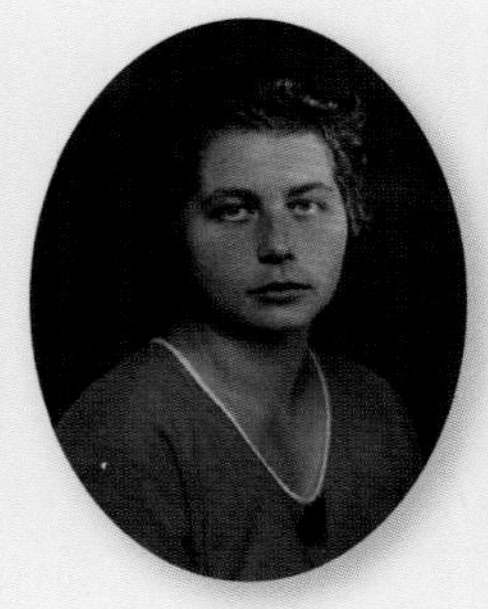

Born
Munich, Germany, 1897

Profession
Weaver

Manifesto
'The watchword of the new epoch was models for industry.'

> **'Gunta Stölzl was the most important weaver at the Bauhaus, supporting the transition from pictorial individual pieces to modern industrial designs.'**

MAGDALENA DROSTE, *Bauhaus 1919–1933*, 2006

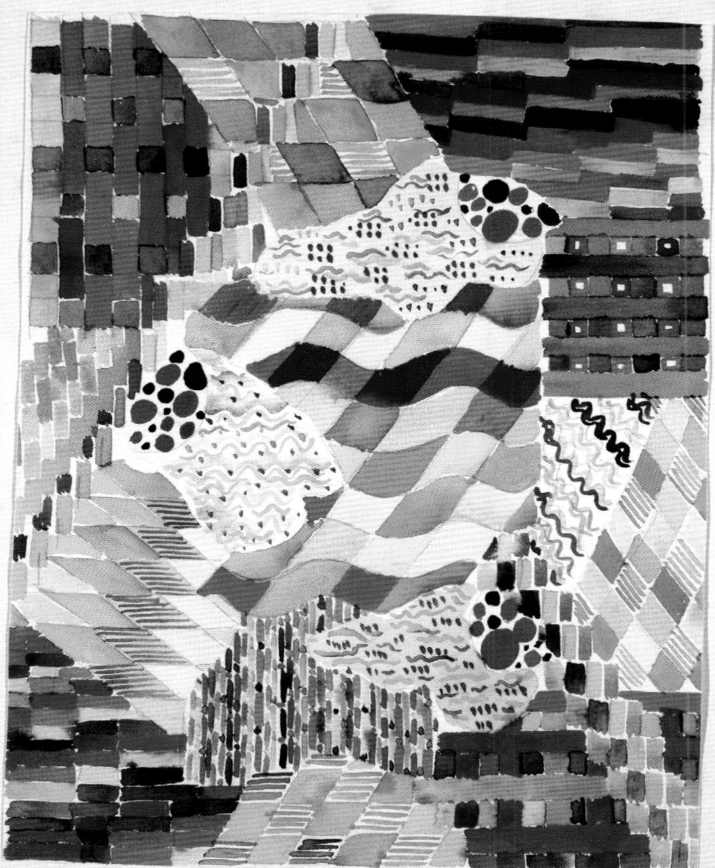

She enthusiastically experimented with new materials, constantly exploring new colour and design concepts and their industrial applications.

Stölzl reorganised the weaving department by creating a teaching workshop separate from the factory floor. She encouraged her students to experiment with their materials to create new hard-wearing fabrics that could be manufactured at low cost and sold on the everyday market. She drew up books of patterns for woven materials to supply to manufacturers in order to streamline the production process. The design and texture of furnishing textiles had to comply with the idea of the construction of modern style from architectural principles, the main concern of the Dessau Bauhaus.

Stölzl's work was inspired by Klee's use of colour and form and by Kandinsky's theory on abstraction: that the more artists use abstract form, the more confident and creative they will become. In accordance with the Bauhaus philosophy of design, she transformed the weaving workshop from a producer of personally expressed decorative work to a maker of utilitarian textiles with simple, abstract geometric patterns for home use and industrial application. Stölzl developed new structures for woven materials, innovative ways of using synthetic fibres and alternative techniques for dyeing fabrics. She concentrated on new properties such as reversible fabrics; upholstery woven from rayon, cellophane and cotton; and the effect of textiles on acoustics in a room – problems of design that were in sympathy with the new objectivity of Bauhaus industrial studies. Under Gunta Stölzl's management, the weaving workshop became the most prolific and profitable department at the Bauhaus.

Design for tapestry, 1927, *Munich, Germany*
This vibrant design for a tapestry combines rich colour and geometric shapes in complex combinations. The Bauhaus basic formulaic shapes of the triangle, square and circle are applied in creative ways as pattern groups, some of which are animated by a wave formation that reflects the woven medium of undulating textile. The weaving structure of the warp and weft grid is also referenced by the arrangement of colour shapes in alternation, threading over and under each other like a tartan.

PATTERN IN DETAIL

Patterns of the Hindu Temple
Early 20th Century

The Jagannath (Vishnu) Temple

The Jagannath Temple at Puri, on the coast of Orissa in eastern India, is represented on this early 20th-century painted cloth as the vibrant centre of Hindu gods in their decorative domain. The huge ancient temple complex itself, built in 1174 CE by Ananga Bhima Deva, is famous for its legendary foundation, for the distinctive stepped stone courses on the walls, typical of the region's medieval temple style, and the magnificent tall beehive form of the *shikara* (main temple tower).

The decorated temple
The centre of the Jagannath Temple is filled with ornaments, as the actual temple would be. The gods sit on an ogee-backed throne and are covered with jewelled adornments, which would be changed with the season. The temple space above has decorative stripes and hatching leading up to a floral scroll below the curving top of the temple.

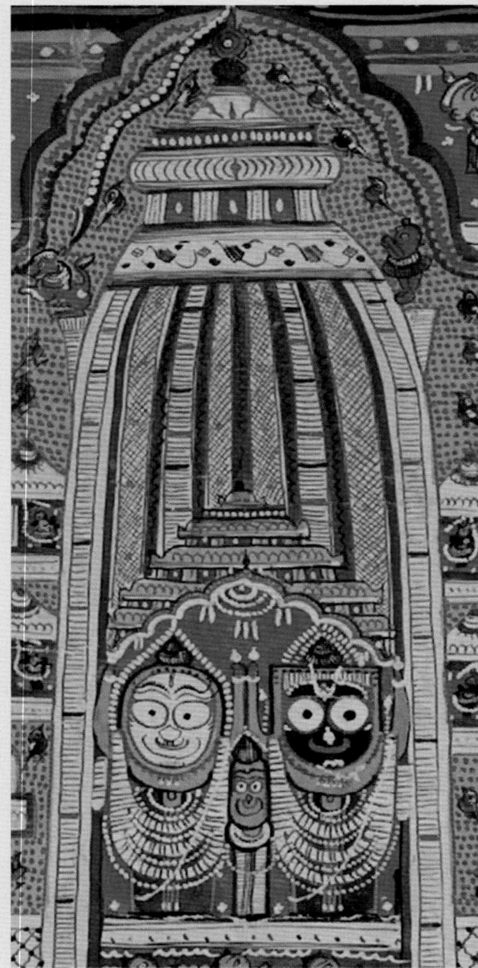

Gods and shrines
The central structure of the temple is surrounded by the stepped outer wall, represented here with a dotted surface covered with little birds and also with a latticework balcony. The area around the temple is filled with compartments containing the smaller shrines, temples and representations of gods within the temple complex. These have decorated backgrounds and are separated by colourful patterned bands of waves and dots.

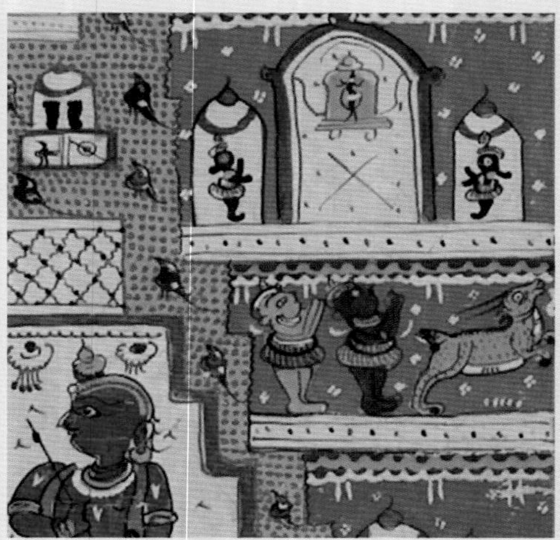

Rampant lions
At the bottom of the cloth, two rampant lions guard the Singhadwara, the main entrance to the Jagannath Temple. A low stepped-roof temple can be seen behind with a small shrine. This temple is covered with decorative sculptural details and ornamentation, typical of the region's style, represented by the small arched patterning on each level of the temple roof.

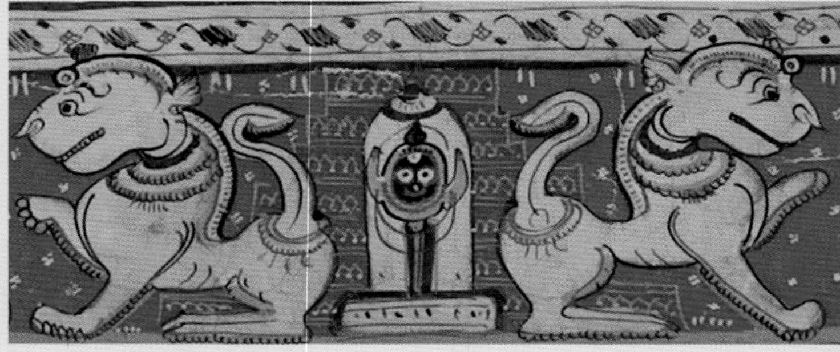

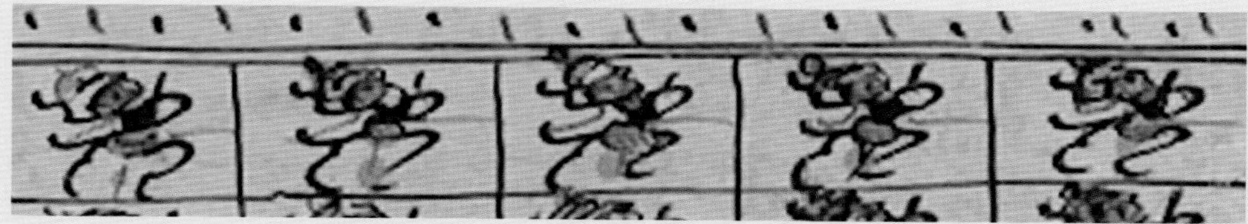

Temple dancers
The temple is an important pilgrimage site, holding festivals and events for worshipping the idols of the gods. The compartments contain devotees celebrating at these festivals, including a group of dancers formed into a pattern. The whole cloth and the different decorative elements comprise a pattern of devotion in which the colourful scenes, figures and designs all play their part.

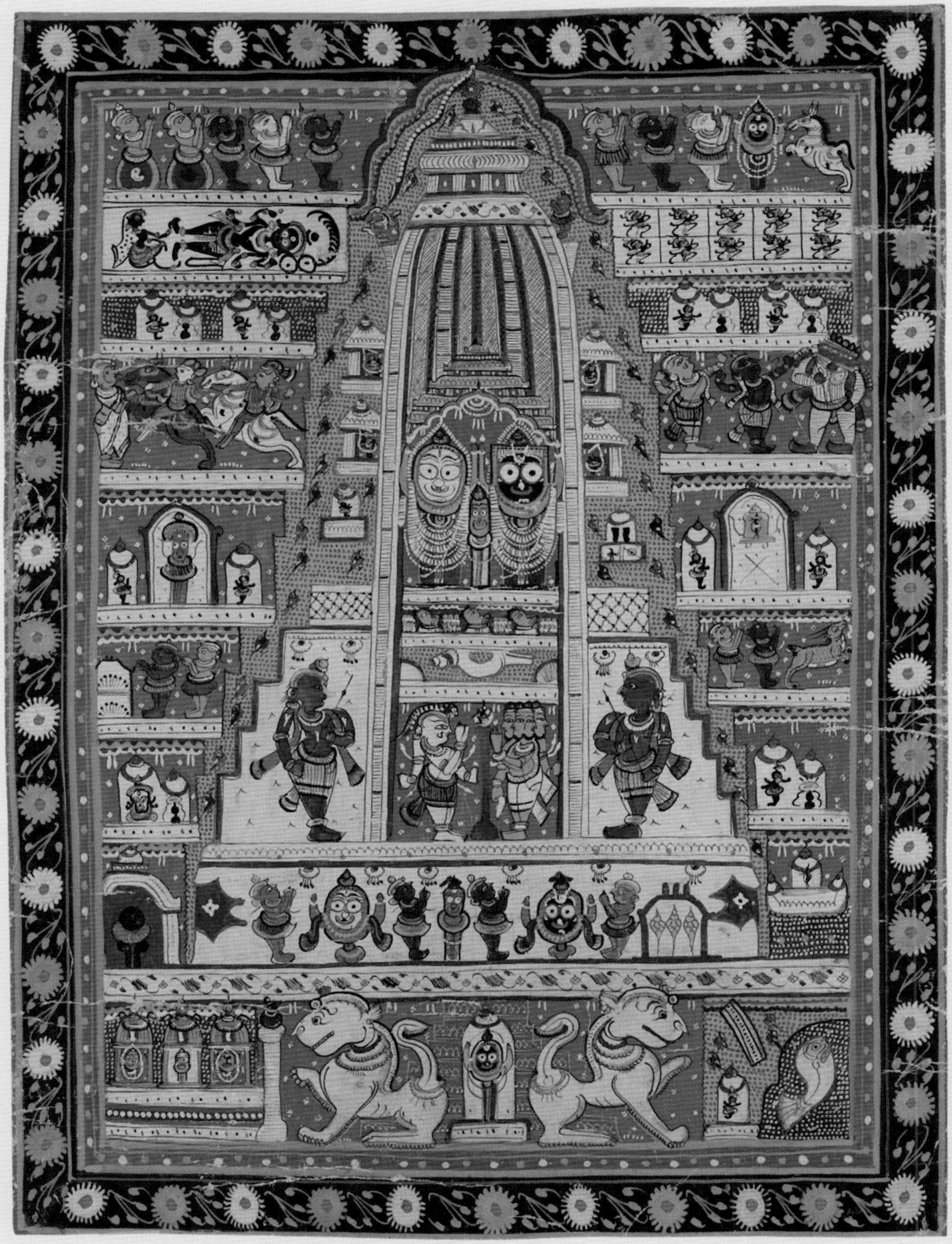

The Jagannath Temple, painted cloth, *Puri, India*
The cloth shows the temple in section with the idols of the Hindu gods Jagannath and Balabhadra and the goddess Subhadra in the centre. Beneath them is many-headed Brahma with Shiva and surrounding the temple are supplementary shrines, other gods and their devotees. The overall hierarchical composition conveys vitality, with bright colours and incidental patterns, encompassed by a floral motif in the border that echoes the '*srichakra*' (eight-spoked wheel) of Vishnu.

Maps, Flowers & Mirrors c. 1900–1940

Fabric designs before the Second World War

Developments in design associated with Constructivism, the Bauhaus and Art Deco in Europe had not only introduced many more abstract patterns but had also stimulated innovation. In the period before the Second World War, the range of patterns available in textiles was very wide. Strikingly simple geometric or stylised organic patterns contrasted with more traditional but vibrantly coloured florals. Idiosyncratic subjects were turned into patterns while the legacy of the previous 75 years of design was adapted and advanced. Although the modernist principles of the 1920s and 1930s – including that form should follow function alone – implicitly rejected ornament for its own sake, patterns continued to evolve in new and imaginative ways.

'The necessity of ornament is psychological. There exists in man a certain feeling which has been called *horror vacui*, an incapacity to tolerate empty space.'

HERBERT READ, 'The Function of Decoration' IN *Art and Industry. The Principles of Industrial Design*, 1934

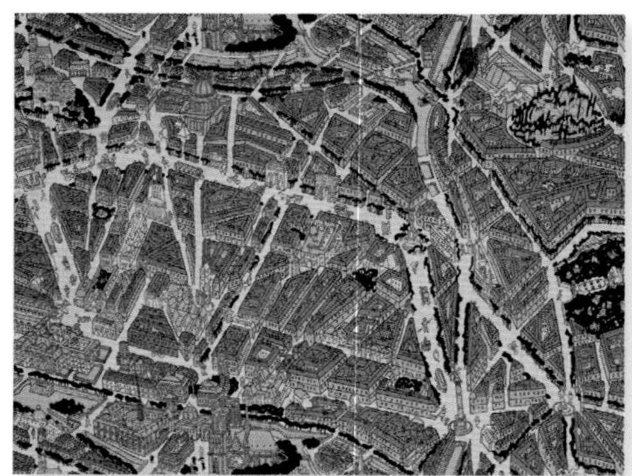

Dress fabric, Ralph Barton, 1927, *New York, USA*
This 'Map of Paris' pattern originated at the time of the 1925 Paris Exhibition and was produced as a fabric print in a range of designs that depicted contemporary American life. The buildings and boulevards simultaneously captured the vibrant modern city and presented a distinctive abstract pattern. The wearer and viewer could appreciate the chic greys, black and cream and spot the famous landmarks.

Obi* (fabric length), 1900–40, *Japan
This traditional Japanese design, of decorative octagons overlaid with floral and tree motifs, patterns an *obi* – a sash used to fasten a kimono. The octagons are filled with a range of wavy, lozenge and banded patterns emphasised by the textured surface of the silk and metallic fabric. The overlaid design includes the significant elements of chrysanthemums and blossoming trees.

ELEMENTS OF PATTERN

- *bold colours and designs against pallid patterns*
- *idiosyncratic subjects such as maps*
- *continued popularity and significance of florals*
- *geometric and octagonal patterns*

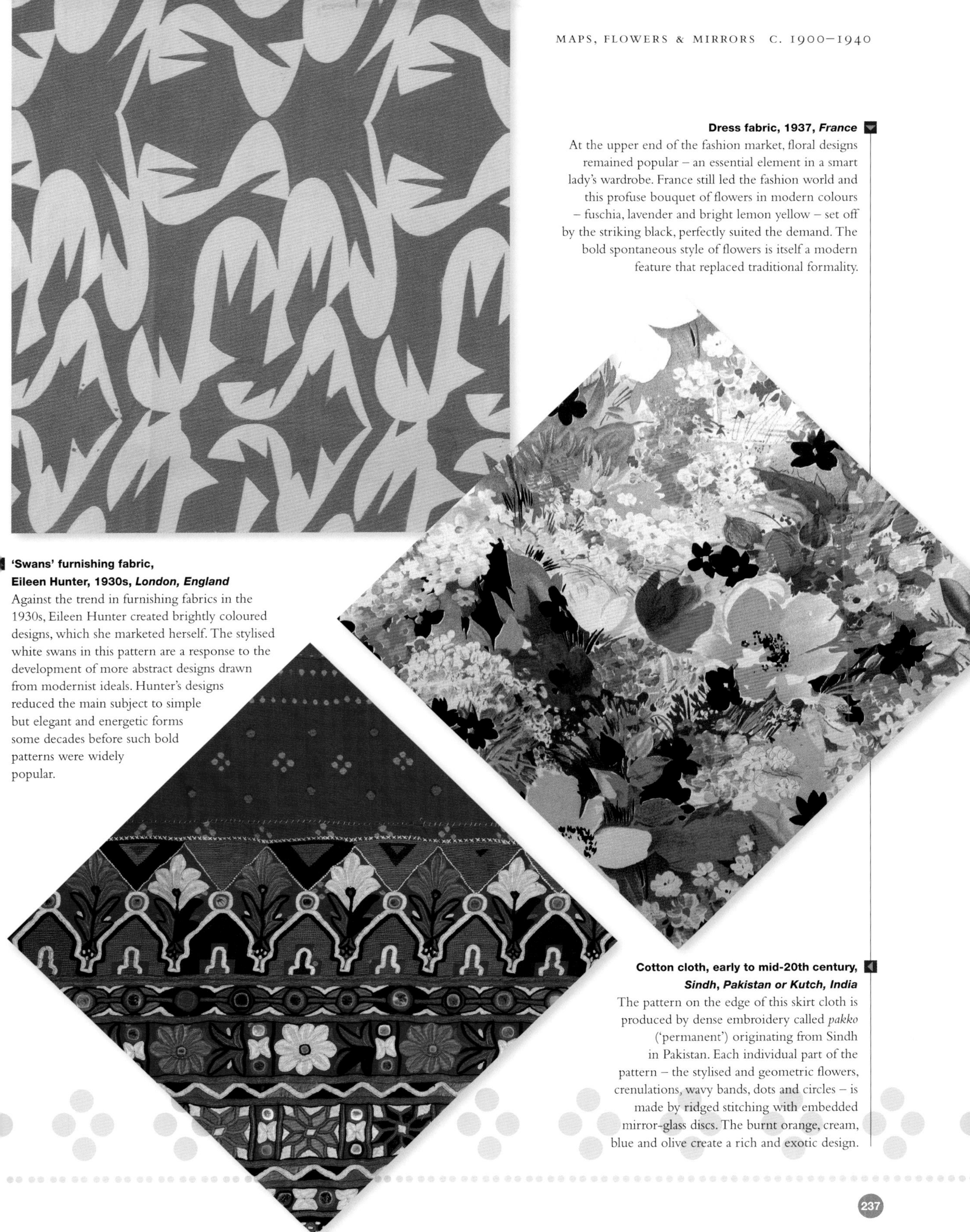

Dress fabric, 1937, *France*

At the upper end of the fashion market, floral designs remained popular – an essential element in a smart lady's wardrobe. France still led the fashion world and this profuse bouquet of flowers in modern colours – fuschia, lavender and bright lemon yellow – set off by the striking black, perfectly suited the demand. The bold spontaneous style of flowers is itself a modern feature that replaced traditional formality.

'Swans' furnishing fabric, Eileen Hunter, 1930s, *London, England*

Against the trend in furnishing fabrics in the 1930s, Eileen Hunter created brightly coloured designs, which she marketed herself. The stylised white swans in this pattern are a response to the development of more abstract designs drawn from modernist ideals. Hunter's designs reduced the main subject to simple but elegant and energetic forms some decades before such bold patterns were widely popular.

Cotton cloth, early to mid-20th century, *Sindh, Pakistan or Kutch, India*

The pattern on the edge of this skirt cloth is produced by dense embroidery called *pakko* ('permanent') originating from Sindh in Pakistan. Each individual part of the pattern – the stylised and geometric flowers, crenulations, wavy bands, dots and circles – is made by ridged stitching with embedded mirror-glass discs. The burnt orange, cream, blue and olive create a rich and exotic design.

Patterns of Utility
1939–1945

Wartime dress and furnishing

With the coming of the Second World War, what was officially and publicly thought to be necessary in the visual environment changed fundamentally in Britain. The manufacturing of bullets and bombs was prioritised, diverting material resources and labour into a collaborative war effort. Social distinctions were less visibly displayed by the ubiquitous wearing of Utility clothing made to restricted types of style, patterns and colours. Designs for household textiles were woven and printed in small-scale patterns, both for economy and ease of application to furniture. Muted colours and wartime motifs were incorporated into patterns to instil a sense of unity and patriotism.

Furnishing textile, 1941, *Manchester, England*
This cotton textile, printed with the design 'Victory V', was designed and manufactured by the Calico Printers' Association. Shaded with a negative effect, V-shaped motifs as pairs of pointing female hands and letterforms are deployed in rows among different types of fighter aircraft and bombers at varying inclinations. Large V-shapes are filled with falling bombs and planes. The background is filled with the word 'VICTORY'. The border comprises a band of opposed letter Vs between trios of small circles alternating with bars, based on the Morse code of three dots and a dash for 'victory'.

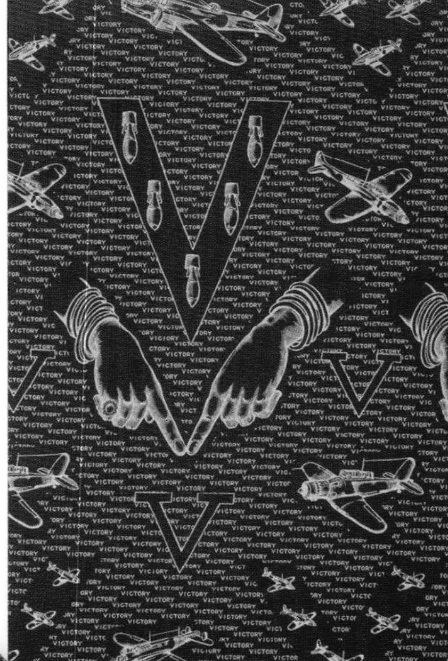

ELEMENTS OF PATTERN

- *muted reds, blues, greens and natural white*
- *war-like motifs*
- *coded geometric forms*

Furnishing textile, c. 1939, *Carlisle, Cumbria, England*
This rayon and cotton fabric has been woven with a pattern of interspaced doves in flight called 'Avis', designed by Marion Dorn. The alternating left- and right-facing rows of birds and slanting parallel lines representing feathers contribute to the effect of fluttering motion. The simple white shapes of the doves' bodies, dark wings and mid-tone of the background give a layered effect to a two-dimensional design. The textile was manufactured by Edinburgh Weavers.

Furnishing textile, 1945, *Carlisle, Cumbria, England*
Entitled 'Spot and Stripe', this furnishing textile pattern in woven cotton was designed by Enid Marx. Roundels with simplified Union Flag crosses on a diagonal grid are arranged over a background of broad vertical stripes. The alternating colours of the stripes are crossed with contrast-colour diagonal lines that form close-set chevrons across the width of the pattern. The muted red, white and blue scheme is a patriotic choice. The fabric was woven by Morton Sundour Fabrics.

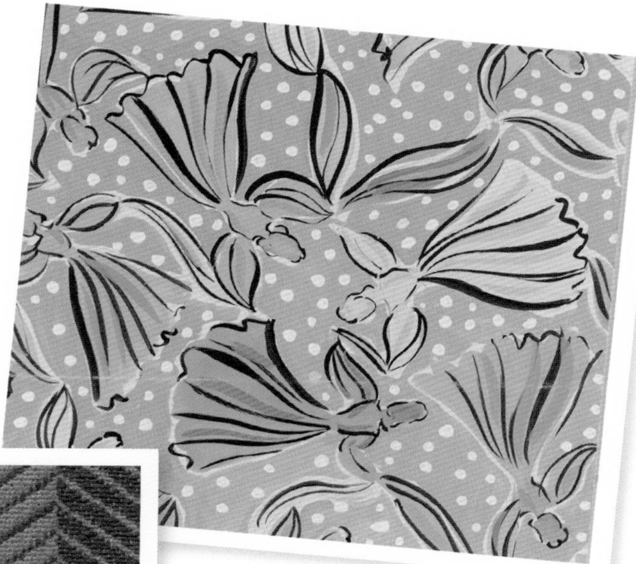

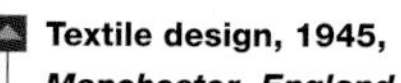

Dress, 1942–45, *London, England*
The economy in the amount of fabric used in this day dress designed by Norman Hartnell for Berketex's Utility range is reflected in its pattern. Pairs of fine parallel lines draw attention to the simple style and drape of the sections of the garment, which have been cut out in straight lines, but shaped to the form of the body with darts and gathers. A pair of lines emphasise the function of the belt that covers the seam at the waist.

Textile design, 1945, *Manchester, England*
Stylised female figures in full-length dresses with billowing sleeves and skirts swirl in dance formation against a shifting background of freely drawn dots. The figures rotate through the pattern and are linked by long curving scarf shapes held between their outstretched arms. The expressively drawn black lines contrast with the soft colours of the figures and anchor the design.

'The constraints imposed when designing Utility furnishing fabrics were: a restricted number and range of available looms; the need for small, economical pattern repeats; and a limited colour range.'

CYNTHIA R. WEAVER, *Utility Reassessed*, 1999

Désirée Lucienne Day 1917–2010

In the austere days after the end of the Second World War, existing designs were perceived as drab. Into this world came an innovative designer, Lucienne Day, whose stylish, colourful and vibrant patterns brightened 1950s Britain. Day combined organic and abstract forms to create new patterns, which dominated British interiors for several decades and influenced fabric design around the world.

Lucienne Conradi, born of a Belgian father and British mother, was brought up in a relatively wealthy world and showed poise and confidence from an early age. Studying first at Croydon School of Art and later at the Royal College of Art (1937–40), she was drawn to working with printed fabric design. In 1942 she married Robin Day (*photo, right*), who would become a renowned furniture designer, and throughout their life they shared a passion for modern design. Day set up her own practice in textile design in 1946 and at first worked on dress fabrics. Dissatisfied with the seasonal fashion business, she changed to furnishing fabric design and began to sell her work commercially in 1948. Her first patterns were printed by Edinburgh Weavers, which attracted the attention of Heal's, the most powerful and prestigious furnishings retailer of the time.

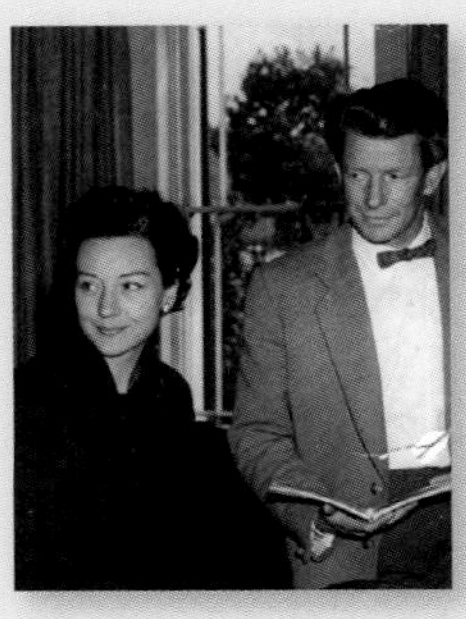

Born
Coulsdon, Surrey, 1917

Profession
Textile designer

Manifesto
Good design should be affordable

In 1951 Lucienne and Robin exhibited their work in a room setting at the Festival of Britain and their modern designs caused a sensation. The modern furniture – with its strikingly simple clean lines and functional, but stylish, forms – provided the perfect context for the 'Calyx' patterned curtains with their elegant, spidery plant motifs, delicate patterning and bright colours. The organic designs drew on the developments in modernist painting from earlier in the century. 'Calyx' was a hugely successful design, a best-seller at Heal's and widely copied, winning an American Institute of Decorators Award.

Lucienne Day's designs were original and radical, encompassing an extensive range of colours, motifs and compositions. Geometric and organic forms were often combined, drawn in fine lines and highlighted by bright and rich colours. The motifs often included plants, one of Day's design sources, but

'The apparent casualness of her designs was misleading: seemingly simple, they were highly sophisticated, many being composed of multiple layers of pattern ...'

LESLEY JACKSON, 'Lucienne Day: Textile designer whose work brightened up Fifties Britain', *The Independent*, 13 FEBRUARY 2010

also the complex forms of shells and seeds. Sometimes the motifs were witty and they always had a feeling of fun. One design, 'Spectators' (1953), was a crowd of thin stick-like figures with eyes and spectacles. In black and red, this design looks sharply abstract from a distance, but close up the eccentric little figures appear. Colours were bright and clean. Fresh lime green and lemon yellow, glowing orange, warm rich red and coral, pale pinks and teal were offset by muted brown, beige, black and cream. Sometimes a motif was reproduced more naturalistically but this would be contrasted with bold geometric forms. The appeal of Day's designs centred on their bold yet delicate compositions, which brought colour and refinement into many homes. Modernity in interior design was epitomised by these patterns, which dominated for 25 years.

In the 1950s, Day produced furnishing designs for many of the most important retailers of the time, transforming the range of fabrics for John Lewis, who ran her lines until 1987. She also worked for Liberty of London. As the popularity of her designs grew, she extended her range into wallpapers, other household and furnishing accessories and ceramics.

In the 1970s, when the taste for modern design began to change, Lucienne Day moved from industrial fabric design to work in a new medium of mosaic silk hangings. These rich works continued Day's ideals of modern and strikingly colourful design with combined organic and abstract forms.

In 1993, the Whitworth Art Gallery put on a major solo exhibition of her work, and in 2001 a retrospective of both Lucienne's and Robin's works was held at the Barbican Art Gallery, entitled 'Robin and Lucienne Day – Pioneers of Contemporary Design'. The exhibitions confirmed that Lucienne was an outstanding fabric designer and that her elegant, colourful and joyful patterns had irrevocably changed interior design of the 1950s and 1960s.

'Calyx' furnishing fabric, 1951, *Britain*
Unveiled at the Festival of Britain in 1951, 'Calyx' was a huge success, which made Day the leading British textile designer in the 1950s. Day loved plants and used their delicate forms as the foundation for a sophisticated pattern. The calyx and stem motif is given added vitality by the bright colour combinations and the organic patterned details.

Biba
1964–1974

Reshaping retrospective

Biba embodied a comprehensive style for clothes and interiors inspired by the rich patterns of the end of the 19th century combined with the Art Deco glamorous cinematic style of the 1930s. A large range of printed textiles for clothing and furnishings were produced through the 1960s with styles changing from futuristic to retrospective. By 1967 fabrics were patterned in Art Deco colours of eau-de-nil, cream, rust and maroon. Geometric patterns of zigzags and eclectic psychedelic patterns were printed on to high fashion clothing in vibrantly contrasting colours or in signature colour palettes.

ELEMENTS OF PATTERN

- *Art Nouveau line*
- *Art Deco colours*
- *geometric zigzags*
- *psychedelia*

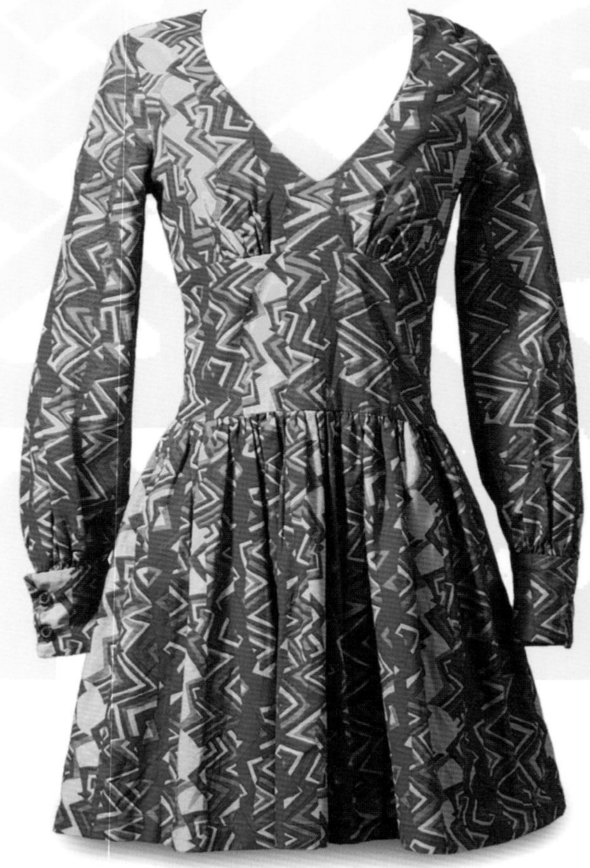

Clothing fabric, 1974, *London, England*
A pattern of florals, including roses in full flower, has been printed on to this cotton fabric. Rich pinks with subtle greens and natural tones are set off against a layer of deep blue shadowed leaves and a dark background. This pattern on printed cotton was made up into a trouser suit with a fitted jacket and flared trousers, a concept for female clothing that combined vintage pattern with contemporary cut. The suit belonged to Petra Siniawski, a leading actress in musicals.

Dress, 1967, *London, England*
This minidress in cotton fabric has been printed in purple, yellow, blue and tan combined in a dramatic intercutting zigzag pattern. Purple, with its rich, muted and retrospective qualities, was a colour that came to typify the Biba label. The restless pattern of angled geometric lines in vibrant colours is combined with a contemporary dress style with a deep panelled waist, short gathered skirt and sleeves tapering from narrow shoulders to wide buttoned cuffs.

Sandals, 1972–73, *London, England*
Designed for Biba by Emma of London, these platform-sole sandals are patterned in contrasting zigzags of silver, green, gold, purple and blue glittering lurex. The dramatic pattern of shifting geometric angles and lines complements the towering heels and platform soles of these high-fashion sandals.

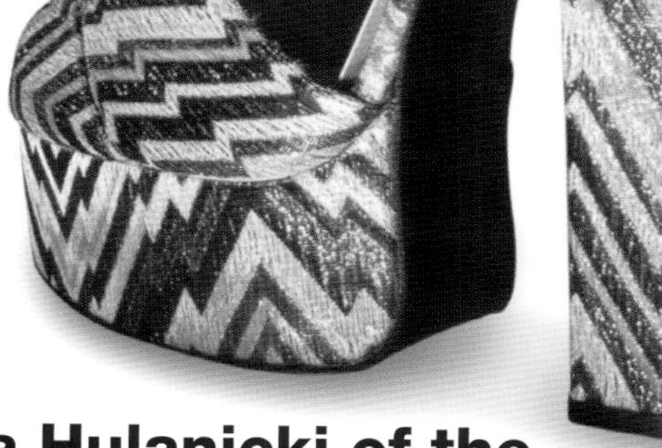

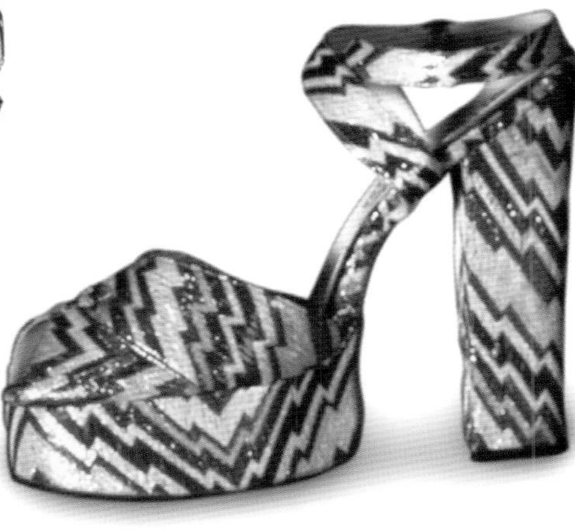

Dress and pinafore, 1971, *London, England*
Printed on Viyella fabric, this pattern of swirling motifs is coloured in a typical retrospective Biba palette of purples, pinks and reds. Pairs of slender paisley shapes patterned with chevrons curl amid serrated and scrolling leaves, Eastern-inspired shapes and dots in this exotic psychedelic design. A sleeveless shorter pinafore is worn over the dress, and both garments are fitted to the body with a high-waisted silhouette. The sleeves of the dress are gathered at the shoulder and into deep cuffs.

'Barbara Hulanicki of the iconic boutique Biba was one of the first designers to recognise the appeal of the colours and patterns of 19th-century design.'

MARNIE FOGG, *1960s Fashion Print*, 2008

Label, 1960s–70s, *London, England*
The logo encapsulates the Biba store's visual aesthetic that was inspired by Art Nouveau and American Art Deco style. This printed label displays opposed pairs of Biba knots separated by the company name. The symmetrical knot is composed of two looping tendrils ending in lozenges, interlacing with a third that ends in stylised leaves, all with thickening curves. The logo was designed by John McConnell of the design practice Pentagram.

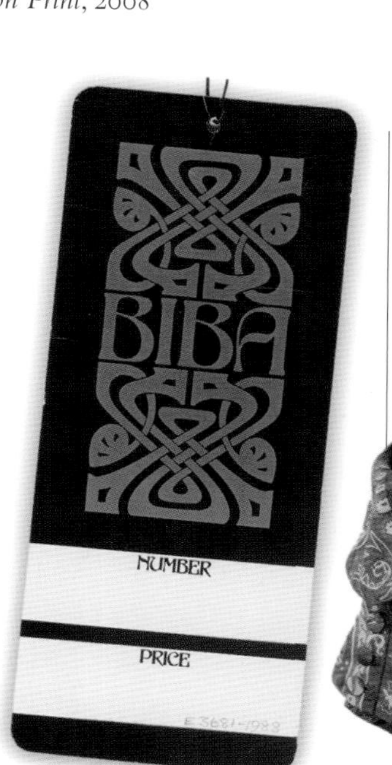

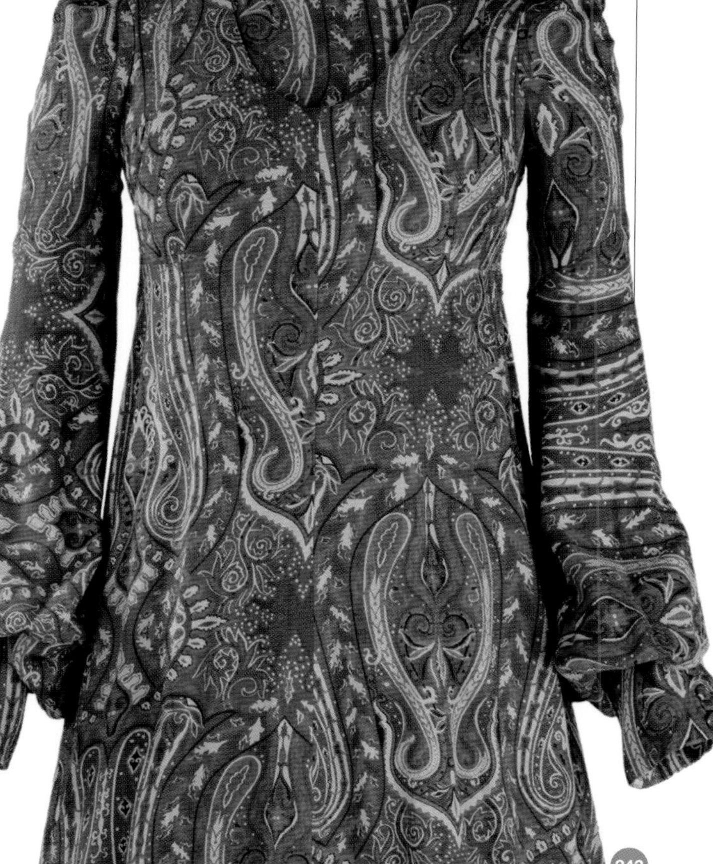

Zandra Rhodes
b. 1940

The innovation and perceived freedoms of the 1960s revolutionised fashion, providing the context in which flamboyant, colourful and outrageous designs would emerge in the 1970s. In the mid-1960s, as Zandra Rhodes began her career in textile design, the miniskirt, bold bright colours and striking patterns were all the rage. Rhodes's early textile designs, though initially too outrageous for the established British fashion industry, would define the styles of the 1970s and continue to be cutting edge and influential into the 21st century.

Rhodes had early contact with the fashion industry in Paris, where her mother worked for the House of Worth. She studied textile design at Medway College, now the University of the Creative Arts, and at the Royal College of Arts in the early 1960s. After receiving a discouraging response to her textile designs from established manufacturers, she opened the Fulham Road Clothes Shop in London in 1967 with Sylvia Ayton, and in 1969 her own shop where she sold her designs made with her textiles.

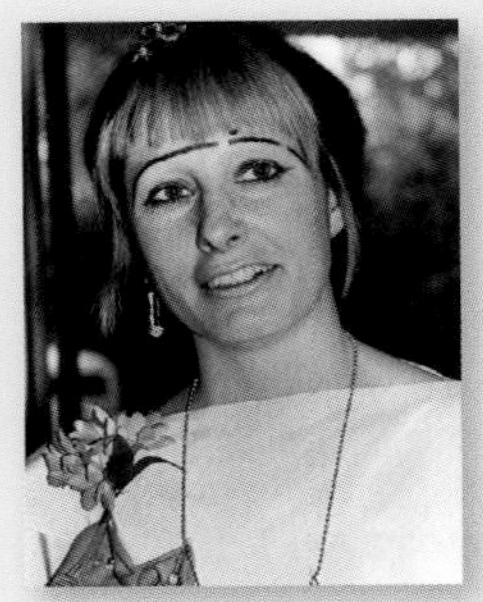

Born
Chatham, Kent, 1940

Profession
Fashion and textile designer

Manifesto
Dramatic, glamorous and extrovert

Her first innovative collection consisted of a range of kaftan-style dresses, made from printed chiffon silks with patterns inspired by knitting and embroidery, called 'Knitted Circle'. The pattern motifs included rippling and straight lines imitating wool or embroidery stitches, sometimes ordered into zigzags, triangles or randomised groups. These were occasionally interspersed with floral and organic forms and contained within large sweeping circles and smaller rosettes bounded by chains and pattern bands. Colours were bright – blues, oranges, golds, reds, yellows and greens – or more muted – grey, black and cream – but all were made ethereal by the translucence of the chiffon fabric. The dress styles derived from the textile designs, so circles formed bodices, yokes and hoods, and sleeves and skirts were voluminous to contain the full patterned circles.

'I had designed in a circle, now I cut in circles and at last the creative circle was complete. I made swirling, dramatic shapes with no concessions to the saleable, the acceptable or the ordinary. The true Rhodes style came into being.'

ZANDRA RHODES, 1969

Rhodes took her first collection to New York, featuring in American *Vogue*, and receiving Design Awards in 1970 and 1972. Through the 1970s, her designs were extremely popular – a fashion item of choice for the wealthy and chic – on sale at Fortnum and Mason, and continuing to be innovative and outrageous. In 1974 she set up her shop in Bond Street, London.

Zandra Rhodes's designs encompass a huge joyous range of forms, colours and patterns. These include swirling, wiggling lines on rich silks in bright colours – especially pink, scarlet, gold, electric blue, emerald green, purple, often in exotic, dramatic and theatrical combinations. Spots, radiating stripes and circles provide framing and contrasting forms for floral or organic motifs combined with geometric and abstract elements. Dresses have frills and floating fabrics; sparkles, satin ribbon rosettes, cabbage-crinkling and lace edgings and appliqué; embroidery and gauze; gold-printed scrolls and trellises; Eastern and Chinese-inspired motifs; and flamboyant colourful jewellery and edgings.

In the late 1970s, Rhodes's shocking-pink and black jersey outfits with beaded safety pins led to her nickname, the 'princess of punk'. She has designed costumes and outfits for Freddie Mercury of the rock group Queen, Diana Princess of Wales, the actresses Elizabeth Taylor and Helen Mirren, the pop-star Kylie Minogue and many other style icons. She has recently produced costume designs for opera in Britain and America. In the last few years some designs have been created with patterned black and white fabrics, but Zandra Rhodes's most recent designs have returned to her iconic long, floating chiffon designs in bold colourful patterns. Some patterns echo aspects of the geometric and organic forms in African textile designs but others reprieve motifs from throughout her career.

She received a CBE in 1997 and was inaugurated as the Chancellor of the University of the Creative Arts in 2010, an appropriate link to her college roots and acknowledgement of the lasting legacy of her work for British design.

Silk chiffon evening dress, 'Knitted Circle' Collection, 1969, *Britain*
This kaftan-style dress became highly fashionable in the 1970s. With a high-waisted bodice, long sleeves and long, floating skirt and motifs from knitting and embroidery stitches, this dress was part of Rhodes's first independent collection.

Tartan Grids
1923–1994

Future nostalgia

The infinite pattern-making of woven tartan is based on the combination of 'setts', the number of threads required to weave a sequence of coloured bands. The sett is repeated vertically across the loom until the width is complete and then interwoven horizontally at right-angles to produce the tartan. This identifying sequence is common to all tartans, whether simple or complex. A symmetrical tartan is woven with the sett repeated in reverse order, while an asymmetrical tartan has a sett repeated in the same order. This interweaving of colours produces a shaded and tonally subtle grid design. The overall effect becomes more muted as the number of colours is increased and similar shades of colour visually mix, with the vibrancy of some colours only seen when viewed close up.

'The immediately recognisable visual element of a tartan pattern – a grid effect ... is conservative and radical, oppressive and liberating.'

JONATHAN FAIERS, *Networks of Design*, 2009

Dress, 1923–26, *Paris, France*
Hand-sewn in silk taffeta with a fashionable dropped waistline, this design for a day dress by Paul Poiret is patterned with broad pink, grey, white and black stripes. This style of 'picture dress' was more romantic and formal than the straight-cut shift dresses of the 1920s, and this dress has been complemented with a contemporary fantasy version of an historic pattern style.

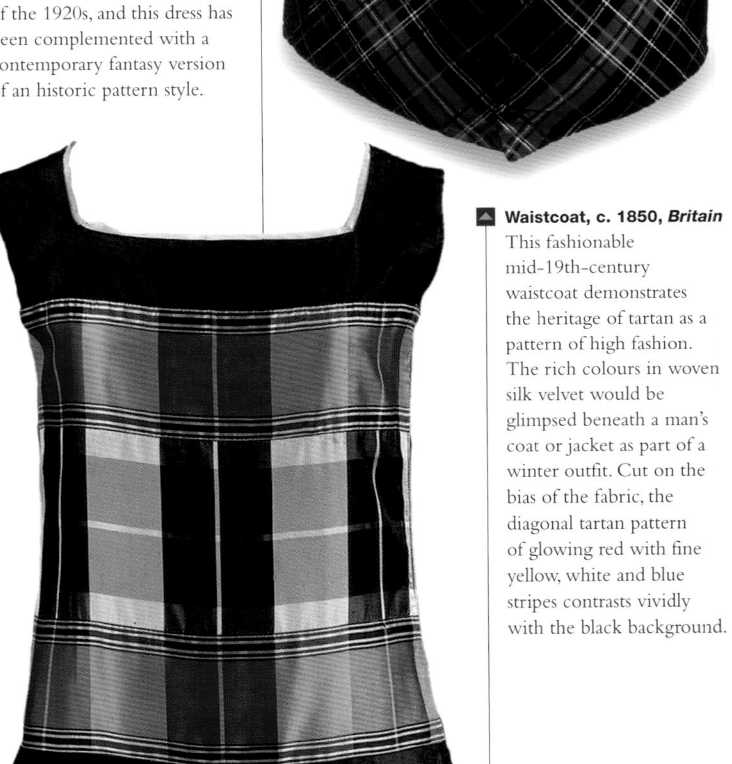

Waistcoat, c. 1850, *Britain*
This fashionable mid-19th-century waistcoat demonstrates the heritage of tartan as a pattern of high fashion. The rich colours in woven silk velvet would be glimpsed beneath a man's coat or jacket as part of a winter outfit. Cut on the bias of the fabric, the diagonal tartan pattern of glowing red with fine yellow, white and blue stripes contrasts vividly with the black background.

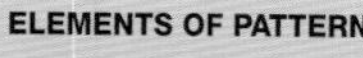

ELEMENTS OF PATTERN

- *grid structure*
- *bold colour contrasts or muted shades*
- *traditional and radical*
- *infinite variation*

Suit, c. 1976, *Britain*
Made of brushed-wool tweed cut in a formal style, this woman's suit designed by Bill Gibb is strongly horizontally banded with red, green and white. The vertical elements of the tartan are woven in paler colours to maintain this focus. The square style of the jacket reflects the structure of the pattern, emphasised by the lines of red piping.

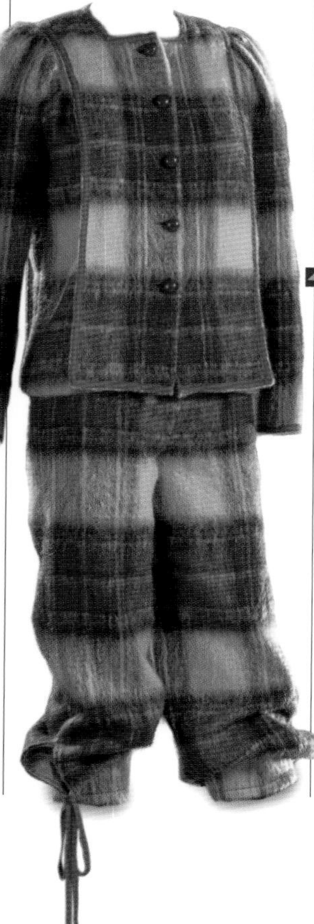

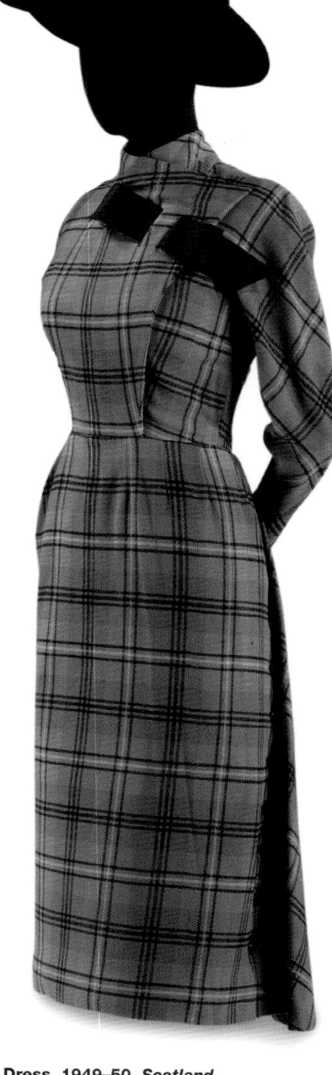

Dress, 1949–50, *Scotland* and *Paris, France*
The long lines of this dress clearly display this traditional Johnston tartan. The dress belonged to Lady Alexandra Howard-Johnston, wife of the naval attaché to Paris at the end of the 1940s. She acquired all her outfits for official functions exclusively from the French couturier Jacques Fath in Paris. This day dress was one of the most fashionable styles of the 1949–50 season, which she commissioned to be made up in her husband's Johnston family tartan, buying the hand-woven fabric, coloured with natural vegetable dyes, from Scotland herself.

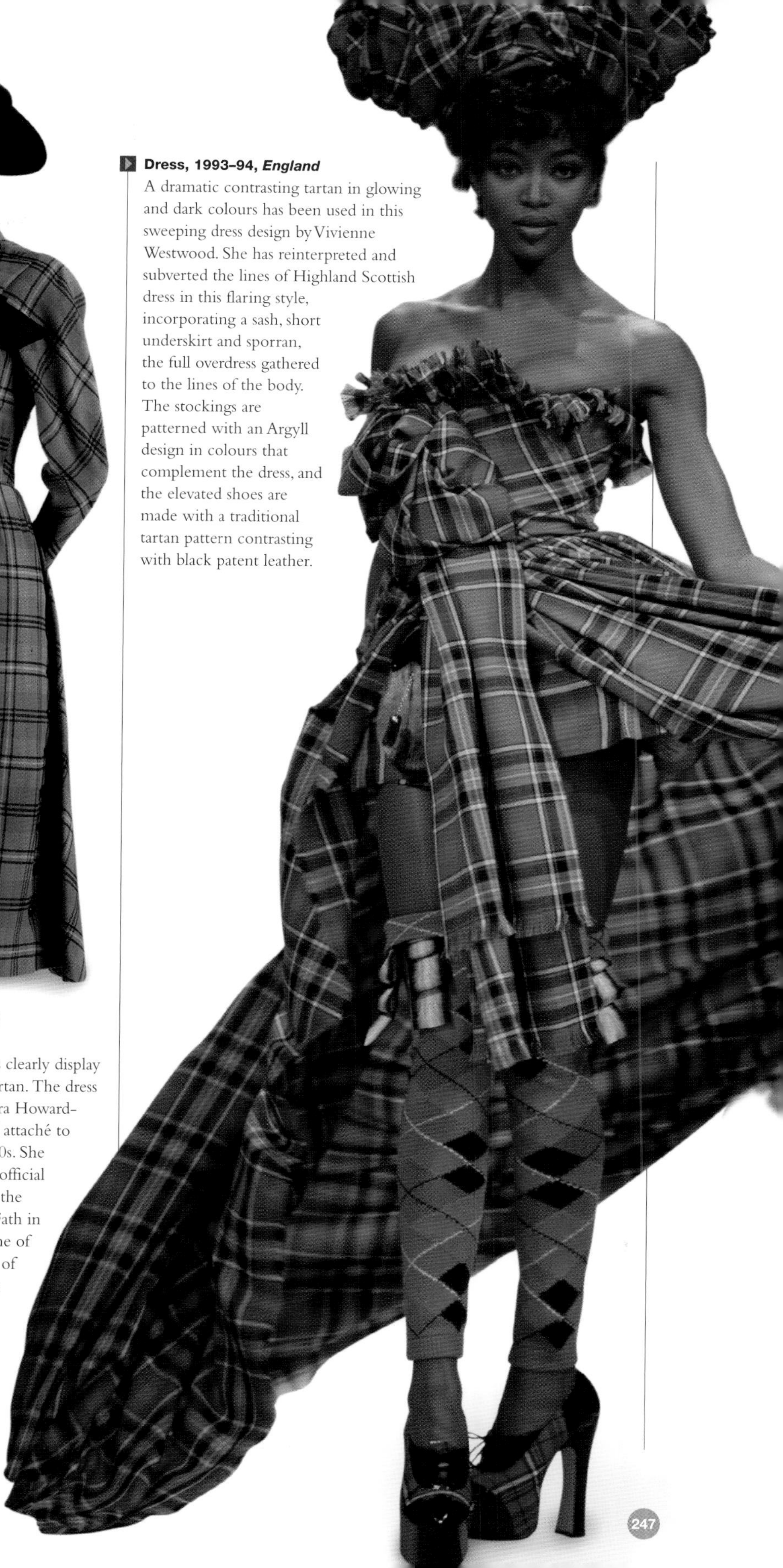

Dress, 1993–94, *England*
A dramatic contrasting tartan in glowing and dark colours has been used in this sweeping dress design by Vivienne Westwood. She has reinterpreted and subverted the lines of Highland Scottish dress in this flaring style, incorporating a sash, short underskirt and sporran, the full overdress gathered to the lines of the body. The stockings are patterned with an Argyll design in colours that complement the dress, and the elevated shoes are made with a traditional tartan pattern contrasting with black patent leather.

Flowers Reborn 1980–2010

The revival of the floral

The popularity of floral motifs, although never totally lost, saw a revival in the last decades of the 20th century. During the 1960s and 70s, Laura Ashley (1925–85) drew on Victorian designs to create popular floral designs for interiors and dress fabrics. The design retailer Liberty's of London maintained iconic floral patterns in its trademark cottons, and designers such as Tricia Guild, Anna French and Cath Kidston promoted flower designs. Rejecting the anti-decorative principles of modernist design and adopting the postmodern ironic referencing of past motifs, flowers remain a powerful pattern form in lush naturalistic blooms or colourful stylised sprigs.

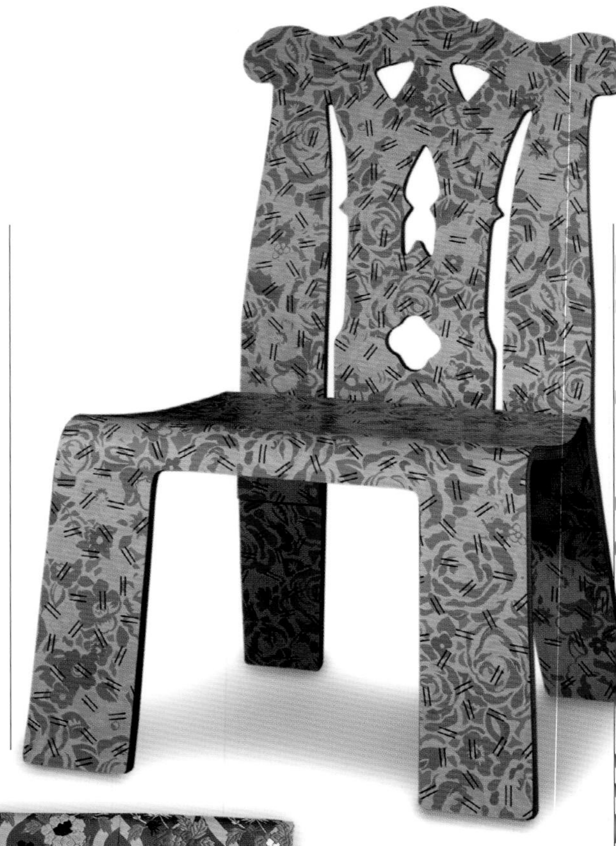

Chippendale chair, Venturi & Scott Brown, 1984, *New York*
Robert Venturi is well known for incorporating past iconic decorative elements into his architecture. Venturi and Denise Scott Brown produced this functional modernist chair using contemporary plywood and laminating techniques. However, the design is covered with a retrospective flower design and the chair-back is pierced with the traditional form used by the 18th-century designer, Thomas Chippendale.

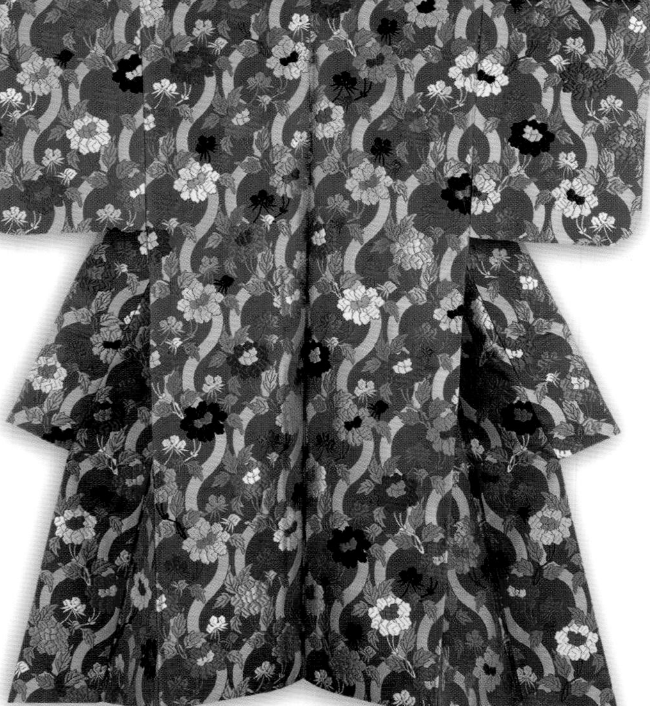

Karaori* robe, Yasujiro Yamaguchi, 1980, *Kyoto, Japan
This *karaori*, 'Chinese weave', robe was designed for a woman's role in classical Japanese *Noh* theatre. In Japanese design, flowers have always been auspicious motifs and this *karaori* is covered in vibrantly coloured silk peonies set against a silver wavy band on a green background. The fabric is woven on a jacquard loom, creating the contrasting textures of the satin flowers and band on a matt background.

Liberty Print 'Mark', 1999, England
The paisley design, probably originating in Iran and becoming extremely popular on 18th- and 19th-century shawls made in India (see pages 204–5), has continued to be part of the textile design repertoire throughout the 20th century. This in-house Liberty design has a range of curling paisley forms filled with floral and geometric patterns based on Islamic designs in vibrant bright colours.

ELEMENTS OF PATTERN

- *simple flower heads and colourful stylised sprigs*
- *revivals of 18th- and 19th-century florals*
- *lush naturalistic blooms*
- *symbolic flowers*

'One of the first was a printed ironing board cover – practical, quirky and with a distinctive floral print, it has come to epitomise the Cath Kidston look.'

CATH KIDSTON, FLORAL FABRIC DESIGNER, WWW.CATHKIDSTON.CO.UK, 2010

Batik design, Iwan Tirta, 2010, *Indonesia*
Batik textiles are made by the traditional technique of wax-resist dyeing. From Indonesia, China, India and Africa, the patterns may represent Hindu deities, concepts of the Universe, royal status or ordinary themes of life. The bands of vibrant tropical flowers and rippling alternating leaves in this dress capture these traditions. Tirta sought to revive and promote the cultural values of traditional batik in the fashion world and based many of his textile patterns on designs from the Javanese Court.

Laura Ashley screenprint wallpaper, 1989, *England*
The two-coloured, scrolling, climbing rose design typifies the pretty delicate floral patterns of Laura Ashley. Modelled on 18th- and 19th-century wallpapers and fabrics in the Victoria & Albert Museum, Laura Ashley's designs have a universal appeal, bringing colour and pattern without overpowering motifs. This pattern, based on an 18th-century silk fabric, features the spiky leaves, rosehips and simple flowers of the dog-rose.

Neo-Baroque Style 1988–2009

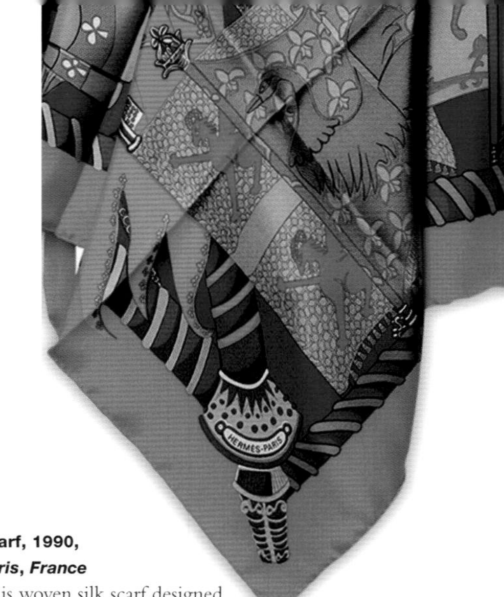

Scarf, 1990, *Paris, France*
This woven silk scarf designed by the French high-fashion house Hermès has been screen-printed with flags and motifs inspired by military trappings such as twisted silk cords. The flags are patterned with heraldic devices such as lions, swans and fleur-de-lis. The design is richly coloured to complement the neo-Gothic style motifs. Such luxury scarves are signature articles of the Hermès brand.

Theatrical flamboyance

The theatricality of the neo-Baroque style is expressed with rich and varied patterning on all types of surfaces in a comprehensive approach to design and colour. The style places a high value on appearance and the incorporation of references to its historical and contemporary design sources. The neo-Baroque can be compared with the historic Baroque style of the late 16th to early 18th centuries in its confidence and dynamic movement of pattern and presentation. The neo-Baroque is perfectly suited to all social levels of the lifestyles market with its ability to be ubiquitously applied in endlessly creative ways.

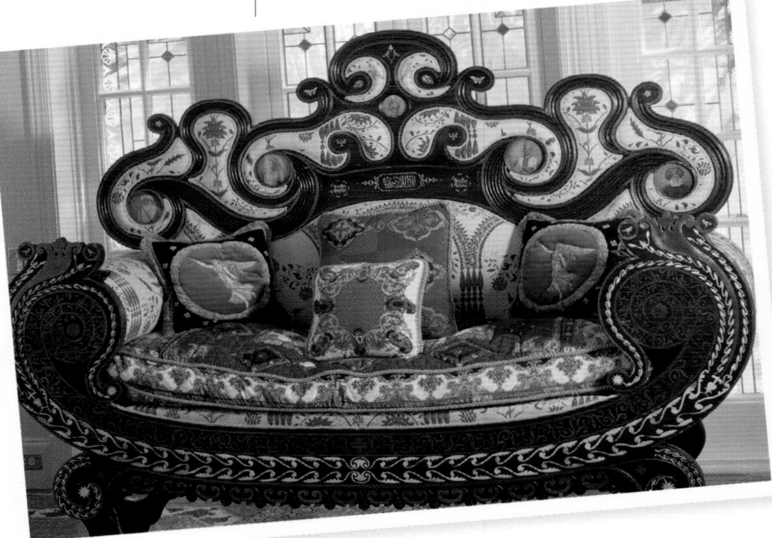

Couch, c. 1980–92, *Italy*
This flamboyant couch, from the home of Italian fashion designer Gianni Versace in Miami, Florida, has a scrolling form elaborately expressed in a symmetrical but rhythmically curling effect. The dominant motif is the pelta, a curve with scrolled ends. The front woodwork is pelta-shaped and patterned with leafy shoots interlinked in a rhythmic double line centring on opposed palmettes, each within a pelta motif. Above is a running leaf-tendril pattern, ending in a tight scroll on the arms, and the lower edge is decorated with a row of peltae. The fabric is patterned with richly coloured florals on a white background in the style of neoclassical interpretations of Roman frescoes.

‘The Baroque must be understood as the aesthetic counterpart to a problem of thought that is coterminous with ... modernity, stretching from the sixteenth century to the present.’

WILLIAM EGGINTON, *The Theater of Truth*, 2010

ELEMENTS OF PATTERN

- *customising of high-status brands*
- *eclectic historicism*

Outfit, 1991, *Milan, Italy*
The jacket and vest of this outfit from the Italian fashion house Versace are patterned with a kaleidoscopic design of retrospective florals in rich colours on a dark background, patterns of peltae and scrolling leaf elements, and clouded colour effects. The trousers are printed with a similar concept of undulating bands of floral, scrolling leaves and geometric key patterns in vivid colours. The eclectic effect of this outfit reflects Gianni Versace's wide-ranging and flamboyant approach to pattern design.

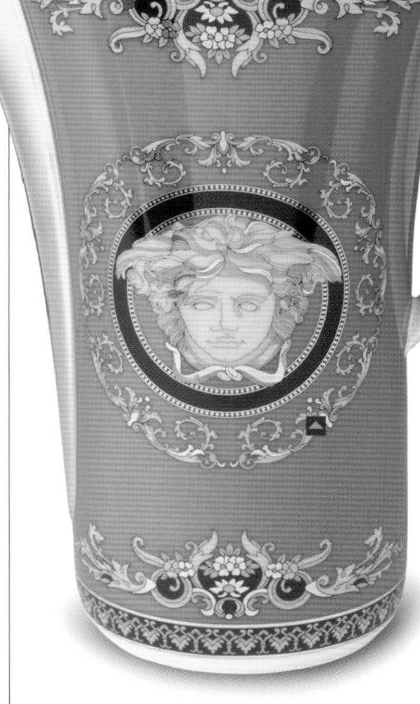

Coffee pot, 2008–09, *Selb, Germany*
Silkscreen-printed in a design called 'Red Medusa' by Gianni Versace, the shape of this porcelain coffee pot, 'Ikarus', was designed by Paul Wunderlich. Emulating the rich colour of red enamel, the pot is decorated with theatrical patterns derived from neoclassical devices. A male mask is encircled by a black ring with pelleted edges, and a pattern of repeated acanthus-like florals centred on pairs of scrolling fronds, between formalised garlands of flowers and curling leaves. A band patterned with alternating geometric lotus and palmette motifs borders the rim and the foot. The coffee pot was manufactured by Rosenthal.

Jacket, 1988, *USA*
This design is from the back of a jacket, part of a man's fashion tracksuit made of leather and nylon. The fake high-fashion design reflects the 'B-Boy' ('Break-Boy') style, named after the young African-Americans associated with urban rap and hip-hop. Inspired by branded sportswear, the style incorporated trainers, baseball caps and heavy gold jewellery. Brand consciousness was expressed by customising the designs and logos of famous clothing chains. The pattern behind the Gucci name and in the logo below comprises a lozengical grid with abstracted double-G motifs at the intersections.

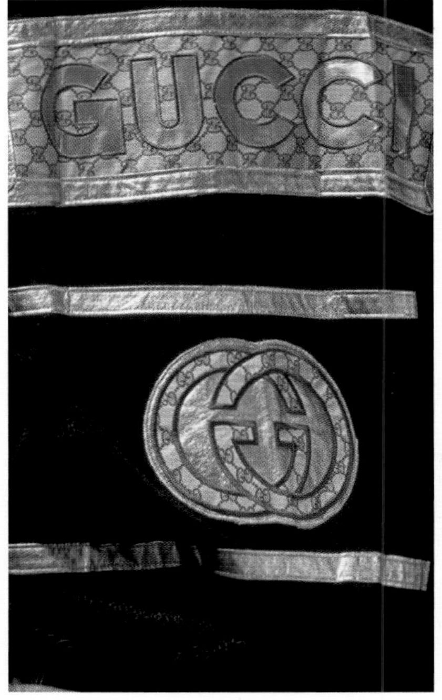

Geometrics & Organic Oppositions 1984–1995

Patterns in designs of life

The legacy of modernism provided many stimuli for late 20th-century design. Abstract geometric and organic motifs remained dominant, while the concern for utilising the qualities of modern materials continued to influence pattern forms. However, the pluralistic and eclectic concerns of so-called 'postmodern' design have produced innovative and radical pattern concepts. In fashion and interiors, geometric patterns, sometimes combined with floral motifs, remain popular with designers. In architecture, regular and irregular geometric patterns have become fundamental to building design. Late 20th-century designers and architects consciously place their designs within a global context.

'[Materials] create physical sensations through their warmth and coolness, smoothness and roughness, and visual impressions through color, grain, scale, pattern, texture, and finish in ever-changing light.'

KELLY CARLSON-REDDIG, 'Students consider architecture's materiality' IN *Journal of Architectural Education*, 1997

Teapot, Ralph Bacerra, c. 1984, *USA*
This pyramid teapot and stand were made of cut sections of earthenware modelled into the required form. The pattern and motifs – textured earthenware, stripes and abstract patterning have been created by inlaid clays and colours. The simple lines of the design are deconstructed by the cut-off corner of the stand, the curved handle and spout and the contrasting rigid and morphing patterning.

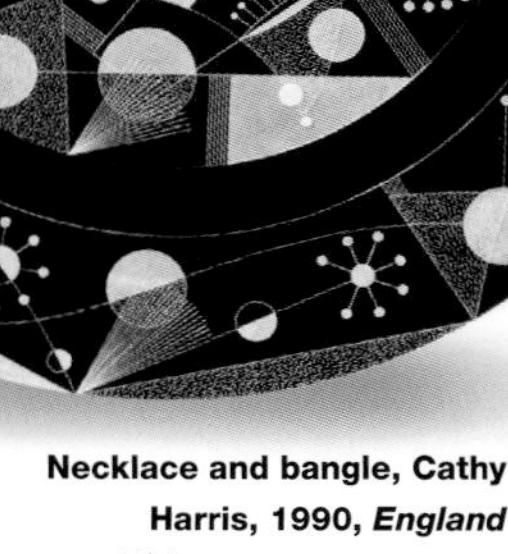

Necklace and bangle, Cathy Harris, 1990, *England*
This transparent perspex necklace and bangle are incised using a metal point to create opaque patterning. The fine lines, circles, curves, ellipses and granular motifs have geometric precision as well as rhythmic balance reminiscent of Lucienne Day's designs (see pages 240–1). Cathy Harris's premature death cut short a promising design career of creating colourful and striking jewellery in non-precious materials.

ELEMENTS OF PATTERN

- *circles, triangles and lines*
- *curving staircases and sweeping pipes*
- *pyramids and stripes*
- *curves and checks*

Evening dress, Gianni Versace, 1995, *Paris, France*
More familiar for his neo-Baroque fashion (see pages 250–1), Gianni Versace's Paris Atelier 1995 collection contained this bold geometric design. The bodice of this dress is made of silver lamé appliquéd with geometrics in black and scarlet sculpted to the figure, balanced by the dress's scarlet and white chequer-board pattern skirt. Versace has included geometric patterns in textures, quilted and appliquéd designs.

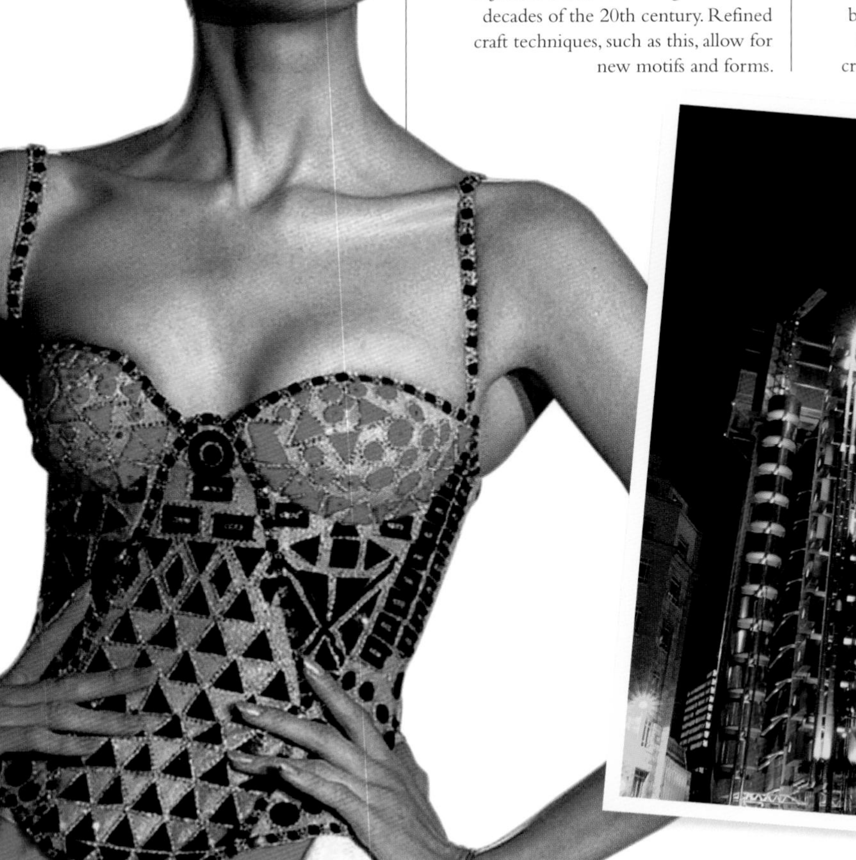

Octagonal glazed stoneware bowl, c. 1990, *Aida, Japan*
The feather design on this bowl is created using five shades of cream to brown coloured stoneware, formed into a wave pattern and then shaped in a press mould. The innovative ways in which pattern is created and applied to objects is a feature of design in the last decades of the 20th century. Refined craft techniques, such as this, allow for new motifs and forms.

Lloyds of London building, Richard Rogers, 1984, *London, England*
Richard Rogers is renowned for designing buildings where the utilities – such as lifts, framework and pipes – are placed on the outside of the structure. Lloyds of London and the Pompidou Centre in Paris (1977) break with modernist exteriors where form was determined by building function. With Rogers's buildings, the curves of the staircases, sweep of the pipes and regularity of the floor structure create an original and unique patterned design.

2000
2011

Twenty-First Century

Introduction

Patterns have always been deeply informed by people's ever-changing experience of the natural and cultural worlds they live in. Rich in codes and signifiers, pattern-making is the language with which people articulate meaning in order to explore and interrogate their relationships with each other, their surroundings and their spirituality. These connections are created through the clothing they wear, the items they own and exchange with each other, and the buildings they construct, in a continuous dialogue of visual experience between person and object.

Digital technology has profoundly altered pattern-making, extending its construction techniques and its application into virtual space. People are now able to view patterns interactively on webpages and in portable document format (pdf) on a surface without physical form. Designers are able to explore, experiment with and manipulate colour and form rapidly, free from the restraints of physical media, opening up their creativity in new ways. This allows pattern-makers to process the interrelationships of colour and form into design solutions for wide-ranging applications in virtual or physical media.

In 21st-century pattern design, a postmodern sense of pleasure underlies the manipulation of colour and tone in infinitely varied treatments of motif and background. Ambiguity and fantasy have become important qualities in the visual experience of reading pattern, informed by devices and themes from palaeontology, prehistory, history and astronomy. These themes are treated in intriguing combinations as designers manipulate information, light and sound to produce innovative conceptual patterns that reflect the contemporary age of multimedia design. The choices and cross-fertilisation of themes and motifs in patterns are reflected in 21st-century consumer culture. A deep referencing of the past is combined with a reanimation of everyday and ephemeral objects to inform new pattern design in ways that dramatise their juxtapositions.

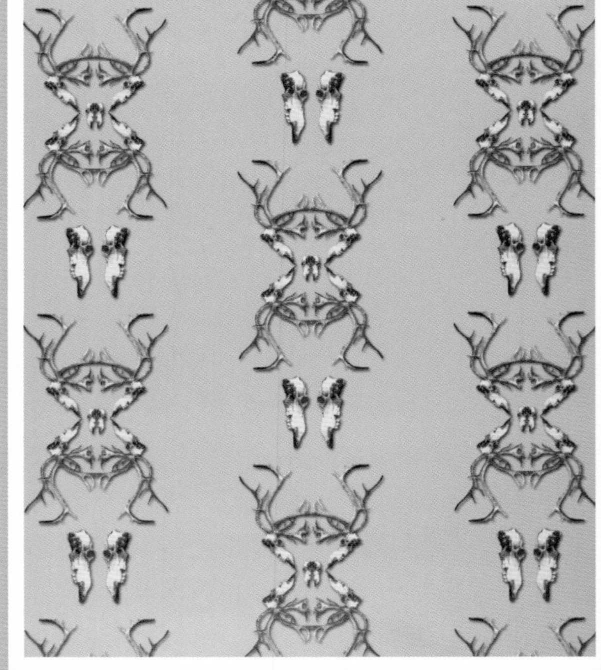

This 'Antler' wallpaper design by Abigail Lane extends the vocabulary of the medium. Promoting their individual style and approach of incorporating unusual objects into interior surroundings, the design group Showroom Dummies reveal their unconventional identity in this aesthetically adventurous design.

With the infinite possibilities of computer software, individuality in pattern design has come to the fore. This has prompted and enabled designers to explore and express issues of their own individual identity in unprecedented ways. Craft traditions and technology have integrated to produce new fabrics and materials to reflect lifestyle changes and the complexity of modern times. Reactions among the consumers of design have also changed. With an increasing demand for innovation, pattern-makers use their intuition to exploit their materials in a limitless working space in order to reveal further creative virtuosity. The development of global markets has spread experience and knowledge of pattern design to the public domain more widely than ever before. The creation of niche markets for objects patterned in individual and unusual ways has lead to personal styles flowing into the mainstream of fashion, a process which constantly renews the desirability of innovative and original design.

Entitled 'Ammonite Interpretation', this textile design by Lizzie Hingley references the palaeontological forms of ammonite fossils. Complementary colours of blue and orange combine with the dynamic rhythm of this pattern to create a vibrant and animated design.

The primacy of craft in 21st-century design is underlined in this coat by Missoni. Dynamically juxtaposed panels of knitted patterns interplay in bold combinations of scale. The technical processes of knitting and hand-stitching involved in the making up of this garment are explicitly highlighted in this composition.

Transnational Modernity 2004–2010

Global clothing

The internationalisation of the fashion industry has resulted in the spread of patterns with complex intercultural histories to a wide global market, from high-fashion catwalks to high-street chains. Historical, indigenous and regional forms and colours have been changed and enriched by the vision of contemporary fashion designers in their creative exploitation of fast-changing technologies. Geometric, organic and ethnically derived patterns are assembled in rich combinations, reflecting the 'historical modernity' of 21st-century fashion design.

Coat, 2004, *Italy*
Created by the Italian fashion house Missoni, this coat is made up of geometric patchwork panels in knitted wool. The panels are patterned with rippling colours contrasted with black, shaded broken bands, shallow zigzag textures, lattices of lozenges and paisley swirls, all in a subtly varied colour palette. Missoni is noted for its innovative approaches to the knitting process – here the interaction between the technical and creative processes involved is clearly shown.

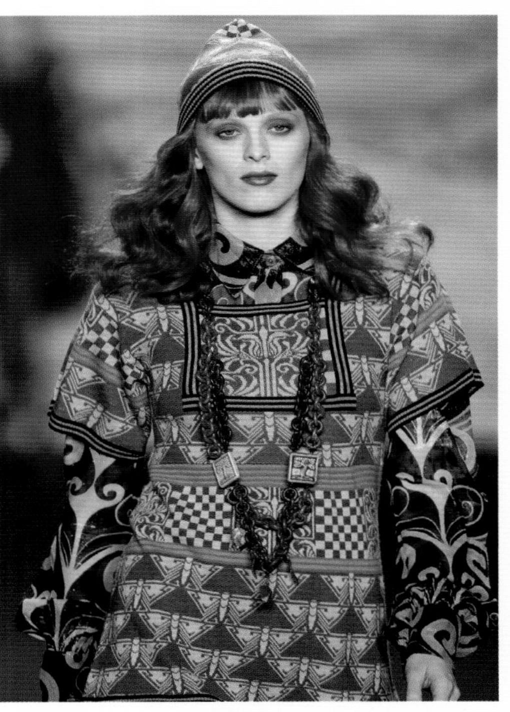

Shirt and tunic, 2010, *USA*
This layered outfit by American fashion designer Anna Sui is dominated by patterns interrelated by form and colour. The cut and pattern of the shirt strongly reference Biba, with sleeves gathered into deep cuffs and a swirling organic pattern in flat colours. The tunic is panelled with Art Deco three-stemmed floral designs alternating with checked squares in the same two colours, and a triangle grid varied by the addition of light blue. Innovative and fresh, historical and ethnic patterns are bordered with a 1960s-style braid effect.

'Fashion is a global enterprise and an international language that crosses ethnic and class boundaries.'

SUE JENKYNS JONES, *Fashion Design*, 2010

Dress, 2010, *USA*
This Biba-style dress by Anna Sui is made up from three patterned fabrics printed in three colours, cut and sewn up both with the weave and on the bias to give a dynamic effect. The three patterns are Chinese-style half-florals with curling stems and delicately decorated leaves contrast strongly with a black background; bands of flowers with four scroll-ended petals alternate with lozenge-shaped flowerheads; and a grid of discs shaded blue with a floral motif.

Coat-dress, 2005, *France*
Designed by the French fashion house Louis Vuitton, the style of this streamlined coat-dress references the classic lines of Chanel in its cut and black banding that describe the lines of the body. The geometric pattern of the garment is informed by the shapes of the LV monogram of this luxury designer brand.

Dress, 2010, *USA*
Nostalgically patterned with garlands of florals in zigzag formation on a white background, the upper body and placket of this dress by Anna Sui contrast with the dark colours of the Far Eastern paisley and floral motifs on the skirt. The sleeves are patterned in two shades of blue with sweeping and intersecting fan-shaped forms reminiscent of Chinese porcelain decoration.

ELEMENTS OF PATTERN

- *combinations of patterns*
- *geometrics*
- *organic forms*
- *ethnic references*

Paul Smith
b. 1946

While he initially had an ambition to become a professional racing cyclist, Paul Smith was persuaded by his father to take a job as an errand boy at a local Nottingham clothing warehouse. While cycling to work, he was involved in a road accident that ended his dream of cycle racing. By chance, he met students from the local art college who stimulated his interest in art and fashion with discussions of modern artists, photographers, and rock and jazz music. Smith observed the practical cut and fabrics of working men's clothes and the elegant tweeds of the local Nottinghamshire gentlemen. He began to design and build displays in the warehouse showroom, impressing his employer, who appointed him buyer for menswear.

Smith decorated and managed a fashion boutique in Nottingham for an art college friend and, in 1970, opened his own shop, Paul Smith Vêtement Pour Homme. He enrolled in evening classes for tailoring, where his designs were noticed by Harold Tilman, chairman of Lincroft Kilgour in Savile Row, London. In 1974 Smith opened his first London clothing shop in Floral Street, Covent Garden, where he also sold unusual accessories for men, including the Filofax, a leatherbound personal organiser from Norman & Hill, a small company in East London, which was to become an inconic 1980s object. In 1976 Smith presented his first menswear collection in Paris and began to sell his own designs based on traditional menswear, made up by local Nottingham manufacturers. In his London shop he sold comfortable, well-made, good-quality suits and American jeans of the type that he himself wore.

Smith bought the premises next door with its old wooden fittings to display clothes alongside the more idiosyncratic objects from his travels – first-edition books, comicbook annuals, and Japanese toys and gadgets. The windows were dressed with furniture designed by friends such as Tom Dixon, and new technology such as James Dyson's vacuum cleaner.

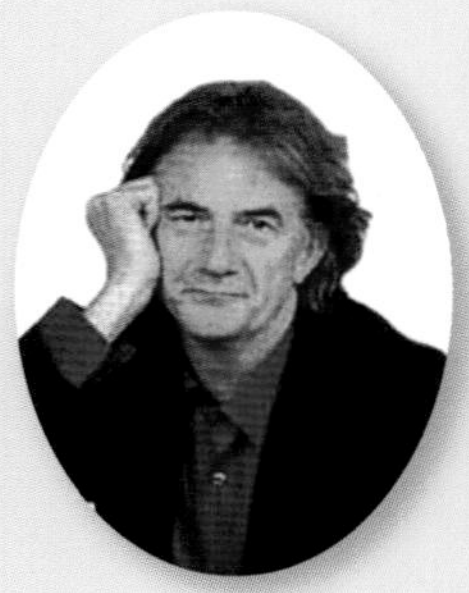

Born
Beeston, Nottinghamshire, England, 1946

Profession
Designer

Manifesto
'You can find inspiration in everything.'

‘It is as though he possesses some inner equivalent of the Houndsditch Clothes Exchange – not a museum, but a vast, endlessly recombinant jumble sale in which all the artefacts of his nation and culture constantly engage in a mutual exchange of code.’

WILLIAM GIBSON, NOVELIST, 2003

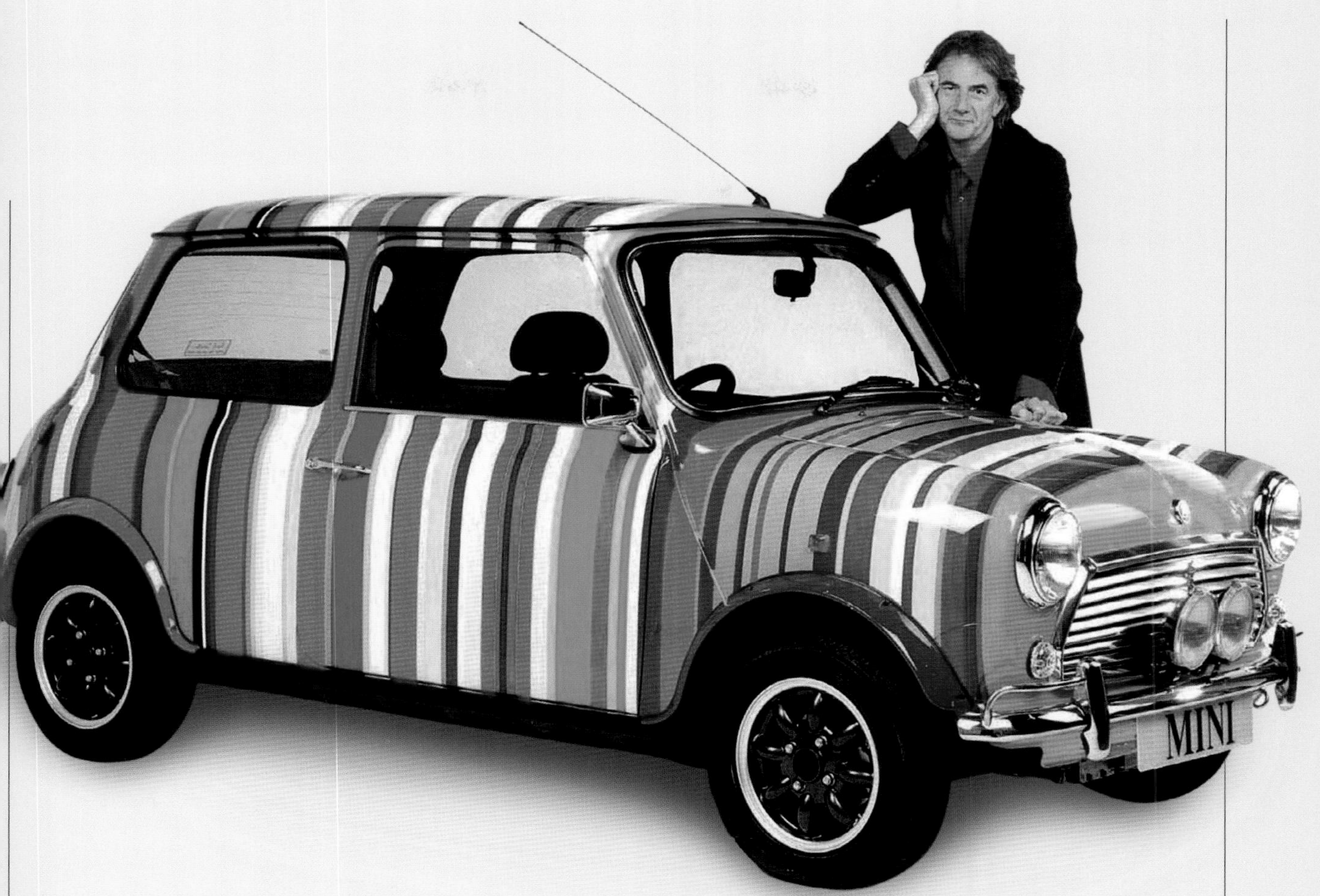

Multi-striped Mini Cooper, 1998
Paul Smith is pictured here with an icon of modern car design, the Mini Cooper, a reference to his love of racing and classic motors. His multi-stripe identifier pattern has been applied in vibrant colours to the bodywork of the car, over which it rhythmically ripples with a classic sense of fun.

In his clothing designs for men and women, which he calls 'classic with a twist', Smith draws on the high-quality tailoring of hand-made suits and combines them with something more frivolous, such as printed floral patterns inspired by old-fashioned seed packets, flamboyantly coloured silk linings or classic styles in unusual colours. He has shops in Europe, Asia and the USA, which showcase his clothes among books and intriguing old and new objects, and has diversified into a wide range of branded goods including jewellery, spectacles, perfume, home accessories and furniture. His ubiquitous signature multi-stripe pattern appears widely on his clothes and products. Paul Smith collections are designed in Nottingham and London and mainly produced in England and Italy, with British, French and Italian materials.

Paul Smith is a businesslike designer who oversees every development of his company, one that is globally successful but that nevertheless resonates with his personal, highly individual touch.

Global Design 2004–2010

Politics and display

Historical referencing, craftwork technologies and digital processes all combine in designs for the early 21st-century. Theatricality and humour are often interwoven in a rich array of patterns expressed in all types of media for clothing, personal accessories, commercial interiors and architectural structures. From international luxury icons to activist aesthetics, patterns have been deeply integrated with both the materials they are expressed in and the forms they define.

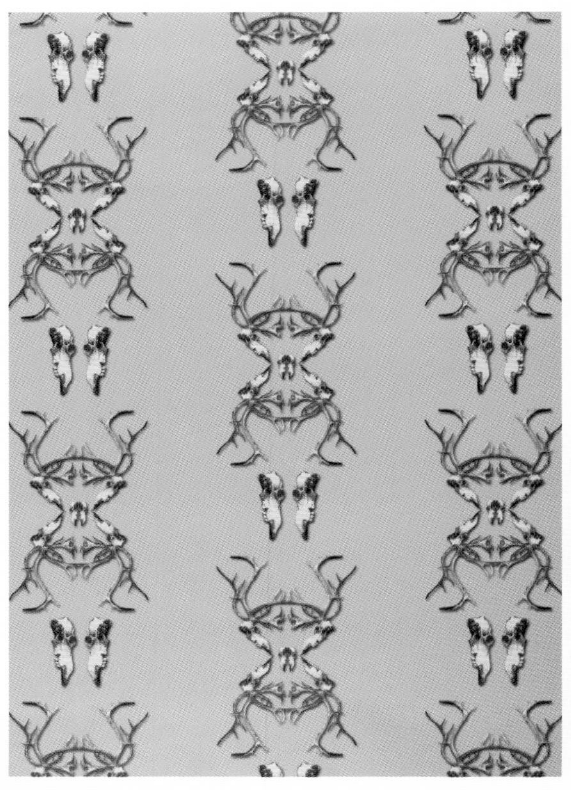

Wallpaper, 2004, *London, England*
This 'Antler' wallpaper design produced by photogravure comprises delicate reindeer bones arranged in a rhythmical pattern of discrete groups and pairs. With elements modelled in grey and white on a soft sea-blue background, the composition has the effect of a Rococo-style pattern. By Abigail Lane of the design group Showroom Dummies, this wallpaper was produced as a Christmas shop commission from The Mulberry Company, along with transparent screens printed with life-sized reindeer.

ELEMENTS OF PATTERN

- *reflections of historical interior design*
- *integration of craft process and art subject matter*
- *political expression*
- *pattern as object*

Textile, 2004, *Seki, Gifu, Japan*
Entitled 'Blue Mountains and Green Rivers', this woven silk pattern for a kimono was inspired by the crisp air and clear streams of Mount Qingcheng in Sichuan Province in China. Coloured with natural vegetable dyes, this design by Tsuchiya Yoshinori undulates with colours of the uplands and watercourses of the Japanee landscape. The structured grid on which this flowing pattern is based is composed of groups of rectangles graded in size across the diagonal, in graduating shades of blue to green.

'Technology and production, consumption and commercialism, craft and esthetics, and social and global responsibility ... a synthesis that may yet remain vital, dynamic, and enriching.'

DAVID RAIZMAN, *History of Modern Design*, 2003

Luggage, 2010, *Paris, France*

In 1896 the Parisian craftsman Louis Vuitton began to authenticate his canvas-covered cases by printing his initials on the material. The LV logo and the two flower motifs inspired by Japanese florals have become associated with personal luxury and refinement in a world of mass-production. Their application as a pattern to luggage denotes excellence of craftsmanship and distinction of style, drawing on the nostalgia for a time when comfortable travel was a privileged adventure for the affluent few.

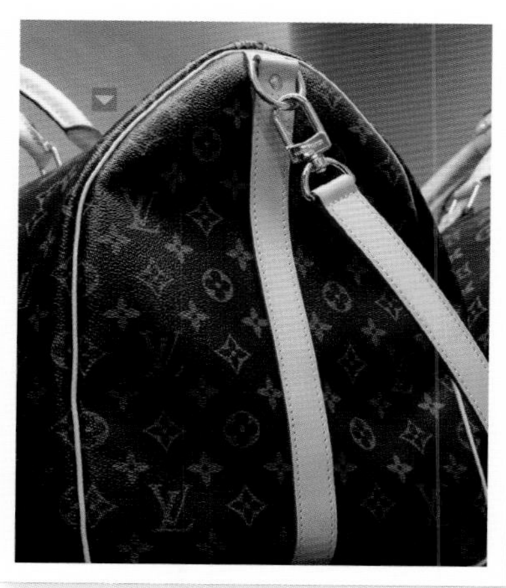

Collage, 2006, *London, England*

In this collage pattern entitled 'Morris/ Honeysuckle, Rodchenko/ Hard Currency', David Mabb contrasts the socialist philosophy of William Morris (see pages 200–1) with that of the Russian Constructivist Alexander Rodchenko (see pages 228–9). Morris's hand-printed romantic 'Honeysuckle' pattern, representing his idealism in the workplace, is combined with Rodchenko's machine-printed everyday motifs of 10-kopek coins. Mabb references the craft aesthetic of Morris in the hand-blocked florals, and the machine aesthetic of Rodchenko in the digitally printed coins.

Stadium, 2008, *Beijing, China*

Originating in a study of Chinese ceramics, the low, rounded form of the 'Bird's Nest' Olympic stadium was designed by Swiss architects Jacques Herzog and Pierre de Meuron in collaboration with the noted Chinese artist and activist Ai WeiWei. It is defined by a network of steel bands, originally designed to conceal the supports for a retractable roof, that create an intricate interplay of surface patterning and spatial shapes.

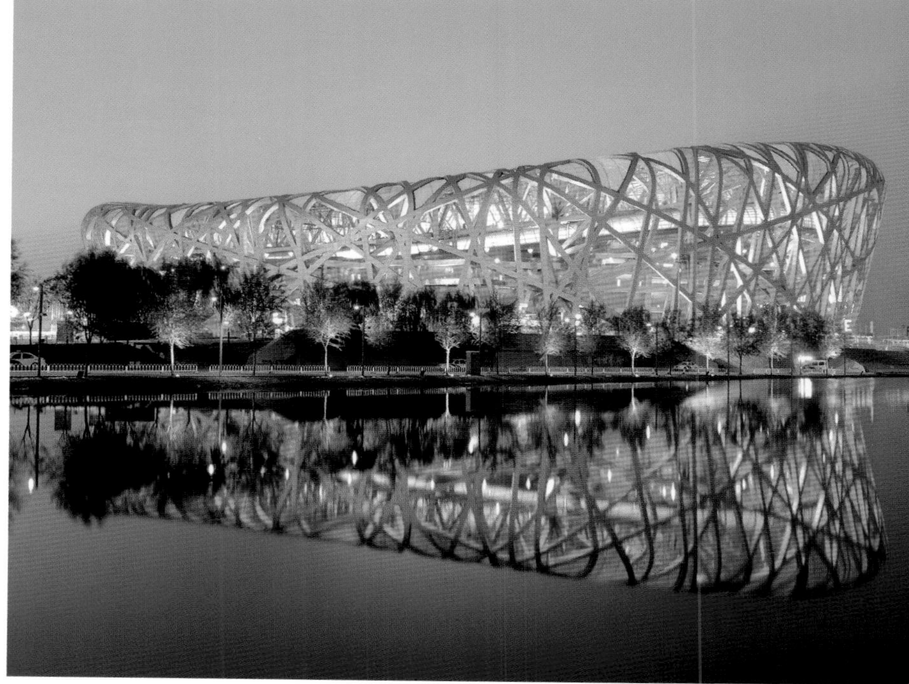

The Potential for Print 2008–2010

The next generation – experiments in techniques and motifs

Contemporary designers are not afraid to experiment with techniques and motifs from across time and space, blending past and present cultural influences on a global stage. The range of processes available to the printer, including the digital creation, enhancement or distortion of patterns and motifs, means that the potential is virtually unlimited. However, an attention to detail and quality in both the creation of designs and the production of prints gives these patterns vibrancy, originality and a sense of fun. It is noticeable that subjects for motifs continue to range from the geometric to the organic, but the designer also combines and plays with them in imaginative and visually exciting ways.

‘My work is largely influenced by a desire to explore ... techniques and processes. In the print room, where the scope for experimentation continually excites and inspires, I am absorbed by layering different processes – devoré, discharge, dyes, pigment and foiling – to discover how they react to each other.’

MEGAN DOW, PRINTED TEXTILES DESIGNER, 2011

Screen print, Hester Simpson, 2010, *London*
The concept for this screen-printed tiled textile design in black and white draws on many traditions in pattern-making. Inspired by an exhibition of vintage quilt fabrics, the design has turned a range of individual patterned tiles into a layered tile pattern. The juxtaposition of alternating black and white with a variety of bold floral and geometric motif tiles creates striking new shapes.

ELEMENTS OF PATTERN

- *fruits, insects and ferns*
- *triangles and dots*
- *vintage quilting fabrics*
- *nomad bird*

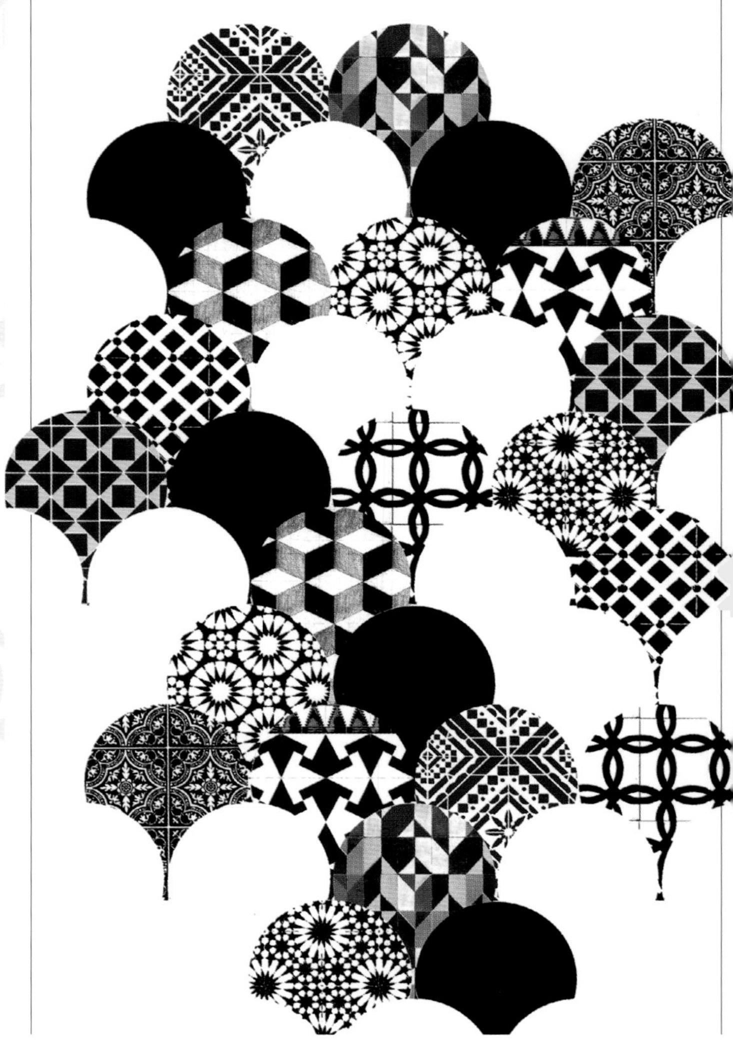

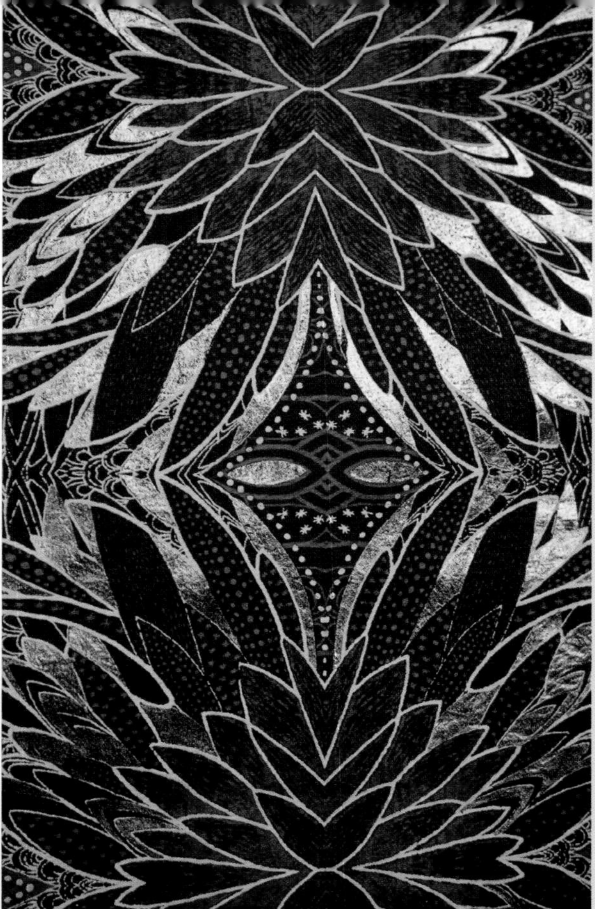

'Carnival Cockerels', dyed silk, Megan Dow, 2008, *Brighton*
The mixing of different textures and forms derive from 'playing' with recipes and techniques. Drawing on experiences in India and influenced by Art Nouveau (see pages 216–17), the design uses decorative elements and animal symbolism. Modern design technology provides the ideal means for experimentation and the fine feather-forms in dark tones and silver foil create a rich tactile fabric design.

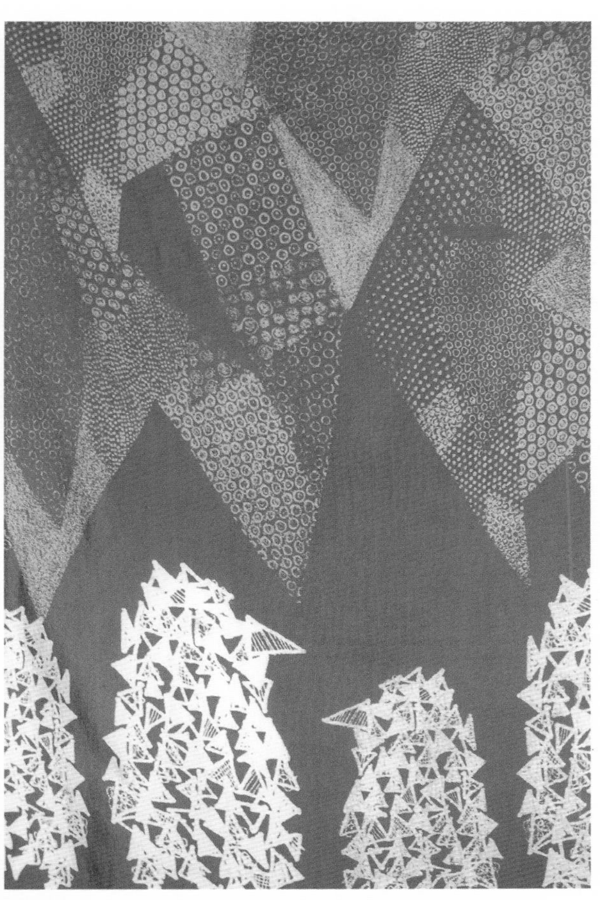

Fruits, insects and ferns design, Mee Rhim Song, 2010, *London*
The warm, luscious, natural colours of these fruits set within open rosettes contrast with the regularity of the pattern. The quirky choices of fruits, insects and ferns capture the 'uncanny shapes of nature' and their isolation echoes the display of single items of jewellery such as a pendant or brooch. The traditions of fine botanical painting are used to create precise representations for a fun-loving, young fashion design.

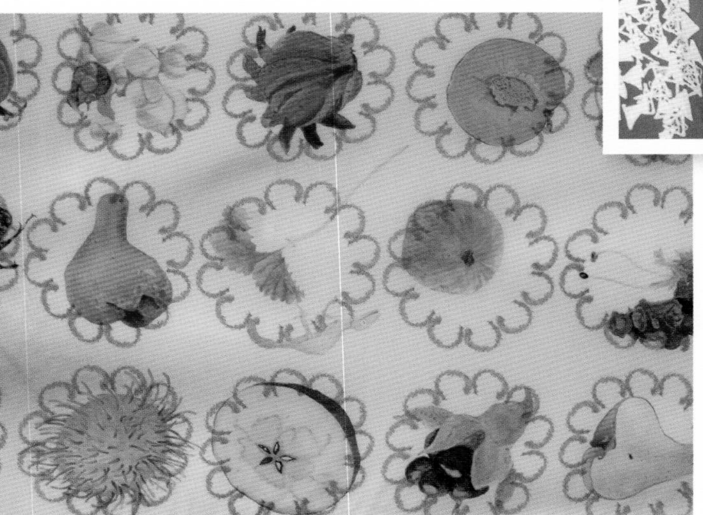

'Nomad Bird' design, Mee Rhim Song, 2009, *London*
The basic elements of this design, aimed at fashion or interiors, are triangles and dots built up into larger motifs, especially a collaged bird form. Although these basic elements are geometric, the subtlety of arranging and patterning the triangles and dots creates organic forms of birds and trees or leaves. The colours used – cream, green, purple, chestnut and navy – emphasise the naturalism.

Motion, Fluidity & Flowers 2010–2011

Next generation – natural and exotic inspirations

Today, courses in textile and surface pattern design inspire designers in new methods and contexts for pattern-making. The layering and combining of motifs is made possible by powerful image manipulation software and computer-aided design tools. Patterns are inspired by organic forms, a wide range of visual stimuli, and colours and designs from different cultures. Colour and the combination of contrasting and complementary hues continue to be vital to the visual impact of a design, but the playful use of forms – often juxtaposing the structural, organic, innovative and traditional – provides depth and energy.

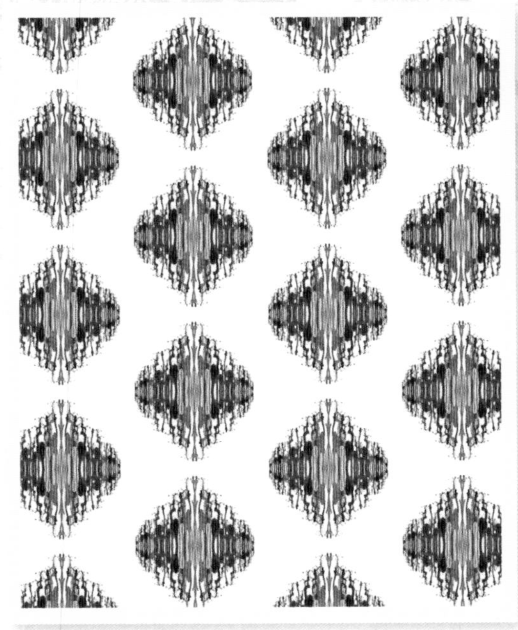

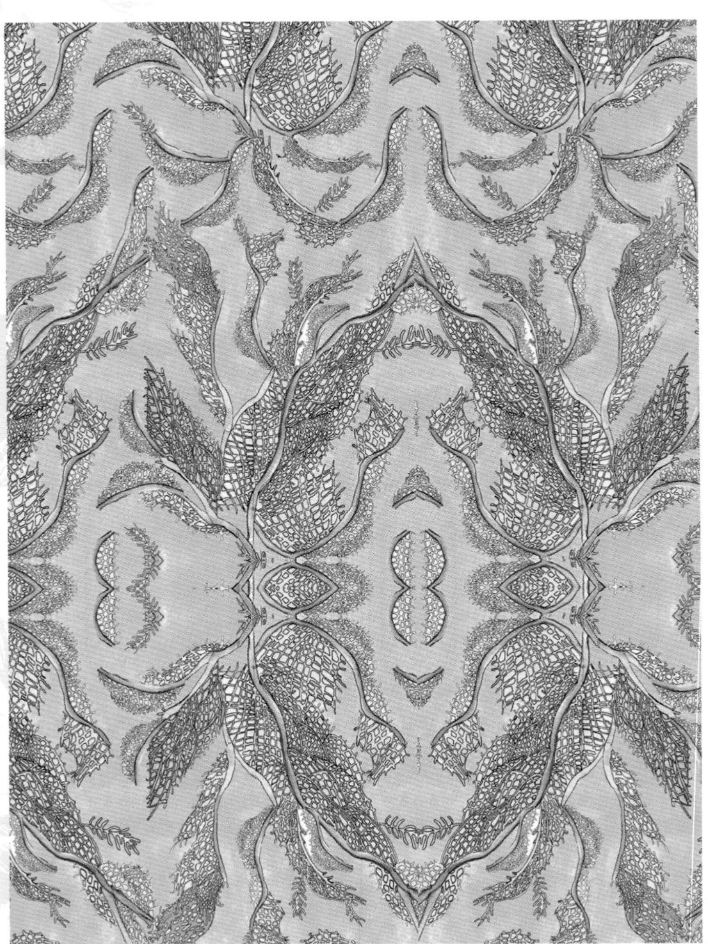

'Jazz', textile design, Hayley Brinsford, 2010, *London*
Initially influenced by the idea of motion, this pattern was developed from original photography of headlights of motor vehicles in the darkness of night, taking the sharp movements and reworking them until they represented something unorthodox. The pattern is formed by repeating the initial motif using the traditional half-drop repetition. This structured repeat was specifically chosen as a contrast to the fluidity and vivacity captured in the motif.

Silk fashion textile design, Jessie Brewin, 2011, *Bristol*
This design was influenced by natural facetted objects such as coral and sea plants. The shapes and texture of the motif were drawn and then manipulated digitally. The motif takes inspiration from the flattened branching form of a type of coral called gorgonian, also known as a sea fan or sea whip, which lives on tropical reefs. The waving forms that separate and rejoin provide the ideal motif for a flowing pattern.

'Tia', fashion textile design, Nikki Strange, 2010
This print is a painterly vibrant floral design representing tropical flowers in candy colours. The strong graphically drawn petals and blooms contrast with the translucent watercolour background creating a dreamy yet energetic surface design. The motifs are transparent and layered, giving the impression of a three-dimensional bouquet of blooms. The colours have been skilfully selected to offset soft pinks, purples and blues with splashes of lemon and grass green.

'Lola', fashion textile design, Nikki Strange, 2010, *London*
This design, inspired by the rich textures and colours of Goa in India, combines sporadic hand-drawn florals, which have been manipulated and clashed with more structural and traditional patterns. The composition echoes the woven and embroidered textiles of South India. The design contains four contrasting elements – semi-abstract florals, the strong cell-like motif overlaid with bright pink flowers and delicate linked rosettes.

ELEMENTS OF PATTERN

- *vibrant colours of electric blue, fuchsia and lemon yellow*
- *flowing sea-plant forms*
- *Indian-inspired florals, colours and motifs*

'These days, when fashion patterns glow, fade or disappear altogether, they probably tell us more about the future than they do about the present.'

BRADLEY QUINN, *Textile Designers at the Cutting Edge*, 2009

'Hari', fashion textile design, Nikki Strange, 2010, *London*
This design incorporates symbolism from bridal costumes through the inclusion of feminine Indian *bindi* motifs – the forehead decoration worn in South Asia. These are synchronised into blooming floral shapes and decorative jewellery, including the *panja* – Indian hand jewellery of a bracelet and ring – to create an intricate yet strong pattern repeat. The exotic and playful colour palette of purple and yellow is synonymous with an Indian summer.

Earth, Moon & Space 2010–2011

Next generation – future design skills and concepts

Digital technologies offer huge potential for creating, manipulating, mixing and refining visually stunning and vibrant designs, in some cases even without human intervention. However, hand-drawing and colouring remain a powerful creative force. These processes can draw on almost any inspirational form, colour or concept, exemplified on these pages by volcanoes, fossils, gardens, children's toys, protective powers, a secluded space and escapism. Fundamentally, the success of a pattern lies its visual impact built up from colours, forms, textures and surface effects. Contemporary design's eclecticism is its strength, ensuring the continuing importance and centrality of patterns to everyday life.

'Factors like the depletion of natural resources and climate change are compelling designers to be environmentally aware.'

CHRISTIAN BOUCHARENC, *Design for a Contemporary World*, 2008

'Pink Lava Florals', textile or ceramic design, Hannah Trask, 2010, *Guildford*

This pattern was designed for a project named 'Space scapes' and was inspired by planet surfaces and molten rocks. The dark and blue greys are offset by bright flushes of crimson red and fuchsia pink suggesting lava flows, which morph into a feminised floral print. The design would be suitable for a silk fashion textile but its versatility could also see it applied to upholstery textiles, and ceramics.

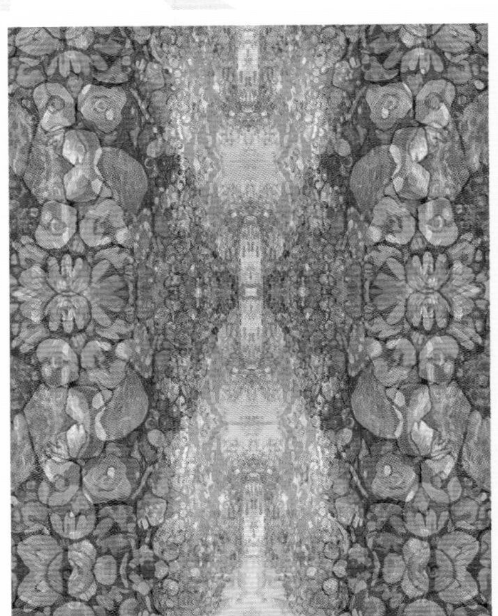

'Acrylic Garden', silk design, Hannah Trask, 2010, *Guildford,*

A refreshing stream flows through a beautiful garden of blooming flowers in the height of summer. This vibrant pattern is inspired by artists such as Gustav Klimt, in whose work thickly applied paint creates pattern and texture. Hot orange and pink flowers capture the shimmering texture of petals reflecting the summer heat, and contrast with the pastel undertones of cool blues and pale aqua greens in the sparkling water.

'Ammonite Interpretation', Lizzie Hingley, 2010, *Brighton*
This pattern draws on the abstraction of the organic form of an ammonite, simplifying the outline and creating sections and patterns within it. It is structured using two different interlocking shapes, represented in the oppositional warm and cool colours. The pattern is intended for use on fabric, for the lining of a bag or coat, creating a bright playfulness within an otherwise neutral piece.

'Eyeprint', fashion textile design, Moon Hussain, 2010, *London*
'Escapism from Reality' was the starting point for this design, which draws on the idea of the shaman's use of ritual objects in exorcism. The simple black on green colouring produces a striking design. The hand-drawn, swirling, open and closed shapes, which might be eyes, faces or flowers, sweep across the surface of the design forming a random and fugitive pattern.

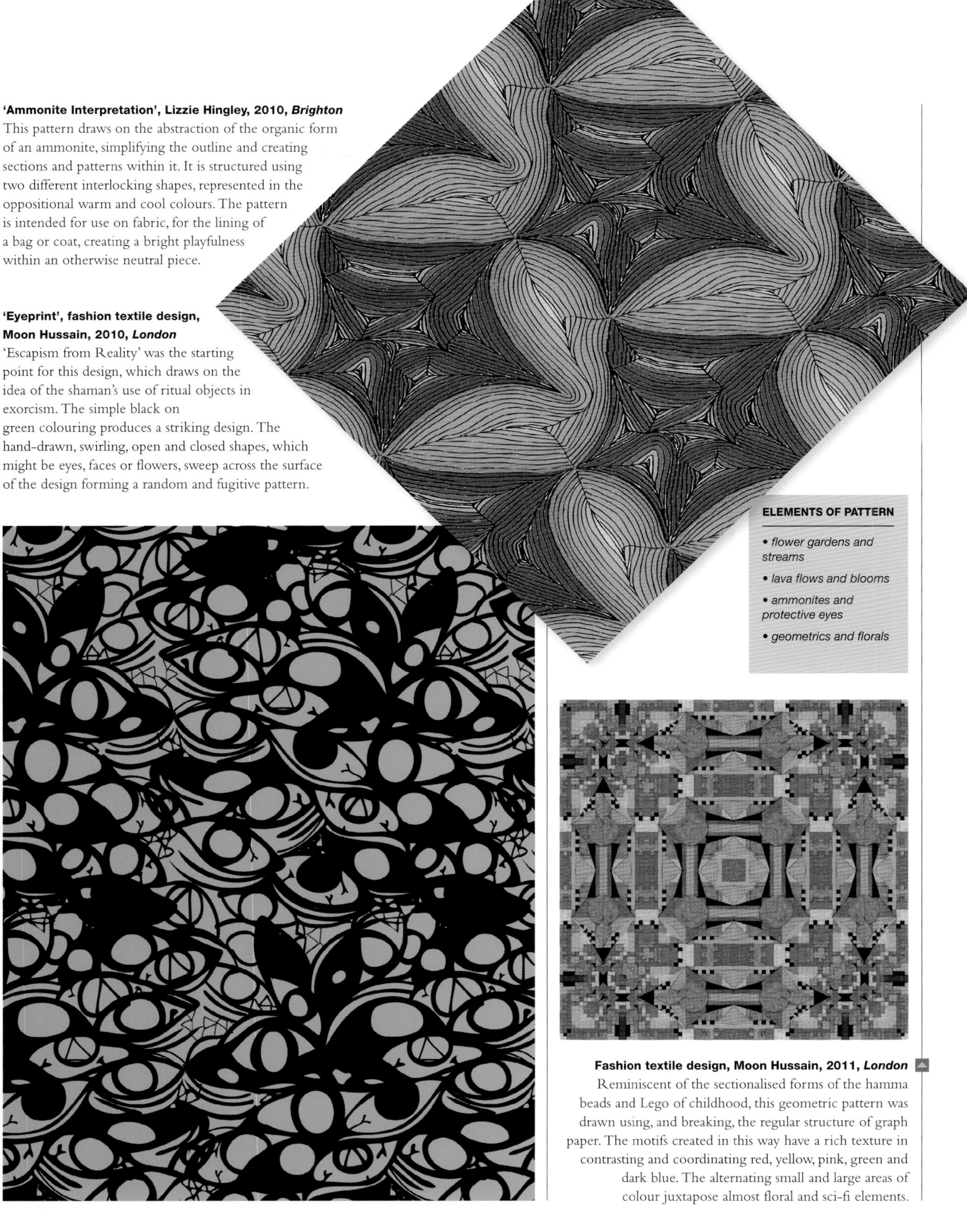

ELEMENTS OF PATTERN

- *flower gardens and streams*
- *lava flows and blooms*
- *ammonites and protective eyes*
- *geometrics and florals*

Fashion textile design, Moon Hussain, 2011, *London*
Reminiscent of the sectionalised forms of the hamma beads and Lego of childhood, this geometric pattern was drawn using, and breaking, the regular structure of graph paper. The motifs created in this way have a rich texture in contrasting and coordinating red, yellow, pink, green and dark blue. The alternating small and large areas of colour juxtapose almost floral and sci-fi elements.

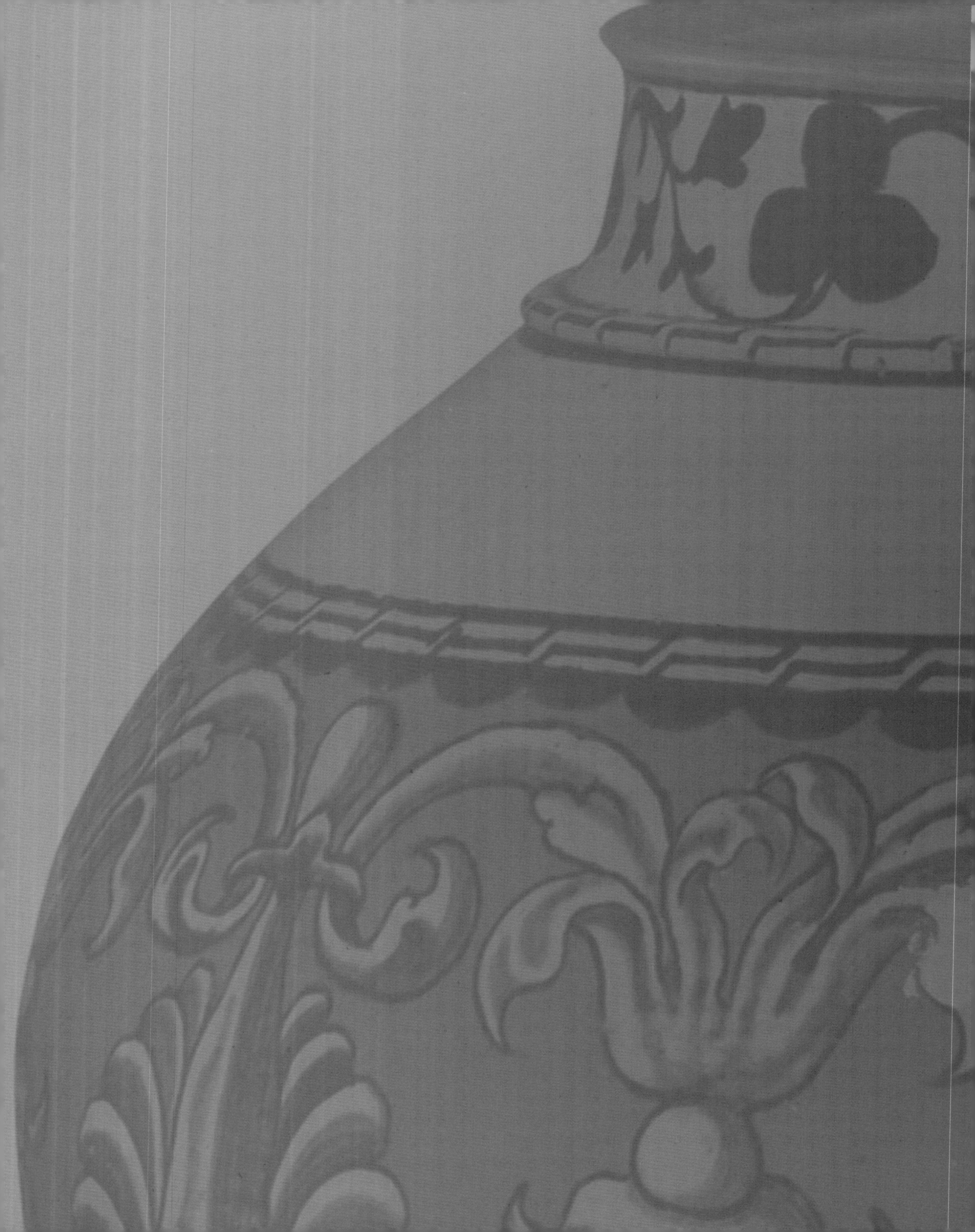

Appendices

Timeline
c. 3050 BCE–1622

c. 3050–332 BCE
Lotus and papyrus are universal motifs and symbols in ancient Egypt.

1100 BCE–100 CE
Cast-bronze vessels with *taotie* motifs, Shang and Zhou dynasties.
see page 24

c. 1000 BCE
Water birds and wheels decorate Late Bronze Age vessels.

704 BCE
'Sacred tree' forms on carved pavement, Nineveh.
see page 22

79 CE
The eruption of Mount Vesuvius in Italy covers Pompeii, Herculaneum and Stabiae in lava and ash, preserving Roman interiors with richly patterned walls and floors.

100–700
Lotus and other plants are symbols of Buddhism. Chinese cloud patterns develop.

400–650
Anglo-Saxon metalwork with patterns of interlace, glass and semi-precious stones.

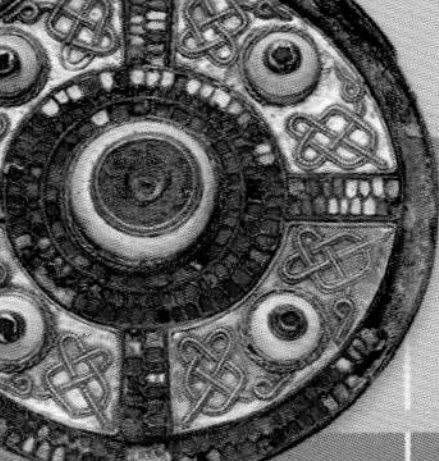

692
Building of the Dome of the Rock (Qubbat As-Sakhrah) begins; it is decorated with mosaics of Paradise.

800
Charlemagne is crowned emperor of the Romans by Pope Leo III on Christmas Day.
see page 49

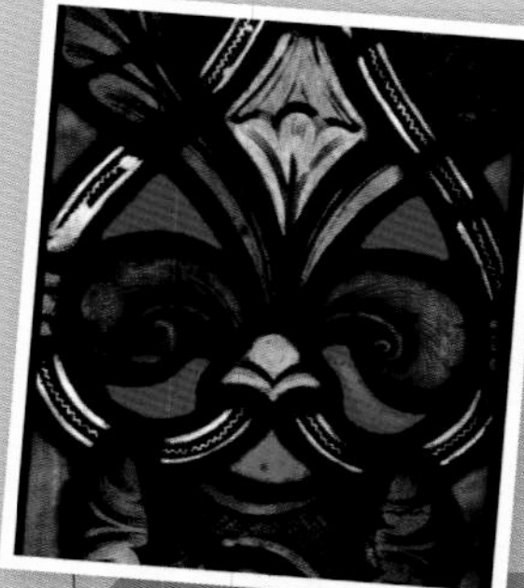
see page 73

1144
New Gothic style introduced in the ambulatory of the Abbey of Saint-Denis, Paris, France.

1190–1303
The Cosmati family working in Rome produce complex mathematical patterns for church buildings.

1297–1300
In Italy, Giotto paints the frescoes in the Upper Church of St Francis of Assisi with scenes containing decorative textiles, mosaics and architectural details.

1320–40
The Luttrell Psalter's decorative borders and illuminated patterned pages philosophise on earthly life.

1413
Illumination by Christine de Pizan shows heraldic and courtly patterns in the rooms of the Queen of France.

1430–1500
Spanish and Italian pots decorated with floral and foliage patterns.

1456–59
Andrea Mantegna uses classical patterns, designs and motifs in the Zeno Altarpiece, Verona.

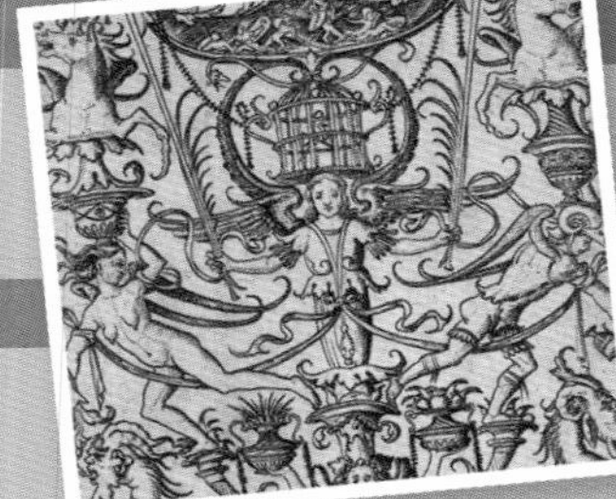
see page 120

1500–20
Nicoletto da Modena produces designs of 'grotesques' based on the decoration of Nero's *Domus Aurae* in Rome.

c. 1500
Blue and white patterned ceramics popular in China.

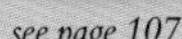
see page 107

1545–90
Iznik ceramics develop in the Ottoman Empire. The walls of the new Palace of Topkapı in Constantinople are covered with polychrome tiles.

1590–96
Akbarnama – the illustrated Book of Akbar – shows the decorative style at the Indian court.

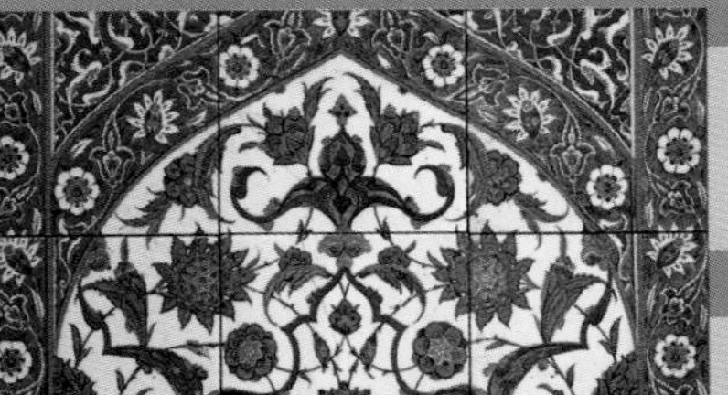
see page 127

c. 1600–c. 1650
Shah Abbas I promotes trade and builds a new market city in Isfahan with decorated mosques and palaces.

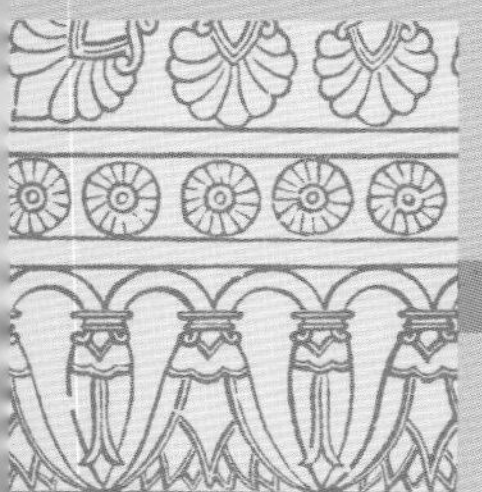

520–500 BCE
Lotus, palmette and key patterns on Greek vases.
see page 28

c. 500 BCE
Lotus and palmette motifs transformed and spread across Europe as new designs.

300–50 BCE
Patterns comparable with styles on bronze vessels dating from 300 to 100 BCE in China are developed in Britain.

527–65
Justinian the Great is emperor of Byzantium. Highly decorated surfaces in the churches of Hagia Sophia in Constantinople and San Vitale in Ravenna.

600–800
Assimilation of Near Eastern and Roman styles into Germanic traditions of patterns in Frankish Europe.

650–1000
Medallion-style silks possibly originating in the Byzantine Empire or Sasanian Iran spread from Europe to China.

c. 800
Lindisfarne Gospels are decorated with colourful complex spiral scrolls and interlacing panels.

800–1100
Scandinavians travel across Europe and beyond, reinventing animated interlace patterns in their new Viking homelands.

c. 850–1279
Tang and Song dynasties in China use vegetal scrolls and begin to decorate ceramics.

c. 1200
Enamel techniques from Limoges and Byzantium ornament sacred objects.

1200–1300
Decorative scrolling and early arabesque patterns in Iran.

1290–1450
Heraldry encodes family identity and status as patterned devices.
see page 79

1395–99
The Wilton Diptych represents King Richard II of England robed in lampas-patterned silk.

see page 86

1400–1500
Gothic styles of pattern and design continue to be influential across Europe.

c. 1400–1533
The conquest of Meso- and South America brings several rich cultures to an end – their patterns of stylised birds and animals in textile forms survive.

1456–70
Leon Battista Alberti develops classically balanced architectural designs and façades.

1459–61
The frescoes in the Medici Chapel, Palazzo Medici-Riccardi, Florence, show figures costumed in rich gold and silver brocades.

c. 1490–1574
Islamic ceramic techniques are imported from Spain to Italy for 'maiolica'.

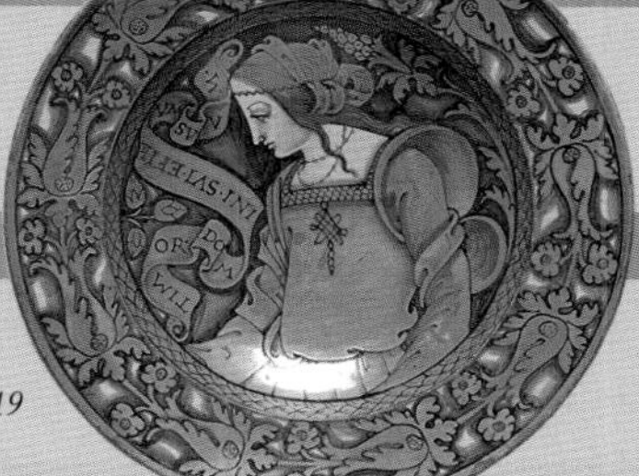

1500–1600
The royal court in Benin possesses brass and bronze plaques richly decorated with patterns derived from nature.

1539–40
The Ardabil Persian carpet made with 25 million knots reflects new floral patterns in carpet design.

see page 119

1570–1600
Fashionable garments are patterned with flowers, leaves and fruits, and with embroidered bands and strapwork.

see page 129

1570–1629
Luxury wall hangings with velvet patterns in scrolling florals and foliage furnish the interiors of wealthy merchants' homes.

1600–1700
In the Dutch Republic wealthy merchants decorate their houses and wear rich lace and silk fabrics.

1600–1700
In Europe and India, passion for flowers and gardens is also expressed by wallpapers and clothing covered in flora and fauna.

1619–22
The Banqueting House, designed by Inigo Jones, is the first fully Italian Renaissance architectural project in England.

Timeline
1637–2011

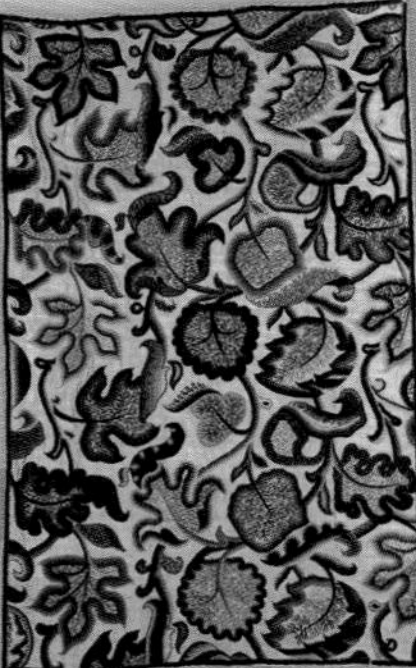

see page 153

1637
In the Dutch Republic a passion for tulips reaches its peak, decorating gardens, interiors and textiles.

1644
The Qing dynasty encourages innovation in crafts and design while symbolic motifs remain powerful.

1660–1700
The restoration of the English monarchy under Charles II leads to a resurgence in luxury interior designs.

1725–78
In Britain and Europe a fascination with Far Eastern designs fuels imitation called 'Chinoiserie'.

1730–40
At Lyons in France, Jean Revel designs naturalistic patterns with shading in silver and gold threads.

see page 168

1740–45
Extraordinarily rich floral and botanical designs are embroidered on dresses worn at the English and French courts.

1760–92
Georgian England has a taste for antiquarianism and the exotic Far East.

see page 178

c. 1770–c. 1800
In Rome, Grand Tourists visit classical sites and acquire souvenirs of an imaginary Rome created by Giovanni Piranesi.

1820–80s
Indian design traditions are adapted for British India. The paisley shawl is highly popular in Britain.

1830–39
The tradition of American quilt designs is a significant movement in the 19th century.

see page 201

1850–80
The patterns of the Salting Carpet from Iran combine early poetry, arabesques and Chinese dragons.

1855–93
Paris design dominates European fashion with self-patterned and machine-made textiles.

1861–96
William Morris stimulates the Arts and Crafts movement to develop natural patterns of native plants coloured with natural dyes.

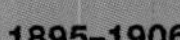

1895–1906
Art Nouveau designs develop naturalistic and floral patterns with new exaggerated and stylised forms.

c. 1900–17
Russian avant-garde design draws on peasant traditions, inspiring the patterned costumes for Diaghilev's Ballets Russes.

1902–25
Fabric patterns are influenced by Art Nouveau and new developments in modernist and geometric design.

see page 242

see page 230

c. 1925–30
Art Deco combines geometric and organic forms.

c. 1927–c. 1940
Fabric design becomes increasingly eclectic and idiosyncratic with geometrics, florals and maps.

1964–74
Biba brings a new vibrancy to patterns, reflecting Art Nouveau, American Art Deco and psychedelic design.

see page 225

1969–2011
Zandra Rhodes creates unified designs of floating chiffon garments with stitch-like patterns.

1984–90
Geometrics are expressed in patterns of bold shapes and colours.

1980s–2011
Paul Smith is known for his ubiquitous multi-coloured striped and retrospective floral patterns for clothes.

2000–10
Contemporary designers use a wide range of pattern forms, combining florals and abstract motifs, and drawing on extensive sources and influences.

1670–90
The opulent decoration of the *Trianon de Porcelaine* expresses the French Baroque.

c. 1700
Thorbjörg Magnúsdóttir completes her bedcover design in Iceland.

c. 1700
Churches in colonial Mexico develop a local extravagant form of Baroque sculptural decoration.

c. 1700–95
Three Qing emperors promote analysis and innovation in ceramics and textile design, resulting in technical and aesthetic refinements.

1740–66
Rococo designs using shell and flower motifs develop eclectic fantasy patterns.

1758–92
Robert and James Adam create a new passion for interiors based on the designs in newly discovered Pompeii.

1759–95
Josiah Wedgwood founds his highly successful ceramics business with designs emulating classical forms and patterns.

c. 1800
Spanish ornament features festive and rustic figures.

1800–1900
The first American and Pacific North-west motifs represent local and mythic animals in stylised designs.

1811–74
The revival of Gothic, Baroque, Renaissance and neoclassical forms in Europe is reflected in buildings, furniture, textiles and jewellery.

see page 171

1835–52
Augustus Welby Northmore Pugin promotes stylised natural forms and collaborates in the design of the new Houses of Parliament.

see page 217

c. 1850–1900
Japanese designs have naturalistic, narrative and symbolic patterns, which become popular in Europe.

1879–1924
The 'father of modernism', architect Louis Henry Sullivan, decorates the façades of his innovative skyscrapers with vegetal and geometric patterns.

1880–1910
The Arts and Crafts movement revives handcrafts and patterns derived from natural forms.

1883–1926
Catalan architect Antonio Gaudí creates organic architectural forms and decorative patterns in Barcelona, Spain.

1903–28
Interiors are dominated by organic natural designs by designers such as Charles Rennie Mackintosh in Scotland and Frank Lloyd Wright in the USA.

1923–24
Russian Constructivist textile design experiments with functional geometric designs.

1925–67
Gunta Stölzl develops functional stylised geometric textiles at the Bauhaus school of design in Germany.

1939–45
In England, designers create universal and economic patterns during the Second World War.

1976–94
Tartan's history and seditious attributes continue to appeal to designers, who adapt them for fashion in challenging new ways.

2008–09
Neo-Baroque designs reflect, respond to and react against modernist and minimalist designs.

see page 251

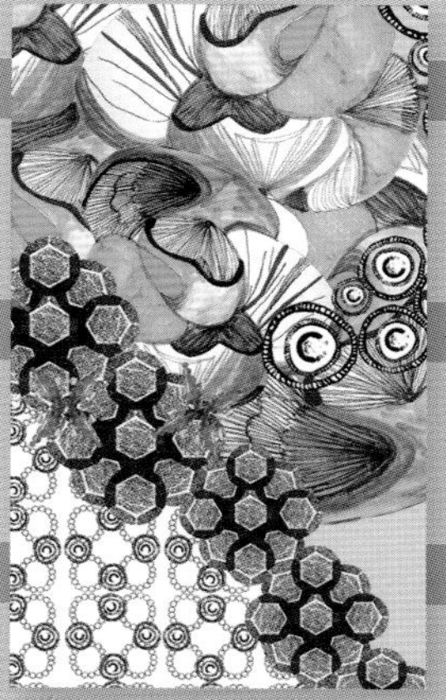

see page 267

1948–90s
After the Second World War, the joyous colourful modern designs of Lucienne Day are very popular.

1980–99
Florals continue to be significant in patterns, such as in the nostalgic designs by Laura Ashley and Cath Kidston.

2011 onward
The next generation of designers explore digital technologies to extend the range and applications of future patterns.

Glossary

ACANTHUS a stylised representation of the leaves of the Mediterranean acanthus plant, originally used for scrolls and ornament in classical architecture.

AMBO a raised, screened platform accessed by steps used for reading the Gospels or the Epistles. First employed in early Christian basilicas, it was later superseded by the pulpit.

AMPHORA a two-handled pottery vessel with a neck narrower than the body, used for storage. One of the main types of vessel seen in classical Greek pottery.

ANTHEMION a honeysuckle-type motif of radiating petals in which acanthus leaves were added to a palmette or lotus. Developed by the ancient Greeks and principally used to decorate pottery and architecture.

ARABESQUE a curvilinear repeating motif incorporating intertwined foliage, tendrils, animals and geometric designs formed into interlocking patterns. It became a significant feature of Islamic decoration.

ART DECO a style of decorative art typical of the 1920s and 1930s, characterised by sleek, streamlined forms and geometric patterns.

ART NOUVEAU a style of decorative art in the late 19th/early 20th centuries that was particularly associated with sinuous flowing lines, often featuring organic plant forms, among other abstracted or formalised motifs.

ARTS AND CRAFTS a British art movement in the late 19th century, particularly associated with William Morris, that sought to return to the ideals of medieval craftsmanship, with designs drawing heavily on the natural world.

BAROQUE an exuberant, dynamic artistic style, characterised by flamboyance and ornamentation, designed to appeal to the emotions; it became fashionable in Europe in the 17th and early 18th centuries.

BAUHAUS (German for 'building house') a German school of art and architecture founded by Walter Gropius in 1919. It aimed to integrate art and technology in design through the skill of the craftworker-designer, and paid particular attention to techniques of mass production.

BEAD-AND-REEL a decorative motif, principally used in architecture, mouldings and furniture design, that takes the form of a line consisting of alternating bead-like forms and cylindrical elements that resemble reels.

BEAUX-ARTS an elaborate 19th-/early 20th-century architectural style characterised by classical forms, rich ornamentation, symmetry, and a grand scale. It reflected the principles taught at the École des Beaux-Arts in Paris.

BROCADE a heavy silk fabric, often velvet, with a woven textured design, sometimes with gold and silver thread.

BRYONY FLOWER a decorative pattern applied to ceramic ware in 15th-century Spain and Italy featuring interwoven tendrils, leaves and flowers. Named after the long-tendrilled climbing vines of the *Bryonia* genus.

CALLIGRAPHY the art of producing beautiful handwriting with a pen or brush and ink.

CELADON a pale sea-green colour; the term is used to refer to a pottery glaze that originated in China and which became popular in Europe in the 17th century.

CHAMPLEVÉ an enamelling technique whereby metal is incised and the resulting troughs and cells are filled with pulverised vitreous enamel (*champlevé* is French for 'raised field'). The piece is then fired until the enamel melts and, when cool, the surface is polished.

CHARGE a heraldic term to signify the particular object or emblem that is depicted on the background 'field' of the escutcheon (or shield) of a coat of arms.

CHEQUY a heraldic term signifying that the 'field' of the escutcheon is divided vertically and horizontally into small squares of alternating colours.

CHEVRON an inverted V-shape or zigzag pattern that runs horizontally across a shape.

CHINOISERIE a European style of decoration, popular in the 18th and 19th centuries, based on Chinese design.

CHIP-CARVING a late Roman technique of working metal with angled knives or chisels to remove small chips from the flat surface. The resulting faceted surface catches the light and thus glitters.

CINQUEFOIL an ornamental design resembling a leaf with five leaflets.

CLASSICAL referring to artistic styles that originated in ancient Greece or Rome or which are influenced by those traditions.

CLOISONNÉ a technique for decorating objects in which cut glass, stones or other materials are inlaid into metal-framed cells (*cloisons* in French) of thin wire strips edge-fused to a metal base. Powdered glass enamel placed in the cells melts when the metalwork is fired and hardens, then is polished to form brilliant, lustrous pools of colour.

CONSTRUCTIVISM a Russian art movement in the 1920s advocating the use of industrial materials, machine production and constructed geometric forms.

CORNICE a horizontal projecting moulding which crowns a building or part of a building; particularly the uppermost part of an entablature (the horizontal structure above the capitals of columns in a classical building).

CORNUCOPIA a decorative element deriving from ancient Greece showing a curved goat's horn overflowing with flowers, fruit and grain to represent fruitfulness and plenty.

COSMATESQUE a style of geometric ornamental inlaid stonework characteristically found in medieval Italy, and especially in Rome. The name derives from the Cosmati family, the leading group of marble craftsmen in Rome during the 12th and 13th centuries.

CREAMWARE a cream-coloured type of earthenware created by Staffordshire potters in the mid-18th century as a cheaper alternative to Chinese porcelain.

CROSS-HATCHING a method of decorating a surface by drawing or inscribing sets of parallel lines, particularly used to suggest shading.

CRUCIFORM having the shape of a right-angled cross; cross-shaped.

DELFTWARE tin-glazed (i.e. covered with an opaque, usually white, glaze) earthenware pottery first made in Delft in the Netherlands in the 17th century.

DENTIL one of a row of small blocks, resembling the end of roof beams like a row of teeth, used as a repeating ornament in the bedmould of a cornice.

DEVORÉ a technique whereby areas or layers of a fabric (often velvet) are etched away by use of a caustic agent to create decorative designs (from the French word meaning 'eaten away').

DIAPERING in heraldry, the decoration of plain areas with arabesques or florals (from medieval Latin *diasprum* or 'patterned cloth'). The term is also used to describe the decorative treatment of a surface, such as a glass window or stonework, with a repeat pattern.

EGG-AND-DART an ornamental device in which a repeating pattern consists of alternate ovoid forms (egg-shaped) and vertical points (dart-shaped).

ENCAUSTIC a method of producing designs in ceramic tiles with different coloured clays, popular in the 19th century.

FAMILLE ROSE 18th-century Chinese porcelain in which the overglaze is painted in rose shades, mainly pinks and purples.

FAMILLE VERTE Chinese porcelain of the Kangxi dynasty (1662–1722) characterised by a colour range including yellow, blue, red, purple and green.

FESTOON an ornament resembling a chain or garland of flowers hanging in a curve between two points.

FLEUR-DE-LIS a stylised lily motif, found especially in medieval heraldry, with three upright petals. It has a long association with the French monarchy.

FOLIATE decorated with, or having the shape of, a leaf or leaves.

FRIEZE a decorative horizontal band, especially the central component of an entablature in architecture.

FRITWARE a type of pottery in which frit (a mixture of sand and fluxes) is added to clay to reduce its fusion temperature, so that it can be fired in low-temperature ovens. It originated in China and is particularly associated with the Iznik pottery of Ottoman Turkey.

GEOMETRIC a style of decoration in which regular patterns are formed from repeating and intersecting straight and curved lines.

GOTHIC a European decorative style, dating from c. 1150 to c. 1500, characterised by pointed arches, ribbed vaults and foliate motifs.

GROTESQUE decoration composed of foliage, bands, tendrils, swags, scrolls, strange animals etc., combined in intricate arrangements. The word derives from the Italian *grotteschi*, referring to the grottoes in Rome where examples were found in c. 1500.

GRYPHON a mythical beast resembling a winged lion with an eagle's head.

GUILLOCHE two or more bands twisting around each other in a repeating pattern of interlacing shapes, often forming circles.

HEXAGRAM a six-pointed star shape formed by the interlocking of two equilateral triangles.

INFILL material used to fill spaces between the component parts of a framework.

INTAGLIO a style of printing in which the ink for the design lies in recessed areas that are cut, scratched or etched below the surface of the plate; the reverse of relief printing.

INTERLACE a decorative element in medieval art in which motifs are joined by lacing, braiding or by crossing over one another in intricate geometric patterns.

IZNIK a form of Turkish pottery-making that flourished in the 16th and 17th centuries, famous for its symmetrical designs of flowers, leaves and tendrils arranged into ordered abstract and linear motifs.

JUGENDSTIL a late 19th-century German decorative style related to Art Nouveau.

KEY PATTERN a running fretwork pattern of interlocking lines and right angles often used for border decoration.

KRATER a large two-handled vessel in which wine and water were mixed in ancient Greece; these vessels were often inscribed or elaborately ornamented.

LAMPAS a type of fabric typically woven in silk with gold and silver thread enrichment created by additional weft threads being brought to the front of the cloth.

LATTICE a design created by a network of straight strips crossing over each other at regular intervals.

Glossary

LEAF-AND-DART a pattern of alternate leaf-like forms and darts, found especially on Ionic capitals.

LOBATE having or characterised by lobes – broad, usually round projections from a larger object.

LOZENGE a diamond-shaped device. In heraldry, used as a charge (q.v.) or repeated as a pattern (lozengy); also used to display the arms of a single woman or peeress.

LUNETTE a semicircular or crescent-shaped space, often including a window, above a door or below a ceiling vault.

LUSTREWARE a type of pottery with a lustrous tin-glazed metallic surface; it originated in the Middle East in the 9th century and spread around the Mediterranean through Spain to Italy through the influence of Islamic culture.

MAIOLICA a type of tin-glazed earthenware pottery (typically using the colours blue, yellow, red, green and purple), mainly associated with Italian Renaissance pieces.

MANDORLA an almond-shaped halo of light around the figure of Christ.

MEANDER another name for the Greek fret or key pattern (q.v.) in which a continuous line forms a repeated right-angled linear motif.

MEDALLION STYLE a style of decoration in which images are organised into repeated roundels (q.v.), developed in 7th-century Byzantium for richly patterned textiles.

MILLEFIORI (Italian for 'a thousand flowers') a background pattern composed of representations of many small flowers. Also a kind of ornamental glass with a flower-like pattern made by fusing together glass rods of different sizes and colours and cutting into slices.

MODERNISM an artistic period from c. 1860 to c. 1960 when artists rejected realistic traditions of representation and increasingly focused on the intrinsic qualities of their media. The subject became subordinate to texture, shape and colour; in architecture, decoration became subordinate to function.

MOSAIC a picture or pattern made up of small individual pieces, or tesserae (q.v.), of coloured glass or stone.

MOTIF a decorative design element that may be repeated in a pattern.

NATURALISTIC the accurate representation in art of the forms found in the natural world, in contrast to stylised forms.

NEOCLASSICISM a movement in 18th-century art which revived the ordered forms of classical antiquity in reaction to the perceived frivolity of the Rococo style.

NIELLO a black paste of metallic alloys used to fill engraved designs in metalwork; the metal is heated and the niello melts and flows into the engraved channels. The technique was particularly popular during the medieval and Renaissance periods.

OGEE an arch shape consisting of a double curved line which is convex above and concave below.

OPUS SECTILE a type of mosaic work in which the component materials, often marble, glass or mother of pearl, are cut into larger pieces than the individual tesserae of a conventional mosaic. Sometimes these pieces are cut and shaped to follow the outline of the design and to delineate it.

ORPHREY a type of detailed, richly patterned embroidery. Also refers to ornamental bands of embroidery attached to ecclesiastical vestments.

PAISLEY a stylised pattern with characteristic motifs of flowers and curved abstract forms. It originated in India, where it was called *boteh*, and was widely used in printed and woven fabrics. Named after the Scottish town of Paisley where cloths with the design were manufactured.

PALLADIAN the style of the Italian architect Andrea Palladio (1508–80), and those who emulated him, whose principles of architectural design were drawn from study of classical Roman buildings.

PALMETTE a type of decoration seen in ornamental designs showing stylised leaves in a fan shape, usually arranged in rows with the stems pointing downwards. It originated as an Assyrian decorative motif.

PAPYRUS an important plant and motif represented extensively in Egyptian culture. It is a tall grass-like aquatic plant *Cyperus papyrus*, with soft-fringed flowers.

PARTERRE a division of garden beds into a formal ornamental pattern.

PATERA a dish-shaped ornamental round motif often resembling an open flower.

PELTA (pl. peltae) shield-shaped motif, named after the small light shields carried by ancient Greek warriors.

PERCALE a closely woven cotton fabric.

PIETRA DURA (Italian for 'hard stone') a mosaic technique whereby polished coloured stones are cut to shape and fitted together on a backing panel to create images and patterns.

PILASTER an architectural element of a column-like form attached to a wall.

POMMEL a round boss; also the knob at the end of the hilt of a sword or dagger.

POSTMODERNISM an artistic movement during the second half of the 20th century that deliberately turned away from modernism. It drew instead on an eclectic mix of styles from several different periods, often with irony or an element of knowing pastiche.

PUTTO (pl. *putti*) artistic representation of a plump young cherub-like child, usually a boy, often winged and naked, that has been a common decorative motif since classical antiquity.

QUATREFOIL (from the Latin meaning 'four leaves') a four-lobed shape consisting of four arcs separated by cusps, sometimes enclosed within a circle or arch; characteristic of Gothic decorative patterning.

QUINCUNX a pattern made of five elements, four occupying the corners and the fifth centrally placed within a rectangular arrangement, such as the pattern of the number 5 on a dice.

RENAISSANCE meaning 'rebirth', the period variously applying in European countries from the 15th to the 17th century which saw a revival of interest in classical learning and practice in the arts and literature.

RETICELLA an open or grid-like pattern used in lace- or fabric-making, from the Italian for 'little net'.

RING-CHAIN an interlocking repetitive pattern of circular rings that extends in a linear fashion, typically found on Viking objects.

ROCOCO a decorative style popular in the 18th century, characterised by shell-work, scrolls, swirls, and C- and S-shaped curves.

ROMANESQUE the architectural style prevalent in Europe c. 1000–1200 before the Gothic style evolved, typified by rounded arch forms, barrel vaults, thick walls and piers, and linear stylisation, emulating Roman architecture.

ROSETTE a decorative element in the shape of a stylised round flower.

ROUNDEL a circular device.

RUMI symmetrical arabesque scrollwork found on Turkish Iznik pottery.

'SACRED TREE' an important religious motif in the Assyrian Empire (934–609 BCE) which incorporated various decorative motifs, such as palmettes, pine cones and pomegranates.

SAZ a type of design using a serrated leaf motif that was employed in Ottoman Turkish ceramic decoration from the 16th century.

SCROLL a ribbon-like motif that resembles a partially rolled-up scroll of paper.

SIMURGH a mythical creature in early Sasanian art having the form of a giant dog-headed bird.

STRAPWORK a form of ornamentation consisting of interlaced or pierced bands resembling roll-ended straps of leather or metal.

STUCCO a fine plaster used to cover walls that can be shaped into sculptural ornamental forms.

SWAG a representation of a festoon of flowers, foliage or drapery.

SWASTIKA an angled cross symbol used since prehistoric times as a symbol of prosperity and good luck. The arms of the cross are of equal length and each is bent at a right angle in the same rotary direction. The name derives from the Sanskrit *svastika* meaning 'bringing good fortune'.

TAOTIE the stylised face of a fierce monster commonly found on ritual bronze vessels from the ancient Chinese Shang and Zhou dynasties.

TENDRIL a motif resembling the thin, spirally coiling stem of plants.

TESSERA (pl. tesserae) a small piece of glass, stone or marble used as a component part of a mosaic pattern.

TINCTURE a term used in heraldry to refer to the colours used to emblazon a coat of arms.

TIN-GLAZED *see* **DELFTWARE**

TORUS a semicircular or roll moulding.

TRACERY the narrow decorative stonework ribs that support the glass in a Gothic window; also applied to similar intricate line patterns used in relief on walls, screens and panels.

TREFOIL an ornamental figure resembling a trifoliate leaf (i.e. one having three leaflets).

TRI-FORM MOTIF a motif composed of three parts.

TRI-LOBE a decorative motif similar to a trefoil consisting of three clover-leaf-like lobes often seen in a repeating pattern.

TRISKELE a motif consisting of three curving extensions radiating from a central point (e.g. the Isle of Man's symbol of three running legs).

TROMPE L'OEIL a work of art that gives the illusion that the viewer is seeing the actual objects depicted, rather than a representation of them (from the French meaning to 'deceive the eye').

VEGETAL of, or relating to, plants.

VITRUVIAN SCROLL ornament consisting of a series of repeating wave-like scrolls.

VOLUTE architectural term for the spiral ornament found on each side of an Ionic capital; more generally, a spiral scroll shape.

VORTICISM style associated with a group of British artists during the early 20th century. They used sharp geometric forms in an asymmetric manner, with a whirling dynamism that suggested the energy of a vortex.

WYVERN a mythical dragon-like animal depicted with wings, two legs like an eagle and a barbed tail.

Resources

ALPERS, SVETLANA, *The Art of Describing: Dutch art in the seventeenth century*, University of Chicago Press (1984)

AMENT, H. 'The Germanic tribes in Europe', in *The Northern World*, DAVID M. WILSON (ed), Thames & Hudson (1980)

ANDERSON, MIRANDA (ed), *The Book of the Mirror: an interdisciplinary collection exploring the cultural story of the mirror*, Cambridge Scholars Publishing (2007)

ARNASON, H. H. with KALB, PETER, *History of Modern Art, Painting, Sculpture, Architecture, Photography*, Prentice Hall (2004)

ART INSTITUTE OF CHIGACO, 'The Fifteenth Century Art' *Institute of Chicago Museum Studies*, Vol. 30, No. 2, 'Devotion and Splendor: Medieval Art at the Art Institute of Chicago' (2004), pp. 64-84+94-96

ATTFIELD, JUDY (ed), *Utility Reassessed: the role of ethics in the practice of design*, Manchester University Press (1999)

BEARD, MARY and HENDERSON, JOHN, *Classical Art: From Greece to Rome*, Oxford University Press (2001)

BENTON, TIM, 'Architecture: theory and practice' in *Making Renaissance Art*, KIM W. WOODS (ed), Yale University Press and the Open University (2007)

BLOOM, JONATHAN and BLAIR, SHEILA, *Islamic Arts*, Phaidon Press Limited (1997)

BOARDMAN, JOHN, GRIFFIN, JASPER and MURRAY, OSWYN (eds), *Greece and the Hellenistic World*, Oxford Illustrated History Series, Oxford University Press (1988)

BOUCHARENC, CHRISTIAN, *Design for a Contemporary World*, University of Singapore Press (2008)

BREWARD, CHRISTOPHER, *The Culture of Fashion*, Manchester University Press (1995)

BREWARD, CHRISTOPHER, CONEKIN, BECKY and COX, CAROLINE, *The Englishness of English Dress*, Berg (2002)

BREWARD, CHRISTOPHER, and EVANS, CAROLINE, *Fashion and Modernity*, Berg (2005)

BUTLER, CORNELIA and SCHWARTZ, ALEXANDRA (eds), *Modern Women: women artists at the Museum of Modern Art*, Museum of Modern Art (2010)

CAMILLE, MICHAEL, *Mirror in Parchment: the Luttrell Psalter and the making of medieval England*, University of Chicago Press (1998)

CARANDELL, JOSEP MARIA and VIVAS, PERE, *1998 Park Güell: Gaudí's utopia*, Triangle Postals (1998)

CARIATI, CHRISTINE, *http://entianred.net/2009/10/31/gunta-stolzl-master-weaver-of-the-bauhaus/* (2009)

CARLSON-REDDIG, KELLY 'Students Consider Architecture's Materiality' in *Journal of Architectural Education (1984–)* Vol. 51, No. 2 (1997)

CAROSCIO, MARTA, 'Lustreware production in Renaissance Italy and influences from the Mediterranean' in *Medieval Ceramics* 28 2004, Journal of the Medieval Pottery Research Group (2004), pp. 99–115

CHEVALIER, MICHEL, and MAZALOVO, GÉRALD, *Pro Logo: brands as a factor of progress*, Palgrave Macmillan (2004)

CHU, HSAIO-YUN, 'Art eco' in H. SHEWMAKER and S. T. WAIDA (eds), *Material Culture in America: understanding everyday life*, ABC-CLIO (2003)

CLUNAS, CRAIG, *Art in China*, Oxford University Press, Oxford (1997)

COBB, HAROLD M., *The History of Stainless Steel*, ASM International (2010)

COLL CONESA, JAUME, 'Cobalt blue in medieval ceramic production in the Valencian workshops: Manises, Paterna and Valencia, Spain' in *Medieval Ceramics* 31, Journal of the Medieval Pottery Research Group (2010), pp. 11–24

CONAN, MICHAEL (ed), *Bourgeois and Aristocratic Cultural Encounters in Garden Art*, Dumbarton Oaks (2002)

CONNOLLY, ANNALIESE FRANCES and HOPKINS, LISA, *Goddesses and Queens: the iconography of Elizabeth I*, Manchester University Press (2007)

COOPER, J. C., *An Illustrated Encyclopaedia of Traditional Symbols*, Thames & Hudson (1978)

CORMACK, ROBIN, *Byzantine Art*, Oxford University Press (2000)

CORMACK, ROBIN and VASSILAKI, MARIA (eds), *Byzantium 330–1453*, Royal Academy of Arts Exhibition Catalogue (2008)

DAVIES, HOWARD JOHN, *John Evelyn: the diary*, Book Guild Publishing (2009)

DEHEJIA, VIDYA, *Indian Art*, Phaidon Press Limited (1997)

DESIGN MUSEUM *http://designmuseum.org/design/paul-smith*

DROSTE, MAGDALENA, *Bauhaus, 1919–1933*, Taschen (2002)

DUITS, REMBRANDT, 'Figured Riches: The Value of Gold Brocades in Fifteenth-Century Florentine Painting' in *Journal of the Warburg and Courtauld Institutes*, Vol. 62 (1999), pp. 60–92

DURANT, STUART, *Ornament A Survey of decoration since 1830 with 729 illustrations*, Macdonald & Co (Publishers) Ltd (1986)

DURRANT, WILL, *The Story of Civilisation Volume 4: The Age of Faith*, Simon & Schuster (1950)

EARNSHAW, PAT, *A Dictionary of Lace*, Constable and Company (1999)

EGGINTON, WILLIAM, *The Theater of Truth: the ideology of (neo)baroque aesthetics*, Stanford University Press (2010)

ERLER, MARY C., 'Sir John Davies and the Rainbow Portrait of Queen Elizabeth' in *Modern Philology* 84, No. 4, (1987), pp. 359–71

EVANS, SÎAN, *Pattern Design: a period design sourcebook*, National Trust Books (2008)

FAIERS, JONATHAN, 'Tartan: set and setting' in *Networks of Design* in Proceedings of 2008 Annual International Conference of the Design History Society (UK), Universal Publishers (2009), pp. 159–63

FAIRCHILD RUGGELS, D., *Islamic Gardens and Landscapes*, University of Pennsylvania Press (2008)

FISHBOURNE ROMAN PALACE, 'Decoration and demon traps – the meanings of geometric borders in Roman mosaics', Research Paper, *www.fishbourneromanpalace.com* (2007)

FITZPATRICK, MARTIN, JONES, PETER, KNELLWOLF, KRISTA and MCCALMAN, IAIN, *The Enlightenment World*, Routledge (2004)

FOGG, MARNIE, *1960s Fashion Print: a sourcebook*, Batsford (2008)

FONTANA, DAVID, *The New Secret Language of Symbols: an illustrated key to unlocking their deep and hidden meanings*, Duncan Baird Publishing (2010)

FOUNET, JEAN-PIERRE, 'Old gilt leather in France', International Council of Museums Committee for Conservation Newsletter 3 (2005), pp. 4–8

FOWLER, PENNY and WRIGHT, FRANK LLOYD, *Frank Lloyd Wright: graphic artist*, Pomegranate Europe, Maldon (2002)

GELL, ALFRED, The technology of enchantment and the enchantment of technology, in *Anthropology, Art and Aesthetics*, J. COOTE and A. SHELTON (eds), Clarendon Press (1992)

GELL, ALFRED, *Art and Agency: an anthropological theory*, Clarendon Press (1998)

GRABAR, OLEG, 'Islamic Art and Byzantium', Dumbarton Oaks Papers, Vol. 18 (1964), pp. 67–88

GRAY, CAMILLA, *The Russian Experiment in Art 1863–1922*, Thames & Hudson (1962 and 1986)

GUILMAN, JACQUES 'The enigmatic beasts of the Lindau Gospels lower cover' in *Gesta* Vol. 10, No. 1, International Center of Medieval Art, New York (1971)

HALL, JAMES, *Dictionary of Subjects and Symbols in Art*, John Murray (1974)

HALL, JAMES, *Illustrated Dictionary of Symbols in Eastern and Western Art*, John Murray (1994)

HANKS, DAVID A. *The Decorative Designs of Frank Lloyd Wright*, Dutton (1979)

HARDING, DENNIS W., *The Archaeology of Celtic Art*, Routledge (2007)

HARRIES, KARSTEN, 'Theatricality and Re-Presentation' in *Perspecta*, Vol. 26, 'Theater, Theatricality, and Architecture' (1990), pp. 21-40

HARTT, FREDERICK and WILKINS, DAVID G., *History of Italian Renaissance Art: Painting, Sculpture, Architecture*, Prentice Hall (1987, 1994, 2003, 2007)

HILLENBRAND, ROBERT, *Islamic Art and Architecture*, Thames & Hudson (1999)

HOOK, MOIRA and MACGREGOR, ARTHUR *Tudor England*, Ashmolean Museum (2000)

HUTTON, EDWARD, *The Cosmati: the Roman marble workers of the XIIth and XIIIth centuries*, Routledge and Kegan Paul (1950)

HYDE, ELIZABETH 'Flowers of distinction: taste, class and floriculture in seventeenth-century France' in CONAN, M. (ed) *Bourgeois and Aristocratic Cultural Encounters in Garden Art*, Dumbarton Oaks (2002), pp. 77–100

HYDE, MELISSA, and BOUCHER, FRANÇOIS, *Making up the Rococo: François Boucher and his critics*, Getty Publications (2006)

IRWIN, DAVID, *Neoclassicism*, Phaidon Press Limited (1997)

JACKSON, LESLIE *Twentieth-Century Pattern Design*, Mitchell Beazley (2002)

JACOBSON, DAWN, *Chinoiserie*, Phaidon Press Limited (1993)

JACOBY, DAVID, 'Silk Economics and Cross-Cultural Artistic Interaction: Byzantium, the Muslim World, and the Christian West' *Dumbarton Oaks Papers*, Vol. 58 (2004), Dumbarton Oaks (2004), pp. 197–240

JAMES, DAVID and HOPKINS, FRANCIS, 'An Irish Visitor to the Court of the Shah of Persia in 1835: Extract from the Unpublished Diary of Sir Francis Hopkins of Athboy' in *Studies: An Irish Quarterly Review*, Vol. 60, No. 238 (Summer 1971), pp. 139–154

JAMES, SIMON, and RIGBY, VALERY, *Britain and the Celtic Iron Age*, The British Museum Press (1997)

JANSON, HORST WOLDEMAR and JANSON, ANTHONY F., *History of Art: the Western tradition*, Pearson Education (2003)

JAYNE, HORACE H. F., 'Peruvian Textiles' in *Bulletin of the Pennsylvania Museum*, Vol. 17, No. 70 (Feb 1922), pp. 5–7

JENKINS, DAVID (ed), *The Cambridge History of Western Textiles I*, Cambridge University Press (2003)

JENKYN JONES, SUE, *Fashion Design*, Laurence King Publishing (2010)

JONES, OWEN, *The Grammar of Ornament*, Omega Books Ltd (1986)

JOY, JODY, 'Reflections on Celtic Art: a re-examination of mirror decoration' in GARROW, D., GOSDEN, C., and HLLL, J. D. (eds), *Rethinking Celtic Art*, Oxbow Books (2008), pp. 78–99

KAPLAN, WENDY (ed), *Charles Rennie Mackintosh*, Glasgow Museums and Abbeville Press (1996)

KERMANN-SCHWARZ, BRIGITTE, 'Gothic stained glass' in TOMAN, ROLF (ed), *Gothic: architecture, sculpture, painting*, Konigswinter, Ullmann & Könemann Tandem Verlag GmbH (2007)

KERR, ROSE, *Chinese Art and Design: The T.T. Tsui Gallery of Chinese Art*, Victoria and Albert Museum (1991)

KIDSTON, CATH *http://www.cathkidston.co.uk*

KING, BRENDA M., *Silk and Empire*, Manchester University Press (2005)

KING, MONIQUE and KING, DONALD, *European Textiles in the Keir Collection 400 BC to 1800 AD*, Faber and Faber (1990)

Resources

KIRKHAM, PAT, 'Fashion, femininity and "frivolous" consumption in World War II Britain' in J. ATTFIELD (ed), *Utility Reassessed: the role of ethics in the practice of design*, Manchester University Press (1999), pp. 143–56

KLEINER, FRED S., *Gardner's Art through the Ages: the Western perspective*, Wadsworth Cengage Learning (2010)

KOEHN, NANCY FOWLER, *Brand New: How entrepreneurs earned consumers' trust from Wedgwood to Dell*, Harvard Business School Publishing (2001)

KOSUDA-WARNER, JOANNE with JOHNSON, ELIZABETH (eds), *Landscape Wallcoverings*, Scala Publishing Ltd (2001)

KRAHL, REGINA and HARRISON-HALL, JESSICA, *Chinese Ceramics Highlights of the Sir Percival David Collection*, The British Museum Press (2009)

LAVER, JAMES, *A Concise History of Costume*, Thames & Hudson (1969)

LEAF, WILLIAM and PURCELL, SALLY, *Heraldic Symbols: Islamic insignia and western heraldry*, Victoria & Albert Museum (1986)

LEHNER, ULRICH L. and PRINTY, MICHAEL O'NEILL, *A Companion to the Catholic Enlightenment in Europe*, Brill Publishing (2010)

LEIDY, DENISE P., SIU, WAI-FONG ANITA and WATT, JAMES C. Y., 'Chinese Decorative Arts', *The Metropolitan Museum of Art Bulletin*, New Series, Vol. 55, No. 1, 'Chinese Decorative Arts' (Summer, 1997), pp. 1–3 + 5–71

LICHT, M. M., 'A Book of Drawings by Nicoletto da Modena', *Master Drawings*, Vol. 8, No. 4 (Winter 1970), pp. 379–387 + 432–444

LODDER, CHRISTINA, *Russian Constructivism*, Yale University Press (1983)

LUCIE-SMITH, EDWARD, *The Dictionary of Art Terms*, Thames & Hudson (1984)

MACNAIR, PETER L., HOOVER, ALAN L. and NEARY, KEVIN, *The Legacy*, Vancouver BC and Seattle WA (1984)

MCLANE, PAUL E., *Spenser's 'Shepheardes Calendar': a study of Elizabethan allegory*, University of Notre Dame Press (1961)

MCNEIL, PETER, 'The Appearance of Enlightenment: refashioning the elites' in FITZPATRICK, MARTIN, JONES, PETER, KNELLWOLF, KRISTA and MCCALMAN, IAIN (eds), *The Enlightenment World*, Routledge (2004), pp. 381–400

MILLER, LESLEY ELLIS, 'Jean Revel: Silk Designer, Fine Artist, or Entrepreneur?' in *Journal of Design History*, Vol. 8, No. 2 (1995), pp. 79–96

MOFFETT, MARIAN, FAZIO, MICHAEL and WODEHOUSE, LAWRENCE, *A World History of Architecture*, Laurence King Publishing (2003)

MUKERJI, CHANDRA, 'Reading and writing with nature: a materialist approach to French formal gardens' in BREWER, J. and PORTER, R. (eds), *Consumption and the World of Goods*, Routledge (1993), pp. 439–61

MURRAY, PETER, *The Architecture of the Italian Renaissance*, Thames & Hudson (1969 and 1986)

NEAL, DAVID S. and COSH, STEPHEN R., *Roman Mosaics of Britain. Volume III South-East Britain, Parts 1 and 2*, The Society of Antiquaries of London (2009)

NEEDHAM, STUART, *Twelve Centuries of Bookbindings 400–1600*, Oxford University Press (1979)

NICKEL, LUKAS (ed), *Return of the Buddha: The Qingzhou Discoveries*, Royal Academy of Arts Exhibition Catalogue (2001)

OAKESHOTT, EWART, *European Weapons and Armour: from the Renaissance to the Industrial Revolution*, Boydell Press (2000)

ORMISTON, ROSALIND and WELLS, NICHOLAS MICHAEL, *William Morris: Artist, craftsman, pioneer*, Flame Tree Publishing (2010)

OSBAND, LINDA, *Victorian Gothic House Style*, F&W Publications (2003)

OSBORNE, ROBIN, *Archaic and Classical Greek Art*, Oxford University Press (1998)

PAJARES-AYUELA, PALOMA, *Cosmatesque Ornament: Flat Polychrome Geometric Patterns in Architecture*, W. W. Norton (2001)

PARPOLA, SIMO, 'The Assyrian Tree of Life: Tracing the Origins of Jewish Monotheism and Greek Philosophy' in *Journal of Near Eastern Studies*, Vol. 52, No. 3 (Jul 1993), pp. 161–208

PASOLODOS SALGADO, MERCEDES, 'Printed gloves, elegant hands' in *Datatèxtil* 20, 16–42, Centre de Documentacio i Museu Textile de Terrassa (2009)

PAUL SMITH DESIGN MUSEUM *http://paulsmith.co.uk/paul-smith-world/history/*

PEVSNER, NIKOLAUS, *Pioneers of Modern Design: from William Morris to Walter Gropius*, 4th edition, Yale University Press (2005)

PILE, JOHN, *A History of Interior Design*, Laurence King Publishing (2000 and 2005)

POOKE, GRANT and NEWALL, DIANA, *Art History: The Basics*, Routledge (2008)

POPPELIERS, JOHN C., AND CHAMBERS ALLEN S., *What Style is it? A guide to American architecture*, John Wiley and Sons (1984)

PROCTOR, RICHARD M., *Principles of Pattern Design*, Dover, Mineola (1990)

QUINN, BRADLEY, *Textile Designers at the Cutting Edge*, Laurence King Publishing (2009)

RAIZMAN, DAVID, *History of Modern Design: graphics and products since the Industrial Revolution*, Laurence King Publishing (2003)

RAWSKI, EVELYN S. and RAWSON, JESSICA, *China: The Three Emperors 1662–1795*, Royal Academy of Arts Exhibition Catalogue (2005)

RAWSON, JESSICA (ed), *The British Museum Book of Chinese Art*, The British Museum Press (1992)

RAY, ANTHONY, *Spanish Pottery 1248–1898*, V&A Publications (2000)

READ, HERBERT, 'The Function of Decoration' in *Art and Industry. The principles of industrial design*, 1934, reprinted Horizon Press (1984)

READE, JULIAN, *Assyrian Sculpture*, The British Museum Press (1983, 1998)

REYNOLDS, HELEN, 'The Utility garment: its design and effect on the mass market 1942–45', in J. ATTFIELD (ed), *Utility Reassessed: the role of ethics in the practice of design*, Manchester University Press (1999), pp. 125–45

RHEAD, G. W. and F. A., *Staffordshire Pots and Potters*, Hutchinson (1906)

RHODES, ZANDRA *http://www.zandrarhodes.com*

RIPA, CESARE, *Iconologia overo Descrittione Dell'imagini Universali cavate dall'Anchità et da altriluoghi*, Rome (1593)

ROBIND, GAY, *The Art of Ancient Egypt*, The British Museum Press (1997)

SCHAEFER, LUCIE, 'Die Illustrationen zu den Handschriften der Christine de Pizan', *Marburger Jahrbuch für Kunstwissenschaft*, 10. Bd. (1937), pp. 119–208

SCHNEIDER, LAURIE, 'Leon Battista Alberti: Some Biographical Implications of the Winged Eye', *The Art Bulletin*, Vol. 72, No. 2 (Jun 1990), pp. 261–270

SCHÖNFELD, CHRISTINE, *Practising Modernity: female creativity in the Weimar Republic*, Verlag Königshausen & Neumann (2006)

SEDDING, JOHN WILLIAM, 'Our art and industries' in *Art and Handicraft*, London (1893)

SEKULES, VERONICA, *Medieval Art*, Oxford University Press (2001)

SHANKS, MICHAEL, *Art and the Early Greek State: an interpretive archaeology*, Cambridge University Press (1999)

SHANKS, MICHAEL, 'Nine archaeological theses on design' *http://documents.stanford.edu/michaelshanks/260*, Stanford University (2007)

SHEWMAKER, HELEN and WAIDA, SHIRLEY TERESA (eds), *Material Culture in America: understanding everyday life*, ABC-CLIO (2008)

SMITH, PAUL, *You Can Find Inspiration in Everything: and if you can't, look again*, Violette Editions (2009)

SPENCER-CHURCHILL, HENRIETTA, *Classic Georgian Style*, Collins and Brown (1997)

STEELE, VALERIE, *The Berg Companion to Fashion*, Berg (2010)

STEVENSON, ROBERT B.K., 'Aspects of Ambiguity in Crosses and Interlace (The Oliver Davies Lecture for 1981)' in *Ulster Journal of Archaeology*, Third Series, Vol. 44/45 (1981/1982), pp. 1–27

SUMNER SMITH, JOAN, 'The Italian Sources of Inigo Jones's Style', *The Burlington Magazine*, Vol. 94, No. 592 (Jul 1952), pp. 200–205 + 207.

SUTHERLAND HARRIS, ANN, *Seventeenth-Century Art and Architecture*, Laurence King Publishing Ltd (2005)

THORNTON, PETER, *Authentic Décor: the domestic interior 1620–1920*, Weidenfeld & Nicholson (1993)

TOMAN, ROLF (ed), *Gothic: architecture, sculpture, painting*, Könemann (2007)

TREGEAR, MARY, *Chinese Art*, Thames & Hudson (1980)

TRILLING, JAMES *The Language of Ornament*, Thames & Hudson (2001)

VAN GENNEP, A., *The Rites of Passage*, Routledge and Kegan Paul (1960)

VERRI, GIOVANNI, COLLINS, PAUL, AMBERS, JANET, SWEEK, TRACEY and SIMPSON, ST JOHN, 'Assyrian colours: pigments on a neo-Assyrian relief of a parade horse', *British Museum Technical Bulletin*, Vol. 3 (2009)

WATKIN, DAVID *A History of Western Architecture*, Laurence King Publishing (2005)

WATSON, WILLIAM (ed), *The Great Japan Exhibition: Art of the Edo Period 1600–1868*, Royal Academy of Arts Exhibition Catalogue, Weidenfeld & Nicholson (1981)

WEAVER, CYNTHIA R., 'Enid Marx: designing textiles for the Utility Furniture Design Advisory Panel' in J. ATTFIELD (ed), *Utility Reassessed: the role of ethics in the practice of design*, Manchester University Press (1999), pp. 171–80

WERNER, MARTIN, 'The cross-carpet page in the Book of Durrow: the cult of the True Cross, Adomnan, and Iona' in *The Art Bulletin* Vol. 72, No. 2 (June), New York, College Art Association (1990)

WILLET, FRANK, *African Art*, Thames & Hudson (1971 and 1993)

WILLIAMSON, PAUL, *The Medieval Treasury: The Art of the Middle Ages in the Victoria and Albert Museum*, V&A Publications (1986)

WILSON, DAVID M., *Anglo-Saxon Art: from the seventh century to the Norman Conquest*, Thames & Hudson (1984)

WILSON, ELIZABETH, 'Biba' in V. STEELE, *The Berg Companion to Fashion*, Berg (2010)

WILSON, EVA, *8000 Years of Ornament: an illustrated handbook of motifs*, British Museum Press (1994)

WOODCOCK, THOMAS and ROBINSON, JOHN MARTIN, *The Oxford Guide to Heraldry*, Oxford University Press (1990)

WOODS, KIM W. (ed), *Making Renaissance Art*, Yale University Press and the Open University (2007)

ZERST, RAINER, *Antoní Gaudí*, Taschen (2002)

ZREBIEC, ALICE, WOLK-SIMON, LINDA and PHYRR, STUART W., 'European 16th–19th Centuries' in *The Metropolitan Museum of Art Bulletin*, New Series, Vol. 53, No. 3 (Winter, 1995-1996), pp. 3–4 + 10–12 + 14–15 + 45–58

Index

Index

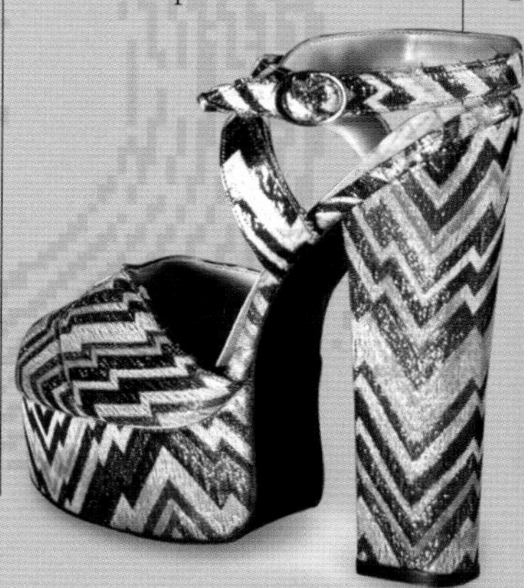
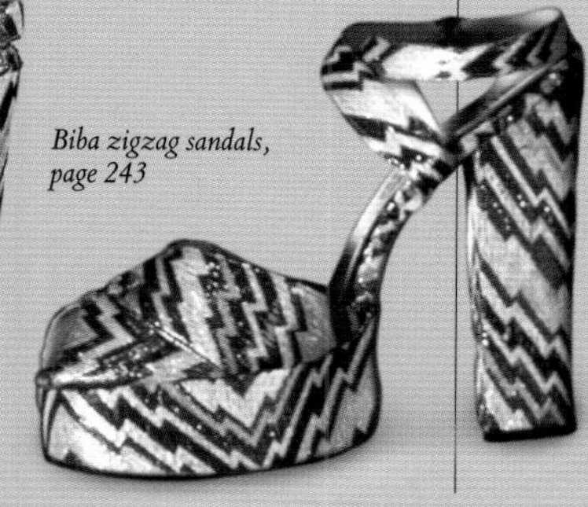

Biba zigzag sandals, page 243

Acknowledgements

Author acknowledgements
Grateful thanks are owed to Durham University's Dr Penny Wilson for her invaluable advice on Egyptian imagery, Dr John Chapman for his thoughts on mobility in Late Bronze Age Society, and Dr Tom Moore for his eloquent quote on the La Tène art of the European Iron Age. Dr Jody Joy, Curator of European Iron Age at the British Museum, kindly forwarded his latest paper on the Iron Age mirror style. Emeritus Professor of Archaeology Rosemary Cramp of Durham University provided stimulating insights into Anglo-Saxon art styles. Expert advice on medieval textiles was contributed by Frances Pritchard, Textiles Curator at the Whitworth Art Gallery, University of Manchester. Thom Richardson, Keeper of Armour and Oriental Collections at the Royal Armouries in Leeds, provided valuable information for the analysis of patterning in 16th-century armour style.

We would like to especially thank Caroline Earle, Editorial Director at Ivy Reference, for her professionalism and patience in managing this challenging and enjoyable project.

Our thanks also go to Dr Grant Pooke and Professor Richard Hingley for their support during our work on this book.

Picture Credits

Special thanks to Elaine Lucas, Christopher Sutherns, Roxanne Peters and Fiona Grimer at V&A Images, for all of their effort and support.

All images courtesy of and © V&A Images, Victoria and Albert Museum, except for the following:

AKG Images: Album/Oronoz: 22BL; Archives CDA: 60T; British Library: 57BL, 88, 89; Cameraphoto: 47; André Held: 125BL, 125TR, 125BR; Erich Lessing: 18B, 20, 21, 29BL, 31R, 31T, 42T, 43T, 48R, 48B, 61TL, 62B; Joseph Martin: 49BL; Ullstein Bild: 214; Vozenesky Collection: 213T.

Alamy/Todd Bannor: 211; CuboImages Srl: 81; Pete Jenkins: 261B; Fergus Mackay: 223TL; Photos12: 58BL.

Art Archive/British Museum: 19BR.

Bauhaus-Archiv Berlin: 232.

© Biba/V&A Images, Victoria and Albert Museum: 243BL.

Jessie Brewin: 266TR.

Hayley Brinsford: 266BL.

British Museum Images: 19BL, 31BL.

Corbis/Andreea Angelescu: 259BL; Michel Arnaud: 247R; Bettmann: 210; Pierre Colombel: 41TR, 67T; Angelo Hornak: 141, Hulton-Deutsch Collection: 244; Massimo Listri: 250C; Edward Le Poulin: 258B, 259T; Werner Forman: 213R.

© DACS 2011: 233.

Megan Dow/www.megandow.com: 265TL.

Jonathan Dresner: 25TL.

Fotolia/Digitalpress: 216; photographicdesign: 215; Rafael Ramirez: 160, 161; yuri4u80: 196B.

Getty Images/Hulton Archive: 82TR, 194; James Keyser/Time Life Pictures: 250T; Pierre Verdy/AFP: 253L.

Herzog Anton Ulrich-Museums Braunschweig, Kunstmuseum des Landes Niedersachsen: 55L.

Lizzie Hingley: 257T, 269T.

© Richard Hingley: 54R.

David V. Hoffman: 222TR.

Moon Hussain: 269BL, 269BR.

iStockphoto/Robin Krauss: 186; Atbaei: 136R, 143T.

Courtesy of Liberty Ltd: 249TL.

© David Mabb/V&A Images, Victoria and Albert Museum. Purchased through the Julie and Robert Breckman Print Fund: 256, 263.

The Marquess of Sailsbury: 132, 133.

BEV Norton flickr.com/catchesthelight: 223TR.

Photolibrary/Gala: 31B.

David J. Radcliffe: 58TR.

Rex Features: 259R, 260, 261T; Alex J. Berliner/BEI: 263R; Daniel Buxton: 49TL; Bill Johnson/Associated Newspapers: 240; Paul Massey: 251BL.

Scala Archives: 76, 77, 102, 103, 228, 229B, 229L, 229T, 229R; BPK, Bildagentur fuer Kunst, Kultur und Geschichte, Berlin: 19T; CM Dixon/Heritage Images: 18R; Fondo Edifici di Culto - Min. dell' Interno: 80; Heritage Images: 34, 35, 94, 95; The Metropolitan Museum of Art/Art Resource: 26, 27, 109BR; Courtesy of the Ministero Beni e Att. Culturali: 32L, 33T, 97TR; Pierpont Morgan Library/Art Resource: 44B.

Shutterstock/Eastimages: 263B.

Hester Simpson: 254, 264.

By Permission of the Society of Antiquaries of London/V&A Images, Victoria and Albert Museum: 65.

Mee Rhim Song: 265R, 265BL.

© Rodchenko & Stepanova Archive, DACS 2011: 229B.

Nikki Strange: 267.

Thinkstock Photos: 253BR.

Thomas Fisher Rare Book Library, University of Toronto: 140.

Iwan Tirta: 249BL.

Topfoto/The Granger Collection: 212.

Hannah Trask: 268.

Christina Unwin: 61TR, 78B.

Werner Forman Archive/Field Museum Chicago: 213B.

York Museums Trust (Yorkshire Museum): 54B.

Every effort has been made to acknowledge the copyright and source of pictures; however, the publisher apologises if there are any unintentional omissions.